KU-548-820

INTELLECTUAL PROPERTY:
PATENTS, COPYRIGHT, TRADE MARKS
AND ALLIED RIGHTS

AUSTRALIA
The Law Book Company Ltd.
Sydney : Melbourne : Perth

CANADA AND U.S.A.
The Carswell Company Ltd.
Agincourt, Ontario

INDIA
N.M. Tripathi Private Ltd.
Bombay
and
Eastern Law House Private Ltd.
Calcutta and Delhi
M.P.P. House
Bangalore

ISRAEL
Steimatzky's Agency Ltd.
Jerusalem : Tel Aviv : Haifa

PAKISTAN
Pakistan Law House
Karachi

INTELLECTUAL PROPERTY:

PATENTS, COPYRIGHT, TRADE MARKS
AND ALLIED RIGHTS

Second Edition

By

W. R. CORNISH, F.B.A.
Professor of English Law,
London School of Economics and Political Science
Professor-Elect of Law,
(University of Cambridge)

LONDON
SWEET & MAXWELL
1989

First Edition 1981
Second Impression 1982
Third Impression 1984

Published by
Sweet & Maxwell Limited of
South Quay Plaza
183 Marsh Wall, London E14 9FT

Laserset by
LBJ Enterprises Limited
Chilcompton, Somerset

Printed in Scotland by Thomson Litho

Hardback edition published by
Matthew Bender Ltd., New York, U.S.A.

British Library Cataloguing in Publication Data

Cornish, W. R. (William Rodolph), *1937–*
Intellectual property : patents, copyright,
trade marks and allied rights. – 2nd ed.
1. Great Britain. Intellectual property. Law
I. Title
334'1064'8

ISBN 0–421–37970–7
ISBN 0–421–37980–4 Pbk

All rights reserved. No part of this publication
may be reproduced or transmitted, in any form or
by any means, electronic, mechanical, photocopying,
recording or otherwise, or stored in any retrieval
system of any nature, without the written permission
of the copyright holder and the publisher, application
for which shall be made to the publisher.

©
W. R. CORNISH
1989

FROM THE PREFACE TO THE FIRST EDITION

The various branches of intellectual property law—patents, trade marks, registered designs, copyright, confidence and so on—confer legal exclusivity in the market-place. The right to prevent others from using ideas or information to their own commercial advantage is not easily delineated. Legal techniques of some sophistication are called for and this has until recently made intellectual property a somewhat esoteric specialism. But, particularly in industrial, free-market economies, these intangible property rights are becoming increasingly valuable in the fight to secure and retain shares of a market. A widening circle of people need some knowledge of what they involve.

This book deals with the British law of intellectual property, in the new setting provided by EEC membership and a growing encrustation of international conventions. I have not written it for the person who understands the main characteristicts of the law: specialist lawyers and professional advisers, such as patent and trade mark agents, are well supplied with detailed practitioners' texts. I am seeking rather to help the relative novice who wants something more substantial than a purely introductory account of the subject.

I have, indeed, had three types of reader in mind. First, students in universities and polytechnics, whether they are studying law in general or specialising in business law or training for one of the intellectual property professions. In Britain and the Commonwealth, an increasing number of students are tackling the subject each year. For them, I have described not only the current state of British law but have sketched in the political and economic debates which always surround the subject.

Secondly, there are lawyers, business executives and civil servants who come in contact with the field in the course of their careers and need to look at its structure systematically. Thirdly, there are specialists in the subject abroad who are looking for a relatively succinct presentation of United Kingdom law. International negotiation about intellectual property proliferate; but legal protection is still at base a matter for the domestic laws of national states. As trans-national business grows so does the expert's need to have some acquaintance with the intellectual property laws of all major industrial countries. Within the EEC, with its special market objectives and its great interest in securing Community-wide or harmonised regimes of intellectual property, there is a real need to understand the British legal position. Both the independent development of the common law and Britain's long industrial history have given the country a distinctive experience which deserves to be better understood among our continental collaborators.

W.R.C.

October, 1980

PREFACE TO SECOND EDITION

This book has had to wait more than eight years for revision, even though a great deal has happened to the subject in the interim. Throughout the period, the British government has been considering how it should revise UK copyright law and the parasitical growth upon it relating to industrial designs. In 1983, the Green Paper by Sir Robin Nicholson, *Intellectual Property Rights and Innovation,* broadened an already wide prospect for reform by questioning the capacity of the current types of protection to foster scientific and technological progress in British industry. Out of the domestic debates has come the Copyright, Designs and Patent Act 1988 and suddenly the need for this second edition has shifted from pending to urgent.

The Act restates general copyright law in various ways, adds something to the panoply of moral rights, seeks to foster the collective enforcement of copyright in face of new, much-enhanced technology and, above all, creates a new, complex scheme for industrial design. The Act also contains changes relating to patent and trade mark agents, patent litigation, the compulsory licensing of certain pharmaceutical patents, and trade mark piracy, but it does not touch the heart of patent or trade mark law. Accordingly revision on those fronts has been more interstitial than in relation to copyright and design. Nonetheless there has been a flow of important case-law, so there is new material at many points of the book.

On the European scene, progress has been made towards the institution of an EC Trade Mark, but final issues (including siting of the Community Trade Mark Office) are still in the balance. Implementation of the scheme, as of the Community Patent Convention, now becomes part of the drive to 1992. They continue to be mentioned in the book as important developments for the future.

In international fora, the impetus behind the New International Economic Order, so fervently desired by developing countries, has faltered. The tensions generated by this movement have meant the abandonment of attempts to revise the Paris Industrial Property Convention. More recently, reaction against it has taken the form of pressure within the current round of G.A.T.T. negotiations to secure a much improved level of recognition and enforcement of intellectual property rights. Something of this rather abrupt reversal, led by the United States, finds its way into these pages. But it is early yet to see much of its potential effect upon legal practice.

My thanks once again to those who have provided research and secretarial assistance and to the publishers for the despatch with which they have processed the necessary work.

W.R.C.

May, 1989

CONTENTS

PART V TRADE MARKS AND NAMES

APPENDICES

TABLE OF CASES

TABLE OF STATUTES

TABLE OF ABBREVIATIONS

1. The following abbreviations are used for case-report series and journals that specialise in intellectual property.

Bull. U.S. Cop. Soc.	Bulletin of the United States Copyright Society
C.P.R.	Canadian Patent Reports
CIPA	Journal of the Chartered Institute of Patent Agents (formerly Transactions of that Institute)
E.I.P.R.	European Intellectual Property Review
E.P.O.R.	European Patent Office Reports
F.S.R.	Fleet Street Patent Law Reports
Fox P.C.	Fox's Patent Cases
I.I.C.	International Review of Industrial Property and Copyright
J.P.O.S.	Journal of the Patent Office Society
Mac C.C.	Macgillivray's Copyright Cases
O.J. EPO	Office Journal of the European Patent Office
R.P.C.	Reports of Patent, Design and Trade Mark Cases
R.I.D.A.	Revue Internationale du Droit d'Auteur
T.M.R.	Trade Mark Reporter
U.S.P.Q.	United States Patent Quarterly
W.P.C.	Webster's Patent Cases

2. The main United Kingdom legislation and international treaties and conventions are abbreviated as follows.

Berne Convention	Berne International Copyright Convention (1886, with revisions)
CA 1911, CA 1956	Copyright Acts 1911, 1956
CDPA	Copyright, Designs and Patents Act 1988
CPC	Community Patent Convention (1975)
CPCr	Implementing Regulations to the CPC
EPC	European Patent Convention (1973)
EPCr	Implementing Regulations to the EPC
PIP	Paris Convention for the Protection of Industrial Property (1883, with revisions)
PA 1949, PA 1977	Patent Acts 1949, 1977
PAr 1977	Rules under the PA 1977
PCT	Patent Cooperation Treaty (1970)
PCTr	Rules under the PCT
RDA	Registered Designs Act 1949
TMA 1938	Trade Marks Act 1938
TMAr 1938	Rules under the TMA 1938
UCC	Universal Copyright Convention (1952, with revision)

3. In the footnotes leading works on intellectual property and competition law are abbreviated as follows:

Bellamy and Child	C. Bellamy and G. Child, *Common Market Law of Competition* (3rd ed., 1987)
Blanco White (1974, 1983)	T. A. Blanco White, *Patents for Inventions and the Protection of Industrial Designs* (4th ed., 1974; 5th ed., 1983).
Copinger	*Copinger and Skone James on Copyright* (12th ed., 1980) by E. P. Skone James, J. F. Mummery and J. E. Rayner James)
Dietz	A. Dietz, *Copyright in the European Community* (English edition, 1978)
Dworkin and Taylor	G. Dworkin and R. D. Taylor *Copyright Designs and Patents Act 1988*
Ency. PL	T. A. Blanco White, J. Jeffs, R. Jacob, W. R. Cornish and M. Vitoria, *Encyclopedia of United Kingdom and European Patent Law* (1978, with supplements)
Kerly	*Kerly on Trade Marks* (10th ed., 1972) by T. A. Blanco White and R. Jacob
Korah	V. Korah, *Competition Law in Britain and the Common Market*
Laddie *et al.*	H. Laddie, P. Prescott and M. Vitoria, *The Modern Law of Copyright* (1980)
Lahore	J. Lahore, *Intellectual Property Law in Australia* (1977, with supplements).
Reid	B. C. Read, *A Practical Guide to Patent Law* (1984)
Ricketson (1984)	S. Ricketson, *The Law of Intellectual Property* (1984)
Ricketson (1987)	S. Ricketson, The Berne Convention for the Protection of Literary and Artistic Works: 1886–1986 (1987)
Russell Clarke	*Russell-Clarke on Copyright in Industrial Designs* (5th ed., 1974) by M. Fysh
Walton and Laddie	A. M. Walton and H. I. L. Laddie, *Patent Law of Europe and the United Kingdom* (1978, with supplements)

Part 1

COMMON GROUND

CHAPTER 1

STARTING POINTS

1. GENERAL

(1) "Intellectual property"

Patents give temporary protection to technological inventions and   1-001
design rights to the appearance of mass-produced goods; copyright gives
longer-lasting rights in, for instance, literary, artistic and musical creations; trade marks are protected against imitation so long at least as
they continue to be employed in trade. These and similar rights are the
subject-matter of this book. There is no single generic term that satisfactorily covers them all. "Industrial property" is not uncommonly used in
the common law world, but many would hold this to exclude copyright,
particularly if they want to emphasise the special importance and
vulnerability of the creative artist. "Intellectual property" is the term used
in this book for the whole field. It scarcely describes trade marks and
similar marketing devices; but it has now acquired a degree of international acceptance.[1] As a title it may sound rather grandiloquent. But
then, at its most serious, this is a branch of the law which protects some
of the finer manifestations of human achievement.

The various aspects of the subject differ in purpose and in detailed
rule. Nonetheless there is good sense in studying them together. Each is
concerned with marking out, by means of legal definition, types of
conduct which may not be pursued without the consent of the right-
owner. The rights thus delimited are enforced in similar ways[2] and all are
dealt with by broad analogy to property rights in tangible movables.[3]
Frequently the objective of controlling the activities of competitors and
licensees is achieved by use of a number of forms of intellectual property
conjointly. Where their deployment comes in conflict with other policies,
such as has happened recently under the impact of EEC law, comparisons
between the different forms of intellectual property need to be made.[4]

(2) Organisation of the material

The main branches of intellectual property each have a Part devoted to   1-002
them in the course of the book. Those concerned with the protection of
ideas—patents, breach of confidence and copyright—are treated before

[1] As in the title of the UN organ, World Intellectual Property Organisation (WIPO).
[2] See Chap. 2.
[3] An analogy that nonetheless is not straightforward: see, e.g. the discussion of damages
for breach of confidence (below, § 8-042).
[4] See further, below §§ 1-023—1-027 and the references given there to other parts of the
book.

3

those which deal with trade marks, trade names and the like. Before reaching this stage, however, there are a number of themes that can usefully be pursued in common and they are explored in this introductory Part.

In the remainder of this chapter three distinct topics are raised: the use of statute and judicial decision as means of defining intellectual property rights and the interrelation between these two sources of law; basic economic considerations underlying the objectives of the law; and the two most relevant policies of the EEC. Chapter 2 deals with matters more immediately practical: the remedies and procedures generally available in the enforcement of intellectual property rights.

The subject has grown in a number of directions over the past decade. To contain it within a single book has called for a considerable measure of selection. This has involved a number of strategic choices, which it is worth listing at the outset:

1-003   (i) Each of the subjects has spawned enough detailed law to merit very substantial texts for specialist practitioners. This book does not try to cover all the detailed points of statute or case-law to be found in them. Some attempt has been made to include cross-references to them where they carry a point further.[5] Beyond this the reader in search of all the available knowledge must be prepared to refer to them without explicit guidance from this book. In particular, the account here tends to concentrate on substantive rules rather than on matters of procedure, both in the acquiring and the enforcement of rights.

(ii) The Patents Act 1977 introduced an elaborate law which relates to applications filed on or after June 1, 1978, and patents that result. The law of "old" patents—contained in the Act of 1949, as modified by the 1977 Act—will continue therefore to have its own importance until 1998. The Part on Patents, however, concentrates on the new law; only brief guidance (in Appendix 2) has been included on "old" patents.

(iii) The most substantial legal changes introduced by the Copyright Designs and Patents Act 1988 create a new regime for protecting the design of industrial products: to a strictly limited degree through copyright, but more substantially through the twin systems for registered and unregistered design rights. The distinctions and overlaps between these are complex and are the subject of Chapter 14.

(iv) The special regime for the protection of plant varieties is dealt with only in outline (see Appendix X).

(v) With membership of the EEC, the rules of competition and allied principles in the Treaty of Rome have come to play a prominent role in the whole subject. This difficult and often imprecise field of law deserves study as a whole and on its own. Here all that can be examined is the impact of competition rules on the different types of intellectual property. To this end: (a) the relevant policies of the EEC are outlined in this introductory Part[7]; (b) the impact of these policies (together with the

---

[5] Most are referred to in abbreviated forms: see the Table of Abbreviations.
[6] Below, § 13-001.
[7] Below, §§ 1-021—1-027.

occasional provision of British statute law) is discussed in each of the Parts on patents, copyright and trade marks[8]; (c) Appendix 1 gives some further crucial clues to the administration of EEC competition policy; and (d) the same Appendix says something about native British competition law, which has had a less dramatic impact upon intellectual property rights.

(vi) The law contained in this book is largely based on statutes applicable to the United Kingdom as a whole. By contrast, most of the case law has been decided in English courts. Nonetheless there are three separate jurisdictions to which litigants may on occasion resort. While the procedures and remedies available in Northern Ireland closely resemble those of England and Wales, the Scottish system is often distinct in substance or in nomenclature. The special characteristics of Scottish litigation, however, are not pursued here.

(vii) For readers who come to this subject without much legal background, it is important also to say that knowledge of the structure of both the English legal system and that of the EEC is assumed.

2. Sources of the Law and Pressures for its Development

Intellectual property protects applications of ideas and information that **1-004** are of commercial value. The subject is growing in importance, to the advanced industrial countries in particular, as the fund of exploitable ideas becomes more sophisticated and as their hopes for a successful economic future come to depend increasingly upon their superior corpus of new knowledge and fashionable conceits. There has recently been a great deal of political and legal activity designed to assert and strengthen the various types of protection for ideas. There have been a succession of campaigns for new rights. For instance, new plant varieties are now protected in a number of countries (including the United Kingdom)[9]; the circuit of a silicon chip has been afforded its own regime[10]; the best method of protecting computer programs is as yet far from settled.[11]

No country favours conferring on the creator of an idea a perpetual property in it against imitators. The political and economic implications of such a privilege would be remarkable. Instead a set of limited forms of protection are fashioned against some types of exploitation by others. The root issue to which we constantly return is whether the balance achieved by this approach is broadly appropriate to the economic needs of the country and to the prevailing sense of what is just. While the legal protection that is provided varies for the different types of subject-matter, there are some useful preliminary points to make: about the way, historically, that developments have occurred, about the kinds of justification for adopting one or other course of action, and about the

[8] Below, §§ 7-030—7-048; 12-026—12-033; 18-001—18-019.
[9] Below, App. 4.
[10] Below, §§ 14-034—14-035.
[11] Below, §§ 5-046—5-050; 13-015—13-024.

foundations from which arguments about ends and means ought to proceed. These are taken up in what follows.

(1) Legislation and judicial decision

1-005   As a regime is developed for protecting a form of intellectual property a number of basic decisions have to be made: What types of subject-matter are to be included? Is the right to be conferred only upon application to a government office? How long is it to last? Is it to be a right good only against imitators (as with copyright and unregistered designs), or is it a "full monopoly" that even affects independent devisers of the same idea (as with patents for inventions, registered designs and trade marks)? The operative rules vary because each type of subject-matter calls for a different balance of public and private interests—the interests of the society as a whole in its economic and cultural development, and the interest of the individual to secure a "fair" value for his intellectual effort or investment of capital or labour.

The marked tendency under modern conditions is to reach answers about the proper scope of protection by political decision expressed primarily in legislation. Partly this is because the interest groups concerned are expected to make out their case sufficiently to a responsible body; and party because a complex set of rules is required which cannot satisfactorily be fashioned from the vagaries of litigation.

1-006   In Britain, the majority of intellectual property rights are today founded upon Acts of Parliament. The patent system had its origins in royal grants under the prerogative, which from the Statute of Monopolies 1624 onwards came to be conditioned by legislation.[12] In the complex evolution of the copyright system a strategic decision was reached in 1774: to the extent that Parliament had entered the field, statutory copyright was not to be supplemented by more embracing common-law rights.[13] And in the modern period, the ability to adhere to the principle of legislative creation has been much enhanced by the willingness of Parliament to use "copyright" as a catch-all for the protection of new subject-matter, such as records, films, broadcasts and cable-casts, and to act with expedition enough for the judges to reserve their creative urges mainly for ancillary matters, such as remedies.[14]

But this is not the unvarying history. In the early industrial period the judges fashioned the tort of passing off to meet an evident commercial need; and when Parliament did introduce a system for registering trade marks this was regarded as a supplement, and not a displacement, of common-law rights.[15] More recently the courts have extended the action against breach of confidence unassisted by legislative intervention and in response to another strong demand that the law should act against dishonest business practices.[16]

[12] Below, §§ 3-003—3-009.
[13] *Donaldson v. Beckett* (below, § 9-003).
[14] Below, § 9-009.
[15] Below,§§ 17-001, 17-002.
[16] Below, §§ 8-001, 8-002.

In all these developments there are distinctively British characteristics, **1-007**
which are the product of a particular economic development and political
history. What is perhaps most striking of all, however, is the absence of
any basic conception that "unfair competition" or the "misappropriation
of trade values" should be treated as an underlying principle of liability
by which the judges can extend protection to new types of subject-matter
and business relationships as they see fit.

In 1918 a majority of the United States Supreme Court in principle
adopted a misappropriation doctrine. The well-known *INS* case[17] arose
out of the French government's refusal to allow the Hearst press facilities
to report the war in Europe. So one way in which the Hearst news
agency procured its war reports was from first editions of Associated
Press's newspapers on the American East Coast. It telegraphed the
information to its West Coast papers in time for reports to appear in
competition with Associated Press newspapers there. This keen bit of
acquisition was held a tortious form of competition even though it lay
outside the confines of statutory copyright. Noting that "the news has an
exchange value to one who can misappropriate it," Pitney J. characterised the defendant's conduct thus:

> "Stripped of all disguises, the process amounts to an unauthorised
> interference with the normal business operation of complainant's
> legitimate business precisely at the point where the profit is to be
> reaped, in order to divert a material portion of the profit from those
> who have earned it to those who have not; with the special advantage
> to defendant in the competition because of the fact that it is not
> burdened with any part of the expense of gathering the news."[18]

Significantly, however, Holmes J. would have restricted relief so that it
covered only the implied misrepresentation that the news was Hearst's
own (through failure to acknowledge source); and Brandeis J. insisted
that legislation alone was the proper medium for fashioning new legal
rights in information.

Some years later Dixon J. summarised developments elsewhere in the **1-008**
common law world in a way that showed a close affinity to Brandeis J.'s
position:

> "[The courts] have not in British jurisdictions thrown the protection of
> an injunction around all the intangible elements of value, that is value
> in exchange, which may flow from the exercise by an individual of his
> powers or resources whether in the organisation of a business or
> undertaking or in the use of ingenuity, knowledge, skill or labour. This
> is sufficiently evidenced by the history of the law of copyright and by
> the fact that the exclusive right to invention, trade marks, designs,
> trade names and reputation are dealt with in English law as special
> heads of protected interests and not under a wide generalisation."[19]

[17] *International News Service* v. *Associated Press* 248 U.S. 215 (1918). On what follows,
see also Cornish (1972) 12 J.S.P.T.L. 126; Heydon, *Economic Torts* (2nd ed., 1978),
Chap. 4 and pp. 134–138.
[18] Above, n. 17, at p. 240.
[19] *Victoria Park Racing* v. *Taylor* (1937) 58 C.L.R. 479 at p. 509 (H.C. Australia).

The evidence for this lay in a succession of decisions. For instance, the House of Lords had refused to subject untruths in comparative advertisements to the discipline of civil action, save in extreme cases of malicious falsehood.[20] Another of its decisions apparently prevented misrepresentation about the quality of one competitor's goods from being actionable at the suit of a rival.[21] In the case being discussed by Dixon J., it was no tort for a broadcasting station to run a commentary on a race meeting from a stand erected outside the course but looking onto it.[22]

The contrast lay not only with the emergent misappropriation doctrine in the United States (which did not prosper particularly in its early years) but also with most countries of Western Europe. There, starting either from general provisions on tortious liability in civil codes[23] or from separate proscriptions of unfair competition,[24] the judges tended to develop a broadening series of precedents concerning unfair business practices in the market place. Under such a rubric, advertisements that made, or even implied, comparisons were treated as actionable; and various types of seller's enticements, such as additional "gifts," were treated as unfair ploys. There was also some tendency to consider slavish copying of the details of products as a form of actionable misappropriation—notably when new technology, such as the apparatus which made it possible to copy records and broadcasts, allowed piracy that fell outside the scope of existing copyright laws.[25] Protection against the direct imitation of products began to assume the character of a sub-species of intellectual property.

1-009   It is worth trying to divine why British common lawyers resisted a demand from business litigants that was being met in comparable countries—places indeed whose industrial and commercial development had only followed the British. A complex set of justifications and underlying motives seem to have been at work. To have adopted a broad principle such as "unfair competition" would have been foreign to the traditional conservatism of the common law courts. Their long-implanted

---

[20] *White* v. *Mellin* [1895] A.C. 154 (H.L.); and see *Hubbuck* v. *Wilkinson* [1899] 1 Q.B. 86 (C.A.); *Alcott* v. *Millar's Karri* (1904) 21 T.L.R. 30 (C.A.); and generally, below, § 00. These cases put a stop to the more generous attitude suggested in *Western Manure* v. *Lawes* (1874) L.R. 9 Ex. 218.

[21] *Native Guano* v. *Sewage Manure* (1891) 8 R.P.C. 125 (alleged representation that "native guano"—human excreta converted into a fertiliser—was made by the plaintiff's process, when it was not); see also *Cambridge U.P.* v. *University Tutorial Press* (1928) 45 R.P.C. 335. The decision in the *Guano* case has now been deprived of much of its effect by remarks upon it in the "Advocaat" case (below, n. 34) at pp. 408–409, 418.

[22] Above, n. 19. This was one of the earlier instances of "misappropriation" admitted in the U.S. under the *INS* doctrine: *Pittsburgh Athletic Club* v. *K.Q.V. Broadcasting* 24 F.Supp. 490 (1938).

[23] As in the case of France: see, *e.g.* Derenberg (1955) 4 Am.J.Comp.L. 1; Krasser, *Rèpression de la concurrence dèloyale: France* (1972).

[24] As in the case of Germany: see, *e.g.* Rowland (1968) 58 T.M.Rep. 853; Reimer, *Rèpression de la concurrence dèloyale en Allemagne* (1978).

[25] Unfair competition doctrine in the U.S. expanded for the same reason and at much the same time: *e.g. Waring* v. *WDAS* 327 Pa. 433 (1937); *Jackson* v. *Universal* 36 Cal. (2d) 116 (1950); *Metropolitan Opera* v. *Wagner-Nichols*, 199 Misc. 786 (1950); *Capitol* v. *Mercury*, 221 F. (2d) 657 (1955).

preference for development only by close and necessary analogy had formerly been expressed through the forms of action, and even the abandonment of that technique in the judicature reforms of the 1850s and 1870s had done little to modify the basic attitude.[26] The nineteenth century had given flesh to one great (indeed over-broad) generalisation, the concept of contract. But the sanctity of bargains, so much a part of the Victorian *Zeitgeist*, was inimical to legal obligations imposed *ab extra*, as distinct from those reached by voluntary agreement. Large generalisations about rights—unjust enrichment, the right to privacy and unfair competition, just as much as the duty to one's neighbour to take care—found little favour.

Another recurrent fear was of a flood of litigation[27]—a matter of serious concern to a court system (with its underlying professional structure) in which a small number of superior judges held the power to make law through precedents. In the case of unfair competition, this threat was linked with a concern that the courts should not become a forum for justifying the advertising claims of one business competitor against those of another.[28] At the same time, the emergence of Parliamentary democracy provided new reason for the judges to appear as objective administrators of established law, rather than as wholesale makers of new principle; the more so in the various fields of intellectual property where the legislature was increasingly active.

How far, then, were the judges also expressing a clearly reasoned preference for freedom to compete, even if it involved making use of the ideas or goodwill of others? Did they, in particular, consider that the public interest in an improved economic future was best served by as little legal interference as possible, and that accordingly rights of intellectual property should be confined to the exceptional categories marked out in the existing law? Whatever their ultimate motives may have been, it is hard to find evidence that they worked out their decisions explicitly from such a premise. If they had felt strongly the need to encourage competition they ought to have been active in turning the law against a different form of unfair business practice from the "excessive" competition in which we are primarily interested. They should have been ready to refuse to enforce agreements amongst competitors not to compete but rather to link together in cartels and other restrictive agreements that would preserve to each his existing market share. Yet in a succession of judgments, they showed considerable reluctance to intervene.[29] The

1-010

---

[26] With the conjoint system of judicial administration introduced by the Judicature Act 1873 rather more contact came about between the traditions of common law and equity. But where equity's penchant for large moral generalisations produced results that would make "mercantile men cry out" (Lord Bramwell, *Derry* v. *Peek* (1889) 14 App.Cas. 337 at p. 350) its excesses were curbed. For our purposes, note the tendency to confine breach of confidence to liability in contract: below, § 8-007.

[27] See, *e.g. White* v. *Mellin* (above, n. 20) at p. 164.   [28] *Ibid.*

[29] See especially *BUSM* v. *Somervell* (1906) 95 L.T. 711; *USM Canada* v. *Brunet* [1909] A.C. 330; *A.G. for the Commonwealth* v. *Adelaide Steamship* [1913] A.C. 781 (J.C.); *North Western Salt* v. *Electrolytic Alkali* [1914] A.C. 461 (H.L.); *English Hop Growers* v. *Dering* [1928] 2 K.B. 174 (C.A.); *cf. Evans* v. *Heathcote* [1918] 1 K.B. 418 (C.A.); *McEllistrim* v. *Ballymacelligott Coop.* [1919] A.C. 548 (H.L.). Note also the refusal to hold tortious a cartel's indirect pressure upon an outsider: *Mogul Steamship* v. *McGregor Gow* [1892] A.C. 25.

watchword was provided by Fry L.J.: "to draw a line between fair and unfair competition, between what is reasonable and unreasonable, passes the power of the Courts."[30] In truth, in the quarter century before World War I, free-trade Britain, facing the growing competition of protectionist Germany and America, had reason to think that there was competition enough.[31] Her judges could afford to place themselves apart for the sorts of motive mentioned earlier. In a world that was having to accept enterprises of the size and strength of the modern business corporation, they showed little desire to become embroiled in the obviously political business of settling the rules of competition.

1-011 Over recent decades, there has been some modification of the courts' approach. But when compared with developments of unfair competition doctrine in parts of Western Europe and the United States,[32] the continuing attraction of late Victorian attitudes remains apparent. Most developed economies have responded to "consumerism" and the fear of business coalitions by introducing anti-trust laws which draw considerably on American inspiration. Likewise they have tried to improve the standards of information and legal protection that traders must meet in advertising and selling goods and services. In some countries,[33] it has been possible to adapt the action for unfair competition so as to allow competitors and consumer groups equally to enforce these standards. The particular advantage of these civil proceedings is that they make available the potent weapon of injunctive relief.

In Britain, as we shall see, over much of the field, criminal law sanctions and administrative enforcement alone perform the same tasks. However, in its "Advocaat" decision,[34] the House of Lords has offered some encouragement towards a broader conception of unfair competition: one that would bring to account new forms of misrepresentation, if not of misappropriation.[35] Even so, it remains unlikely that common law doctrine will develop rapidly.

(2) Statutes and their interpretation

1-012 The first Parliamentary interventions in the creation of intellectual property—the Statute of Monopolies 1624, the Copyright Act 1709 and their successors—left much for the courts to work out in terms of principle. Over the past century, as legislation has become broader in range and more complete in content, judicial influence has increasingly been felt through the interpretation of statute. Here the attitudes of the

[30] *Mogul* case (1889) 23 Ch.D. 598 at pp. 625–626.
[31] Attitudes in Britain, France and Germany contrasted strongly with those in the U.S.: see Cornish in *Law and the Big Enterprises in the 19th and early 20th Centuries* (Horn and Kocka eds., 1979), p. 280.
[32] But in the U.S., there was a significant "liberal" reaction against uses of the misappropriation doctrine: see *Sears-Roebuck v. Stiffel*; *Compco v. Daybrite*, 376 U.S. 225, 234 (1964). Argument centred upon the constitutional power of state legislatures and courts, but it carried more general overtones. In turn the full effect of this has been tempered: see especially *Goldstein v. California*, 412 U.S. 546 (1973); *Kewanee v. Bicron*, 416 U.S. 470 (1974).
[33] West Germany is a significant example.
[34] *Erven Warnink v. Townend* [1980] R.P.C. 31; see below, § 16-003.
[35] *cf.* Holmes J. in the *INS* case (above, § 9).

judges have much in common with their caution towards the creation of new common law rights. The preference for taking the meaning of a statute apparently expressed by Parliament, rather than searching for some "true" intent; the refusal to fill in gaps in legislation; the readiness to insist that it is for Parliament to remedy unsatisfactory results—these are all part of an approach that abjures obvious intervention in the political process.

It is an approach in no way peculiar to the field of intellectual property and its consequences in this field have, as we shall see, been varied. What should be appreciated is the effect of the general approach upon the style of statutory draftsmanship practised in the United Kingdom and countries which follow its lead. The tendency to proliferate detail and to make complicated cross-references has a long history. It is rooted in the assumption that the judges cannot, will not or should not work out the implications of statutory directives for themselves. We shall have occasion enough to wrestle with provisions that neglect the statement of general principle in favour of dealing elaborately with relatively special circumstances.[36]

Today, however, there are influences at work—and nowhere more so than in the intellectual property field—that are inducing change.[37] To these we shall return under the next heading.

(3) Recent developments—international, European and domestic

The growth of trade competition over the last quarter century has brought ever-increasing advantages to those in the van of innovation. Intellectual property rights, which help to sustain the lead of those with technical know-how, with successful marketing schemes, with new fetishes for pop culture, have come to foster immense commercial returns. The increasing numbers of patents granted and trade marks registered, particularly in industrial countries, and the upsurge of publishing, record-producing, film-making and broadcasting, stands as some measure of this development. But in some of these fields particularly, success has been accompanied by advances in copying techniques which make piracy possible on a scale that is just as new. The resources of existing legal techniques are under considerable strain. This is one reason why today there is a profusion of different and sometimes conflicting demands, some for new and some for improved rights.

The growth of international organisations, particularly within the frame of the United Nations, has provided one forum for the discussion of such claims.[38] Industries and professional experts have produced a

1-013

---

[36] Lord Diplock has recently found occasion to remark upon the "unhappy legacy of this judicial attitude" (*Fothergill* v. *Monarch Airlines*, below n. 48 at 222). See further, below, § 300, n. 34.

[37] Their influence has given the Copyright Designs and Patents Act 1988 a novel clarity of organisation and expression.

[38] The World Intellectual Property Organisation (WIPO) which (*inter alia*) administers the Paris Convention on Industrial Property, the Berne Convention on Copyright and the Patent Co-operation Treaty, is one of these UN organs; UNESCO administers the Universal Copyright Convention and deals with other copyright matters; for the role of UNCTAD, see below, § 3-013.

plethora of interest groups which seek to further their own political
ambitions at the national and international level. At the same time, other
pressures for change have been at work. The expansion of bureaucracies,
such as national patent offices, has brought in its train plans for
rationalising their activities. Partly this goes to standardising procedures
such as classification for indexing purposes. But it also aims to reduce
overlaps in the work that they do.[39] Thus it is a basic object of the Patent
Co-operation Treaty that the acceptance, searching and even examination
stages of applying for a patent should be conducted on an international
basis before proceeding to the grant of national patents.[40] In Western
Europe it has been possible to link this desire to eliminate repetitious
waste with the desire to strengthen the bonds of the EEC and EFTA. One
result has been the opening of the European Patent Office, another the
Convention (signed, but still not implemented) for a unified EEC patent.[41]
In the field of trade marks, the drive by EEC authorities to eliminate
distortions in the Common Market is fast advancing a project for a
Community-wide system of registration.[42] Discussions have been initiated
on the harmonisation of aspects of copyright within the EEC.[43]

1-014   The end product of much of this activity must be domestic legislation,
particularly given the rule which requires an Act of Parliament to turn
the international obligations of the United Kingdom into municipal law.
This may be done either by re-enacting a Convention in a paraphrase
which a British draftsman deems suitable for legislation here, or it may
be done by making the Convention text itself part of United Kingdom
law. The latter technique is used for the legal enactments of the EEC.[44]
The British enabling statute is then no more than a conduit pipe for texts
which will likely have been drafted with a Continental preference for the
statement of general principle—relatively uncomplicated in language, but
more or less indeterminate in scope. The former technique may be
adopted at least partly in the belief that British courts must be provided
with more specific guidance than the Convention text affords.[45] If not,
they may be led by their traditional approaches to interpretation into
destructive readings that would do little for comity between the contracting states concerned. The fear is not without foundation. The courts'
preference for literal interpretation has given rise to the rule of construction that, unless a British statute is ambiguous, its meaning must be
accepted, however much this results in inconsistency with the convention

[39] The urge to rationalise is all the greater when budgetary overseers notice that an office is
being run as a service below cost. As recent experience of the British Patent Office shows
only too clearly, the other weapon against this sort of extravagance is a steep increase in
official fees.
[40] See below, §§ 3-001, 3-015—3-017. cf. also the arrangements for international collaboration in registering trade marks, in which Britain has not so far participated: below
§§ 15-010—15-011.
[41] See below, §§ 3-001, 3-018—3-022.
[42] Below, §§ 18-014—18-018.
[43] Below, § 9-016.
[44] In general, see European Communities Act 1972. For specific examples, see Patents Act
1977, s.86, making the CPC part of the U.K. law.
[45] In taking over principles of the PCT and EPC, the Patents Act 1977 provides numerous
examples of this approach. This seems particularly curious in an Act which (see previous
note) also adopts an EEC Convention in virgin form.

from which it derives.[46] But the point at which ambiguity is considered to arise is itself a matter of judgment. Certainly once the meaning of a provision is deemed uncertain, the courts have recently shown a new willingness to resort to the convention text (or texts, if more than one language has been used).[47] In searching for the most acceptable meaning in such a case, the House of Lords has endorsed the adoption of a purposive approach to interpretation, rather than a literal one.[48] Equally, the House is willing to take account of the decisions of foreign courts on the convention's meaning, the writings of experts on the subject and even (with caution) the *travaux préparatoires* which led to the agreement of the final text,[49] at least if they have been published[50] and were intended to resolve doubts about its meaning. This, clearly, is important in dealing with law that comes from the EEC. British courts are expected to take heed of the EC Court of Justice's approach to the interpretation of legislative texts. This is characterised by Lord Diplock as teleological rather than historical, seeking "to give effect to what the Court conceives to be the spirit rather than the letter of the treaties; sometimes, indeed, it may seem to the exclusion of the letter."[51] This, as we shall see, is likely to be equally important whether the text has become United Kingdom law in its original form, or whether it has been adapted to the purpose by the British draftsman.[52]

(4) Challenges to intellectual property

As on the one hand the demand for increased protection has arisen, so on the other has the level of suspicion and criticism of intellectual property protection. Two sources of this are particularly noteworthy.   1-015

First, the developing countries, which are only beginning to exploit intellectual property of their own, often find themselves with an inheri-

---

[46] *Ellerman Lines* v. *Murray* [1931] A.C. 126; *Soloman* v. *Commrs. of Customs and Excise* [1967] 2 Q.B. 116 at p. 143, *per* Lord Diplock; *Warwick Films* v. *Eisinger* [1969] 1 Ch. 508; *cf. James Buchanan* v. *Babco Forwarding* [1978] A.C. 141 at p. 153, *per* Lord Wilberforce. But note also the tendency to stress that, if there is room for manoeuvre, a court will strive to achieve consistency between statute and convention: *e.g. Post Office* v. *Estuary Radio* [1968] 2 Q.B. 740; *The Jade* [1976] 1 All E.R. 920 at p. 924, *per* Lord Diplock; *Smith Kline and French* v. *Harbottle* [1980] R.P.C. 363; *E's Applications* [1983] R.P.C. 231.

[47] The H.L. has refused to accept that a foreign text may only be referred to if expert evidence about its meaning is led; there are no precise rules and a judge may rely on his own knowledge of the foreign language, dictionaries or expert opinion, when it is appropriate to do so: see Lord Wilberforce, *Buchanan* case (above, n. 45) at p. 152; Lord Fraser of Tullybelton, *Fothergill* case (below, n. 48) at pp. 709-710.

[48] *Fothergill* v. *Monarch Airlines* [1980] 2 All E.R. 696.

[49] Lord Diplock has stressed that this is not an invitation to resort to *Hansard* in resolving ambiguities in domestic legislation, though it is permissible to look to the reports of official commissions and committees in order to determine what mischief consequential legislation was intended to remedy: *Fothergill* case (above, n. 48) at pp. 705-706.

[50] It is Lord Fraser's view that, where the issue affects a private citizen, the preliminary document must have been published to the same extent as the ensuing Act: *Fothergill* case at p. 711.

[51] *R.* v. *Henn and Darby* [1980] 2 All E.R. 166 at p. 196.

[52] Note, in particular, the appreciation of the need to bring uniform interpretation to the EPC and its national derivatives, demonstrated on the "second medical use" question: below, § 5-053.

tance of "protectionist" laws from colonial days. These can all too easily appear a legal pretext for foreign industry, technical and cultural, to cream off scarce resources in royalty payments. Yet in the race for development, there is a real need to acquire technology from the advanced nations and there is often strong popular demand for products bearing the allure of Western prosperity. Patent, copyright and trade mark laws therefore tend to be kept because they give the security that will continue to attract foreign enterprise. But their operation may well be modified. There may be compulsory licence requirements, curbs on the manner in which royalties may be paid, or official examination of the terms on which foreign right-owners establish their own local operations or grant licences to local enterprises.

The developing countries have striven to secure the international acceptability of such derogations from unfettered rights of "property." They base their claim upon their need of freer access to technical and educational materials and of self-sufficiency and independent initiative for national business concerns. Of this movement, which had its first major impact during the revision of the Berne Copyright Convention in Stockholm in 1967 and continued particularly at the meetings of UNC-TAD, and the abortive attempts to revise the Paris Industrial Property Convention, there will be more to note at later stages. But now it is being countered by demands that developing countries cease to harbour intellectual property pirates. The United States is leading other industrialised countries, particularly in the current (Uruguay) round of GATT negotiations, in a demand that these countries adopt adequate laws and provide the infrastructure for their enforcement.

Secondly, there is the tendency, amongst the developed capitalist states, led by the United States, to limit the monopolistic tendencies of successful private enterprise by anti-trust laws (or competition laws as they are coming to be known in Britain). Intellectual property rights have often enough been one basis for powerful anti-competitive collaborations. Since their very purpose is to confer rights to exclude competitors, it is inevitable that they should have been combined into wider accretions of market power. But legislatures, competition authorities and courts have felt the need to impose restrictions upon at least the most evidently excessive arrangements of this kind: patent pools, copyright collecting societies, international or regional divisions of marketing territories achieved by the splitting of rights and the suppression of the initiative and independence of licensees.

As we shall see later,[53] the competition law sketched out in the Treaty of Rome for the EEC has been read in tandem with the basic principle of the free movement of goods within the Common Market. The consequence has been that traditional ways of using intellectual property rights to divide up markets country by country has been severely curtailed; and licensing agreements, particularly when exclusive, have been subjected to detailed scrutiny which has aroused considerable controversy.[54]

[53] See below, §§ 10-023—10-027.
[54] See below, §§ 7-030—7-040.

3. MARKET POWER: ECONOMIC APPROACHES

No serious student of intellectual property law can today afford to ignore 1-016
the economic arguments for and against the maintenance of these rights.
Patents, copyright and trade marks each have a different form of
economic impact, so a good deal must be reserved for later discussion.[55]
Underlying the whole, however, is a theoretical approach to the question
of monopoly power in a market. Full analysis of this must be sought in a
textbook on economics,[56] but a word of non-technical explanation may at
least be suggestive. There are two main issues: how does the economic
behaviour of the monopolist differ from that of competitors? And on
what grounds is this behaviour open to objection?

(1) Monopolist behaviour

The typical circumstance in which monopoly power is acquired con- 1-017
cerns a commodity which the consumer already needs or desires: a
monopolist's power can be thought of in terms of his ability to restrict
the supply of the commodity; this has a consequential effect on its price.
Everyday experience of prices for (say) petrol, food or land suggests the
effect of cutting down the quantity of such a commodity on the market.
Some purchasers will be prepared to devote more of their resources to
buying what there is of it. If therefore a supplier is in a position to
reduce the quantity of something that the public wants, he will be able to
effect an increase in its price: he then behaves as a monopolist. If, on the
contrary, he has competitors enough it will not avail him to reduce his
output, because they are likely to be able to expand their output to fill
the small shortfall that he would otherwise bring about. And of course to
raise his prices unilaterally would be merely to invite his customers to
take their business to a cheaper competitor. This is equally true whether
the competitors offer precisely the same products or things more or less
similar which the public will treat as substitutes.

The profit that any trader makes depends upon three principal factors:
the number of things sold, their price and their cost per unit to produce.
Assuming that unit costs do not vary significantly, there is a relationship
between number and price which is crucial to an understanding of why a
monopolist may benefit from selling fewer units at higher prices. Suppose
that the first producer of a video cassette recorder is setting his price for
a year in which he can expect no competition from other manufacturers.
He knows that if he limits his production run to a given number, he
should be able to increase his price to the level that this number of
purchasers is willing to pay. (How far the level of demand will regress as
price increases is something that he will have to guess from such market
indicators   as   he   can   amass.)   But   he   must   appreciate

---

[55] See especially below, §§ 3-023—3-035, 9-023—9-030.
[56] Particular help may be derived from Lipsey, *An Introduction to Positive Economics* (5th
  ed., 1979), Part IV, especially Chap. 20; Samuelson, *Economics* (11th ed., 1980), Part III,
  especially Chap. 25; Scherer, *Industrial Market Structure and Economic Performance*
  (2nd ed., 1980), especially Chaps. 2, 14-16.

that, if demand can be accurately forecast, there is an optimum number and correlated price to find. Suppose the calculation looks like this:

Number	Price per unit £	Cost per unit £	Profit (total revenue less total cost) £000's
1,000	700	400	300
2,000	600	400	400
3,000	550	400	450
4,000	500	400	400
5,000	475	400	375
6,000	450	400	300

A rational producer under these conditions will market 3,000 at £550.

(2) The presumption against monopoly

1-018   In any economy which is to a substantial extent unplanned by government, there are good reasons for fearing the market power of the monopolist, or at least for making sure that there are countervailing justifications, general or specific. Four arguments may be mentioned:

(i) The basic theoretical objection taken by economists concerns those who were not prepared to buy at the monopoly price, though they would have paid the competitive price or something in between. These consumers are left by the monopolist's behaviour to buy something else less valuable to them and in this sense there is a "misallocation of resources": too little of society's resources by this criterion are being put into the production of the goods monopolised. This objection is in fact a complex argument turning upon a number of assumptions: in particular that competition, or conditions equivalent to it, prevails in the market for similar or connected goods. Such qualifications are enough to make some economists doubt the relevance of this theory to the problem of monopoly.

(ii) Compare with this the common objection—socio-political rather than economic in nature—which looks rather at the position of those who do pay the monopolist's price. The latter thereby acquires his monopoly profit at their expense. A redistribution of wealth takes place which may be regarded as unjustifiable.

(iii) The monopolist is able to determine factors about goods in addition to their price: the kinds of service supplied, continuity of supply, the number of different versions, the amount of research and development into future products or services. This may have deleterious effects, immediate or consequential, for the consumer.

(iv) The monopolist loses the incentive to keep down costs that comes from competition. For only if his costs are constantly pared can a competitor hope to maintain or enhance his market share against those of his rivals.

Monopoly, or at least some measure of market power, nonetheless has its advocates. At one extreme lie cases where economies of scale are such that the most efficient production will be procured from a single source.

Few people would argue against the advantages of this sort of "natural monopoly." But if it is to remain in private hands it may be desirable to make it in some way publicly accountable. We shall see that copyright collecting societies present a special instance of such a phenomenon.[57] More equivocal are cases where, for instance, it can be said that only with the security of monopoly profits will a firm make sufficient investment in research to secure the really advantageous break-throughs for the future.[58] This sort of consideration becomes particularly germane to the justification of the patent system.

Advanced industrial societies engage in a continuing debate about the advisability of taking steps to curb or restrain the dangers set by monopolists, oligopolists and cartels within the private economic sector. The current growth of "anti-trust" laws is an indication of an increasing concern over the scale of profit and economic power of private enterprise. The tendency in these laws to treat certain manifestations of market power as at least prima facie unjustifiable demonstrates the force that experience gives to the theoretical objections to monopoly; equally, the provision that is made to allow firms to justify their practices is some admission that there may well be a countervailing case to be made out.

(3) Intellectual property and monopoly

All intellectual property consists in the exclusive right to perform some   1-019
defined activity, in the main productive or commercial. But this is not at all the same thing as the ability to exert monopoly power within a market. A market for goods has to be conceived in terms of all the goods that consumers will treat as substitutes for one another: will they switch from one to another if, for instance, the price of the first is raised? The extent to which purchasers want the product that is the subject of intellectual property and not some alternative is often difficult to determine. It may depend on the technical advance that has been made (particularly in the field covered by patents), or upon the dictates of fashion (as with many of the most popular copyright works) or upon the effect of repeated advertising (as with well-known trade marks).

The degree of market power that may be secured in these different areas by the deployment of intellectual property is a matter that we will take up topic by topic. Here it is appropriate merely to bring out two underlying considerations:

(i) The fact that much intellectual property has very little capacity to   1-020
generate market power leads to considerable difficulty in arguments over the proper scope of rights. On the one hand there is the potential disadvantage of power over a market in the few really successful cases—a power which may sometimes be unjustifiably great even given the special public policies (such as the encouragement of invention) which may underlie the creation of the right in the first place. On the other, if the investment of resources to produce ideas or convey information is left unprotected, it will be prey to the attentions of a competitive imitator

---

[57] Below, §§ 12-021—12-026.
[58] Below, §§ 3-024—3-031.

who will not be obliged to pay anything for what he takes. There will accordingly be no incentive to invest in the ideas or information and the consumer may be correspondingly the poorer. The only way out of this dilemma is, on the one hand, to make the best practicable estimate of the dangers that unjustified monopolies may produce; and, on the other, to assess the degree to which the claimant's investment will be open to dissipation if he is not accorded his right.

(ii) To the extent that intellectual property is capable of generating market power, it offers its owner (and his associates) the opportunity to reduce output and raise prices. What it does not bring about is the condition in which the monopolist behaves as though he were the only competitor on the market. Yet the more naive arguments in favour of one or other exclusive right often imply that this alone will be the effect of according the right sought. This intermediate condition can indeed be aimed at: through mechanisms such as direct price control, or through one or other of the forms of compulsory licensing. Accordingly it is no surprise to find that economists who doubt the justifiability of unconstrained intellectual property turn to the compulsory licence as a moderating technique.[59] In theory at least it provides machinery for obliging the right owner to accept a return (the royalty officially set under the licence) at a rate below that which he would have accepted if left to exercise his market power unfettered (hence the need for compulsion). Whether in practice this mechanism can be made to work without creating its own run of administrative expense depends on the legal form in which it is clothed. We shall have occasion to study a number of different examples in the course of the book.[60]

4. Division of Markets and the EEC

(1) Dividing markets

1-021   The obvious purpose of intellectual property is to give protection against rival enterprises which would otherwise sell goods or provide services in direct competition. In international trade, however, these rights have acquired a separate significance. In many cases, by adopting the appropriate legal technique, goods produced by a single organisation or associated enterprises can be prevented from moving from one territory to another; a barrier of private rights can be set up against imports or exports which is as effective as an embargo or tariff imposed by a state.[61] The procedure is often more effective than limitations on movement imposed only by contract.

Accordingly a middleman (known in Community jargon as a "parallel importer") cannot buy A's goods in cheap State No. 1 and transport

---

[59] Good instances are the Report of the Economic Council of Canada, *Report on Intellectual and Industrial Property* (1971), Chap. 5 and Penrose, *The Economics of the International Patent System* (1951).

[60] Below, §§ 7-049—7-056.

[61] The customs authorities of a state may be used to arrest the importing of goods that infringe an intellectual property right: for the British position, see below, § 2-012.

them to expensive State No. 2 for resale at a profit. But A's ability to discriminate in his pricing between different territories is only one reason for restraining parallel importing. In countries other than his home territory it may be economically desirable, or sometimes legally necessary, to manufacture and sell through the medium of a local licensee; or at least to sell imported goods through a local distributor. Difficulties with the local language, local contacts or local labour relations may be overcome by such arrangements. It may, however, be hard to find a local licensee or distributor unless he can be assured of exclusive rights to market in his own territory; for he will have his own investment in promoting a foreign product to protect. An intermediate case is the transnational corporation which has reasons (often involving taxation and foreign exchange) for operating in different territories through national subsidiaries. Again, each may be given exclusive rights to restrain imports of products emanating from the others—in order to protect price differentials, or to monitor performance comparatively within the group.

(2) Exhaustion of rights

The manner in which intellectual property can be deployed to divide   1-022
markets has been dependent upon the particular form of a right, and so it derives ultimately from the national policies behind the creation of the right in the first place. Since this varies with the kind of right held, the question is one to which we must return at later points.[62] But one general concept can usefully be introduced here. In every intellectual property law it is necessary to decide which steps in the chain of production and distribution of goods require the licence of the right-owner: manufacture, first sale by the manufacturer, subsequent sales and other dealings, export and import, use. In the past, legislators have often left the answer to the courts. In many cases, both in British and in foreign laws, the rights are "exhausted" after first sale by the right-owner or with his consent. But mostly this is confined to first sales within the territory covered by the right—it amounts to a principle of domestic, rather than international, exhaustion. Accordingly, national rights that are subject to such limitation can still be used to prevent the importation of goods sold abroad by the national right-owner or goods which come from an associated enterprise.

In Britain, the relation between rights and distribution of goods has not in the past been dealt with by any general concept of exhaustion. The approach has varied with the subject-matter. In the case of patent law (in contrast with other major patent systems), the British traditionally adopted the contrary position to "exhaustion": in principle subsequent uses and sales continued to require the patentee's licence. This, as we shall see,[63] is an approach that is in process of being dismantled in all save exceptional cases. For this basic policies of the EEC are primarily responsible.

[62] The discussion of exhaustion is taken up at §§ 6-011—6-012, 7-040—7-048 (patents), §§ 12-028—12-032 (copyright) and §§ 18-001—18-012, (trade marks). see generally, Korah; Bellamy and Child; Oliver, *Free Movement of Goods in the EEC* (1982); Gormley, *Prohibiting Restrictions on Trade Within the EEC* (1985); Horner, *Parallel Import.*
[63] See below, §§ 6-011—6-012.

(3) The idea of a common market

1-023   A common market is the product of a political decision to promote trade competition without the interposition of legal or fiscal barriers. It is a normal consequence of political unification (the United Kingdom) or federation (the United States, Canada, Australia) and it may be established by independent states that are concerned with economic integration (the EEC). How far legal measures are introduced to help in achieving a common market have varied with time and place. But as far as intellectual property rights are concerned, it has been usual to work towards a unified law for the whole territory.

In the EEC, the absence of political union has made any movement towards unified or harmonised laws of patents, copyright and trade marks a complex business.[64] Yet in the past intellectual property rights have played a major role in preventing the movement of goods from one part of Common Market territory to another. In the eyes of Community authorities the need to put an end to this has correspondingly been urgent. Indeed this was initially seen as the prime reason for studying the unification of intellectual property laws. But action has not waited upon the outcome of these investigations. The EC Court of Justice and the EC Commission have interpreted provisions of the Treaty of Rome as limiting the scope of national intellectual property laws in certain circumstances where they give rise to a conflict with two policies expressed in the Treaty: the elimination of restrictions upon the free movement of goods between Member States, and the establishment of a system to prevent distortions of competition in inter-state trade.[65]

The provisions of the Treaty which give specific content to these objectives are Articles 30-36 (free movement of goods) and Articles 85-90 (competition). At this stage, these provisions can be introduced in general terms, while leaving their effect upon the different types of right to later chapters.

Both sets of provisions are directly enforceable, and so may generate rights and obligations in individuals, as well as in Member States, which may be enforced, or pleaded in defence, in litigation before national courts.[66] Accordingly, it should be noted that decisions on the content of EEC law may reach the ultimate court of reference, the EC Court of Justice, by way of appeal from the Commission—*e.g.* in respect of a violation of the rules of competition; or by way of Article 177 reference in the course of national litigation—as where the enforcement of an intellectual property right is allegedly in conflict with the free movement of goods policy or the rules of competition.

(4) Free movement of goods

1-024   Article 30 of the Treaty prohibits quantitative restrictions on imports "as between Member States," and all measures having equivalent effect.

---

[64] On this theme, see below, §§ 3-018—3-022, 9-016, 18-014—18-018.
[65] Other policies of the Treaty—notably the freedom to provide services and the right of establishment—contain some potential for conflict with intellectual property. See below, §§ 12-027—12-033.
[66] For the extent to which the provisions afford direct rights of action to individuals, see below, §§ A1-002—A1-004.

The EC Court of Justice has held that national industrial property rights may amount to "measures having equivalent effect" when they are directed to preventing acts of importation.[67] Accordingly such actions should not be allowed to succeed unless justified by Article 36. This permits prohibitions or restrictions on imports if they are justified on various grounds, including the protection of industrial and commercial property. But this exemption itself does not apply where the "prohibitions or restrictions . . . amount to a means of arbitrary discrimination [or] a disguised restriction of trade between Member States."[68]

As we shall see, there are a wide range of circumstances in which the Court of Justice has ruled that national intellectual property rights should not be used to restrain parallel imports so as to defeat the free movement of goods policy. Article 36 has not been allowed to stand in the way, any more than has Article 222 which provides that the Treaty is not to prejudice the rules in Member States pertaining to form or type of ownership. The court has characterised some assertions of these rights as going to their very existence (and therefore properly made), while other assertions have been labelled mere exercises of the right (and therefore not within the exemption of Article 36).[69] The distinction has been made to turn upon a "definition" of the specific subject-matter of the particular right.[70] But, as with the basic dichotomy between existence and exercise, these definitions have the appearance of being formulated only in the wake of a policy decision to give preference to EEC policies beyond a certain point. All of this may seem an exercise in legal obscurantism, but the basic intent is not hard to grasp: intellectual property rights are properly exercised when used against goods that come from independent competitors in trade; but they are not to be used against the movement from one Member State to another of goods initially connected with the right-owner.

Intellectual property is not the only form of legal embargo that can affect the free movement of goods. The Court of Justice has been equally strict in appraising other forms of legal barrier, some of which have related objectives. Thus regulations under the German Wine Act 1971, which allowed "Sekt" and "Weinbrand" to be used only on German sparkling wine and brandy, were held equivalent to a restriction on imports. In Germany at least, the words were not specific designations or indications of origin but simply general descriptions of types of goods, and as such not within any exemption provided by Article 36.[71] One

[67] But not when the right applies to some other action within the territory (e.g. hiring or selling), irrespective of whether the articles in question are of local manufacture or are imported from another member state.

[68] See the final sentence of Art. 36, see further Wyatt and Dashwood, *The Substantive Law of the EEC* (2nd ed., 1987); Chap. 7.

[69] The distinction was first applied in connection with the competition policy (from the *Consten/Grundig* case (below, § 18-006) onwards); but it was treated as equally relevant to free movement of goods (from the *Deutsche Grammophon* case (below, § 12-028 et seq. onwards).

[70] This refinement was first introduced, for trade marks, in the *Hag* and *Winthrop* cases (below, §§ 18-007—18-008), and for patents, in the *Sterling Drug* case (below, § 7-042).

[71] *Re German Sparkling Wines and Brandies* [1975] 1 C.M.L.R. 340. For *appellations d'origine*, etc., see below, Appendix 5. See also *Eggers v. Bremen* [1979] 1 C.M.L.R. 562; and generally, Wyatt and Dashwood (above, n. 68), Chap. 10.

permitted ground within that article is the protection of life and health. But still the measure must be a matter of imperative necessity.[72] A Dutch Decree which had the effect of restricting importation of a drug to the enterprise which secures its clearance from the Dutch health authorities was deemed in this respect unduly restrictive.[73]

The conjoint policy concerning the free provision of services, outlined in the Treaty of Rome by Articles 59-66, may also have an impact upon intellectual property rights, as for instance in the broadcasting or cable-casting of copyright material. This, however, occurs only occasionally. Article 59 has required the abolition of restrictions on the freedom to provide services within the Community "in respect of nationals of Member States who are established in a State . . . other than that of the person for whom the services are intended." The Articles do not explicitly refer to justifiable exceptions; there is no provision equivalent to Article 36. Nevertheless, the Court of Justice interprets these provisions as open to reasonable limitation.

(5) Rules of competition

1-025   The Rules of Competition in the Treaty that apply to private undertakings hang upon two conjoint pegs. Article 85 deals with restrictive practices between enterprises, Article 86 with abuse by one or more firms of their monopolistic position. A particular commercial practice could well be prohibited under both heads. Without these rules there would be little point in lowering customs and other barriers to trade imposed by states. They are vital machinery in insisting that resources should be allocated by market forces—forces that will cause efficient firms and sectors to expand at the expense of others.

Article 85(1) prohibits agreements between undertakings, decisions of associations of undertakings and concerted practices "which may affect trade between Member States and the object and effect of which is to prevent, restrict or distort competition within the Common Market."[74] An agreement which falls within this prohibition may nevertheless be exempted for a limited period where it can be economically justified: if it contributes towards improving the production or distribution of goods, or towards promoting technical or economic progress, whilst allowing consumers a fair share of the resulting benefit; provided also that it does not (a) impose on the undertakings concerned restrictions which are not indispensable to the achievement of these objectives, nor (b) afford them the possibility of eliminating competition in a substantial part of the products in question. The EC Commission, which is the body chiefly charged with the enforcement of the rules of competition, alone has power to grant such an exemption under Article 85(3).

---

[72] See esp. *Rewe* v. *Bundesmonopolverwaltung für Branntwein* [1979] E.C.R. 649 ("Cassis de Dijon").

[73] *Officier van Justitie* v. *De Peijper* [1976] 2 C.M.L.R. 271. For a similar decision that regulations were unduly restrictive of parallel imports, even though their object (protecting the genuineness of "Scotch" for whisky) was proper: *Procureur du Roi* v. *Dassonville* [1974] E.C.R. 837; [1974] 2 C.M.L.R. 436; *cf. EC Commission* v. *Belgium* [1979] E.C.R. 1761; *Commission* v. *Ireland* [1982] E.C.R. 4005 ("Buy Irish").

[74] A list of examples is then set out. Art. 85(2) declares such agreements and decisions to be "automatically void".

Article 86 prohibits any abuse by one or more undertakings of a dominant position within the Common Market (or a substantial part of it) in so far as it may affect trade between Member States.[75] There is here no explicit power to exempt a practice for its countervailing benefits, but this is implicit in the requirement that the deployment of dominant position be abusive.

To re-emphasise: some basic points about the enforcement of the competition rules are contained in Appendix 1. Their impact upon the exploitation of the various forms of intellectual property is taken up in later Parts.[76]

(6) Relation between the two policies

The policy of securing the free movement of goods between Member 1-026
States is an objective distinct from that sought by the rules of competition. Accordingly there are two basic differences in the scope of the relevant provisions of the Rome Treaty which call for mention at once:

(a) Trade between Member States

The provisions on the free movement of goods relate specifically to the import and export of goods between one Member State and another. They do not apply where the goods are being moved between a non-Member and a Member State. In *EMI* v. *CBS*,[77] the EC Court of Justice held that trade mark rights in any member state could be used to prevent the importation of goods from the United States without offending Article 30. But in the rules of competition, the requirement that there be an effect on trade between Member States need only be consequential. Thus if the reason why imports of CBS's records from America could be kept out of any EEC country by virtue of trade mark rights was that the various EEC marks had been put into EMI's hands in pursuance of an agreement, the object and effect of that agreement would have to be examined. If it brought about a significant distortion of competition in the Common Market by keeping out goods that otherwise would be sold somewhere within it, Article 85(1) would be offended.[78] It seems that in applying this Article it is not necessary to ask for proof that the goods would, if sold in part of the market, have been purchased for resale in another part; this may instead be assumed.[79]

---

[75] Again a list of examples is attached.
[76] See below, §§ 7-032—7-040, 18-011—18-012.
[77] [1976] E.C.R. 811; [1976] 2 C.M.L.R. 235; see Judgment § 8-12; also *Re Tylosin* [1977] 1 C.M.L.R. 460 (West German S.C.); Hay and Oldekop (1977) 25 Am.J.Comp.L. 120. Note that the association agreements between the EEC and six EFTA countries and Iceland contain provisions for the elimination of measures having equivalent effect to quantitative restrictions. These do not prevent the reliance on intellectual property rights in order to prevent the importation of goods into an EEC country from an EFTA country: *Polydor* v. *Harlequin Record Shops* [1982] E.C.R. 329.
[78] Judgment, §§ 25-39.
[79] *cf.* Judgment, §§ 28, 29 with the observations of Warner, Adv.-Gen. [1976] 2 C.M.L.R. at pp. 258-259; and, see generally, Bellamy and Child, *Common Market Law of Competition* (3rd ed., 1987), § 2-126, 2-129.

(b) *The economic counter-balance*

1-027   From another perspective, the free movement of goods policy, when it
does apply, may be more categorical. The competition rules of Articles
85 and 86 allow the economic impact of an apparently impermissible
practice to be viewed as a whole. If there are countervailing benefits, it
may nevertheless be permitted—under Article 85(3) by way of exemption, under Article 86 by finding the deployment of dominant position
not, after all, to be abusive. By contrast, the manner of reading Article 36
that was initially developed did not take account of economic justifications for using industrial property rights in ways that may result in
division of markets within the totality of the EEC. More recent decisions,
however, are beginning to bring a new measure of differentation to this
task, national laws of intellectual property and unfair competition being
examined to see whether their application affects imports from another
member state disadvantageously in comparison with domestic products,
thus showing the "arbitrary discrimination" referred to in Article 36,[80]
and to determine whether the exploitation is a normal means of realising
their economic potential.

[80] See below, § 7-046.

CHAPTER 2

THE ENFORCEMENT OF RIGHTS

This chapter deals with the forms of relief available to the owner of   2-001
intellectual property rights and with a variety of procedural factors
affecting their enforcement. Although there are variations between the
different specific fields, there is enough common ground to justify
treating these matters in one place: a good deal of repetition can be
dodged and various comparisons pointed up.

There is a more basic reason for prefacing the discussion of the
different rights with some consideration of how they are turned to
practical account. Most commercial law is facilitative in character. It
determines the effect of consensual dealings between individuals and
limits their freedom of contract only where some exception of public
policy is overriding. Accordingly, for much of the time, commercial law
provides a safety-net for the execution of contracts. When the net is
needed, it is frequently the contract which provides one party with a self-
help remedy. Intellectual property rights are, of course, the basis of many
contractual dealings. But their fundamental characteristic is their power
to constrain those who have no relationship with the right-owner. They
are rights that depend for their effectiveness, to a peculiar degree, upon
the speed and cheapness with which they can be enforced. This explains
why, so often in the modern law, it is cases in this field that test the
procedures and remedies provided by the courts.

These are matters typically within the province of the judges, who
receive only a modicum of direction from Parliament. Many of the issues
raised in particular cases have large implications. To give one plaintiff a
more effective method of proceeding is to give it to all who can claim to
be in comparable case. Amongst them must be reckoned those whose
claims are dubious or downright false—a particularly telling consideration where the rights are intangible and may depend on complex value
judgments. Accordingly there are delicate balances to be struck in most
of the issues that call for examination.

1. TYPES OF PROCEEDING

This section takes up some basic characteristics of the different methods   2-002
of protecting intellectual property. It treats in turn civil actions, criminal
proceedings, administrative procedures and measures of self-help. Of

these, civil actions are the most central and many additional aspects of them are dealt with elsewhere in the book. The other three categories have resonances only occasionally at later points.

(1) Civil causes of action

For the most part, the acts of infringement with which we are concerned are treated as tortious invasions of property.[1] Questions accordingly arise about which people have title to sue and whom they may proceed against. These are dealt with first. Then some consideration is given to the more general economic torts, particularly where they may help plaintiffs who otherwise have no sufficient basis for action.

(a) *Owners and licensees of intellectual property*

The obvious person to bring proceedings for infringement of one of the statutory types of intellectual property is the owner at law (or one of them). A person with a purely equitable title (under a trust or a specifically enforceable contract) is permitted to bring a motion for interlocutory relief, but he may not proceed further without joining the legal owner.[2]

Where the right is the subject of a grant by the state the fact that the proprietor is not registered as such may introduce complications. In the case of patents, the true owner is entitled to sue but risks failing to secure damages or an account of profits through not registering.[3] In the case of registered designs and registered marks, registration of an assignment of title is a pre-requisite.[4]

In the case of patents, copyright and unregistered design right, an exclusive licensee is entitled to bring the proceedings, joining the proprietor as a defendant if he will not be joined as plaintiff.[5] In the case of registered trade marks any registered user may require the registered proprietor to institute infringement proceedings and after two months' default he may do so himself.[6] In other cases, licensees cannot themselves sue for infringement of intellectual property,[7] but must rely upon their licensors to take action. This can be difficult and cumbersome, particularly for an organisation which exists to provide right-owners with collective protection.[8]

[1] Breach of confidence, however, requires special consideration: see Chap. 7.
[2] *PRS* v. *London Theatre of Varieties* [1924] A.C. 1; but note the modern rules on the assignment of future copyright: below, § 12-007.
[3] See below, § 7-017.
[4] RDA 1949, s.7(1); TMA 1938, s.4(1).
[5] PA 1977, s.67, CDPA 1988, s.101, 102, 234, 235 (but, oddly, not registered designs). The licence must exclude even the licensor and must exist when the writ is issued: *Proctor & Gamble* v. *Peaudouce* [1989] 1 F.S.R. 180 (C.A.). In the case of copyright and design right, it must comply with the formalities prescribed in ss.92, 225. Beyond this it is a matter of interpreting each licence to decide whether, and, if so in what respect, it is exclusive: *Morton-Norwich* v. *Intercen (No. 2)* [1981] F.S.R. 337. In each case there are provisions concerning the assessment of damages; in the case of copyright and design right these are elaborate.
[6] TMA 1938, s.28(3). For registered users generally, see below, §§ 7-058—7-059.
[7] They may, however, be able to sustain an action for the tort of unlawful interference with trade: *PCUK* v. *Diamond Shamrock* [1981] F.S.R. 427.
[8] See below, § 2-006.

A representative action may be pursued, for instance, against a defendant who has allegedly been selling pirated tapes of copyright sound recordings. The association of British record producers, British Phonographic Industries Ltd., could proceed in the name of one member, suing on behalf of itself and all other members. In the circumstances, the court would order not only an injunction but an inquiry as to damages suffered by all the members.[9]

(b) Defendants

The law relating to each form of intellectual property defines the nature of the exclusive right in terms of content and business activity. For instance, the invention that is the subject of a patent is defined principally in the claims of the patent specification; it is then infringement to make, sell or use this invention in the various ways prescribed in the Patents Act. A person who performs such an infringing act is liable in respect of it and anyone else who collaborates in a common design to do the act will be liable as a joint tortfeasor.[10] A director of a company will be personally liable for torts committed on his company's behalf where he has ordered or procured their commission.[11] 2-003

In addition an employer is vicariously liable for torts committed by an employee in the course of his employment.[12] But a person who commissions work from an independent contractor is not normally placed under the same responsibility.[13] The distinction is often important where the production of some species of intellectual property is concerned. Many authors, composers and artists, and some inventors, work in some degree of independence from those who take up their ideas for exploitation. In the field of copyright, as we shall see, the absence of vicarious liability in such cases is compensated for by other means: to "authorise" an act of infringement is there treated as itself amounting to infringement.[14]

It is not always easy to determine whether a person is employed, nor whether he is acting within the course of his employment. Employment may be a part-time, as well as a full-time, relationship. Traditionally the governing characteristic has been that the employer is entitled to control the work that is done in detail. But many types of work relationship are now treated as employment even though the employee exercises man- 2-004

---

[9] *EMI Records* v. *Riley* [1981] F.S.R. 503. Equally an action may be pursued against a represented class in which an *ex parte* interlocutory injunction and associated relief may be ordered: *EMI Records* v. *Kaidhail* [1985] F.S.R. 36.

[10] *Morton-Norwich* v. *Intercen* [1978] R.P.C. 152; *Ravenscroft* v. *Herbert* [1980] R.P.C. 193 (copyright). *Crystal Glass* v. *Alwinco* [1986] R.P.C. 259 (C.A., N.Z.); *C.B.S. Songs Ltd.* v. *Amstrad* [1988] 2 W.L.R. 1191. For the significance of claims and for the definition of types of patent infringement, see below, §§ 4-028—4-039; 6-002 *et seq.*

[11] *Evans* v. *Spritebrand* [1985] F.S.R. 267 (C.A.). Where a particular state of mind is a requisite of the tort, the director must be shown to have had it.

[12] Vicarious liability of the employer in no way exempts the employee from his personal liability. There may be consequential questions of ultimate liability between employer and employee, for which see below, § 70; and generally, *Clerk and Lindsell on Torts* (16th ed., 1989) Chap. 3.

[13] For the exceptional cases (not of significance to intellectual property), see *Clerk and Lindsell*, Chap. 3, Pt's. 3 & 5.

[14] See below, §§ 11-016, 11-017; *cf.* "indirect" infringement of a patent, §§ 6-013, 6-014, and the general tort of incitement or procurement, below, § 2-007.

agerial or professional skills under no regular supervision. In those cases other indicators are relied upon. Typical attributes of employment today are: payment of regular sums as a wage or salary, rather than lump sums for given jobs; income tax deductions under Schedule E on the P.A.Y.E. basis; joint contribution to a pensions scheme; and joint national insurance contributions as for an employed person.[15] Much is accordingly determined by the relationship that the two sides set out to establish. Tribunals have to settle the issue where the practical arrangements still leave ambiguities. A composer who is obliged to supply a music publisher with one song a month will be an independent contractor if his return is to come solely from royalties and none of the other attributes of employment are present. But the contrary will likely be the case if he receives a monthly salary subject to P.A.Y.E. and national insurance deductions, even though he is entitled to copyright royalties in addition.

What an employee does in the course of his employment is determined by what he is employed to do. The employer may not restrict the scope of vicarious responsibility by instructing the employee not to commit torts in the course of those duties.[16] If a broadcasting organisation employs a commentator who makes a defamatory statement, the organisation remains liable however firm its rule against defamation. But, as we shall see, not everything that a journalist or business executive writes is done in his employment.[17] There must be sufficient connection between his job and what he has written.

(c) General torts covering economic loss

2-005   The common law developed a number of heads of liability which are usually grouped together as economic torts. Two of these—passing off and injurious falsehood—are directly germane to our subject and are dealt with in Part V.[18] Here, however, mention must be made of torts which may effectively broaden the range of people who can be held responsible when someone interferes with intellectual property or proposes to do so. In particular, the torts have some capacity to go beyond the rules on plaintiffs and defendants which have just been discussed. Their general characteristics are that the defendant must be acting intentionally or recklessly; that the plaintiff must suffer (or be about to suffer) damage; and that they will not apply if some ground of justification is open to the defendant.[19]

2-006   (i) **Conspiracy.** It is tortious for two or more people to agree to secure the commission of an infringement of intellectual property, as of other

---

[15] On the question generally, see *Clerk and Lindsell*, Chap. 3 Pt. 1; Hepple and O'Higgins, *Encyclopedia of Labour Relations Law* I, §§ 1-041 — 1-053.
[16] See generally, *Clerk and Lindsell*.
[17] See below, § 12-003. The same question arises in deciding whether intellectual property belongs to an employee or his employer.
[18] Below, Chap. 16.
[19] No attempt can be made to present a systematic analysis of the torts that are mentioned. Good descriptions can be found, *e.g.* in Heydon, *Economic Torts* (2nd ed., 1978); *Clerk and Lindsell*, Chap. 11.

unlawful acts.[20] This may occur equally if one or more of the conspirators is to perform the infringing act or if a third party is to be induced to do so.[21]

(ii) **Inducing or procuring breach of contract.** This could occur, for instance, if a licensee of intellectual property were persuaded to depart from the limits of his licence and so to infringe. In particular it is a form of liability that may affect indirect recipients of confidential information.[22]

(iii) **Wrongfully interfering with business relations.** This tort, now established as a separate head,[23] has grown up as an adjunct of inducing breach of contract. It covers, for instance, cases where a contracting party is persuaded to do something contrary to another party's expectations which is nevertheless not a breach of the contract.[24] It can also apply outside contractual relationships to circumstances, for example, where a defendant's misrepresentation induces a third party to act in a way which harms the plaintiff's business relations. It is necessary to show that one intention of the defendant's action (even if it is not the predominant motive) is to injure the plaintiff; and that there is a sufficient causal link between action and injury. It does not have to be shown that an inducement or other act towards a third party constitutes a complete tort against that party.[24a]

Thus, before the recent introduction of performance rights, the Court of Appeal applied it in two cases concerned with musical recordings.[25] In *Carlin* v. *Collins*,[26] the defendant was infringing the copyright in music by importing records of it; but the court allowed a collecting society, Mechanical Copyright Protection Society, which did not own the copyright, to sue on the basis of a purely contractual interest: its members, who were the copyright owners, had undertaken to pay the society commission on the royalties that it collected. Here the "interference" tort extended the range of plaintiffs in a manner that was clearly convenient to the owners and their society.[27] In *Island Records* v. *Corkindale*,[28] the defendant's records were of performances in which no

---

[20] For what may constitute "unlawful means," see Heydon (above, n. 19), 67-68. There is authority that abuse of confidence is one form: *Spermolin* v. *Winter, The Guardian*, June 22, 1962. The other form of the conspiracy tort—a combination to inflict damage on a person without using unlawful means but without any legitimate interest in doing so—is not specially relevant to intellectual property: but note *Jarman & Platt* v. *Barget* [1977] F.S.R. 260 at 277-282 (C.A.).

[21] For the application of this tort where the wrong is infringement of a patent, see below, § 6-013.   [22] For its relevance in that field, see below, § 8-006.

[23] See, *e.g. Acrow* v. *Rex Chainbelt* [1971] 1 W.L.R. 1676 (C.A.) *Merkur Island Shipping* v. *Laughton* [1983] 2 All E.R. 189 and the cases in nn. 24, 24a, 26 and 28, below.

[24] See *National Phonograph* v. *Edison-Bell* [1908] 1 Ch. 335 (C.A.) (undermining resale price maintenance arrangements for records); *Torquay Hotel* v. *Cousins* [1969] 2 Ch. 106 (C.A.).   [24a] *Lonrho* v. *Fayed* (to be reported, C.A.).

[25] Both were concerned with *ex parte* applications for *Anton Piller* orders: for this potent weapon, see below, §§ 2-030—2-033. For performance rights see below §§ 13-033—13-036.   [26] [1979] F.S.R. 548; Dworkin (1980) 2 E.I.P.R. 28.

[27] There is of course no difficulty if the owners are prepared to assign the relevant part of their copyright to the collecting society. But M.C.P.S. members were not prepared to do this.

[28] [1978] F.S.R. 505; [1978] 3 All E.R. 824.

copyright was claimed at all; the performers were then protected only by criminal offences against unauthorised reproduction.[29] Yet the "interference" tort was held to provide a civil cause of action. To the consequences of this we return when considering the relations of criminal and civil liability below.[30] If the House of Lords does eventually accept that interference with business relations by unlawful means is a notion of general import, the judges will have adopted with a conceptual tool of considerable potential.

2-007   (iv) **Inciting or procuring commission of a tort.** While there has been recent recognition that such a basis for liability exists, it appears that it is not a conception appreciably wider than that of joint tortfeasance.[31] It is necessary to show more than that the defendant facilitated the doing of an act. He must, generally speaking, induce, incite or persuade an individual infringer and must indentifiably procure a particular infringement.[32]

In the *Amstrad* case, a company was manufacturing and selling a twin-deck tape-recorder, knowing the likelihood of its use for home-taping which would infringe copyright. The company was nonetheless not a procurer of any infringement,[33] any more than that it was a joint tortfeasor, or a person who incited the commission of crime.[34]

We shall see that in the law of copyright there is a statutory proscription against "authorising" and "permitting" types of infringement[35]; and in the Patents Act 1977 there is now a rather elaborately defined notion of "indirect" infringement.[36] In their particular fields, these act as extensions of the strictly limited common law conception.

(v) **Intimidation.** A person is liable for threatening to commit an unlawful act, if it induces another to do something that causes the plaintiff damage. The early instance of *Tarleton* v. *McGawley*[37] showed the relevance of this tort to competition between traders: one shipper of goods induced an African people to deal with him rather than a rival by firing warning shots. He was held liable in damages to the other. It is not settled what other threats of unlawful conduct are actionable, but they include threats to commit torts, crimes and, in some circumstances, breaches of contract.[38]

(vi) **Duties of care.** In addition to the recent discussion of intentional economic torts in the sphere of our subject, there have also been attempts to argue that failure to prevent others from infringing intellectual

---

[29] Under the Performers' Protection Act 1958-1972. For the new legal position, see below, §§ 13-034—13-036.

[30] Below, §§ 2-040, 2-041.   [31] For which, see above, § 2-003.

[32] *Lavender BV* v. *Witten Industrial Diamonds* [1979] F.S.R. 59 at 00, *per* Buckley L.J.; *Dow Chemical* v. *Spence Bryson* [1982] F.S.R. 397 (C.A.); *Kalman* v. *P.C.L. Packaging* [1982] F.S.R. 406; *Cadbury* v. *Ulmer* [1988] F.S.R. 385.

[33] *CBS Songs* v. *Amstrad* [1988] 2 All E.R. 484 at 496-497.

[34] *Ibid.* at 497.

[35] Below, § 11-016—11-017. In the *Amstrad* case (above, n. 33), the selling of the tape-recorders did not amount to "authorising" infringement.

[36] Below, § 6-013, 6-014; but there was already some authority concerning the common law tort in the patents field: *ibid.*

[37] (1794) Peake 270.   [38] Heydon (above, n. 19), 66-67.

property amounts to the tort of negligence. Such well-known decisions as Dorset Yacht v. *Home Office,*[39] *Anns* v. *Merton LBC*[40] and *Junior Books* v. *Veitchi*[41] accept that there are circumstances in which one person owes a duty of care to prevent the deliberate conduct of another, if it may injure the plaintiff (physically or even economically); and that this duty arises once the injurious effect on the plaintiff can reasonably be foreseen, unless there is an overriding reason for not imposing it. But so far the duties of care which have been asserted in an attempt to impose liability beyond the scope of intellectual property infringement and the economic torts already discussed have not succeeded. A printer who produced labels for a skin cream to the order of a customer without knowing or inquiring about the latter's proposed use of them, would be liable for any infringement of copyright; but he did not have an additional duty to discover whether the customer would engage in passing off skin cream as the plaintiff's.[42] Likewise, in the twin-deck cassette recorder case, Amstrad owed no duty to ensure that those who purchased its tape-recorders did not make infringing copies on them. Those who merely facilitate infringement by others, without controlling what they do or positively encouraging it, are not to be brought within the bounds of legal responsibility by this route.[43]

(2) Criminal proceedings

It is a distinctive characteristic of the English judicial system that civil and criminal modes of redress are largely kept separate.[44] In our field of interest, most claimants make use of the civil process, partly because its technique and atmosphere are appropriate to the assertion of private property rights amongst businessmen, and partly because the types of remedy—in particular the injunction (interlocutory and permanent) and damages—are more useful than punishment in the name of the state.

2-008

But for the very power that civil remedies generate has been one reason for circumspection in conferring civil rights. Accordingly there are some activities on the periphery of our sphere where the relevant statutes only specify criminal sanctions. This has been true, until very recently, of a performer's ability to object to unauthorised recording, filming or broadcasting of his performance (under the Performers' Protection Acts)[45]; and it remains true of various forms of misdescriptive advertising and labelling that may be injurious to competitors as well as consumers (and constitute offences under the Trade Descriptions Act 1968 and allied

[39] [1970] A.C. 1004 (H.L.).   [40] [1978] A.C. 728 (H.L.).
[41] [1983] 1 A.C. 520 (H.L.).
[42] *Paterson Zochonis* v. *Merfaken Packaging* [1983] F.S.R. 273 (C.A.).
[43] *Amstrad* case (above, n. 33) at 497-98; see also *Western Front* v. *Vestron* [1987] F.S.R. 66.
[44] If anything this tendency became more marked from the late nineteenth century onwards. There is now some movement back. Under the Powers of Criminal Courts Act 1973, ss.35-38, a court, on convicting an offender, may order him to pay compensation in respect of personal injury and other loss or damage. Magistrates' courts may order up to £1,000 compensation; and a Crown Court has the alternative of making a criminal bankruptcy order (ss.39-41). Compensation orders have been made with some regularity in favour of consumers misled by false trade descriptions. In *R.* v. *Thomson Holidays* [1974] Q.B. 592, it was held that a series of orders could be made in favour of different customers misled by the same travel brochure.
[45] See now below, §§ 13-033 *et seq.*

legislation).[45a] In this connection it is worth noting the competence of any citizen (in England and Wales, and Northern Ireland) to institute criminal proceedings.[46] Under the Trade Descriptions Act this means that a competitor who objects to a misdescription on a rival's product may institute a prosecution, just as may a consumer, a police officer or a trading standards inspector.

There are some criminal offences that cover the same ground as rights of intellectual property. In these cases the right-owner usually prefers the civil route—for the reasons already mentioned, and because of two further factors:

(i) There is no possibility in criminal procedure of securing an interim order to desist from conduct pending the trial (which will take weeks or months to mount); nor are there pre-trial procedures, such as discovery, for the extraction of information from a defendant.

(ii) There is a high burden of proof on the prosecution in criminal proceedings: the defendant must be shown to be guilty beyond reasonable doubt, and not merely (as for most civil issues) on a balance of probabilities. This quantum of proof may be specially hard to demonstrate if the type of offence requires proof of *mens rea* in the defendant, *e.g.* that he knew, or had reason to believe, that he was committing an infringing act or other offence.

(a) *Offences specifically concerning intellectual property*

2-009   These are most prominent in the copyright field, where, as we shall see, there is a long history of conferring special remedies against pirates.[47] The Copyright, Designs and Patents Act 1988, creates a series of summary offences concerning infringements of copyright. These cover the same sphere as "secondary infringement"of copyright, and in the case of the more serious instances may now be prosecuted either summarily or on indictment.[48]

While they do not cover everything that is actionable as infringement in civil proceedings its ambit is much wider than anything applicable to patents, registered trade marks or registered designs. Since they are all forms of protection which depend upon official grant or registration, there are specific offences relating to this. It is in each case an offence to secure false entries in the register[49] and to make an unauthorised claim to the rights.[50] But no criminal liability attaches specifically to the activity of an infringer, as is equally the case with the new unregistered design right.

[45a] Discussed below, § 16-003.
[46] But some crimes are exceptional in requiring the consent of the Attorney-General or Director of Public Prosecutions. For an example, see below, n. 59.
[47] Below, § 9-003.
[48] Below, § 11-022.
[49] See PA 1977, s.109; TMA 1938, s.59; RDA 1949, s.34.
[50] See PA 1977, s.110 (s.111 covers false claims to have applied for a patent); TMA 1938, s.60; RDA 1949, s.35. There are also offences connected with secrecy directions in PA 1977, ss.22(9), 23(3); RDA 1949, s.34.

(b) *Conspiracy to defraud*[51]

To some extent the lacuna just noted may be filled by the general   2-010
crime of conspiracy to defraud.[52] This may be committed not only where
those agreeing together are proposing to acquire property dishonestly but
also when they seek to obtain some other pecuniary advantage or try to
deceive a person into acting contrary to his duty. Thus in *Scott* v.
Metropolitan Police Commissioner[53] there was a conspiracy to defraud
the owners of film copyright by bribing cinema employees to hand over
films so that they could be surreptitiously copied and returned. The
House of Lords confirmed that the owners were defrauded by this
practice even though no one was deceived by the operation.[54] The
decision does not depend upon the fact that the actual copying was itself
a summary offence,[55] and so it might apply if the subject-matter were
some form of intellectual property other than copyright.

There is some doubt where the subject-matter is confidential information.[56] In *DPP* v. *Withers*[57] the accused conspirators induced bank officers
to provide information about their customers by pretending to be acting
for another bank; they then supplied the information to their own clients.
This may be chargeable as a conspiracy to defraud, either if the
information is itself treated as close enough to property to be in the line
of *Scott's* case; or because persons are being actively deceived into
breaking a duty. But it is not clear whether the latter approach extends
beyond deceiving public officers and covers deceiving those acting for
private institutions such as banks.[58]

(c) *Crimes and civil relief*

The mere fact that a person is the victim of a crime does not entitle   2-011
him to civil relief such as damages or an injunction. He must show that
he has a distinct cause of action.[59] In our fields of interest the courts have
been reluctant to follow one route that would result in the imposition of
civil liability. It is difficult to persuade them that by imposing criminal
liability Parliament intended that an offender should owe a civil duty to a
person injured[60] Until recently this posed problems in the protection of

---

[51] See generally, *e.g.* Williams, *Textbook of Criminal Law* (2nd ed., 1983), Chaps. 13, 28.
[52] For the preservation of this common law form of conspiracy (*pro tem.*), see Criminal
Law Act 1977, s.5.
[53] [1975] A.C. 819; see further Cornish (1975) 6 I.I.C. 43 at 57.
[54] Relying upon a line of authority, especially *Welham* v. *DPP* [1961] A.C. 103 at 123-124.
[55] Conspiracy to commit this offence was also charged: it would now rank as a statutory
form of conspiracy: Criminal Law Act 1977, s.1(1), and could only be charged with the
consent of the DPP: see s.4(1).
[56] See also below, § 8-032.
[57] [1975] A.C. 842 (H.L.). The Prosecution failed because the accused were charged with
conspiracy to effect a public mischief, an offence held to be unknown to the criminal law.
[58] In *Scott* (above, n. 57) Lord Diplock thought that, if there was no element of economic
loss, a public officer must be deceived; but other members of the House were more
equivocal.
[59] See, in relation to injunctions, *Emperor of Austria* v. *Day* (1861) 3 De G.F. & J. 217;
Springhead Spinning v. *Riley* (1868) L.R. 6 Eq. 551; *CBS Songs* v. *Amstrad (No. 2)*
[1987] R.P.C. 429 (C.A.).
[60] The cases in which a court will imply civil duties from criminal law proscriptions are
concerned with personal safety in employment and elsewhere: see, *e.g. Cutler* v.
Wandsworth Stadium [1949] A.C. 398.

performers against illicit recordings of their concerts.[61] In our field, it remains the case that the Trade Descriptions Act 1968, while imposing a series of criminal penalties on those who mis-advertise and mis-describe goods and services, does not of itself impose statutory duties for which either a consumer or a competitor could sue by civil action.[62] However, Lord Diplock has encouraged the judges to look to the range of the criminal law in determining the scope of equivalent civil redress—in this instance, the extent of the tort of passing off.[63]

A further possibility should be noted. If the criminal offence is imposed in order to confer a "public right," the Attorney-General may secure an injunction to restrain its commission. He has an unfettered discretion over intervening, which the judges will not review; it makes no difference whether the Attorney-General considers the case upon his own motion or at the relation of some person interested.[64] He has refused to intervene in order to protect the interests of particular performers under the Performers' Protection Acts.[65] But under the Trade Descriptions Act, where there is a threat to the interests of consumers in general, the chances of obtaining his co-operation could be greater even where the relator is an interested competitor.

(3) Administrative procedures

(a) Customs prohibition

2-012   Both the Copyright, Designs and Patents Act 1988, ss.111 and 112, and the Trade Marks Act 1938, s.64A, provide a special procedure for arresting imports at their point of entry into the United Kingdom. The right-owner may notify the Commissioners of Customs and Excise[66] of his right and request that they treat certain imports as prohibited.[67] The imports in question, in the case of copyright, must be infringing copies of literary, dramatic or musical copyright work (in print), or of copyright sound recordings or films. In the case of trade-marked goods, it must be a potential infringement to use the mark in United Kingdom trade in relation to them.[68] The Commissioners will then exclude such goods as

---

[61] Now resolved by conferring explicit civil rights on performers and those who have exclusive contracts with them: CDPA 1988, Part II; below, § 13-027—13-030. Before this, the increased "bootlegging" of performances led to a contorted line of cases. These eventually conceded that the criminal provisions of the Performers Protection Acts 1958-72 created a civil right of action in performers (*Rickless v. United Artists* [1987] F.S.R. 362 (C.A.)) though not in recording companies (*RCA v. Pollard* [1983] F.S.R. 9 (C.A.)).

[62] *Bulmer v. Bollinger* [1978] R.P.C. 79 (C.A.).   [63] Below, § 16-003.

[64] See especially *Gouriet v. Union of Post Office Workers* [1978] A.C. 435; Feldman (1979) 35 M.L.R. 369. For repeated breaches of the criminal law an injunction may be granted: *Att.-Gen. v. Harris* [1961] Q.B. 74 (C.A.).

[65] See *Island Records v. Corkindale* (above, n. 28).

[66] In due form, for which see Copyright (Customs) Regulations 1982; Trade Mark (Customs) Regulations 1970.

[67] As regards sound recording and film copyright and trade-marked goods, the notice has to specify where and when the improper consignment is expected to arrive: CDPA 1988, s.111(3)(*b*), *cf.* s.111(1); TMA 1938, S.64A(1)(b).

[68] TMA 1938, s.64A(1)(*c*). This may give rise to difficult questions where the goods are "parallel imports": for which, see below, §§ 18-002 *et seq. cf. Textiles House v. Carmody* [1976] 9 A.L.R. 58; *Pioneer v. Reg. of T.M.* (1978) 52 A.L.J.R. 79 (both H.C. Australia).

they can identify. But the right-owner must indemnify them against any liability and expense.[69] It seems that the system is little used.[70] However, so far as goods bearing a counterfeit trade mark are concerned, their powers have been somewhat fortified by an EEC Regulation covering similar ground.[71]

The same system is not open to the owners of other intellectual property rights. But an action may be brought against the Commissioners for discovery of the names of (say) patent infringers, where customs records reveal that infringing imports have been taking place.[72]

(b) *Trading standards authorities*

The measures of consumer protection that have been developed under the modern law are now enforced principally by the trading standards departments of local authorities. In particular a positive duty to act was placed upon these authorities by the Trade Descriptions Act 1968. To this end they are armed with powers to make test purchases and to seize goods and documents for the purposes of the Act.[73] The extent to which the criminal offences contained in that Act may protect competitors against unfair practices has already been noted. The executive powers of the local authorities may sometimes provide a lever in the process of securing evidence or in informally putting a stop to some relatively minor injury.   2-013

(c) *Independent Broadcasting Authority*

The content of television and radio advertising on the commercial channels and stations is supervised by the I.B.A. It administers a detailed code on a great variety of matters, including such points of concern to competitors as comparative advertising.

(d) *Advertising Standards Authority*

Outside the field of broadcasting, the advertising industry has averted the creation of a public body to supervise it by setting up a voluntary organ of its own. To this Authority (half of whose members are drawn from outside the industry) complaints about the content of advertising may be made and these are judged against the British Code of Advertising Practice, which is drawn up by the industry. The proponents of the system claim for it the advantages of co-operation and quick action that are certainly possible within an organisation of this kind. But there have been criticisms of the effectiveness of the A.S.A., to which we shall come later.[74] The system is mentioned here in order to point the contrast with the public institutions that work in cognate fields.

(4) Self-help

Those entitled to possession of chattels have a right of recaption which entitles them to take the things, using no more force than is reasonably   2-014

---

[69] CDPA 1988, s.112(2), TMA 1938, s.64A(4); security may be required in advance.
[70] See the Whitford Report, Cmnd. 6732, § 721; Noackles (1979) 1 E.I.P.R. 103.
[71] Regulation 3842/86, in effect from January 1, 1988. See Billings [1988] E.I.P.R. 346.
[72] See below, § 2-034.
[73] s.26(1); see generally, Cornish (1974) 5 I.I.C. 82-84. The role of the Office of Fair Trading in this field is also discussed there: *ibid.* 84-85.
[74] See below, § 18-019.

necessary.[75] The rights in intangible property which we are discussing give rise to no equivalent remedy by self-help, with one new exception. The Copyright Designs and Patents Act 1988 creates such a power, subject to specified conditions, which is exercisable against the lowest rung in the piratical heirarchy, but only in relation to copyright.[76] The right-owner, or anyone whom he authorises, may seize and detain infringing copies that are "exposed or otherwise immediately available for sale or hire," provided,first, that a local police station is duly notified and, secondly, that the seizure is in a public place, or is on public premises from a person who does not have a permanent or regular place of business there.[77] Notice of what has been seized has to be given in prescribed form.[78] No force may be used,[79] so, if the police will not accompany, the remedy is probably only good against the feeblest suitcase-salesman. The seller will mostly be committing a relatively minor offence, which is non-arrestable. But a police officer present might be able to use his discretionary power to arrest, on the ground, for instance, that he cannot ascertain the name, or the true name, of the offender.[80]

2. REMEDIES IN CIVIL ACTIONS

2-015   The precise value of a right must be measured in terms of the remedies that lie for its enforcement. The range of relief provided by civil courts for the protection of property is wide and that is one of the most significant consequences of characterising patents, copyright, trade marks and the like as property. The subject must be approached with a weather eye upon history. Before the mid-nineteenth century reforms that culminated in the Judicature Acts, the award of damages (assessed by a jury) was the remedy of the courts of common law. Remedies such as the injunction, which laid constraints upon a defendant beyond the mere payment of money, were developed by the Chancellor in equity. In addition, some causes of action arose at common law, others in equity. Each attracted the remedies available in its own court. Furthermore, while purely equitable actions could not lead to an award of common law damages, equity might supplement the relief in a common law action by granting an equitable remedy. But frequently Chancery judges would require first that the opinion of a common law court be taken on the substance of the matter.[81]

2-016   In the 1850s, statutes began the process of making the remedies of each jurisdiction available more readily in the other. In particular: courts of common law could award equitable forms of relief including injunctions[82]; courts of equity were to grant injunctions for breach of common

[75] *Clerk & Lindsell on Torts* (16th ed., 1989), § 23-28.
[76] As originally introduced, the power was to have been much broader.
[77] CDPA 1988, s.100.
[78] s.100(4).
[79] s.100(3).
[80] See Police and Criminal Evidence Act 1984, ss.24, 25.
[81] Not that the Lord Chancellor necessarily considered himself bound by the jury's verdict.
[82] Patent Law Amendment Act 1852, s.42; Common Law Procedure Act 1854, s.79 *et seq.*

law rights without first requiring a common law trial[83]; and by Lord Cairns' Act 1858, damages might be awarded in a court of equity "in lieu of or in addition to" an injunction (and other equitable relief).[84] This cross-fertilisation laid a basis from which to achieve the coalescence in administering civil law that was brought about by the Judicature Acts.[85]

The main intellectual property rights, whether they arose out of statute or judicial decision, were early in their existence accepted as rights enforceable at common law. This meant that damages were available, though as the jury was gradually dropped from the trial of civil actions,[86] their assessment fell to the judge trying the action. But as the consequence primarily desired by most right-owners was the cessation of the competing wrong, an injunction was commonly sought, even in the days when it was necessary to pursue the case through two courts. Only the action for breach of confidence does not conform to this straightforward pattern. It grew as a comparatively recent manifestation of equity's power to put down impropriety by means of injunction, and its exact status is still in some measure opaque. To this special case we shall return later.[87]

(1) Injunction

An injunction looks to the future. It is an order of the court directing a party to litigation to do or refrain from doing an act.[88] Wilfully to disobey is contempt of court, punishable by fine, imprisonment or sequestration of assets.[89] The law of injunctions is beset with over-general propositions that require qualification in particular areas of application. In the intellectual property field an injunction is almost always prohibitory (as opposed to mandatory) since it enjoins the threatened commission[90] or continuance of wrongful acts. It can be granted after a trial establishing infringement of the plaintiff's right, when it is called "final" or "perpetual." But it may also be sought in "interlocutory" form, not to enforce an established right, but to maintain the status quo until a trial of the merits can take place. This latter type of injunction contributes a

2-017

---

[83] Chancery Procedure Act 1852, ss.61, 62; Chancery Regulation Act 1862, ss.1-3.

[84] The jurisdiction established by Lord Cairns' Act continues in force, though by a somewhat circuitous route: see *Halsbury's Laws of England* (4th ed.), Vol. 24, § 934, n. 3.

[85] But substantive rights were not in consequence expanded or altered in nature. Thus an attempt to argue that the Acts gave a house-owner a new right to an injunction to restrain his neighbour from calling his house by the same name was firmly rejected: *Day* v. *Brownrigg* (1878) 10 Ch.D. 294.

[86] Because of the length and difficulty of patent actions, the right of a party to a jury was restricted in 1883: see below, § 3-008.

[87] See below, Chap. 8.

[88] The order may restrain the defendant by its directors, employees or solicitors from doing the prohibited act: the latter, and any others who deliberately engage in the conduct, will be liable in contempt: *Seaward* v. *Paterson* [1897] 1 Ch. 545 (C.A.); *Marengo* v. *Daily Sketch* [1948] 1 All E.R. 406 (H.L.); *Att.-Gen.* v. *Newspaper Publishing* [1987] 3 All E.R. 276 (C.A.); *cf. Chelsea Man* v. *Chelsea Girl (No. 2)* [1988] F.S.R. 217.

[89] Sequestration is the form appropriate to contempt by a company. And see *Hospital for Sick Children* v. *Walt Disney* [1968] Ch. 52 (C.A.).

[90] An injunction may be granted *quia timet* against a proposed course of action that will infringe the plaintiff's rights, if there is a strong probability that the injury will be committed: see *Halsbury's Laws of England* (4th ed.), Vol. 24, § 932.

great deal to the practical efficacy of intellectual property rights and we shall discuss it first.

(a) *Interlocutory injunction*

2-018   An interlocutory injunction, ordering the defendant not to continue or not to embark upon a course of action until trial of the issue with the plaintiff, is a rapid and relatively cheap way of procuring temporary redress. Its effect against a business competitor may be to cut off for good the road to commercial success. Even without this, businessmen frequently treat the outcome of the interlocutory proceedings as settling the matter in dispute.

Whether such an injunction will be granted has always been a matter of discretion.[91] The motion to procure it must be proceeded with as soon as the plaintiff learns of the alleged infringement of his rights; even short periods of delay may debar interlocutory relief if there is no reasonable explanation.[92] An injunction will normally be granted to a plaintiff, other than the Crown,[93] only if he gives a cross-undertaking to make good any damage suffered by any defendant from the injunction, should the plaintiff fail at the trial.[94] The interim period will inevitably be a matter of months and, in a patent action, probably two years or more. The defendant's competitive losses over such a period may well be considerable. The cross-undertaking cannot be lightly given.

The injunction granted is typically in the form that the defendant be restrained from infringing the plaintiff's right as asserted, an injunction which will cover variations of what the defendant has been doing if they too would amount to infringement.[95-99] It is open to the defendant to obtain a declaration that his altered product is outside the injunction; and he will protect himself better if he chooses that course than if he puts the variation on the market without telling the plaintiff.[1]

Beyond this, the usual approach was, until 1975, first to consider whether the plaintiff has made out a prima facie case of infringement, taking account of the apparent merits of any defence that the defendant proposed to establish at the trial.[2] Each side normally supported its case with written evidence in affidavits.[3] If a prima facie case was estab-

---

[91] It is a discretion difficult to challenge on appeal: *Elan Digital* v. *Elan Computers* [1984] F.S.R. 374 at 384, 386.

[92] *cf.*, *e.g. Bourjois* v. *British Home Stores* (1951) 68 R.P.C. 280 (C.A.); *Versil* v. *Cork Asbestos* [1966] R.P.C. 76; *Quaker Oats* v. *Alltrades* [1981] F.S.R. 9 (C.A.).

[93] The cross-undertaking will not usually be required of the Crown where it seeks the injunction to enforce the law: *Hoffmann-La Roche* v. *Secretary for Trade* [1975] A.C. 295 (see below, § A1-012).

[94] See *Harman Pictures* v. *Osborne* [1967] 2 All E.R. 324 and *Halsbury's Laws of England* (4th ed.), Vol. 24, §§ 1072-1078. The cross-undertaking does not found an independent cause of action, but is a discretionary order: *Fletcher Sutcliff* v. *Burch* [1982] F.S.R. 64.

[95-99] This assumes that the right as alleged can be substantiated at the trial: *Spectravest* v. *Aperknit* [1988] F.S.R. 161; but note Scott J.'s doubt whether such an assumption can properly be made: *Staver* v. *Digitext Display* [1985] F.S.R. 512; *cf. Video Arts* v. *Paget Industries* [1988] F.S.R. 501.

[1] *Spectravest* v. *Aperknit* above, n. 1.

[2] For a latter instance, see *Hubbard* v. *Vosper* [1972] 2 Q.B. 84 (C.A.).

[3] Witnesses were summoned to give oral evidence only when it appeared crucial to test their credibility at this preliminary stage.

lished, the court then considered whether the balance of convenience lay in favour of restraining the defendant until the trial or in leaving the plaintiff to recover damages at the trial for any infringements by the defendant in the intervening period.

In *American Cyanamid* v. *Ethicon*,[4] the House of Lords modified this 2-019 approach. It did so in patent litigation, insisting however that the new principles were in no way special to this field. According to Lord Diplock, the correct approach is as follows: The court must first be satisfied that there is a "serious question to be tried."[5] Thereafter, it should not try to assess relative merit by looking for a prima facie case in the affidavit evidence; it should instead turn at once to the balance of convenience.[6] If it appears that damages awarded at the trial will adequately compensate the plaintiff, and that the defendant is likely to be able to pay them,[7] interlocutory relief should not normally be granted. If damages will not be adequate to compensate the plaintiff, it becomes necessary to consider whether, on the other hand, the defendant would be adequately compensated by damages upon the plaintiff's cross-undertaking, should the plaintiff not make good his claim at trial; if damages would be adequate, the injunction will be granted. Where there is doubt about the adequacy of damages to one or both,[8] any factor which may affect the balance of convenience is brought into account—in particular, whether the defendant has yet started on his allegedly infringing course of action[9] (it being "a counsel of prudence . . . to preserve the status quo"). If the balance remains substantially even, some account can ultimately be taken of the relative strength of each party's case as revealed by the affidavit evidence. "This, however, should be done only where it is apparent upon the facts disclosed by evidence as to which there is no credible dispute that the strength of one party's case is disproportionate to that of the other party."[10]

How substantial a reorientation is effected by this directive is open to 2-020 question.[11] Because a court is no longer to consider whether, if the case

---

[4] [1975] A.C. 396; [1975] R.P.C. 513.
[5] *i.e.* that the claim was not "frivolous or vexatious" or "disclosed no real prospect of succeeding in his claim for a permanent injunction at the trial." Lord Diplock uses all three phrases, apparently as synonyms, and subsequent courts have varied in their understanding of the standard which the plaintiff must satisfy: see Megarry V.-C. in *Mothercare* v. *Robson* [1979] F.S.R. 466 at 471-474, in whose own view the plaintiff must show more than "an honest but hopelessly optimistic case." (This, however, is what "frivolous or vexatious" means when an order to strike out of action is being sought under R.S.C. Ord. 18, r. 19(1)).
[6] A weakness of the judgment is that it did not deal with *Stratford* v. *Lindley* [1965] A.C. 269 in which the House of Lords adopted a "prima facie" case approach: see pp. 338 (Lord Upjohn), and 325, 331 and 342.
[7] See, *e.g.* *Belfast Ropeworks* v. *Pixdane* [1976] F.S.R. 337 (C.A.).
[8] *John Walker* v. *Rothmans* [1978] F.S.R. 357; *Combe* v. *Scholl* [1977] F.S.R. 464.
[9] See *Beecham Group* v. *Bristol* [1967] R.P.C. 406 at 416 (C.A.); *ibid.* [1968] R.P.C. 301 (H.C. Australia).
[10] [1975] R.P.C. at 542.
[11] Judges have varied in their readiness to follow the new approach religiously. Lord Denning M.R. and Pennycuick V.C. were early doubters: see *Fellowes* v. *Fisher* [1976] Q.B. 122; *Hubbard* v. *Pitt* [1975] 3 All E.R. 1 at 10 and see *Dunford* v. *Johnston* [1978] F.S.R. 143 at 150. The change was also rejected abroad: *Firth* v. *Polyglas* [1977] R.P.C. 213 (H.C. Australia); *Beecham Group* v. *BM Group* [1977] R.P.C. 220 (P.D.S. Africa).

went to trial on the affidavit evidence, the plaintiff would probably succeed, it can cut short any invitation to evaluate rival contentions presented in elaborate affidavits.[12] In this way, substantial trials-before-trials can be eliminated. But short of this, because so many cases that are fought at the interlocutory stage involve substantial uncertainties, it is difficult for the court to exclude all consideration of relative merits—the factor given such prominence in the former "prima facie case" approach. Thus some considerations that previously went to the prima facie case may be given weight in deciding whether there is a serious case to be tried[13]; and they may appear equally relevant to the adequacy or otherwise of damages. Consider, for instance, the question whether the defendant's trade mark or name is close enough to the plaintiffs to constitute passing off.[14] In other cases again, because the adequacy of damages remains in doubt, some judges have taken advantage of the statement that as a last resort they may balance the merits.[15]

2-021   The new formulation has given greater prominence to the balance of convenience, although no appreciable change has been needed in the manner of assessing it. Three factors in particular are of recurrent importance. First is the degree to which plaintiff and defendant are successfully established in business: for loss of market share during the interim period until trial may well be thought to have wide-ranging effects that cannot be easily quantified in damages. If the defendant has not yet set up in production, but the plaintiff is already on the market, the balance may well be in the latter's favour.[16] If both are marketing and the plaintiff is struggling to gain a foothold with a new product, again the special danger to him may lead to grant of the injunction. But the contrary may well apply if he is already well-established and the defendant is unlikely to offer major competition in the interim.[17] In such cases, it is generally easier to assess the loss to the plaintiff from actual sales by the defendant than loss to the defendant by being enjoined from competing.[18]

[12] The *Ethicon* case posed just this threat.

[13] Thus an important question of law was decided under this rubric in *Revlon* v. *Cripps & Lee* [1980] F.S.R. 85; see below, §§ 18-002—18-005. See also *Mothercare* v. *Penguin Books* [1988] R.P.C. 113; *Mail Newspapers* v. *Express Newspapers* [1987] F.S.R. 90.

[14] *Sirdar* v. *Mulliez* [1975] F.S.R. 309; *John Walker* v. *Rothmans* [1978] F.S.R. 357; *Morning Star* v. *Express* [1979] F.S.R. 113; *Newsweek* v. *BBC* [1979] R.P.C. 441.

[15] *Constable* v. *Clarkson* [1980] F.S.R. 123 (C.A.); *Quaker Oats* v. *Alltrades* [1981] F.S.R. 9 (C.A.) and *cf. Great American Success* v. *Kattaineh* [1976] F.S.R. 554. If, however, the result of the interlocutory proceedings is likely to dispose of the dispute, the court will consider the relative chances of success: see Lord Diplock, *NWL* v. *Woods* [1979] 3 All E.R. 614 at 625-626: applied in *Athletes Foot* v. *Cobra Sports* [1980] R.P.C. 343; *BBC* v. *Talbot* [1981] F.S.R. 228.

[16] *Belfast Ropework* v. *Pixdane* [1976] F.S.R. 337 (C.A.); but see below.

[17] *Catnic* v. *Stressline* [1976] F.S.R. 157 (C.A.). If the dispute is worldwide the damage to each must be considered in that context; if the plaintiff has been unable to secure interlocutory protection through his patents in other countries, this may militate against a grant in England: *Polaroid* v. *Eastman Kodak* [1977] F.S.R. 25 (C.A.). If the effect of an injunction would be to deprive the defendant of his usual means of earning, this weighs against grant: *Raindrop Data* v. *Systemics* [1988] F.S.R. 354.

[18] It is no argument that failure to grant the injunction effectively licenses invasion of the right: *Hunter* v. *Wellings* [1987] F.S.R. 83 (C.A.).

Secondly, if either party appears to lack the financial ability or backing to meet any ultimate liability in damages this may operate against him.[19] Thirdly, unnecessary delay on the plaintiff's part will weigh against him, at least if the defendant has materially altered his position in consequence.[20]

Beyond this, for all its alleged universality, the manner in which the *American Cyanamid* rule is applied needs to be separately considered in relation to particular intellectual property rights.[21]

(b) *Final injunction*

Even after the plaintiff has established his right at trial of the action, an injunction is said to be subject to two considerations: it lies in the discretion of the court; and it is available at the instance of a private litigant only if he has some proprietary right or interest to protect. As regards intellectual property the following can be said in amplification: 2-022

  (i) Against proven infringement of patent, design, copyright, trade mark and any other right that has acquired the status of "property" at common law, an injunction will be granted in the absence of something special in the case—such as imminent expiry of the right, no likelihood of repetition by the defendant, or some conduct on the plaintiff's part that leaves him with unclean hands, such as a representation that he would not seek an injunction.[22] In the general run of circumstances, to leave the plaintiff to a remedy in damages[23] would in effect be to compel him to license his right to all comers.

  (ii) To protect confidential information, injunctive relief is more evidently at the court's discretion. The relevant case law is discussed later.[24]

  (iii) A private party may not procure an injunction against violation of the criminal law unless he has a special interest in its enforcement greater than that of the ordinary citizen.[25] Even if he has this interest, the statute creating the offence must not have been drawn with the intention of restricting its enforcement to criminal law procedures.[26]

(2) Delivery up

In order to ensure that injunctions are properly effective, courts of equity and their successors maintain a discretion to order delivery up of infringing articles or documents for destruction, or else to require their destruction under oath by the defendant or some equivalent step such as   2-023

---

[19] *Standex* v. *Blades* [1976] F.S.R. 114 (C.A.).
[20] *Sirdar* v. *Mulliez* (above, n. 14); *Radley Gowns* v. *Spyrou* [1975] F.S.R. 455; *Great American Success* v. *Kattaineh* (above, n. 15); *cf. Belfast Ropework* case (above, n. 7).
[21] See below, §§ 6-020, 8-037.
[22] An intermediate possibility is for the court to give the plaintiff leave to apply for an injunction should it prove necessary in future.
[23] Whether by refusing an injunction under the general discretion or under Lord Cairns' Act.
[24] See below, § 8-039.
[25-26] See *Gouriet* v. *UPOW* (above, n. 68).

erasure of a trade mark.[27] In a breach of confidence case, however, the defendant was ordered to deliver up when he was not trusted to destroy under oath.[28] In the case of copyright and unregistered design right this jurisdiction is now governed by statute and extends both to infringing copies and to apparatus, etc., specifically designed to make infringing copies.[29] Here the courts discretion is wider than in general, for it may, in order to compensate the right-owner, forfeit the things to him rather than order destruction or other disposal.[30]

(3) Damages

(a) Bases for assessment

2-024   The normal aim of an award of damages is to compensate the plaintiff for the harm caused him by the legal injury.[31] In the case of breach of contract, damages generally seek to put the plaintiff in the position that he would have occupied had the contract been carried out; and so (subject to the exclusion of losses that are unforeseeably remote) he may recover profits that he anticipated making from the contract.[31] Damages in tort (again subject to exclusion of the unforeseeably remote)[32] aim to put the victim back to his position before the tort.[33] Generally, if a tortious action is also a breach of contract, the law allows the claim to be put on either basis; and occasionally the different assumptions for calculating damages may make this significant.

Contrary to the older view, exemplary damages may not be awarded to punish the plaintiff for wrongful conduct, however aggressively or insultingly deliberate. But there is an exception where the defendant's conduct has been calculated by him to make a profit for himself which may well exceed the compensation payable to him by the plaintiff; for "it is necessary for the law to show that it cannot be broken with

---

[27] See, e.g. Mergenthaler Linotype v. Intertype (1927) 43 R.P.C. 381; Slazenger v. Feltham (No. 2) (1889) 6 R.P.C. 531 at 538 (trade mark); Peter Pan v. Corsets Silhouette [1963] 3 All E.R. 402.

[28] Industrial Furnaces v. Reaves [1970] R.P.C. 605 at 627-628.

[29] CDPA 1988, ss.99, 230. There is in general a time limit on such an order of six years from making the article. In criminal proceedings for copyright infringement, similar orders may be made: s.108.

[30] ss. 114, 231. Industrial Furnaces v. Reaves [1970] R.P.C. 605 at 627-628.

[31] Not some other cause: see United Horse Shoe v. Stewart (1888) 5 R.P.C. 260 at 267. But is no excuse that the defendant might have injured the plaintiff as much by some non-infringing act: ibid.

[31] See, e.g. Chitty on Contracts, Vol. I, §§ 1551 et seq., McGregor on Damages (14th ed., 1980), §§ 24-47, 175-207.

[32] This concept is semble somewhat narrower in contract than in tort: Koufos v. Czarnikow [1969] 1 A.C. 350, at 422-423 (H.L.).

[33] See, e.g. Clerk and Lindsell on Torts (16th ed., 1989), Chap. 5, Pt. 3 and McGregor on Damages (14th ed., 1980), §§ 48-55, 100-174. The extent to which original profits would have been taxed is brought into consideration, but—in the other direction—not intervening inflation (save to the extent that interest is awarded).

impunity."[34] But it is still open to courts to award aggravated damages, adding compensation for injury to the plaintiff's feelings or reputation to a sum for the breach which otherwise may only be nominal.[35]

In arriving at the measure of damages in the various fields of **2-025** intellectual property, courts have to deal with recurrent circumstances. But the similarities are often of broad outline rather than of detail. Accordingly statements about the proper approach to assessment provide general guidelines, not strict rules. In particular the judges resist being saddled with any single test for all cases.[36] The fact that a particular assessment is difficult and must be rather rough-and-ready is not a reason for refusing to attempt it.[37]

There are many ways in which particular copyrights and patents may be exploited. A starting point in assessing damages is accordingly to ask whether the plaintiff and defendant are in actual competition.[38] Where this is so, the next question is whether the defendant might have had the plaintiff's licence if only he had sought it. Then the measure of damages will likely be what the plaintiff would have charged for a licence.[39] The award for infringements already perpetrated may well be based on a royalty for each infringement.[40] But the plaintiff is not normally under any compulsion to grant licences.[41] If he would not have done so, the court will look to his losses through the defendant's competition. It is only where the plaintiff's and defendant's anticipated profits are the same in the same market that the defendant's gain will be the plaintiff's loss. To take an obvious example: the plaintiff may be exploiting his copyright by selling small numbers of high-priced hardback books, and the defendant may infringe with large quantities of low-priced paperbacks. The issue is the loss to the plaintiff, and this may include not only the lost profits on hardback sales (taking account of any price reduction

---

[34] *Rookes* v. *Barnard* [1964] A.C. 1129 at 1220-1231, *per* Lord Devlin. The other recognised exception concerns the acts of government servants. See also *Cassell* v. *Broome* [1972] A.C. 1027 (H.L.); *Morton-Norwich* v. *Intercen (No. 2)* [1981] F.S.R. 337.

[35] Notice also the power in a copyright or unregistered design case to award additional damages: CDPA 1988, s.97(2), 229(3); below, § 11-044.

[36] *Meters* v. *Metropolitan Gas* (1911) 28 R.P.C. 157 at 161, 163 (C.A.); *Watson, Laidlaw* v. *Potts Cassels* (1914) 31 R.P.C. 104 at 117-118 (H.L.); *Interfirm Comparison* v. *Law Society* (1975) 6 A.L.R. 445 at 446-447 (S.C., N.S.W.).

[37] *Chaplin* v. *Hicks* [1911] 2 K.B. 786; *Watson, Laidlaw* case (above, n. 36) at 118; *General Television* v. *Talbot (No. 2)* unreported; see *Ricketson* (1980) 2 E.I.P.R. 149.

[38] Taking account of competition by the plaintiff's licensees, if any.

[39] *General Tire* v. *Firestone* [1976] R.P.C. 197 at 212 *et seq.* (H.L.).

[40] A plaintiff who has fought his case to judgment may not then be bound by the royalty rate that he gave before the validity of his right was established: it depends on whether the rate was a standard one or not: *General Tire* case (above, n. 39); and see *Caxton* v. *Sutherland* [1939] A.C. 178 at 203 (H.L.). If no injunction is to be granted for the future, damages may take the form of a capitalised royalty. See also *British Thompson-Houston* v. *Naamloose* (1923) 40 R.P.C. 119 at 127-128 (I.H.).

[41] As far as trade marks and the like are concerned, he may indeed jeopardise his own rights, if he grants a licence, unless certain conditions are complied with: see below, §§ 17-056 *et seq.* At the other extreme. *cf.* the possibility of compulsory licensing for patents and designs: below, §§ 7-049 *et seq.*

forced on him by the defendant's conduct),[42] but also the damage to his future prospects—his chance of putting out paperbacks, and possibly even the fact that infringement has enabled the defendant to build up a strong position in other competitive lines.[43]

2-026   When it comes to non-competitive infringements, the courts have held that a reasonable royalty for non-competing use will be awarded upon a principle "of price or of hire."[44] Otherwise the right might be invaded with impunity.[45]

A different question also goes to the nature of the "property." Suppose that the infringement (even if competing) is only one contributory factor in the profit that the defendant has made: a copyright work has been included in a larger compilation; an invention forms one part of more complex plant, or it is a machine or process that is used in making a non-patented article. In which of these cases, if any, is the plaintiff only entitled to some proportion of the whole amount otherwise arising under the principles just discussed? If the damages represent lost sales to the plaintiff[46] he is entitled to the whole lost profit.[47] But where this is not so a royalty may be the appropriate basis of calculation at a rate which takes into account the proportional contribution of the right infringed.[48]

(b) *Innocence*

2-027   Normally rights that rank as common law property are enforceable even against those who unwittingly interfere with them. But this aspect of the property analogy in our field has not always appealed to Parliament and the courts. They have not, it is true, refused injunctions against the continuance of an infringement simply on the ground that a defendant in all innocence expended money on a production system—a change of position that will bring him loss if he is then obliged to desist. But there has been some reluctance to oblige him to pay damages for infringements committed during a period of "innocence." Thus in the patents, designs Acts relating to patents, designs and copyright it is explicitly provided that no damages are payable for a period in which the infringer did not know, and had no reasonable grounds for supposing, that the right existed.[49] However a genuine belief that there was no infringement or

---

[42] See *Meters* case, above, n. 15 at 48; *Manus* v. *Fullwood* (1954) 71 R.P.C. 243; *cf. United Horse Shoe* v. *Stewart* (1888) 5 R.P.C. 260 at 269 (H.L.).

[43] *cf. Alexander* v. *Henry* (1895) 12 R.P.C. 360 (trade mark); *Khawam* v. *Chelaram* [1964] R.P.C. 337 at 342-343 (J.C.) (registered design).

[44] Lord Shaw, *Watson Laidlaw* case (above, n. 36) at 119-120; and see Fletcher Moulton L.J., *Meters* case (above, n. 36) at 163-165.

[45] ". . . what would have been the condition of the Plaintiff, if the Defendants had acted properly instead of acting improperly?" Page Wood V.-C., *Penn* v. *Jack* (1867) L.R. 5 Eq. 81 at 84.

[46] Because the plaintiff would have produced an end product competing with the defendant's.

[47] *United Horse Shoe* v. *Stewart* (1888) 13 App.Cas. 401, 3 R.P.C. 139 (patented machine saved expense in making nails).

[48] *cf. Meters* v. *Metropolitan* (above, n. 15).

[49] PA 1977, s.62(1), RDA 1949, s.9(1), CDPA 1988, s.97(1), 233 (also affecting "secondary infringement").

that the right had been properly licensed is not an excuse.[50] The requirement of reasonableness moreover means that a defendant who copies a new product ought to inquire whether it is patented,[51] and one who copies a literary work or the like should look for any indications that it is in copyright.[52] Where statute has not intervened there is less certainty. The view that an innocent defendant is not liable to pay substantial damages for passing off has considerable support,[53] but has been left open.[54] There is no exception of this kind for infringement of a registered trade mark—perhaps because any reasonable defendant would consult the register in advance.

We shall see that the uncertain status of confidential information—is it property, and if so is the property legal or equitable?—is bound up with the question whether any form of relief should be given against "innocent" defendants.[55] In this connection the comparison with the rules for the established form of intellectual property needs to be remembered; it has sometimes been ignored in the past.

(4) Account of profits

Equity never trespassed so directly upon the prerogatives of the common law courts as to award damages for common law wrongs. But, as a corollary of the injunction, it might order a defendant to account to a plaintiff for profits made from wrong-doing such as the infringement of an intellectual property right.[56] This is not a notional computation as with damages, but an investigation of actual accounts, which may incidentally afford the plaintiff a sight of customers' names and other information about the defendant. Nonetheless it is a laborious and expensive procedure and is infrequently resorted to. If the protected subject-matter is part of the article sold, or a mark used to sell it, the plaintiff is entitled to the whole profit on each infringement.[57] But if his wrong merely enables him to save expense in production he may only be entitled to the amount by which the saving increases the profit.[58]

2-028

---

[50] See, e.g. Byrne v. Statist [1914] 1 K.B. 622 (belief that someone other than plaintiff owned copyright did not excuse).
[51] Lancer Boss v. Henley Fork-Lift [1975] R.P.C. 307. But note the provision that (in the case of patents and registered designs) it is not enough to mark goods "patent," "registered," etc., without adding the number.
[52] Byrne v. Statist (above, n. 50).
[53] Draper v. Trist [1939] 3 All E.R. 513 (C.A.); Henderson v. Radio Corp. [1969] R.P.C. 218 at 229; but cf. 244.
[54] Marengo v. Daily Sketch (1948) 65 R.P.C. 242 at 247, 251, 252, 253 (H.L.).
[55] See below, §§ 8-030—8-031.
[56] This was treated as accepted by Lord Eldon, Hogg v. Kirby (1803) 8 Ves.Jun. 215 at 223.
[57] Peter Pan Mfg. v. Corsets Silhouette [1963] 3 All E.R. 402. In a trade mark case, the plaintiff is entitled to the profit on each item wrongly sold—he does not have to prove that the sale was to a deceived customer: Lever v. Goodwin (1887) 36 Ch.D. 1 (C.A.); if necessary the number may have to be reached by approximation: My Kinda Town v. Soll [1982] F.S.R. 147; House of Spring Gardens v. Point Blank [1985] F.S.R. 327 at 345.
[58] United Horse Shoe v. Stewart (above, n. 47) at 266-267. cf. the calculation of damages on the basis of actual sales lost, where the plaintiff can claim the whole of his own lost profit: see above, § 2-025.

In principle, the account will give a better recompense than damages when the defendant has been making profits that the plaintiff would not himself have made.[59] But if the case is an exceptional one, exemplary damages may achieve much the same result.[60] It used to be said that the plaintiff must elect either for damages or an account, upon the theory that by seeking an account the plaintiff adopted the defendant's acts as his own.[61] But this explanation is now dubious.[62] The better principle is merely that in respect to any one infringement the plaintiff should not be entitled to be both reimbursed and compensated.[63]

(5) "Franking"

Intellectual property rights relate to a series of stages in the commercial life of products—their creation and preparation for sale, their distribution down the chain to ultimate users; and in some cases also to their use, their resale second-hand, etc. The question accordingly arises whether monetary payments for infringement, paid on goods in respect of an early step in the chain, "franks" them as legitimate thereafter. It has been held, both in relation to damages and an account of profits for patent infringement, that no such legal effect is brought about. Actions may be maintained in relation to later wrongful acts.[64] Where there has been a settlement, any payment will not be understood to "frank" infringement unless this is an agreed term.[65]

3. SECURING EVIDENCE OF INFRINGEMENT

2-029   Intellectual property litigation is mostly governed by the general principles of civil procedure[66] and no attempt can here be made to review the whole gamut of relevant rules.[67] But given the great significance of the law's machinery in this field, two things can be attempted. In this section, attention is given to procedures developed to help the plaintiff in amassing evidence for his case. Often enough it is difficult for him to

---

[59] As far as the innocent defendant is concerned, there are curious differences: the patent infringer is protected to the same extent as he is from paying damages, whereas the opposite applies in the case of copyright and unregistered design right (above, n. 49). Since an account is discretionary, the innocence of the defendant may always be a reason for refusing it: e.g. Seager v. Copydex [1967] R.P.C. 349 (C.A.); but cf. Edelsten v. Edelsten (1863) 1 De G.J. & S. 185.

[60] For the conditions, see above, § 2-024.

[61] e.g. Neilson v. Betts (1871) L.R. 5 H.L. 1; De Vitre v. Betts (1873) L.R. 6 H.L. 319; Sutherland v. Caxton [1936] Ch. 323 at 336.

[62] cf. the House of Lords' rejection as fictitious of the same theory for waiver of tort: United Australia v. Barclays Bank [1941] A.C. 1; Street, Law of Damages (1962) 263-266.

[63] This appears to follow from the formula in PA 1977, s.61(2).

[64] Catnic Components v. Evans [1983] F.S.R. 401; Codex v. Racal-Milgo [1984] F.S.R. 87.

[65] Lewis Trusts v. Bamber Stores [1982] F.S.R. 281; Rose Records v. Motown Records [1983] F.S.R. 361.

[66] It should be noted however that patent and registered design actions receive their own treatment in the Rules of the Supreme Court; see especially Ord. 104.

[67] Reference should be made to the standard texts on the various intellectual property rights.

know whom to sue or to discover what a particular competitor or pirate is doing. In the next section we look from the opposite direction—by considering what a defendant can do against a plaintiff who turns litigation into a war of nerves.

This section, then, is concerned with three aspects of the plaintiff's armoury. It concentrates particularly on recent developments designed to increase the strength of his position.

(1) Ex parte order for inspection and other relief

In *Anton Piller* v. *Manufacturing Processes*,[68] the Court of Appeal approved a procedure that is of major practical importance to some owners of intellectual property rights. The plaintiff applies to the High Court *in camera* without any notice to the defendant,[69] for an order that the defendant permit him (with his solicitor) to inspect the defendant's premises[70] and to seize, copy or photograph material relevant to the alleged infringement. The defendant may be required to deliver up infringing goods,[71] keep infringing stock or incriminating papers,[72] and even to give information, for instance, about his sources of supply, or the destination of stock passing through his hands. An injunction against infringement may be part of the order.

The order will be made if the plaintiff (i) provides an extremely strong prima facie case of infringement, (ii) shows that the damage, actual or potential, to him is very serious, and (iii) provides clear evidence that the defendant has in his possession incriminating documents or things and that there is a real possibility that this material will be destroyed before any application *inter partes* can be made.[73] There are certain safeguards which are said to distinguish this sort of order from a search warrant[74]: the plaintiff's solicitor, who is an officer of the court, must attend[75]; the defendant must be given time to think and must be informed of his right to consult his own solicitor and to apply to discharge the order.[76] The

2-030

---

[68] [1976] Ch. 55; [1976] R.P.C. 719; approving *EMI* v. *Pandit* [1975] 1 All E.R. 418. A slender line of earlier precedent existed; *e.g. East India Co.* v. *Kynaston* (1821) Bli.P.C. 153; *Hennessy* v. *Bohmann* [1877] W.N. 14.

[69] R.S.C. Ord. 29, r. 2 which allows orders for the preservation or inspection of property in dispute, is (significantly) limited by the requirement that notice first be given.

[70] Orders covering any premises under the defendant's control are made only in exceptional circumstances: *Protector Alarms* v. *Maxim Alarms* [1979] F.S.R. 442. Orders have also been made against those who have no premises, or whose names are not known. Against some of these, the new self-help remedy will be available in copyright cases: see above, § 2-014.

[71] *Universal City* v. *Mukhtar* [1976] F.S.R. 252.

[72] *EMI* v. *Sarwar* [1977] F.S.R. 146 (C.A.).

[73] *Anton Piller* case (above, n. 68).

[74] Ormrod L.J., *Anton Piller* case (above, n. 68), R.P.C. at 726; and see Lord Denning M.R. (at 752) who adds that the inspection must do no real harm to the defendant or his case. On the basic requirements, note also the *Island Records* and *Carlin* cases (above, § 2-006). It seems unlikely that *ex parte* orders concerning premises out of the jurisdiction (even in Scotland) will be made: see *Protector* v. *Maxim* (above, n. 70); but *cf.* the *inter partes* proceedings in *Cook Industries* v. *Galliher* [1979] Ch. 439.

[75] *Anton Piller* case (above, n. 68), R.P.C. at 724, 726.

[76] An *ex parte* application to discharge the order will not, however, be granted in the absence of strong evidence: *Hallmark Cards* v. *Image Arts* [1977] F.S.R. 150 (C.A.). As to an appeal against the order, see *Bestworth* v. *Wearwell* [1979] F.S.R. 320.

plaintiff must also give a cross-undertaking in damages. Subject to these, the defendant's refusal to allow the inspection is contempt of court (as well as in itself being evidence against him) and will be dealt with according to the circumstances.[77]

2-031   "Anton Piller" orders have been a response to growing concern over the current volume of sound recording, video and other copyright piracy and the imitation of popular trade marks, but they are equally available, for instance, in breach of confidence cases.[78] Although the reassurance was at first given that the orders would be rare,[79] in the event it has proved that the procedure is "in daily use"[80] and it has considerably increased the speed and effectiveness of civil process. Yet it raises the spectre which previously made the courts so fearful of the general warrant to search. The proceedings turn upon the plaintiff's evidence alone and they occur in camera. If a single judge is satisfied prima facie that there is infringement and the likelihood of serious injury, the defendant knows nothing until the inspection is demanded. It takes considerable temerity then to challenge the findings on which the order was made. The process has been labelled "draconian and essentially unfair" in that it condemns a defendant without having been heard.[81]

Accordingly the courts strive to be watchful for plaintiffs who go to excess, seeking for instance, a means of shutting out the defendant from all business, legitimate as well as illegitimate. The ground on which defendants have challenged orders with some regularity is the plaintiff's failure fully to disclose all material circumstances. This it has been said, should err on the side of excess; for it is for the court, not the plaintiff's advisers, to decide whether the order is justified.[82] It is no answer to a charge of inadequate disclosure that enough was shown to justify the making of the order.[83] Moreover, if business records have been seized, they should not be retained until trial, but should be returned after necessary information has been extracted from them; and where infringing material has been seized it should be handed over to the defendant's solicitor, once he is on the record, upon his undertaking to keep it in safe custody and produce it, if required, at the trial.[84]

2-032   Even if the order is open to challenge, for instance because of inadequate disclosure, it is for the court, not the defendant, to decide whether it should be discharged.[85] Accordingly it remains contempt of

---

[77] Even a defendant whose contempt is not very serious may have to pay the plaintiff's costs on the application on an indemnity basis: *Chanel* v. *Three Pears* [1979] F.S.R. 393; *cf.* the *Hallmark* case (above, n. 76).

[78] *Anton Piller* itself concerned copyright and confidential information in a machine; and see *Vapormatic* v. *Sparex* [1976] F.S.R. 461—confidential list of customers ordered to be removed.

[79] Ormrod L.J., *Anton Piller* case at 725.

[80] Lord Denning M.R., *Island Records* v. *Corkindale* [1978] F.S.R. 505 at 512.

[81] *Columbia Picture* v. *Robinson* [1986] 3 All E.R. 338 at 371.

[82] *Ibid.* at 372. See also *J. Rogers Knitwear* v. *Vinola* [1985] F.S.R. 184.

[83] *Wardle Fabrics* v. *Myristis* [1984] F.S.R. 263.

[84] *Columbia Picture* (above n. 81) at 371. It is also wrong to procure wider seizure than the order allows without the defendant having a solicitor's advice.

[85] *Ibid.,* at 372-375. Even if a wrongly obtained order has been executed, it will be discharged: *Booker McConnell* v. *Plascow* [1985] R.P.C. 475 (C.A.); unless that would amount to an empty gesture without practical effect: *Columbia Picture,* at 377-379.

court to refuse to comply with the order.[86] The defendant is protected only by the discretion on costs and the plaintiff's cross-undertaking in damages. If the order was not justified—whether or not it is subsequently discharged—the defendant will be entitled to compensatory damages for injury to his business; and possibly also to aggravated damages for the "contumely or affront" in the way the proceedings were used against him, and even to exemplary damages. The last are justified under the special case concerning wrongs committed by government servants, given that the plaintiff's solicitor is acting as a court officer.[87]

The acute difficulties of balancing efficacy against fairness have surfaced equally over the element of "instant discovery"[88] in any *Anton Piller* order which requires answers on sources of supply or customers. Since these answers would in many cases furnish evidence of criminal conduct, defendants at first sought to plead in response a privilege against self-incrimination. The House of Lords upheld this plea in any case where there was more than a remote or fanciful chance that a serious charge, attracting heavy penalties, might result.[89] This meant that the privilege was available to those who ran substantial piracy operations and so were likely to be charged with conspiracy to defraud, as distinct from (say) a summary offence under the copyright or trade descriptions legislation, which might be appropriate against a street trader. Because the upshot was to offer a haven to those apparently most culpable, Parliament proved willing to intervene. By the Supreme Court Act 1981, s.72, in proceedings for infringement of intellectual property rights[90] or passing off, a defendant may after all be compelled to answer a question or comply with an order which would tend to expose him or her to proceedings for a related offence or recovery of a related penalty.[91] It is, however, not possible to use any statement or admission so procured in any equivalent criminal proceedings.[92]

The development of the *Anton Piller* order has coincided with another, more general evolution in interlocutory procedure: the *Mareva* injunction is directed, not to the uncovering and preserving of "fragile" evidence, but to the retention of assets belonging to the defendant which may be needed to satisfy judgment in the action, particularly if they may otherwise be removed from the jurisdiction.[93] Orders are frequently made

2-033

---

[86] *Wardle* (above, n. 83); *Columbia Picture* (above, n. 81) at 368.

[87] *Columbia Picture* (above, n. 81) at 379-380.

[88] Bridge L.J., *Rank Film* v. *Video Information* [1980] 2 All E.R. at 283.

[89] *Rank Film* v. *Video Information* [1982] A.C. 380.

[90] This, the first statutory use of the term, encompasses "patent, trade mark, copyright registered design, technical or commercial information or other intellectual property": s.73(5).

[91] The privilege is taken away more generally where proceedings are being brought against apprehended infringement, rather than against acts which have already occurred: s.73(5); *Universal City* v. *Hubbard* [1984] R.P.C. 43 (C.A.). But it seems that documents wrongly seized, where the privilege should still have been upheld, do not have to be returned: Cumming-Bruce L.J. at 47-48.

[92] *i.e.* such proceedings as are no longer a justification for upholding the privilege against incrimination by virtue of the section.

[93] A number of cases have manifested a desire to aid a plaintiff in searching for the defendant's assets world-wide. See, *e.g.* *House of Spring Gardens* v. *Waite* [1984] F.S.R. 277; *Altertext* v. *Advanced Data* [1986] F.S.R. 21.

which contain both *Anton Piller* and *Mareva* terms.[93a] These may relate to bank accounts and other financial assets.[94] Equally, there have been orders directed to the seizure of specified valuables, such as cars, in which, according to evidence, the proceeds of infringement have been invested. Just as a defendant is permitted an allowance for living expenses out of financial assets that are subject to a *Mareva* order, so also, where the order relates to other assets, he will not be deprived of things needed for living and conducting legitimate trade.[95]

(2) Discovery of names

2-034   Sometimes the only lead that a right-owner can pick up about infringing goods is that they are passing through the hands of some person in the course of transit. That person may however not be infringing and may not even know that others have infringed or are likely to do so. The court may order such a person to disclose the names of the consignors or consignees responsible, if this is the only way for the plaintiff to discover whom he should act against and if the person against whom the order is made is shown (however unwittingly) to be facilitating the wrongful acts. On this basis an order was even made against the Commissioners of Customs and Excise to reveal the names of importers of a patented drug, which their published records showed to have been imported.[96] The order, which is discretionary, is not confined to such circumstances. For instance, a television company has been ordered to reveal the name of a "mole" within British Steel, who was acting in admitted breach of confidence in revealing how the Board was opposing against strikers. The admitted purpose of the proceedings was to procure the mole's dismissal, not to sue him.[97] Where the goods are still being held, an injunction restraining their removal may also be granted.[98]

(3) Discovery, interrogatories, inspection

2-035   English courts have generally been careful to protect defendants against speculative suits that are no more than "fishing expeditions"—proceedings begun to find out what, if anything, might really be claimed.[99] Accordingly, in our field, infringement actions cannot be launched effectively unless the plaintiff can specify in his statement of

---

[93a] Equally they may well contain an interlocutory injunction.
[94] In order to ensure efficacy, the court may allow cross-examination on affidavits in defence: *House of Spring Gardens* v. *Waite* [1985] F.S.R. 173 (C.A.).
[95] *CBS United Kingdom* v. *Lambert* [1983] F.S.R. 123 (C.A.).
[96] *Norwich Pharmacal* v. *CCE* [1974] A.C. 133; [1974] R.P.C. 101 (H.L.) The costs of the proceedings may be recovered as damages from the infringers thus exposed: *Morton-Norwich* v. *Intercen (No. 27)* [1981] F.S.R. 337. An importing or exporting agent might equally be subject to such an order: see *Orr* v. *Diaper* (1876) 4 Ch.D. 23; *Upmann* v. *Forester* (1885) 24 Ch.D. 231.
[97] *British Steel* v. *Granada.*
[98] See Buckley L.J., *Norwich Pharmacal* case [1972] R.P.C. 743 at 771.
[99] While power exists to order discovery before delivery of a statement of claim, it will not be exercised readily: *RHM Foods* v. *Bovril* [1983] R.P.C. 275; likewise with inspection: *Unilever* v. *Pearce* [1985] F.S.R. 475.

claim particulars of at least one act of infringement.[1] If he does not give them and does not comply with any order for further and better particulars he will be unable to defend himself on a motion to strike out pleadings or action.[2]

Provided that he can show enough to repel attacks on his pleadings, the plaintiff will carry his case forward to the stage of pre-trial preparations. As in other types of civil litigation, discovery of documents and the administration of interrogatories are steps which on occasion may provide important evidence or admissions.[3] In the United States of America such steps have been inflated into a form of discovery that allows wide-ranging preliminary cross-examination of party by party.[4] That has yet to occur in England, but some expansion has occurred of the range of documents which must be made available during discovery in a complex patent action.[5] If the documents discovered contain confidential information the other party may be restrained from using the information for other purposes such as revelations in the press[6] or further litigation.

Beyond this there are special procedures for cases involving industrial techniques. The plaintiff may need to discover what the defendant is doing; but the defendant may fear that inspection by him will reveal the defendant's own secrets—a fear that, in the race to get ahead, is sometimes acute. The court has power to order inspection even against this sort of objection. But while it will not require first to be satisfied prima facie that the defendant is infringing,[8] it may need to be shown

---

[1] Equally if a defendant ripostes with a defence or counterclaim which turns on issues of fact, he may be required to give particulars of allegations; for instance, that the plaintiff's alleged trade mark is in fact common to the trade. If his response in a patent suit is to seek revocation of a patent he will be obliged to give particulars of his objections to validity: see Ency. PL, § 10-107.

It has been said that a plaintiff who brings a motion for interlocutory relief is entitled, on seeing the plaintiff's evidence, to apply to stand the motion over until trial of the action without costs being immediately awarded against him: *Jeffrey* v. *Shelana* [1976] F.S.R. 54. But this may invite a form of fishing and a later court has held that the award of costs is always a matter of discretion: *Simons Records* v. *W.E.A. Records* [1980] F.S.R. 35 at 36. See also *Rockwell* v. *Serck* [1988] F.S.R. 187.

[2] Equally he will not be permitted to seek discovery or deliver interrogatories: *AG für Autogene Aluminium* v. *London Aluminium* [1919] 2 Ch. 67.

[3] Discovery concerning the whole of a defendant's trading operation, in order to secure evidence going purely to his credit, is oppressive and will not be allowed: *Ballatine* v. *Dixon* [1975] R.P.C. 111; *E.G. Music* v. *S.F. (Film Distributors)* [1978] F.S.R. 121; *cf. Mood Music* v. *de Wolfe* [1976] Ch. 119.

[4] For the impact of this procedural development in patent actions, see White, *Patent Litigation: Procedure and Tactics* (1979), § 5.01/06.

[5] *American Cyanamid* v. *Ethicon* [1977] F.S.R. 593 at 602 (C.A.).

[6] *Distillers* v. *Times Newspapers* [1975] 1 All E.R. 41; *Home Office* v. *Harman* [1983] A.C. 280; *Wilden Pump* v. *Fusteld* [1985] F.S.R. 581. This applies equally to prejudicial material uncovered under an *Anton Piller* order, which carry an implied undertaking not to use it for a collateral purpose; but the court has an ultimate jurisdiction in the matter: *Crest Homes* v. *Marks* [1987] F.S.R. 305 (H.L.); *CCE* v. *Hamlin Slowe* [1986] F.S.R. 346. It is proper to use the material to arrest assets in another jurisdiction: *Bayer* v. *Winter (No. 2)* [1986] F.S.R. 357.

[7] *Medway* v. *Doublelock* [1978] 1 All E.R. 1261; *Riddick* v. *Thames Board* [1977] 3 All E.R. 677 (C.A.).

[8] *British Xylonite* v. *Fibrenyle* [1959] R.P.C. 252 (C.A.). To hold that there was a prima facie case might embarrass the trial judge.

that there are "formidable grounds," rather than a mere suspicion.[9] It may try to alleviate the defendant's anxieties by requiring an independent expert to make the inspection.[10] If such a person could not make a properly informed inspection, then it may have to be done by the plaintiff and his advisers; but possibly on condition that nothing is copied or taken away and that all involved are placed under obligations to respect confidence.[11]

4. DELAYED AMBUSH AND SELECTIVE ACTION

2-035   In the main it is not isolated acts of infringement but runs of production that provoke the owner of intellectual property rights into taking action. Accordingly, a defendant's stake is likely to be high; and it may well become higher if proceedings against him are delayed until he has established commercial production and tied himself to distribution arrangements. While there are incentives that will induce right-owners in many circumstances to move as quickly as possible (in particular, the chance to secure interlocutory relief)[12] these may for some reason have little or no force. Not only may there be tactical advantages in delay, it may also seem more damaging to proceed not against the manufacturer who is the source of the alleged infringement, but against his wholesale or resale distributors or even the ultimate users or consumers. In all this, the legal limitations upon a plaintiff's freedom of action can have great importance, and the most important of these limitations, many of them matters of general law, deserve to be sketched in.

(1) Limitation of actions

2-036   The question here is: within what period after a particular infringement has been perpetrated must a writ be issued? The various infringement actions in our field, being tortious in character, must normally be begun within six years, of the wrongful act.[13] The same applies to actions based upon breach of contract. Only the action for breach of confidence may differ (when not founded in contract) because of its equitable origin: probably the only principle is that a period of too great delay (laches) must not be allowed to lapse.[14]

An action which is commenced within the limitation period, but then allowed to stagnate, may be struck out for want of prosecution. But under current practice, this will only be done if there is real prejudice to the defendant, as well as inordinate delay.[15] Such prejudice might arise if

[9] Wahl v. Buhler-Miag [1979] F.S.R. 183.
[10] cf. Printers & Finishers v. Holloway [1964] 3 All E.R. 54 (inspection of plaintiff's plant for defendant: elements claimed to be secret must be pointed out).
[11] Centri-Spray v. Cera [1979] F.S.R. 175.
[12] See above, § 2-018.
[13] Limitation Act 1939, s.2(1). There are exceptions for cases of mistake and fraud: see generally, Halsbury Laws, Vol. 28, §§ 16 et seq. The rule applies to amendments alleging additional acts of infringement: Sorata v. Gardex [1984] F.S.R. 81.
[14] See § 2-037.
[15] Birkett v. James [1978] A.C. 297 (H.L.); Compagnie Française de Télévision v. Thorn [1978] R.P.C. 735 (C.A.); Bestworth v. Wearwell [1986] R.P.C. 527; Department of Transport v. Smaller (1989, H.L., to be reported).

witnesses in a patent action would have to testify to the state of an art
which has receded a considerable distance in time.[16]

(2) Acquiescence

Beyond the limitation periods for particular wrongs, lies a further   2-037
question: if a defendant has been left to pursue a course of infringement
for a substantial period of time, can the right-owner be taken to have
consented to its continuance? If so, no part of his activity, even the most
recent, is actionable. This consent may be expressly given or it may be
implied from the circumstances; it may occur before, at the time of, or
after the infringing act. Conduct alone can create an implied licence in
some circumstances. Where the plaintiff represents, expressly or
impliedly, that the defendant's conduct is not an infringement, he will
thereafter be estopped from asserting his right.[17] Where he both knows of
his right against the defendant and that the defendant mistakenly believes
that he is entitled to do what he is doing, yet he stands by without
asserting his right, he will be taken to have acquiesced in the wrong.[18] If
all this can be proved, there is no need to show any element of delay.

At least when the question is whether an injunction should be granted
in support of a legal right, it may be enough to prove delay by itself if
the delay is "inordinate"; or delay coupled with "something . . . to
encourage the wrongdoer to believe that he does not intend to rely upon
his strict legal rights, and the wrongdoer must have acted to his prejudice
in that belief."[19]

(3) Estoppels of record (res judicata)[20]

In order to give finality and to prevent a person from repeatedly   2-038
asserting either an unsubstantiable right or the freedom to act in
contravention of another's right, estoppels of record may be raised
against him in various circumstances. Three kinds should be
distinguished.

(a) *Judgment in rem*

Certain types of judgment bind all persons and not merely the parties
to the action. In our field an order revoking a patent, registered design or
registered trade mark—the rights that depend upon grant—may be relied
upon by all the world against the former right-owner. By contrast a
decision that a plaintiff has no copyright, that a patent is valid or that a

[16] *Horstman Gear v. Smiths Industries* [1979] F.S.R. 461.
[17] Cotton L.J., *Proctor v. Bennis* (1886) 36 Ch.D. 740 at 758-761.
[18] See Fry J., *Willmott v. Barber* (1880) 15 Ch.D. 96.
[19] Goff L.J., *H.P. Bulmer v. Bollinger* [1978] R.P.C. 79 at 134-136 referring especially to
Electrolux v. Electrix (1954) 71 R.P.C. 23; *Cluett-Peabody v. McIntyre* [1958] R.P.C.
335. In *Vine Products v. Mackenzie* [1969] R.P.C. 1 at 25-26, Cross J. held that the
defence might arise, even though the plaintiff did not appreciate that the law afforded
him any civil remedy; but *cf. Willmott v. Barber* (above, n. 18). For acquiescence as a
reason refusing an account of profits, see *International Scientific Communications v.
Pattison* [1979] F.S.R. 429.
[20] This is a complex subject. See generally, Spencer Bower and Turner. *The Doctrine of Res
Judicata* (2nd ed., 1969); *Halsbury's Laws* (4th ed.), Vol. 15, §§ 1527 *et seq.* The term
res judicata, commonly applied to one or other aspect of the subject, is here avoided
because of its ambiguous meaning.

trade mark is properly registered can only have a binding effect on the other parties to the action and their privies.[21] The judgment is *in personam* and falls for consideration under the next heads.

(b) *Cause of action estoppel*

If A sues B alleging a particular cause of action upon pleaded facts and he loses, he will subsequently be estopped from suing upon the same cause of action. Suppose, for instance, the action is for passing off and A fails to provide sufficient evidence that the public were likely to be deceived by the defendant's acts into believing that it was getting goods of the plaintiff; or he unsuccessfully claims a reputation with the public as manufacturer when he might have succeeded on a claim to be known as a distributor; or a general rule of law is held to preclude his claim. In each of these circumstances, a second case based on the same facts would be precluded, if the first judgment was final and not interlocutory. Thus this category of estoppel may debar attempts to put the same case more persuasively, whether in point of evidence or legal argument; but it operates only where cause of action is the same.[22]

(c) *Issue estoppel*

2-039　　If a dispute about facts has been distinctly put to a court and a final judgment given, the loser is estopped from raising the issue a second time even upon a different cause of action.[23] In the case of such an issue estoppel, both the initial parties and their privies will be bound. But the range of this "privity" is not wide. Where a number of enterprises are engaged in the evolution of a product from conception to marketing, and a question of (say) copyright infringement arises, the successors in title and the employees of any business will be treated as its privies, and probably also an assignee of its rights. But a design-creating firm and the manufacturer which it commissions to execute its designs are not privy.[24]

The manner in which issue estoppel may go further than cause of action estoppel is illustrated by this: if it were decided that A and not B is the successor in title to a business by proceedings to establish the ownership, in subsequent passing-off proceedings by A against B for misappropriation of the marks of the business, B could not reopen the question of A's ownership. But the issue must have been raised and not

---

[21] But certificates of contested validity may be granted for patents and registered designs: PA 1977, s.65; RDA, 1949, s.25. An unsuccessful challenge subsequently risks an award of solicitor-and-client costs (designs), or even solicitor-and-non-client costs (patents).

[22] In general, any matter is *res judicata* which is raised on the pleadings and falls within the terms of the order; but exceptionally, an explicit qualification in the judgment may be taken account of to limit the scope of the estoppel: *Patchett* v. *Sterling* (1954) 71 R.P.C. 61 (C.A.).

[23] See generally, *Carl Zeiss* v. *Rayner & Keeler (No. 2)* [1967] 1 A.C. 853; *Unilever's Trade Marks* [1987] R.P.C. 13 at 20-21. Under the law before 1978, the conditional character of a decision to allow a patent application to proceed to grant despite opposition (see below, § 4-022) meant that it was not final (see *Bristol Myers* v. *Beecham* [1978] F.S.R. 553 (Israel S.C.)). Now that a third party may challenge only after grant it may well be that an unsuccessful attack on validity before the comptroller or in an EPO opposition would raise an estoppel. On the difficult questions which may arise when only one issue is appealed, see the *Bristol Myers* case (*cf.* 562-563, 568-571).

[24] *Gleeson* v. *Wippell* [1977] F.S.R. 301.

allowed to go by default—in this respect issue estoppel is narrower. In its wider aspect, issue estoppel has special importance for intellectual property. In this sphere, defendants frequently repeat the allegedly infringing act in the course of producing or marketing goods. Each new act may give rise to a distinct cause of action, so the cause of action estoppel may be too narrow to achieve the objective that the law sets itself.

Both cause of action and issue estoppel may be raised in English proceedings upon the judgment of a foreign court.[25] As intellectual property grows in significance as a supra-national commodity, so does the impact of this rule: litigating the same issue in several jurisdictions can be just as harassing as litigating it several times in one. Equally, the courts are likely to approach this form of issue estoppel with caution, taking care to see that the issue was a basis for the foreign decision, rather than being merely collateral or obiter, and avoiding prejudice to a party who found it impracticable to fight the issue properly in the foreign jurisdiction.[26]

The main intellectual property rights are territorial in character. A French judgment, therefore, on (say) infringement of a French patent or copyright cannot give rise to a cause of action estoppel between the same proprietor of the equivalent British rights and the same defendant who is performing equivalent acts in England. Whether it might found an issue estoppel is less certain: the question remains unexplored in the case-law.[27] Since the actual activities must be different, the issue would be concerned with the application of the law to equivalent facts. A finding of estoppel could scarcely be made unless the court was satisfied that the same legal principle fell to be applied. Given such arrangements as the European Patent Convention, it may now be possible to meet this criterion in some circumstances (*e.g.* on the validity of a European patent in light of a prior publication or use).

(4) Actions on foreign infringements

Estoppel may prevent an issue from being re-litigated in different jurisdictions. This leads to a correlative question: may a plaintiff sue in an English court for infringements committed abroad?[28] The growth of international trade, and in its wake the development of supra-national institutions for granting intellectual property rights, suggests that it may become increasingly important to know the answer. Two aspects must be considered. First, the jurisdiction question: when will an English court hear an action seeking an injunction, damages, or both for an injury which, if it were committed here, would amount to a tort?[29] Secondly, the choice of law question: according to what law (or laws) must the act be wrongful?

2-040

---

[25] *Carl Zeiss* and *Bristol Myers* cases (above, n. 23).

[26] *Carl Zeiss* case, at 917-918, *per* Lord Reid; and see 948-949 (Lord Upjohn), 972 (Lord Wilberforce).

[27] The Israel S.C. in the *Bristol Myers* case (above, n. 23), however, assumes the possibility in appropriate circumstances.

[28] With or without also alleging infringement of equivalent British rights.

[29] The contractual and equitable background to the action for breach of confidence introduces special considerations, which cannot be pursued here.

In deciding whether to assume jurisdiction over such a case, the courts are guided by three main considerations: whether the proceedings are likely to lead to an efficaceous result; whether they will be unduly burdensome to the defendant; and whether they will interfere with the autonomy of another sovereign state. Two points in particular may be made. First, it must be possible to bring the defendant within the court's jurisdiction: by serving the writ on him in England, by getting him voluntarily to submit to the jurisdiction or by securing an order for service out of the jurisdiction, for instance on the ground that he is domiciled or ordinarily resident in England or that an injunction is being sought against things done in England.[30] In the first two cases the court will exercise its jurisdiction unless to do so would be oppressive; but in the last it is very much a matter of discretion. Secondly, where an injunction is sought, it would be unlikely to be granted unless a personal defendant were to remain present in the jurisdiction or a personal or corporate defendant were to retain assets there: otherwise there would be no way of enforcing it.[31] As to the place of performance of the forbidden acts: there is no particular difficulty over banning acts in England which are in preparation for a foreign infringement; and there have been cases where an injunction has been granted to restrain acts abroad which are shown to be wrongful in that place.[32]

Where a defendant is domiciled in another EEC jurisdiction the operation of the normal jurisdiction rules is to be constricted by the EEC's Judgments Convention.[33] There is of course no change in the principle that, if the infringement is committed in England, an English court may assume jurisdiction.[34] On the other hand, under the Convention a national court has jurisdiction to hear an action upon a foreign wrong only where the defendant is domiciled in the country or submits to the jurisdiction voluntarily.[35] Residence or a passing visit is not enough

[30] See Dicey and Morris, *The Conflict of Laws* (11th ed., 1987), Rules 20, 21, 23. This problem arises equally when the alleged tort is committed in England: for examples see *Burland's T.M.* (1889) 41 Ch.D. 542, 6 R.P.C. 482; *Dunlop* v. *Cudell* [1902] 1 K.B. 342, 19 R.P.C. 46 (patent infringement: German company's agent properly served in England). But in that case the fact that the tort is committed in the jurisdiction is a separate justification for allowing service out of the jurisdiction: *cf. Badische Anilin* v. *Johnson* (1897) 14 R.P.C. 919.

[31] *Marshall* v. *Marshall* (1888) 38 Ch.D. 330 (C.A.); *cf. Burland's* case (above, n. 5).

[32] *Alfred Dunhill* v. *Sunoptic* [1979] F.S.R. 337 (C.A.: interlocutory injunction against acts of alleged passing off in Switzerland); and see *John Walker* v. *Ost* (below, n. 11) (contrast the second injunction with the others, which are restricted to acts in the jurisdiction). *cf. "Morocco Bound" Syndicate* v. *Harris* [1895] 1 Ch. 534.

[33] Convention on Jurisdiction and the Enforcement of Judgments in Civil and Commercial Matters (Brussels Convention of 1968, as amended by the Convention of Accession by the U.K., Ireland and Denmark).   [34] Art. 5.3.

[35] Art. 2. Domicile is a technical notion distinct from nationality and residence; its meaning differs in the law of different states: for the English concept, see Dicey and Morris, *Conflict of Laws* (11th ed., 1987), Chap. 7; Cheshire and North, *Private International Law* (11th ed., 1987), Chap. 7. Under the Convention, an English court (for instance) is to apply its own law in order to decide whether a person is domiciled in England, and the law of (say) France to decide whether a person is domiciled there; but a person's national law shall apply if it makes his domicile depend on that of another person or the seat of an authority: Art. 52. Non-natural persons are domiciled in the place of their seat (Art. 53) but actions concerning the activities of a branch, agency or other establishment may be launched where it is situated: Art. 5.5. Note also Art. 5.4 on civil claims in criminal proceedings; Arts. 21, 22 on *lis pendens*; Art. 17 on jurisdiction agreements.

to give the court power,[36] whereas this remains the case, if the defendant is domiciled outside the EEC.

Turning to the choice of law question[37]: the normal rule is that an action can be maintained in England concerning a wrongful act committed in a foreign country if two conditions are satisfied: (i) it must have been one that would have been actionable as a tort in England had it been committed there; (ii) the act must have been actionable (though not necessarily in tort) in the foreign country.[38] Where the English tort in question is conceived to be part of the general private law—as with the common law tort of passing off—there seems to be no obstacle to the application of this principle.[39] Possibly copyright, which arises automatically, can be similarly treated.[40] But when it comes to rights that are granted after official examination—as with patents, registered designs and registered marks—it is possible to say that the state's act, giving rights only for the territory in question, makes them subject-matter which should be litigated only in the courts of that place (the so-called "principle of territoriality").[41] Certainly proceedings for revocation of the grant could only be brought effectively in the country concerned; if successful, they must result in an order to officials to cancel the rights; and those officials are answerable only to their own tribunals.[42] In a country such as Britain which allows an infringement suit to be answered either with a defence that the right is invalid or a positive counterclaim for revocation, it may seem particularly inappropriate to admit any proceedings concerning equivalent rights arising in a foreign jurisdiction.[43] If this is the real objection, then exceptionally when questions of invalidity were not involved it might be possible to try the issue of infringement in England. But arguably, it should be considered enough to preclude the action that the defendant is entitled to plead invalidity as a defence.

2-041

---

[36] See Art. 3.
[37] The traditional approach is to treat what follows as a choice of law rule. But there is some argument in favour of its being another jurisdictional rule; see Cheshire and North, pp. 526-531.
[38] For the intricacies of this rule, following the opinions expressed by the House of Lords in Boys v. Chaplin [1971] A.C. 356, see Dicey and Morris, Chap. 35; Cheshire and North, pp. 519-521 Exceptions may arise because of the status of the parties, or because the court considers itself not a proper forum.
[39] Hence the Scotch whisky producers successfully sued a defendant in England for selling an admixture of whiskies as Scotch in Ecuador: John Walker v. Henry Ost [1970] R.P.C. 489 at 509-513.
[40] Complications might arise over notice or registration if U.S. copyright was in issue; or over such matters as the liability of distributor defendants or the award of conversion damages: see below, pp. 372-373.
[41] This conclusion can be expressed in terms of the general rule by saying that its first requirement is not satisfied: the infringement of (say) the foreign patent is not actionable in England because the patent does not extend to England. But that is so only if one assumes that the act occurred in England but not that the patent covers England. Is this reasonable in the case where in fact there is an equivalent English patent? See the difference of opinion on how to apply the rule which is found in Potter v. Broken Hill Pty. (1905) 30 V.L.R. 612 (S.C. Victoria).
[42] Potter v. Broken Hill (1906) 3 C.L.R. 479 (H.C. Australia).
[43] cf. Norbert, Steinhardt v. Meth (1960) 105 C.L.R. 440 (threats action similarly treated because normally it develops into a patent action: for this, see below, § 2-045).

The EEC Convention appears to have no effect on this choice of law principle. The Convention acknowledges that any revocation proceedings may be brought only in the territory concerned.[44] But it has nothing to say about special principles which may affect actions concerning intellectual property infringement or invalidity elsewhere. It does not abrogate the requirement that the act in question be tortious if done in England.[45] Accordingly, one competitor could not sue another for an act of unfair competition committed in Germany (and actionable as such there) if it would give rise only to criminal liability (*e.g.* for affixing a false trade description) in England.[46]

(5) Making others responsible

2-042   A defendant to an action who wishes to establish the responsibility of another solely or jointly for the alleged wrong may do so by issuing him with a third party notice.[47] If two or more defendants in an action are liable in respect of the same damage and one meets the liability he will have a claim to contribution from the others.[48] The same is true where the second and subsequent persons have not been sued by the victim of the tort.[49] The amount of contribution due is that found to be just and equitable having regard to the person in question's responsibility for the damage.[50]

A contract to indemnify for loss suffered through legal liability will displace this principle. These indemnities are common in intellectual property dealings: for instance, where an inventor assigns the rights in what he claims to be his invention, or where an author, in entering a publishing agreement, undertakes that he infringes no one else's rights. The obligation to indemnify is indeed implied in some contracts. If a person purchases a machine and is then obliged to pay damages for its use because it infringes a patent, the vendor will be in breach of his implied warranty of quiet possession[51] and accordingly obliged to make good the loss. Where one person commissions another to carry out work for him and the other thereby unwittingly commits a patent or copyright infringement there is arguably a similar implied undertaking to indemnify for any loss through liability. But the matter has never been decided.

[44] Art. 16.4. This does not extend to questions of ownership: *Duijnstee* v. *Goderbauer* [1985] F.S.R. (E.C.J.).

[45] This in itself may be employed as a reason for disallowing an action on the infringement of rights created by grant of registration: see above, n. 91.

[46] On this difference of approach, see below, §§ 586–587. For the subject in general, see Ulmer, *Intellectual Property Rights and the Conflict of Laws* (1978).

[47] R.S.C. Ord. 16. Equally a manufacturer may intervene in proceedings against his customer under R.S.C. Ord. 15, r. 6(2): *Tetra Molectric* v. *Japan Imports* [1976] R.P.C. 547 (C.A.).

[48] Civil Liability (Contribution) Act 1978, s.1. The legal basis of liability may be tort, contract, trust or otherwise: s.6(1).

[49] When the victim's action against the others has become time-barred the payer may still seek contribution: *ibid.* s.1(3). But there is also a limitation period for the contribution claim: see Limitation Act 1963, s.4. For the subject in detail see, *e.g.* Goff and Jones, *Law of Restitution* (2nd ed., 1978), 232–235; *Clerk and Lindsell on Torts* (16th ed., 1989). §§ 2-57–2-61 Dugdale (1979) 42 M.L.R. 182.

[50] 1935 Act, s.6(2).

[51] Sale of Goods Act 1979, s.12(2)(*b*). But to the extent that this obligation is limited in accordance with s.12(3), (5), the responsibility will be reduced.

(6) Establishing freedom from liability

A person who fears that he will be sued can only have the issue   2-043
brought to a head if he has some countervailing right; if a procedure
exists for annulling the right on which the other party may eventually
claim; or if the claim against him is imminent.[52] In the case of patents,
registered designs and registered trade marks, statutory procedures exist
for attacking the validity of the right, and these are open to competitors
and others with sufficient interest to bring them.[53] Even then, the
question whether a person is infringing lies outside these procedures: the
alleged infringer must proceed by way of an action for a declaration that
he is not doing so.[54]

In intellectual property litigation generally, this possibility is a recent
development. In the case of patents, special provision was earlier made. A
person may apply in writing to a patentee[55] for an undertaking that a
particular act does not infringe the patent.[56] If this undertaking is not
forthcoming he may seek a declaration from the court to the same
effect.[57] In the course of the proceedings, questions of the patent's
validity, as well as of infringement, may now be raised.[58]

(7) Threats to sue

If a potential plaintiff chooses to do what damage he can merely by   2-044
threatening to sue, again those affected may find it difficult to force his
hand. Apart from instituting revocation or rectification proceedings in the
cases mentioned under the last head, a person who suffers by the threats
may not be able to prevent them, save in exceptional cases. In general the
common law has not limited the freedom to institute claims or to
threaten that they will be begun. Rather it insists that those who choose
to succumb to a claim instead of fighting must abide by the consequences
of their faint-heartedness. If the claim was in fact groundless, they are
not in general permitted to re-open the controversy by having the
settlement rescinded, by claiming back money paid or by suing for loss
suffered because of their submission.[59]

The same approach applies in general even where the threats cause
injury indirectly. For instance, A, a promotion firm, imported toy bricks
to be used as free gifts in a campaign being organised for a client, B. C
threatened B with an action for infringement of design copyright if the
campaign went ahead. In consequence C refused to participate, leaving A

[52] In *Vine Products* v. *Mackenzie* [1969] R.P.C. 1 it was assumed that after an exchange of
letters before action, the person threatened with liability could himself institute the
proceedings for a declaration of freedom from liability. *Bulmer* v. *Bollinger* [1978] R.P.C.
79 (C.A.), followed the same course.
[53] See below, §§ 122–123, 206–207, 544–545, 611. For certificates of contested validity, see
above, n. 21.
[54] As in the cases mentioned in n. 53.
[55] Or exclusive licensee.
[56] He is not obliged to show the alleged infringement to the patentee, only to describe it:
Plasticisers v. *Pixdane* [1979] R.P.C. 327.
[57] PA 1977, s.71.
[58] This is a change introduced in 1977.
[59] For these rules and exceptions to them, see, *e.g.* Goff and Jones, *Law of Restitution* (3rd
ed., 1986), especially pp. 213–215.

with the stock of toys on its hands. An action by A against C for wrongful interference with contractual relations was struck out as disclosing no cause of action.

However the tort of injurious falsehood will lie for the *malicious* statement that a right of action exists and will be sued upon.[60] Malice will be present if the threatener knows that his claim is groundless; likewise, if he draws attention to his success in proceedings against another defendant without saying that the court saw fit to stay the injunction pending an appeal.[61] Nonetheless the requirement of malice severely limits this form of tortious relief.

2-045   In the case of patents, where the expense and uncertainty of infringement and validity proceedings has long been thought to be acute, and the threat to sue is accordingly grave, an exception exists by statute.[62] In the version included in the 1977 Act, a person aggrieved by the threat that he himself or someone else (such as a customer) will be sued for patent infringement may claim relief in civil proceedings in the form of a declaration that the threats are unjustifiable, an injunction against their continuance and/or damages for any loss that they cause (*e.g.* because a customer switches his orders to the threatener).[63] But threats relating either to making or importing a product for disposal, or to using a process, are now outside the scope of this special provision.[64]

To avoid liability the threatener may show either that what he said did not amount to a threat, or that the threat was justified.[65] The patentee is entitled to draw attention to the existence of his patent.[66] But to go further is to court danger.[67] It is actionable, for instance, for a patentee to say to a competitor's customers that he is going to apply for an injunction against the competitor and that the customers are to see that there are no further infringements.[68] In the case of circulars to customers or notices in trade journals (common ways of giving notice of rights claimed) a person suing for threats must show that potential customers of

[60] The scope of injurious falsehood is discussed in detail, below, §§ 16-037—16-043.
[61] *Mentmore* v. *Fomento* (1955) 72 R.P.C. 157 (C.A.).
[62] Threats to enforce registered and unregistered design rights are similarly treated: RDA 1949, s.26; CDPA 1988 s.253, Sched. 3, § 15. The Whitford Committee's proposal (Cmnd. 6732, 1977, § 198) that the same form of relief should apply to copyright has not been acted upon.
[63] PA 1977, s.70. For orders restraining the institution of vexatious proceedings against customers see *Landiden Hartog* v. *Sea Bird* [1976] F.S.R. 489; *Jacey* v. *Norton* [1977] F.S.R. 475.
[64] s.70(4); and see CDPA 1988, s.253(3), RDA 1949, s.2A; *Neild* v. *Rockley* [1986] F.S.R. 3; s.70(4) permits threats against acts of importing that are allegedly acts of indirect infringement (for which see s.60(2)): *Therm-a-Stor* v. *Weatherseal* [1981] F.S.R. 579 (C.A.).
[65] Interlocutory relief may be available even where the defendant proposed to justify; the rule in defamation does not apply: *Johnson Electric* v. *Mabuchi-Motor* [1986] F.S.R. 280.
[66] PA 1977, s.70(5); RDA 1949, s.26(3).
[67] For examples of statements held to be threats (and not to be) see Ency. PL § 10-402. A letter before action, which solicitors commonly regard as proper practice, may give rise to threats proceedings in the case of patents. But if the letter is followed by a writ, it is doubtful whether a counterclaim for threats could then succeed, since it is not clear how the person threatened is aggrieved: see Evershed M.R., *Benmax* v. *Austin* (1953) 70 R.P.C. 284 at 295 (C.A.). As to circumstances in which interlocutory relief should be granted against threats, see *HVE Electric* v. *Cuffin* [1964] R.P.C. 149 (C.A.).
[68] *Berkeley & Young* v. *Stillwell* (1940) 57, R.P.C. 291.

his would understand the circular or notice to be referring to his goods.[69]

A threat can be justified only if the threatener shows that the acts of which he complains do constitute infringement of some patent, and the person suffering by the threats cannot establish that the relevant patent claim is invalid.[70] Thus in the case of a serious fight the threat gives the alleged infringer a springboard equivalent to an action for a declaration of non-infringement from which to launch the contest.

[69] *Reymes-Cole* v. *Elite Hosiery* [1965] R.P.C. 102 at 120 (C.A.).
[70] Frequently these issues are raised by counterclaim for infringement and counter-counterclaim for revocation of the patent.

Part II

PATENTS

CHAPTER 3

GROWTH AND PURPOSE OF PATENTS

1. THE NEW LAW

With the Patents Act 1977, the British patent system received the largest   3-001
culture shock in its history. The Act provides machinery for collaborating
in three supra-national ventures:

(i) Since June 1, 1978, it has been possible to secure a patent for the
United Kingdom either by the traditional route of an application
to the British Patent Office or by applying to the new European
Patent Office (EPO), established under the European Patent Convention 1973 (EPC). The EPO grants a bundle of national patents
in common form, of which one may be a European patent (U.K.).[1]
Its headquarters are in Munich.

(ii) From the same date it has been possible to initiate international
patent applications in a number of countries throughout the world
by a single procedure under the Patent Cooperation Treaty 1970
(PCT). The PCT system provides for a single application and
search, and in some cases a single preliminary examination; but
thereafter it transmits applications to national offices for them to
decide upon the grant of a patent for their territories.[2] It is
administered by WIPO, Geneva.

(iii) From a date to be fixed, an application to the EPO for a patent in
an EEC country may mature into a single Community patent
covering the whole Common Market. The main provisions of this
scheme are contained in the Community Patent Convention 1975
(CPC), which has been the subject of substantial revision, agreed
in principle in 1985.[3]

In addition to all this, the substantive and procedural law governing
patents for the United Kingdom was extensively altered by the 1977 Act.
This was for various reasons. The EPC arrangements require each
contracting state to treat a European patent granted by the EPO for that
territory in accordance with standard rules on basic matters such as term,
validity and scope of protection; there was a strong case for subjecting
patents granted by the national system to the same substantive regime
and for modelling the application procedure on similar lines to the

[1] See below, §§ 3-019, 3-035—3-037, 4-001—4-004.
[2] See below, §§ 3-015—3-018, 3-037, 4-001—4-003.
[3] See below, §§ 3-019—3-022.

European granting system.[4] The Report of the Banks Committee on the British system also awaited implementation[5]; and the government had plans of its own on the subject of inventions by employees.[6]

3-002   The new edifice is byzantine in complexity. At least it can be said that the building blocks from which it is constructed are not themselves a novelty. These have been formed out of the experience of national patents; and in their turn national systems are a characteristic by-product of a country's "take-off" into industrialisation. In private enterprise economies a patent system represents a judicious compromise. On the one hand it is a recognition that technological innovation, which is seen as the key to economic growth and social prosperity, cannot be left to the stimulus of market competition alone. On the other hand it leaves the added incentives to be determined by demands of the market rather than by the apparatus of the state, through rewards or grants of some kind. But because the idea is a compromise on a vital ground, it has long been the subject of controversy—particularly in the mid-nineteenth century and again in our own time. Indeed the arguments today are an appendage to larger questions: about the possibility and desirability of pursuing innovation, and the need to avert its more damaging consequences for people and their environment.

          This Chapter accordingly contains, first, an historical sketch of the British patent system and its relations with those of other countries. This leads to an account of the international developments that stand behind the 1977 Act. Finally, there is some introduction to the range of current debate about patent systems, national and international.

2. THE BRITISH PATENT SYSTEM: HISTORICAL DEVELOPMENT

(1) Beginnings
3-003   The idea of conferring a market monopoly as an incentive to innovate has old roots.[7] In England, as in other parts of Europe, it emerged as one minor form of state patronage.[8] James I was partial to rewarding his political creditors with trading monopolies granted by letters patent. For this there were precedents enough from the illustrious hand of Elizabeth.[9]

[4] See below, §§ 4-001, 5-001.
[5] *The British Patent System*, Cmnd. 4407 (1970).
[6] The government's plans were developed in a White Paper, Cmnd. 6000 (1975) and accompanying Consultative Document (Green Paper).
[7] The growth of guilds and boroughs with exclusive trading privileges was to some extent connected with the desire to introduce and support new industries: see, *e.g.* Fox, *Monopolies and Patents* (1947), Chap. 2.
[8] A Venetian law of 1474 went so far as to establish a positive system for granting 10-year privileges to inventors of new arts and machines. See generally, Penrose, *The Economics of the International Patent System* (1951) 2 *et seq.*; Phillips (198.). J.Leg.Hist. 71.
[9] Even she, at the end of her reign, had to face considerable pressure which led to her issuing the Proclamation concerning Monopolies of 1601. Subsequent litigation declared the invalidity at common law of a patented monopoly granted by her in playing cards; expediently, the case was not brought to judgment until after her death: *Darcy* v. *Allin* (1602) 11 Co.Rep. 84b; see Fox Chaps. 7, 8; Davies (1938) 48 L.Q.R. 398.

But James lacked her command. In 1624 Parliament sought to declare these exercises of royal prerogative void.[10]

The Statute of Monopolies which it enacted suggests not only the growing significance of trade in the country's economy and the beginnings of the long political campaign to favour competition at the expense of monopoly,[11] it also shows the readiness of the political forces represented in Parliament to challenge policies of convenience to the Crown. In its own way it reflects some of the conditions which gradually coalesced to make England the first country to leap forward into industrial production.

Section 6 of the Statute of Monopolies, which exceptionally allowed patent monopolies for 14 years upon "any manner of new manufacture" within the realm to the "true and first inventor," has its own character. The English were already feeling their relative technical backwardness— in comparison with France and Holland—and an "inventor" was accordingly understood to cover not only the deviser of the invention but also one who imported it from abroad. The appeal of patent systems to countries that are set to catch up in the race for technology is a continuing one and one that makes the international aspects of patents, if anything, more important than domestic considerations. Section 6 also expressed the desire to impose some qualification upon the system in the name of higher public interests. The protected manufactures were not to be "contrary to the law nor mischievous to the state, by raising prices of commodities at home, or hurt of trade, or generally inconvenient." The difficulty of finding either criteria or language that could more precisely curb excesses in the system remains as perplexing today. More generally the terms of the section make it plain that an act of economic policy was intended: the objectives were the encouragement of industry, employment and growth, rather than justice to the "inventor" for his effort. The patentee's "consideration" for the grant was that he would put the invention to use and the 14-year period may well represent two cycles of seven-year apprenticeships.

(2) The coming of industrialisation

The seventeenth century provided no more than a germ of a functioning patent system. Even the patent specification, the kernel of today's practice, made its appearance only in the early eighteenth century. Then patentees started to enrol statements of their inventions with the court of Chancery. Initially this practice may have been a device to help prove against infringers what the protected invention was.[12] But a half-century later the courts were requiring the patentee to make a sufficient statement of his conception as "consideration" for the monopoly granted to him.[13]

3-004

---

[10] This was the culmination of a battle on the subject that ran throughout James's reign and continued against his successor, Charles I: see Fox, Chaps. 8-10.

[11] The idea is more completely expressed in the case of the *Cloth Workers of Ipswich* (1615) Godb.R. 252; see further, Fox, pp. 219-232.

[12] Hulme (1897) 13 L.Q.R. 313; but *cf.* Adams and Averley (below, n. 13) at 158-160.

[13] Hulme (1902) 18 L.Q.R. 280, claiming Lord Mansfield's judgment in *Liardet* v. *Johnson* (1778) to have been decisive; but *cf.* Adams and Averley (1986) 7 J.Leg.Hist. 156; see also Adams (1987) 8 J.Leg.Hist. 18.

In the pre-industrial world, the notion that patents should be used as a regular source of technical information was not an obvious one. As long as competition in international trade remained primitive, each country might hope to keep its technical advances to itself. Britain was to be first in learning the economic rewards of exporting technology, but not before she had attempted a policy of national conservation[14] which accorded ill with the notion of patents as a source of technical information. But the requirement of an adequate description was often pressed,[15] not only because patents could then teach an industry what its liveliest members were doing, but because it provided competitors with ammunition against the patent; the sufficiency of the disclosure could itself be attacked, and also the usefulness of the invention. There was a correlative shift in the conception of novelty which would justify the patent grant: the question had been whether anyone was already practising the invention in the country; now another issue was added, did the trade already know of it through publication?[16]

3-005   These changes of emphasis coincide with the first steps towards mechanised factory production and with a decisive increase in the number of patents.[17] Probably these concerned many more home-grown inventions than before, but the role of the patent system in this first remarkable stage of industrial development was somewhat tangential, if not as irrelevant as some economic historians have supposed.[18] Among the famous, Boulton and Watt secured large sums from their steam-engine patents, but these came partly from a special extending Act.[19] Arkwright's main patent threatened the whole industry but proved to be too obscurely drawn to survive the attack on its validity.[20] Crompton had to be given a parliamentary reward of £5,000 since he had virtually no commercial return from his spinning jenny.[21] It is likely that patents provided equally sporadic encouragement for those with less celebrated improvements.[22]

[14] A succession of Acts (not completely repealed until 1843) forbade the export of British machinery, parts or plans and the emigration of skilled workers. Arkwright attempted to defend the obscurity of one specification by claiming that the invention was kept from foreigners: Mantoux, *The Industrial Revolution in the Eighteenth Century* (1961), pp. 227-228.
[15] As in Arkwright's case; see below, n. 20.
[16] A doctrine also propounded in *Liardet* v. *Johnson* (above, n. 13). Half a century later it seems to have been thought that one act of communication to a third party, without any condition of confidence, would rank as an anticipation: Select Committee (below, n. 24) at p. 9. This became firm law later: see below, § 5-011.
[17] In the 1750s less than 10 patents a year were begin granted: in the 1760s that number more than doubled. By the 1810s the average was 110 p.a. and in the 1840s 458 p.a. The figures are tabulated in Boehm, *The British Patent System: 1. Administration* (1967), pp. 22-23: later periods: pp. 33-34.
[18] H. Dutton, *The Patent System and Inventive Activity during the Industrial Revolution 1750-1852* (1984) is an admirable assessment of the evidence.
[19] And after laborious litigation: *Boulton* v. *Bull* (1795) 2 Hy.Bl. 463; *Hornblower* v. *Boulton* (1799) 8 T.R. 95.
[20] See *R.* v. *Arkwright* (1785) 1 W.P.C. 64. Subsequently Arkwright considered publishing all the details of his machine so that foreigners could have it as well: Fitton and Wadsworth, *The Strutts and the Arkwrights 1758-1830* (1958), p. 88.
[21] See Mantoux (above, n. 14), pp. 237-238.
[22] See Boehm (above, n. 17), pp. 22-26.

Part of the explanation must lie in the inefficiencies and uncertainties that surrounded the procedures for securing and enforcing patents.[23] Despite vociferous complaints to a Select Committee in 1829,[24] the process of patenting was to remain one of those obscure pockets of grasp, if not graft, which were able to resist longest the demands of bureaucratic reform. Change finally came just as the Great Exhibition of 1851 marked the vast commercial success of Britain's technical pre-eminence. But the reforms in the patent system were earnest of purpose rather than complacent. The rifts in industrial society were to be filled by providing the working man with every opportunity for self-improvement; and what more significant contribution could there be than to help finance his inventive schemes?[25]

The new patents system,[26] cheap and simple in concept, was designed **3-006** to attract capital for the small ventures and out-of-the-way ideas being generated on the fringes of industry, as much as at its centre. For reasonable fees,[27] an applicant could in effect secure grant merely by registering his specification; and he might take advantage of the new arrangement for first filing a provisional, and then within a year, a complete specification, thus gaining time to work out his ideas more fully. The amount of patenting activity at once increased markedly.[28] Perhaps it was invention at a relatively minor level that was particularly encouraged—it has often enough been said that this is the point where the system has most impact.

But easy patenting had other, less happy consequences. Patent litigation had always been notably protracted and costly. This might deter the genuine inventor from seeking protection, but it left the swashbuckler plenty of room to brandish dubious patents, hoping that competitors would find it simpler to treat shadow as if it were of substance. In the high age of economic liberalism, one school of thought reacted by demanding abolition of the whole system, another by proposing that the alleged invention should, at least in some measure, be the subject of an official examination before any patent was granted.[29]

---

[23] Separate patents had to be secured for England, Ireland and Scotland (until 1852) and a large number of officials had to give their approval. There were some (inevitably) who thought this disincentive a useful filter, but active reform groups kept up agitation. Dickens provided some telling parodies of the inventor's lot (*A Poor Man's Tale of a Patent; Little Dorrit*). See Dutton (above, n. 18), Chaps. 2, 3.

[24] B.P.P. 1829 (332) III.

[25] The same motivation impelled a contemporaneous movement for companies with limited liability.

[26] Introduced by the Patent Law Amendment Act 1852; and see the Report of the Select Committee on Patents B.P.P. 1851 (486) XVIII.

[27] The initial cost of securing U.K. protection was reduced from some £300 to £25.

[28] Net sealings: 1852—891; 1854—2,113: see Boehm (above, n. 17).

[29] The critics had opportunities to put their cases before a Royal Commission (B.P.P. 1864 [3419] XXIX) and then a Select Committee (B.P.P. 1871 (368) X, 1872 (193) XI); and a bill imposing very severe constraints on the system was even passed by the House of Lords. A similar anti-patent movement arose in Western Europe; it lost headway in face of the adoption of the German Patent Law of 1877 and the movement for international patent co-operation: see Machlup and Penrose (1950) 10 J.Econ.Hist. 1.

3-007   Even so modification only came slowly. In 1883,[30] the modern Patent Office replaced the Commissioners of 1852 and it began to examine applications, mainly for formal defects and for sufficiency of description.[31] Successive governments remained reluctant to create a bureaucracy that would search the prior literature and examine against the search results; and this despite the fact that the United States Patent Office had done so since 1836. It was not until 1901, when the Fry Committee demonstrated that 40 per cent. or more of the patents granted were for inventions already described in earlier British specifications, that the change became irresistible.[32] The Office began to search British specifications of the previous 50 years in 1905,[33] but the examination (contrary to the United States example) was confined to the issue of novelty. From this point onwards novelty is generally to be understood in its limited modern sense—as excluding any inquiry into the obviousness of the alleged invention. But equally, it is by this time accepted that a patent once granted might be attacked for its obviousness or lack of inventive step.[34] This additional criterion, which casts such a miasma of uncertainty around patents, is one expression of concern over the consequences of making patents "too easy" to obtain.[35]

3-008   Two other changes in 1883 are linked: juries were excluded from trials of patent actions in favour of a single judge[36]; and patentees were obliged to include in their specifications at least one claim delineating the scope of their monopoly.[37] The question whether the defendant was infringing, so often marginal in contested cases, ceased to be weighed upon a private moral balance in the jury-room and was instead subjected to that nice form of linguistic inquiry so natural to the Chancery mind. Buoyed up by a certain suspicion of monopoly grants, the judges soon insisted that claims marked out the full range of protection: alternative embodiments outside the scope of the words used in the claims were not covered,[38] any more than were the separate parts of machines claimed as mechanical combinations.[39] As we shall see, this use of claims as "fence-posts,"

[30] Patents Designs and Trade Marks Act 1883. Again the initial fees were reduced and the number of patents granted rose from under 4,000 p.a. to some 9,000 p.a.: Boehm (above, n. 17).
[31] The new Comptroller-General was also given a limited power to hear third-party oppositions to applications for patents, a jurisdiction somewhat expanded in 1902. Right of appeal was to the Solicitor- and Attorney-General until 1932, when the Patents Appeal Tribunal (consisting of a Chancery Division judge) was established.
[32] B.P.P. 1901 [Cd. 506, Cd. 530] XXIII.
[33] See Patents Act 1902.
[34] Fox traces the beginnings of this doctrine (which it is his object to denounce) to *Crane* v. *Price* (1842) 1 W.P.C. 393 at 411. By the end of the century Brett M.R. could treat it "generally with amused contempt" (*Edison Bell* v. *Smith* (1894) 11 R.P.C. 389 at 398; and see him also in *Hayward* v. *Hamilton* (1879-81) Griff P.C. 115 at 121). But thereafter the doctrine was at most looked at with suspicion *e.g.* by Fletcher Moulton, L.J. in *British Westinghouse* v. *Braulik* (see below, § 5-032, n. 20).
[35] Obviousness secured an earlier foothold in U.S. law (see *Hotchkiss* v. *Greenwood* 52 U.S. 248 (1850)), but patents were then more readily available in that country.
[36] Complaints about the difficulty of presenting technical matters to juries can be found in the various Parliamentary investigations.
[37] Patents, etc., Act 1883, s.5(5): "a distinct statement of the invention claimed."
[38] *Nobel* v. *Anderson* (1895) 12 R.P.C. 164 (H.L.).
[39] *British United* v. *Fussell* (1908) 25 R.P.C. 631 (C.A.).

rather than as "guidelines," affects a great deal else in the basic law of patents. And since it is a development that has not been paralleled in some other industrial countries, it has presented an obstacle in the way of modern plans for collaboration, such as the European system for granting patents.[40]

With these developments, the essential features of the modern admin-   3-009
istrative system were settled in a way that was not to be disturbed until the events of the 1970s. The statutory revisions of 1907, 1919, 1932 and above all 1949, put the law more in the form of a code and altered it in many details, but attempted nothing really drastic. Apart from certain international considerations dealt with below, events worth recording were the restrictions upon claims to chemical substances that were introduced in 1919 and removed again in 1949 as having little real value[41]; and the introduction in 1949 of obviousness as a ground of pre-grant opposition—an objection which, however, it proved very difficult to substantiate in these proceedings.[42]

3. THE "INTERNATIONAL" PATENT SYSTEM

(1) Foreign impact upon national systems

Many countries have been attracted to introduce a patent system by   3-010
the hope that it will act as a lure to foreign technology. The same concern has induced them to open their system to foreign applications. The United States, for instance, allowed foreigners to apply for patents well before it offered copyright to foreign authors.[43] Equally the patenting countries of the nineteenth century were led to a modest union, under the Paris Industrial Property Convention of 1883,[44] which guaranteed the nationals of each member state the same treatment in others as was given to their own nationals.[45] The union also established the system of Convention priority, under which an application in one of the states gave a period (eventually 12 months) in which to pursue an application in any of the others; this would bear the same priority date as the first.[46]

---

[40] See below, §§ 4-030—4-031.
[41] See below, §§ 4-036—4-037.
[42] See below, §§ 5-026—5-028.
[43] In 1836 and 1891 respectively. The British, having greater interest in securing rights for themselves abroad, were in both fields prepared to extend protection to foreigners; even so, in copyright it took reciprocal agreement to establish that publication in another country could found British copyright: see below, § 9-008.
[44] Subsequently revised in 1900 (Brussels), 1911 (Washington), 1925 (The Hague), 1934 (London), 1958 (Lisbon) and 1967 (Stockholm). The U.K. ratified the latest version in 1969. For the debates leading to the Convention see Ladas, *The International Protection of Industrial Property* (1930); Penrose, *The Economics of the International Patent System* (1951), Chap. 3. For the latest attempt at revision, see below, § 3-012. In 1989, the Convention had 99 members of its Union. See generally Beier (1984) 15 I.I.C. 1.
[45] The point of this formula was that countries without a patent law could join the Union and get benefits for their own nationals abroad. On this basis the Netherlands and Switzerland joined and the strategy proved useful in getting them to adopt patent systems of their own. The present provisions (Arts. 2, 3) provide equal treatment on a basis of domicile and place of business as well as nationality.
[46] See below, §§ 4-008—4-010.

In this century, the international exchange of technology has been the chief point of maintaining patent systems in countries whose socialised economies provide little reason for offering market power as a reward to domestic inventors. Within a planned economy it is logical to encourage innovation by systems of state rewards[47]—the very notion which is most often posed as the alternative to a patent system even for capitalist countries.

3-011   As in seventeenth century England, any country which offers patents to foreigners will want the invention to be exploited to the advantage of its own economy. It may indeed take measures to make the patent more than a cover protecting the import of foreign-made goods. If it has a domestic industry that competes with the foreign patentee there may be particular cause for jealousy. This certainly was the motive force behind the introduction into the British system of provisions allowing the grant of compulsory licences on the ground that the invention was not being worked domestically[48]: the success of the German and Swiss chemical industries in the late nineteenth century was built to a substantial degree on the holding of key patents.[49] The French originally went even further, making revocation of the patent the penalty for importing patented articles from abroad; lifting this draconian sanction was made a precondition of membership of the Paris Convention.[50] The majority of patenting countries now have some form of compulsory working requirement,[51] which the Paris Convention allows to be sanctioned by compulsory licensing once three years have elapsed from grant[52]; and by revocation if compulsory licensing fails after two years to produce the required result.[53] Provisions of this kind in national law are not only offensive to notions of international comity supposedly underlying the Convention; they are also economically unsound in any case where efficiencies of scale demand production in one place for international markets.

(2) Hostility to patents

3-012   Countries which are well enough organised to bargain hard for the foreign technology that they buy, and technically advanced enough to build for themselves upon what they learn, are likely to be reasonably satisfied with what they get out of patents. By keeping their patent systems alive, Comecon countries have created some sense of security for Western enterprises selling them technology. Today, they also provide a convenient route to reciprocal rights for their own technology in foreign states. The U.S.S.R., it may be noted, joined the Paris Convention in 1964.

[47] For such inventors' certificates see, *e.g.* Soltisynski (1969) 32 M.L.R. 408; Boguslavsky (1979) 18 Ind.Prop. 113; accompanying the new interest in market forces in the Eastern bloc are signs that patents will be made available to domestic inventors.
[48] Tentatively introduced in 1883 without reference to foreign working, the provisions were made much more specific in 1907. But, as elsewhere, they did not lead to frequent applications: see below, §§ 7-050 *et seq.*
[49] Haber, *The Chemical Industry during the Nineteenth Century* (1971), pp. 166-167, 198-204.
[50] See Penrose (above, n. 44), pp. 74-77; PIP Art. 5A(1).
[51] But the U.S. has always, by geography and economic position, been able to remain aloof from this sort of requirement.
[52] Or four years from application if this is longer.
[53] PIP Art. 5A(2)-(5).

Indeed, it is in countries where the patent system remains part of an unplanned or partly planned economy that its effects upon the international trade of the state are more likely to be called in question. To take two very different examples among common law countries: in Canada, the patent system came under careful, but sceptical scrutiny from a team of economists.[54] To them it seemed to operate largely as a shield for the imported products of foreign owners (mainly from the United States), while doing very little to encourage the development of home-based industry. However, plans drastically to curtail the scope of the patent monopoly in the wake of these criticisms met with hostile reception from industry there and abroad— some measure at least of the very considerable value that substantial owners do attach to patents.[55] In India, where the government became intent on rapid intervention in industrial ownership and policy, wide powers were actually taken to grant compulsory licences on "reasonable" terms.[56] One result was a marked reduction in the amount of patenting by foreign enterprises in that country.

For countries even less advanced, the disadvantages may seem still graver. Yet they will likely be under pressure from industrialised countries and trans-national enterprises to have a patent system, whether or not one has been inherited from a colonial past. Increasingly the developing countries have been searching for a *via media* by which they can use patents to attract foreign technology, while at the same time influencing by bureaucratic intervention the terms on which their own firms collaborate with foreign enterprises. In the 1970s a number of experiments were made in domestic legislation, particularly in Central and South America.[57] In international circles there was increasing discussion about acceptable models. This focused particularly on two negotiations: one was the formulation of UNCTAD's Code of Conduct for the Transfer of Technology, which was a practical expression of the search for a New International Economic Order. The other was the Revision Conference of the Paris Convention, which also grew out of UNCTAD criticisms of the current operation of patent systems internationally. The Transfer of Technology Code was taken by 1980 to a point where detailed drafts existed; but it was a point of high controversy, with different versions; preferred by the Group of 77 (developing countries) the industrial countries and the socialist countries.[58] It was never settled

3-013

---

[54] Economic Council of Canada, *Report on Intellectual and Industrial Property* (1971) (with additional background studies); Firestone, *Economic Implications of Patents* (1972). For a similar appraisal in Australia, see Manderville *et al.* (below, n. 88).
[55] Working Paper on Patent Law Reform (1976).
[56] Patents Act 1970 (India); Vedaraman (1972) 3 I.I.C. 39; Kunz-Hallstein (1975) 4 I.I.C. 427 at pp. 438-440.
[57] Following, in particular, resolutions of the Andean Pact countries in 1970 and the Argentine law on technology transfer of the same year: see, *e.g.* Soberanis (1977) 7 Georgia J.Int.L. 17 (on Mexico).
[58] For these developments, see, *e.g.* Anderfelt, *International Patent Legislation and Developing Countries* (1971); Vaitsos (1972) 9 J.Dev. Studies; Penrose (1973) Econ.J. 768; Lall (1976) 10 J. World Trade Law 1; Kunz-Hallstein (above, n. 55); Laird (1980) 9 CIPA 276; Wilner and Fikentscher in *Legal Problems of Codes of Conduct for Multinational Enterprises* (Horn ed., 1980), pp. 177, 189; Fikentscher, *The Draft International Code of Conduct on the Transfer of Technology* (1980); Cabanellas, *Antitrust and Direct Regulation of International Transfer of Technology Transactions* (1984); Blakeney, *Legal Aspects of the Transport of Technology to Developing Countries* 1989.

whether any final form of the Code would have legal effect or would be regarded as a voluntary code of good practice. Immediately after this, the Revision Conference of the Paris Convention held three sessions, but then adjourned *sine die* in 1982. The eventual sticking point proved to be demands from the Group of 77, for example, that their countries have power to impose *exclusive* compulsory licences on patentees in respect of failure to work the invention in the national territory.[59]

3-014   Against such revisions, the United States took a particularly strong position, urging the importance at the least of maintaining the Convention's existing standards of protection.[60] Subsequently, it has proposed that "trade-related" aspects of intellectual property should become part of the Uruguay Round of GATT negotiations, which are currently in progress. This is a determined initiative against a group of 20 or so countries which fail to give any real protection to American intellectual property (or so it is claimed). The hope is to secure a GATT Agreement on Intellectual Property, which would require a high level of protection and adequate sanctions over a wide range of subject-matter. On the technical side, it is sought to cover biotechnical processes and products, patents for microorganisms and products, trade secrets and integrated circuit designs, together with copyright for computer programs. Through GATT machinery, techniques for dispute settlement between countries would be provided, which are present only in the most shadowy form in the Paris Convention.[61] Since such an agreement would emerge as part of a package of mutual concessions on access to markets, it has given a new conspectus to diplomacy in the intellectual property field, which hitherto had found its main focus in the activities of the World Intellectual Property Organisation (WIPO). The outcome could be highly significant to the industries of advanced countries, but its legal effects are most likely to be felt in countries of Third World that are evidently on the way to development.

(3) Co-operation in patenting: world-wide linkages

3-015   Before 1977, there was nothing that could be called an international patent system, at least in legal and organisational terms. The Paris Convention was largely restricted to basic principles for securing readier access to the national systems maintained by the different Member States. It made no arrangements beyond its priority system for standardising or simplifying the process of applying for patents and it required the substantive law to conform to its standards only on such collateral matters as the compulsory licensing requirements.[62]

The experience of many industrial countries has been that unexamined patents lead to nuisance. The answer to this was to institute some form of pre-grant examination of the substantive merits of the case in the light of a search of earlier technical literature. Serious examination is not

---

[59] On this particular campaign compare, P.A. 1977, s.49(3), now quietly removed by CDPA 1988, Sched. 5, § 13.
[60] It stood alone in resisting demands that the present unanimity rule for amending the Convention become a qualified majority rule.
[61] See generally, Beier and Schricker (eds.) *GATT or WIPO?* (1989, forthcoming).
[62] See above, § 3-011.

cheap; and, as the number of countries demanding an examination rose, so did the cost. The applicant seeking a patent in several countries saw his case processed in a roughly similar way, but subjected to a search of a varying range of literature and judged accordingly to varying criteria, in a series of offices operating quite independently. Accordingly patentees (whatever the interests of their patent departments and professional advisers) and governments (whatever the bureaucratic pretensions of their patent offices) began to appreciate that "internationalising" the patenting process might increase efficiency and reduce costs.

On a world-wide basis,[63] a system of international patent applications **3-016** under the Patent Cooperation Treaty (PCT) has reached fruition. The Treaty was signed in Washington in 1970 and put into effect from June 1, 1978, its central administration being provided by WIPO in Geneva.[64] The Treaty is of interest to any country which is not content to have a pure registration system but instead opts for some form of examination. For its main chapters provide, after the submission of a single international application designating the PCT countries in which patents are wanted,[65] for two things. Chapter 1 creates an international search conducted by one of a handful of International Search Authorities (the Australian, Japanese, Russian and United States Patent Offices, the European Patent Office and to a more limited extent the Swedish and Austrian Offices)[66]; Chapter 2 establishes an International Preliminary Examination. Participating states are not obliged to adhere to both Chapters[67]; nor is an applicant obliged to have the preliminary examination.

The Treaty is not founded upon any international agreement about the **3-017** grounds of validity for a patent. The Preliminary Examination accordingly leads to a report on a number of basic questions (patentable subject matter, novelty, inventive step and industrial applicability) in accordance with criteria that are defined only generally in the Treaty.[68] Nevertheless, for countries which have no examining system, the report may provide a basis upon which a national patent office, applying its own law, can decide whether or not to grant a patent. In the hope of opening this opportunity to developing countries, it was hastily decided to introduce the second Chapter along with the first in 1978.[69]

Apart from this, the main advantage of the Treaty is practical: it allows an applicant to institute applications in numerous countries by a

[63] Another collaboration of importance is the Strasbourg Convention concerning the International Patent Classification 1971 (not yet ratified by the U.K.).

[64] Records of the Diplomatic Conference are published. See generally Pfanner (1979) 1 E.I.P.R. 98.

[65] National or regional patent offices are appointed receiving offices for applications from given countries.

[66] The range of material open to search is broadly defined: PCT Art. 15(2), PCT Rules, 33; but each Search Authority will work upon a different body of material, depending upon its collection and linquistic capacity. For the consequences in the EPO, see below, § 4-003.

[67] The Member States adopting Chapters I and II, the search authorities and examining authorities at any time may be ascertained from the latest number of the PCT Gazette.

[68] PCT Art. 33, PCT Rules, r. 64.

[69] Accordingly a number of African states from the start took advantage of both Chapters

single procedure; and to delay his final decision to apply in a number of countries (with the official fees, agents' fees and translation costs that this entails) for a period of 20 months (or, where Chapter II can be employed, for 25 months) after his priority date.[70] What the Treaty does not provide is an "international patent," since in the end each national office, or regional office such as the EPO, decides what patents to grant for its own territory.

In 1989, 41 states were participating in the PCT. Over its first decade in operation, the Convention attained a moderate degree of success with users: in 1987, over 9,000 international applications were filed.

(4) Co-operation in patenting: Western Europe

3-018   Europes industrial renaissance after the Second World War pointed up the considerable differences that existed in the systems of patent administration in the different countries. West Germany, Holland and Switzerland, for instance, undertook extensive examination of patents before grant and permitted third-party interventions; but the first two countries had introduced arrangements allowing this to be deferred for up to seven years.[71] France, Belgium and Italy had registration systems, though in the French law of 1968 a search, with examiner's commentary, was introduced.[72] Britain occupied a mid-way position, providing for a limited search and examination, together with the possibility of third-party opposition on somewhat wider grounds.

It was appreciated very early in the life of the EEC that patents would pose a substantial barrier to intra-Community trade in "legitimate" goods.[73] In 1959, a Working Group was convened to consider solving the problem by instituting an EEC patent. Its plan for the purpose[74] was put aside in the wake of Britain's first failure to secure entry to the EEC; for the desirability of having the British in such an enterprise was widely acknowledged. When, however, the United States took the lead in promoting the Patent Cooperation Treaty, France sought refuge in a revival of the EEC plan. With only the beginnings of an examination system, she found reason to fear the advent of international applications for France which would carry the impress of a PCT search and preliminary examination.

3-019   The revived negotiations now involved a double package: first, a Convention for a single granting system through a European Patent Office; second, a convention for a Community patent which would be one product of this system. The first Convention was concerned, not with

---

[70] See below, §§ 4-008 et seq.
[71] See below, § 4-015.
[72] This "documentary report system" survives in the 1978 legislation which gave effect to the new conventions, but the opportunities for intervention have increased: Vianès (1979) 18 Ind.Prop. 220; Lecca (1979) 9 CIPA 282.
[73] See above, § 1-023.
[74] The "Haertel Draft" of 1962. This was followed by the Strasbourg Convention on The Unification of Certain Points of Substantive Patent Law (Council of Europe, 1963), which has proved of great influence in settling the law of validity in the EPC and CPC. Its entry into force was, however, delayed until 1980 (the U.K. being one of the initial ratifying states). For the history of the European Conventions, see further Van Empel (below, n. 76), Chap. 1; Banks Report (Cmnd. 4407, 1970, Chap. 3).

freedom of EEC trade, but with providing a less wasteful, but nonetheless substantial, examination of applications. It was accordingly to be open to a wider range of West European states, including the United Kingdom. A successful applicant would secure at the end of the process a bundle of national patents, normally in common form, for such participant countries as he designated in his application. The system would only provide an alternative route to a patent in those countries, each of which would be left free to maintain its own national system.[75] On this basis the European Patent Convention (EPC) was signed at Munich in 1973.[76] That city became the headquarters of the European Patent Office (EPO),[77] which opened its doors for applications on June 1, 1978.[78] In the first 10 years of operation, the EPC has had considerable success in attracting applications. In 1987, the total number of European applications (including those via the PCT) was nearly 46,000; and in that year over 17,000 European patents were granted.[79] While there are now 13 countries participating in the system, the EEC states which face continuing political difficulty in joining are Denmark and Ireland. This casts a certain shadow over an otherwise bright picture.

The second part of the arrangement, the Community Patent Convention (CPC), was signed two years later in Luxembourg by the EEC states (including, by then, the United Kingdom).[79] Its principle is that, at the end of the European granting procedure, if a patent is sought for any EEC state, a single patent for the whole Community will be granted.[80] This Community patent will thus come in the "bundle," together with national patents for such non-EEC States as are also designated. It is possible that the CPC will take actual effect as part of the completion of the internal market by 1992.

3-020

There have been two main reasons for the long delay in introducing the CPC. The chief advantage which the single Community patent would bring would be the ability to enforce it throughout the Common Market by a single main proceeding.[81] But since such a process would involve national courts, the matter is inevitably complex and was left by the original Convention for further discussion. In 1985 an Agreement, resulting from a Luxembourg Conference, was initialled (but not signed) by member states. This provided that, for an indefinite period, certain national courts,[82] would have jurisdiction to consider both the infringe-

3-021

---

[75] Proceedings of the negotiations have been published and form a source which is considered in deciding how to interpret the EPC.

[76] See Van Empel, *The Granting of European Patents* (1975); Beier (1981) 14 Vanderbilt J.Trans.L. 1.

[77] The main sub-branch is at the Hague where the Search Division of the EPO is situate; the Office took over the former International Patent Institute there.

[78] Originally the fields in which it would examine were restricted, but progress towards the complete range was completed by December 1, 1979; see EPC Art. 162.

[79] EPO, Annual Report, 1987, which contains much else by way of interest on the European system.

[80] CPC Art. 3. The Community Patent is to be "unitary" in the sense that it can be granted, transferred, revoked or allowed to lapse only in respect of the whole Common Market: Art. 2(2). It seems, however, that an applicant will retain the right to opt for national patents.

[81] This would include the possibility of interlocutory orders having Community-wide effect.

[82] There was agreement that in some countries the range of courts able to hear these proceedings would be much more restricted that for national patents at present. See generally, Groves [1987] 8 Bus.L.R. 170.

ment and validity of a Community patent. Alternatively, validity could be raised before a special Revocation Division of the EPO.[83] In addition, a Common Appeal Court (COPAC), with judges from all member states, would act as the effective appeal court from the national courts and the Revocation Division.[84] The EC Court of Justice would only consider references involving possible conflicts with the Rome Treaty and on questions of jurisdiction arising under a special Protocol which will determine the member state in which proceedings may be launched.

3-022   The second problem has been political: since the CPC is a Convention distinct from the Rome Treaty, Community organs possess no power to impose its terms on member states. Denmark and Ireland both face serious obstacles in securing the national mandate necessary to ratify the Convention and its proposed amendments[85]. There have been discussions over the possibility of implementing the CPC for less than the whole Community but that seems a decidedly second-best solution.[86] This explains why the prospect of a Community patent still remains obscure, even amid the rhetoric of "1992."

Ironically, the starting point of these negotiations—the desire to stop national patents from limiting the free movement of goods within the Common Market—became much less significant with time. For the EC Court of Justice has interpreted the Treaty of Rome in a way that achieves much of what is necessary. The provisions touching the question that were finally included in the CPC do little to provide answers on those issues which are still outstanding.[87]

4. JUSTIFYING THE PATENT SYSTEM

(1) Basic objectives

3-023   In the course of time, both "private" and "public" justifications have played prominent roles in the arguments in favour of patents for invention, as for other kinds of intellectual property.[88] At various periods

---

[83] Originally, after a transitional period, invalidity was to be restricted to the Revocation Division (and above it a Revocation Board, now abandoned).

[84] In appeals from national courts, overall conduct would be in the hands of a second instance national court, which would be required to refer questions of infringement and validity to the COPAC.

[85] Likewise for ratification of the EPC (see above).

[86] See generally, S.C.(H.L.) on the European Communities, *A European Community Patent* (H.L. 17, 1986).

[87] See below, §§ 7-042 *et seq.* It should be noted that the CPC is expressed to be subject to the Treaty of Rome: see Art. 93.

[88] What follows builds upon the ideas introduced above at §§ 1-016—1-020. The best-known modern discussion of the justifications for patent systems, sceptical in tone, is Machlup, *An Economic Review of the Patent System* (US Senate Committee on the Judiciary, Sub-Committee on Patents, Trademarks and Copyrights, Study No. 15). And see Plant (1934) 1 Economica 30; Scherer, *Industrial Market Structure and Economic Performance* (2nd ed., 1980), Chap. 15; Economic Council of Canada, *Report on Intellectual and Industrial Property* (1971), Chaps. 3, 4; together with Hindley, *Background Study on Economic Theory*, Chap. 1; and Firestone, *Economic Implications of Patents* (1971); Taylor and Silberston, *The Economic Impact of the Patent System* (1973) Chap. 2; Bowman, *Patent and Antitrust Law* (1973), Chap. 2; Kitch (1977) 29 J. Law & Econ. 265; Manderville, Lamberton and Bishop, *Economic Effects of the Australian Patent System* (1982).

the idea of a patent as an instrument of justice to the inventor has proved attractive, and the power of this sort of argument to persuade is by no means politically exhausted.[89] But, looking at the matter with any degree of sophistication, it is hard to see that rewarding inventive ingenuity is anything more than an incidental consequence of modern patent systems. They do not protect each inventor who conceives an invention; only the first-comer is entitled—in most systems, indeed, it is the first to apply for a patent, rather than the first to invent, who is given priority. The protection is then good not only against those who derive their information from that patentee but also against those who work it out independently. The period of protection, moreover, is very short compared with other forms of "property." If a major object were to give the inventor his just reward, a system more closely akin to copyright—with its "property"-like duration and its protection of all original creations, but only against copying—would seem more appropriate. In this connection, the intrusion of artistic copyright into the sphere of industrial production after 1968, and its major modification twenty years later, provides a telling comparison.[90]

Today the bulk of debate over patent systems concentrates upon their role as a "public" instrument of economic policy. Patents are looked upon to provide two kinds of aid towards the technical efficiency, and hence the growing wealth, of the community as a whole. They are intended to encourage the making of inventions and the subsequent innovative work that will put those inventions to practical use; and they are expected to procure information about the invention for the rest of the industry and the public generally, which otherwise might be withheld, at least for a period that could be crucial. These incentives and the informational objectives deserve separate consideration.

(2) Patents as incentives to invent and innovate

Discussion about the efficacy of incentives has a practical, utilitarian   3-024
flavour which is lacking when the argument is about the demands of justice for the individual. Even so, it is very difficult to measure or assess the effects (if any) that a patent system is producing. It is widely felt that some sort of intervention is needed if inventions are to be made and introduced at anything like an optimal rate. But whether this should be done by a patent system, rather than by giving legal protection against breach of confidence or copying, or by direct investment on the part of the state, is more controversial. And if it is to be by a patent system, there are many questions about its exact nature which may affect its performance.

Modern patent systems, it should be observed, offer a standard formula to all who have "inventions" to protect. They contrast with systems of research grant and reward, whether funded by the state or private organisations.[91] These usually depend upon a decision by the

---

[89] For instance, the introduction of compensation for employee-inventors reflects this attitude: see below, §§ 7-008—7-014.

[90] See below, Chap. 14.

[91] Compare also recent suggestions for systems of "innovation patent" and "innovation warrant," both of which require a state office to play a deciding role in determining the term and other incidents of the right granted: see Kingston [1981] E.I.P.R. 131, 207; Kronz [1983] E.I.P.R. 178, 206.

paymaster to concentrate resources upon particular objectives. Assessing a patent system, accordingly, means taking a view of its effects across the board—and that adds considerably to the difficulty. Two aspects of its range which make useful starting points in the discussion are the types of inventor for whom today it provides its incentive; and the types of invention to which it is applied.

(a) *Types of inventor*

3-025   One persistent argument against patents in the nineteenth century controversy was this: since inventions are there to be discovered, industries that have progressed to a certain point will inevitably make them, and so artificial aids are unnecessary.[92] It was a line of argument that carried some conviction when the bulk of inventions concerned relatively simple mechanical contrivances that were often worked out as by-product of ordinary manufacturing. In the face of increasingly systematic organisation or research and development, and the extensive process of education which precedes it, this point of view is harder to maintain. If anything, the development of this characteristic of modern industry turns the issue on its head: is the only question now, whether patents are needed to produce the optimal degree of investment in research and development organised on a "corporate" scale? It seems not. One perceptive account of the historical record suggests that the individual inventor, and the small organisation centred around individuals of outstanding quality, continue to contribute a significant, even perhaps a disproportionate, number of the most important inventions that have been made over recent decades.[93] This type of inventor certainly cannot be ignored in any assessment of patents.

In any case, there is no clear evidence that corporations are not influenced in their research and development decisions by their chances of securing and taking advantage of patent protection. Invention, and its subsequent development, still occur across the whole spectrum of industrial organisation from giant troop to one-man band. One of the more attractive arguments for a patent system is that, because of this very diversity, a range of different incentives is desirable.[94] Patents then have their place as the technique aimed at those who feel the attraction of market rewards.[95]

[92] See Machlup and Penrose (above, n. 29). Further, it could be said that there was injustice in giving the reward to the man who stumbled upon the solution first, since he probably owed a great deal to what he had learned from his precursors. Note in this connection the recent refusal of a patent to a genetic engineering firm because it merely won a race to a known goal by known methods; below, § 5-036.

[93] Jewkes, Sawers and Stillerman, *The Sources of Invention* (2nd ed., 1969), Chap. 9. It does not follow that individual inventors are necessarily spurred by the patent system. Many academic scientists, for instance, are moved more by the desire for knowledge and the recognition that invention may bring; they may well have the comfort of secure employment already.

[94] *Ibid.*

[95] There is some evidence that the expenditure of really large firms on R & D does not produce proportionately as much invention as that of smaller firms. But it is hard to weigh the significance of this, since it requires an evaluation of the merits of different inventions; nor, even if it is true, has it any clear consequence for the future of patent systems.

(b) *Levels of invention*

Patent systems protect a wide variety of technical novelties, from **3-026** breakthroughs that will found new industries, to quite minor improvements in established products. The chance of behaving to any striking degree as a monopolist is in fact reserved to a small proportion of all patentees.[96] Two characteristics of the invention will determine how far this is possible: the extent to which it fulfils a demand from consumers that was previously not met at all, or met only by something much less satisfactory (television in place of sound radio); and the degree to which it is cheaper or leads to more efficient operations in comparison with the substitutes which preceded it (power-driven tool replacing one hand-operated). Occasionally, as with a drug that had no real precursor, a patentee may be able to withhold supplies so as to charge the price which will give him the largest return from estimated demand. So also when he is able to cut costs of production so much that he can still reach this level of profit at a price below that at which competitors can sell any substitute products and stay in business. More often, however, he cannot achieve so drastic an effect. His room for manoeuvre is then limited by the need to sell at a price just enough below that of competitors to cut into their market shares.[97]

Some of this century's most significant inventions were only put to **3-027** productive use long after their discovery, which suggests the system is not always a noticeably efficient mechanism for procuring commercial innovation.[98] But equally the long gaps indicate the need for some artificial intrusion into the competitive process. The barriers that may stand in the way of introducing completely new ideas, however striking their ultimate commercial success, are numerous. The difficulties may be innovative— the investment and time needed to arrive at a viable product may be unpredictable. The problems may be financial—the cost of setting up new plant, and often of writing-off old, or the cost of persuading distributors to stock and consumers to buy, may seem forbidding. The inhibitions may be organisational—the very size of an enterprise may mean that risky ideas are abandoned in face of well-reasoned argument from one or other quarter. Of course there are industries where the leading firms become seized by a determination to innovate. Pharmaceutical producers are one outstanding recent example, the computer industry another. But in others again, major technical change may be held up until individuals with flair and determination can secure the independence (within or outside a larger organisation) that they need to override the well-meaning caution of others less adventurous. In particular, if the dominant firms in

[96] See also above, §§ 1-019; 1-020.

[97] This puts in very summary form some crucial conclusions to be drawn from the standard economic analysis of the patent system: for which see, *e.g.* Baxter (1966) 76 Yale L.J. 267, 358-370 (Appendix).

[98] Individuals or industries have an obvious motive for suppressing highly efficient inventions of the long-lasting razor-blade variety. However, there is not much evidence that this object can actually be achieved: that it can be brought about by patenting, as distinct from swearing all concerned to secrecy, seems highly unlikely, though it is sometimes suggested.

3-028   an industry are few, there is a danger of complacent sluggishness; of this a number of illustrations exist.[99]

Patent systems ought to help in lowering the psychological barriers to major innovation, particularly since the limited period of protection imposes a penalty for being dilatory. But the practical operation of the system introduces elements that diminish this impact. An innovator who is successful either demonstrates that there is a new market to be tapped, or he begins to cut substantially into the market shares of established competitors. No one is more obviously exposed to envious imitation. It becomes vital for competitors to examine the innovator's patents for weaknesses. Since the protection a patent gives depends primarily on the language used to define the claims in the specification, a rival may well spend a good deal on finding other ways of doing much the same thing, which the draftsman of the specification did not contemplate (and did not inadvertently manage to cover). Any competitor with fight in him must be expected to look for methods of "inventing round" the specification.[1]

3-029   As far as the validity of a patent is concerned, the difference between making the invention and succeeding in innovation is crucial. There may have been various suggestions in the literature and practice before the patent which reached more or less the same invention. Even if none of these led to successful production, they may nevertheless provide a plausible basis for attacking the patent.[2] A patentee who appreciates this when he is deciding whether to manufacture may be obliged to treat his exclusive right as a weapon that can be tested only in prolonged and exhausting legal skirmishes.

In terms of objectives, the implications are straightforward: if the patent system is to provide a useful incentive for the making and commercial introduction of major inventions, it must give sound rights of clear scope. The current movement to strengthen the examination procedures of patent offices should accordingly be pressed ahead. If in consequence a few significant inventions are mistakenly refused protection, this should be accepted as an inevitable risk in the pursuit of a greater good.

3-030   Looking across the whole range of industry, however, a measure of doubt must continue to surround the role of patent systems in encouraging the exploitation of major inventions. Even with pharmaceutical products, where patents do appear to provide a significant amount of protection, it is evident that this strength arises from a combination of forces: in particular, the fact that many countries now require lengthy testing of new products substantially increases the "lead-time" of a novel drug over the substitutes and alternatives that competitors may then develop. It may well be that the incentive effect of patents is of more significance when it comes to marginal ideas—concepts that do not hold hope of more than minor improvements in the existing art. Although a patent cannot in such a case promise a major run of monopoly profits,

---

[99] e.g. Jewkes et al. (above, n. 93), pp. 166-168 on the extraction of iron from laconite.

[1] "Inventing round" a patent, and the patentee's counter-ploy of himself fencing off the alternatives in order to block others, may sometimes produce valuable information. But this is scarcely a rational way to allocate scarce resources; see Plant (above, n. 88 at 45); Machlup (above, n. 88, at 51).

[2] See further, below, § 5-031.

nonetheless it offers the chance to explore and exploit free of direct imitation; and competitors may not feel the same compulsion to find equivalents or to attack validity. With major inventions, moreover, the advantage of being first in the field may well be a perfectly adequate incentive, whereas lesser improvements may well be neglected in the absence of a protective stimulus. And, of course, there is no telling when something that looks small will turn out big.

One practice question which stems from such considerations is how to define the minimum inventive content that will justify the grant of a patent. This breaks down into two major issues. First, should the general patent system adopt a requirement of inventive step (or "non-obvious-ness"), and, if so, how should its level be set? Most modern patent systems (including the British) have such a test, and we shall discuss later the search for verbal formulae which seek to specify the elusive quality in question.[3] Here it should be emphasised that the issue creates uncertainty about the validity of many patents and is one significant cause in lowering the practical value of the system as an incentive to innovation. 3-031

Secondly, a country must decide whether to introduce a special regime of "petty patents" or "utility models," giving a shorter period of protection without preliminary examination for minor technical advances. A number of countries have taken this road,[4] but so far Australia is the only member of the British Commonwealth among them.[5] One type of petty patent system restricts its protection to the design features of industrial articles which assume their appearance for functional reasons. The right is then useful in stopping direct imitations of mechanical novelties during their early years on the market. In Britain, a broadly similar result is to be achieved through the unregistered design right now being introduced in place of a deployment of artistic copyright.[6]

(c) *Optimum term for patents*

The consensus in the European convention negotiations was that patents deserve to last for 20 years from filing. A single period for all patents has an arbitrary appearance[7]; but the British experience of granting extensions in deserving cases demonstrated the practical hurdles in the way of introducing individual variations. If one term must be chosen as a maximum how can the most desirable be ascertained? The answer must be given in terms of incentives, and in particular of the encouragement needed for inventions of commercial importance enough 3-032

---

[3] Below, § 5-024.
[4] For the well-known West German system of *Gebrauchsmuster* (utility models), see, *e.g.* Popp (1978) 7 CIPA 368. A similar solution for the U.K. was adumbrated, *e.g.* in the Green Paper, *Intellectual Property Rights and Innovation* (Cmnd. 9117, 1983) 20-22; but was rejected in the Government's White Paper (Cmnd. 9712), pp. 15–18
[5] Patents Act Amendment Act 1979; see Halford [1979] Ann.I.P.L. 40.
[6] Below, §§ 14-026 *et seq.*
[7] Thus the pharmaceutical industry constantly point out that scrupulous official testing of new drugs to establish their safety may delay their introduction for several years; hence the demand for a longer period of protection in their case. But within the EPC net, that would now have to be by agreement of the participant states, and that is diplomatically unlikely.

to last for the whole period. It may be that the recent increase in the British period from 16 to 20 years is large enough to have real impact on the willingness to spend on invention and innovation of this potential kind. Nonetheless the present value of a return of investment from a point so far in the future is small.[8] Additions even of this magnitude to the term can have little predictable effect on incentives. Yet each year that is added increases the social cost of having the invention available only through the channel of the patent monopoly. Certainly any further extension should be made only after most careful consideration.

(3) Patents as an information system

3-033   In Britain the policy of making the patent system a source of technical information has been deliberately pursued since the early industrial revolution.[9] For many years the results have justified treating this aspect of the system as more than a useful by-product. Patents do make available a large quantity of information about the latest technical advances, and they are regularly consulted by those concerned with development in many industries. Nevertheless exaggerated expectations need to be avoided. If the inventive concept is one that has to be embodied in a marketed product the patent may give earlier access to the information and perhaps a more explicit statement of what the invention is. Only if the invention is one that need never be revealed to the rest of the industry in the course of exploiting it does the patent provide a clear long-term gain in terms of publicity. But this, of course, is the case where secrecy offers a real alternative—a route that, despite the danger of leaks, may seem simpler and cheaper to pursue.

3-034   The information aspect of patents is not a policy that is altogether easy to implement.[10] There is an obvious temptation to any patentee to omit from his specification information that may seem incidental but is in fact useful or important to commercial success. When this effect can be achieved, the patent system is reduced to an index of sources from which further information may be had on application and payment. This leaves the policy maker, whether legislator, patent office administrator or judge, with a choice: either to recognise that the system cannot hope to provide more information, or to insist that it should by declaring such patents invalid. Countries with examining offices have arrived at rather varied results in their approach to this dilemma. The typical American specification is noteworthy for its dogged attention to pedestrian detail; a West German specification may be hazy about practical steps but is more likely to reveal basic concepts. One decision of the English Court of Appeal leans in the former direction: it holds that a specification about basic ideas in a new technology should teach its principles to second-rank technicians rather than to leading researchers in the field.[11] This sort of

---

[8] For a technical demonstration of this, see Machlup (above, n. 88) at 66-73.

[9] Above, § 3-004.

[10] See generally, Beier and Straus (1977) 8 I.I.C. 387; Eisenschitz and Oppenheim in Phillips (ed.) *Patents in Perspective* (1985) Chaps. 5, 6. On the important practical question of how the British Office should classify its material there has been a substantial debate: see, *e.g.* Arnot (1979) 8 CIPA 287, 381; Oppenheim (1980) 9 CIPA 217.

[11] *Valensi v. British Radio* [1973] R.P.C. 337; and see generally, below, §§ 4-032—4-033.

insistence carries with it the danger that really significant developments may be the subject of invalid patents. Yet to give up any real effort to police the disclosure requirement may be to surrender the one public advantage of the patent system that remains relatively uncontroversial.

The notion of patent collections as an index of where to apply for   3-035
more information at least gives some clue to the businessman's continuing interest in the patent system. Of course specifications are read by competitors who are at roughly the same stage of advance and who then seek licences in order to avoid impediments in the way of their own development work. But a great deal of licensing is of an information package to a firm which lacks the background to set up production for itself. In this sort of case the basic concept is frequently patented while much crucial incident exists only as know-how that has to be transmitted under terms of confidence. For this sort of case, the patent system may alert potential licensees about people who have interesting ideas on offer; and the licensor will be interested in having a patent, not only for the publicity that may follow but also because it may provide a measure of security. If his only protection lies in confidence obligations, he has to ensure that all personnel have given adequate undertakings and he may well have to contemplate proceedings against them if they appear to be in breach. Resources ought not to be devoted to ensuring that people keep their bargains wherever this can be avoided.

5. THE PATENTS ACT 1977: STRUCTURE AND INTERPRETATION

This Chapter ends with a bridge passage. The international and European   3-036
antecedents of the Patents Act 1977 make it a complex measure which deserves a more technical outline than has yet been given. Part I sets out the new domestic law. So far as this is concerned with the making and processing of applications, it only affects applications to the British Patent Office as such[12]; European applications are governed by the EPC so long as they are being dealt with by the EPO (*i.e.* up to grant and during post-grant opposition before the EPO). But the other main provisions apply to British patents granted by either route. These concern patentability,[13] term, restoration and surrender[14]; property rights and employees' inventions[15]; abuse of monopoly and Crown use[16]; infringement, revocation and associated issues[17]; and amendment.[18]

Part II provides the incorporative machinery for the EPC, CPC and   3-037
PCT. International applications under the PCT may evolve into applications to the British Office under the Act by virtue of section 89. By

[12] See ss.14-21; to this s.13(3) is an exception. The provisions on secrecy (ss.22, 23) can affect European and foreign applications generally.
[13] ss.1-6.
[14] ss.24-29.
[15] ss.30-43.
[16] ss.44-59.
[17] ss.60-74.
[18] ss.75, 76.

section 77, European patents which designate the United Kingdom fall to be treated as patents under the 1977 Act from publication of the mention of grant in the *European Patent Bulletin*; and there follow a number of consequential provisions on European applications, authentic texts, conversion into a national application, jurisdiction over the right to apply for a European patent, professional representation and evidence for EPO proceedings.[19] By contrast, when the CPC takes effect, Community patents will be governed by that Convention. The main purpose of section 86 is therefore to make the Convention itself part of United Kingdom law and to give the Secretary of State an implementive power to make regulations. It is important to note that a Community patent will not become a patent under the 1977 Act and so will not be governed by the provisions of Part I which affect a European patent (U.K.). Thus infringement of a Community patent will be determined by the CPC's provisions, not the Act's[20]; and the rules on patentability will be the relevant Articles in the EPC since these are incorporated into the CPC. But because there is still no immediate prospect of the CPC being implemented, the law governing Community patents will be mentioned only incidentally in the following Chapters.[21]

3-038   Part III deals with a variety of general matters: legal proceedings, including the creation of the Patents Court within the frame of the Chancery Division[22]; criminal offences[23]; patent agents[24]; administrative provisions[25]; the power to make Patent Rules[26]; a provision attempting to elucidate what is meant by the scope of a patented invention (taking account of the Protocol to the EPC, Article 69)[27]; and interpretation.[28] Sections 127 and 128 and associated Schedules[29] determine how far "old" patents—*i.e.* those already granted on June 1, 1978, or resulting from applications for which a complete specification had been furnished before that day—are still governed by the Patents Act 1949, and how far they are affected by the 1977 Act. Despite the considerable practical importance of these variations at the present, there is no room for an extended discussion of "old" patents in this book. An outline is given in Appendix 2.

3-039   Some parts of the new domestic law have been inspired in a general way be legal developments elsewhere. Thus the restructured application system in the British Patent Office is to a considerable extent modelled on the arrangements for the PCT and the EPO. Yet the derivation is not direct in the sense that help in construing Patents Acts provisions can be

---

[19] ss.78-85.
[20] *cf.* the *Harbottle* case, below, n. 33.
[21] Part II also provides machinery for declaring countries to be Convention countries for the purpose of the Parish Convention arrangements on priority (s.90(1)) and on evidence, judicial notice and other matters in relation to the more recent conventions (ss.91-95).
[22] ss.96-108.
[23] ss.109-113.
[24] ss.114-115.
[25] ss.116-123.
[26] s.124.
[27] s.125.
[28] s.130.
[29] Scheds. 1-4.

had from specific provisions of the international and European conventions. The opposite is true, however, of a number of crucial provisions, since section 130(7) declares that they are "so framed as to have, as nearly as practicable, the same effects in the United Kingdom as do the corresponding provisions" of the EPC, CPC and PCT in the territories too which they apply. These provisions concern: patentability and the requirements for description and claims of the specification; revocation at the behest of the person properly entitled to grant; non-working as a ground for granting a compulsory licence; infringement and the extent of monopoly; grounds of revocation; and certain supplemental provisions.

The particular importance of this declaration arises because, in so much of the new law, provisions from the conventions are not taken into domestic law by repeating the same language. The legacy of strict, grammatical interpretation by British courts led the draftsman of the Act to make many variations of expression in the hope (presumably) of giving British judges directions that would unambiguously produce the legal result aimed at by the Convention text.[30] But there are two dangers in this technique. One is that the draftsman may not spot new ambiguities in his revised version and so introduce his own uncertainties.[31] The other is that if a variation in language produces a clear difference in meaning, this may, despite section 130(7), be treated as intentional.[32]

There have now been a number of occasions on which the terms of   **3-040**
section 130(7) have been used in order to reach an interpretation of the Act which is considered consistent with a convention text.[33] Whitford J. has remarked that "it is of the greatest importance that in this jurisdiction we should take note of the decisions of the EPO and that, so far as may be possible in all those countries which are now bound by the common interest created by the Convention, an attempt should be made to give the same meaning to relevant provisions, whichever the jurisdiction which is being invoked."[34]

The significance of that statement lies in the fact that there is no ultimate court of appeal to which questions of interpretation can be referred for final settlement. Within the EEC this will to a large extent be rectified once the amended CPC is brought into effect, since this will create a Community Patent Appeal Court.[35] But even so, this will not provide a complete solution for the whole network of authorities established through the Conventions. For this "Copac" will hear appeals from national courts trying proceedings for infringement or revocation of Community patents. But it will not be a Court of Appeal from decisions

[30] See above, § 1-012; and Ellis in M. Vitoria (ed.), *The Patents Act 1977* (1978), pp. 21-34.
[31] For an example, see below, § 5-013 on the disclosure of information in breach of confidence.
[32] Note in this connection the authorities on the interpretation of statutes derived from convention texts, above § 1-014.
[33] *e.g. Smith Kline* v. *Harbottle*, below, § 6-009, n. 38; *Schering's and Wyeth's Applcns.*, below, § 5-053, n. 19.
[34] *B. & R. Relays' Applcn.* [1985] R.P.C. 1 at 6.
[35] See above.

of the EPO taken in the course of its granting procedure[36]; nor will it have jurisdiction over tribunals in the non-EEC states (Austria, Sweden, Switzerland) which have dealt with the equivalent European patents for their country.[37] Accordingly, even at that stage, Whitford J.'s spirit of cooperation will remain essential. It is currently fostered by biennial meetings of judges concerned with patent matters from the EPC states, which began in 1982.

Over time the judges' willingness to collaborate may be tested, for one reason in particular. It is widely considered that a meeting to revise the EPC would be an extremely difficult occasion and one better avoided for the foreseeable future. This accordingly places considerable strain upon the judiciary concerned to read the existing text in a manner which will allow for reasonable adaptation. Already there are a number of points at which the decisions embodied in the text of 1973 seem no longer to fit the needs and wishes of particular industries and there has been one major issue (over the so-called "second medical use" exception) which has for now been resolved by decisions which impose a highly "purposive" interpretation on the actual terms of the EPC.

Over the next few years, other controversial questions will fall inevitably to be settled by judicial interpretation. Somehow the present edifice must be kept in position without an appellate keystone to its vaulting.

---

[36] These will continue to go to the EPO Boards of Appeal, with ultimate reference to the Enlarged Board of Appeal: see above, § 3-021.
[37] On the need for harmonisation, Gall [1988] E.I.P.R. 38.

CHAPTER 4

THE PATENT: GRANT AND CONTENT

1. OBTAINING A PATENT

(1) General

(a) *Parallels*

A patent may now be secured for the United Kingdom either through the   **4-001**
British Office or the EPO; with the additional possibility of entering either
system by means of International Application under the PCT. Native British
procedures have been substantially remodelled to resemble the new European granting system. Accordingly the major steps through which an
application proceeds to the stage of grant in each office can be represented
in a common diagram (see p. 94).

A European patent designating the United Kingdom falls to be treated as
a patent under the 1977 Act as if it had been granted by the British Office.[1]
For a variety of purposes the European application ranks as if it were a
British application.[2] But there remains one significant difference: the European patent as a whole is open for a limited period to opposition
proceedings before the EPO, and the European patent (U.K.) will be subject
to revocation proceedings before British tribunals. Obviously a patent
granted by the British Office can be subject only to the latter form of
attack.[3]

(b) *Competition between the systems*

The new international arrangements have provided a measured compe-   **4-002**
tition which ought to benefit patenting industries. The greater efficiency
that is their chief attraction turns on a number of variables. As far as the
PCT is concerned much depends on the trust that is accorded to the
international search.[4] At present a measure of mutual suspicion remains.
The EPO, for instance, currently makes its own search (with extra fee) to
supplement international search reports emanating from most of the
other PCT search authorities.[5]

---

[1] PA 1977, s.77.   [2] PA 1977, s.78.
[3] See below, § 4-022.
[4] PCT Rules, r. 34 lays down the minimum documentation that an International Search
Authority must cover. There are transitional difficulties, particularly in making Japanese
and Russian material available elsewhere. See generally, Perrott [1982] E.I.P.R. 67.
[5] EPC Art. 157; EPO Official Journal, 1979, p. 50. This supplementary search takes place
during the six months in which the applicant has to decide whether to ask for
examination: see Ency. PL § 11-101; see also PA 1977, s.18(3A), introduced in 1988.

4-003   With the EPO, the matter is more complex. For the applicant with a strong case, already confirmed perhaps by a private search in advance, the single procedure before the EPO will look more attractivè if cover is wanted in three or four participant countries (or more). It is at this point that the considerable fees and other expenses of a European application begin to fall below the cost of national fees and the other costs of separate applications.[6] But if the expenditure of patenting is justified at all, it is worth paying for the course that is more likely to give the desired protection. The EPO route, moreover, has an all-or-nothing outcome in terms of geographical coverage. In the early years the EPO has sought to examine applications in a reasonably helpful spirit.[7] The choice may well turn on the countries for which protection is most needed: thus the possibility of deferring examination in the Netherlands and West Germany for seven years may in some cases be important, or the absence of any examination in Belgium or Italy or of a power of rejection in France. In some cases, it will be considered worthwhile pursuing both European and national patents. The only consequence of covering an invention to the same extent by both procedures, as far as the United Kingdom is concerned, is that the comptroller must then revoke the patent granted by his own office.[8]

(c) *Languages*

4-004   One particular advantage offered by the international conventions concerns languages. This is not just a matter of saying translation costs, considerable though these often are. In an art so tied to linguistic skills, every translation is fraught with dangers of error and inaccuracy. What the PCT provides is the longest chance to delay preparing translations during the crucial months after an initial application has been lodged.[9] The international application must be in the appropriate PCT language[10]; but translations are not needed until the application is transferred into the national (or regional) offices: normally after the international search (up to 20 months from the priority date)[11] or (if applicable) after the international preliminary examination (up to 25 months from the priority date).[12]

[6] Notably the costs of professional representation and translation: for the latter, see below, § 4-004.

[7] The aim has been to achieve a standard mid-way between the severity of the Dutch and the lenience of the Austrian and British approaches: the German standard was thought to be "about right": Van Benthem and Wallace (1978) 9 I.I.C. 297 at 298; see also Pagenberg, *ibid*.. 1, 121; Casalonga (1979) 10 I.I.C. 412.

[8] PA 1977, s.73(2) (as amended by CDPA 1977, Sched. 5, § 19). The British patent must be "directed to the same invention": see *Maag Gear's Patent* [1985] R.P.C. 572.

[9] See also below, n. 12.

[10] *i.e.* the language that is used by the International Search Authority to which an application from the particular receiving office will be referred: English, French, or German where the EPO will search, English for the U.S. Patent Office, Japanese for the Japanese Patent Office and so on. The Search Report and abstract will be translated into English, if in another language: PCT Rules, r. 48.3.

[11] PCT Art. 22.

[12] This is possible only for a country which has adopted the PCT Chap. II; and the request for the International Examination must be made within 19 months of the priority date, if the need to start the national examination within 20 months is to be averted: PCT Art. 39(1); and see PCT Rules, rr. 46.1, 52.1 for the time allowed for making voluntary amendments.

In the EPO an applicant may proceed in any of the official languages, English, French, or German.[13] When his application is published, he will need to translate the claims, as they then stand, into the languages of his designated states if he wants to bother with securing protection to the period of grant[14]; and when his patent is accepted for grant he must translate the claims into the other official languages.[15] All the participant states except Luxembourg and West Germany require translation of the whole specification into their language.[16] The authentic text remains that of the language of the proceedings before the EPO; but some protection is provided for a person misled by a narrower translation.[17]

(2) Persons entitled to grant

The Paris Industrial Property Convention ensures that nationals of any 4-005 one Union country have the same right to secure patents in each other Union country as do nationals of the latter.[18] Both the United Kingdom and the EPC systems go further, making access open to all without consideration of nationality, residence or other status.[19]

In the new British system, the right to be granted a patent[20] is given to the inventor or the inventors[21] unless (i) at the time when the invention is made a general rule of law or an enforceable agreement gives that right[22] to someone else; or (ii) the person entitled when the invention was made (under (i)) later assigns his right, or it has been otherwise disposed of to a successor in title (through death, bankruptcy, winding up, etc.[23]) Under (i) the most likely person to supersede the inventor by virtue of a rule of

[13] EPC Art. 14(1). Nationals of states (such as Italy) which do not have English, French, or German as an official language are entitled to file in their own language and supply a translation, the original document being treated as the document filed, in cases of variance: see Art. 14(2), (4) and further, Ency. PL §§ 11-301—11-304.
[14] If this is not done, states are permitted to treat the application as ineffectual: EPC Art. 67(3). Most have done so, but not so far the U.K. (note the power given by PA 1977, s.78(7), (8).
[15] EPC Art. 97(5), EPC Rules, r. 51(4).
[16] EPC Art. 65 leaves the matter optional. Power to require this translation is to be found in PA 1977, s.77(6)-(9) and was exercised in 1987.
[17] See PA 1977, s.80; EPC Art. 70.
[18] PIP Art. 2(1).
[19] See EPC Art. 58; cf. PCT Art. 9: PCT Rules, r. 18 (resident or national). There was a stage in the EPC negotiations when the exclusion of foreign nationals was seriously contemplated. This was intended as retaliation against the U.S.: foreign applicants there were considered to suffer certain disadvantages in comparison with domestic applicants. Nobler sentiments prevailed: see Van Empel, *The Granting of European Patents* (1975), pp. 72-80.
[20] Formerly, the limitations were placed upon the right to apply, but that is now unrestricted: PA 1977, s.7(1); this follows the EPC approach, see below, § 7-001.
[21] *i.e.* the actual deviser of the invention: s.7(3). The hallowed notion of the importer of an idea as inventor (see above, § 3-003) finally disappeared with the 1977 Act. Its only recent value had been in overcoming technical difficulties that could affect applications from abroad.
[22] But "the whole of the property (other than equitable interests)" must be given to the preferred person; which may lead to complications where there are joint inventors.
[23] PA 1977, s.7(2). But the applicable rule may arise by foreign law, treaty or convention (s.7(2)(*b*)) because this is the appropriate rule to apply by virtue of the private international law of the British jurisdiction invoked: see further below, n. 33.

law is his employer[24]; this is a matter treated more fully in Chapter 7.[25]

The Act creates a presumption that the applicant or applicants are the persons entitled to be granted the patent.[26] But it provides channels through which someone else may claim to be properly entitled—alleging, for instance, that the applicant stole the invention from him, or that he revealed it to the applicant without transferring any right to secure grant of a patent. Such questions of proprietary right can always be raised in declaratory or other proceedings in the High Court.[27] But in addition the comptroller is given special jurisdiction to decide upon the right to be granted not only the British patent, but also European and foreign patents and allied rights, provided that the question is referred to him before the relevant patent is granted.[28] He can also entertain references concerning the right to be granted the United Kingdom patent even after its grant (by either route).[29]

4-006   If a challenger shows that he, and not an applicant, is properly entitled to the patent, for all or some part of the subject-matter covered by the specification,[30] the tribunal has a wide discretion to do what it thinks fit. The proper claimant may be allowed to join in, or take over, the existing application[31]; or, if the patent has already been granted, to be registered as proprietor. Or he may be allowed to start afresh, taking for himself the date of filing of the displaced application (provided that he does not add to its disclosure),[32] but after grant this course is open only if proceedings are begun within two years.[33] There is also power to grant and transfer licences, and to register transactions and instruments relied upon by the claimant.[34]

As far as European applications are concerned, the EPO does not undertake investigations of true entitlement[35]; that is left to national tribunals.[36] So long as the EPO has not granted the European patent, the proper forum for deciding who is entitled to the grant is dealt with in a

---

[24] PA 1977, s.39.   [25] Below, §§ 7-001—7-002.   [26] s.7(4).

[27] See below, § 7-002. Where the comptroller has jurisdiction, he may decline to exercise it upon the ground that the court is the more suitable tribunal: see ss.8(7), 12(2), 37(8).

[28] ss.8, 12. Note that the question can be raised before any application has been made: leading to a declaration over entitlement to grant.

[29] s.37 (as amended by CDPA 1988, Sched. 5, § 9). A reference received before grant by the British office is treated as continuing under this section: s.9.

[30] The jurisdiction conferred on the comptroller also allows him to deal with disputes where one co-applicant is objecting to the transfer or granting of any right to any other person. In addition, there is a separate power to give directions to joint applicants if they cannot agree upon how a British application is to be proceeded with: s.10.

[31] Where the rights of licensees may be affected, they are afforded at least some measure of protection: see ss.11, 38; Ency. PL §§ 8-108—8-109.

[32] Semble, he may not also annexe any earlier priority claimed for the original: Georgia Pacific's Applcn. [1984] R.P.C. 469.

[33] See ss.8(2), (3), 37(2). In the case of "non-British" applications—apart from the special cases dealt with in s.12(6)—the comptroller is left to determine the question as far as he is able and makes such order as he thinks fit: see s.12(1). The court's jurisdiction and the jurisdiction to order revocation on the ground that the patent was granted to a person not entitled are similarly limited in time: ss.37(9), 72(1)(b) (as amended by CDPA 1988, Sched. 5, § 18), 72(2).

[34] s.37(5).

[35] EPC Art. 60(3); see Ency. PL § 13-102.

[36] In the EPO the application will, on request and subject to limitations, be stayed: see EPC Rules, rr. 13, 14. British applications are not stayed in the same way: see n. 29, above.

special protocol to the EPC.[37] Once the patents have been granted, however, the question is one for each designated country. Where a challenge is successfully made to a European application, the challenger may, in appropriate circumstances, continue the application, have it withdrawn, or file his own application (as to the whole or a part), with a claim to the earlier priority date if he is adding nothing of substance.[38]

(3) Patent specification

It should by now be plain that the crucial document in the whole process of securing and relying upon a patent is the specification. In the British and European systems it has two main parts[39]: the description (which may be accompanied by diagrams or drawings) and the claims. The former must disclose the invention sufficiently for it to be performed by an appropriately skilled person, the latter will mark out the scope of monopoly rights. There will be a good deal to say about both aspects of the specification. The reader who has not had an opportunity to study specifications would do well to look at a representative sample.[40] In particular, it is useful to note how far the draftsman has referred to the "prior art" in an effort to bring out the character of the invention; the degree to which specific examples are used to give explicit description of how the invention can be performed; the generalisations used in the claims (particularly the broadest); and the manner in which a succession of claims cover increasingly specific areas (for fear that the wider may prove invalid).

4-007

(4) Priority

Today more than ever, those engaged in research may be competing to solve a scientific or technical problem. The "first-to-file" basis of most patent systems exacerbates the pressure to reach the patent office as soon as feasible.[41] It may be necessary to file a series of applications as, on the

4-008

[37] This Protocol on Jurisdiction and Recognition gives jurisdiction first to the Contracting State agreed by the disputants; if not agreed, then, in employer-employee disputes, to the State where employed (see Art. 60); and in other cases, to the applicant's State; or otherwise to the claimant's State; and if none of these tests provides a Contracting State, then to West Germany. PA 1977, ss.82 (jurisdiction) and 83 (recognition) give effect in the U.K. to this Protocol. See further Ency. PL § 8-111; *Kakkar* v. *Szelke* [1989] F.S.R. 225.

[38] EPC Art. 61.

[39] It must also have a title and name the inventor. The abstract, which is used for patent office search purposes and to notify the public at once of the fact and nature of the application, is separate: this notification is made in the issues of abstracts that accompany the British Patent Office journal, the EPO Bulletin, or the PCT Gazette.

[40] If no other source is ready to hand, the reported case law often sets out in full the specification in dispute. Good examples for beginners: *Carroll* v. *Tomado* [1971] R.P.C. 401 at 402-404 (clothes horse); *Reeves* v. *Standard Fabrics* [1972] R.P.C. 47 at 48-62 (bonding polyurethane foam); *Bugges Insecticide* v. *Herbon* [1972] R.P.C. 197 at 198-202 (weedkiller); *Minnesota Mining* v. *Bondina* [1973] R.P.C. 491 at 493-503 (scouring pads); *Illinois Tool* v. *Autobars* [1974] R.P.C. 337 at 339-351 (nestable cups for vending machines); *Letraset* v. *Rexel* [1974] R.P.C. 175 at 177-188 (transfers—2 specifications); *Proctor & Gamble* v. *Peaudouce* [1989] F.S.R. 180 (nappy holders).

[41] The new regimen takes a severer attitude than ever before on the need to reach the patent office without prior publication, yet with an application complete enough to support the eventual patent: the elements that are compounded in this attitude are considered together in §§ 6-022—6-025. On the comparison with "first to invent" systems, see Nicolai (1972) 3 I.I.C. 103.

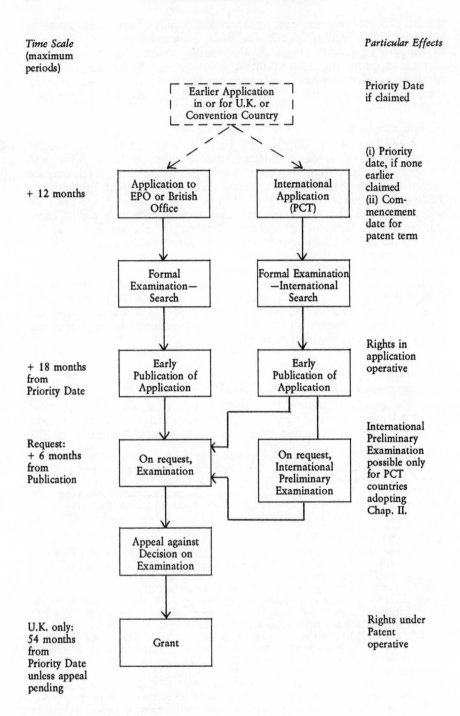

Time Scale
(maximum
periods)

Particular Effects

Priority Date
if claimed

Earlier Application
in or for U.K. or
Convention Country

(i) Priority
date, if none
earlier
claimed
(ii) Com-
mencement
date for
patent term

+ 12 months

Application to
EPO or British
Office

International
Application
(PCT)

Formal
Examination—
Search

Formal Examination
—International
Search

+ 18 months
from
Priority Date

Early
Publication of
Application

Early
Publication of
Application

Rights in
application
operative

Request:
+ 6 months
from
Publication

On request,
Examination

On request,
International
Preliminary
Examination

International
Preliminary
Examination
possible only
for PCT
countries
adopting
Chap. II.

Appeal against
Decision on
Examination

U.K. only:
54 months
from
Priority Date
unless appeal
pending

Grant

Rights under
Patent
operative

one hand, more is discovered about how the invention works, and, on the other, more is appreciated about alternatives that might be deployed by competitors outside the scope of the initial application. On top of this, the question of which foreign patents to pursue imposes its own pressures, since foreign applications often involve collaboration with patent agents abroad and the making of translations.

This brings us to the initiatory steps on the Table (p. 94). It has long been recognised that an applicant should have some room for manoeuvre in these matters. Within one year, he is given a limited opportunity to amplify his application without losing his priority. And through the machinery of the Paris Convention, he is able to keep the priority of his first application for other applications filed within a year in or for other Convention countries.[42] Most industrial countries, with a few important exceptions in the Far East, belong to this Convention, and the European system is also within its net. To secure this advantage, then, the earlier "informal" application need only satisfy the basic requirements for a filing date: an indication that a patent is sought, identification of the application, a description of the invention, and, for a European or International application, at least one claim and the designation of at least one state.[43]

The "priority date" of a patent is the date on which it is tested against "the state of the art"[44]; and it is the date on which it, or any application claiming priority from it (provided that it is subsequently published), becomes part of the art, when assessing the novelty (but not the obviousness) of later applications.[45] This crucial date will be the filing date of the application unless the date of an earlier application in the United Kingdom, the EPO, or a Paris Convention country is claimed.[46] As already noted, the earlier application must have been made within the previous 12 months. And so far as the British Act is concerned, it must "support" the invention in the later application by the matter it discloses.[47] Generally also it must be the applicant's first disclosure of the invention in a patent application.[48]

---

[42] For the tendency nonetheless to favour national applicants at the expense of Convention applicants in some Member States, see Wieczorek (1975) 6 I.I.C. 135; Gansser (1980) 11 I.I.C. 1.

[43] PA 1977, s.15(1), EPC Art. 80, PCT Art. 11. For the full requirements of a "formal" application, see below, § 00. It is not permissible to derive priority from a registered design application: *Agfa-Gevaert's (Engelsmann) Appln.* [1982] R.P.C. 441 (C.A.).

[44] See below, § 5-003.   [45] See below, § 5-012.

[46] PA 1977, s.5(1), (2); EPC Art. 7(1)-(3), and note Art. 89.

[47] The EPC Art. 87(1) requires that the later application be "in respect of the same invention" as the earlier; and this may sound like the former British rule for convention priority—that the prior application had also to claim the invention. Art. 88(4), however, says that if elements of an invention are not claimed in the earlier specification, it is enough that they should have been "specifically disclosed." According to the EPO Guidelines C V 2.2, specific disclosure, rather than inclusion in a claim, will be taken as the criterion. If the priority is claimed from a British "informal" application there may well be no claims in it.

[48] Disclosures in a first application can be disregarded only if that application was unconditionally withdrawn, abandoned or refused without having been made available to the public before filing of a second application from which it is now sought to derive priority and without having been the basis of any claim to priority: PA 1977, s.5(3), EPC Art. 87(4), giving effect to PIP Art. 4C(4).

4-009   The basic question—has there been a "supportive disclosure?"—
resembles the question under the 1949 Act—were the claims of the later
specification "fairly based" on the disclosure in the earlier document?[49]
Probably the courts will read the new phrase in much the same sense as
the old. In paraphrasing the earlier notion, Buckley L.J. said that the
addition of features that are "developments along the same line of
thought which constitutes or underlies the invention described in the
earlier document" may be fairly based upon it; it is otherwise where "the
additional feature involves a new inventive step or bring something new
into the combination which represents a departure from the idea of the
invention" earlier described.[50] Thus in the case where greater detail has
been added in the later document—a statement of specific temperatures,
say, in place of a simple instruction to heat—the earlier disclosure will be
sufficient if the new limits do not involve any unexpected and significant
new discovery. Where the later document is seeking to make more
general something that was earlier confined to the particular, it will be
necessary to ask whether the potentialities of the feature in question were
appreciated in the earlier document. In one instance, the earlier description of a method for the electrolytic production of titanium called for a
titanium nitride anode and a molten metal cathode. The disclosure was
held insufficient to justify a generalisation which covered all other
cathodes, because that depended upon an appreciation of the efficiency of
the anode, which was not to be found in the earlier document.[51] Of
course each case turns upon an understanding of all the particular
circumstances: there can be no rules of thumb.

4-010   The 1977 Act allows an applicant to claim multiple priorities, based on
different earlier applications, not only for different claims but even for
different aspects of a single claim.[52] If, in the example used in the last
paragraph, a first document discloses molten metal cathodes, a second
document other cathodes and the application or suit in one claim refers
to the two classes separately, then the different priority dates can easily
be assigned. But if the cathodes are claimed only in general a tribunal
may not be willing to split a claim into separate parts.

The system of priorities eases the pressure of an applicant to decide
whether in Europe to proceed in the EPO or in national offices, since he
may use an application in any one office to give priority in the others. It
is not necessary to designate (say) the United Kingdom in a European
application in order to secure priority for a subsequent national application in the United Kingdom.[53]

[49] PA 1949, s.5(2), (4).
[50] *Stauffer's Application* [1977] R.P.C. 33 at 54. Or as Lloyd Jacob J. put it: "Is the
invention claimed broadly described in the [priority document]? Is there anything in the
[priority document] which is inconsistent with the invention as claimed? Does the claim
include as a characteristic of the invention a feature not mentioned in the [priority
document]": *ICI's Applcn.* [1960] R.P.C. 223, following *Mond Nickel's Applcn.* [1956]
R.P.C. 189.
[51] *ICI's Applcn.*, above, n. 50.
[52] PA 1977, s.125(2), EPC Art. 88(2), (3). This reverses the restricted approach concerning
Convention applications apparently adopted in *Union Carbide's Applcn.* [1968] R.P.C.
371; and see *SCM's Applcn.* [1979] R.P.C. 341 (C.A.).
[53] It would in practice be unusual to use a European application in order to secure priority
for national applications.

(5) Secrecy: national interest

Applications under the EPC and PCT may be lodged with the United   **4-011** Kingdom Patent Office. One purpose of this arrangement is to allow the national office, in collaboration with the Ministry of Defence, the Atomic Energy Authority and other Government Departments, to vet applications in the interests of national security and public safety. British residents, indeed, are obliged (under criminal law sanction) to lodge applications with the British office six weeks before applying abroad.[54] If the comptroller considers that any application contains information prejudicial to the defence of the realm[55] or the safety of the public he may make a secrecy direction.[56] So long as it remains, the application cannot be sent on through the EPC or PCT routes,[57] and foreign applications may be made only through restricted arrangements, for instance within NATO.[58] It may be processed in the British Office, but without any publication, to the point where it is ready for grant. No patent will be granted but the applicant is entitled to compensation for any Crown use[59]; and—as a matter of departmental favour—he may also be compensated for hardship resulting from the secrecy direction: taking account, for instance, of lost commercial opportunities and foreign patent rights.[60] The government department involved must review the need for secrecy from time to time.[61]

(6) Unity and division

Two patents are not to be had for the price of one. One invention per   **4-012** patent, moreover, simplifies the classification of specifications and the process of searching which is the reason for classifying. Accordingly, as the EPC has it, an application must "relate to one invention only or to a group of inventions so linked as to form a single general inventive concept."[62] It is possible to have claims for a process, the apparatus to operate it and its products; or for products, processes for making them and use of the products.[63] Beyond this what will be allowed is a matter of judgment, and one that is left to the examiner(s) of the patent office in question.[64]

[54] PA 1977, s.23; the Comptroller's permission may be sought to file abroad without filing first in Britain. See generally, Ency. PL §§ 6-118—6-120.
[55] By reference to a list of subject-matter supplied by the Ministry.
[56] PA 1977, s.22(1).
[57] Provided that the U.K. is a designated country, an EPC application may be converted into a British application; a PCT application is similarly treated: see EPC Arts. 75(2), 77(4), (5); PCT Arts. 11(3), 12(3); PA 1977, s.81(1)(b).
[58] PA 1977, s.23(1)(b).
[59] Following the general rules: see below, § 7-055—7-056.
[60] PA 1977, s.22(7).
[61] PA 1977, s.22(5): i.e. on the making of the secrecy direction, then at least at the ninth month from the filing date and annually thereafter.
[62] EPC Art. 82; PA 1977, s.14(5)(d) (omitting "general"). See, e.g. Bayer's Applcn. [1983] O.J. EPO 274.
[63] EPC Rules, r. 30, PA 1977 Rules, r. 22.
[64] In the past the Appeal Tribunal in Britain has been exceedingly reluctant to interfere with the Office's discretion. And it is no objection to a granted patent that it lacks unity: s.26. In the EPO, where Search and Examining Divisions are separate, and only the latter may refuse an application, the Search Division may require a second fee to search parts of an application which it considers separate; with power in the examining division to remit the fee if it finds unity: EPC Rules, r. 46 (note also r. 45; search not possible, as a whole or in part).

An applicant may cope with an objection that he is seeking to patent more than one invention by dividing his single application into two (or more). Provided that he adds no new matter and keeps to the prescribed time schedule, he may keep his priority date for the "new" applications.[65] Division is permitted even where there is no objection to unity: it may be requested, for instance, where new claims are wanted which might give rise to an objection to unity.[66]

(7) Formal examination

4-013   We now reach the step of Application on the Table (p. 94). If the applicant does not ask for a preliminary examination and search the only value of an application will be that it may found priority for a later application. But, once the request is made (and fee paid), the office will make its preliminary examination to ensure that there is a request for grant; a description and one or more claims; any drawings referred to; identification of the applicant(s); identification of the inventor(s); an abstract of the invention described; and compliance with various formalities.[67] In the EPC, the states for which a patent is sought have also to be designated: these designations may afterwards be withdrawn but never added to.[68] An application will, of course, normally be drawn to meet the much more stringent standards of the substantive examination, and these will be discussed later.

The inventor or inventors must be named as a matter of "moral right."[69] Now that employee-inventors are entitled on occasion to "compensation," there may be considerable evidential value in being named as an inventor.[70]

The abstract is required as an aid to those conducting searches, giving them preliminary assistance in deciding whether a specification is relevant to their investigation. Its terms may ultimately be settled by the patent office concerned, and it is disregarded when treating the specification as part of the art. Probably it is not to be used in interpreting the claims.[71]

(8) Search and examination

(a) *Introductory*

4-014   At the heart of the European and the new British systems lies a compulsory examination before grant, not only of the novelty but also of

---

[65] *Kiwi Coders' Applen.* [1986] R.P.C. 106. But he may not set up a "cascade" of priorities: *Hydroacoustic's Applen.* [1981] F.S.R. 538; and see *Van der Lely's Applen.* [1987] R.P.C. 61.

[66] For time limit see Ency. PL §§ 6-111, 13-202.

[67] PA 1977, ss.14(1)-(3A), 17(1)-(3); EPC Arts. 78, 90, 91. Only in relation to drawings is there a special rule in effect allowing post-dating. If drawings referred to are not provided, reference to them can be deleted; or they may be filed within a limited time, the date of filing being postponed until this is done.

[68] EPC Art. 79. A mistaken failure to designate may, however, be remedied under EPC Rules, r. 88: [1980] O.J. EPO 293.

[69] PA 1977, s.13, PA 1977 Rules, rr. 14, 15; EPC Arts. 62, 81; EPC Rules, rr. 17-19 in implementation of PIP Art. 4*ter*. For the concept of "inventor", above, § 4-005. See *Nippon Piston Ring's Applen.* [1987] R.P.C. 120.

[70] See below, §§ 7-007—7-014.

[71] PA 1977, s.14(2), PA 1977 Rules, r. 19; EPC Art. 85, EPC Rules, r. 33.

the inventiveness of the alleged invention. To this there are three important preliminaries: a substantial search; "early publication" of the application in the form that it has by then reached; and the opportunity within a short period after that for the applicant to decide whether or not he wants his application to proceed to examination.

British practice under the 1949 Act was very different: the Patent Office's examination only went to novelty and prior claiming, judged against a search of British specifications for the previous 50 years. It took place without the applicant's first considering the search result and before the industry was acquainted with the content of the specification. The detailed content could be kept dark for as much as four years from the priority date. Before grant, obviousness could only be brought in issue by an outside party in separate opposition proceedings, but upon whatever prior art he put to the tribunal. However, this ground of opposition was narrower than that available in post-grant attacks on the validity of the patent before the High Court; and the same restriction applied in "belated oppositions" launched before the office within one year of grant.

Under the EPC approach, both the British Office and the EPO examine for obviousness as a matter of course in proceedings before grant that are *ex parte*.

Neither the European nor the new British system has adopted the technique of deferred examination. This was introduced into the "full examination" systems of the Netherlands, West Germany and Japan in order to lift some of the burden on their patent offices in the great patenting boom of the 1960s. Quite apart from bureaucratic considerations, this arrangement has one advantage. Many patents that are applied for prove to have no lasting commercial value; even if granted they would be allowed to lapse. Delaying examination for up to seven years, while allowing a provisional form of protection after publication of the application, means that this swill of unwanted patents can filter away without wasting resources on examining the applications.[72] In the councils where the EPO was negotiated, however, a different principle triumphed. The importance of trying to ensure that an industry was saddled only with valid patents was held to require a rapid pre-grant examination.[73] Accordingly, the applicant was given only six months from early publication in which to decide whether to seek examination. It should be noted, however, that neither the Dutch nor the West Germans have got rid of deferred examination in their own systems. This remains one factor which may attract an applicant in Europe to the national systems, particularly if he is not sure how he will fare under examination or if he doubts the commercial potential of the patent. **4-015**

(b) *Search*

A search undertaken by one of the PCT authorities, or by the EPO for itself, will cover a considerable body of patents from major patenting **4-016**

---

[72] See, *e.g.* Hoffman (1972) 3 I.I.C. 423.
[73] The Banks Committee's firm rejection of deferment was influential: Cmnd. 4407, §§ 100 *et seq.*

countries and a range of the most important technical literature.[74] If the British Office is searching for itself, the material covered is narrower,[75] even though the British system now is concerned with the prior art throughout the world (and not only in Britain, as formerly.[76])

(c) *Early publication of application*

4-017   The new systems aim to publish the application, for the benefit of outsiders, at 18 months from priority date.[77] References to the prior art cited in the search report are also published.[78] From this point in time the patent office file (subject to a variety of exceptions) falls open to inspection[79]: outsiders may thus trace how an applicant has reacted to the results of the search and objections that examiners may subsequently put.[80]

If at this point an applicant using the PCT does not opt for the International Preliminary Examination,[81] his application must pass into the national systems (or the EPO).[82]

(d) *Amending during prosecution*

4-018   In the successful prosecution of an application, much may turn on the degree to which a specification and claims originally filed can be amended, and the points in time at which this can be done. The applicant is offered his freest opportunity in the period after receiving the search report and in his response to the first report of the examiner; thereafter, amendments require leave.[83] Even when making amendments of his own volition, however, the applicant is constricted by general rules. As far as the description of the invention is concerned, he may not add to his original disclosure; if he does, the examiner may reject the amendment, or subsequently (even if the examiner allows it) the patent may be revoked.[84]

Equally with claims: although they may be broadened in the course of prosecution, they must continue to be supported by the description—as

---

[74] For the range covered by the EPO, see its Guidelines B IX.

[75] It is still largely confined to prior British specifications.

[76] See below, § 5-003.

[77] PA 1977, s.16, PA 1977 Rules, rr. 27, 28; EPC Art. 93, EPC Rules, rr. 48-50; PCT Art. 21, PCT Rules, r. 48. Until publication, the application may be withdrawn without jeopardising the novelty of its contents. In the UK Office, this may be done until allotment to a printing contractor and collection: *Intera's Appln.* [1986] R.P.C. 459 (C.A.).

[78] In the European system if the search report is not available at the date of early publication it may be published later; in which case the time for requesting examination is extended: EPC Art. 93(2); *cf.* PCT Rules, r. 48.2(g).

[79] PA 1977, s.118, PA 1977 Rules, rr. 92-96; EPC Art. 128, EPC Rules, rr. 92-95; PCT Art. 30 (but note Art. 38—confidential nature of International Preliminary Examination).

[80] For the significance of this, see below, § 4-034.

[81] Or cannot do so, because a country has not ratified Chap. II.

[82] PCT Art. 20; PA 1977, s.89 (requiring a translation into English if necessary); EPC Art. 158 (requiring a version in one of the three official languages). For supplementary search in the EPO, see above, § 4-003.

[83] PA 1977, s.19, PA 1977 Rules, r. 36; EPC Art. 123(1), EPC Rules, r. 86: PCT Arts. 19, 28; PCT Rules, rr. 46, 52.

[84] Amendment is considered further below, §§ 4-023—4-025.

well as being clear and concise. As we shall see, objections to claims can be raised after grant only indirectly.[85] So examiners ought to take this requirement particularly seriously. But without the stimulus of outside criticism, it will be tempting for them to let the applicant's drafting stand.

(e) *The course of examination*

The purpose of the examination is to decide whether the application   **4-019** meets all the criteria for the grant of a patent: whether the subject-matter is within the patentable field, whether in the light of the search report, the invention is novel and inventive, whether there is a sufficient description and the claims meet the criteria mentioned above. Examining the application in the light of the search report proceeds with relative informality. The examiner in charge sets forth any objections in a letter and states the time within which amendments may be submitted in order to overcome the objections. If applicant and examiner cannot agree, the issue may be raised in a formal hearing—in the United Kingdom Office before a senior examiner, in the EPO before the full Examining Division[86]; in either case, with a right of appeal.[87] Formal proceedings at this stage are infrequent in the British system, even with obviousness now on the agenda.[88]

Although outsiders have no right to present a case in opposition to grant before it takes place, they may make observations on patentability, drawing attention to prior art or even prior use which may not be known to the office.[89] Even though there are enhanced opportunities for competitors to monitor the progress of applications after early publication,[90] this remains an occasional strategy. Its tactical disadvantage is that the competitor cannot put a case on how the information should be regarded.

(f) *Time limits*

The EPO and the British Office and courts have seen a procession of   **4-020** cases about failure to comply with the requirements of the application system within due time. The fact that such errors occur with frequency is one measure of the growing complexity of the whole structure.[91] Thus a noticeable proportion of those arising in Britain have concerned the process of converting an international application under the PCT into a national application, either after search or after preliminary international examination.[92] Where the default is in part a consequence of a failure in

[85] Below, § 5-064.
[86] *i.e.* three examiners of whome one has been primarily responsible from the outset.
[87] *i.e.* in the British office, to the Patents Court and in some cases to the Court of Appeal (PA 1977, s.97); in the EPO, to a Board of Appeals: EPC Arts. 106(1), 21(3); Paterson [1987] E.I.P.R. 221.
[88] Unless an appeal is pending, the period for completing the examination in the British Office is 4½ years from priority: PA 1977, s.20, PA 1977 Rules, r. 34. The EPO has no such prescribed limit.
[89] PA 1977, s.21; EPC Art. 115.
[90] See above, § 4-017.
[91] For details, see, *e.g.* Encyc. PL. §§ 6-002, 13-005.
[92] See, *e.g.* *E's Applcns.* [1983] R.P.C. 231 (H.L.); *Mitsui's Applcn.* [1984] R.P.C. 471; *Matsuda's Applcn.* [1987] R.P.C. 37; and see also PA 1977, ss.89, 89A, 89B (as amended by CDPA, 1988, Sched. 5, §§ 24, 25). For equivalent questions in the EPO, see Gall [1984] E.I.P.R. 302.

communication from the patent office concerned, the tendency has been to discount it.[93] In the EPO there may be further help under the arrangements for restitution of an out-of-time application where due care has been observed.[94] But there are some dates crucial to the whole procedure—such as the six-month period for requesting examination—to which that special concession does not apply. They require the most scrupulous watching.

(9) Grant and renewal

4-021   The patent grant is formally effective from the date when notice of it is officially published.[95] The maximum term for which it may last is then 20 years from the filing date,[96] the effective period for a claim to damages running from the date of early publication.[97] Grant is also the point at which the European application matures into a bundle of patents for the designated contracting states (including, once the CPC is brought into operation, a Community patent). A patent continues for the full 20 years only upon payment of the annual renewal fees. In the United Kingdom these start with the fifth year and increase with age: the one official price of success. The fees may be paid up to six months late under penalty.[98] After that time the patent will lapse for non-payment, but may be restored within a further prescribed period subject to a measure of protection for those who in the meantime begin in good faith to work within the patent.[99] If the comptroller finds it proper, a patentee may formally surrender his patent.[1] He may also secure a 50 per cent. reduction of renewal fees, if he has the patent endorsed "licences of right"[2]; in which case he must license all-comers on terms which, if they cannot be agreed, must be fixed by the comptroller.

(10) Objections to validity after grant

4-022   The EPC, drawing inspiration from the "belated oppositions" of the former British procedure, allows an outsider to launch an opposition in the EPO within nine months of grant.[3] Objections may be taken on three

---

[93] See PA 1977 Rules r. 100; *M's Applcn.* [1985] R.P.C. 249 (C.A.); *Mills' Applcn.* [1985] R.P.C. 339 (C.A.).   [94] EPC Art. 122.
[95] When the patent is in order, the fees due must be paid; in the case of the EPO, the Examining Division has also to notify the applicant of the final terms of the grant. Translations of the claims into other official languages have to be filed; see EPC Art. 97(5), EPC Rules, r. 51(4); see Teschemacher [1986] E.I.P.R. 149.
[96] See above, § 4-008.
[97] EPC Art. 63, PA 1977, s.25(1). Nothing remains of the former sytem of granting extensions for war loss or lack of adequate remuneration on a case-by-case basis. The EPC allows general extensions on account of a state of war or similar emergency conditions; and the British Act gives a rule-making power that would include such cases.
[98] PA 1977, s.25(3)-(5), Sched. 1, PA 1977 Rules, r. 39.
[99] PA 1977, s.28, 28A. The liberalising amendments introduced by CDPA 1988, Sched. 5, §§ 6, 7, were a response to a set of difficult cases about failure to renew on time.
[1] PA 1977, s.29. The surrender would likely not be accepted if it prejudiced a licensee; *cf.* CPC Art. 50.
[2] PA 1977, s.46, which contains further conditions.
[3] EPC Arts. 99 *et seq.* The opponent need establish no special interest to oppose. Even after the time for launching an opposition has expired, any person who has been sued or threatened with infringement proceedings personally may intervene in an opposition: Art. 105. See generally, Turner (1978) 7 CIPA 316; Meller (1979) 61 J.P.O.S. 550.

grounds[4]—unpatentable subject-matter,[5] inadequate disclosure[6] and unallowable amendment.[7] If it succeeds, the whole "bundle" of European patents will be revoked, or granted only in amended form, save in exceptional cases.[8] So the procedure offers an outsider a unique chance of attack and is therefore being used more than the old British opposition. Because of the thorough consideration now given at the application stage, an opposition based on the material in the search report and nothing else is not likely to succeed. Contrary to the British "accusatorial" tradition, which applied as much to oppositions as to High Court proceedings, Opposition Divisions of the EPO are expected to play a more directive part in resolving issues raised before them—deciding what evidence to take, and possibly securing information from sources not nominated by the parties, appointing experts to give opinions and conducting inspections.[9] Since High Court proceedings will allow questions of infringement and invalidity to be tried together, the Court may well refuse to stay them pending an EPO opposition—an approach which the English courts are not alone in adopting.[10]

The new British system continues to offer the outside party an opportunity of attacking a patent[11] by a largely documentary procedure originating in the Patent Office[12]; this is intended to be cheaper and more expeditious than a challenge to validity in the High Court.[13] This chance does not now arise until after grant, but it is then available throughout the life of the patent and the grounds are the same as those on which an attack may be launched in High Court proceedings. It is an alternative to the latter, rather than an intermediate course.[14] Accordingly the applicant for revocation ought not to face any specially high standard of proof; though he must still make out his case.

---

[4] EPC Art. 100.
[5] See below, §§ 5-039—5-057.
[6] See below, §§ 5-058—5-063.
[7] *i.e.* that the amendment extends the subject-matter beyond the application as filed: see below, § 4-026.
[8] If the state of the art differs for different states, because prior applications do not designate them all (as to which see below, § 5-012), a patent may be available only in some; alternatively, it may be granted subject to amendment for some. Or if proprietors differ, amendments may vary from state to state.
[9] For these procedural matters, see further Ency. PL § 13-002/014; Gall (1983) 14 I.I.C. 229.
[10] *Amersham* v. *Corning* [1987] R.P.C. 53; *Pall* v. *Commercial Hydraulics* [1988] F.S.R. 274; and see [1988] O.J. EPO 357-362 (cases from France, Netherlands, Switzerland).
[11] Including, of course, a European patent (U.K.): if the patent is also being opposed in the EPO, the British proceedings are likely to be stayed: see Ency, PL § 12-102.
[12] PA 1977, s.72; as to amendments in such proceedings, see below, §§ 4-024—4-025.
[13] See Ency. PL §§ 6-201 *et seq.*
[14] As indicated by this: if the comptroller refuses to revoke, the applicant may apply to the court only with leave: s.72(6). The comptroller may always certify that the case would be more suitably determined by the court: s.72(7). The Court will in its discretion decide whether High Court proceedings ought to be stayed in favour of those in the Office: *Hawker Siddeley* v. *Real Time* [1985] R.P.C. 395; *cf. Gen Set* v. *Mosarc* [1985] F.S.R. 302.

2. AMENDMENT

(1) Introductory

4-023   The fact that a specification may be amended adds finesse to the art of patenting. In the course of securing the grant, the description, the claims or both may be substantially rewritten, either to take account of prior art or some other objection to validity, or to reflect the growing understanding of the invention by those prosecuting the application. Nevertheless amendments have to comply with important ground rules and these can conveniently be set forth here. Some illustrations of what can be achieved by amendment will, however, be found in the discussion of validity in Chapter 5.

The legal provisions in point distinguish between, on the one hand, alterations that are intended to introduce new ideas, or at least new expression of existing ideas; and on the other, corrections that remove mistakes in expressing what was originally intended. The bulk of amendments, proposed and allowed, are of the first kind. But the two categories are not always easy to distinguish, and there may be advantages in trying to justify a change under the second head: this is discussed below.

(2) Amendment: general

(a) *Legal requirements*

4-024   The rules governing amendment distinguish between alterations in the description of the invention and in the claims. The description must not be amended so as to introduce matter extending beyond that disclosed in the specification as filed.[15] This applies whether the amendment is sought during the application or after.[16] If such an amendment is improperly allowed, this may ground a suit for revocation of the patent, in whole or in part.[17]

If the claims are amended during application, they have still to satisfy the basic rules that they must be clear and concise, be supported by the description and satisfy the requirement of unity of invention. But it is primarily for the patent office concerned to see that this principle is observed.[18] Amendments that are themselves sought after grant[19] may not alter the claims so as to extend the scope of protection; if wrongly admitted, they may provide cause for revocation.[20] If they are proper, they have a retroactive effect.[21]

---

[15] PA 1977, s.76(2) (as amended by CDPA 1988, Sched. 5, § 20); EPC Art. 123(2).

[16] PA 1977, ss.19, 27, 75; and see above, § 4-023.

[17] PA 1977, s.72(1)(d); EPC Art. 100(c).

[18] How far the content of the claims is open to challenge after grant is considered below, §§ 5-064—5-068.

[19] Either in the course of proceedings for infringement or revocation (s.75); or, if none are pending, in an application to the comptroller to amend (s.27); or in opposition proceedings before the EPO (EPC Art. 123(2), (3)).

[20] PA 1977, s.27(1)(e); and see EPC Arts. 123(3), 138(d); *Raychem's Appln.* [1986] R.P.C. 521.

[21] PA 1977, ss.27(3), 75(3).

In many cases, the aim of an amendment is to cut down the scope of **4-025** what is claimed, because a piece of prior art is discovered which makes the original claim cover unjustifiably broad territory. Sometimes this can be achieved by amending the claims alone: the broadest may have to be deleted; or features of subsidiary claims may have to be added to it; or claims for different aspects of the invention may have to be coalesced. In a well-known example,[22] the broadest claim originally related to a tool for crimping together electrical wires and connectors, which had a ratchet and pawl device to prevent premature release of the tool before crimping was complete. In order to side-step prior art, the patentee was allowed to add to this a device that was mentioned in the description incidentally as an additional feature—a stop designed to prevent crimping from going too far. Under the new law, this amendment would remain allowable.[23]

If the description must also be amended, the issue may be nicer. In the crimping tool case,[24] if the stop device had not originally been mentioned, to add it by amendment would in most circumstances be barred as "extending" the matter disclosed. The same would probably apply if originally a particular kind of stop was mentioned and the amendment sought to refer to all kinds of stop. Again, suppose that stops were mentioned in general and the amendment sought to refer to one particular kind of stop. It may be objected that this is to give prominence to something not previously pointed up in the description.[25]

(b) *The discretion*

Amendment in the course of application is frequent; after grant, much **4-026** less so. But if leave to amend is sought from comptroller or court after grant, not only must the applicant show that it is within the legal requirements just discussed; he must also satisfy the tribunal that it should in its discretion allow the amendment to be made.[26]

In the past, the discretion has been used to subject the patentee's conduct to critical scrutiny. This contrasts with the approach to most other issues, where the applicant or patentee is obliged to meet specific requirements but not in addition to show that he has behaved properly, honestly and candidly.[27] Patentees who have delayed their application to amend for long periods after appreciating the need, or who have insisted first in maintaining an invalid claim, have been denied leave.[28] To some extent, the new willingness to see virtue in the patent system[29] seems to

---

[22] *Amp* v. *Hellerman* [1962] R.P.C. 55 (H.L.).
[23] PA 1977, s.76(2).
[24] Above, n. 22.
[25] See *Ward's Applcn.* [1986] R.P.C. 54. The EPO Guidelines C VI 5.3-6 direct the examiner to consider whether there has been an overall change in the content of the application; and he is to object to greater specificity (*e.g.* "mounted on helical springs" in place of "resilient supports") unless the substitution is an obvious one.
[26] PA 1977, ss.27(1), 75(1); leave to amend may be conditional, requiring possibly that no proceedings be brought for past infringement (but note the relevance here of s.62(3) (restriction on damages)).
[27] But *cf.* the duties associated with the requirement of disclosure: see below, § 5-063.
[28] For examples, see Ency. PL § 7-205.
[29] Put in these terms by Salmon L.J., *Ethyl Corp's Patent* [1972] R.P.C. 169 at 193 (C.A.); *cf. ICI's (Small) Applcn.* [1979] F.S.R. 78.

have made the judges and the Patent Office reluctant to refuse amendments that fall within the legal requirements. But still judgments are given which insist that the onus that the applicant has to discharge is a heavy one and that he must put before the court the whole story leading to the application to amend.[30]

(3) Correction of errors

4-027   The British Office and the EPO each has power itself to correct errors of translation, transcription, clerical errors and mistakes in all documents.[31] But in the case of specifications, the correction has to be obvious in the sense that it is immediately evident that nothing else would have been intended than what is offered as the correction. This is a severe limitation: under the previous law, the question whether there had been an "obvious mistake" was judged by the standard of the person skilled in the art, who was taken merely to have perused the specification.[32] The standard is likely to remain applicable.

Errors of translation are particularly liable to occur. But the rule seems to allow little scope for their correction, since so often translations leave obscure what the original must have meant. Only in the case of European patent applications may a special rule apply. If the United Kingdom at any time requires the claims of the published application and the whole of the granted patent to be translated from French or German into English,[33] these can be corrected so as to achieve the meaning of the original.[34] There is however intermediate protection for those who rely on the earlier version.[35] Claims of the European patent have to be translated into the other official languages; but it is the original which governs[36] and in this case there seems to be no special protection for a person who relies on a more narrowly formulated translation.

3. CLAIMS

(1) Claims and infringement: an introduction

4-028   In Britain, the United States and countries which have taken their patent laws from these sources, the purpose of claims in the patent specification is to delimit the scope of the monopoly. "Fence-posts" are set up, most often by the use of words, but commonly also by chemical and mathematical symbols; sometimes by reference to drawings. Activities within the territory thus defined require the patentee's consent

---

[30] *S.C.M. Corp's Applcn.* [1979] R.P.C. 341 (C.A.); *Western Electric v. Racal-Milgo* [1981] R.P.C. 253; *Waddington's Patent* [1986] R.P.C. 158.

[31] PA 1977, s.117, PA 1977 Rules, r. 91(2); EPC Rules, r. 88. In the EPO there must first be a request (though not necessarily from the proprietor of the patent).

[32] *Union Carbide's (Hostettler) Applcn.* [1969] R.P.C. 530 at 543; *Chevron's Patent* [1970] R.P.C. 580; *General Tire's (Frost) Patent* [1972] R.P.C. 259, approved in *Holtite v. Jost* [1979] R.P.C. 81 (H.L.).

[33] *i.e.* making use of powers in PA 1977, ss.77(6), 78(7); see above, § 4-004.

[34] PA 1977, s.80, following EPC Art. 70(3), (4).

[35] PA 1977, s.80(3), (4).

[36] s.80(1), following EPC Art. 70(1).

if they are not to infringe.[37] Whether activities which all but fall within the area also infringe has been the subject of a certain flux in British case-law. There was a period in the 1960's when the House of Lords seemed intent on keeping the patentee strictly to his claim, at least when the invention consisted only of a modest improvement over what was already known.[38] During the European Convention negotiations, this undoubtedly aroused a mistrust of the British way of doing things. Using the claims in this way has two crucial consequences. First, draftsmen must perfect the art of legitimate generalisation—in part this is an exercise in imagining alternative forms for the inventive idea, in part in finding descriptions that will cover all the variants concisely. Secondly, disputes about the interpretation of claims become of central significance, both in deciding what constitutes infringement and in determining the validity of the patent itself.[39]

"Fence-post" claiming is to be distinguished from the "sign-post" claiming which has been favoured by some patent systems. "Sign-post" claims aim to specify the essential inventive concept in the specification: an important part of this accordingly is to distinguish what is new from what is old, and the claims are generally put into a form which is designed to achieve this.[40] The relation between claim and protected territory is then less direct: to some extent it is left to the court to work out the proper scope of the monopoly from the description of the invention, the claims merely showing what the patentee considers is his inventive step. In the more extreme applications of this approach the court is in effect deciding whether, given the description of the invention, a "fence-post" claim could have been written that would cover the alleged infringement.

With the introduction of the EPC and PCT examining arrangements **4-029** this difference of emphasis suddenly became something much more immediate than an occasional trap in patenting across a spectrum of countries. For it affects not only infringement but also questions of validity. In the new European system, so far as statutory texts go, the "fence-post" approach has been preferred. By EPC Article 69(1), the extent of protection is determined by "the terms of the claims," using the description and drawings to interpret them; and this formula is in effect repeated for United Kingdom patents in the 1977 Act, section 125.

Even so, qualification looms, in the ungainly form of the Protocol on the Interpretation of Article 69.[41] This requires Article 69 to be read as defining a middle position which combines a fair protection for the patentee with a reasonable degree of certainty for third parties. Two

---

[37] The concept of infringement is dealt with in detail below, § 6-001.
[38] For these cases, see below, §§ 6-003—6-006.
[39] For the general principles of construction, see below, §§ 4-030—4-031.
[40] The influence of this thinking is to be found in the form that European patent claims are to be given "wherever appropriate": the features shared with the prior art must first be described, and then the inventive additions emphasised in a phrase starting "characterised by . . .": EPC Rules, r. 29(1).
[41] The Protocol also applies to the principle in PA 1977 that the patented invention is that specified in a claim, as interpreted by the description and drawings, and the extent of protection is to be determined accordingly: see s.125(1), (3). On the whole question see Winkler (1979) 10 I.I.C. 296; Sijp. *ibid.* 433; Armitage (1983) 14 I.I.C. 811.

extremes are disapproved: using the strict, literal meaning of the claims to define the scope of protection, with resort to description and drawings only to resolve ambiguities (a caricature of the British approach); and using the claims only as a guide-line, the scope of protection covering "what, from a consideration of the description and drawings a person skilled in the art, the patentee has contemplated" (an exaggeration of the German approach). While the Protocol has not perhaps had explicit effect on British attitudes to interpretation,[42] there has come in the last few years to be a new emphasis on "purposive construction" which seems in result to honour its directive.[43]

If it achieves anything at all, the Protocol may help courts in other countries to realise that they ought not to mark out their own bounds for the monopoly; and it may stimulate patent draftsmen in other countries into imagining alternatives and drafting claims to cover them. For if Britain or another EPC country with a similar approach to claims is among those designated for a European patent, the claims must be drawn to meet their more exacting standards.

(2) Interpretation of specifications

4-030   Since the claims are the principal determinant of the scope of the monopoly, how they are to be interpreted is frequently the nub of a dispute. In so far as this goes to infringement, the patentee will generally be arguing for a wide construction. But if it goes to validity, he may well want a narrow reading. Sometimes he finds himself pinioned upon this dilemma: the defendant will allege that what he is doing is something anticipated in the prior art or obvious from it. In which case, if the claim covers the activity, it is bad; if not, there is no infringement.[44]

The construction of claims is not something that can be considered in isolation from the rest of the specification. Claims are intended to be pithy delineations of the scope of monopoly, and they are drafted in light of the much more detailed text of the description.[45] A specification must always be read as a whole, just as any other document is.[46] It must moreover be read as having been addressed to a person acquainted with the technology in question. So it must take account of his state of knowledge at the time. Terms which then have a special meaning in the art, or are given a special definition by the specification, will be read in their particular sense. Otherwise they will be understood in their ordinary meaning.[47]

4-031   The direction in EPC Article 69 that description and drawings are to be used to interpret the claims[48] simply reflects British practice. It has not been proper to construe claims in isolation unless and until some

[42] See below, § 6-002.
[43] For this notion, see below, §§ 6-003—6-006.
[44] This is the so-called "Gillette" defence, after Lord Moulton, *Gillette* v. *Anglo-American Trading* (1913) 30 R.P.C. 465 at 480; it requires strict proof: *Hickman* v. *Andrews* [1983] R.P.C. 147.
[45] See Lord Russell, *EMI* v. *Lissen* (1939) 56 R.P.C. 23 at 40-41.
[46] *Ibid.*; and see *Ransburg* v. *Aerostyle* [1968] R.P.C. 287 at 297 (H.L.).
[47] See Lord Russell, above, n. 45.
[48] See above, § 4-029.

ambiguity emerges in the course of doing so. What British courts have insisted on is that the claims are there to mark out the monopolised territory; Article 69 says the same. If they clearly do mean one thing, arguments that they nevertheless mean something else will be rejected. It is in this sense alone that Lord Russell of Killowen's well-known dictum is to be understood:

> "I know of no canon or principle which will justify one in departing from the unambiguous and grammatical meaning of a claim and narrowing or extending its scope by reading into it words which are not in it; or will justify one in using stray phrases in the body of the specification for the purpose of narrowing or widening the boundaries of the monopoly fixed by the plain words of a claim."

As will be emphasised later, claims are to be construed purposively, to determine how they would be understood by those skilled in the relevant art as indications of the scope of monopoly claimed.[49] This modern approach is apposite not only when the question is whether it is infringed, but also on issues of validity, such as novelty and adequate disclosure.[50]

(3) The addressee of the specification

4-032 The complexity of some modern technologies, and the fact that some fields—notably organic chemistry[51]—have lost the precision of earlier, simpler days, makes the task of interpreting specifications increasingly difficult. Some assumption, however, has to be made about the persons to whom it is addressed. As we shall see, essentially the same question arises when assessing whether the invention is obvious and whether the disclosure is adequate,[52] though in those cases there is likely to be more concern over what conclusions the reader would draw from what he is told, and whether he would likely be misled by positive misstatements and misleading implications.

4-033 In *Valensi* v. *British Radio*,[53] the Court of Appeal felt constrained by venerable authority to hold that, even in a new and still experimental field (colour television in 1939), a specification must be looked upon as addressed to skilled technicians, rather than to leading experts (*i.e.* those in the few research teams then tackling the problem) or to manual workers. But they did find that such an intermediate group must have existed in fact and that it would have included representatives from the different technical fields whose knowledge was being pooled in the research.[54] If specialist and highly skilled workers are the only ones who

---

[49] *Catnic* v. *Hill & Smith*, below, § 6-005, n. 15.
[50] See *Dow Chemical* v. *Spence Bryson* [1984] R.P.C. 359 (C.A.); *Van der Lely* v. *Ruston's Engineering* [1985] R.P.C. 461 (C.A.); *Warin Pipe* v. *Hepworth Iron* [1984] F.S.R. 32.
[51] See R. D. Satchell (1970) 1 I.I.C. 179, on the serious practical problem of defining inventions in macro-molecular chemistry. See also *Fernholz's Appln.* [1984] O.J. EPO 555; *Bayer's (Wagner) Appln.* [1982] O.J. EPO 149.
[52] See below, §§ 5-029, 8-061—8-062.
[53] [1973] R.P.C. 337. See further below, §§ 5-061—5-062.
[54] *Ibid.* at 375-377.

exist at the priority date, the specification may, it seems, be treated as addressed to them.[55] The judges have been careful to preserve the general rule that they interpret the words of a document.[56] But expert witnesses may be asked what technical words, phrases and even sentences mean in context to them.[57] It is the general responsibility of the judge, before he construes the claim, to acquaint himself with the art concerned as it would have been understood by the notional addressee at the priority date.[58]

(4) The application file

4-034   In the course of prosecuting an application, substantial amendments are frequently made.[59] In the past, outsiders were not entitled to inspect the official file and so could not know of amendments before publication.[60] Now they may do so at the EPO and the British Office.[61] This may well provide evidence, for instance, of why a claim was limited in a particular way, or what construction the applicant said ought to be put upon a claim when he persuaded the examiner to drop an objection. Such "file-wrapper" estoppels are used as an aid to the construction of claims in the United States.[62] Now it has also been accepted in English proceedings that if an applicant relied on a narrow meaning of a term in order to secure grant, he cannot subsequently argue for a wide view of the same term.[63]

(5) Types of claim

(a) *General*

4-035   In modern patent systems a certain amount turns on the kind of claim in question. The basic distinction is between, on the one hand, product or substance claims and, on the other, process, method or use claims. The first of these categories comprises claims to things. Such claims are infringed primarily by making, selling or using the things claimed. The second category concerns procedures for conducting activities. Here

---

[55] *American Cyanamid* v. *Ethicon* [1979] R.P.C. 215 at 245-246.

[56] See especially Lindley L.J., *Brooks* v. *Steel* (1897) 14 R.P.C. 46 at 73; Lord Tomlin, *British Celanese* v. *Courtaulds* (1935) 52 R.P.C. 171 at 196. In origin, construction of documents was a matter for literate judges, not jurors of uncertain education. The same attitude is not maintained in respect of drawings and photographs: *Van der Lely* v. *Bamfords* [1961] R.P.C. 296 at 306 (C.A.); [1963] R.P.C. 61 at 71 (H.L.).

[57] See Lindley L.J.; *American Cyanamid* v. *Ethicon* [1979] R.P.C. 215 at 251-255.

[58] *Boyd* v. *Horrocks* (1892) 9 R.P.C. 77 at 82 (H.L.); *British Dynamite* v. *Krebs* (1896) 13 R.P.C.190 at 192 (H.L.). but it has been firmly denied that the specification should be construed specifically in the light of an alleged anticipation in the prior art, with an eye to avoiding it: *Dudgeon* v. *Thomson* (1877) 3 App.Cas. 34 at 53-54. *Molins* v. *Industrial Machinery* (1938) 55 R.P.C. 31 at 39 (C.A.). Equally, no account is taken of the alleged infringement: *Dudgeon* v. *Thomson* (above); *Nobel* v. *Anderson* (1894) 11 R.P.C. 519 at 523 (C.A.).

[59] See above, §§ 4-024—4-025.

[60] Publication previously took place after examination and acceptance by the Office.

[61] EPC Art. 128, EPC Rules, rr. 93-95; PA 1977, s.118, PA 1977 Rules, rr. 93-95. There are various exceptions and procedural requirements.

[62] See Chisum, *Patents* (1978) IV, § 18.05; the judges have differed in their willingness to look beyond amendments to the reasons for requiring, proposing or resisting them.

[63] *Fürr* v. *C. D. Trüline* [1985] F.S.R. 553.

infringement consists primarily of performing the activity. There are overlaps. Consider a claim to an article which is some form of mechanical apparatus: since the monopoly includes using the apparatus, it must cover a process. Conversely, we shall see that a process claim may be infringed by dealing in its products in certain circumstances.[64] There are also refinements: a "product-by-process" claim gives a monopoly in an article only when made by the defined process. But the basic distinction is the one to watch: a claim to a thing gives a monopoly over it whatever it is to be used for—and is correspondingly broad; when the prior art precludes such a claim, it may still be possible to secure a method claim to protect the invention of a particular use for the known thing—but then the monopoly is restricted to that use alone. Sometimes claims are drawn in such a way that it is difficult to decide which kind they are. This has to be settled by interpretation.[65]

(b) *Chemical inventions*

The distinction just made is particulary important in the application of the patent system to chemical inventions—rather more so than in the case of mechanical inventions. Indeed, the adaptation of the patent system so as to accommodate the various branches of chemical industry has proved a difficult matter, and one on which some sort of international consensus has only recently begun to emerge.[66] Speaking very broadly, inventive activity in the chemical field sometimes consists of making or in analysing compounds whose existence could not even have been theoretically predicted in advance. More often it involves devising ways of making substances more successfully or cheaply. But the largest part of the ground is concerned with searching for the values that substances may have in use. This sort of work is frequently concerned either with substances which are new (in the sense of never having been made before) but can be made from known starting materials by known methods; or with substances which are known, either as laboratory playthings or as functional products, and which are then tested for initial or further practical uses.　　4-036

The first difficulty in the chemical field is whether patents should ever be granted for a chemical substance itself. Substances may prove to have a variety of values: well-known examples are dyestuffs which prove to have valuable pharmaceutical properties.[67] (By contrast, mechanical things less readily assume new functions, at least without adaptation.) Accordingly, many systems have at some time required chemical claims to be for "substance-by-process." The British system contained such a constraint between 1919 and 1949.[68] But it was found, as in other countries, that　　4-037

[64] Below, §§ 6-010—6-011.
[65] For instance, claims to a thing "for" a purpose: see below, § 5-053.
[66] cf., e.g. the papers by Satchell (above, n. 46) and Robinson and Nastelski (1972) 3 I.I.C. 139, 267; Lawrence (1973) 2 CIPA 385; Gaumont (1982) 13 I.I.C. 457; Klöpsch (1982) 13 I.I.C. 457.
[67] See for instance the adventures of the phenothiazines: *Olin Mathieson* v. *Biorex* [1970] R.P.C. 157 at 185 *et seq.*
[68] See Final Report of the Swan Committee, Cmd. 7206, 1947, §§ 92-95.

this only introduced a game of seeing whether the patentee could think of all the possible processes for producing the substance and therefore claim them; while still leaving him the difficulty of showing that the defendant was using one of them.

In Britain from 1949 onwards, and now elsewhere in EPC states,[69] it has been accepted that claims to chemical substances of all kinds, including pharmaceuticals, are admissible. It seems that they may be validly granted whenever the substance itself is not part of the prior art.[70] This is then treated as any other article claim: the patentee's permission is needed to make the article for any purpose. If a second use for the substance is found during the life of his patent, his permission is needed just as much to make, sell and use for that purpose as for the purpose that he worked out. This is not so overweening as it may sound, because there are ways in which the second inventor can secure patents, by means of use claims or through the special rules for "selections."[71] In the main, therefore, the first patentee is given the chance of a share in the monopoly for the second discovery, provided that it comes during the life of his patent.[72] Any injustices arising from this compromise have not aroused chemical industry circles to major protest.

4-038   A second problem concerns the breadth of monopoly allowable. Much investigation into the properties of organic substances involves testing a few substances in a family of compounds that may have thousands or millions of members. The basic structure of the family has a defined molecular form which can be varied by attaching atoms or chains at particular positions of the molecule. Experience shows that in many cases, the whole group of compounds will have similar characteristics, though in different degrees and with different consequences. The dilemma then is this: if the patentee is restricted to claims upon the substances that he has used in his experiments, his rival is free to take up the next nearest in imitation. If, however, he is given a claim to the whole family of compounds, his monopoly may appear unduly wide. Authorities in different countries have reacted with greater or less caution in seeking some compromise, looking in the main at the degree of certainty with which it can be predicted that the whole class will share the discovered advantages. On a strict view, for instance, it can be insisted that either end of a range of compounds be tested, together with a representative sample of those in between. But it is difficult to reach a formula like this which seems reasonable in every case.[73] In Britain, by contrast, it has been held that it is enough, in the absence of positive proof that some members of the class do not work at all,[74] to base a claim to the class simply upon a sound prediction that all members will show the advant-

[69] See Michaelis (1983) 14 I.I.C. 372; Gruber and Kroher (1984) 15 I.I.C. 588, 726.
[70] But see further below, § 5-068.
[71] See below, §§ 5-018—5-020.
[72] Should he obstruct the second application by refusing permission, a compulsory licence could be secured: see below, § 7-051.
[73] An attempt by the German Patent Office to require this was rejected by the courts: see Nastelski (above, n. 66).
[74] Whether this factor remains of any significance under the new law is questionable, since inutility is no longer a distinct ground of objection to validity: see below, § 5-065.

ageous property in some degree.[75] The test finds a place in the EPO Guidelines; and it has been espoused by the Supreme Court of Canada in place of an earlier, more grudging approach.[76]

Chemical patents present a number of other difficulties. With the   4-039 macro-molecular substances that play such a part in modern plastics and other chemistry there are major obstacles to finding a sufficiently clear description for a claim.[77] There is a problem when the substance claimed has itself no use but may prove a useful intermediate in the production of something that does turn out to be valuable.[78] The continued preclusion of patents for methods of human and animal treatment poses problems which are growing with the current expansion of biotechnology.[79] These are particular difficulties which can be left for later discussion. But they are symptomatic of a larger truth.

[75] Graham J., *Olin Mathieson* case (above, n. 67) at 193: see below.
[76] EPO Guidelines, CIII 6.2; *Monsanto's (Coran and Kerwood) Applcn.* [1980] F.S.R. 50.
[77] See above, § 4-032 n. 51.
[78] See below, § 5-068.
[79] See below, §§ 5-051—5-053.

CHAPTER 5

VALIDITY

5-001　This Chapter investigates the substantive law of validity of patents. A number of ideas introduced in the last Chapter form an essential background. First, the challenges that may be made to validity, and the persons who may make them, differ for applications and granted patents. Secondly, if a patentee seeks to enforce his rights, he may be met by the defence that his patent is invalid or a counterclaim for its revocation. Thirdly, the claims, which define the monopoly, are the starting point of various issues about validity.

European patents must meet the criteria of validity specified in the EPC. But a national state for which a European patent is granted may not add further requirements by its own law.[1] The Patents Act 1977 accordingly adopts the EPC grounds of invalidity for United Kingdom patents whether granted by the European or the British Office.[2] But to some extent the language of the EPC is revamped, with attendant uncertainties.[3] In outline the grounds are these: the invention must be patentable, *i.e.* (i) it must be novel, (ii) it must involve an inventive step, (iii) it must be capable of industrial application, and (iv) it must not belong to one of the categories of excluded subject-matter.[4] The specification must satisfy the "internal" requirement of adequate disclosure,[5] and during the application stage the claims must meet a number of standards.[6] There are certain other objections relating to the right to grant and to unallowable amendments.[7]

The grounds of invalidity are formulated in general terms. Yet the issues that are hardest fought often lie at their perimeters. There remains much for the courts and other tribunals to do in determining the precise application of law to particular cases. In this, decisions under the former British law must be treated as suggestive rather than authoritative, for they were concerned with statutory texts that were differently formulated. Also now significant are decisions on the EPC and national law

---

[1] One basic limb of the so-called "maximum" approach adopted in drafting the Convention: see EPC Art. 138.
[2] PA 1977, s.72.
[3] These difficulties are, if anything, compounded by s.130(7): see above, § 3-039.
[4] EPC Arts. 52-57; PA 1977, ss.1-4; below, § 5-003.
[5] EPC Arts. 83, 100(*b*); PA 1977, ss.14(3), 72(1)(*c*); below, § 5-058.
[6] Below, §§ 5-064—5-065.
[7] Above, §§ 4-023—4-027.

114

deriving from it which are reached by the EPO and the courts of contracting states.[8]

An important objective of the new regime is that patents should be granted only after a more extensive examination than previously. The former British approach deliberately and rather indiscriminately set a low standard for applicants to satisfy before grant: if doubt existed about an objection it was to be resolved in the applicant's favour, full investigation being reserved for proceedings after grant.[9] We shall see that there are inherent reasons for taking a cautious approach to some objections, notably obviousness, at an early stage in the life of an invention. But a firmer hand may be applied to other questions, such as whether categories of subject-matter (computer programs, micro-organisms, etc.) fall within the system or not. For these are issues of policy and interpretation that do not depend on evidence in the particular case.[10]

5-002

1. NOVELTY

(1) Introduction

No system grants valid patents for inventions that are already known: that would be to encumber industry with constraints upon the use of information without any sufficient return. Accordingly, the present law requires a patented invention to be new in the sense of forming no part of the state of the art, *i.e.* it must not be found at the priority date in any "matter (whether a product, a process, information about either, or anything else) which has at any time been made available to the public (whether in the United kingdom or elsewhere) by written or oral description, by use, or in any other way."[11] This concept draws no distinction between information published by the inventor and by someone unconnected with him: if the inventor were protected from prejudicing himself, he might delay his patent until it was commercially most advantageous to apply.[12]

5-003

In most cases the assessment of novelty is relatively straightforward. Here are a few examples which illustrate the nature of the inquiry and point towards some of the problems requiring further discussion.

5-004

(a) (*Van der Lely* v. *Bamford*[13]: mechanical product.) The patentee claimed a hayraking machine in which the rake-wheels were turned not by engine but by contact with the ground. The patent was held to have been anticipated by a photograph in a journal which showed a hayrake with this feature (the issue was whether the photograph was clear enough to reveal the invention to an informed person.)

[8] Also, when the CPC takes effect, the European Court of Justice and the proposed Community Patent Appeal Court.
[9] The approach stems from the *Swift* case (below, § 5-055, n.34.).
[10] For examples, see below, §§ 5-039 *et seq.*
[11] PA 1977, s.1(1)(*a*), s.2(1), (2), based upon EPC Arts. 52, 54. For the special problem of prior patent applications subsequently published (s.2(3), Art. 54(3)), see below, § 5-012.
[12] But see below, § 5-007.
[13] [1963] R.P.C. 61 (H.L.). For anticipation in a drawing, see, *e.g. Charbonnages' Applcn.* [1985] O.J. EPO 310.

(b) (*Fomento* v. *Mentmore*[14]: mechanical process/product). The patentee claimed a ball-point pen in which the housing around the ball had a groove running in a ring below the equatorial plane of the ball; this produced a smooth flow of ink. The alleged anticipation (a patent specification[15]) was found to describe a method of enclosing the housing around the ball by "peining," *i.e.* by hitting the open housing with a tool shaped like a candle-suffer. Before there could be anticipation, however, it was necessary to show that peining would inevitably produce the desired ring-like groove in the correct position; and the earlier document, it was held, only gave instructions that "might well" produce this effect.[16]

(c) (*Shell's Patent*[17]: chemical combination.) The patentee claimed a petrol with three additives: a lead anti-knock component (one of a class of chemicals), an ordinary scavenger and an additional scavenger (from a specified class of esters) in certain proportions. The scavengers were added to prevent the fouling of spark plugs and corrosion of exhaust pipes. In one example, the anticipating document (a published patent application that was not pursued to grant) described a petrol containing one member of the class of special scavengers within the patentee's proportions. The advantage alleged for this addition was different (preventing fuel tank corrosion) and most likely did not produce that result. Nevertheless, the patentee was obliged to disclaim this one instance in order to save the rest of the claim from anticipation. Because the one anticipation did not concern the patentee's problem, and so was "accidental," the rest was not obvious and the amendment permissible. (To other difficulties raised by this case we shall come later.[18])

5-005   From these examples it may be seen that novelty involves an essentially factual investigation: has the same invention already been made public? There is little room for the sort of evaluation that arises where the issue is obviousness: is the step over what is already known significant enough to be called inventive? As Example (c) above suggests, there are circumstances in which, if an anticipation cannot be shown, there is no room for an attack on the grounds of obviousness.[19] It is therefore important to know what counts as lack of novelty. It is worth introducing some of the problems in historical and comparative terms.

---

[14] [1956] R.P.C.87 (C.A.).
[15] In which at least one plaintiff had an interest.
[16] For the effect of this on the law, see below, §5-015. There was also a prior use point: below, § 5-012.
[17] [1960] R.P.C. 35 (C.A.) The EPO scrutinised the earlier disclosure very carefully, when anticipation is supposed to have arisen by chance: *AMP's Applcn.* [1984] O.J. EPO 551.
[18] Below, §§ 5-017, 5-019—5-021.
[19] Another instance is the rule concerning matter in prior specifications, discussed below, § 5-012.

(2) Publication and use

The British patent system originally treated prior use as the principal **5-006** objection to the validity of a patent, the first purpose of the system being to encourage the introduction of inventions into British manufacture.[20] Even when prior publication evolved as a distinct ground of objection, prior use kept its independent status—for instance, in the principle that even a secret use was in some circumstances a ground of invalidity; and in the rule that a prior use which did not reveal the invention to the world but which involved no deliberate secrecy could found an objection under the general provision relating to novelty, rather than the more limited secret use provision.[21]

In the new law, use has lost its independence as an objection to **5-007** validity. An invention is new if it does not form part of the state of the art; and the state of the art comprises all matter made available to the public before the priority date of the invention "by written or oral description, by use or in any other way." Use founds an attack on novelty if it effects a public release equivalent to publication. If a product is marketed whose mechanics, circuitry or chemical composition can be worked out by an appropriately skilled person this will suffice for "publication"[22]; if the invention is a process which can be understood only by observing it and not by inspecting or analysing the end product, it is a question of fact whether enough of the public have been allowed an adequate chance of seeing it in operation to understand it.[23] But to make batches of one chemical substance that are then mixed with others so as to be undetectable when the mixture is sold[24] would not be to "publish" the substance. Under the new law, novelty is concerned with the patent system as a source of information, not as a stimulus to use. The prior user who does not reveal his invention is confined to a limited measure of protection against being held an infringer.[25]

While prior use was a distinct objection, it was not open to an inventor of (say) a process exploitable without revelation first to use it until it became a success and then to patent it at the most advantageous moment. If he can do so, the patent system suffers as an incentive to early revelation in the very case where it ought to have greatest effect. However, the devisers of the EPC chose not to provide separately against this danger. Certainly in a system which is strictly "first-to-file," an inventor who intends to patent can risk delay only if he sees no serious hazard of others publishing or applying for a patent before he does.

---

[20] See above, § 3-003.
[21] See PA 1949, ss.32(1)(e), (c), 32(2); there had, however, to be prior use and not merely prior invention: *Catnic* v. *Evans* [1983] F.S.R. 401.
[22] *Stahlwerk Becker's Patent* (1919) 36 R.P.C. 13 (H.L.) held that to market a steel was to publish its composition, since this could be deduced by chemical analysis. See also *Fomento* v. *Mentmore*, above, n. 14.
[23] The question of how many must be informed, now more important than ever, is discussed below, §§ 5-010—5-011.
[24] As in *Bristol Myers' (Johnson) Appln.* [1975] R.P.C. 127 (H.L.), the leading case on "prior use" under the former law; see Ency. PL, § 2-013.
[25] Below, § 6-016.

(3) Material available for consideration

A patent system has to define the material which it will take into consideration in assessing novelty, using broad criteria relating to time, place and form. Each element can be separately considered:

(a) *Temporal factors*

5-008   The British system has long taken the priority date of the patent as the point in time for deciding whether there has been an anticipation and this (subject to fewer exceptions than before[26]) continues to be the rule: there is no general period of grace.[27] The special difficulty created by applications with earlier priority which are published only after the later priority date of another application receives new treatment as far as British law is concerned: the earlier specification is added to the state of the art for purposes of novelty but not obviousness. To the problems that this may cause, we return subsequently.[28]

(b) *Territorial factors*

5-009   Traditionally the British system, with its emphasis on the encouragement of national industry, only looked at anticipations within the United Kingdom.[29] Other countries have taken greater account of the growing internationalism of technical knowledge. But in the various solutions adopted, there has been some tendency to distinguish between anticipations by documentary publication and by use: in some systems the former is considered upon a worldwide purview, while the latter has to take place within the territory.[30]

The EPC and the 1977 Act pursue an uninhabited internationalism in the matter, apparently imposing no territorial constraints at all. The British Act refers specifically to material "made available to the public (whether in the United Kingdom or elsewhere)."[31] But this liberality offers temptations to the unscrupulous to produce instances of anticipation from highly obscure foreign sources. If a British court or tribunal has doubts about genuineness of the evidence, it may find that the attacker has not sufficiently proved his case. Alternatively, it may be attracted to hold that the anticipation must have been made available to a public which includes at least some persons from British industry. Certainly on this basis material could be disregarded which, because of a legal embargo in a foreign country, could not be consulted by a British technician or research scientist; more doubtfully in the case of material which could only be obtained by such a person after laborious and expensive persistence.

[26] For the previous law, see below, §§ A2-003—004.

[27] Periods of grace covering material published by the patentee (or deriving from him) have been found in various systems. Disregard of material, published or used within a period before the priority date, is typically associated with the "first to invent" systems of the U.S. and Canada; see Chism, *Patents* I, §§ 3.04-3.07. There is now much discussion of the need to introduce more extensive grace periods, particularly

[28] Below, § 5-012.

[29] See above, § 3-003.

[30] For countries which prefer this "relative" novelty, those which allow "absolute" novelty and those which adopt the "local" novelty formerly found in British law, see Baxter (above, n. 27), pp. 84-87.

[31] s.2(2). The EPC Art. 54(2) has nothing equivalent to the phrase in brackets.

(c) Form

In the past, prior publication of an invention has normally been found **5-010** in a document, while prior use has required proof that the use has taken place. The new law admits prior matter irrespective of its form. It may be made available to the public "by written or oral description, by use or in any other way."[32] This too may give rise to difficult questions of proof.

(d) Degree of dissemination

Underlying the rules about place and form is a general question of **5-011** degree. How far must information have been communicated, or at least put at the disposal of others, before it can be said to be available to the public? Under the 1949 Act, the law called only for a minimum that was, in a sense, artificial: it was enough that information about the invention (or the means of discovering it from a concrete embodiment) was put in the hands of a single person who might use it as he liked, free from obligations of confidence and similar duties.[33] Likewise it sufficed that a document was placed in a library or other place in the United Kingdom for consultation as of right by any person with or without paying a fee[34]; and this latter proposition, at least remains the rule.[35] These liberal rules not only simplified an attacker's task in procuring evidence. They also side-stepped the difficult question: how much publicity would make a thing "known?" So long as novelty was confined to anticipations within the United Kingdom, and the Patent Office made only a limited search as the basis for its *ex parte* examination, the artifice of the rule had its merits. But, as already remarked, the "absolute novelty" of the new law will lead to the citation of much more obscure documents, to say nothing of oral communications and uses. If the actual circulation of them, or the potential availability of information from them, is very limited it is possible that they may be discounted.[36] But at least it must be assumed that the contents of patent specifications, no matter where or when published,[37] belong to the art.

(e) Matter in prior specifications

If competitors make the same invention at much the same time (by no **5-012** means an uncommon phenomenon in today's race for innovation) there is a special aspect of the principle under which the first to secure a priority date is preferred. Once the earlier applicant has his specification published, it of course becomes part of the state of the art. But without special provision it would not have that character in the period between securing the priority date and publication of the specification. Yet if nothing is done, "double patenting" may result, and that has long been

---

[32] See EPO Guidelines D V 3 1. Demonstrating in specialist training courses or on television are given as examples of "other ways."

[33] *Humpherson* v. *Syer* (1887) 4 R.P.C. 407, at 413-414 (C.A.); *Fomento* v. *Mentmore* (above, n. 14) at 99; *Monsanto's (Brignac) Appln.* [1971] R.P.C. 127. But criticism of the rule was noted by Sachs L.J., *Laguerre's Patent* [1971] R.P.C. 384 at 399.

[34] PA 1949, s.101(1). See further Ency. PL, § 5-114.

[35] PA 1977, s.130(1) "published."

[36] *cf. Badowski* v. *U.S.* 118 U.S.P.Q. 358 (1958) (Russian document available only through diplomatic channels is not an anticipation).

[37] Unlike the former rule which discounted U.K. specifications more than 50 years old.

thought unacceptable. Previously, British law sought to deal with the problem in the way that would least jeopardise the chances of the later patentee: by preventing him from also claiming protection for inventions within the claims of the earlier patent, provided that they were valid. But under the 1949 Act this process of comparing claims in order to exclude overlap bred highly recondite judicial decisions which militated against continuing this approach.[38]

Instead, the material in a patent specification is now given a priority date, which is determined in the same way as the priority date of a claim. Provided that it is subsequently published, it is treated as having formed part of the state of the art in the intervening period for the purpose of assessing the novelty of later inventions; but not, let it be stressed, for ascertaining inventive step.[39] In applications to the British office this applies to the contents of prior British applications[40]; in the EPO to the contents of prior European applications, but only to the extent that the same states are designated in the earlier and later applications[41] (hence the European patents granted for various states may differ.) Correspondingly, after grant of a British patent by either route, the comptroller or court must take account of earlier applications for United Kingdom patents by either route.[42] It is not required of applications that they must mature into granted patents, a pre-condition which would conjure echoes of "prior claiming."[43]

This "whole contents" approach applies not only between rival applicants but also to successive applications by the same person. Hence the danger of "self-collision," which is particularly apparent in the case of mechanical inventions. In that field, one piece of research may produce a succession of broadly interrelated inventions, each of which calls for a separate application either as a matter of tactics or because of the requirement of "unity of invention."[44] Each application will need a sufficient description and this may well call for mention of the other parts of the whole concept. If the applications are not filed on the same day, it is only too easy for the first to describe matter for which the second seeks protection. It was just this hazard that the old "prior claiming" approach avoided; but by making the earlier material part of the art only for novelty and not for obviousness (until it is actually published) the danger is to some extent reduced.

[38] For the debate, see the Banks Report (Cmnd. 4407, 1970), Chap. 10.

[39] PA 1977, s.2(3), EPC Art. 54(3). The Banks Committee had proposed the contrary (Chap. 10) but this was not accepted for the EPC or the PA 1977. Switzerland is one EPC member which continues to adopt a "prior claiming" approach in its own law: see EPO Bulletin 1979, p. 14.

[40] As far as the Act is concerned (see s.78(1) (2)), this could also include prior European applications designating the U.K. But no regular machinery exists for searching these applications. A third party "observation," however (see above, § 4-021), could provide the notification.

[41] EPC Art. 54(3), (4).

[42] PA 1977, s.2(3), s.78(1) (2). S.73(1) gives the comptroller special power to revoke upon his own initiative, in order to take account in particular of late information about prior European patents (U.K.). Under s.73(2) a British-granted patent will be revoked if a European patent (U.K.) for the same invention bears the same priority date.

[43] See now PA 1977, s.78(5A), inserted by CDPA 1988, Sched. 5, § 22.

[44] See above, §§ 4-011—4-012.

(f) *Special exclusions*

A patentee faces the risk of anticipation from two sources: from   **5-013**
independent inventors and from those whose information comes from the
same inventive source as his own. In a modern business organisation risks
of the latter kind may arise because its research staff are eager for
recognition, because an employee has turned disloyal, or because an
outsider to whom the invention was revealed in confidence breaks his
undertaking. Against such hazards as these, the 1977 Act affords some
measure of protection, but it is more limited than under the old law. For
instance inventors are no longer free to describe the invention in a paper to
a learned society.[45] So it is crucial to keep their natural desire to share ideas
with colleagues under rein until all relevant priority dates have been
secured.

In two circumstances, according to the British Act,[46] a disclosure does
not count in determining novelty for a period of six months after it is
made:

(i) if the information was obtained unlawfully or in breach of
confidence; or if it was disclosed in breach of confidence.[47]

(ii) if the disclosure resulted from display by the inventor at a
prescribed "international exhibition" and the applicant files proper
notification of this.[48] Only exhibitions to educate the public (not
trade fairs) are within the exception and they must last between
three and 26 weeks and must occur no more than once in every
20 years.[49]

These exceptions, particularly the former, do not follow the equivalent
EPC provisions,[50] apparently because "it will not do"[51] to have English
judges wrestle with the Convention's vague language ("evident abuse in
relation to the applicant or his legal predecessor"). One consequent
difference is that the British provisions appear to exempt the disclosure of
an invention even if it has also been made by an inventor who is quite
independent of the applicant or his predecessor, and the information
comes from this separate source.

(4) Relations between anticipation and invention in suit

(a) *The comparison*

Novelty involves a comparison between the invention, in any of its   **5-014**
embodiments, and the thing that is revealed by the prior publication or

[45] *cf.* PA 1949, s.51(2)(*d*), and note the other exceptions in ss.50, 51; below, §§ A2-003 —
004. See Lesser [1987] E.I.P.R. 81.
[46] PA 1977, s.2(4). See also s.6.
[47] s.2(4)(*a*)(*b*). This abbreviates highly elaborate provisions, which apparently cover the
various possible situations. On the burden of proof, see *Dunlop's Appln.* [1979] R.P.C.
523 (C.A.).
[48] s.2(4)(*c*). The exhibition has to be one within the Convention on International Exhibitions 1928: see PA 1977, s.130(1), (2). For the notification required, see PA 1977 Rules,
r. 5; EPC Rules, r. 23.
[49] Unlike the much more generous provisions in the previous law: see Ency. PL § 5-122,
[1979] O.J. EPO 159; Vitoria (1978) 1 E.I.P.R., October 29.
[50] EPC Art. 55.
[51] J. C. H. Ellis, in *The Patents Act 1977* (Vitoria ed.), p. 23.

use. Under the old law at least, the question was whether anything within the claims has already been published or used. Or, standing the question on its head: would the earlier thing fall within the later claims for purposes of infringement (assuming that other conditions for infringement were fulfilled)?[52] For instance, in *Van der Lely* v. *Bamfords* (Example (a), § 5-004), if the photographed hayrake were made in the United Kingdom after publication of the patent application, would it fall within the terms of any claim? If it would, then the photograph was an anticipation. Given the new emphasis on the purposive construction of claims, the result may be a correspondingly enlarged scope for anticipation.[53] Thus a claim to a windsurfer of the now familar modern type included as one element, "a pair of arcuate booms", by which was meant the wishbone-shaped grip held by the surfer. An earlier model made by a young amateur and used publicly, had a pair of straight booms. Since in use these deformed flexibly into arcs, they were held to anticipate.[54]

(b) *The anticipation: clarity*

5-015   Not infrequently a question of anticipation centres on whether the prior document or use does sufficiently disclose the later invention. This may be so when the alleged anticipation is "unintentional"; but the issue is by no means confined to such cases. For instance, in *Fomento* v. *Mentmore* (Example (b), § 5-004), actual examples were put in evidence of pens produced according to the allegedly anticipatory instructions. Virtually all showed the crucial deformation of the housing of the ball. Yet the Court of Appeal still found, on the evidence as a whole, that, while this "might well" occur from following the instructions, yet it would not do so "necessarily," or "inevitably," or "in 99 cases out of a hundred."[55] This then is the test: if the claim is for a method of use or a process, the anticipation must give "clear and unmistakeable directions to do what the patentee claims to have invented"[56] if it is for an article, apparatus or substance the qualified reader must be enabled "at once to perceive and understand and be able practically to apply the discovery without the necessity of making further experiments."[57] Instructions or descriptions may, however, anticipate even if they fall short of the

---

[52] See, *e.g. Harwood* v. *GNR* (1865) 11 H.L.C. 654 at 681; *General Tire* v. *Firestone* [1972] R.P.C. 457 at 486, 496 (C.A.).

[53] See above, § 4-031.

[54] *Windsurfing International* v. *Tabur Marine* [1985] R.P.C. 59 (C.A.); see also *Dow Chemical* v. *Spence Bryson* [1984] R.P.C. 359 (C.A.).

[55] A statement, later shown to be incorrect, that something would not work can scarcely be an anticipation: see *Nestlé's Appln.* [1970] R.P.C. 88; but a statement that something has been tried and did not work is more doubtful; a statement that something works for a purpose when it does not anticipates a claim to the thing, even though it is found to have a different advantage: *Shell's Patent* (above, n. 17).

[56] Parker J., *Flour Oxidising* v. *Carr* (1908) 25 R.P.C. 428 at 457. Subsequently much cited, *e.g.* Lord Dunedin, *Metropolitan Vickers* v. *British Thomson-Houston* (1927) 45 R.P.C. 1 at 22-23. *Beecham Group's (Amoxycillin) Appln.* [1980] R.P.C. 261 (C.A.). "A signpost, however clear, upon the road to the patentee's invention will not suffice. The prior inventor must be clearly shown to have planted his flag at the precise destination before the patentee." Sachs L.J., *General Tire* v. *Firestone* [1972] R.P.C. 457 at 486.

[57] Lord Westbury, *Hill* v. *Evans* (1862) 4 De G. F. & J. 288 at 300; cited in *Van der Lely* v. *Bamfords* [1963] R.P.C. 61 at 71 (H.L.).

detailed description that it would be needed to support a valid patent.[58] But—and here obviousness must be distinguished—it is not permissible to read two documents together one does not positively cross-refer to the other.[59]

(c) The anticipation: appreciation of significance

Certainly under the previous law, in order for there to be an anticipation, the prior revelation did not have to show the same understanding of the advantages of the invention, nor did it have to offer so adequate an explanation of why the invention worked. It was enough, to anticipate a claim to a chemical substance, for a chemistry textbook to state that it had been made, even though its characteristics were still under investigation.[60] A claim to stockings made with a tuck in the toe (giving the advantage of a better-shaped toe end) could not survive proof that machines already sometimes produced stockings with such tucks, despite the fact that the tucks were previously thought a disadvantage.[61]

5-016

At its most extreme, this approach means that "unintentional" anticipations can be employed to invalidate later patents. In *Molins* v. *Industrial Machinery*[62] the patent concerned a way of ensuring an even distribution of tobacco in cigarettes formed on a high-speed machine: the trick lay in giving the tobacco a preliminary push in the same direction as the paper in which it would be wrapped. Bonsack's much earlier specification, dealing with a low-speed machine, described a device which would give this movement. Accordingly it anticipated, although it was not directed to solving the patentee's problem.

(5) New use of an old thing

The principle that once a thing has been made public, no one may have a patent for it, must be understood as a ground rule to which a number of qualifications are admitted. These certainly go some way towards giving patentees a monopoly commensurate with the novelty of their invention. But not in every case; for the system does not aim to reward merely for creative effort.

5-017

Many of the difficulties in the basic rules arise from the fact that an inventor may discover a new use for something already known. He may, for instance, discover that a well-known chemical can be added to water in a boiler so as to reduce scaling. To allow him to claim the chemical as a substance, would give him a monopoly over all its uses, not just in boilers; this would be more than he is entitled to. But if no one has found a use for the chemical in boilers before, he is entitled to claim "a method for preventing scale in boilers in which. . . . " Such a claim limits his monopoly to what he has discovered: only those who use the chemical in this way, or who induce its use, will infringe.[63]

[58] Lord Watson, *King, Brown* v. *Anglo American Brush* (1892) 9 R.P.C. 313 at 320; cited *Ransburg* v. *Aerostyle* [1968] R.P.C. 287, 299 (H.L.).

[59] See below, § 5-032.

[60] *Gyogyszeripari's Applcn.* [1958] R.P.C. 51; and see *Adhesive Dry Mounting* v. *Trapp* (1910) 27 R.P.C. 341; *Smith Kline & French's Applcn.* [1968] R.P.C. 415.

[61] *cf. Reymes-Cole* v. *Elite* [1965] R.P.C. 102 (C.A.) (where, in light of the evidence, the case was treated as one of obviousness).   [62] (1938) 55 R.P.C. 31 (C.A.).

[63] The 1977 Act provides more extensively than in the past for "indirect" infringement of method claims by supplying materials for carrying out the process: see below, §§ 6-013—6-014.

However, if his discovery is only of an advantage, in the sense of something which involves no change in actual construction or procedure for use, a problem remains. For instance, in *Shell's Patent* (Example (c), above § 5-004) both the claimed invention and the anticipation were engine fuels, even though the same mixtures were proposed for different purposes (prevention of spark-plug fouling, prevention of tank corrosion.) The later patentee could not alter this by adding to his claim a statement of purpose which emphasised his discovered advantage.[64] He had to confine himself to mixtures not claimed in the earlier specification or to those which he could claim by selection.

The rule which confines a later inventor's claim to his newly discovered use also causes difficulty when a separate policy debars claims for the kind of method in question. The main instance of this concerns claims to medical treatment of the human or animal body. To the special considerations raised by this we shall come in a later section, but it should be noted here that a special provision allows substances or substances-in-compositions to be claimed as such, where a new medical use for them has been discovered.[65]

(6) Selection patents

5-018   In certain types of case, mainly concerned with chemical substances and mixtures,[66] claims to a selection have been allowed. Where a class of things is already known from a general description of some kind, it has been possible to claim specific things within that class, or a sub-class, provided that these latter are stated to have an advantage over the class as a whole. This special approach is of considerable value, particularly since recent decisions have shown some willingness to apply the idea flexibly in favour of patentees.

Du Pont's (Witsiepe) Application[67] was a case broadly similar to *Shell's Patent* (Example (c), § 5-004): a co-polymer comprising three elements, including as its second 1,4-butanediol, was claimed for its quality as a rapidly hardening plastic. A much earlier I.C.I. specification had claimed a similar plastic for its capacity to absorb dye. Its second element had to be one of a list of nine possibilities, including 1,4-butanediol; but this was named only as a prospect on paper, the experiments recorded having been with other substances on the list. The House of Lords refused to treat this disclosure as one which precluded the possibility of selection of Du Pont's co-polymer for the newly discovered purpose. It is

---

[64] See [1960] R.P.C. 35 at 48-49. The way in which a claim is formulated may make it doubtful whether it is to be read as a claim to an X for purpose Y or as a claim to carrying out activity Y using an X: if the first gives a monopoly in X, it will be bad once X is known; the second requires Y to be known for it to fail: see generally *Adhesive Dry Mounting* v. *Trapp* (1910) 27 R.P.C. 341.

[65] See below, §§ 5-051—5-053; EPC Art. 54(5); PA 1977 s.2(6).

[66] Only occasionally is selection possible in a mechanical case. See generally, Jeffs [1988] E.I.P.R. 291.

[67] [1982] F.S.R. 303 (H.L.), approving the classic formulation of the requirements for a selection is that of Maugham J. in *IG Farbenindustrie's Patents* (1930) 47 R.P.C. 289, 321. See also *Shell's Patent* [1960] R.P.C. 35 at 53 (C.A.). *Beecham Group* v. *Bristol Laboratories* [1978] 521 at 579, *per* Lord Diplock.

by such a response that the patent system has adapted to fit the needs of the chemical industry.[68]

The special treatment of selections needs to be viewed in light of the **5-019** rules discussed in the previous paragraphs. First, the need for it only arises if the earlier description does disclose the later subject-matter sufficiently. It is not enough that the later thing in a sense fits within earlier language that is too general to describe any clear result. It has been common practice, when a novel chemical substance (or a few related substances) are shown to have a particular use, to refer to derivative and analogous compounds (sometimes totalling millions in number) which may be expected to show similar characteristics in some degree.[69] This is treated as revealing the whole class sufficiently to raise prima facie an objection of novelty against claims anywhere within the class. Those members of the class which have been specifically named as the subject of experiment may not be claimed again as substances even if an advantage previously undetected has been discovered for them; only if this advantage calls for the substance to be put to a new use can a claim to the new method be secured. But because, apart from these specific cases, the earlier reference to the class has been general, the "selection rules" allow claims to be made to substances (or sub-classes of the whole) and not merely to methods, and this by virtue of the advantages as such and not only because the advantages result in a new use. So where selection is possible, it is free of the difficulties of proving infringement of a method claim. In the field of human and animal treatment, where a method claim is not possible, the ability to secure a selection claim is often essential in order to get any patent at all.[70]

The "selection rules" allow the anticipatory effect of general revela- **5-020** tions to be discounted where special advantage is stated by way of quid pro quo: this is the "consideration" and so goes to the sufficiency of the disclosure. Equally it may be looked upon as the quality which provides the incentive subject-matter. Selections, accordingly, are one occasion upon which a patentee is obliged to state the usefulness of his idea over the prior art. The new law calls for both adequate disclosure and inventive step, and so this aspect of the selection "rules" seems likely to survive. In their "classic" form, it was also required that substantially all the selected group should show the special advantage, and that substantially only those selected should show it.[71] In *Shell's Patent* the Court of Appeal showed little inclination to attach any precise meaning to the

[68] Lord Keith and Lord Simon expressed some disquiet that the result would keep I.C.I. from using one of its named alternatives. But they did not insist that Du Pont's claim be limited to the new purpose: [1982] F.S.R. at 316; *cf. Beecham Group's (Amoxycillin) Appln.* [1982] F.S.R. 202, where the New Zealand C.A. insisted that a pharmaceutical selection patent be restricted to a composition for oral administration to humans; see below, § 5-053.

[69] If, however, specific compounds or sub-classes have alone been mentioned and a later patentee is concerned with other compounds or sub-classes, the only issue normally is obviousness: a well-known instance of the problem is *Sharpe & Dohme* v. *Boots* (see below).

[70] For this, see below, §§ 5-051—5-053; PA 1977, s.3(6), now admits a significant qualification.

[71] See Maugham J., *IG Farbeninstrie's Patents* (above, n. 67).

latter[72]: probably the rule is only that the advantage must not be one shared by virtually the whole class.[73] As to the former requirement, now that the objection of inutility has been abandoned, there may be a rather generous tendency to excuse the inclusion of some examples which do not have the advantage[74]: but claims that go too far in this direction would undoubtedly appear grasping; the selection would likely be disallowed for its failure to tell others when they will get the alleged advantage.

(7) Exclusion by amendment

5-021   Where one of the alternatives covered by a claim is anticipated by a previous description, it may be possible to save the rest if the particular case is disclaimed by amendment. The amendment, giving what is often referred to as an "n-1" claim, will not however be allowed if the result would still be objectionable. In most cases, if one alternative has been described, others are likely to be held obvious.[75] But if the earlier description covered the later only by chance and not as a result of an effort to solve the same problem the objection of obviousness will not arise: hence the amendments allowed in such examples as *Molins* and *Shell*.[76]

2. INVENTIVE STEP

(1) Introduction

5-022   Patents are constantly sought for inventions which vary from the known only in some more or less minor detail. For instance, when a new kind of material is put on the market, claims will likely follow which attempt to patent the making of well-known articles out of the material (plastics have provided a welter of examples in recent years).[77] Sometimes at the outset the applicant will know that he is seeking protection for a thing that is not greatly different from what is known already. Sometimes he is pushed into that position by the unearthing of prior art which he did not appreciate. The difficulty is increased by the need to mark out broad "fence-post" claims.

It is in order to draw a line excluding some claims of this kind that many patent systems have come to require the presence of an inventive step.[78] In the EPC and the 1977 Act, an inventive step[79] is considered to

---

[72] The patentee's Claim 2, after amendment, covered proportions of ester up to two "theories" (a proportional measure). It was admitted that the new advantage would attach to mixtures up to four theories; but this was not allowed to prevent the selection; the court's sympathy for a deserving patentee faced with an unintended anticipation was evident. See also *Du Pont* (above, n. 67); and in the EPO, *Hoechst's Appln.* [1985] O.J. EPO 209.

[73] If it were, the claim would come under the edict against allowing a claim to a substance merely for having found it a new advantage: above, §§ 5-017—5-018.

[74] For this, see further below, § 5-061.

[75] Now that obviousness is a regular objection in the two patent offices, there is less scope for amendment by the exclusion of numbers of particular anticipations, resulting in claims for "n-m."

[76] Above, § 5-017.

[77] See below, § 5-026.   [78] See above, § 3-007.

[79] Which is a requisite of "patentability": EPC Art. 52(1), PA 1977, s.1(1). See generally, Beier (1986) 17 I.I.C. 301.

be present if, having regard to the state of the art, the invention is not obvious to a person skilled in the art.[80] The state of the art is the same broad conception that operates in assessing novelty,[81] save that no account is taken of any prior specifications subsequently published.

The evaluative issue that this introduces is the largest single cause of uncertainty about the validity of patents and hence a frequent inflator of the scale and length of patent disputes. The assessment it calls for is often labelled a jury question[82]; which means, amongst other things, that firm rules (such as define the factual comparison called for in determining novelty) are replaced by a vaguer, qualitative yardstick. In trying to describe how this yardstick is deployed there are some basic points that can usefully be taken in an introductory way, before looking at the essence of the inquiry.

(a) Terminology

It has become customary to treat "inventive subject-matter" and "non-obviousness" as largely synonymous with "inventive step." But cases occur where what the patentee is suggesting is pointless (at least at the time.) If there is no reason for it, the step is scarcely an obvious one to take: yet if nothing useful is being added to the sum of human knowledge there ought to be no inventive step.[83]

5-023

(b) Paraphrases

Some judges have been tempted to seek other synonymous phrases that will somehow make clearer the nature of the basic inquiry; others dislike such efforts. Certain paraphrases of "obvious" carry the implication that the threshold for an inventive step is a very low one: "very plain," the obvious and natural suggestion of what was known," a mere "workshop adjustment," an idea that "would . . . in effect suggest itself."[84] These deserve to be read with the repeated emphasis upon the absence of "any inventive step whatever," of "a very small advance," of a "scintilla of invention."[85] But to a judge trying to envisage how an average technician would set about solving the problem (if, indeed, he would have predicated it at all), obviousness may cover rather more. One test that has been thought appropriate to some cases is: would a person versed in the art assess the likelihood of success as sufficient to warrant actual trial?[86] It

5-024

[80] EPC Art. 56, PA 1977, s.3.
[81] See above, § 5-003.
[82] e.g. Jenkins L.J., *Allmanna Elektriska* v. *Burntisland Shipbuilding* (1952) 69 R.P.C. 63 at 69; *Johns-Manville's Patent* [1967] R.P.C. 479 at 491, 496 (C.A.).
[83] cf. Lord Shaw, *British Thomson-Houston* v. *Duram* (1918) 35 R.P.C. 161 at 184; Jenkins J., *May & Baker* v. *Ciba* (1948) 65 R.P.C. 255 at 281; Lloyd-Jacob J., *Anxionnaz* v. *Rolls-Royce* [1967] R.P.C. 419 at 467.
[84] See respectively, *General Tire* v. *Firestone* [1972] R.P.C. 457 at 497; Lopes L.J., *Savage* v. *Harris* (1896) 13 R.P.C. 364 at 730; *Cincinnati Grinders* v. *BSA* (1931) 48 R.P.C. 33 at 75 (C.A.); Harman L.J., *Technograph* v. *Mills & Rockley* [1969] R.P.C. 395 at 404.
[85] Respectively, *Martin* v. *Millwood* (1954) R.P.C. 458 at 466 (C.A.); Ormerod L.J., *Killick* v. *Pye* [1958] R.P.C. 366 at 377; Tomlin J., *Parkes* v. *Cocker* (below, n.45).
[86] Lord Diplock, *Johns-Manville's Patent* [1967] R.P.C. 479 at 494 (at the same time warning against the dangers of general paraphrases; and see 496); Lord Reid, *Technograph* v. *Mills & Rockley* [1972] R.P.C. 346 at 356; *Tetra Molectric* v. *Japan Imports* [1976] R.P.C. 547 (C.A.). See also *Alsop's Patent* (1907) 24 R.P.C. 733.

would be easy to carry this a long way. In fact, where numerous lines of further research were suggested by a given result and nothing marked the patentee's subsequent discovery out as the line to follow first, the step has not been held obvious.[87] Equally, this test has been held appropriate only where the skilled man would have had a particular problem in mind.[88]

It will be apparent from this, how difficult it is to establish a consistent line on the degree of severity which is to be brought to the testing of obviousness. Amongst the countries now collaborating in the EPC, a particularly stringent test of "inventiveness" seems previously to have prevailed in the Netherlands and Switzerland; while in West Germany talk of a "level of invention," together with the separate protection of utility models (a form of petty patent) that in theory at least need not reach the same inventive level, creates an impression that there too rather more has been required.[89] The EPO has indicated that it aims for a middle level (roughly equivalent to that of German practice), rather than adopt the particularly favourable attitude towards applicants that has characterised British pre-grant procedure under the 1949 Act.[90]

(c) Objective test

5-025   The comparison called for is between two objective conditions: the state of the art and what the patentee claims to have invented. It is not an inquiry into how easy or difficult it was for him personally to take the step. The patent system makes no attempt to exclude protection for accidental, lucky or sudden inventions, however little its incentive effect may seem to be responsible for such discoveries.[91] Equally it is of no relevance to consider whether the person responsible thought that he had made an invention[92]: he may well have worked out independently what others knew already. Nonetheless it is relevant to the ultimate assessment to know how the alleged inventor reached his result and accordingly discovery may be ordered of notes and other documents concerning his research. This may assist the defendant in cross-examining the inventor and other witnesses, in obtaining expert evidence of what a skilled man would or should have done, and in comparing what was actually done with the state of the art at the priority date.[93]

(d) Advance in the art

5-026   There is no distinct requirement in the new law, any more than in the old, that an invention should show "technical progress" over the prior

---

[87] Graham J., Olin Mathieson v. Biorex [1970] R.P.C. 157 at 187; and see Dow Corning's Applcn. [1969] R.P.C. 544; American Cyanamid v. Ethicon [1979] R.P.C. 215 at 266-267. A very limited view of what it is obvious to try is taken in I.C.I.'s (Pointer) Applcn. [1977] F.S.R. 434 at 456-457.

[88] Beecham's (Amoxycillin) Applcn. [1980] R.P.C. 261 at 290.

[89] On the nuances that may attach to EPC Art. 56 in its various linguistic versions, see Pagenberg, (1974) 5 I.I.C. 157.

[90] See above, § 4-003, below, § 5-028.

[91] Crane v. Price (1842) 1 W.P.C. 393 at 411.

[92] Fletcher Moulton L.J., B.U.S.M. v. Fussell (1908) 25 R.P.C. 631 at 652; Allmanna Elektriska v. Burntisland (1952) 69 R.P.C. 63 at 70.

[93] SKM v. Wagner Spraytech [1982] R.P.C. 497 (C.A.); Wellcome Foundation v. VR Laboratories [1982] R.P.C. 343 (H.C. Australia).

art, *i.e.* that it should in some practical sense be a better way of doing things.[94] However, considerations of technical advance, as of commercial value, become points of reference in the search for an inventive step. For if the idea is a real step forward in technique, yet it is an obvious one, why was it not made before?[95] And in the case of "selection" from a larger class, the particular advantage which the specification must describe and which alone avoids the objection of anticipation,[96] must also be one that is not obvious: the selection must be more than a mere verification that particular properties would be found in the sub-group.

"Technical progress," which was previously a requirement of German patent law and which has been actively debated in the United States, in fact involves two sorts of consideration: substantive (whether there is any advance at all, whether it is so large that there must be invention), and formal (whether the specification must describe the advance.) Accordingly it is an issue to which we turn again when discussing sufficiency of description.[97]

(e) *New advantage and new use*

The discovery of a new advantage in a thing already known does not in general save it from objection. So equally a thing that it is obvious to make for one purpose should not become the less so just because a further, unexpected, advantage is discovered.[98] If this advantage allows a "new use" method claim to be formulated that may well be inventive.[98] The point is to confine the patentee to a properly limited monopoly.

5-026

(f) *Perception of problem*

The inventive step may lie in seeing that a particular solution to a problem should be adopted: it does not have to be found in the technical means that are then employed.[99] Consider, for instance, "the problem of indicating to the driver of a motor vehicle at night the line of the road ahead by using the light from the vehicle itself. As soon as the problem is stated in this form the technical solution, *viz.* the provision of reflective markings along the road surface, appears simple and obvious."[1]

5-027

---

[94] But *cf.* Warrington L.J.: "a step which is useful and not merely one which results in some immaterial and futile improvement": *Teste* v. *Coombes* (1923) 41 R.P.C. 88 at 104 (C.A.).

[95] See, *e.g. British Vacuum* v. *L.S.W.R.* (1912) 29 R.P.C. 309 at 328-330, 333. In *Moulinage de Chavonoz's Appln.* [1961] R.P.C. 279 at 295, Lloyd Jacob J. distinguishes between the perception of the advance in the art and its evaluation in terms of inventive ingenuity. The former, being "susceptible of reasonably precise expression" is more readily open to review on appeal.

[96] For the rules concerning selection patents, see above, § 0-000. They need to be considered not only in relation to obviousness but also in relation to sufficient disclosure: see next note.

[97] Below, §§ 5-058—5-063.

[98] But this point was neglected in *Cleveland Graphite* v. *Glacier Metal* (1950) 67 R.P.C. 149 (H.L.): see Ency. PL § 5-224.

[99] *Hickton's Patent Syndicate* v. *Patents & Machine Improvements* (1909) 26 R.P.C. 339 (C.A.) (inventive to see that a process of "shogging," already used in net machines, could be used in lace machines for the purpose, there important, of equalising the bobbin threads).

[1] EPO Guidelines C IV 9.4(i). The whole chapter is full of useful examples for the student.

(g) *Onus of proof*

5-028   Since obviousness has become a matter for patent office examiners to judge upon the material arising from the search (and their own general knowledge,) much is likely to turn on the onus and quantum of proof employed during the examination stage. The past practice of the British Office and tribunals was to resolve doubts about inventive step in the applicant's favour,[2] because, although these proceedings had to arise out of the opposition of an outside party, the evidence was not tested as thoroughly as it would be in court, where oral witnesses would be examined as a matter of course.[3] In the new law this procedural difference in essence, even when the legal tests have become the same.

(2) Assessing obviousness[4]

(a) *The notional skilled worker*

5-029   The tribunal assessing obviousness is expected to trace out the mental processes of a determinedly prosaic individual, one who, according to recent British case-law, has the following characteristics[5]:

  (i) He is a skilled technician who is well acquainted with workship techniques. "Technician" may probably be contrasted both with the highly-qualified research staff who in industry today are set to solve many of the more complex technical problems; and also with the "ordinary workmen" who frequented the earlier case-law.

  (ii) He will read the relevant literature carefully,[6] showing an unlimited capacity to assimilate it but none in making even a "scintilla" of invention from it.[7] Such indefatigable but uninspired individuals do not wittingly give evidence themselves; for the most part, tribunals are left to make their own assessment after hearing what cleverer people have to say.

(b) *The uninventive technician's knowledge*

5-030   Like novelty, obviousness is judged by the state of the art, excluding, it must be supposed, the same material published in breach of confidence and at international exhibitions.[8] Accordingly, the notional technician

---

[2] See above, § 5-003. "At this stage in the lifetime of an application there exists in addition to the two verdicts, so to speak, of obviousness and non-obviousness, an interim stage of non-proven": Lloyd-Jacob J., *Bakelite's Appln.* [1958] R.P.C. 152, 160.

[3] *General Electric's Applcns.* [1964] R.P.C. 413 at 452-453, treating the differently worded standards of obviousness before and after grant (PA 1949, s.14(1)(e), s.32(1)(f)) as merely reflecting the difference of approach necessitated by the different procedures. The 1977 Act no longer draws this verbal distinction but that may not prove the governing consideration.

[4] See generally, Asquith (1978) 8 CIPA 19; Walton and Laddie, II, §§ 700 *et seq.*; Reid, 43-61.

[5] See Lord Reid, *Technograph* v. *Mills & Rockley* [1972] R.P.C. 346 at 355; followed in *General Tire* v. *Firestone* [1972] R.P.C. 457 at 504.

[6] See below, §§ 5-032—5-034.

[7] He bears considerable resemblance to the ordinary skilled worker by whose powers of comprehension the adequacy of disclosure is tested: see below, § 0-000. But it has recently been doubted whether, in determining obviousness, his powers of perception must be regarded as quite so limited: *Genentech* v. *Wellcome Foundation* [1989] (to be reported), *per* Mustill L.J.

[8] This is not made explicit in the relevant provisions; see above, § 5-013.

will be taken to have in mind, first, the common general knowledge of his art at the priority date and, second, whatever he would learn from the existing literature when seeking an answer to the problem at issue.[9] Frequently a case of obviousness is built up by referring to specific documents (such as patent specifications, learned articles, and items in the general press) and to specific instances of use; and generally these belong to the second category. Common general knowledge (which may be shown from such sources as standard texts and expert evidence) is then used to explain why it would be obvious to take the patentee's step from the specific sources that have been cited.[10]

In one instance,[11] the patent was for a steel tip to a shoe heel so made that the bottom of the heel fitted the tip, thus solving the problem of aligning the two parts. At the time, this seemed inventive to shoe repairers. But shoe manufacturers were already using very similar heels, which were thus part of the trade's general knowledge. In addition, some of these heels were illustrated in cited documents. The attack might well have succeeded even if one or other class of evidence had not been available. Note, however, that the general knowledge arose from actual use of the interlinking tips. It is much more difficult to show that a "mere paper proposal" is part of the ordinary technician's standard mental equipment. Even as specific citations, unworked proposals—mere "laboratory toys"—are treated with suspicion.[12] Occasionally they may form the basis for a finding of obviousness, perhaps because they come very close to being anticipation.[13] But they demand answer to the standard questions: Are they addressed to the same problem which the patentee solved? If so, they did they not lead to earlier discovery of his solution?

5-031

It is in relation to such cases that the judges have warned against viewing the matter with the advantage of hindsight. The EPO, in particular, seeks to formulate, on objective criteria, the technical problem which the inventor was addressing. The prior art may then be examined to see how far it suggested answers to that problem (the so-called) "problem-and-solution approach").[14] In this connection, Buckley L.J. has drawn a useful distinction.[15] There will be the situation where the

---

[9] It is resort to the second category of information (which was carried so far in decisions such as *Allmanna Elektriska* v. *Burntisland* (below, n. 92) that arouses controversy and difficulty. In *Minnesota Mining* v. *Beiersdorf* (1980) 144 C.L.R. 253, the High Court of Australia has decided that obviousness should be judged purely on common general knowledge. This is in broad contrast with much of what follows in the text. It introduces its own difficulties but seems essentially realistic in a system which does not have the question of obviousness regularly examined in application proceedings.

[10] Common general knowledge is not pleaded: *Holliday* v. *Heppenstall* (1889) 6 R.P.C. 320; *British Thomason-Houston* v. *Stonebridge* (1916) 33 R.P.C. 166. Now that the state of the art is not limited to what is known and used in the U.K., the question arises whether what is common general knowledge in any other country will suffice; presumably it does: *cf. Lucas* v. *Chloride Batteries* [1979] F.S.R. 322 (Fed.Ct., Australia).

[11] *Colburn* v. *Ward* (1950) 67 R.P.C. 73. See also *Fives Babcock's Appln.* [1982] O.J. EPO 225: if a problem concerning a suitable substitute material for making scrapers would have been put to materials specialist, the issue must be judged from his perspective.

[12] Basic scientific principles may attract rather different treatment: *Sonotone* v. *Multitone* (below, n. 37).

[13] See below, § 5-036.

[14] *Bayer's (Baatz) Appln.* [1982] R.P.C. 321.

[15] *Beecham case* (n. 16, below) at 291.

uninventive but skilled man has a particular problem or need in mind, in
which case the testing carried out by him may amount to no more than
obvious verification, though it could be inventive if the result is unexpected in kind rather than degree. Equally there will be the case where
the skilled man has no particular problem or need in mind. Then,
selecting a particular course for further research which provides unexpected results is likely to be inventive, for he is then on "a voyage of
discovery" rather than "a mere exercise of ingenuity" in *Beecham
Group's (Amoxycillin) Application*,[16] Buckley and Browne L.JJ. were
prepared to classify the case before them as falling within the second of
these categories, even though the prior art indicated that work should be
done on six further substances in the search for better semi-synthetic
penicillins. Accordingly the applicant was entitled to a patent for one of
them, upon making the anticipated discovery of its outstanding ability for
absorption into the blood-stream.

(c) "Mosaicing"

5-032   Obviousness is judged by viewing the invention as a whole[17] against the
state of the art as a whole.[18] Cited documents do not have to be treated
in isolation (as normally they would be when assessing novelty.) They
may be read in the light of one another—but only if it is obvious to do
so.[19] Even so, James L.J. disparagingly called this making a "mosaic of
extracts,"[20] and it remains difficult to build up such a case. Again doubts
surface which are hard to refute. Why, if it is obvious to combine two
pieces of knowledge, has no one done so before? Is the case not one
where the precursors were able to think out everything except the crucial
bridge from failure to success? It is in this context that some judges have
been particularly hard on paper proposals.[21]

(d) Obscure sources: publication

5-033   Obviousness calls for inquiry whether the invention in suit could have
been straightforwardly derived from what was already known. Accordingly difficult problems are set by the fact that a prior publication or use
would have been difficult for the average skilled worker to find, or to
understand.
        First, on the difficulties of unearthing sources: it is possible to treat the
state of the art as being the same for obviousness as it is for novelty (save

[16] [1980] R.P.C. 261; and similarly in New Zealand: [1982] F.S.R. 218.
[17] A combination should not be picked apart into its components: Lord Romer, *Non-Drip*
v. *Strangers* (1943) 60 R.P.C. 135 at 145 (H.L.).
[18] Lord Simonds, *Martin* v. *Millwood* [1956] R.P.C. 125 at 133-134; *Illinois Tool* v.
Autobars [1974] R.P.C. 337.
[19] " . . . a mosaic which can be put together by an unimaginative man with no inventive
capacity": Lord Reid, *Technograph* v. *Mills & Rockley* [1972] R.P.C. 346 at 355.
[20] *Von Heyden* v. *Neustadt* (1880) 50 L.J.Ch. 126 at 128; and see Fletcher Moulton L.J.,
British Westinghouse v. *Braulik* (1910) 27 R.P.C. 209 at 230; *cf.* the EPO's greater
willingness to read documents together if they show a tendency to look elsewhere for
technical solutions: *Mobey's Appln.* [1982] O.J. EPO 394.
[21] *cf.* Gratwick (1972) 88 L.Q.R. 349, Blanco White (1973) 89 L.Q.R. 16. But in *Allmanna
Elektriska* v. *Burntisland* (1952) 69 R.P.C. at 68-69, the Court of Appeal refused to hold
that there could never be a mosaic of documents, as distinct from actual uses; and
proceeded (surprisingly) to read together descriptions different in date and language.

for the special case of subsequently published specification)—*i.e* anything made freely available to even a single person will be treated as published.[22] On the other hand it is possible to limit the state of the art for obviousness to whatever a diligent searcher would have uncovered.

In the case-law on the 1949 Act each approach had its adherents, Lord Diplock emerging as protagonist of the former, Lord Reid of the latter.[23] The former approach had the merit of not attributing different meanings to the same statutory formula.[24] And it eliminates one dimension of evaluative judgment—a dimension which it may be particularly difficult for patent office examiners to handle on a regular basis. The latter approach aims to make the inquiry into the activities of the unimaginative technician somewhat more realistic. But it may be doubted whether, even on its own terms, it helps much. For the diligent searcher still has to be treated as having found some things that in reality would have been unlikely to have reached him by the priority date: a description in a patent specification published only a few days before, for instance[25]; or, given the new definition of "the state of the art," a use which has occurred only in a remote place. There seems little point in striving to decide what revelations are so exceedingly remote that they should be discounted.[26]

(c) *Obscure sources: comprehension*

In *Woven Plastics* v. *British Ropes*, it was accepted by counsel that 5-034 utility model specifications, available only in Japanese and apparently never worked, were to be treated as known. Harman L.J. regretted that such "recondite" publications should have to be brought into account.[27] In the new world of supra-national patenting, however, the notional technician presumably has acquired, at least passively, the gift of tongues.

Language difficulties aside, the notional technician's reading of the literature will be "careful."[28] If after this it appears that a document expresses its ideas obscurely it is unlikely that obvious inferences are to be drawn from it. But there is the further case where, although (with hindsight, particularly) a highly suggestive reference can be found in a prior document, it is for some reason masked, perhaps by the abundance of other documentation, or by prevailing opinion that other avenues of inquiry would be much more hopeful. These are factors which in the past

[22] *i.e.* assuming that the test under the old law applies equally under the new: see above, § 5-011.
[23] *Technograph* v. *Mills & Rockley* [1972] R.P.C. 346 at 361, 355. In the Court of Appeal ([1969] R.P.C. 395 at 408), Sachs L.J. even suggested that the searcher might confine his reading of prior specifications to the claims and perhaps the drawings; Lord Diplock specifically disapproved this and certainly Lord Reid did not go so far. See also *General Tire* v. *Firestone* [1972] R.P.C. 457 at 499 (C.A.); *I.C.I.'s (Pointer) Applcn.* [1977] F.S.R. 434.
[24] *i.e.* previously "known or used . . . in the United Kingdom"; now "the state of the art," as defined.
[25] As in *Du Pont's (Holland) Applcn.* [1971] R.P.C. 7.
[26] Consider, for instance, the prior patent specification that has been inadequately indexed. In *Asea's Applcn.* [1978] F.S.R. 115, this was held no reason for disregarding it when assessing obviousness.
[27] [1970] F.S.R. 47 at 48; and Widgery L.J. said that it went "beyond the bounds of reason" (at 58).
[28] See *Johns Manville* (above p. 22) and *Technograph* (above, n. 33).

have weighed against a finding of obviousness.[29] Thus, even if it is proper to treat the technician as having read everything in the state of the art,[30] these further considerations may modify the effect of particular documents.

(3) The basic comparison

5-035   We may now return to the crux of the issue: was it for practical purposes obvious to the appropriate skilled technician, armed with all the specific information and general knowledge deemed relevant, that he could or should do what the patent proposes?[31] Part of the answer may depend on the proximity of the idea to the prior art, part on the extent to which the idea is a technical or a commercial success. Each of these factors deserves exploration.

(a) *Proximity to the prior art*

5-036   Novelty and inventive step are different questions. Even so, the fact that an idea escapes being anticipated only by the shortest remove will often jeopardise the chances of its being found inventive. Indeed, if the claimed invention is a "mere collocation"—where two known devices are to be placed side-by-side without any working inter-relationship—it will be more likely to be treated as a claim to discrete things separately anticipated. The traditional example of such a case is the "sausage-machine patent": a claim to a known cutting-machine and a known filling-machine placed in juxtaposition.[32] Another example is a pill containing two known therapeutic substances which have no interactive or heightened effect when taken together.[33]

Beyond this point, "near anticipations" have to be considered for inventive step.[34] They may well fail the test, being discounted under one of the following axioms:

(i) There can be no patent for the analogous use of a thing or process; or, as it is sometimes put, for the mere new use of an old

[29] See, e.g. Whitford J., *I.C.I.'s (Pointer) Appln.* [1977] F.S.R. 434 at 454.
[30] *i.e.* accepting Lord Diplock's view (above, n. 23). *cf.* Whitford J. (previous note) who, despite a nod in Lord Diplock's direction, appears in substance to favour Lord Reid's approach.
[31] This derives from the "Cripps question," first formulated by Sir Stafford Cripps (as counsel) in *Sharpe & Dohme* v. *Boots* (1928) 45 R.P.C. 153 at 173 (C.A.), and subsequently adapted in various cases: *e.g. Allmanna Elektriska* v. *Burntisland* (above, n. 21); *Olin Mathieson* v. *Biorex* (above, n. 87). As originally put, it contained a reference to the object of the alleged invention ("Was it obvious . . . to any skilled chemist . . . that he could manufacture valuable therapeutic agents by . . . ?"). But that does not allow for two cases: (i) where it was allegedly obvious to do the thing for a different purpose (see above, § 5–026); (ii) where at the date of the prior art, what was proposed in it had allegedly no usefulness at all (as in *Killick* v. *Pye* [1958] R.P.C. 366 (C.A.)). See further, Ency. PL, § 5-213.
[32] *Williams* v. *Nye* (1890) 7 R.P.C. 62: in fact there was just enough interrelation of parts for the C.A. to deal with the question as one of inventive step. See further Ency. PL, § 5-107.
[33] *cf.* also *Beecham Group's (Amoxcyllin) Appln.* [1980] R.P.C. 261 (selected substance not anticipated (or obvious) when claimed as a pharmaceutical composition).
[34] A typical example is *Seiller's Appln.* [1970] R.P.C. 103: toy bells—the prior version differing in a minor detail of construction which could amount only to a theoretical scientific advantage bearing no practical relationship to the purpose for which the invention was intended.

thing. For instance, it was held unpatentable to coat boot eyelets with celluloid when this was already done to hooks and studs[35]; or to keep drinks hot or cold in vacuum flasks when they had already been used for liquids in laboratories.[36]

(ii) There can be no patent for the mere application of a known principle to a use or subject-matter admittedly within its scope. Thus there was no invention in applying a basic principle of electrical amplification to bone-conducting hearing aids, even though this had not previously been suggested in the considerable period since the principle's first formulation.[37]

(iii) There can be no patent merely for verifying previous predictions. Where it was already known that polyesters for electrical insulation could be made from reagents that were members of a chemical series, it was not inventive to demonstrate that satisfactory results ensued from substituting other members of the same series.[38] The particular choice "would sooner or later inevitably have attracted attention" and no unexpected result was demonstrated which might have justified a selection. Likewise in genetic engineering: where the substance to be made is known through its occurrence in the human body, and the relevant procedures of recombinant DNA technology are also known, there is nothing inventive in working them through, even though this involves considerable labour by specialists in a new field, and specific knowledge is procured in the course of the work. The person or team which first produces a successful result has only won a race down an established track to a known goal.[39]

These should be regarded today as no more than ways of stating emphatically that no inventive step has been taken.[40] Like most such aphorisms, they have their counter-propositions—for use in cases that are considered to fall on the other side of the evaluative line. Thus a use is not a mere analogy, or the mere application of a principle, if it calls for some ingenuity to overcome a practical difficulty in the adaptation or application.[41] For instance, to adapt a suction pump for the purpose of supplying petrol in an engine from fuel tank to carburettor was held to involve more than merely putting a well-known thing to a new use.[42] Likewise, a patent covers more than mere verification if others have been able to do everything except take the last crucial step.

---

[35] *Riekmann* v. *Thierry* (1897) 14 R.P.C. 105 (H.L.).

[36] *Thermos* v. *Isola* (1910) 27 R.P.C. 388.

[37] *Sonotone* v. *Multitone* (1955) 72 R.P.C. 131 (C.A.); but *cf. BASF's Appln.* [1989] O.J. EPO 74.

[38] *General Electric's Appln.* [1964] R.P.C. 413 at 436 (C.A.); and also *Sharpe & Dohme* v. *Boots* (above, n. 31).

[39] *Genentech* v. *Wellcome Foundation* (1989) (to be reported).

[40] Formerly there was some distinction (not easily identified) between whether something was a manner of new manufacture and whether it involved an inventive step. The Patent Office itself had power to refuse an application if it could be said not to involve new manufacture.

[41] See especially Lindley L.J., *Gadd* v. *Mayor of Manchester* (1892) 9 R.P.C. 516 at 524; *cf. Lister's Patent* [1966] R.P.C. 30 at 35-37 (D.C.); *Mutoh's Appln.* [1984] R.P.C. 85.

[42] [1956] R.P.C. 125 (H.L.).

(b) *Technical advantage and commercial success*

5-037   From time to time the courts are called upon to judge the inventiveness of a technical improvement which brings a real cutting of costs, with the result that it is popular with customers. Evidence about this sort of success is unlikely to be available at the application stage, which is one reason for then dealing circumspectly with the question of inventive step. In such a case, the unavoidable question is, why was so desirable a thing not discovered before? Indeed, the very simplicity of the solution in such circumstances tends to confirm its inventive character.[43]

Commercial success can help to demonstrate inventive character only if the invention is the cause of the success. There may well be other explanations: in *Martin* v. *Millwood* the success of the patentee's ballpoint pens was found to turn not upon the patented nib construction but upon the discovery of an adequate ink reservoir, which was not the subject of the patent[44]; in *Parkes* v. *Crocker* the patentee's clip device became a sudden success some 11 years after the patent grant because all the railway companies agreed to adopt it and more than a million were then sold.[45]

Because other causes may exist, courts have said that they will take account of commercial success only if the need for the patentee's invention has long been felt, "so that men's minds were likely to have been engaged upon a mode of remedying" the pre-existing defect. The vigour with which Lord Herschell makes this point in *Longbottom* v. *Shaw*[46] would suggest that the person attacking validity is not obliged to show some other explanation of the patentee's commercial success so long as the latter has not clearly demonstrated the "long-felt want" to which his invention is the answer. But arguably, the absence of other explanation, the fact of commercial success should itself be taken as at least a persuasive indicator of inventiveness. Certainly there have been judges to whom the success has been at least one reason for upholding the patent despite the absence of long-felt want or the presence of some other explanation. *Parkes* v. *Cocker* was such a case, and it is with this in mind that Tomlin J.'s much-repeated dictum on the subject deserves to be read:

" . . . once it has been found . . . that the problem has waited solution for many years, and that the device is in fact novel and superior to what had gone before, and has been widely used, and used in preference to alternative devices, it is, I think, practically impossible to say that there is not present that scintilla of invention necessary to support the Patent."[47]

[43] *BASF's Applcn.* [1988] O.J. EPO 12.
[44] [1956] R.P.C. 125 at 139.
[45] (1929) 46 R.P.C. 241 (C.A.).
[46] (1891) 8 R.P. C. 333 at 336 (H.L.).
[47] Above, n. 45 at 248; see generally, Bouly (1970) 89 Trans. CIPA B99.

3. INDUSTRIAL APPLICATION

The requirement that a patentable invention be "susceptible" or "cap-   5-038
able" of industrial application had no direct counterpart in previous
British statutes.[48] In part, the concept is concerned with the categories of
subject-matter that fall within the sphere of the patent system.[49] It is used
to indicate that agriculture is an industry for patent purposes; and to
exclude methods of treating humans and animals.[50] To these we shall
return in the next section.[51]

The capacity of an invention for industrial application raises other
questions. First, can objections that used to be dealt with under the
notion of inutility[52] instead be treated as showing lack of industrial
applicability? The EPO uses the concept for the purpose of excluding
some aspects of the lunatic fringe: attempts patent ideas which evidently
do not achieve the claimed ends, such as machines to produce perpetual
motion.[53] In the past the British system, partly because of its approach to
claims, found occasion to deploy inutility much more extensively. It was
an effective objection not only when the patentee's basic idea did not
work, but also when one of the variants specifically pointed to in a claim
proved ineffective. In the standard example, the patentee explicitly
mentioned, among chemicals that could be used as reagents in a copying
process, some alternatives that were ineffective, as well as several that
worked: the claim was nonetheless bad.[54] It made no difference that the
skilled man would recognise the duds and so would not waste time trying
them out.[55] The defects could be cured only by amendment and that
would depend upon being able to find an acceptable form of words in
light of the original disclosure.

While this was considered by the Banks Committee to impose too
severe a sanction,[56] and had been abandoned in 1977, tribunals may feel
the need to take a wide view of what constitutes "industrial applicability" so as to require unduly wide claims to be limited to what
actually works.[57]

---

[48] EPC Art. 52(1), PA 1977, s.1(1)(c).
[49] This was apparently considered its main function during the drafting of the EPC; for this
    and its origins in German law, see Ullrich, *Standards of Patentability in European
    Inventions* (1977), pp. 7-9.
[50] EPC Arts. 52(4), 57, PA 1977, s.4(1).
[51] Below, §§ 5-039 *et seq.*
[52] For this objection under the 1949 Act, see Blanco White, §§ 4-401 *et seq.*
[53] EPO Guidelines C IV 4.1. Note the connection with inadequate disclosure: a claim to the
    machine without reference to its purpose would be disallowed by the EPO on this latter
    ground, which is discussed below, §§ 5-058—5-062.
[54] *Norton* v. *Jacobs* (1937) 54 R.P.C. 271 (C.A.). Applied to claims to a chemical class
    some of which did not work: *Mineral Separation* v. *Noranda* (1952) 69 R.P.C. 81 (J.C.).
    See Blanco White, § 4-409.
[55] See cases in previous note and Lord Westbury L.C., quoted by Fletcher Moulton L.J. in
    Vidal Dyes v. *Levinstein* (1912) 29 R.P.C. 245. If possible, however, ambiguities were
    resolved so as to avoid including an evidently useless embodiment: *e.g. Henriksen* v.
    Tallon [1965] R.P.C. 434 (H.L.).
[56] Report, Cmnd. 4407, 1970, § 376.
[57] For objections to claims after grant, see below, § 5-064.

A second issue which might be related to the requirement of industrial applicability, is whether a patent can be granted for a thing or process which, however interesting or suggestive it may be to scientists, has no known practical application at the priority date. But the same issue may be raised by asking whether the specification concerns an invention or a mere discovery. At this point we note it for later discussion.[58]

4. PATENTABLE SUBJECT-MATTER

5-039   Patent law has to define the types of subject-matter to which it accords protection. The issues of policy involved are varied. Nice distinctions seem unavoidable. Decisions in particular cases have to be left to the courts and patent offices. But there is still the question, how far can they be guided by general propositions laid down in legislation or case-law?

Before the 1977 Act in Britain, the judges dealt with the matter, guided only by the Jacobean catch-phrase, "manner of new manufacture."[59] Increasingly in recent years, this was treated as an invitation to decide what properly fell within the scope of the patent system, rather the occasion for investigating the real meaning of "manufacture."[60]

In the new Act there are lists of things which are not to be granted patents, or are not "as such," to be taken as inventions, or are not to be taken as capable of industrial application.[61] This stems from a list in the EPC which represents a fairly conservative consensus of European opinion on the subject in 1973. In large measure, the list involved no departure from previous British understanding. It is in very general terms, so the earlier case-law provides suggestive illustrations. The continued applicability of these decisions, however, turns on whether or not the new statutory provisions are found to have introduced some change.

5-040   Two main ideas recur in distinguishing the categories of subject-matter that may and may not be patented. One is that intellectual conceptions become patentable only to the extent that they have been embodied in technical applications. The other is that techniques which relate to living organisms, animal or vegetable, may call for special treatment: either because the public interest demands that their use should not be restricted or because a special legislative regime is needed for their protection. We shall first consider the specific cases associated with these two ideas, and then turn to other miscellaneous problems.

[58] Below, § 3-041.
[59] See generally, Blanco White, § 5-118.
[60] This became especially true after the judgment of the High Court of Australia in *NRDC's Applcn.* [1961] R.P.C. 134.
[61] PA 1977, s.1(2) (with power to extend by order: s.1(5)), ss.1(3), (4), 4; EPC Arts. 52(2)-(4), 53.

(1) Intellectual conceptions

(a) *Discoveries*

The list of things excluded from invention in the 1977 Act starts with **5-041** discoveries, scientific theories and mathematical methods[62]; but these are excluded only to the extent that the patent relates to the conception "as such." The distinction is well-known in many patent systems: discovery is the unearthing of causes, properties or phenomena already existing in nature; invention is the application of such knowledge to the satisfaction of social needs.[63] For instance, in an internal combustion engine, the idea of putting a cushion of air in the cylinder between the fuel and the piston in order to cushion the explosive effect of ignition was said not in itself to be patentable; but a machine devised to do so was.[64]

At this point we meet a question of interpretation that is strategic for all the exclusion discussed under this head: must the excluded subject-matter be disregarded in assessing whether there is invention in a claim involving an application of it in (say) a production process or a machine. In relation to a claim for an application of a computer program, Falconer J. held that invention must be found in some aspect of the application apart from the program.[65] But in *Genentech* v. *Wellcome Foundation* the Court of Appeal has since ruled that approach to be incorrect.[66] Discoveries concerning the structure of the DNA of a given protein could contribute the element of inventiveness in a claim to the employment of that knowledge in producing the protein by genetic engineering: patentability of the discoveries was excluded only "to the extent that" they are claimed "as such."

In chemical research the matter raises an issue of general importance: is it more than discovery to make a substance without also finding a use for it? It might be said that to give a new thing to the world is in itself sufficiently useful to merit protection; and that argument will doubtless seem stronger where technical difficulties are overcome in order to produce it.[67] Moreover, if mere making is not invention, yet discovery of one use allows a patentee to claim the substance itself in all its uses, an evident imbalance results: only if the first identifier of a use can patent for that use alone would it seem reasonable to deny any protection to the first maker of the substance. But both issues for the moment remain unresolved.

[62] For the evolution of this in the EPC, see Kolle (1974) 5 I.I.C. 140, 147-148.
[63] Kolle (above, n. 62). And see Buckley L.J., *Reynolds* v. *Smith* (1913) 20 R.P.C. 123 at 126: "Discovery adds to the amount of human knowledge, but it does so . . . only by disclosing something . . . Invention necessarily involves also the suggestion of an act to be done." *cf.* also the use of "mere discovery" to preclude from patentability the discovery of a new advantage for an old thing": above, § 5-017.
[64] Jessel M.R., *Otto* v. *Linford* (1882) 46 L.T.(N.S.) 35 at 39.
[65] *Merril Lynch's Appplcn.* [1988] R.P.C. 1 at 12.
[66] [1989] (to be reported); repeated in the *Merrill Lynch* case on appeal (below, n. 71).
[67] It may also seem stronger where the substance is an intermediate which may be useful in making further substances, even though they are at the time of unknown usefulness. *cf. Smith's Applcns.* [1971] R.P.C. 31, where it was said that the question of the value of the ultimate products was irrelevant to the assessment of obviousness; but the more fundamental issues was not addressed.

5-042   In the bulk of cases, where discovery and invention can be distinguished, the two stages are part of a single development by one person or team. Even so, as invention has become less the product of trial and error on the job, and more a matter of systematic research, the possibility of the two steps being taken by different people has increased. It is likely to have practical consequences, first between individuals, since only "inventors" are entitled to an employee's rights in an invention[68]; and secondly, between commercial rivals, as in the case where one is first to discover but only second to invent.

The case in favour of treating the conceptual stages in research and development as involving "invention," rather than "discovery," is broadly that these are the points at which the system should do more: by encouraging "pure" rather than "applied" work and by affording early protection that will stimulate the investment for innovation.[69] But unless all theoretical work is to lead to patents for whatever practical uses may subsequently be found for it, the approach raises formidable difficulties. How would it be possible to characterise information coming close enough to practical application to be patentable? And unless further requirements were built into the system, it might result in information about practical applications never being made publicly available.[70]

(b) *Schemes for performing mental acts; presentation of information*

5-043   Similar in essence to the previous category is the exclusion "as such" of schemes, rules or methods for performing mental acts, playing games or doing business; likewise presentations of information.[71] There have been many instances of attempts to patent ideas which involve some association between a technical device and the collation, interpretation or deployment of information.[72] In such cases the usual inquiry has been whether the novelty or usefulness lies in the former or the latter aspect.[73] If the latter, the idea is likely to be labelled a "mere scheme or plan" and placed outside what is patentable.

Contrast the following[74]: colouring fertilisers in order to distinguish them from one another (unpatentable),[75] and colouring a squashball a

[68] For which, see below, §§ 7-007—7-014.
[69] See Neumeyer (1975) 14 Ind.Prop. 348; Beier (1975) 6 I.I.C. 367; *cf.* Kitch (1977) 20 J. Law & Econ. 265 at 288.
[70] As to this, *cf.* the U.S. Supreme Court's requirement that there be "specific utility" before scientific information is patentable: *Brenner* v. *Manson* 383 U.S. 519 (1966). Douglas J. (at 534): "Until the process claim . . . has been reduced to production of a product shown to be useful, the metes and bounds of that monopoly are not capable of precise delineation. It may engross a vast, unknown and perhaps unknowable area. Such a patent may confer power to block off whole areas of scientific development without compensating benefit to the public."
[71] PA 1977, s.1(2)(*c*), (*d*); EPC Art. 52(2)(*c*), (*d*). "Presentations of information" comes from PCT Rules, r. 39.1(*v*) and 67.2(*v*) and needs to be read in a limited sense: see Kolle (above, n. 62) at 152-153; *Merrill Lynch's Appln.* (1989), C.A. (to be reported).
[72] Cases where there is no technical aspect are clearly not patentable: for instance, methods of musical notation (*C's Appln.* (1920) 37 R.P.C. 247) or of learning a language (see EPO Guidelines C IV 2.1); *cf.* however *Pitman's Appln.* [1969] R.P.C. 646 (material printed in a form suitable for use in a reading machine).
[73] The distinction is common to most patent systems: Kolle (above, n. 62) at 150.
[74] For the many other examples, see Blanco White, § 1-211.
[75] *Johnson's Appln.* (1930) 47 R.P.C. 361.

particular shade of blue to make it specially visible (prima facie patentable)[76]; a system of marking buoys in a channel in order to show ships where to go (unpatentable),[77] and a system of devices on vehicles which would co-operate on approach to avoid dazzle (patentable)[78]; the rules of a new game (unpatentable), and new card-packs and similar equipment for a game (patentable)[79]; a record on which the music is new (unpatentable), and a new way of forming grooves on a record so as to transmit stereophonic sound (patentable)[80]; printed forms for a "home shopping club" (unpatentable),[81] and a new way of printing a newspaper so that it could be folded crossways as well as longways (patentable).[82]

On the whole, the existing British decisions have looked to the essence of the matter, not taking account of the form in which the invention is claimed. Thus a scheme for arranging the supply of water, electricity and other services to a set of houses was held to be merely a layout plan not affecting the technical means of supplying any of the things; it made no difference that the rejected claim read: "In an underground installation for distribution of utilities . . . the improvement characterised by . . . [a specified layout]."[83]

Mostly the judicial decisions that distinguish between novelty in 5-044 schemes and novelty in mechancial means offer by way of explanation the merely reiterative statement that the concern of the patent system is with technical advances alone.[84] The real justification for the distinction seems to lie partly (as with "discoveries") in concern lest monopoly powers of potentially great scope may be conferred, partly in the belief that the encouragement of industry through a market monopoly is an effective medium only in the sphere of industrial production, and partly in a fear that it would be difficult to determine what constitutes anticipation and infringement if the range of the system were broadened.[85] The effect of the current approach can be measured by what is excluded: in particular, new ways of organising businesses and of testing their efficiency are not patentable even though they are often the subject of considerable investment in today's economic conditions. They may be copied by others, save to the extent that contract or confidence operates to the contrary.

(c) *Aesthetic creations*

The exclusion "as such" of literary, dramatic, musical and artistic 5-045 works and any other aesthetic creations[86] can be justified by the existence

---

[76] *ITS Rubber's Applcn.* [1979] R.P.C. 318.
[77] *W's Applcn.* (1914) 31 R.P.C. 141; *cf. de Beers' Applcn.* [1979] F.S.R. 72 (C.A.).
[78] *F.M.M.'s Applcn.* (1941) 58 R.P.C. 115.
[79] See Official Ruling 1926 (A) 43 R.P.C. 1; *Cobianchi's Applcn.* (1953) 70 R.P.C. 199.
[80] See EPO Guidelines C IV 2.1.
[81] *Littlewood's Applcn.* (1954) 71 R.P.C. 185.
[82] *Cooper's Applcn.* (1902) 19 R.P.C. 53; and see *Fishburn's Applcn.* (1940) 57 R.P.C. 245.
[83] *Hiller's Applcn.* [1969] R.P.C. 267; *cf.* also *Quigley's Applcn.* [1977] F.S.R. 373.
[84] Formerly this was expressed in the proposition that a "manner of manufacture" required the making, improvement or repair of a "vendible product," an approach in effect abandoned after the *NRDC* case (above, n. 49).
[85] See on these factors, Lloyd Jacob J., *Rolls-Royce's Applcn.* [1963] R.P.C. 251 at 255.
[86] PA 1977, s.1(2)(*b*), EPC Art. 52(2)(*b*); *cf. Tetra Molectric's Applcn.* [1977] R.P.C. 290 (C.A.).

of copyright system for their protection.[87] The kinds of distinction already discussed pertain equally here: where the element of creativity lies in the aesthetic ideas expressed there is no room for patent protection.[88] But the contrary will apply where a new technical process or article is devised for its pleasurable appeal—for instance, a new method of making candles,[89] or a novel perfume.

(d) *Computer programs*[90]

5-046   It was decided, against the pleas of some interest groups, specifically to exclude programs for computers "as such" from the ambit of what is patentable under the EPC.[91] Given the speed at which the computer industry is advancing, "computer program" is a term that may describe a wide range of phenomena, from basic algorithms capable of application in an indefinite number of more specific uses[92] to detailed instructions for the solution of particular problems.[93] A different complication is this: the result of actually using programmed computer is to produce information which may be taken for itself, or may immediately be put to some further use, as where a computer controls a step in the operation of a production process.[94] To add to the complexities, there is, for instance, the possibility that principles that might be written into programs are instead given expression in the circuitry of the computer, and the possibility of writing programs that will bring about the co-operation of network of computers.[95]

5-047   A computer uses mathematical instructions to select information from "input" data and, frequently, to perform mathematical manipulations with what is selected. It goes through processes that could theoretically be undertaken by the human brain unaided. If what is claimed to be patentable is a way of making a known machine operate upon data to produce desired results, then in essence it seems that nothing other than

---

[87] There has been much recent discussion of the extent to which technical designs should be protected by copyright (see below, Chap. 14) but none of whether the patent system should offer protection to the essentially aesthetic. The registered design system, however, offers comparable monopoly protection; cf. the U.S., where the same kind of protection is actually incorporated within the patent system.

[88] Where they take the form of instructions (plays, music) they are methods of performing mental acts in the sense discussed in the previous paragraph.

[89] cf. the German decision to this effect: 1972 Mitt. 235 (BGH).

[90] cf. the discussion of copyright protection for programs, below, §§ 13-016—13-020. And see generally, Tapper, *Computer Law* (1978) Chap. 1; Banks Report, Chap. 17; Bender (1968) 68 Col.L.R. 241; (1973) Soltisynski 3 Rutgers J.Comp.L. 1; Nimtz (1979) 61 J.P.O.S. 3; Morland (1980) 9 CIPA 386.

[91] EPC Art. 52(2)(c); hence PA 1977, s.1(2)(c) to the same effect. For the evolution, Kolle (above, n. 99) 150-152.

[92] Some of the cases presented to test the patentability of programs have involved ideas of this type: *Slee & Harris's Applcns.* [1966] R.P.C. 194 (claim to computer as programmed accepted in the U.K.); [1968] F.S.R. 272 (refused in Australia). cf. *Gottschalk* v. *Benson* 406 U.S. 63 (algorithm for conversion of binary code into pure binary: refused).

[93] In the U.S. Supreme Court's view, if the only novelty in the process is the added efficiency brought about by the way the computer is programmed, the case falls to be treated as if it were a claim to a program without the technical consequence: *Parker* v. *Flook*, 437 U.S. 584 (1978).

[94] This at least is more than a computer program "as such."

[95] As in the *Burroughs* case (below, n. 98).

an instruction about how to perform intellectual tasks is being given. But the case is not a precise analogy to the instruction to the pilot to fly a plane in a certain way in order to reduce noise.[96] For no human is obliged to interpret the instructions each time a computer uses its program. Computer programs accordingly lie exactly at the boundary of what previously has been thought to separate the patentable from the non-patentable: to some, even the most detailed operational programs remain nothing else than instructions for performing intellectual exercises; to others, the conversion of the operation into a technical process capable of constant repetition carries it over into the patentable sphere.[97]

In Britain, under the 1949 Act, claims to methods of programming a computer have been allowed to reach grant by reasonably liberal analogy to cases where new contrivances have been held patentable.[98] The computer with its special instructions was regarded as a different machine from one without, and that made it patentable, whether the claim was for a computer as programmed, means for programming (tape, cards, etc.), or a method of programming it.[99] Among EPC countries, France by statute apparently excluded such patents[1] and in other countries the courts showed themselves reluctant to adopt so favourable a position as in Britain.[2] With the introduction of the EPC provisions excluding computer programs as such from patentability, the question has required consideration in the EPO and under the revised national legislation. That process is currently in course of resolution. It is being conducted against the rapid transformations of the computer industry towards the sophistications of artificial intelligence and the remarkable variety of applications possible in micro-processors. In this febrile state, investment in novel programs is often very large, and major procedures have greatly increased their interest in procuring patent protection for programming techniques. They have begun to press for favourable treatment. For major advances in technique, copyright, confidence and contract is unlikely to accord them the breadth of legal protection that they now desire.[3]

A willingness to explore accommodations within the Convention framework was indicated by the EPO when it amended its Guidelines in 1985.[4] The change made it clear that that Office would allow claims involving use of a program if overall the invention made a contribution to an art that was technical. The scope of what is now permitted may be judged by contrasting the following examples:

[96] Held unpatentable in *Rolls-Royce's Appln.* [1963] R.P.C. 251.
[97] See the *Burroughs* case (below, n. 98) at 159-160.
[98] *Burroughs' (Perkins) Appln.* [1974] R.P.C. 147; 1.
[99] The first cases attempted to draw distinctions between different ways of formulating claims (contrary to the usual approach to such problems: see above, p. 171). But this approach was abandoned in *Burroughs* as pure casuistry.
[1] Patent law of 1968, treating as creating a broad exclusion by two decisions reported in *Propriètè Industrielle Bulletin Documentaire* 1973 III 197; 1975 III 349.
[2] See generally, Pagenberg (1974) 5 I.I.C. 253.
[3] See generally, §§ 13-015 *et seq.*
[4] Guidelines C IV 2.2.

5-049   (i) A claim to a process for producing a chemical in which a program of defined content is used to control production and this provides the element of novelty and inventiveness. Here the program is used in a production process and so clearly has technical consequences. From the outset there has not been much doubt that such a claim is patentable.

      (ii) A claim to a computer so programmed (or provided with hardware) as to be able to process digital images in accordance with a given mathematical procedure expressed as an algorithm; the effect being to increase processing speed over previously known processes. In its principal decision to date, *Vicom Systems' Application*,[5] the EPO has accepted this claim to an operating program concerned with the general functioning of a computer rather than the execution of a particular task. Clearly the value of patent protection for some programs of this type is very considerable.

      (iii) A claim to a data processing system for making a trading market in at least one stock exchange security in which a set of "means" were to be provided for analysing customers' buy and sell orders against given criteria; those which qualified would then be executed. This was a program which could be introduced into any suitable computer in any encoding language to cause data to acted upon so as to effect legal transactions, not technical production or machine functioning *per se*. In *Merrill Lynch's Application*,[6] it was refused protection under the new British law (though it would presumably have been allowed under the old law.) While Falconer J's interpretation of section 1(2)'s proviso has since been held incorrect,[7] his actual conclusion on the facts before him has been approved.[8] Such a program could accordingly be protected only to the extent that copyright in its expression was infringed, or some obligation of contract or confidence was broken. None of these offer the same potential scope as would have stemmed from a patent.

5-050   The line which emerges from these examples seems if anything to be rather more generous than that observed in current United States law and practice.[9] On a question which is inherently difficult to resolve, it is desirable that leading industrial countries with substantially similar interests should move in step. It cannot be predicted with any certainty that the present law, which is very much in the process of evolution, will continue to grow according to current indications. New instances will arise in the borderland between examples (ii) and (iii) which may well make it impossible to maintain the boundary now set. In the end, the

[5] [1987] O.J. EPO 14.
[6] [1988] RPC 1.
[7] See above, § 5-041.
[8] *Genentech* v. *Wellcome Foundation* [1989] (to be reported).
[9] In the U.S. there were a series of restraining decisions of the Supreme Court: *Gottschalk* v. *Benson* (above, n. 92); *Parker* v. *Flook* (above, n. 93); *Diamond* v. *Diehr*, 450 U.S. 175 (1981).

new system may well be pushed to the position reached in Britain in the 1970s under the 1949 Act.

(2) Biological subject-matter

(a) *Living organisms*
In the past, tribunals have handled rather uneasily a number of 5-051
questions over patenting inventive ideas that involve the use or treatment
of living matter. Yet the post-war years have seen a rapid growth of
procedures in this sphere which resemble techniques traditionally patentable. Agriculture, horticulture and animal husbandry have been trans-
formed by artificial procedures in which natural growth is affected by
chemical additives or special physical conditions. Useful substances are
frequently produced by the agency of micro-organisms. At the same time
the advance of biological knowledge, with its revelation of the complex
physical and chemical foundations of living matter, has provided a
common scientific foundation for the explanation of animate and inani-
mate phenomena.

The EPC embodies a consensus that does not favour the admission into
the patent fold of all contenders in this general group. It is little more
adventurous than British practice as it evolved after 1962.

(b) *Methods of treating the human or animal body*
An invention that has to be claimed as a "method of treating the 5-052
human or animal body by surgery or therapy or of diagnosis practised on
the human or animal body" is unpatentable.[10] The explanation continues
to be that its application is not "industrial." If it has a justification, it is
either that public policy demands the free dissemination of new techniques of medicine,[11] or that the patent system should not properly
intrude into the realm of a leading liberal profession, where rewards
other than those of monopoly in a particular procedure are the accepted
norm.[12]

But the British system, along with many others, has at this point 5-053
allowed a technical distinction of crucial importance: a new substance or
composition—one that has not previously been known in the art—may
be claimed "as such" and therefore does not come within the exclusion.

[10] PA 1977, s.4(2), (3); EPC Art. 52(4). As regards human treatment, the rule was long
observed before it was upheld by an appellate court: see *Upjohn's (Robert) Applcn.*
[1977] R.P.C. 94 (C.A.). Although some discontent about it was expressed in *Schering's
Applcn.* (below, n. 20), Parliament apparently accepted the exclusion by not listing
methods of medical treatment in the special compulsory licensing provision, PA 1949,
s.41. The Supreme Court of Israel refused to accept the exclusion (*Wellcome Foundation
v. Plantex* [1974] R.P.C. 514) and such doubts were cast on it in Australia (in the *Joos*
case, below, n. 21) as to lead the Australian Office to begin allowing applications for
methods of human treatment. But the New Zealand C.A. followed the approach in the
Upjohn case: *Wellcome Foundation's (Hitching) Applcn.* [1983] F.S.R. 593. In the U.K.
the exclusion did not extend to methods of treating animals (see *U.S. Rubber's Applcn.*
[1964] R.P.C. 104); so in this respect the new law is severer.
[11] It is moreover, not a field in which there is a serious danger that new ideas will be
exploited secretly.
[12] "The exclusion of methods of surgery and other processes for treating the human body
may well lie outside the concept of invention because the whole subject is conceived as
essentially non-economic." *NRDC* case (above, n. 60) at 145.

Hence it is only with a thing already known,[13] where the claim must be confined to the method of using it, that the exclusion begins to bite.[14] Because research to discover new medical properties of known substances is so similar to the testing of new substances to the same end, this exception has now been expanded in one important respect by the EPC and its derivatives: an invention consisting of a substance or composition for use in an excluded method of medical treatment remains novel, despite the fact that the substance or composition is itself known, "provided that its use in any [such] method . . . is not comprised in any the state of the art."[15] The natural meaning of this special exception is that only for the first discovery of a medical use for a known product can a claim be made to it for that use which will be regarded as novel. So left to itself would the Patents Court have read it.[16] But the Enlarged Board of Appeal of the EPO, faced with numerous applications for second and subsequent discoveries of medical use showed its determination to confine the medical treatment exception strictly to what it described as "non-commercial and non-industrial medical and veterinary activities." In *Eisai's and other Applications*,[17] it decided that in addition to the exception for first medical use, it was legitimate to recognise claims to use of a substance for making up into a medicament for pharmaceutical administration in pursuit of the discovered use (provided, of course, that a patent for the use itself would be debarred as a method of treatment.)[18] In the interests of common progress, the Patents Court proceeded to accept the same casuistry.[19] It remains to to be seen whether higher courts here and courts in co-contracting states are prepared to accept the EPO's lead. If they do in this instance, a highly significant precedent will have been set in making up for the difficulties of revising the EPC and national laws and for the lack of any ultimate jurisdiction to provide definitive interpretations of the Convention text. The exclusion of medical treatment from the system has by no means become devoid of content. For instance more efficient or less harmful dosages, in known treatment, the administration of a bacterium to secure immunity from a disease[20] and the employment of known medical equipment to new ends, still remain unpatentable. At the margins there are certain possibilities of avoiding the prohibition. First, the precedents

[13] The important practical question arises: when is a pharmaceutical composition of more than one known substance itself new? The British Office's answer has been that there is novelty only if the substances have a "synergistic" effect—*i.e.* they must produce an unexpected enhancement when taken together. The common practice of mixing an active ingredient with an inactive carrier will not do. The practice resembles that for a "selection" patent: see Satchell (1970) 1 I.I.C. 179, 188; *cf.* also *Beecham Group's (Amoxycillin) Applcn.* [1980] R.P.C. 261 (C.A.); [1982] F.S.R. 202 (N.Z. C.A.).

[14] The distinction is explicitly recognised in PA 1977, s.4(3) and (less clearly) EPC Art. 52(4).

[15] PA 1977, s.3(6), EPC Art. 54(5).

[16] See *Schering and Wyeth*, below, n 19).

[17] [1987] O.J. EPO 147; and see *Duphar's Applcn. (Pigs II)* [1989] O.J. EPO 24. White [1984] E.I.P.R. 62.

[18] This is known as "the Swiss form of claim," the Swiss Patent Office being the first perspicaceous enough to appreciate its potential; *cf.* the earlier, wider decision of the German Supreme Court (*Hydropiridine* [1984] O.J. EPO 26).

[19] *Schering's and Wyeth's Applcns.* [1985] R.P.C. 545 (in banc).

[20] *Unilever's (Davis) Applcn.* [1983] R.P.C. 219.

have confined methods of treatment to "the arrest or cure of a disease or diseased condition or the correction of some malfunction or the amelioration of some incapacity or disability"[21] and the new statutory formula suggests the same limitation. So patents will remain available for a method of oral contraception by smaller dosages than previously known; for the use of a known substance to remove lice from the skin; the use of a chemical to improve the growth of hair or nails; and the insertion of a radio receiver in a tooth as a hearing aid.[22]

Secondly, under the 1949 Act, the Patent Appeals Tribunal once allowed a "pack claim" as a way of patenting the discovery of an improved a dosage: the claim was for a pack giving the daily dosages of two pharmaceuticals (oral contraceptives) together with instructions about the days on which each should be taken in relation to the female menstrual cycle.[23] The particular way of conveying this specific information was held to justify an exception. It can, however, be said that the pack only conveyed information designed to direct the course of human conduct; certainly the Court of Appeal has prevented the proliferation of "pack claims" where the method of display does not help particularly in transmitting the new information.[24]

(c) Agricultural inventions

The field of "industrial application" includes agriculture.[25] Thus it seems clear that patents will continue to be granted for those uses of chemical substances in the production of plants and animals for commercial purposes which were first given patentable status in the 1960s.[26] There is instead a narrow exception which covers plant and animal varieties, and essentially biological processes for the production of plants and animals other than micro-biological processes and the products thereof.[27]

5-054

---

[21] Barwick C.J., *Joos v. Commissioner of Patents* [1973] R.P.C. 59 (H.C. Australia), building upon *Schering's Appln.* [1971] R.P.C. 337. Recently the EPO has confined "method of diagnosis" to the assessment for medical treatment, thus keeping prior tests which gather information within the patent system: *Bruker's Appln.* [1988] O.J. EPO 308.

[22] Respectively: *Stafford-Miller's Appln.* [1984] F.S.R. 269. *Schering* case, *Joos* case (above, n. 21) and *Puharich's Appln.* [1965] R.P.C. 395; *cf. Oral Health's Appln.* [1977] R.P.C. 612; *Wellcome's Appln. (Pigs I)* [1989] O.J. EPO 13.

[23] *Organon's Appln.* [1970] R.P.C. 574; *Blendax-Werke's Appln.* [1980] R.P.C. 491; *cf. L'Oreal's Appln.* [1970] R.P.C. 565, where a reason (putting creases in material) existed for wanting to combine the two chemicals which the applicant claimed in a pack for a different purpose (treating human hair); accordingly the claim was refused.

[24] *Ciba-Geigy's (Dürr) Appln.* [1977] R.P.C. 83; and see *Wellcome Foundation's Appln.* [1981] F.S.R. 72 (H.C. Australia). The importance of "pack claims" in catching infringers is now reduced with the introduction of the new law of indirect infringement: see below, §§ 6-013, 6-014.

[25] PA 1977, s.4(1), EPC Art. 57.

[26] Mentioned below, nn. 33-35.

[27] PA 1977, s.1(3)(b), EPC Art. 53(b).

In the case of plant varieties, this is because a separate, limited system of protection exists.[28] For new breeds of animal there is no equivalent and the EPC is more cautious than the former law of at least one of its Member States.[29] For the United Kingdom, however, the exclusion represents no change.[30]

Where the inventive step lies not in evolution of the variety itself, but in a new technique for producing a given plant or animal it is not patentable if it consists of an "essentially biological process."[31] Patents have been refused in the past for a method of improving clove trees by a particular form of pruning coupled with chemical sterilising; and for a method of producing better poinsettias by exposing them to artificial periods of light and dark.[32] Such examples may be contrasted with cases where chemicals are used to modify growth or the end product; patents have since 1961 been allowed for using a selective weedkiller,[33] and for injecting animals with a meat "tenderiser" before slaughter.[34] Some such distinction is likely to continue. But the EPO, at least, has indicated that it will not treat the pruning example as non-patentable: the essence of this invention is said to be technical, not biological.[35]

5-055   These are considerations which go to relatively traditional techniques for stimulating and altering the production of living matter The sudden development over the last decade of genetic engineering procedures is opening a range of additional prospects whose horizons are as yet still shrouded.[36] Enough can be seen to suggest, both that the existing regime for plant variety protection (under an international convention which precludes patent protection from its territory) is rapidly becoming an outmoded impediment to a logical framework of protection[37] and that this is likewise true of the exclusions in the EPC, turning upon the concepts of "plant and animal varieties" and "essentially biological

---

[28] Plant Varieties and Seeds Act 1964; see below, App. 4. It exists only to the extent that a scheme has been introduced for a species. The rights given do not extend to trade in the products of a variety (fruit, flowers) as distinct from reproductive material (seeds, tubers, bulbs, plants, etc.).

[29] Thus in West Germany a new procedure for breeding was in principle held patentable but it had to be capable of repetition if it was to satisfy the criterion of sufficient disclosure. It was not enough that the breed could be bought from the inventor: see "Rote Taube" (1970) 1 I.I.C. 136.

[30] The Irish Patent Office has allowed a claim to a method of rearing salmon (*Unilever's Appln.* (1979) 1 E.I.P.R. D-27); such a claim might be allowed under the new British law.

[31] See n. 27 above.

[32] *Lenard's Appln.* (1954) 71 R.P.C. 190; *N.V. Philips' Appln.* (1954) 71 R.P.C. 192; both were accepted as good in the *NRDC* case (above, n. 49). Note also *Rau's Appln.* (1935) 52 R.P.C. 362 (selective cultivation of lupin seeds: patent refused).

[33] *NRDC's Appln.* (above, n. 49) (H.C. Aust., but accepted by the C.A. in *Ciba-Geigy's (Dürr) Applcns.* [1977] R.P.C. 83 at 88).

[34] *R. v. P.A.T., ex p. Swift* [1962] R.P.C. 37.

[35] EPO Guidelines C IV 3.4.

[36] See Byrne (1985) 16 I.I.C. 1, (1986) 17 I.I.C. 324; Crespi [1986] E.I.P.R. 262; Grubb, *Patents in Chemistry and Biochronology* (1986); Bent, Schwaab et al., *Intellectual Property Rights in Biotechnology Worldwide* (1987); Roth (1987) 18 I.I.C. 41; Crespi, *Patents: a Basic Guide to Patenting in Biotechnology* (1988); Teschemacher (1988) 19 I.I.C. 18.

[37] For the UPOV Convention of 1961 and its impact on contracting states, see below, § A4-002. The Revision Conference for the Convention, currently being organised, ought to consider whether the regime has a viable future. See Adler (1986) 17 I.I.C. 195; Straus (1987) 18 I.I.C. 723.

processes for the production of plants and animals." It can be predicted that the EPC provision will be progressively pared down by interpretation, on the ground that it imposes unwarranted barriers against some of those who invest in biotechnical and agricultural research and wish to have patents for their successful results.

Thus there is currently much concern over recombinant-DNA techniques which allow the insertion in plant and animal genes of disease-resistant or insect-repellent sequences or other important improvements. To do this is not to create a new variety, but to do something that may be viewed as either greater or less: if the new sequence can be successfully applied to a whole genus or species, it is a larger modification; if it does not produce physical changes of (say) shape or colour, it is a change less than the creation of a variety (and to take that illustration is to hint at the practical difficulties of deciding when indeed a new variety has emerged—in traditional breeding, as much as in laboratory tinkering.)[38] There are other indications of the EPO's readiness to mould the EPC so as to encompass new fields of activity. So it may be that the EPC system will be extended in the agricultural sphere, without leaving too many exceptions which might have the effect of re-channelling the natural flow of research. Nonetheless, there is no point at which the difficulties of interpreting and reforming the Convention pose greater hazards for the future.

(d) *Microbiological processes and micro-organisms*

Microbiological ferments, such as yeasts, have a long history of usefulness. Particular bacteria are now employed in many production processes conducted under industrial conditions similar to those used in other parts of the chemical industry. Claims to methods of production which deploy micro-organisms have accordingly been treated as patentable.[39] This is confirmed in the new legislation, which provides special procedures for depositing samples of micro-organisms in culture collections, in order to satisfy the requirement of sufficient disclosure.[40]

In chemical research most new substances are artificially made before being tested for useful properties. In the exploitations of micro-organisms, the particular bacterial strain may first be isolated in a natural sample and thereafter reproduced by laboratory cultivation. In the course of this it may be manipulated, for instance so as to purify the strain or to bring about genetic mutations in it. The strain when thus modified by a specified process[41] is likely to be patentable.[42] While this is not made

5-056

[38] See Christie (1988) 19 I.I.C. 646. In future, the production of entirely new animals or plants, if by "technical" rather than "biological" means, may become patentable; likewise the growth of new parts for animals (arms? legs?) and the production of tissue on which research can be conducted (obviating the use of animals for some experiments).

[39] *American Cyanamid* v. *Berk Pharmaceuticals* [1976] R.P.C. 231.

[40] See below, § 5-059, n. 54.

[41] The British practice was doubtless affected by the former provision (PA 1949, s.4(7)), that substance claims were not to be construed as extending to the substance as found in nature; *cf.* White (1980) 2 E.I.P.R. 37.

[42] In Ireland a distinction has now emerged between an engineered micro-organism (patentable) and one occurring naturally (unpatentable): see *NRDC's Applcn.* [1986] F.S.R. 620; *Rank Hovis McDougall's Applcn.* [1978] F.S.R. 588. This could be taken up elsewhere. Note also Teschemacher (1982) 13 I.I.C. 27; Marterer (1987) 18 I.I.C. 666. See *Szuecs' Applcn.* [1956] R.P.C. 25 (claim allowed to production of mushroom tissue by artificially manipulating a mushroom culture).

explicit in the EPC the current tendency to read all exclusions narrowly supports this view. The point at which micro-organisms and micro-biological processing divide from plants and essentially biological processing is far from plain. But whatever can be put into the former category is not excluded from the patent system.

(3) Miscellaneous

5-057   Since the developments of the 1960s there is little left of the former test that for patentable subject-matter, a method must result in a "vendible product," made, improved or altered. That rule prevented patents for the use of known things to produce a negative result, such as the extinguishing of an incendiary bomb; and patents purely for methods of testing in the course of manufacture.[43] It is highly likely, following more recent authority, that patents for producing a fog-free atmosphere,[44] or for generating radio waves with particular characteristics[45] will be acceptable, as well as methods of testing that are used in industrial production or such associated fields as the extraction of minerals.[46]

The 1977 Act excludes from the range of patentability inventions the publication or exploitation of which would be generally expected to encourage offensive, immoral or anti-social behaviour. This is a variant of an EPC provision excluding inventions contrary to "ordre public" or morality.[47] Neither is likely to have much practical significance, but occasionally—perhaps over the question of contraception—differences of moral attitude may lead to European patents being held invalid in some states but not in others.[48]

5. CLEAR AND COMPLETE DISCLOSURE

(1) General

5-058   The specification must disclose the invention clearly enough and completely enough for it to be performed by a person skilled in the art.[49] It is this requirement that aims to extract the essential "consideration" for the patent grant—revelation of the invention for the information of the rest of industry and any others interested. When the invention consists of a step forward that then needs only routine development to make it a commercial success, the question of disclosure is usually straightforward. But where a succession of inventions is needed, as in

---

[43] See, e.g. GEC's Applcn. (1943) 60 R.P.C. 1; R.H.F.'s Applcn. (1944) 61 R.P.C. 49; methods of testing were specifically admitted by PA 1949, s.101 ("invention")—they are not explicitly mentioned in PA 1977.
[44] Elton's Applcn. [1957] R.P.C. 267. Treated as patentable in the EPO Guidelines C IV 4.1.
[45] Rantzen's Applcn. (1947) 64 R.P.C. 63.
[46] See n. 19 above.
[47] PA 1977, s.1(3)(a); EPC Art. 53(a). The EPC goes on to emphasise that mere prohibition by law or regulation in some or all member states is not enough, and this falls to be considered in implementing the British provision. It suggests that the former practice of requiring a disclaimer of potentially illegal applications of the invention will be appropriate only in extreme cases.
[48] See Van Empel, The Granting of European Patents (1975), pp. 68-69.
[49] PA 1977, s.14(3), 72(1)(c); EPC Art. 83, 100(b) (ground of opposition).

the evolution of most new technologies, the issue is more complex. Obviously it would be wrong to reserve the patent for the person lucky enough to take the last step towards the most successful version of the article or process. Witness to the contrary the long-settled practice of granting patents for "basic" inventions and then for improvements upon them and selections within their range. But if there are to be patents for inventions on the road to ultimate success, they must be kept for steps that are not only non-obvious, but also which work well enough to contribute something useful to what is already known; and this the instructions for performance must reveal. How the law seeks to do this we consider in the next subsection.

Beside these considerations arise two associated problems. First, is the patentee to be bound by obligations of good faith—bound for instance to reveal the best way of performing his invention at the time of his application? It is by no means clear how far this is a requirement of the new law.[50] Secondly, how much broader may the claims be than the specific examples of the invention that are described, given the special function of claims in the specification? This relationship we shall consider when we turn in the next section to the criteria governing claims.[51]

The former law contained a number of specific requirements covering the sorts of issue just mentioned: sufficient and fair description, utility, disclosure of best known method, fair basis for claims.[52] Now, after grant, the only relevant objection, apart from those going to amendments,[53] is absence of complete and clear disclosure.[54] There are indications that this provision is to be read in a broad sense. Thus where micro-organisms are used an invention there may be no *disclosure* if the samples are not publicly available and are not deposited in a specified Culture Collection and made available on request. Under the former law, the House of Lords held that the requirement of *description* could not be read to impose an obligation to make available a micro-biological culture[55] (or, for that matter, any starting material not otherwise procurable.)[56]

5-059

---

[50] See below, §§ 5-060—5-061.
[51] See below, §§ 5-067—5-068.
[52] See especially PA 1949, s.32(1)(g)-(i); below § A2-008—010.
[53] Above, § 4-024.
[54] PA 1977, ss.14(4), (8), 72(3), 125A; PA 1977 Rules, r. 17; EPC Rules, rr. 28, 28a. Under the new British legislation, this is apparently an absolute requirement. The EPC Rules have, however, been amended so as to exclude the requirement of deposit if the micro-organism can be described in such a manner as to enable a skilled person to carry out the invention. But it should be remembered that, once granted, a European patent (U.K.) must satisfy the standards of the Patents Act. For the conditions imposed on the recipient of a sample from a culture collection, see Ency. PL, § 13-111A; Van Empel, above, n. 48, pp. 148-152.
[55] *American Cyanamid's (Dann) Patent* [1971] R.P.C. 425.
[56] *Quaere*, whether there is now any obligation to "disclose" rare starting material by making it available (and if not self-producing, how much?). One argument against, presumably, is that special regulation would be needed: *cf.* Lord Wilberforce, *Dann* case, above n. 55 at 450.

(2) Making the disclosure

5-060   In the case of mechanical contrivances the patentee normally seeks to fulfil his obligation of disclosure by describing at least one embodiment of his concept, giving details about how it is to be made wherever that is not obvious. He may, of course, resort to such abbreviations as "any suitable material" or "general methods," whenever these will be readily understood by addresses. Likewise in a chemical case he will provide at least one example of the procedures involved in his invention. One embodiment may suffice if it contains a feature present in one or other of all the claims. Where alternatives are claimed, other examples may well be necessary.[57]

In his examples, the patentee will often use specific measures: of size, weight, volume, temperature and so forth. But in cases where nothing turns on finite limits, he may confine his description to general relationships between component parts. This is permissible if it will take only simple experiments for someone else to carry out the invention successfully. In the leading case, the invention was a "smokeless ashtray" consisting of a receptacle with a tube at the top and a deflector at the bottom, so placed that butts would give off smoke only into the enclosed space above. This was properly described in terms of interrelationships that would produce the desired result (and claims in equivalent terms were also allowed).[58]

5-061   Whether disclosure is sufficient has always been treated as a question of fact.[59] A court must judge the issue from evidence about how the skilled addressee would have understood the specification at the date from which it speaks—presumably that when the application is published.[60] The purpose is not to instruct the uninitiated in the whole art. Those who have been working in a field soon build up a web of assumptions and understandings about how things can be made to work which will not be shared by outsiders. They may know, for instance, about the necessary quality of starting materials, suitable catalysts, effective ranges of temperatures. Typical issues about disclosure concern the failure to specify a limiting condition that is crucial to success. For instance, suppose that a chemical reaction will work only in an iron autoclave, but this the patent fails to require.[61] In such a case, the patentee will seek to argue that the notional addressee would have known to use the right vessel; the objector to the patent will claim that there was no such understanding. He will, moreover, emphasise any

---

[57] It has never been an absolute requirement of British practice that even one example be provided. In the case, for instance, where the invention consists in discovering a use for a new material that is made from known materials by known methods, an example to illustrate its making may be superfluous. But in the EPO detailed description of at least one way of performing the invention is required, and more examples may be needed in many cases claiming a broad field: EPC Rules, r. 27(1).

[58] *No-Fume* v. *Pitchford* (1935) 52 R.P.C. 231 (C.A.).

[59] *British Dynamite* v. *Krebs* (1896) 13 R.P.C. 190 (192) (H.L.).

[60] Thus later knowledge cannot be used to cure inadequacies: *Nicholls* v. *Kershaw* (1910) 27 R.P.C. 237 (250) (movement for bringing plate carrier closer to lens in camera let in light; this defect later cured by self-capping focal lens, but this was not on market at the time.)

[61] Example drawn from *Badische Anilin* v. *Usines de Rhone* (1898) 15 R.P.C. 359, (C.A.) where the patentee did not in fact appreciate the significance of iron to the reaction, and the instructions were held insufficient.

passages which appear to suggest that any autoclave will do; for positive suggestions that something can be done which will in fact not work are likely to be fatal.[62] Since patent office examiners and patent agents tend to share a similar level of expertise, they are likely to take much the same view of what can be assumed and what must be spelled out. It is when the matter goes into court (and particularly before non-specialist judges on appeal) that this sort of issue becomes chancy.

Much may depend on the court's picture of the proper addressee. It **5-062** was in considering sufficiency of description that the Court of Appeal held a "pioneer" patent in the field of colour television to be addressed to skilled technicians rather than to members of leading research teams. What is more, those technicians could not be expected to make "prolonged study of matters which present some initial difficulty."[63] These are high standards which pursue a categorical view of the patent system's informational role. For they were used to deny the sufficiency of a patent otherwise valid, which at first instance had been held adequate to instruct the research leaders in a novel art.

(3) Good faith in disclosing?

It is only to be expected that some patentees may try to secure effective **5-063** patent cover and at the same time keep to themselves crucial pieces of information about how the invention works best. How to make a patentee describe his invention sufficiently was a preoccupation of the early case-law, and pronouncements that he must act in utmost good faith, that he must be "fair, honest and open" have been repeated often enough in modern times.[64] This attitude used to be reflected in the statute law, which required the description to be fair and to disclose the best method known to the patentee.[65] Now all that is called for is that the disclosure be clear and complete.

To prove an objection that the best method had been withheld was never easy. But, given the necessary proof, how would a court now react? If it found that the disguising had taken the form of deliberately obscure passages in the description, it would doubtless hold the disclosure insufficiently clear or complete.[66] But suppose that the description leads to a perfectly acceptable, but not necessarily optimal, version of the invention, and the patentee knew this at the date of the application. The new form of the law may be intended to allow him to do just this. Arguably, under conditions of modern research, patentees can no longer be expected necessarily to give full instructions for performance. Instead

---

[62] Likewise, positive suggestions that a selected sub-group has a particular advantage (subject to *de minimus* exceptions). For the requirement that a selection patent must state as part of its disclosure the special advantage involved, see above, § 5-018. However, an erroneous explanation of why an invention works will not be objectionable, unless it is misleading to someone trying to achieve performance: *"Z" Electric v. Marples* (1910) 27 R.P.C. 737 (C.A.).

[63] *Valensi v. British Radio* [1973] 3 R.P.C. 337 at 377 (C.A.). See generally, above, §§ 4-032, 4-033.

[64] See, *e.g. Morgan v. Seaward* (1836) W.P.C. 170 at 174; *Vidal Dyes v. Levinstein* (1912) 29 R.P.C. 245 at 269 (C.A.); *Raleigh v. Miller* (1948) 65 R.P.C. 141 at 147 (H.L.).

[65] PA 1949, s.32(1)(*h*).

[66] See below, n. 84.

it should be enough if they indicate clearly the problem to which they have found some solution, and upon which they are likely to be pursuing further research; the patent then names the person to whom application can be made for further information and the patentee is left free to keep his extra knowledge for his own "head-start" or to sell it as know-how.[67] Certainly he will be allowed to do this if he acquires the extra knowledge only by later research.[68] Yet in Britain it has long been the chief "public" purpose of the patent system to secure the release of information about inventions as rapidly as possible. It is by no means clear the revisionism ought to go so far as to allow a patent for as much about an intention as will give the public something while leaving the patentee ahead to an undisclosed degree. The Court of Appeal's recent insistence (admittedly under old law) that a specification must be addressed to the technicians of leading researchers[69] suggests that old standards are not readily to be abandoned.[70]

6. REQUIREMENTS FOR CLAIMS

(1) Pre-grant requirements

5-064   The claims of the specification, so crucial to the whole patenting process under a "fence-post" regime, must comply with four criteria: they must define the protected matter, be clear and concise, be supported by the description, and related to one invention.[71] During the application stage, the examiner must consider all these. Unity of invention has always been a matter which cannot afterwards be brought in question.[72] It is required in the interests of orderly classification and it is something which has simply to be settled one way or other at an early stage. But the other requirements are fundamental and used to be open to objection once the patent was granted. There is now no distinct ground of invalidity relating to them; nor is it possible to read such a ground into the Patents Act 1977, s.72(1) by inference.[73]

At least in the EPO, failure to make a sufficiently clear and complete disclosure of the invention is being treated as a basis upon which objection to the undue breadth of claims could be taken.[74] On this view "disclosure" requires an adequate delineation of all those things which are claimed, since the claims specify what is the invention. It may well follow that the disclosure is deficient if general descriptive words are used

---

[67] On this see the arguments of Beier and Kitch (above, n. 69), and generally above, §§ 5-041, 5-042).
[68] Or to secure an improvement patent, if the extra knowledge constitutes an invention over that in the first patent.
[69] Above, § 4-033.
[70] See also *Hakoune's Appln.* [1986] O.J. EPO 376: no adequate disclosure where applicant omitted details in order to make copying difficult.
[71] PA 1977, s.14(5); EPC Art. 84.
[72] See above, §§ 4-011, 4-012.
[73] *Genentech v. Wellcome Foundation* [1989] (to be reported).
[74] EPO Guidelines D III 5; to the same effect, see Intergovernmental Conference for the EPC, Luxembourg 1971, p. 68 (Report of Working Party I).

in a claim and only substantial experiment can determine which of the things described by the words will actually work. Thus considerations which under the old law were thought of as questions of inutility, are likely to remain open. Its unlikely that the specification will be bad if it suggests that an alternative will work, when a skilled person will know that this cannot be or can find out quickly and easily. Formerly an objection of inutility would nonetheless have lain[75]; but that penalised innaccuracy in perhaps an unnecessary degree.[76]

(2) Ambiguous claims

The requirements that the claims define the invention and that they be clear should be read in the same sense as the similar objection under the old law.[77] Their essence is disciplinary; they insist that the draftsman should not use language that is avoidably obscure and ambiguous. While this is supposed to apply whether the obscurity was deliberate, careless or simply the result of lack of skill, a court is most likely to take offence at attempts unnecessarily "to puzzle a student and frighten men of business into taking out a licence."[78] The advance of science has brought increasing difficulties of definition. The old precision with which chemical formulae could be used to define the structure of substances, for instance, can no longer always be used for macro-molecules of today.[79] Where the difficulty is genuine, a draftsman who does the best the case admits of will not be penalised.[80]

The courts have not insisted, in the name of precision, that patentees adopt strict dimensional and other limits, if to do so would likely offer competitors a simple route around the patent and they will not be seriously embarrassed in trying to decide whether or not they are performing within the claims. Thus claims limited by result (such as for the "smokeless ash-tray" mentioned in connection with sufficient disclosure)[81] are allowed if only simple experiments with the feature called for by the claim will determine what works. In similar vein, patentees may be permitted to use general words, that are comparative in import, like "large." Thus in *British Thomson-Houston* v. *Corona*,[82] a claim to a new type of electric light filament was held valid even though one characteristic required in the relevant claim was that the filament should be "of large diameter." This was read in the light of knowledge about filaments previously in use and was sufficiently clear to allow an informed worker to know when he was achieving the invention.

Judges have not been unanimous about how hard to strain in the search for definite meaning in a claim. On the whole, modern courts

5-065

5-066

---

[75] *Norton & Gregory* v. *Jacobs* (1937) 54 R.P.C. 271 at 276 (C.A.); *Mineral Separation* v. *Noranda* (1952) 69 R.P.C. 81 at 95 (J.C.).
[76] See above, § 5-038.
[77] PA 1949, s.32(1)(i); see Blanco White, at §§ 2-218 *et seq.*
[78] See especially Lord Loreburn, *Natural Colour Kinematograph* v. *Bioschemes* (1915) 32 R.P.C. 256, 266, 269.
[79] For the considerable difficulty that these present, see above, § 4-032.
[80] For the assorted dicta, see Blanco White, § 2-219.
[81] Above, § 5-060.
[82] (1922) 39 R.P.C. 49.

have proved readier to find some meaning rather than none, and indeed to prefer meanings that will avoid absurd results.[83] This will not necessarily redound in the patentee's favour: for if he is trying to make his case by having his claims read in an unexpected sense (by virtue perhaps of some passage in the body of the specification) he may find the "plain" meaning preferred.[84] Altogether it has proved more difficult than in the past to sustain an attack based on the ambiguity of claims. There is no reason to suppose that this reflects a rise in standards of draftsmanship; indeed, the current readiness to be accommodating positively invites imprecision. Rather it is that patents are no longer looked upon with that suspicion of monopoly which underlay all the insistence upon accuracy in claiming.

(3) Claims and disclosure

5-067   A patentee will want claims that generalise the particular embodiments of his invention described in the specification. Yet, at least before the Patent Office,[85] description must "support" claims. A good starting point is this distinction: the invention may lie in proposing a new thing (reflecting cat's eyes as guides to night drivers[86]) or in improving an old thing (better reflectors.) The first inventor should be allowed to claim all ways of reaching his "idea," for that is what is inventive; the second should be confined to his particular technique and not permitted to claim all ways of reaching the result.[87]

Rather similar to the conception of an "idea" is the discovery of a principle: there the discoverer ought to be allowed patents for the practical embodiments of the principle: his new theory supplies a measure for the proper scope of the claim.[88] Contrast with this the empirical discovery, where experiment shows that particular instances give useful results. One success, say with a new chemical compound or micro-organisms, will suggest, even to the uninventive, that closely related alternatives may be as good or better. There would thus be little value in a patent confined to the examples worked upon. Yet if the inventor is to be allowed to generalise, it is not easy to suggest any rational basis for settling the scope of his claims. As already noted, it has been held that a claim to a very large class of organic substances is justified, wherever a sound prediction can be made from the experiments on a few numbers that all the class will have the beneficial property discovered (in some degree); beyond this a claim will be disallowed as merely speculative.[89] For want of anything better, this has seemed a

---

[83] See, especially Henriksen v. Tallon [1965] R.P.C. 434 (H.L.) (claim to ball-point pens with "jumbo" and "capillary" tubes read so as to exclude variants that would not work).
[84] See, e.g. Mineral Separations v. Noranda (1951) 69 R.P.C. 81 at 93-94 (J.C.).
[85] See above, § 5-064.
[86] For this example, see above, § 5-027.
[87] See Ency. PL, § 3-404.
[88] cf. above, § 5-017.
[89] Olin Mathieson v. Biorex [1970] R.P.C. 157 at 192-193; see above, § 5-024. Note Blanco White, § 2-304, suggesting, inter alia, that the inventor should be allowed to claim anything that he predicts will work until proved wrong in any instance; but inutility is no longer a separate objection.

usable test in a number of patent systems and it has been adopted by the EPO.[90] Because those who carry out further work on different members of the class will be able to have selection patents for the non-obvious successes, the result will frequently be to give the initial inventor a monopoly share in the ultimate successes, while his patent remains alive.

There is a further aspect of such difficulties: when a distinction is drawn between an idea and a mere improvement it is being assumed that the thing has only one purpose. But suppose that actually this is not so or that predictable it may not remain so: there are examples enough of substances originally found to have one use, later showing quite different properties. In British practice under the 1949 Act, there were practical reasons for allowing the first person to propose a use for a new thing to have a claim to it untied to method of use: in particular, the absence of a doctrine of "indirect infringement" and the embargo on claims to methods of medical treatment. Hence claims to new chemical substances were allowed upon disclosure of a use for the substance, however much its actual making was a matter of routine.[91] Whether or not it was justifiable to ignore the problem of other uses, the practice seems firmly entrenched, and it is likely to survive even in a system which now covers indirect infringement.

More difficult are the cases where the thing is not so evidently "new" as is a class of previously unmade chemical substances. Consider first, a claim to synthetic rubber, *i.e.* to a polymer however synthesised whose chemical structure was already known from the natural product. Where the difficulty was to discover a reaction that would achieve the synthesis and the inventor disclosed one catalyst that would work, the High Court of Australia held the claim too broad.[92] It amounted to a claim to all ways of reaching a desired, but previously unattainable result. The patentee was rightly confined to claims involving his reaction.[93]   5-068

Consider next, the claim in *Mullard* v. *Philco*[94] to a radio valve with three auxiliary electrodes, in which that nearest the anode was connected to the cathode. When used in a radio as the final amplifier in a series, this produced an unexpected advantage, and there could be no objection to a claim limited to this deployment. The actual adjustment in the valve involved no technical difficulty, once a reason for making it had been found (in this case the patent was concerned with an "idea" invention.) But even so, it was not permissible to have a monopoly good against others who might want to put the valve in this novel form to uses other than that for which the design was being suggested. The House of Lords accordingly held that the claim was too broad.

[90] *e.g.* see above, § 4-038.
[91] See Jenkins J., *May & Baker's Patent* (1948) 65 R.P.C. 255 at 281; *Olin Mathieson* v. *Biorex* [1970] R.P.C. 157 at 181. *cf. Upjohn's Appln.* (NZ Patent Office) cited by Blanco White at § 2-304.
[92] *Montecatini* v. *Eastman Kodak* [1972] R.P.C. 639.
[93] *Firestone's Patent* [1966] F.S.R. 366 (C.G.) was decided the other way; criticised by Blanco White, § 2-303.
[94] (1936) 53 R.P.C. 323 (H.L.).

The interrelated issues raised under this heading are fundamental in character. They lay at the heart of the recent *Genentech* case[95] concerning genetic engineering: these claims were to a known protein, human tissue plasminogen activator (t-PA), as produced by recombinant DNA technology. All but the narrowest of the claims were considered by the Court of Appeal to be in unacceptably wide form, and should have been rejected by the British Patent Office for lack of support in the disclosure. In the judgments there are suggestions that this objection may effectively be taken in invalidity proceedings after grant; in particular, by holding that the claims were not for any invention[96]; or that there was no sufficient disclosure in the description of the invention claimed.[97] But these propositions did not command majority support.[98] For the moment, the law stands in a condition of regrettable uncertainty.

[95] [1989] (to be reported); and see §5-041.
[96] Purchas L.J.
[97] Mustill L.J.
[98] In the upshot, the particular research was found by a majority to lack any inventive step: see above, § 5-036.

CHAPTER 6

SCOPE OF MONOPOLY

1. INFRINGEMENT

(1) Introduction

Two sorts of patent infringer may be regarded as typical: the enterprise   **6-001**
which through ignorance or stupidity, imitates the patentee's own product and so falls within the core of the monopoly; and the concern which,
by independent effort or determination to find a way round the patent,
works (if at all) only in the penumbra of the claims. A patent which does
not provide substantial protection against the second kind of infringer is
generally not worth much. Yet if it is for an invention of real value its
precise scope is likely to be the subject of constant questioning. Hence
the importance, in a system of patent law, of how this question of extent
is determined.

The British law before the 1977 Act, with its "fence-post" approach to
the definition of the monopoly, in fact combined scrupulousness over the
question of who was infringing with a wide view of the scope of the
rights affecting acts that did fall within the claims. The initial scrupulousness was found in the rule that, primarily but not quite exclusively, the
monopoly was determined by the scope of the claims; and equally in the
rule that a person who only contributed towards infringement could not
for that alone be held liable. The subsequent breadth was to be found
particularly in the principle that all sales and uses of patented goods
required the patentee's licence; so that if he himself sold goods on terms
restricting their resale or use, those who knowingly broke the conditions
would infringe.

This highly individual blend of severity and generosity has been
substantially changed in the new deal. A contributor may now be held
responsible for "indirect infringement"; and a doctrine of exhaustion of
rights will in future curb the possibilities of limited licensing. Both of
these changes we shall discuss in due course.[1] At the same time,
somewhat more interstitially, the former British approach to the question
of what constitutes "direct infringement" has altered, and this must be
the first subject for investigation.

(2) The role of the claims

The "fence-post" approach of the British to the claims of the specifica-   **6-002**
tion expresses a preference for certainty, however arbitrary it may
sometimes seem, over the inevitably vaguer merits of "fair" protection to
the patentee in the light of his disclosure. It is the approach which in

---

[1] Below, §§ 6-011—6-014.

principle has been accepted in EPC, Article 69,[2] and accordingly no radical re-direction of British practice has been called for. The essential question over the scope of the monopoly remains whether an activity falls within the scope of a claim. This continues to make extent turn upon construction of the claim, in accordance with the rules already mentioned.[3] A thing within the claim remains an infringement, even if further things are added to it and even if those things make it more successful. Likewise it remains an infringement even though further work by the infringer enables him to select the best version of all the alternatives covered by the claims.[4] But a thing will cease to be within a claim if one or more of the essential elements is omitted or substituted by something different—by something which does not fall within the description used by the claim.[5]

Accordingly, the question often in doubt is whether a defendant who is acting in the shadows of meaning on the periphery of a claim still falls within it. In answering this, recent decisions have responded to the injunction not to take too severe an interpretative approach, which is one element in the Protocol to Article 69.[6]

6-003   Before the 1977 Act English case-law did not in fact insist that a person was free to perform any act which did not fall exactly within the language of a patent claim properly construed. It was always law, as the recent leading cases have emphasised, that while an infringer must take each and every one of the essential integers of a claim, "non-essential" integers may be omitted or replaced by mechanical equivalents.[7] That oddly mixed metaphor—taking the "pith and marrow" of the invention—was to be understood in this sense and not as introducing some broader catch-net.[8] There was, however, considerable argument over what differences could be ignored as "insubstantial," "immaterial," "non-essential" (the three adjectives appear interchangeable).

6-004   In the 1960s the House of Lords decided two cases concerning mechanisms where invention lay merely in a new combination of known parts. Both ideas were useful, but not major advances of technology. In *Van der Lely* v. *Bamfords*,[9] the claim in issues was for a mechanical

---

[2] But while the English version says that extent is to be determined by the "terms" of the claims, the other versions use words ("teneur," "Inhalt") which may well convey a looser idea to those likely to use the French or German.

[3] Above, § 4-029.

[4] Even if the selector secures his own patent for his selection, this gives him no right to ignore a still subsisting patent for the wider class from which he selects: see above, § 5-018.

[5] See, e.g. *Birmingham Sound Reproducers* v. *Collaro* [1956] R.P.C. 232 at 245 (C.A.); *Van der Lely* v. *Bamfords* [1963] R.P.C. 61 (H.L.); *Rodi & Wienenberger* v. *Showell* [1969] R.P.C. 367 (H.L.).

[6] The content of the Protocol is described above, § 4-029.

[7] Parker J., *Marconi* v. *British Radio* (1911) 28 R.P.C. 181 at 217; and see the cases cited above, n. 5.

[8] The phrase was used by Lord Cairns in *Clark* v. *Adie* (1877) 2 App.Cas. 315 at 320; and see Lord Reid, *Van der Lely* case (above n. 5) at 75; Lord Upjohn, *Rodi* case (above, n. 5) at 391.

[9] Above, n. 5. The plaintiff was reduced to relying upon this subsidiary claim because the main claims were anticipated (see above, § 5-004). The first filing was in the Netherlands where less exacting standards prevailed towards claims. The case was an object lesson to those charged with British applications to use greater imagination in thinking through obvious alternatives.

hayrake with given characteristics in which the hindmost set of rake-wheels could be moved forward in parallel with the foremost rake-wheels, so as to cover wider areas of ground in some operations. The defendant's hay-rake had means for moving its foremost rake-wheels back in line with the rearmost, which produced no different effect; but a majority of the court refused to consider this infringement: if a claim stated that an integer should have a given characteristic, then this was essential because the patentee had chosen so to describe it.[10] Similarly in *Rodi & Wienenberger* v. *Showell*[11] an expandable watch-strap was required by the claim to have two layers of links which were connected on each side by "U-shaped" bows. The defendant instead used "C-shaped" bows which extended from one side of the strap to the other, thus amounting to a combination of two U-shaped bows. A bare majority of the House took the view that there was no infringement in this substitution, inclining to the opinion that some material change in function had been introduced.[12]

However, in *Beecham Group* v. *Bristol Laboratories*, a claim to a semi-synthetic penicillin was infringed by importation and sale of a chemical substance which did not have the claimed formula but which would nevertheless be converted in the human blood-stream into the claimed substance. The infringing "bio-precursor" was treated as being the claimed substance "temporarily masked."[13] In this case the patented invention was of basic importance, the result of a major research initiative. There was moreover no apparent advantage in using the defendant's bio-precursor form (though in some cases, administration of a drug through a bio-precursor may reduce harmful side-effects).[14]

If this suggested that some liberalisation over the attitude of the 1960s **6-005** was beginning, it has been confirmed by subsequent events. In the leading case of the moment, *Catnic* v. *Hill & Smith*,[15] the House, speaking through Lord Diplock, shifted emphasis in the construction of patent claims. True, his speech first insists that interpretation is the sole issue, and that there is no separate question of "non-textual infringement." But equally he under-scores the importance of "purposive", rather than "purely literal" construction. He disapproves of "the kind of meticulous verbal analysis in which lawyers are too often tempted by their training to indulge" and prefers the understanding of "persons with practical knowledge and experience of the kind of work in which the invention was intended to be used." Would they read a particular descriptive word or phrase as making strict compliance an essential element, excluding any variant, even though it could have no material effect upon the way the invention worked?[16]

[10] Particularly where the claim was a subsidiary one, relating to something more specific than what had gone before: see Lord Radcliffe, at 78; Romer L.J., *Submarine Signal* v. *Hughes* (1932) 40 R.P.C. 149 at 175; Buckley L.J., *Catnic* v. *Hill & Smith* [1979] F.S.R. 619 at 633.

[11] Above, n. 15.

[12] And see below, n. 17.

[13] [1978] R.P.C. 153, esp. at 200, 202.

[14] The discovery of this fact in an appropriate case could give rise to a separate patent:*cf Beecham Group's Appln* [1977] F.S.R. 565.

[15] [1982] R.P.C. 183, see Pendleton [1982] E.I.P.R. 79; Walton [1984] E.I.P.R. 93.

[16] *Ibid.* at 242-243. For dislike of undue meticulousness, see also Lords Reid and Pearce, dissenting in *Rodi* case: above, n. 5, at 378, 388.

In applying this test it is accordingly necessary to decide whether there is a material difference between claimed invention and alleged infringement.[17] But a court would likely ignore an alteration which merely made the invention work less well. It is also necessary to show that the variant was an obvious one to the informed reader at the date of the patent's publication before the difference can be discounted. The "bio-precursor" in the *Beecham* case[18] may illustrate an obvious variation. Contrast the old case of *Heath* v. *Unwin*, where in making cast steel the patentee called for the addition of manganese carburet. The defendant did not infringe by adding manganese oxide and coal tar instead, even though it was afterwards discovered that they converted to manganese carburet during production. They were much cheaper to use and so constituted a significant variation.[19]

6-006   In subsequent decisions there has certainly been some tendency to treat differences from the claim as minor variants which, looking purposively, still infringe.[20] Where the result in individual cases is just has inevitably attracted differences of opinion. The spirit of the Article 69 Protocol, which favours at least some generosity towards the patentee in catching alternatives, appears to have been to an extent absorbed. But still, because the issue remains one of interpretation, the room for manoeuvre is undoubtedly proscribed. In *Van der Lely* v. *Bamfords*,[21] in order to bring the defendant's hay-rake within the claim, it would have been necessary to read the whole claim *mutatis mutandis*, "foremost" and "hindmost." To do so would not be interpretation but re-writing, and there is no indication yet that a British court would go so far, however much it might seem "fair" to the patentee; the Protocol, after all, also adjures a "reasonable degree of certainty for third parties."[22]

(3) Types of infringing activity

6-007   A defendant infringes only if he performs certain kinds of activity, normally industrial or commercial. These are now defined in the Patents Act 1977, section 60, which draws upon CPC, Articles 29-31, but does not always say the same thing.[23] The bulk of patents are concerned with things manufactured or processes of manufacture; accordingly the prohibited acts may usefully be considered under three heads: acts performed during manufacture, acts after and acts before. In all cases there are two qualifications to observe:

[17] For instances, where such differences led to a finding of non-infringement, *Deere* v. *Harrison McGregor* [1965] R.P.C. 461 (H.L.); *Rodi & Wienenberger* v. *Showell* (above, n. 5) particularly as regards the second allegation of infringement in the case.
[18] Above, n. 13.   [19] (1800) 2 W.P.C. 296.
[20] See esp. *Codex* v. *Racal-Milgo* [1983] R.P.C. 383 (C.A.); *Sociètè Nouvelle des Bennes Saphem* v. *Edbro* [1983] R.P.C. 345 (C.A.); *Dow Chemical* v. *Spence Bryson* [1984] R.P.C. 359 (C.A.); *Fairfax* v. *Filhol* [1986] R.P.C. 499 (C.A.); *Harrison* v. *Project & Design* [1987] R.P.C. 151 (C.A.)
[21] Above, n. 5.
[22] See also, Lord UpJohn, *Rodi* case (above, n. 5) at 391-392: "unlike a conveyance or commercial document . . . a patent is a grant of a monopoly forbidding others to enter part of the general commercial territory open to all of Her Majesty's subjects and so in the interests of those subjects that territory must be marked out with reasonable clarity by the claim, construing it fairly in the light of the relevant art."
[23] But remember the conformising injunction to conform contained in PA 1977, s.130(7), see, *e.g. Smith Kline & French* v. *Harbottle* (below, n. 38).

(i) A British patent is infringed only by acts done in the United Kingdom, its territorial waters and "designated" continental shelf.[24] A patentee who wishes to sue for acts done in (say) France must sue upon his French patent and he will normally bring his action in French courts. It is unlikely that an English court would entertain an action for infringement of the French patent.[25]

(ii) Nothing done with the patentee's consent is an infringement; the act is then licensed. Occasionally the question may arise whether the patentee in effect consents either by standing by inactive or by some positive mis-statement to the defendant: delay, acquiescence and estoppel have also been discussed already.[26]

(a) Infringement during manufacture

Making a patented product and using a patented process head the list **6-008** of infringing acts.[27] Most of the problems here concern the issue already discussed: is the defendant's activity within the terms of the claims (or some extension beyond them allowed by law)? A nice point, however, arises over repairs.[28] A person who obtains a patented product from a legitimate source may repair it or have it repaired; but he may not go so far as to make the product anew.[29]

The Act creates exceptions to the range of infringing acts: two of these are general, the rest particular. The general exceptions cover:

(i) acts done privately and for purposes which are not commercial.[30] Note the conjunctive "and": activities of governmental, educational and charitable organisations may not be commercial, but they are also not likely to be private.

(ii) acts done for experimental purposes relating to the subject-matter of the invention.[31] This covers investigations seeking to improve or modify the invention. It does not permit trials to see whether a

---

[24] The U.K. includes the Isle of Man but not the Channel Islands. For the designation of seabeds, important in an age of off-shore extractions, see the Continental Shelf Act 1964; cf. generally, Stauder (1976) 7 I.I.C. 470. There is now developing a need to provide for the patenting of inventions in space, e.g. on satellites: see Beier and Stauder, Space Stations (1985).

[25] Above, § 2-040.

[26] Above, §§ 2-037—2-039.

[27] PA 1977, s.60(1); CPC, Art. 29.

[28] Previously this was regarded as turning on the extent of the patentee's licence to use that was to be implied from unconditional sale. In future it may be better regarded as a limit upon the scope of the doctrine of exhaustion (see below, § 6-011); and consider also the doctrine of non-derogation from grant: see § 14-006.

[29] Solar Thomson v. Barton [1977] R.P.C. 537 (and note the corresponding difficulties over design copyright); Sirdar Rubber v. Wallington (1906) 22 R.P.C. 257 at 266, (1907) 24 R.P.C. 539 at 543. A person who supplies replacement parts for an infringing article may well be an indirect infringer: a person who merely carries such repairs out, although he helps to prolong its life, is less likely to be caught (but does he "keep" the invention—s.60(1)(a)?). cf. Aro Mfg. v. Convertible Top 377 U.S. 476 (1964).

[30] PA 1977, s.60(5)(a); CPC Art. 31(a).

[31] PA 1977, s.60(5)(b); CPC Art. 31(b). Likewise the previous law distinguished between experiments on the invention and using the invention in other experiments: see, e.g. Frearson v. Loe (1878) 9 Ch.D. 48 at 66; Strachan v. Pakcel (1949) 66 R.P.C. 49; Cave-Brown-Cave's Application [1958] R.P.C. 429.

person can produce commercially according to the patent, this includes the conduct of field trials on a weed killer in order to secure government authority for marketing.[32] Nor is it justifiable to use the invention for experiments on unrelated subject-matter.[33]

(b) Infringement after manufacture: general provisions

6-009   The list of infringing acts also covers: disposing of, offering to dispose of, using, importing, and even keeping for disposal or otherwise, either the patented product or a product "obtained directly by means of a patented process."[34] The range of defendants made possible by this extensive list is considerable. Where infringing goods pass down a chain of distributors each person becomes liable: as a "keeper," then as a "disposer." Even the ultimate recipient may be a "keeper," if he is not a "user."[35] A person who acquires or imports goods for the purpose of exporting them to sell abroad will thus infringe, as he did under the previous law.[36] Both sides to a simple hiring agreement will in turn be "keepers."[37] But a mere carrier has not been treated as a keeper.[38]

Again, in addition to the licensing by the patentee of "acts," there are exceptions. For instance, the exclusion from infringement of private, non-commercial acts and experimental acts[39] apply in this post-manufacture phase, but only to protect those who perform the specified acts. The exceptions do not give cover for subsequent "acts" that would otherwise infringe: if infringing apparatus is sold once in a purely private sale, this does not justify its resale in a business deal.[40]

6-010   Where the chain of distribution originates abroad, a person who completes a sale by transferring property in the products in another country does not infringe (because of the restriction to acts done in the United Kingdom),[41] but the subsequent importer will. Even if the foreign exporter at some stage writes to the British purchaser about an order, he

---

[32] Monsanto v. Stauffer [1985] R.P.C. 515 (C.A.); Similarly in New Zealand, [1984] F.S.R. 559; and for further proceedings in England, [1985] F.S.R. 55; Sheppard [1987] E.I.P.R. 116.

[33] Amongst the particular exceptions, the one relating to manufacture covers "extemporaneous" preparations by pharmacists from prescriptions: s.60(5)(c); cf. CPC Art. 31(c).

[34] PA 1977, s.60(1); note that there are a number of trying variations here from the language of CPC Art. 29: for instance, the former uses "disposes of," etc., in place of "puts on the market" and see the following footnotes. When Community patents are eventually introduced, their precise scope may differ somewhat from U.K. patents.

[35] In contrast with (i) the previous law (see, e.g. British United Shoe v. Collier) (1910) 27 R.P.C. 567; and (ii) CPC Art. 29—to which the old authorities on "use" seem relevant (see Blanco White (1974), § 3-204).

[36] Here the different language of s.60 and Art. 29 seems to lead to the same result. And see Hoffmann-La Roche v. Harris [1977] F.S.R. 200; British Motor v. Taylor (1900) 17 R.P.C. 723.

[37] Under the CPC, hiring out is covered, if at all, by "putting on the market." This phrase is also used in the CPC's definition of exhaustion of rights: see Arts. 32, 81. It is a common assumption that if something is hired out a patentee can continue to control its use: but that may be open to question, once this version of exhaustion takes effect. See below, § 6-011.

[38] Smith, Kline & French v. Harbottle [1980] R.P.C. 363; Howe (1979) 1 E.I.P.R. 287.

[39] Above, § 6-008.

[40] For special exceptions covering uses connected with land, sea and air craft, see PA 1977, s.60(5)(d)-(f), CPC Art.31(d)-(f); Ency. PL, §§ 4-310.

[41] Above, § 6-002.

will not thereby be offering to dispose.[42] However, if he positively solicits orders from British customers, he is likely to be infringing on this ground, or as a joint tortfeasor or as one who procures infringement.[43] It is in such cases that infringement of a process patent by dealing in its *direct* product becomes specially important. The commercial value of a process patent can obviously be impaired if the process can be carried out abroad (where there may be no patent) and the product sold in competition in Britain.[44] In the pre-1977 law, English courts had gone some distance in holding a claim to a process to be infringed by the importation of the subsequent product, requiring not that the product be the immediate result of the process (for there might be intermediate steps)[45] but only that the contribution of the process to the final product be important (the "Saccharin" doctrine).[46] One of the successful arguments establishing infringement in *Beecham Group* v. *Bristol Laboratories*[47] arose upon claims to processes for making ampicillin from the organic acid, 6-APA. The defendants used one of these processes to make ampicillin in the United States, then subjected it there to a further chemical reaction and imported the resulting drug—chemically a different substance—into Britain. Under the new Act, it is very doubtful that this would still amount to an infringement of those claims. The further reaction that intervened between conducting the patented process and importing the final product would seem to make the chain of causation an indirect one.

(c) *After manufacture: exhaustion of rights*
Patents used to be the field of intellectual property where most **6-011** evidently no notion of exhaustion of rights applied. As noted already, even when the patentee made or authorised a sale of patented goods, restrictions of their further sale or use could still be imposed as part of the patent right: these would bind not only another contracting party but all recipients of the goods will notice of the restrictions[48] Where the British patentee himself markets patented goods abroad he will be able to prevent their import into Britain only if he attached a clear and express embargo.[49] Where however the sale abroad is by a licensee under the

---

[42] *Kalman* v. *P.C.L. Packaging* [1982] F.S.R. 406, applying to the new Act, *Badische Anilin* v. *Johnson* (1987) 14 R.P.C. 919. Not all West European countries take so restrictive a view: the issue may have to be reconsidered.
[43] See above, § 2-007.
[44] It is possible, of course to take the strict view of the Banks Committee (Cmnd. 4407, § 297) that if a patentee wants appropriate cover he must secure a product-by-process claim; which is all very well if he knows all the relevant products when he applies for his patent. This approach has not been adopted in the 1977 Act.
[45] *Saccharin Corp.* v. *Anglo-Continental Chemical* (1900) 17 R.P.C. 307; extending *Elmslie* v. *Boursier* (1869) L.R. 9 Eq. 217; *Von Heyden* v. *Neustadt* (1880) 14 Ch.D. 230 (C.A.).
[46] Tomlin J., *Wilderman* v. *Berk* (1925) 42 R.P.C. 79, 86, as explained in *Beecham Group* v. *Bristol Laboratories* [1978] R.P.C. 153 at 201, 203, 204.
[47] Above, n. 46.
[48] A *fortiori*, where the claim is to an intermediate "indirect" product, as distinct from an intermediate process. Even in the *Beecham* case, the House of Lords were doubtful about the former: above, n. 46 at 200-204. Any subsequent taker who knows that conditions exist will be bound: *Dunlop* v. *Longlife* [1958] R.P.C. 473; and see *Goodyear* v. *Lancashire Batteries* (1958) L.R. 1 R.P. 22 at 35 (C.A.).
[49] *Betts* v. *Willmott* (1871) L.R. 6 Ch. 239.

foreign patent, the goods cannot enter Britain unless there is a licence (express or implied) from the British patentee.[50]

This principle, which began to be modified by legislation such as the Resale Prices Act 1964, is now in the process of virtual annihilation. Two stages are involved:

(i) *Limitation by the Treaty of Rome.* Until the CPC takes effect, the former British principle would appear to continue in operation. But as well as the qualifications upon it in British legislation, it has been affected since 1973 by the twin doctrines of the Treaty of Rome: the free movement of goods and the rules of competition. Thus in 1972 it was held that where patented drugs were sold on condition that they were not be be exported from the United Kingdom, a sub-purchaser who knew of the restriction could be enjoined from infringing by exporting.[51] So far as such a condition applied to exporting to other Common Market countries, it would now be bad; the same would be true of a condition that the goods could be exported only to part of the Common Market. Each of these constraints inhibits the free movement of goods within the Community.[52] But the old British principle might still uphold restrictions preventing exports to non-EEC countries, or the condition attached to a sale in a non-EEC country that goods are not to be imported into the United Kingdom. To these the free movement of goods policy has no application[53] and the question is whether any aspect of the Community's competition rules is offended.

(ii) *Operation of the CPC.* Once the CPC is put into effect, it will introduce a specific doctrine of exhaustion affecting both Community and national patents within the EEC.[54] This provides that once patented goods have been put on the market in any part of the EEC by the patentee or with his express consent,[55] the rights conferred by the patent or other national patents within the EEC can no longer extend to them, unless Community law admits some special exception. If the ownership of national patents for the same invention has been divided up among patentees economically associated, so that a different legal person must license the initial sale in the different countries, the rights will still be treated as exhausted.[56] These specific provisions are still subject to the Treaty of Rome, and should that Treaty be held to embody severer rules, the CPC could not have the effect of limiting them.

[50] *S.A. des Glaces* v. *Tilghmann* (1883) 25 Ch.D. 1 (C.A.); *Beecham* v. *International Products* [1968] R.P.C. 129; *Minnesota Mining* v. *Geerpres* [1973] F.S.R. 113; above, § 6-010.
[51] *Sterling Drug* v. *Beck* [1973] R.P.C. 915.
[52] Accordingly they would constitute a measure equivalent to a quantitative restriction on imports (Treaty of Rome, Art. 30) which, as a "mere exercise" of industrial property rights operating as a disguised restriction upon intra-Community trade, could not be absolved by Art. 36: see §§ 1-024, 7-041 *et seq.*
[53] See *EMI* v. *CBS* above, § 1-026.
[54] CPC Arts. 32, 81; with specific exception for the case where the goods are first marketed by a compulsory licensee (including in Britain someone within the Crown use exemption): Arts. 46(1), 81(3). PA 1977, s.60(4) makes this the rule that will govern U.K. patents.
[55] For the significance of "express" consent, see below, § 7-043.
[56] Art. 81(2); see further, below, § 7-045.

Because these principles of Community law, present and predicted, directly affect the scope of patent infringement they are mentioned here in brief. But they need to be seen in broader context. This has been introduced in general already and its impact on patent deployment and licensing is dealt with in the next Chapter. **6-012**

We should note that the scope of "exhausted" rights is not free from doubt. Suppose X has a patent claiming (i) chemical Y and (ii) the use of Y in process Z. If X or a licensee sells Y, X ought arguably to be able to control the use of Y in process Z: but, if the two claims are in the same patent, a literal reading of the exhaustion rule suggests that he cannot.[57]

(d) Before manufacture: "indirect" infringement

The former law showed great reluctance to treat as a "contributory infringer" someone who assisted in preparations for acts within the claims, but did not himself perform the acts. Only if the "assister" ordered the full performance,[58] or participated in a conspiracy or common design to secure performance,[59] or knowingly induced another person to perform,[60] would any liability in tort be imposed. In other cases, the courts' caution obliged the patentee to proceed against the actual performer[61]; for one thing he might well deny infringement, claim that the patent was invalid, or claim a licence or Crown authority. The approach had some attraction, particularly where the patentee was attacking a small "assister" who supplied to a larger "performer."[62] But in the contrary case of a large "assister" supplying materials towards infringement by small "performers," the patentee could be placed in considerable difficulty. **6-013**

Following other patent systems and the CPC, the 1977 Act has introduced general principles of contributory infringement.[63] It has become infringement, first, to offer a process for use, knowing that the user will have no licence from the patentee and that the use will be an infringement.[64] Both offer and use must be in the United Kingdom; and the offeror's knowledge is judged objectively, taking account of what is "obvious to a reasonable person in the circumstances."

[57] Perhaps "Community law" would admit an exception for this case: see Arts. 32, 81. It ought to do so, unless the arrangement is part of some larger anti-competitive agreement.
[58] Sykes v. Howarth (1879) 12 Ch.D. 826.
[59] Morton-Norwich v. Intercen [1976] F.S.R. 513.
[60] Innes v. Short (1898) 15 R.P.C. 449; Belegging v. Witten [1979] F.S.R. 59 at 66-67 (C.A.); and see generally above, § 2-005 et seq.
[61] Dunlop v. Moseley (1904) 21 R.P.C. 274 (C.A.).
[62] A good illustration is provided by Slater Steel v. Payer (1968) 55 C.P.R. 61 (Ex.Ct., Canada).
[63] The expression, "indirect infringement," is used in the CPC Art. 30, and there only to describe the second of the instances here described.
[64] A paraphrase of PA 1977, s.60(1)(b); cf. CPC, Art. 29(b). Neither are happily drafted. The offeror must know (objectively) that use of the patent without the proprietor's consent would be infringement; which may excuse the offeror (i) who could not have known of the patent; or (ii) who could not have known that the process would be used in an infringing way; or (iii) who could not have known that the user did not have the licensee's consent or other authority. The last does not easily fit the language used, but would probably be read in. It is not within this provision to direct use in a non-infringing way when it would not be obvious to use the process in an infringing way: Fürr v. C.J. Truline [1985] F.S.R. 553; see also Kalman v. PCL Packaging [1982] F.S.R. 406.

6-014   Secondly, it has become "indirect" infringement to supply (or to offer to supply) "means relating to an essential element of the invention, for putting the invention into effect" to someone not licensed or authorised to work it, knowing that the "means" are suitable for putting and are intended to put it into effect.[65] Again the supplier is treated as knowing what is obvious to a reasonable person in the circumstances.[66] If, however, the means are a staple commercial product, there is no infringement unless the supply is for the purpose of inducing the person supplied to infringe "directly."[67] In these cases the place of supply and the place where it is intended to carry out the invention must be in the United Kingdom. This excludes from "indirect" infringement the foreign supplier of materials or parts which are brought into Britain by the "direct" infringer; and also the British manufacturer who makes up kits of the parts needed for completing manufacture or operating a process abroad.[68] Arguably, in the latter case, a doctrine of indirect infringement ought to cover such an obvious way of assisting towards infringement that is so essentially connected with production in the United Kingdom.[69] But to treat it as a common law tort, such as comspiracy or inducement,[70] would be to subvert an apparent limitation in section 60(2) and CPC Article 30(1).

The former British approach made it important to secure claims, where possible, to parts of mechanical combinations, to intermediates in chemical production, and to the substances that would be applied in methods and processes. There are marks of this upon the inherited law of novelty, obviousness and patentable subject-matter.[71] Under the new law focus shifts to the question, have the conditions for "indirect" infringement been fulfilled? Whether material or apparatus is a "staple commercial product" is likely to depend on whether there exists at least one alternative way in which the product as sold could ordinarily be used. Far-fetched or purely experimental alternatives will doubtless be discounted.[72] On the question of whether a supplier ought to have known that "means" would be put to an infringing use, consider the case where a client orders a particular part to be made up from his specifications. The maker may well not be in a position to know how the part will be

---

[65] PA 1977, s.60(2), CPC Art. 30(1). See *Kalman* v. *PCL Packaging* [1982] F.S.R. 406. One person does not escape being an "indirect" infringer by supplying to another who acts within the exceptions for private use, experiment or pharmaceutical preparation: s.60(6).

[66] Presumably the reasonable person (who is mentioned specifically only in the PA text) is someone in the supplier's position: see Ency.PL, § 4-204.

[67] PA 1977, s.60(3), CPC Art. 30(2). Where the enterprise supplied knows, or must be taken to know the patent position and makes its decision to act as it does independently of anything that the supplier does (as, *e.g.* in the *Slater* case, above, n. 62), there would be neither inducement nor conspiracy.

[68] In *Deepsouth Packing* v. *Laitram* 406 U.S. 518 (1972), the U.S. Supreme Court refused to hold such conduct contributory infringement.

[69] *cf.* Stauder (1972) 4 I.I.C. 491; Kerr (1974) 26 Standford L.R. 893, [1974] Patent L.R. 81.

[70] See above, § 2-006.

[71] For instance in the importance attaching to article claims, as distinct from method-of-use claims (above, §§ 4-035 *et seq.*, and in the attempts to secure "pack" claims (above, § 5-053).

[72] U.S. patent law contains a similar distinction (Patents Act s.271(c) and much case law to this effect: see Chisum, *Patents* (1978) IV § 17.03[3]. Thus if the alternative use calls for sale in much larger quantities than the defendant is putting on the market, his commodity will not be treated as staple: *Johnson* v. *Gore* 195 U.S.P.Q. 487 (1977).

used. It is presumably his (objective) state of mind that is relevant, not that of his client.[73]

(e) *New medical applications*

A substance may be claimed for its first known medical use and a **6-015** composition including it may be claimed for subsequently discovered medical uses.[74] If the claim covers the substance or composition "for" its medical use then only those who administer it or who make or market it for its medical purpose would infringe. If a claim has been allowed to the substance *puro*, proof of the earlier knowledge ought either, for once,[75] to cut down the claim's scope so as to confine it to use in or towards the medical purpose, or amendment by the addition of a "for" phrase ought to be required. If claims are in this instance to be read as limited by the discovered use, why not in other cases? Should claims to entirely new things also be read as limited by the useful application described for them in the specification? This would be one solution to the nagging problem posed by *Mullard* v. *Philco*.[76]

(4) Prior use and commencement of infringement

If a person uses an invention in a way that makes it public before the **6-016** priority date of a patent for it, his anticipation will render the patent invalid. As well as this, he has a defence against infringement, should he continue to use the invention after the patentee's rights take effect.[77] This defence is also open to people who have not provided material for attacking the patent's validity—prior users whose activities have not made the invention available to the public,[78] and those who have in good faith made effective and serious preparations to use the invention (or to do some other act in the list of infringements).[79] The defence, however, is limited: the act done or prepared for before the priority date may be continued[80] or done afterwards by the person concerned, a partner of his or an assignee of the relevant business,[81] but not by a "licensee.[82] Nor is

[73] s.60(2) leaves the matter uncertain; *cf.* above, n. 66.					[74] Above, § 5-068.
[75] Whether suppliers would be direct or indirect infringers is unclear, and could be important: for if "indirect" and the product is a "staple," the limitations in s.60(3) will apply.
[76] It has never been suggested in English courts that the doctrine of equivalents could be used to cut down the apparent scope of claims: *cf. Graver* v. *Linde*, 339 U.S. 605 at 608-609 (1950).
[77] See above, §§5-006, 5-007. PA 1977, s.64 as substituted by CPDA 1988, Sched. 5, § 17; the CPC Art. 38 follows whatever national law allows for national patents: see Østerborg (1981) 12 I.I.C. 447.
[78] Formerly, if their use was "secret," in certain circumstances this formed a ground for attacking validity. But now the principle is that an anticipation must be published rather than merely used: see above, §§ 5-006, 5-007.
[79] Previously such people went unprotected (*cf.* Walton and Laddie).
[80] If a prior user has been using a production process consisting of a series of repetitions, there is a question whether these can all count as continuance of the act. It would be extraordinary if they did not. Those who have only prepared to do the act are given the right to do it, not restricted explicitly to one occasion. Yet they could scarcely be put in a position of greater privilege without the most unambiguous direction from Parliament. The difficulty is more acute in the transitional provision, Sched. 4, § 3(3), and (curiously) is avoided in the provision on the restoration of lapsed patents: s.28(5).
[81] s.64(2).Articles thus produced may be dealt with as if disposed of by the patentee: s.64(3).
[82] *i.e.* anyone to whom the prior user attempts to transfer or license his freedom to continue doing the act, without assigning the business.

there any entitlement to perform variants of the prior "act," such as might arise from improvements to the invention.

The earliest point in time at which infringement can occur is the date of publishing the application—normally some 18 months from the priority date. But proceedings for the period between then and the grant can only be brought after grant; and the defendant's act must infringe not only the claims finally included but those in the published application.[83] There is the difficulty, however, that the claims of the early publication may be clearly objectionable. A potential infringer may have no idea whether the application will ever pass examination so as to leave claims that he will infringe. If it would not have been reasonable to expect this outcome, the court or comptroller is given a discretion to reduce damages.[84]

In the period between priority date and publication of a patent application it is possible for another person to start his preparations and production of something in the claims. Not only will his production after publication be actionable; but articles which he has made before this date will infringe if sold, used or kept by himself or another person after the date. In these circumstances, a seller will then be in breach of his contractual warranty either that he has the right to sell or that his buyer will enjoy quiet possession.[85] These rules constitute a fortuitous hazard which scarcely seems necessary to the patent system.

(5) Proceedings concerning the infringement and validity of patents[86]

6-017　　Proceedings for infringement, revocation and such associated matters as relief from threats to sue for infringement and declarations of non-infringement,[87] are brought either in the Patents Court[88] or, in certain cases, before the Comptroller (with appeal first to the Patents Court).[89] Arrangements have now also been enacted for the creation of a patents jurisdiction in county courts, but they are not yet operative.[90] The Comptroller's jurisdiction in revocation proceedings is now co-terminous

---

[83] PA 1977, s.69(1), (2).

[84] PA 1977, s.69(3). This is somewhat more precise than an alternative allowed by EPC Art. 67(2) under which compensation reasonable in the circumstances may be provided for in national legislation.

[85] *Microbeads* v. *Vinhurst Road Markings* [1976] R.P.C. 19 (C.A.). The warranty now arises under s.12, Sale of Goods Act 1979, which allows for the undertaking to be given in conditional form. Apart from this, liability cannot be excluded: Unfair Contract Terms Act 1977, s.6(1).

[86] For a comparison (Germany, France, Italy, England): Stauder (1983) 14 I.I.C. 793.

[87] For these, see above, §§ 2-043—2-045.

[88] Created as a part of the Chancery Division of the High Court by PA 1977, s.96; for Scottish equivalents see ss.98, 97(4), (5). The Patents Court consists of one or both of the patents judges (ss.96(2), 97(2)) and there is power to appoint scientific advisers (s.96(4); R.S.C. 104 r. 11). In the past this was not used: but the Court of Appeal has done so under equivalent powers.

[89] PA 1977, s.97(1); further appeal only lies in certain cases to the Court of Appeal: s.97(3).

[90] CDPA 1988, ss.288-291; rules detailing the procedure are still awaited. The chief incentive to take small cases to the county court will be in costs: see s.290. This new departure is the product of concern over the high cost of patent litigation and also of a campaign to make the Comptroller's jurisdiction open as of right to some plaintiffs. See Intellectual Property Rights and Innovation (Cmnd. 9117, 1983); Report of the Oulton Committee on Patent Litigation (1987); Gladwell [1989] E.I.P.R. 128.

with that of the court.[91] This marks a considerable extension of his powers. Formerly he could entertain a belated opposition to the grant of the patent only on limited grounds, provided that it was commenced within twelve months of grant.[92] But the nature of the proceedings has not changed, the Comptroller's decision is still normally upon documentary evidence, with lower scales of fees.[93] Attackers who want an exhaustive investigation of the merits, with oral examination of witnesses, should still bring proceedings in court.[94] Questions of infringement can be referred to the Comptroller only by the agreement of both parties[95]; but his power to grant declarations of non-infringement is not conditioned in this way.[96]

We have already noted some general techniques that exist in intellectual property actions to preserve or elicit evidence of what the defendant has been doing. When, however, the patent is for a process, and the alleged infringements are imported, there may be no means of discovering or inspecting how they are made. In such a case it may be that a court will find against a defendant who will not or cannot explain, upon proof of a bare prima facie case of infringement.[97] There is also a statutory presumption that a new product is made by an infringing process.[98] But "new product" can only mean one not previously known for novelty purposes; and in such cases, product claims are allowed. So the provision appears to cope with a spectral difficulty. **6-018**

In proceedings for infringement, the validity of the patent can be put in issue.[99] This may be done purely as a matter of defence, or by way of a counterclaim for revocation: the former will save expense, the latter is more final.[1] There are cases when the two questions are closely related: as where the defendant alleges that what he is doing is anticipated or obvious.[2] And more generally there is a feeling that a broadly just outcome can be reached only if what the plaintiff has tried to annex is set against how the defendant has acted, whether with the patent in mind or in ignorance of it.

But this traditional approach is now controversial. Two EEC countries—West Germany and the Netherlands, each with strong examining offices—require validity to be raised before specialist tribunals, while **6-019**

---

[91] PA 1977, s.72. The Comptroller also has certain powers to revoke upon his own initiative: see above, § 5-012, n. 42.
[92] See PA 1949, s.33. The Banks Committee recommended that the Comptroller be given wider jurisdiction: Cmnd. 4407, 1970, §§ 181-188.
[93] i.e. lower fees for both initial proceedings and any appeal to the Patents Court.
[94] The difference is marked by the rule that the Comptroller's decision creates no issue estoppel against subsequent court proceedings: s.72(5), but note (6).
[95] s.61(3)-(6). He has no jurisdiction over threats.
[96] In each case, invalidity may be raised as a defence: s.74(1). If revocation is sought under s.72, the proceedings would be heard at the same time. See also above, § 4-022.
[97] See above, § 2-035.
[98] PA 1977, s.100; there is a saving clause protecting defendants against "unreasonable" disclosure of secrets.
[99] Likewise both issues may be raised in actions for threats and for declarations of non-infringement; and invalidity may also be raised in disputes about Crown use: see PA 1977, s.74.
[1] Even if there is no counterclaim the court probably has power to order revocation in the public interest: Whitford J., Norprint v. SPJ Labels [1979] F.S.R. 126.
[2] See above, § 4-030.

leaving infringement to ordinary civil courts.[3] For Community patents, the draft CPC originally adopted this division of functions; there was a fear that non-expert tribunals in some countries would not handle revocation questions satisfactorily. But in the light of British objections, the revised version of the Convention will allow the practice to continue without limit of time.[4]

The length, complexity and cost of patent infringement actions have long been notorious. One consequence has been the introduction of special procedures for the protection of potential defendants—the action for a declaration of non-infringement and the action against threats, which were dealt with in Chapter 2.[5] Other aspects of procedure and remedies affecting patent suits are dealt with there, and the reader is reminded particularly of the guidelines that are used to assess damages and the problems of apportionment that may arise where the infringement contributes to the making of a loss or profit for which damages are being awarded or an account taken.[6]

6-020   The one issue that deserves special comment at this stage is the availibility of interlocutory injunctions in patent infringement suits. Because of the grave implications of deciding to carry an action to its full term, much of the real effectiveness of a patent may turn on whether the court will intervene at this early stage. Before *American Cyanamid* v. *Ethicon*,[7] the patentee could rarely hope to succeed. He had to make out a prima facie case and against this the defendant could usually set up a sufficient barrier by averring the invalidity of the patent, particularly on the ground of obviousness. On such an issue it is intrinsically hazardous to form a preliminary view. Accordingly, success was reserved to patents for exceptionally significant or widely acknowledged inventions.[8]

6-021   The *Ethicon* case, however, has transferred emphasis to the balance of convenience.[9] This means that the substantive dispute between the parties is demoted and prime weight is given to their relative commercial positions, with particular stress on the use that each is making, or is intending to make, of the invention covered (actually or allegedly) by the patent. Either party will boost his case, for instance, by showing that this is most or all of his business.[10] A patentee will make ground out of showing that he is struggling to secure a market position for the

---

[3] For the German position, see Pakuscher (1979) 10 I.I.C. 671.

[4] See CPC Arts. 56-63, 68-73, 78, 90.

[5] See above, §§ 2-043—2-044. Note also PA 1977, s.61(1)(2).

[6] Above, §§ 2-024—2-026.

[7] [1975] A.C. 396; (1975) R.P.C. 513 (H.L.) For the new approach to the granting of interlocutory relief established by this case and for its application to intellectual property cases in general: above, §§ 2-018—2-021.

[8] See Blanco White (1974) § 12-113.

[9] The plaintiff's need first to show a serious case to be tried can usually be satisfied in a patent infringement action: questions of law might, however, be decided under this rubric; *cf.* above, § 2-019; Cole [1979] E.I.P.R. 71.

[10] *e.g. Netlon* v. *Bridport-Gundry* (C.A.) [1979] F.S.R. 530; *Potters-Ballotini* v. *Weston-Baker* [1977] R.P.C. 202 (C.A., breach of confidence). The counter-argument that the defendant started knowing that he was likely to be sued may weight against him: *Belfast Ropework* v. *Pixdane* [1976] F.S.R. 338 (C.A.). But the argument that, even if a defendant is enjoined, he will be able to open up other lines of business has been discounted: *Condor* v. *Hibbing* (1978) [1984] F.S.R. 312 (C.A.).

invention and would be impeded by the defendant's direct competition.[11] A defendant will fall back if he has not yet started manufacturing and has not expended much in preparations for doing so,[12] or if he only imports and so has not committed capital to production plant.[13]

A defendant in a small way, moreover, may have difficulty in showing his ability to pay any damages ultimately awarded.[14] One line of argument that may well be to a defendant's advantage, however, is that, if he is allowed to continue, his sales will normally form a reasonable basis for assessing competitive losses to the plaintiff,[15] whereas if he is stopped, what he might have made will remain speculative.[16] There are, of course, many other such considerations which may affect the outcome of particular cases.[17]

The danger of the *Ethicon* approach is that a particular patent's value comes to depend too much on commercial position.[18] Statistically at least, the chance of securing interlocutory relief has undoubtedly improved under the new principles. This is likely to foster the general impression that patents in Britain have become more damaging weapons in competitive industry than was previously the case.

2. THE SPECIFICATION IN LIGHT OF THE LEGAL REQUIREMENTS

Patent specifications are drawn to deal with conflicts. Even where they 6-022 form the basis for licensing, their real significance arises only when the collaboration begins to turn sour. A specification must strive to provide protection against those looking for ways of side-stepping it; at the same time, it must not break any of the validity rules. The basic principles, which we have now looked at in some detail, interact in a complex manner. We have reached the point where it is useful to summarise some crucial points in these interrelations.

[11] cf. *Catnic* v. *Stressline* (above, § 2-021, n. 17. If a patent is nearing the end of its life, the Court of Appeal has been reluctant to refuse an injunction where to do so would provide the defendant with a bridgehead against both the patentee and other competitors: *Corruplast* v. *Harrison* [1978] R.P.C. 761 at 766.

[12] *Hepworth Plastics* v. *Naylor* (C.A.) (see Cole, above n. 9 at 13).

[13] *Belfast Ropework* case (above, n. 10).

[14] e.g. *Belfast Ropework* case (above, n. 10), where even a bank guarantee of £15,000 was not enough to satisfy the Court of Appeal.

[15] Refusal of an injunction may "snowball" by inducing other competitors to follow the defendant; but the Court of Appeal has been reluctant to take this into account: *Condor* v. *Hibbing* (above, n. 10).

[16] *Polaroid* v. *Eastman Kodak* [1977] R.P.C. 379 (C.A.), *Brupat* v. *Sandor Marine* [1983] R.P.C. 61 (C.A.); cf. *SKM* v. *Spraytech* [1982] R.P.C. 497.

[17] Particular difficulties arise with important patented pharmaceuticals. The patentee may argue that doctors and patients may be seriously put out by learning to use the defendant's product only to see it removed from the market after the trial: *American Cyanamid* v. *Ethicon* [1975] R.P.C. at 513. But if there is some difference between the plaintiff's and defendant's products the latter may argue that the public should not be deprived of his version, particularly if it could be life-saving: *Roussel-Uclaf* v. *Searle* [1977] F.S.R. 125.

[18] See Cole, above, n. 9.

(a) *The description*

6-023   There are a variety of pressures upon the draftsman to include in his description of the invention a fair amount of detail, going beyond the minimum that may satisfy the requirement of a complete and clear disclosure:

  (i) There is the danger that if particular versions of the invention are not mentioned, room may be left for a competitor to secure an improvement or selection patent at the very point where thepatentee wants himself to operate; whereas specific description will put paid to this possibility from the moment that the application is filed, provided that the application (or one claiming priority from it) is later published.[19]

 (ii) There is the need (at least before the patent office) to show support in the description for the claims, particularly the broadest.[20]

(iii) A case must be developed to support the present of an inventive step; where the subject-matter is an improvement over known art, rather than a breakthrough with a mechanical principle, chemical substance, or new micro-organism, this means spelling out the advantage that gives inventive character.[21]

 (iv) The limitations upon amendment condition the possibility of introducing changes during prosecution of the application[22]; the governing rule that there must be no new disclosure over the contents of the specification originally filed makes it crucial to start with all that may later be needed. It is important to put enough into any "informal" application to ground priority round the world.[23]

(b) *The claims*

6-024   The aim is to cover all imaginable alternatives, while avoiding the inclusion of things that are anticipated or obvious. In the United Kingdom in the past, this has meant that if, for instance, the inventor has found a way of making a material that is then used in a production process, it has been desirable to include claims for making the material, the material itself, and its use in the subsequent process. To some extent, the introduction of "indirect" infringement[24] has reduced the importance of doing this. But it is plainer to cover the matter directly. At the other end, the rule that a process claim covers only its direct products[25] is stricter than the former British approach; so where, for instance, a series of chemical syntheses are involved, it is important to cover those at the end as well as those at the beginning.

[19] See above, § 5-012.
[20] See above, §§ 5-067, 5-068.
[21] In the case of a selection, advantage is also necessary to disclose what makes the invention novel; see above, § 5-012.
[22] See above, §§ 4-024—4-026.
[23] See above, §§ 4-008—4-010.
[24] See above, §§ 6-013, 6-014.
[25] See above, § 6-009.

(c) *Pitfalls of saying too much*

So much for the pressures to be as complete as possible: now consider   6-025
the dangers inherent in this course.

A would-be patentee may endanger his own chances by any sort of
publicity: we have already noted the severity of the new European
concordat in the matter of "periods of grace."[26] Equally there are dangers
that one of his specifications will prejudice others that come later,
whether they are attempts to cope more successfully with what is
essentially the same invention or they deal with some distinct improvement. It is worth drawing together the points at which earlier applications tell against later:

  (i) The arrangements for according priority are limited by the require-
       ment that the later application or applications be made within 12
       months of the first application to disclose the invention. The only
       exception discounts earliest applications that are totally abnegated
       without having been published.[27]

 (ii) If an application is made for patent protection in the United
       Kingdom (to either the British Office or the EPO) and the
       application reaches the stage of being published, its content is
       treated for novelty purposes as forming part of the art from the
       priority date claimed. So before applicant allows this publication
       to take place, he must consider whether he is prejudicing any of
       his own later applications, not claiming the same priority, which
       attempt to patent any invention disclosed in the published form of
       the application. Gone is the confinement of this issue to a question
       of prior claiming. But it does not, for this interim period, matter
       that the later invention is obvious in the light of the earlier.

(iii) Once an application is published,[28] like any other publication it
       joins the state of the art for all purposes. Improvements that are
       obvious in the light of its revelation cannot be patented. No longer
       is there the old patent of addition, which allowed the engrafting of
       improvements even though they marked no inventive step over the
       main patent.

All in all the patent system calls for acute awareness of the hazards
and the highest attention to getting the whole thing right from the outset.
More than ever, it is a game that only the highly professional can hope
to play with much success.

---

[26] Above, § 5-013.
[27] Above, § 4-009, n. 48.
[28] As to this, see Burnside (1980) 9 CIPA 266.

CHAPTER 7

PROPERTY RIGHTS AND EXPLOITATION

7-001   This Chapter draws together a number of themes concerned with the ownership of patent rights and the exploitation of those rights through consensual dealings. The question of initial entitlement to a patent arises from the making of the invention onwards. It may be important before any application is made, during the application and after grant. The person or persons thus entitled may deal with their rights, disposing of them by assignment or permitting others to act within the scope of the monopoly by giving them a licence to do so. These two aspects of property rights in patents are considered in the first part of this Chapter. The second part deals more specifically with the content of patent and allied licences and takes account of the competition law criteria which they must now meet, particularly the requirements of EEC law. The third part is closely related to this, since it deals with the application of Community law to the importation of patented products. The last two parts move on to other public policy considerations—the provisions seeking to correct under-exploitation by allowing for the grant of compulsory licences; and the provisions which allow for Crown use upon payment of compensation.

1. INITIAL ENTITLEMENT AND PROPERTY DEALINGS

(1) The right to grant: general
7-002   In contrast with the former law, the 1977 Act allows anyone to apply for a patent but restricts those to whom a patent may be granted.[1] At the moment of invention, section 7(2) confers the right to be granted a patent upon one of three categories of persons: (i) the inventor or co-inventors;[2] or (ii) the employer of the inventor when the invention is

---

[1] s.7(1), following EPC Arts. 58, 60(1); PA 1949, s.1, by contrast, defined the classes of persons entitled to apply.
[2] "Inventor" means actual deviser: PA 1977, s.7(3); see above, § 4-005. A person who contributed one of two main ideas in an invention is a co-inventor: *Norris' Patent* [1988] R.P.C. 159; likewise one who contributed an idea thought by the collaborators to be essential, without regard to whether it was known or obvious: *Viziball's Appln.* [1988] R.P.C. 213; and see Lloyd (1979) 8 CIPA 11.

made during employment[3]; or (iii) where foreign law[4] applies by virtue of private international law rules,[5] the person entitled by that law.[6] Whoever is given this initial entitlement to the patent can assign it; or it may devolve upon a successor because of death, bankruptcy and the like. An assignee or successor is then entitled to the grant in place of his predecessor.

(2) The right to grant: employees[7]

(a) *Common law rules*

In capitalist societies it is an assumption by now largely unremarked **7-003** that the products of labour belong to the owner of the business. Even so, it took some time for the first industrial countries to apply this assumption to intellectual property rights without some measure of reserve. In England it was left to Lord Simonds, in the age of corporate capitalism, to declare that "it is an implied term in the contract of service of any workman that what he produces by the strength of his arm or the skill of his hand or the exercise of his inventive faculty shall become the property of his employer."[8] Before that emphasis tended to be placed on the need to show either a positive contract in the employer's favour or an implied duty of trust.[9] Indeed, it was said that the invention might be the employee's even though made in the employer's time and with his materials.[10] The tendency to increase the presumption in favour of his employer probably grew as cases arose in which employees were trying to stop their employer using the invention in his own business. The implied term adopted by English courts may be contrasted with the handling of similar problems by United States courts. There, in cases where the employer's claim to entitlement is doubtful, he is given only a "shop

---

[3] An employer who is only entitled to part of the property right—for instance, because his employee has worked with an outsider to make the invention—should, it appears from s.7(2)(b), take an assignment from his employee so as to acquire a right under s.7(2)(c).

[4] Including rights created in foreign law by treaties or conventions (in countries where, contrary to English law, international obligations may take effect directly upon ratification).

[5] This could be the law of the place of invention, or that governing the inventor's contract of employment. Such a question has never been explored in English private international law; but see below, § 7-010.

[6] The mention in s.7(2)(b) of entitlement by virtue of a "pre-invention" agreement seems meaningless, as far as English law is concerned, since such an agreement can only be to assign future property rights and that can at most create an equitable interest: yet the paragraph specifically excludes equitable interests.

[7] See also Cornish in Vitoria (ed.) *The Patents Act 1977* (1978) 79 and (1978) 1 E.I.P.R. October 4; J. Phillips and M. Hoolahan, *Employees' Inventions in the United Kingdom* (1982), and see J. Phillips (ed.) *Employees' Inventions: A Comparative Study* (1981).

[8] *Patchett* v. *Sterling* (1955) 72 R.P.C. 50.

[9] See *Marshall and Naylor's Patent* (1900) 17 R.P.C. 553 at 555; *Edisonia* v. *Forse* (1908) 25 R.P.C. 546 at 549, both citing *Frost on Patents*.

[10] *Worthington* v. *Moore* (below, n. 16) at 48; *Mellor* v. *Beardmore* (1927) 44 R.P.C. 175 at 191 (I.H.).

7-004   right": he is entitled to a free licence to use himself, but has no general power to stop the employee from licensing his invention to others.[11]

In English law, there have been two kinds of case in which, commonly, an employee has been obliged to hold his invention for his employer. First, where the employee was employed to use his skill and inventive ingenuity to solve a technical problem—where he was "employed to invent." Thus an engineering draftsman who was instructed to design an unlubricated crane-brake was obliged to hold a resulting patent on trust for his employer.[12] An assistant engineer employed to design linings for colliery tunnels was sent at his own request to a particular colliery and in consequence produced an inventive solution to its problem: the arrangement of the visit was held to place him under a duty to make over the consequent patent.[13] But a man employed purely as manager to sell valves and to deal with customer problems in the first instance was not obliged to hold an invention concerning the valves for his employers. They sent on serious difficulties to the Swiss firm from whom they acquired the technology.[14]

Secondly, where the employee occupied a senior managerial position and so owed a general duty of fidelity to his employer.[15] Thus, in *Worthington v. Moore*, an American pump manufacturing corporation put a man in charge of its English business at a high salary and commission and made him a vice-president of the corporation; he was held liable under an obligation of good faith to account for patents relating to developments in pumps.[16] More recently, an employee who was a chief technician, employed *inter alia* to give technical advice on the design and development of soda syphons, but not to design the particular kind of syphon that he actually invented, was held accountable.[17] But the manager of a lampshade business (not a director of the concern) was held entitled to keep a patent for a method or coating wire frames, an idea which amongst other uses could be applied to lampshades.[18] The employee's duty under either head

---

[11] See Stedman in Neumeyer, *The Employed Inventor in the United States* (1971) Chap. 2. An attempt to introduce an apportionment of benefits into the same "grey area" (PA 1949, s.56(2)) was held to have no effect in the absence of a contractual agreement to divide: *Patchett v. Sterling* (above, n. 8).

[12] *British Reinforced Concrete v. Lind* (1917) 34 R.P.C. 101.

[13] *Adamson v. Kenworthy* (1932) 49 R.P.C. 57.

[14] *Harris' Patent* [1985] R.P.C. 19 (decided under PA 1977, s.39—see below); and see *Spirroll v. Putti* (1976) 64 D.L.R. (3d) 280.

[15] Not easily distinguished in scope from the duties imposed in equity upon fiduciaries, such as company directors, to account for profits where there has been a conflict of personal interest and duty: see now, *Canadian Aero v. O'Malley* (1973) 40 D.L.R. (3d) 371 (S.C. Canada); and as to the duty of a managing director to exploit all new opportunities, *Fine Industrial Commodities v. Powling* (1954) 71 R.P.C. 254 at 258.

[16] (1903) 20 R.P.C. 41. Note that there was evidence that the defendant was taking over the work of the employees.

[17] *British Syphon Co. v. Homewood* [1956] R.P.C. 225, 231:
  "Now, would it be consistent with good faith, as between master and servant, that he should in that position be entitled to make some invention in relation to a matter concerning a part of the Plaintiff's business and either keep it from his employer, if and when asked about the problem, or even sell it to a rival, and say: 'Well, yes, I know the answer to your problem, but I have already sold it to your rival'?" Roxburgh J. held not.

[18] *Selz's Application* (1954) 71 R.P.C. 158. It was emphasised that the manager had not tried to keep knowledge of the invention or patent application from his employer.

applied to rights in the invention from its conception onwards. Until a   **7-005**
patent application had been filed, his obligation coincided with his duty
to keep confidential any information about his employment which was
more than mere general knowledge and skill.[19]

The common law principle operated as a presumption within a regime
of free contract; express agreement could alter its operation. But to
exclude it there had to be a positive contract and not a mere "understanding."[20] One common practice was for employers, both industrial and
governmental, to require employees to give over rights in all inventions
made during the time of the employment, rather than just in its course, at
least if the invention related to the employer's business. But recently such
a term has been held ineffective as being in unreasonable restraint of
trade: a vacuum cleaner company could not require a senior storekeeper
to surrender rights in an invention made at home, even though it
consisted of an adapter for vacuum cleaner bags.[21]

(b) *The changes in the 1977 Act*

If the only purpose of the patent system in a private enterprise economy   **7-006**
is to stimulate that economy, it may be logical to exclude employed
inventors from the benefits of employment patents: one has simply to accept
that the incentives—towards instituting research, development and publication—will only affect the employer. In other words, the bait of a patent or
patent share is unlikely to incite the employed inventor to greater effort. As
an assumption this may seem more or less plausible. But the recent shift of
opinion in the employee's favour has not turned upon this sort of
psychological calculation. Rather it expresses a resurgent feeling for the
demands of natural justice—a belief that an inventor should not go
unrewarded for the fruits of his intellectual endeavour. This inspiration has
coalesced with the recent tendency to cast legal protection around contracting parties who as a class may well not appreciate the unfavourable
consequences of their bargains.

The "new deal" in the 1977 Act is, however, a strictly limited
concession to the demand for fairness towards the inventor. Just what
has been given is in any case still obscure, since much of the hard
decision-making is left to the courts and the comptroller.[22] What the Act
does is to lay out a framework of rights, which can nevertheless be
replaced if certain provisions of the scheme are observed.

(c) *Basic entitlement under the 1977 Act*

Section 39 in effect codifies the common law principles which deter-   **7-007**
mine whether employer or employee is initially entitled to an invention.[23]

---

[19] See below, § 8-028.   [20] *Patchett* v. *Sterling* (above n. 8).
[21] *Electrolux* v. *Hudson* [1977] F.S.R. 312. The Banks Committee had recommended
legislation to similar effect, though it wanted no further compulsion to be placed upon
employers: Cmnd. 4407 (1970), Chap. 16; see now P.A. 1977, s.42(2), below § 7-042.
[22] This is in striking contrast with the statutory scheme in West Germany, whose detailed
regulations lay down methods of weighting and calculation. From these there is much of
interest to be learnt: see, *e.g.* Schade (1972) 11 Ind. Prop. 249 and [1979] Ann I.P.L.
169; Schippel (1973) 4 I.I.C. 1.
[23] In *Harris' Patent* above, n. 14, however, Falconer J. refused to accept that this statutory
provision necessarily embodied the common law.

The employer takes the invention (i) when made either in the course of the employee's normal or his specifically assigned duties, provided that an invention might reasonably be expected from carrying them out[24]; and (ii) where the employee has a special obligation to further the interests of the employer's undertaking "because of the nature of his duties and the particular responsibilities arising from the nature of his duties."[25] This reflects the two types of case where the decisions held employers entitled, and they are likely guides to future decisions. In all other cases the employee has the intial rights in his own invention.

(d) Compensation and employers' inventions

7-008   Where the invention belongs to the employer, the inventor may nevertheless have a statutory right to what is called "compensation," *i.e.* a special bonus. This arises when (i) the patent for the invention is of outstanding benefit to the employer, and (ii) it is just that compensation should be awarded; in assessing which, tribunals are under the ambiguous instruction to have regard, among other things to the size and nature of the employer's business.[26] It is the patent, not the invention, which must be of outstanding benefit, and a patent is a right to prevent others from infringing; so the relevant issue would seem to be, how much has the employer made, or how much could he have made, from licensing the patent? This may be difficult to assess, but perhaps explains the sense in which the size and nature of the employer's own business are to be considered relevant. If there are no competitors, or if competitors would use some alternative to the patented invention, then there may be no outstanding benefit from the patent.

Once this basic test is satisfied, the Act directs that the assessment of compensation is to allow the employee "a fair share (having regard to all the circumstances)," treating for the purpose dealings between the employer and a person connected with him as if an "arm's-length dealing" had taken place between them.[27] A number of factors are specified to which the tribunal must have regard, but only among other things: the employee's duties, remuneration and other advantages from employment or "in relation to" the invention; the employee's effort and skill; the effort and skill of others—co-inventors, whether employees or not, other employees who give advice and assistance; and the employer's contribution—by the provision of advice, facilities and other assistance, the provision of opportunities, and managerial and commercial skill and activities.[28]

(e) Compensation and employees' inventions

7-009   Where the patent is the employee's, the employer will be entitled to use the invention only if he has acquired rights from the employee by assignment or licence. "Compensation" falls to be paid by the employer

[24] s.39(1). The invention must accordingly be one expected to be achieved by carrying out the employee's duties: *Harris' Patent* (above n. 14).
[25] s.39(2). By amendment in 1988, the employee entitled to a patent may use material in support of his application in which the employer owns copyright or design right: s.39(3).
[26] s.40(1).
[27] s.41; and note in s.41(3) the further provision governing free licences by the Crown and Research Councils.
[28] s.41(4).

when the consideration for this transaction is inadequate in comparison with the benefit derived by the employer from the patent, and it is just that it should be paid.[29] The general principles for the assessment of compensation are the same as those for employers' inventions. But the list of factors to be brought into account differs somewhat: while account must be taken of the contribution of any co-inventor and the employer, the employee's own employment is not relevant; but conditions in licences (granted, presumably, by the employer) are.[30]

(f) Scope of the new provisions

The new provisions apply to inventions[31] made after June 1, 1978[32] by   7-010
a person who is an employee[33] mainly employed in the United Kingdom.[34]
The provisions on compensation appear to apply only between the employer and the employee at the time of making the invention— something that is likely to cause difficulty, given the lapse of time before a claim is made.[35] They do require that benefits received under foreign patents and equivalent protection be brought into account.[36]

(g) By-passing the Act: collective agreements

A collective agreement may replace the statutory scheme for compensa-   7-011
tion if it is made by or on behalf of a trade union to which the employee belongs and by an employer or an employer's association to which the employer belongs and the agreement is in existence at the time of making the invention.[37] The agreement does not have to procure any particular level of benefit to the employee in order to be effective. The broad definition of "trade union" seems to allow a temporary group (e.g. a research team) to negotiate a collective agreement. This possibility may enable a shop agreement to be reached where (as may well be the case) the research employees are not members of a regular union.[38] With the spread of white-collar unionism, such collective agreements may become commoner. They may well seek to spread bonus moneys amongst all the staff concerned with the development and marketing of the invention.

[29] s.40(2).
[30] s.41(5).
[31] i.e. "inventions for the purposes of this Act," and so not the "things" in s.1(2).
[32] For the question, when is an invention made? see Dupont's Patent [1961] R.P.C. 336 (C.A.); Bristol Myers v. Beecham [1978] R.P.C. 521.
[33] Not an independent contractor, nor a director without a service contract: e.g. Parsons v. Parsons [1979] F.S.R. 254 (C.A.); see above, §§ 2-003—2-004.
[34] Or if not mainly employed anywhere, or it is not possible to determine where he is employed, but he is attached to a U.K. place of business of the employer: s.43(2). This follows the formula in EPC Art. 60(2) for determining which national law shall decide employer-employee questions over European patents. If such a connection does not exist with the U.K. but (exceptionally) English law applies to the question, the common law rules will apply.
[35] Benefits to personal representatives of the employer must be brought into account; and the personal representatives of the employee may claim in his shoes, s.43(4), (5); but these exceptions serve to show that other substitutions are not to be made.
[36] s.43(4).
[37] s.40(3), (6).
[38] The definition of "trade union" is that in the Trade Union and Labour Relations Act 1974, see ss.28, 29.

(h) By-passing the Act: individual agreements

7-012   As with the latter-day extension of the public policy considerations in common law doctrine,[39] the Act renders unenforceable contractual terms which diminish an "employee's rights in inventions . . . or in or under patents for those inventions or applications for such patents."[40] The contracts covered are those that he makes with his employer or any third party at the employer's request or in pursuance of the contract of employment, before the date on which the invention was made.[41] This provision is beset with uncertainty, but, given the recent extension of common-law doctrine, it may well be generously construed. It clearly applies to a provision in an employment contract requiring an employee in advance to give up his rights of initial ownership where there is no distinct consideration for this.[42] But if (say) a reasonable sum is to be paid for these rights, it might well be held that they were not "diminished" (if the sum to be paid were an undervalue, it could in any case be the subject of "compensation").[43]

More important, can the inventor make a pre-invention contract to surrender his rights to compensation when the patent belongs initially to the employer? Not if by doing so, he diminishes his rights "under" the patent; and arguably this is the case. A contract made after the invention is not affected by the statute and so by implication would seem a matter of free bargaining. Certainly, if the invention belongs to the employee he cannot make a contract with his employer, before or after the invention, which deprives him of "compensation" that would adjust the price paid to him.[44]

(i) By-passing the Act by not patenting

7-013   Where the employer has initial ownership of the invention under section 39 and chooses not to patent it, it would seem that the employee is deprived of any right to "compensation." The only hope of arguing to the contrary is by way of a generous construction of the reference in section 43(4) to "other protection": if this were to include the protection of the invention as confidential information or through copyright in designs for it the result might be achieved.[45] A court might be tempted into such a construction if faced with an employer who had set out deliberately to do his employee down by not patenting.

(j) Administration

7-014   Issues between employer and employee—over ownership or "compensation"—can be heard by the High Court or upon a reference to

---

[39] See *Electrolux* v. *Hudson*, above, n. 21.
[40] s.42(2).
[41] s.42(1), (2). Duties of confidentiality owed by employee to employer must be respected: s.42(3).
[42] Equally, an employer could not require the employee to seek his consent to any patent application. But it would not diminish the employee's rights if he were required to notify the employer of the invention and any patent application.
[43] s.40(4).
[44] *Ibid.*
[45] The "other protection" would certainly include foreign protection through utility models, inventors' certificates and the like.

the comptroller. Either may order "compensation" in the form of a lump sum or periodic payments.[46]

Obviously the scope for disputes is very considerable. This potential can only be reduced if at all stages an acceptable record of events is kept: concerning who instituted the research, the making of the invention and its subsequent development and commercial exploitation.[47] At the same time the definition of duties in the contract and employment needs to be clear and to be kept under review.

(3) Dealing in rights

A patent is a right of personal property; so is an application.[48] Both can be dealt with by assignment, mortgage, licence and the like. The new Act indeed provides a code of basic rules about such dealings, introducing at the same time certain modifications of the pre-existing law.   7-015

(a) *Formalities*

The grant of a licence is not required to be in any particular form. "Licence" covers everything from occasional permission to exclusive licence, and it is only right that an informal oral licence should be legally effective.[49] However, assignments or mortgages of patents, applications and rights in patents (including, *e.g.* assignments of patent licences) are void unless in writing signed by or on behalf of the parties (not just the right-giver).[50]   7-016

(b) *The Register*

The system of maintaining a register of all legal interests in a patent is carried over from the previous law, but with some differences. There is now no statutory obligation to register transactions and the like, and indeed, registration only provides prima facie evidence of the things registered.[51] But there are two sanctions for failure to register which are intended to provide greater incentive to do so than in fact has been the case in the past: 7-017

    (i) The person with the unregistered right may lose priority to the holder of an inconsistent later right.[52] Where, for instance, the proprietor executes assignments of his title to different people, or grants an exclusive licence and then assigns his title, the rule is that the person taking under the later of the grants is to be preferred unless at that time the earlier was already registered (or notified to the Comptroller in the case of an unpublished applica-

---

[46] See ss.8, 12, 37, 41(6),(8). There is also power to vary, discharge, revive or suspend orders; and to hear an application despite previous lack of success: see s.41(7), (9)-(11).

[47] Where research is successful and patents are obtained the records should be kept at least for the life of the patent.

[48] PA 1977, s.30(1). They are not, however, things in action; though why not, is a mystery.

[49] See s.30; and for Scots law, s.31. Note that even an exclusive licence does not have to be in writing in order to give the licensee his entitlement to sue for infringement: see PA 1977, ss.67, 69 and note s.58.

[50] See s.30(6).

[51] ss.32(2)(b), 35(1), PA 1977 Rules, r. 46.

[52] s.33.

tion) or the person taking the later right knew of the earlier.[53] This varies the rule which otherwise would have applied to legal proprietary rights in patents: that once granted they would be good against all who take later interests even in all innocence.[54]

(ii) A proprietor or exclusive licensee who does not register within six months cannot claim damages or an account of profits for infringements between his entitlement and registration.[55]

The relationship between equitable interests and the requirement to register is not clear. The comptroller is not to enter notice of trusts— express, implied or constructive—on the register.[56] Where therefore the legal owner of a patent is constituted trustee of the beneficial interest for others,[57] it would seem that the ordinary rules relating to equitable interests apply: their interests are enforceable against all save a person who acquires an inconsistent right in good faith for valuable consideration without actual or constructive notice. But where a contract is made to transfer a legal interest in property and is supported by consideration, this also creates an immediate equitable interest in the property. In the case of patents such an interest has in the past been held registrable.[58]

(4) Co-ownership

7-018   Joint entitlement to ownership of a patent can arise either initially (e.g. where there are co-inventors) or through subsequent dealings.[59] Joint owners are each entitled to operate under the patent by themselves; but they may not transfer, mortgage or license their interest to third parties without seeking the consent of other co-owners.[60] A co-owner who has capacity to set up as a manufacturer himself is thus in a comparatively strong position. He may have an outside business supply him with components for a thing covered by the patent without the outsider becoming liable as an indirect infringer to other co-patentees,[61] though he cannot have the article made up completely by outsiders. He may also use and deal with patented articles made by him as if he had been the sole proprietor, though he may not supply parts for others to use in completing manufacture.[62] He is under no liability to

---

[53] Probably each joint assignee falls to be considered separately.

[54] s.33 deals only ambiguously with cases where subsequent dealings follow the inconsistent transactions; as where A assigns to B, and subsequently assigns to C; then B assigns to D; is D entitled to rely upon being the latest in time, or can C claim under the later of the initial transactions? See Ency. PL, § 8-103.

[55] Unless exceptionally he can claim to be excused: s.68.

[56] s.32(3).

[57] For instance, where an employee secures a patent to which his employer has the better right under s.39 (see above, § 7-007); or vice versa.

[58] Stewart v. Casey (1892) 9 R.P.C. 9 (C.A.).

[59] Where a patent is granted to two or more persons, they are entitled, in the absence of contrary agreement, to equal, undivided shares—i.e. they take as tenants in common, rather than as joint tenants. So the interests of each survives his death as part of his estate: s.36(1). See also Florey's Patent [1962] R.P.C. 186, 188.

[60] s.36(2), (3).

[61] s.36(4).

[62] Note the provisions concerning infringement suits by a co-patentee: s.66; disputes between joint applicants and patentees: ss.8, 10, 12, 37. Ency. PL, § 8-203.

share with his co-patentee what he earns from permissible exploitation. By contrast a co-owner without any manufacturing capacity can only import and sell.[63]

LICENCES OF PATENTS AND ALLIED RIGHTS[64]

(1) Traditional approach

In obeisance to freedom of contract, English courts have generally left **7-019** the parties to patent licences and assignments to determine the scope and extent of obligations by mutual agreement between themselves. Whatever they included in their contract the courts would enforce, resolving any ambiguities by reference to the likely intention of the parties and reading in only such additional terms as might be reasonably necessary to give the agreement business efficacy. In 1875 it was held that the assignor of a patent must honour his undertaking to assign subsequent patent rights covering improvements to the technology. Any public disadvantage in thus discouraging him from further invention was outweighed by the policy that "contracts when entered into freely and voluntarily shall be held sacred and shall be enforced by courts of justice."[65]

Accordingly, a licence gave each party what he was strong enough to demand, or canny enough to include. Because typically it concerned technical procedures that would be used with modifications over a substantial period of time, there was the chance that one or other party would find himself benefited or disadvantaged in an unanticipated fashion: for instance, because a problematic invention licensed for a modest lump sum proved unexpectedly successful; or because a licensee found himself bound not to use alternate technology. There has been no regular technique for adjusting agreements in the name of "fairness,"[66] nor did statute intervene, save exceptionally,[67] to prevent abuse of monopoly.

(2) Types of licence

As a matter of law, there is only one distinction of importance between **7-020** the different types of patent licence. The exclusive licence, by which the licensor undertakes not only to grant no other licences but also not to manufacture or sell within the licensee's province himself,[68] puts the licensee in the special position of being able to sue infringers.[69] In actual

[63] Purchasers and others who acquire patented products, directly or indirectly from one co-owner are treated as having acquired from a sole registered proprietor, s.36(5).
[64] For technical treatment of this complex subject see Melville, *Forms and Agreements on Intellectual Property and International Licensing* (3rd ed., 1979).
[65] Jessel, M.R., *Printing and Numerical* v. *Sampson* (1875) 19 Eq. 462 at 465. See also, *Jones* v. *Lees* (1856) 1 H. & N. 189 (royalty payable on non-patented item); *Brownie Wireless' Application* (1929) 46 R.P.C. 457.
[66] For possible modification of this attitude, see *Schroeder* v. *Macaulay* (discussed below, § 12-018.
[67] See below, §§ 7-027, 7-037, 7-039.
[68] See PA 1977, s.130(1) which defines an exclusive licensee as one whose rights exclude all others, including the proprietor. Where both have rights, the licence is sometimes called "sole."
[69] PA 1977, s.67.

business life, the terms of licences vary greatly. It is vital to understand something of this real world, not only because it forms so significant a part of the lawyer's business in industry but also because increasingly licences have to meet exacting criteria developed by competition law. Accordingly this section first sketches the kinds of consideration that the parties to a manufacturing licence will want to cover if left to their own self-interested concerns. After this, we can turn to the constraints upon them now being imposed in the name of public interest.

(a) *Interests at the start*

7-021   The value of what the licensor has to offer varies greatly from case to case. If the licensor has not already put the invention into production the licensee may have no sure means of judging whether the idea is commercially or even technically viable: this may well be so where he is dealing with an individual inventor, or an organisation devoted to research. If the licensee is an enterprise which also has its own research and development resources, it may be keen to restrict its obligations towards an outside licensor; then its own team remains free to explore ideas beyond and to the side of the patent.

If licensor and licensee are both manufacturing organisations, the purpose of the licence may simply be to transfer rights in one direction, because the licensor alone holds the technical knowledge; or it may that each has technology to exchange—patented or unpatented, competing or complementary. The latter circumstance may have grown out of collaboration in a joint research programme (not infrequently organised by creating a joint subsidiary for the purpose), or a mutual agreement each to conduct research only in complementary fields.[70] The pooling of patents by cross-licensing may be one consequence of a decision to deploy joint strength in the battle against outside competition. What follows is primarily concerned with "one-way" manufacturing licences, where at the outset the technology is all on one side. But it should not be forgotten that the more complex cases of cross-licensing and pooling will raise many of the same issues for the parties, and the mutual restrictions that they are likely to contain will appear more obviously anti-competitive.

(b) *Rights in the technology*

7-022   Where an invention has been worked out into a system of production, the licensor is likely to have on offer not just the invention described in his patent specification but additional information—anything from knowledge of how to adapt the invention for particular tasks to merely incidental tricks that help in putting the invention to best use. If he is selling a whole process, the licensor may collect this know-how into an operations manual; in addition he may provide technical staff to get the plant operating properly and to teach the licensee's staff how to keep it going (so called "know-how"). In such cases the know-how is likely to be imparted upon terms of confidence which will be legally binding.[71]

---

[70] Joint ventures in R & D and specialisation agreements have attracted their share of attention from the EC Commission's Competition Directorate: see further Bellamy and Child, Chaps. 10, 11.

[71] The legal basis of breach of confidence is dealt with below, Chap. 8.

There may be legal reasons for keeping the know-how licence separate from the licence of associated patents: the former may carry fiscal advantages or may avoid provisions directed against abuse of monopoly. But because patents and know-how are so frequently associated in licensing we shall consider aspects of both in this discussion.

It should be added that other forms of intellectual property have often to be included also in licences: the licensee may well want the licensor's designs, whether protected by registration or through copyright, and use of his trade marks. Sometimes the licensor will want to compel the licensee to use either designs or trade marks as part of a strategy for building long-term goodwill with the public.

(c) *Exclusivity*

Particularly when the licensor is seeking to get a technical process used in a new geographical area by finding a manufacturing source there, a basic issue is likely to arise over exclusivity: whether the licensee is to be guaranteed that neither the licensor nor other licensees will manufacture or sell, directly or indirectly, in his territory. The licensee will be interested in shoring up the investment that he will have to make: on the manufacturing side, the plant that he must install and the labour that he must employ; on the selling side, the outlets that he may have to set up, the advertising that he may have to put out, the spare parts and servicing that he may have to provide. If risks such as these are heavy and the licensor is not prepared to help in shouldering them, the licensee may well hold out for complete exclusivity: protection even against potential price differences between territories and the parallel importing that these may induce.

If a licensee is given the security of exclusivity it is frequently on condition that he will respect the exclusivity of others—licensor or exclusive licensees—in their territories. Unlike the restrictions on the licensor mentioned in the previous paragraph, which must be made a term of the licence, the licensee can be kept to his own territory simply by not granting him manufacturing or sales licences under the patents of other territories.[72] This is, of course, protection only so long as the country of import neither treats a first "legitimate" sale beyond its borders as exhausting patent rights, nor assumes that sale abroad by one licensee implies a licence to export to other countries where there are parallel patents. But it has been normal for national patent laws to give the necessary protection. It may therefore be difficult to use rules of competition to object to this form of exclusivity, since there may be no contractual term on which they can bite. Only in the Common Market does the doctrine of free movement of goods[73] qualify patent law at this point. There at least contract is the sole mode of achieving the kind of limitation under discussion (and such an agreement will likely be subject to the competition rules).

Mutual exclusivity in sales may, of course, be achieved indirectly. If the licensor has power to dictate prices, maximum quantities of production

7-023

---

[72] But a determined competition authority such as the EC Commission may treat absence of a licence as the equivalent of an undertaking not to sell in the territory concerned: see *AOIP* case below, n. 92, and *cf. Chemidus Wavin* v. *TERI* [1977] F.S.R. 181 (C.A.).

[73] Or of Community-wide exhaustion, as it will become with the introduction of the CPC: see above, § 6-011.

or even the types of goods for which the technology can be used, this may in practice lead to territorial protection.

(3) Particular terms in licences

(a) *Basic obligations*

7-024   If the licensor undertakes no more than to give the licensee permission to manufacture under his patent or patents, he acquits himself by making the grant. If he is to provide "know-how," then he must make available whatever information has been described in the contract. Giving an adequate description of "know-how" for this purpose can be a difficult business. Since in practice much of it may have to be made known in the course of negotiations, the wise potential licensor insists on a preliminary contract that anything revealed will be kept confidential and used only in accordance with such contract as may be agreed. If the licensee is seeking not just a chance to work under the patent or to use the know-how, but instead wants a fully operative package, he must secure undertakings from the licensor that this is what will be provided; with escape clauses leaving him free of obligation if it is not.

Unless for some reason the licence is to be free, the licensee's first obligation will be to pay for what he has received. This will likely take the form of a lump sum, or a royalty on articles produced (normally calculated as a proportion of their net selling price) or both. If there are special risks in the project—particularly because more technical development needs to be undertaken—a profit-sharing arrangement may prove attractive.

(b) *Duration*

7-025   Equally basic will be the duration of the licence, and the definition of circumstances in which either party is to have power to terminate it. If a patent licence is properly determined while the patent remains in effect, the former licensee falls to be treated like any other stranger.[74] More difficult issues arise upon the ending of a know-how licence; for (subject to public policy) the contract between the parties will settle whether the licensee must give up his use of the information, while continuing to keep knowledge of it from outsiders. If this is provided for expressly, it may well be coupled with an obligation to return all relevant documentary information. If it is not, it will not necessarily be implied, particularly when the information was given in order to get a business established.[75]

In the past, strong licensors have tied their licensees to long-term arrangements by such techniques as requiring the continuance of royalties after expiry of the patents[76]; or requiring royalties on articles whether or not made under any licensed patent; or requiring them whether or not the patent is valid.[77]

---

[74] But there may be difficulties about the obligations which one side owes to the other at the date of termination, *e.g.* to make over rights in improvement patents: *National Broach* v. *Churchill Gear* [1967] R.P.C. 99 (H.L.).

[75] *Regina Glass Fibre* v. *Schuller* [1972] R.P.C. 229 (C.A.); *cf. Torrington* v. *Smith* [1966] R.P.C. 285.

[76] Or requiring royalties so long as any patents relating to the subject-matter of the licence are in force—including those subsequently taken out on improvements.

[77] But, as we shall see (§ 7-039), some attempt to limit this was introduced in 1949.

(c) *Improvements*

Since novel technology is generally subject to further development it is   7-026
important to decide whether new information is to be fed around—from
licensee to licensor as well as vice versa. And if additional intellectual
property rights are acquired by one, the other is likely to want at least a
non-exclusive licence under these rights. It is common practice for the
patentee of a basic invention to set up a net of "one-way" manufacturing
licences, country by country. Since each licensee will be likely to discover
improvements, traditionally the patentee has sought to keep control over
the developing technology by requiring not only "feed-back" of information for distribution to the other licensees but also "grant-back" in the
form of an assignment of consequent patent and allied rights acquired by
the licensee; or if not this, then at least an exclusive licence, with or
without power to grant sub-licences to others within the network. Each
licensee will of course find this arrangement to his advantage only to the
extent that he feels that he is getting at least as much as he is giving. Not
only may he try to drag his own feet in the matter of revelations; he may
not make much effort to find improvements.

(d) *Ties*

The licensor may well want to insist that the licensee acquire non-   7-027
patented goods from him alone as a condition of the patent or know-
how licence. If a process is being licensed, he may in particular want the
exclusive right to supply the starting materials to be used in it. Sometimes
there are technical reasons for this: his material alone may be good
enough to make the process function satisfactorily. For one reason or
another such "ties" have, traditionally, been common.[78] There may also
be "ties" in distributing the licensee's product.[79] The licensor may insist
that it be marketed through his own distribution channels. This may be
so even though the licensed patent only contributed to the course of
production and no patent rights apply to the final article.

(e) *Protection for the licensor*

In exclusive licences for royalties, the licensor needs particularly to   7-028
ensure that the licensee gets the invention into production. If he can
negotiate a minimum royalty or minimum production clause, this will
give him the guarantee of specific amounts. Beyond this he may seek an
undertaking that the licensee will use his best endeavours to exploit the
invention. The courts read this to mean what it says, unqualified by any
notion of "reasonableness,"[80] but the licensor may face grave difficulties
in actually establishing that the licensee has not been as assiduous as he
might have been. Closely allied to this, the licensee may undertake not to
employ competing technology,[81] thus explicitly surrendering one aspect of
his capacity to compete to his own best advantage.

[78] Despite legislation (from 1907 onwards) treating "ties" and exclusions of competitive
technology as abuses of monopoly: see below, § 7-036.
[79] A special case for mention here is the "sub-contracting" out of work on parts for a
machine to be completed by the licensor; as to which see the EC Commission's Notice on
Sub-contracting Agreements [1979] 1 C.M.L.R. 264.
[80] *Terrell* v. *Mabie Todd* (1952) 69 R.P.C. 234; *IBM* v. *Rockware* [1980] F.S.R. 335.
[81] See, n. 79.

A different hazard for the licensor is that, because the licensee becomes closely acquainted with the invention he is in a peculiarly strong position to discover weaknesses in the patent: reasons, for instance, for saying that the disclosure was inadequate or that its subject-matter is obvious in the light of prior art.[82] Even if the licensee cannot mount a sure attack he may be able to cause enough trouble to secure variations of the licence in his own favour. Accordingly, it has been traditional practice for the licensor to require an undertaking that the licensee will not challenge the validity of the patent or know-how during the currency of the licence; or to require the payment of royalties, whether valid or not.[83]

(f) Protection for the licensee

7-029　　The exclusive licensee acquires a position of some independence from his licensor.[84] The non-exclusive licensee, on the other hand, may well be concerned that he is having to pay for permission that others are getting cheaper or for nothing. Against the danger of more favourable licences, he may seek a clause which will reduce his obligations to the best terms at any time granted to any other licensee. To meet the danger that the licensor will simply fail to pursue an infringer, he may seek power to withhold royalties for any period of inaction.

(4) Competition law criteria[85]

7-030　　Modern business history knows examples enough of agreements amongst leading firms in an industry which use the licensing of intellectual property rights as a basis for anti-competitive liaisons—arrangements that will keep out or drive out competition by price, by product, by advertising, or in a host of other ways. A "pool" by leading firms under which they and they alone can use inventions patented by them individually or after joint research can prove a very efficient instrument for such manifestly horizontal links. Pools may increase geometrically the potential market power of the individual patents and there is widespread agreement that competition policy should be used against such "expansions" of patent rights, especially where they cover the competing ways of making a product. Accordingly they find no special exemption from either United Kingdom[86] or EEC competition law.

　　Patent and know-how licences such as those described in preceding paragraphs, however, are frequently concerned with fostering the use of the licensor's technology in the competition against the same and similar products in the market. By themselves, they do not limit "inter-product"

---

[82] Likewise he may be able to show that know-how has become public knowledge from an independent source.

[83] An express "no challenge" clause is arguably invalid as being in unreasonable restraint of trade and so contrary to public policy: see, per Clauson J., *VD Ltd. v. Boston* (1935) 52 R.P.C. 303 at 331; cf. *Mouchel v. Cubitt* (1907) 24 R.P.C. 194 at 200. If this is good law, it may be questioned whether there is room for any implied estoppel, based on the notion (borrowed from landlord and tenant law) that a licensee must not "approbate and reprobate."

[84] Particularly by his ability to sue infringers: PA 1977, s.67; above, § 7-020.

[85] See further Bellamy and Child, *Common Market Law of Competition* (3rd ed., 1987); Korah, *Competition Law of Britain and the Common Market* (3rd ed., 1982).

[86] For their treatment in U.K. law, see App. 1.

competition. If competition authorities are to subject them to critical scrutiny it is because of their inhibiting effect upon the "intra-product" competition that could otherwise exist between licensor and his licensee or licensees. But the use of competition policy to this end is controversial for an obvious reason. A patent is a decision to allow the patentee to behave as a monopolist to the extent that the market admits. When he licenses his rights, albeit on terms that limit the licensee's or his own freedom of action, he would seem prima facie to be doing no more than realising the potential of his economic power. A rational patentee will not grant licences if his best chance of extracting monopoly profits from the market lies in exploiting the patent himself. Accordingly, if a term in such licensing agreements is to be regarded as invalid, there must be an acceptable explanation in economic terms of how it increases the anti-competitive effect of the initial monopoly grant beyond what was intended.

The difficulties of providing such justifications are reflected in United Kingdom competition law. This contains special exceptions relating to patent licences and, to a lesser extent, other intellectual property agreements.[87] Accordingly the only aspects of "local" United Kingdom law that become of concern in what follows are isolated provisions in the Patents Act directed against particular "abuses" of monopoly. Although these have been part of the law for some time they have constituted nothing more than minor traps for the unwary. At root this has been because courts have rarely felt that the provisions embody exigent public policies.[88]

7-031

By contrast, "intra-product" competition has seemed of greater moment to those directing Common Market policy. The prime importance of breaking down barriers to free marketing within Community territories has made the EC Commission critical of exclusive selling rights wherever they occur, and whether they are created directly or as a consequence of some other restriction, such as a maximum production limit in a technology licence. Accordingly, any restrictive licence having significant impact on interstate trade within the Community is now subject to detailed regulation.

(5) Development of Commission policy on patent licences

As early as 1962, in a non-binding notice (the "Patent Notice"),[89] the Commission reserved its position on patent pools, cross-licences and similar forms of mutual horizontal restraint.[90] But it indicated that it would not regard certain limiting terms in "one-way" licences as falling within the prohibition of the Rome Treaty, Article 85(1).[91] Even so there

7-032

---

[87] See App. 1.
[88] See below, §§ 7-037, 7-039.
[89] Announcement on Patent Licensing Agreements, December 24, 1962 (hence known to initiates as the "Christmas Message")—now withdrawn.
[90] In *Video Cassette Recorders Agreements* [1978] F.S.R. 376 the Commission found a patent pooling aspect of the licences in question to be restrictive of competition because any member of the pool was to surrender its rights upon leaving the pool but was obliged to allow continuing members to retain their rights in its patents.
[91] For the main content of Arts. 85, 86, see above, § 1-025; for a note on their implementation, App. 1.

were indications that some clauses (non-essential "tie-ins," exclusive "grant-backs," post-patent obligations) might go too far and towards these commission policy remains unchanged. But within a decade, the Notice permitted clauses ceased to be a reliable guide (particularly over exclusivity in manufacturing or sales, and maximum production limits). For in the 1970s a number of test decisions by the Commission took a severer (and so more controversial) line.[92] Agreements that at first were thought to be outside Article 85(1) were instead treated as needing exemption under Article 85(3); and in the matter of sales exclusivity this has proved particularly difficult to justify.

In consequence of this shift, the Commission eventually, in 1984, formulated a Block Exemption on Patent Licences[93] that specifies the conditions under which a licence need not be individually justified before exemption. To some extent the industrial and governmental objections raised against the drafts of this Block Exemption[94] induced a softening in the Commission's approach, which is indicative of a more general shift away from restrictive regulation under the competition policy. The Exemption applies to patent licences in a reasonably broad sense.[95] However it covers mixed agreements also pertaining to know-how only where the patents are "necessary for achieving the objects of the licensed technology and as long as at least one of the licensed patents remains in force."[96] Where on the other hand, the licensed know-how is not merely ancillary to the patents, or where there are no patents (at least for some member states), a parallel Block Exemption has since been introduced.[97] To come within it, the know-how licensed must be secret and substantial, and also sufficiently identified.[98]

The two Exemptions—on Patent Licences and Know-How Licences— have many features in common, and will here be discussed in tandem.[99] Each contains an Article 1 which is primarily devoted to defining the extent to which exclusivity provisions may protect the licensee, the

[92] See especially *Raymond/Nagoya* [1972] C.M.L.R. D45; *Davidson Rubber* [1972] C.M.L.R. D52; *Burroughs/Delplanque and Geha* [1972] C.M.L.R. D72; *Kabelmetal/ Luchaire* [1975] 2 C.M.L.R. D40; *Bronbemaling* v. *Heidemaatschappij* [1975] 2 C.M.L.R. D67; *AOIP/Beyrard* [1976] 1 C.M.L.R. D14; *Vaessen* v. *Moris* [1979] F.S.R. 259.

[93] Commission Regulaltion 2349/84; see esp. V. Korah, *Patent Licensing and EEC Competition Rules* (1985); Alexander (1986) 17 I.I.C.I. This Exemption runs for 10 years from January 1, 1985. For the Commission's power of enactment, see below, § A1-003.

[94] The change in attitude is easily seen by comparing the final version with the initial draft, as given in [1977] 1 C.M.L.R. D25.

[95] *i.e.* of patents, utility models and the like, and applications for all; but not plant variety rights; also excluded are patent pools, joint ventures and cross-licences between competitors: Arts. 5, 10.

[96] See Recital 9. That the Patent Licences Exemption did not apply to a licences of a number of processes, some not covered by patents at all, others by patents in part, but only in some member states: *Boussois/Interpane* O.J. 1988 L.69/21.

[97] Commission Regulation 556/89, operative for 10 years from April 1, 1989. For the distinction from the Patent Licences Exemption, Arts. 1.1, 1.7(5), (6). Excluded from this Exemption, as well as pools, joint ventures and cross-licences, are bare sales licences and franchising agreements: Arts. 1(5), 5, Recital 5. See V. Korah, *Know-how Licensing and EEC Competition Rules* (1989, forthcoming).

[98] Each of these requirements is defined: see 556/89 Art. 1.

[99] They are footnoted as BEx-P and BEx-K.

licensor and licensees in other territories: an Article 2, comprising a "White List" of permissible clauses; and an Article 3, comprising a "Black List" of impermissible clauses, some of them in direct contrast to clauses on the White List. It is to be remembered that an Agreement which does not come within the terms of either Block Exemption may still be the subject of an individual exemption granted by the Commission, and today such treatment is by no means beyond hope.[1] There is also an interim case: both Exemptions provide an opposition procedure in respect of agreements within their subject-fields which have provisions restrictive of competition that are not within those exempted, but are not on the Black List: if such an agreement is notified and the Commission does not oppose exemption within six months, the relevant Block Exemption applies to it.[2] And as a further qualification, the Commission retains power to withdraw the benefits of the Block Exemption in particular cases which are incompatible with Article 85(3).[3]

The content of the two Block Exemptions, together with two comparable provisions of the British Patents Act 1977, can best be considered under two main heads: provisions relating to exclusivity; and terms restricting the licensee's freedom of action.

(6) Exclusivity

In its decisions of the 1970s on patent licences, the Commission's starting point was that undertakings to ensure the exclusivity of territories were restrictive of competition in the sense of Article 85(1), since they necessarily involved a surrender of freedom.[4] This applied to the licensor's undertaking not to manufacture or sell in the licensee's territory and not to grant licences to others to do so; and it even applied to the licensee's undertaking not to manufacture or sell in a territory which the licensor reserved to himself, or was licensing to another exclusive licensee. The latter was particularly controversial since, but for the licence to him, the licensee would have no entitlement to use the patented technology at all, and so would be even more constrained. The Commission, however, considered that the ultimate objective of unifying the internal market justified treating a licence to manufacture in one country of the Community as a licence to sell in all.

However, proceedings concerning a licence of plant variety rights in a new form of maize seed, to which the Commission applied its approach,

7-033

---

[1] Shortly before adopting the Know-how Block Exemption, the Commission issued a number of individual decisions which indicated how far it was prepared to go on the subject: in addition to *Boussois* (above, n. 96), see *Mitchell Cotts/Sofiltra* [1988] 4 C.M.L.R. 111; *Rich Products/Jusrol* [1988] 4 C.M.L.R. 527; *Delta Chemie/DDD* [1988] O.J. EC C152/2, Korah (above, n. 97).

[2] BEx-P Art. 4; BEx-K Art. 4.

[3] Cases where this is likely to occur are listed, thus constituting a "grey-black" list: BEx-P 9 mentions the effects of an arbitration award; absence of effective competition; no right to terminate exclusivity after five years on ground of non-exploitation by licensee; refusal to meet unsolicited demand unjustifiably. BEx-K 7 adds to these refusal to supply parallel exporters and post-term use bans which extend to previously patented inventions.

[4] See esp. *Davidson Rubber*, *Raymond/Nagoya*, and *Kabelmetal/Luchaire* (above, n. 92). It should be remembered that in the last two of these cases, the Commission took the view that licences for manufacture outside the EEC could infringe Article 85(1) if they excluded a realistic prospect of the licensee selling into the Common Market: see also *Davide-Campari Milano's Agreement* [1978] 2 C.M.L.R. 397.

were taken on appeal to the EC Court of Justice.[5] The developer of the new variety, a French research organisation, INRA, had granted an exclusive manufacturing and sales licence for Germany to a firm there, Nungesser. The Court accepted that, so far as this agreement sought to impose *absolute* territorial protection on Nungesser, by requiring that even a parallel importer should be prevented from obtaining the seed in France and exporting it to Germany, it was bad under Article 85(1) and could not be saved by exemption. The parallel importer is a prime mover in operating the Common Market. But so far as the agreement only secured *open* exclusivity—undertakings that neither INRA nor its French licensees would themselves export to Germany—the matter must be judged in light of the prevailing circumstances in the particular market (in American parlance, by "rule of reason").[6] Given the "specific nature of the products in question," to introduce the newly developed seeds involved such risks in cultivating and marketing that a potential licensee might have been deterred by the prospect of direct competition in the same product from other licensees. Accordingly competition would be prejudiced by the licensor's inability to offer exclusive rights. It was not even a question of exemption; there was no infraction of Article 85(1).

7-034   The decision constitutes a *via media*. Open exclusivity may be useful where price differentials between different parts of the common market are not substantial, or where transportation costs or other factors serve to inhibit parallel importation. But there will be circumstances where the insistence that opportunities for the parallel importer be preserved may prevent the initial producer from supplying a cheap market at all with his product, to the detriment of consumers there. The Court has insisted that such a risk has to be courted, both here and (as we shall see) in relation to the free movement of goods between member states.

The *"Maize Seed"* decision undoubtedly curbed the Commission's enthusiasm against exclusivity provisions. In the Patent Licence Block Exemption it gave up its attempts to limit certain types of exclusivity clause to the protection of small enterprises. Instead it was provided that, in most cases, so long as one of the patents originally licensed remains in force, undertakings to preserve exclusivity are exempted, even where they are not completely clear[7]: this covers

   (i) the licensor's undertaking not to exploit the invention in the licensee's territory either by his own activities or by licensing others—though this, following *"Maize Seed"*, will be no infraction of Article 85(1) if it is needed in order to get new technology introduced;
   (ii) the licensee's undertaking not to exploit the invention in territory explicitly reserved by the licensor for himself; and
   (iii) the licensee's undertaking not to manufacture in the territory of another licensee or to engage actively in selling there (for instance,

---

[5] *Nungesser v. EC Commission* [1982] E.C.R. 2015; Korah (1983) 28 Antitrust Bull. 699.
[6] On the distinction between absolute and open exclusivity, see Hoffmann and O'Farrell [1984] E.I.P.R. 104; *cf.* Korah *ibid.* 206.
[7] BEx-P 1.1.

by setting up a branch or depot, or by advertising)[8]; but, so far as concerns passive selling (responding to unsolicited orders from the other licensees' territories), such exclusivity can last only for five years from the first putting of the licensed product on some part of the Common Market.[9]

In the Know-how Block Exemption,[10] the equivalent provision operates, so far as (i) and (ii) are concerned for ten years from the date of the first licence for the technology in the territory to be protected; and in the case of (iii), for ten years from the date of the first licence to exploit the technology in the EEC, so far as concerns manufacture and active sales; as regards passive sales, the period is (as for patent licences) five years from the first marketing of products in the Common Market.[11]

In support of the Court's disapproval of "absolute" elements in exclusivity, both Block Exemptions place on the Black List terms requiring parallel importers to be refused supply or calling for difficulties to be placed in their way.[12]

(a) Restrictions on production and sale

According to both Black Lists, it is not justifiable to restrict the licensee's freedom, or the licensor's, in reaching certain basic decisions about marketing products made under the licence—in particular, about sale prices[13] or their corollary, maximum quantities of production.[14] Nor is it permissible, directly or indirectly,[15] to divide up the customers that each may serve.[16]   7-035

However, the Commission has accepted that there is sufficient justification in allowing the licensor to restrict the types of application open to the licensee: for patents the licensee may be confined to "one or more fields of application' (an imprecise term)[17]; for know-how, the limitation may also refer to "one or more product markets" (a more workable conception).[18] It has also accepted that an exclusive licensor must be able to build in incentives to ensure himself an adequate return. He may require a minimum level of production by the licensee, or the payment of a minimum royalty.[19] Equally he may impose a requirement that the licensee use his best endeavours to exploit the licensed technology,[20]

---

[8] It is true that the "*Maize Seed*" case does not deal directly with exclusivity between different territorial licensees, so it cannot be said with certainty that its reasoning applies equally to such cases; but it may well carry some outside Article 85.

[9] This last limitation is reinforced by BEx-P 3.10.

[10] BEx-K 1.1.

[11] Reinforced by 3.11. In a mixed agreement, so far as patent give protection the periods in BEx-P 1.1 apply: BEx-K 1.4.

[12] BEx-P 3.11; BEx-K 3.12.

[13] BEx-P 3.6, BEx-K 3.8.   [14] BEx-P 3.5; BEx-K 3.7.

[15] Indirectly: *e.g.* by reference to distribution systems or types of packaging.

[16] BEx-P 3.7. But here BEx-K 3.6 is more limited, imposing the ban only "within the same technological field of use or within the same product market."

[17] BEx-P 2.1.3.

[18] BEx-K 2.1.8.

[19] BEx-P 2.1.2, BEx-K 2.1.9.

[20] Exception to BEx-P 3.3; the equivalent BEx-K 3.9 adds further possibilities: the right to withdraw exclusivity or to cease communicating improvements, if the licensee begins excluded competition.

though he must not go so far as directly to prohibit the production, use or distribution of a competing product, or other forms of competition.[21] Inevitably it must be doubted whether the "blacking-listing" of non-competition clauses has much effect, given the scope of what may be included.

(b) *Technical adequacy* v. *unwanted ties*

7-036   The licensor of new technique has a legitimate interest to ensure that it is adequately used by any licensee. He may, for instance, insist that the licensee should have no power to sub-license or assign the licence to another. In *Erauw-Jacquery* v. *La Hesbignonne*,[22] the Court of Justice has recognised the propriety of such an objective, and the White Lists include such a clause.[23] The licensee may be placed under an obligation (a "tie-in") to procure goods or services from the licensor or his nominee so far as is necessary for a technically satisfactory exploitation of the invention or know-how; to the same end he may be placed under minimum quality specifications and have to undergo checks to see that they are observed.[24] It is also proper for the licensor to require that products be sold under his trade mark or with his get-up, provided that the licensee is not deprived of his ability to indentify himself as manufacturer.[25] But it is improper to oblige the licensee to accept further licences, or other tied goods or services which he does not want[26] (if that can be established, given that he has in fact accepted them).

7-037   As regards tie-ins, the British Patents Act, now by section 44,[27] sets a trickier hazard. A term in a contract to supply a patented product or to license a patented process is void if the supplier or licensor requires anything else[28] to be acquired from him or his nominee.[29] The same provision strikes against terms that preclude a licensee from using or from taking competing technology—whether in the form of articles (either patented or unpatented) or processes (if patented).[30] The sanction is harsh: so long as the term is in existence it constitutes a defence to any infringement action by the patentee.[31] There is no exception for technically necessary supplies. Instead there is a statutory exemption of a "tie-in" where the person supplied or licensed was offered a reasonable alternative without the tie and the tie can be undone on three months'

---

[21] BEx-P 3.3, BEx-K 3.9.
[22] [1988] 4 C.M.L.R. 576.
[23] BEx-P 2.1.5; BEx-K 2.1.2.
[24] BEx-P 2.1.1, 2.1.9; BEx-K 2.1.5.
[25] BEx-P 1.1.7; BEx-K 1.1.7.
[26] BEx-P 3.9; BEx-K 3.3; and note the example given in the Treaty itself—Article 85(1)(e).
[27] Again a version of this provision was first introduced in 1907: see above, n. 35.
[28] The 1977 Act uses "anything" in place of "article"; it may accordingly also cover tied services. See further, s.130(1) ("patent," "patented product," "patented invention").
[29] s.44(1). For an instance (under the 1907 Act) see *Huntoon* v. *Kolynos* [1930] 1 Ch. 528 (C.A.) (patent on collapsible toothpast tubes, licensee to procure all unpatented wire-loops (connecting cap and tube) from patentee; obligation void).
[30] s.44(1).
[31] s.44(3). Apart from this the term is treated as being no part of the agreement: *Hunter's Patent* (below, n. 35) at 427.

written notice with payment of compensation.[32] Beyond this, the case-law shows a marked contrast in attitude. The House of Lords held that no objection could be raised against an agreement which merely offered a financial inducement not to take outside supplies; in this there was no "prohibition" or "restriction" in a legal sense.[33] In other more recent cases, the same determination to adopt a narrow interpretation of the prohibition has been manifest.[34] But the Irish Supreme Court refused to uphold one variety of "label licence": patented machinery (bottling plant) was supplied without licence to use, this being given with each item of non-patented material (bottle caps).[35] Yet here also, there was no "restriction," only permission, if legal appearance rather than economic intent is looked at. Even more difficult to handle is the simplest "label licence" of all—where the licensor does nothing other than supply starting materials with a licence to use them in the patented process.[36] If the patentee has secured claims to a process and its products, is it to be improper for him only to grant licences to use the method with his own materials?

The conundrum posed by that instance suggests that much of the attack on "tie-ins" may be misplaced. Assertions that they necessarily "extend" the scope of the patent monopoly[37] need to be viewed with caution. They may proceed upon simplistic assumptions which do not ask whether the patentee is making larger monopoly profits than he could under his patent alone. Proper investigation of the question calls for economic analysis of some sophistication.[38] But consider at least the following: if a patent covers a copying machine and it is leased on terms that the lessee buys his supply of paper from the patentee (even above market price), the return to the patentee will reflect the amount of use of the machine. It will, in other words, enable him to discriminate in the price he charges different users on an efficient basis. It is hard to see that he is doing anything other than maximising the profit upon the invention.[39]

(c) *Further technical advances*

Manufactures ought to perfect what they are producing: to this end the patent system and the legal protection of know-how act as lures. If therefore a licensee must hand over the licensor any rights in his improvements, the incentive may be substantially dampened.[40] Hence from the outset, the EC Commission has objected to "grant-back"   **7-038**

[32] s.44(4), (5); "compensation" is further described.
[33] *Tool Metal* v. *Tungsten Electric* (1955) 72 R.P.C. 209 at 218-221; but *cf.* Lord Simmonds (dissenting) at 214-216. The 1907 Act, s.38, applied, but the subsequent changes in language scarcely affect the point.
[34] *Fichera* v. *Flogates* [1984] R.P.C. 257 (C.A.).
[35] *Hunter's Patent* [1965] R.P.C. 416 at 426-427; and see *Vaessen/Morris* [1979] 1 C.M.L.R. 511.
[36] *cf. Sarason* v. *Frenay* [1914] 2 Ch. 474, 31 R.P.C. 330 (C.A.).
[37] *e.g.* Romer L.J., *Huntoon* v. *Kolynos* (above, n. 29) at 562.
[38] See, *e.g.* W. S. Bowman *Patent and Antitrust Law* (1973) especially Chaps. 7, 8; Monopolies and Mergers Commission (U.K.) *Tie-in Sales and Full line Forcing* (H.C. 212, 1981).
[39] Monopolies and Mergers Commission (U.K.), *Indirect Electrostatic Reprographic Equipment* (H.C. 47, 1976).
[40] Even more so, if the licensee must grant over rights in competing technology.

clauses which require assignment or exclusive licensing to the original licensor.[41] Even a clause which obliges the licensee to give information and non-exclusive rights is likely to be objectionable if it does not impose a reciprocal obligation on the licensor.[42] Unless such a mutual exchange is agreed, the policy insists that each party should compete with the other in the matter of improvements.[43]

(d) Duration and termination

7-039   Just as, to be capable of exemption, provisions on exclusivity must be limited in duration, so more generally it is improper to include a clause allowing the licensor unilaterally to prolong duration of the licence by adding into it new patents or know-how concerned with improvements to the technology licensed.[44] Rather, the licensee must have the right to terminate the agreement: under the Patent Exemption, annually from the expiry of the last patent initially licensed; under the Know-How Exemption, at initial expiry and then at least every three years (or, in the alternative, a right to refuse the improvements).[45] These limitations are associated with those, already mentioned, precluding a requirement to take unwanted rights and an unduly strong "grant-back" clause.

A provision of the Patents Act 1977 is also relevant here for comparison. To the extent that the agreement covers British patents, once the last of the patents initially licensed has ceased, either party has a statutory right to terminate the agreement (or the relevant part of it) on three months' notice in writing.[46] Once this right to terminate arises, the court may instead vary the agreement on the ground that it would be unjust to require compliance with all the terms.[47] Under this power the court could, presumably, order a reduction of royalty where the British patents have expired but foreign patents continue.[48]

7-040   No licence is necessary, if the patent in question is invalid or the know-how is not capable of protection. A person who nevertheless takes a licence will be working the technique and so will be in a particularly strong position to discover reasons why the rights are in fact invalid. Against that prospect arising to upset the established relationship under the licence, traditional practice was to require the licensee to undertake not to challenge the validity or existence of the rights during the term of the agreement. But the Commission has been steadfast in disapproving of "no challenge" clauses, as seeking to maintain the extraction of royalties

---

[41] Patent Notice, 1962, ID IV. Now "black-listed": BEx-P 3.8; BEx-K 3.2. This approach has now been adopted by the Court of Justice: *Royon v. Meilland* [1988] 4 C.M.L.R. 193.

[42] For permissible feed-back and grant back, see BEx-P 2.1.10; BEx-K 2.1.4.

[43] See also *Davidson Rubber* and *Kabelmetal/Luchaire* (above, n. 00).

[44] BEx-P 3.2; BEx-K 3.10.

[45] *ibid.*

[46] PA 1977, s.45—a new version of one of the 1907 attacks on "abuses of monopoly allegedly committed by United Shoe Machinery of Boston. It is restricted to British patents by definition (see s.130(1)—"patent") and decision (*Advance Industries v. Frankfurther* [1958] R.P.C. 392; *Hansen v. Magnavox* [1977] R.P.C. 301 (C.A.), but applies to licences both to manufacture and to supply, with a special provision for hire-purchase agreements.

[47] s.45(3).

[48] This was the special problem in *Hansen* (above, n. 46).

where none are properly justified.[49] In general, this approach is supported by the Court of Justice.[50] But, it has recently held, in an agreement compromising a genuine dispute over the validity of a patent that a clause may be included to prevent the licensee from reopening the issue which has been compromised.[51] The Commission nonetheless looks attentively at settlements of disputes, and equally at the findings of arbitrators, to ensure that they do not dress up what is really an amicable market-sharing arrangement between competitors.[52] Inevitably it may be slow and costly to decided on which side of the line the "compromise" falls.

The Patent Licence exemption permits the inclusion of a term by which the licence may be for less than the full duration of a patent or patents.[53] When therefore the licence expires, the licensee may not continue to act within the scope of any continuing patent. When this was enacted the Commission's view on whether the licensee must be left free to continue using ancillary know-how was unclear, and the matter was not explicitly covered.[54] But now, in the Know-how Licence Exemption, it has reached the opinion that a post-term use ban relating to know-how is justified, provided that the information remains secret at termination and has not become publicly available through revelation by the licensor or a third party (but not through revelation by the licensee).[55]

3. EXHAUSTION IN THE COMMON MARKET

We turn next to "exhaustion" of patent rights and its relation to fundamental policies of the EEC, in particular that of free movement of goods between member states. These ideas have already been introduced at a number of points and what has so far been said will not be repeated here.[56] But it should be recalled that a particular notion of exhaustion forms part of the CPC. When this Convention is brought into operation

7-041

---

[49] See, e.g., Davidson Rubber, Kabelmetal/Luchaire (above, n. 92); and now BEx-P 3.1; BEx-K 3.4—both of which, however, permit the licensor to take power to terminate the licence in the event of a challenge being launched; see also DuPont's Blades Patent [1988] R.P.C. 479 at 492-493.

[50] IMA v. Windsurfing International [1984] 1 C.M.L.R. 1; Royon v. Meilland [1988] 4 C.M.L.R. 193, J. S. Venit (1987) 18 I.I.C. 1.

[51] Bayer and Hennecke v. Suellhoefer (to be reported); Korah [1988] E.I.P.R. 381.

[52] Bronbemaling (above, n. 92); Sirdar/Phildar [1975] 1 C.M.L.R. D 93 (trade mark dispute); cf. Penney's T.M. [1978] F.S.R. 385 (settlement of trade mark war, parts of which are documented in the report).

[53] BEx-P 2.1.4.

[54] The Commission's earlier view, evidenced in Drafts of the Block Exemption, had been that once know-how had been imparted, it should not be retractable. But it was coming to appreciate that this might truly impede the dissemination of know-how at all.

[55] BEx-K 2.1.3, 3.1

[56] For the basic EEC doctrine, see above § 1-024. For the two-stage introduction of "exhaustion" into U.K. patent law, see, in addition to what follows, above, §§ 6-011, 6-012. The application of the doctrine to copyright and trade marks is discussed under those heads: see below, §§ 12-028—12-031, 18-006—18-012.

it will affect both Community and national patent rights as they apply to trade between the Member States.[57]

Most patent systems—including those of the United States and many European countries—have given the patentee no right to control the use or resale of goods which he has placed on the domestic market or has allowed a licensee to market there. Amongst Common Market countries, Britain and Ireland were previously unique in not adopting a rule of national exhaustion. Instead, the patentee's right to control the use, exercise and vending of inventions was held to extend even to goods which the patentee had himself sold.[58] But at least so far as importation of goods connected with the patentee was concerned, there was no essential difference in result: as with countries that have adhered to a purely domestic doctrine of exhaustion,[59] national patent rights provided a barrier to entry of goods into the country, if (so far as concerned the patentee's own goods entering a common law country) adequate notice of prohibition on importing was given.

7-042   The EC Court of Justice has, in principle, insisted that a Community-wide concept of exhaustion of rights should apply. In *Centrafarm* v. *Sterling Drug*,[60] it derived this from the Treaty of Rome provisions on the free movement of goods. First it wove exhaustion in general terms into its definition of the "specific subject-matter" of a patent: "the guarantee that the patentee, to reward the creative effort of the inventor, has the exclusive right to use an invention with a view to manufacturing industrial products and putting them into circulation for the first time, either directly or by the grant of licences to third parties, as well as the right to oppose infringements." Then it refused to allow a derogation from the principle of free movement of goods "where the product has been put onto the market in a legal manner by the patentee himself or with his consent in the Member State from which it has been imported, in particular in the case of proprietor of parallel patents.[61]

When the right that must be treated as exhausted has a uniform effect throughout the territory in question, the application of the exhaustion concept is straightforward; either the right-owner has or has not consented to the first sale or other marketing (or has undertaken it himself). But the whole difficulty in the Common Market stems precisely from the fact that there is no single decision to grant a patent for the whole territory which will give rise to uniform legal consequences. If there is a price differential which makes parallel importing worthwhile from one EEC country to another, there is often a question whether the higher price in the country of import is not due to the superior character of the

---

[57] See CPC, Arts, 32, 46, 47, 81, 82; *cf.* Art. 43.

[58] See above, § 6-001.

[59] This was the rule in most other EEC countries. For the restricted scope of the patentee's rights in Belgian law, *e.g.* see Joliet (1974) 64 L'Ingenieur-Conseil 197.

[60] [1974] E.C.R. 1147; [1974] 2 C.M.L.R. 480: the particular facts are discussed below, § 7-047. See further, Joliet [1975] C.L.P. 15; van Nieuwenhoven Helbach (1976) 13 C.M.L. Rev. 37.

[61] Judgment, §§ 9, 11. The judgment developed the line of thought already apparent in *Deutsche-Grammophon* v. *Metro* [1971] E.C.R. 487: sound-recording right, discussed below, § 12-028.

right accorded in that country. A difference in patent rights may arise (i) because there is no patent in the country where the goods are first marketed; (ii) because there is a weaker patent in that country; or (iii) because the patents in the two countries are in unconnected hands. Each of these circumstances bears investigation.

(1) No patent in the first EEC country

The absence of a patent means that the marketing there may, on the   7-043
one hand, be by the patentee or an associate, or, on the other, by an enterprise unconnected with him.

If the marketing is by the patentee, a connected subsidiary, a manufacturing licensee or a distributor, movement of the goods cannot be prevented as a patent infringement in the country of import. In *Merck* v. *Stephar*,[62] the parallel importer was moving pharmaceuticals which it had purchased in Italy to the Netherlands against the will of the Dutch patentee. The latter held no equivalent patent for Italy but had sanctioned the marketing of the drugs there. Despite the consequent inability to extract any monopoly profit from sales in Italy, and the damage that introduction of the drugs onto the Dutch market would do to the protected price in the Netherlands, the Court insisted that the free movement be permitted because there was consent to first marketing.[63]

The same approach is adopted in the text of the CPC. By Article 32, Community patent rights will not extend to products once they have been marketed in a Common Market country by the patentee or with his "express consent," unless Community law allows some exception (a matter left undefined and thus to the jurisprudence of the Court). Once the CPC is brought into effect, national patent law of member states is obliged to adopt an equivalent rule.[64] The reference to express consent was included in the hope of ending any argument that failure to acquire a patent in any country was tantamount to consenting to others marketing there.[65] This danger has in any case receded as the Court has developed its notion of what constitutes consent in the subsequent case-law referred to in next paragraph.

Where the marketing in the first territory is by an unconnected   7-044
concern, the patentee derives nothing from the first sale of the goods. Since he acts without the consent of the patentee in the country of import, he may be prevented from moving the goods to that country by virtue of the patent rights enjoyed there. This has been accepted by the Court in *Keurkoop* v. *Nancy Kean Gifts*[66] which was concerned with registered design rights in a handbag granted for the Benelux countries, and must apply also to patents and other equivalent rights. It also

---

[62] [1981] E.C.R. 263; Handoll [1982] E.I.P.R. 26. And see *Dansk Supermarked* v. *Imerco* (below, n. 75—copyright, trade mark, consumer protection).

[63] For the argument that this should not be so because it risks the product being kept off the Italian market: Demaret, *Patents, Territorial Restrictions and EEC Law* (1971), pp. 91-93, 97-102.

[64] CPC Art. 81.

[65] The text could not in any case formally have tied the Court's hands, since it would be interpreting the Treaty of Rome, to which the CPC is subject (see its Art. 93).

[66] [1982] E.C.R. 2853.

follows *a fortiori* from the Court's decision in *Pharmon* v. *Hoechst*.[67] There a drug patented in both the United Kingdom and West Germany was manufactured and sold in the former country by a compulsory licensee. This licence had been imposed upon the patentee by the decision of the Comptroller. The patentee was held not to have consented to the parallel importation into Germany and could use his German patent to resist it. The decision indicates a willingness of the Court now to treat consent realistically, rather than notionally (as was earlier feared). The opposite result had been reached in *Musikvertrieb Membran* v. *GEMA*, which concerned the copyright in musical works embodied in sound recordings[68]; but there, despite the operation of a statutory licence to record under the then British copyright legislation,[69] the records were first marketed under a licence that was, technically "voluntary," for all that the royalty clause followed the rate prescribed in the statutory licence provision.

7-045   Other sight-lines in the Court's view of the free movement of goods policy have emerged in recent decisions concerning patents and similar rights. Where a national law, including an intellectual property provision, has the effect of limiting or restraining trade, the first question must be whether the law discriminates arbitrarily against importation from another Community state. If it does, it must fall outside the exempting provision of Article 36, as the second sentence of the Article states.[70] Thus in *Allen & Hanburys* v. *Generics*,[71] the right in question arose under an "old" British patent, which under the 1977 Act had its term extended from 16 to 20 years, subject to a compulsory designation of licences of right during the extra four years.[72] The patent was for a drug, salbutamol, which was never patented in Italy, and a parallel importer was proposing to get it from an independent supplier there and import it under licence of right into the United Kingdom. The Comptroller and the English courts were prepared to grant the licence only in respect of drugs to be manufactured in Britain because of the importer's lack of substantial business organisation in Britain, the difficulty of checking the origin and quality of foreign goods, either for the purpose of calculating royalties or for maintaining quality control in the interests of public health.[73] But the law and its application were doubly discriminatory: a distinction was being drawn between manufacture in Britain and other EEC countries; and (thanks to the terms of the Act) importers were not

---

[67] [1985] E.C.R. 2281. Earlier the same result was achieved in respect of patent rights in *Parke Davis* v. *Proebel* [1968] E.C.R. 55: but there argument was restricted to holding that neither Art. 85 nor Art. 86 prevented the patent from being asserted in the country of import.

[68] Discussed below, § 12-030.

[69] CA 1956, s.8, prescribing, under given conditions, the payment of a royalty of $6^{1}/4$ per cent. of the net selling price. There was no equivalent provision in the country of import, Germany.

[70] See above, § 1-024.

[71] [1988] F.S.R. 312. See also *Theodor Kohl* v. *Ringelhahn & Rennett* [1984] E.C.R. 3651 (unfair competition law applied only against foreign goods).

[72] For the transitional provision, see below, § A2-002. The designation brings into play PA 1977 s.46 (see below, licences of right).

[73] For these proceedings, see [1986] R.P.C. 203 (H.L.).

entitled to a special exemption which is available to a domestic infringer once he undertakes to apply for a licence of right.[74] Accordingly the refusal of the licence of right was contrary to Article 30.

On the other hand, if the national law applies equally to domestic   7-046
producer and importer, it is possible to balance—by "rule of reason"—the inhibitory effects of the law against its advantages for consumer protection and fair trading: if the latter are "necessary" it will remain operative. Thus in *Dansk Supermarked* v. *Imerco*,[75] a British pottery had produced plates to particular designs for a Danish company, and had undertaken not to allow "seconds" to reach the Danish market. Since the Danish company had consented to the marketing of these "seconds" in Britain it could not use Danish intellectual property (in this case, copyright and trade marks) to prevent importation; but in so far as the goods might be sold in a way which led the public to think that they were perfect when they were not, the Court apparently conceded that the Danish Marketing Law might be enforced. Such confusing of the public would have nothing to do with whether the goods were or were not imported from another state. Equally, a limiting provision in national intellectual property law which has an indiscriminate effect may be applied, because at present (*i.e.* without standardisation or harmonisation) "the determination of the conditions and procedures under which protection . . . is granted is a matter for national rules."[76] Thus in *Thetford* v. *Fiamma*[77] an "old" British patent for a portable lavatory could be asserted against competing products first marketed in other Common Market countries where there was no equivalent patent. The reason for this was that, under the Patents Act 1949, the criteria of novelty were "relative" and inter alia no account was to be taken of British patent specifications more than 50 years old.[78] The rules governing validity are matters for national law, provided that they do not discriminate, so that the patent could be enforced here. It cannot be argued that intellectual property which lacks a particular element (here a doctrine of "absolute" novelty) is not "industrial or commercial property" within the Article 36 exception. Equally it cannot be objected that in the country of import the intellectual property law covers an activity which is not caught in the country of export.[79] The Court has wisely eschewed the task of formulating piecemeal either the minimum or the maximum content of the substantive rights.

---

[74] PA 1977, s.46(3)(a) provides that such a producer is not to be liable to an injunction and can be liable in damages only to an amount double any licence royalty which would be set under the licence of right. The importer is explicitly excluded from this advantage.

[75] [1981] E.C.R. 181.

[76] *Keurkoop* v. *Nancy Kean Gifts* [1982] E.C.R. 2853 (Rule of Benelux registered designs law that applicant for protection did not have to be the creator or his assign not open to objection).

[77] [1988] 3 C.M.L.R. 549; [1989] F.S.R. 57.

[78] PA 1949, s.50(1).

[79] See *Warner* v. *Christiansen The Times*, June 1, 1988 (E.C.J.) (no rental right affecting video-cassettes in U,K., but such a right in Denmark; Danish law would apply to domestic copies and so could apply to imports from U.K.); also *Basset* v. *SACEM* [1987] 3 C.M.L.R. 173.

(2) A weaker patent right in the first EEC country

7-047   In the *Sterling Drug* case,[80] the owner of British and Dutch "parallel" patents was held not entitled to preclude from the Netherlands parallel imports of the drug, "Negram,"[81] which it had marketed in Britain at around half its Dutch price. This was so even though a number of factors combined to explain the lower British price. Two of these limited the potential monopoly power of the patentee: the system of price negotiation with the Department of Health and Social Security was backed, in the case of patented drugs, by the Crown's power to pay reasonable remuneration for use of the invention[82]; and by the power of private competitors to seek compulsory licences almost as of right under the law as it then stood.[83] But there was another, more potent factor: the decline in value of the pound sterling against the Dutch gilder since the prices had first been set.

Proponents of the view that a patentee in the country of import should have his full opportunity to earn a monopoly profit preserved to him, have argued that the Court should not have ignored the differences in patent values in this case.[84] But the facts of the *Sterling Drug* case suggest that this may be to seize upon legal variations whose effect upon the difference in price is more formal than actual. It is plain, in any case, from the even more unequivocal decision in *Merck* v. *Stephar* that "consent" to marketing is the one relevant criterion.[85]

(3) Different ownership of the patents in the two EEC countries

7-048   Occasionally this might arise when those claiming rights from two independent inventors of the same invention each manage to secure the patent for it is one of the relevant EEC States.[86] The Court of Justice has made it clear that in this circumstance each could use his rights to exclude from his own country the goods of the other.[87]

Much more likely is the case where the patents derive from a single act of invention, the rights having been split between the countries by assignment. With this the Court of Justice has not yet dealt. But it has held that if a trade mark has a single origin, the acquirer of it in one EEC country cannot use it to prevent the importing of goods properly marked by the owner in another country.[88] Under the "consent" theory

---

[80] Above, n. 68.
[81] This was the trade mark used by the marketing subsidiaries in the two countries; contemporaneous proceedings against the same parallel imports were considered by the Court of Justice at the same time: see below, §§ 18-007, 18-008.
[82] See below, §§ 7-055, 7-056.
[83] PA 1949, s.41; for its abolition by the 1977 Act, see below, §§ 7-054—7-056.
[84] cf. e.g. Demaret (above, n 72), §§ 87-89.
[85] In the CPC, Arts. 46(1), 81(3), an express exception is provided to Community-wide exhaustion where the goods are first marketed under compulsory licence in one state. See below, § 7-051, n. 10.
[86] Normally the "first-to-file" rule will give one or other precedence. But note the case where the applications are for different states and neither is published before the priority date of the other: see above, § 5-012. See also *Keurkoop* v. *Nancy Kean Gifts* (above, n. 76) which so treats the possibility of independent persons acquiring overlapping design rights in different states.
[87] *Centrafarm* v. *Sterling Drug* (above, n. 68), Judgment, § 11.
[88] *Van Zuylen* v. *Hag* (discussed below, §§ 18-007—18-008).

of free movement this could be justified only by an extended notion of "consent" and then not in a case where the splitting of the right occurred by government intervention. The Court, however, merely stated that the common origin of the rights was justification enough.[89] The Court might be moved to a similar conclusion over assignments of patents by this consideration: if division by assignment still gives protection to discriminatory pricing in different countries which would be denied to a single patentee, it may pay the patentee best to assign in one of them. It is hard to see why, by this one technique, it should be possible to maintain a result that is otherwise the very target of the free movement policy.[90]

4. COMPULSORY LICENCES

A wholehearted patent system will contain nothing that fetters a patentee's power to act as a monopolist if the market allows it: he will be able to hold production of his invention down to the level of maximum profit. But many countries have felt the urge to qualify this full potential in the name of some other political objective, such as local working of the invention or the satisfaction of consumer demand.[91] The technique for this is generally some form of compulsory licence, which will prevent the patentee from acting as sole producer. He will be obliged instead to face direct competition subject only to a royalty or other fee on the licensee's sales, assessed by an outside arbitrator under some criterion of reasonableness.[92] Pressure for this sort of curb tends to follow upon the success of particular patentees, frequently foreigners. The meetings of Paris Convention countries have long been the field for exhausting battles over the principle of compulsory licensing. A stringent requirement of local working, for instance, would seem a means by which one country could give preference for its home inventors, while hoping for no corresponding handicap upon them abroad. In the industrial countries, however, what has seemed vital in an international forum has become purely token in domestic practice: compulsory licensing provisions are commonly enmeshed in such a net of procedures that it is only the threat of invoking them that carries any significant weight. Exceptionally, the compulsory licence has been used severely enough for a serious falling-off of patenting to occur. This is a direction that has recently exercised and led to the breakdown in revising the Paris Convention.

7-049

---

[89] "Consent to first marketing of *goods*" is a notion concerned with the activities of parallel importers after rights have been exhausted. One consequence of abandoning it in favour of "common origin of *rights*" may be the conclusion that Arts. 30-36 permit direct exports by a manufacturer from his own territory into another without any intervening sale (see, as to trade marks, below). If this view were to be adopted for patents, it would make for difficulties in the application of the competition policy to patent licences: see above, § 7-033.

[90] *cf.* Waelbroeck (1976) 21 Antitrust Bull. 99, who offers the proprietary character of the patentee's right as a justification, but he feels the need of a (surely awkward) distinction between "real" assignments and those that are "really" licences.

[91] For the beginnings in the U.K., see above, § 3-011.

[92] "Compulsory licence" in this broad sense extends to the Crown use provisions discussed in the next section. Their similarity is stressed, *e.g.*, in CPC Art. 46(2).

(1) Compulsory licensing under the 1977 Act

(a) *Legal grounds*

7-050   Once a British patent has been granted for three years, the comptroller has power[93] to grant compulsory licences under it[94] on a number of grounds. He then settles the terms as he sees fit.[95] The elaborate provisions first give an extensive list of grounds, and the applicant must show a case within one or more of them. But their breadth is qualified, not simply by the fact that the comptroller's jurisdiction is discretionary, but by the enumeration of various policy considerations which he is expected to balance in assessing the particular case. Under a special provision concerning food and drug patents, which was abandoned by the 1977 Act, compulsory licences were available save exceptionally. The general rules covering compulsory licences (which survive in the latest Act) do not raise the same expectation that once a ground is made out the public interest demands a licence unless there are special circumstances. It is this difference which is the first explanation of why the general provisions result in very few applications and even fewer grants.

Three principal motives have lain behind the creation of the present powers. They form useful heads under which to group the statutory grounds:

7-051   (i) It should not be permissible to hinder the exploitation of other new technology. Hence one ground for granting compulsory licences is that the working of another patented invention in the United Kingdom is being prevented or hindered through refusal to grant licences, at all or on reasonable terms.[96] This could arise, for instance, where one patentee is refusing to licence a "head" patent to another who has a derivative patent for a selection or improvement. The ground is subject to the requirement that the compulsory licensee be prepared to cross-license his own patent on reasonable terms.[97] This power is easy to justify in light of overall objectives of the patent system.

(ii) A patent should not be a pretext for refusing to exploit new technology at all. Thus one ground for compulsory licensing is that United Kingdom demand for a patented product is not being met on reasonable terms.[98] There is a perennial fear that inventions so efficient as to threaten the future of an industry (the long-life light-bulb or razor-blade, for instance) are patented in order to delay their introduction. If that fear is at all justified, this power ought to have some effect. But the effect may only be to make the

---

[93] PA 1977, s.48(1). An applicant may receive a licence in his own favour and in certain circumstances also in favour of his customers (see s.49(1)). A government department may seek a licence for another.

[94] Or to enter a "licences of right" endorsement upon the register—as to which, see above, § 4-021.

[95] s.48(4). The licence may be exclusive even of the patentee and may revoke other licences: s.49(2).

[96] s.48(3)(d)(ii).

[97] s.48(7); cf. *Taylor's Patent* (1912) 29 R.P.C. 296.

[98] s.48(3)(b) and see also the grounds mentioned under (iii) below.

industry more than ever determined to suppress the information entirely.[99] Only very exceptionally could compulsory licensing of patents help: the usual difficulty with inventions is to show that they are a success. Compulsory licence applications in Britain (few as they have been) have mostly concerned things that the patentee or his voluntary licensees have shown to have market potential.

Note that the ground just mentioned covers more than the case of suppression. Its terms are wide enough to support an attack on "unduly high" monopoly prices: of this, more below.

(iii) A patent should result in the invention being worked in the United Kingdom. As the history of the Paris Convention shows, most countries have wanted to use the patent system to induce the actual working of the invention in their home territories.[1] Some countries used to provide harsh sanctions in this endeavour[2] and one role of the Convention has been to secure some moderation: by requiring that compulsory licensing should be tried before revocation, and that it should not be imposed within three years of grant.[3] For many inventions, the scale needed for cost-effective manufacture would make it absurd to expect plant to be established in each country where products are sold. However, it is in such cases that compulsory licences are least likely to be sought.[4] But in less obvious cases, patentees may feel that there is enough danger in failing to work in a country for them to set up facilities at least to finish their products there.[5]

The legal grounds in the British legislation are couched very broadly. The patent may be licensed if the invention is not being worked to the fullest extent that is reasonably practicable in the United Kingdom[6]; if United Kingdom demand for a patented product is not being met on reasonable terms or is being met to a substantial extent by importation[7]; if United Kingdom working is being hindered or prevented by importation[8]; if refusal of licences (at all or on reasonable terms) prevents an export market from being supplied with United Kingdom products or prejudices the establishment or development of United Kingdom industry.[9]

---

[99] The fear is easily fanned in political debate on patents. Evidence on the matter is very hard to come by.

[1] See Ladas, *The International Protection of Industrial Property* (1930); Penrose, *The Economics of the International Patent System* (1951), pp. 78-87. The old notion of the "importer-inventor" reflected the same desire: see above, § 4-005.

[2] See above, § 3-011.

[3] PIP Art. 5A; reflected in the British legislation, see above, § 7-050. The Convention allows revocation as a sanction if compulsory licensing is ineffective, but this has been dropped from PA 1977.

[4] For the economic implications of compulsory working, see Penrose (above, n. 1), Chap. 8.

[5] Thus obscuring the question whether the patent is really being worked in the territory. Pharmaceuticals, for instance, can be conveniently transported in bulk and made into tablet form immediately for supply.

[6] s.48(3)(a).

[7] s.48(3)(b).

[8] s.48(3)(c); this covers the direct products of patented processes.

[9] s.48(3)(d)(i), (iii), (e); where exports are concerned, the countries may be limited: s.48(6).

The policy is thus protectionist. It has been argued that if a compulsory licence were today granted upon an objection to importation from another EEC country, arguably the licence is a measure equivalent to a quantitative restriction on imports between Member States.[10] But this is rejected in *Extrude Hone's Patent*.[11] Certainly once the CPC takes full effect, manufacture anywhere within the Common Market will be sufficient discharge of the patentee's obligation to work the invention.[12]

(b) *The discretion*

7-052   Beside these grounds, the comptroller must balance a variety of considerations in deciding whether and what licence to grant compulsorily. To some extent these make clearer what limits upon monopoly power Parliament considered that it was imposing. Thus in addition to weighing such factors[13] as the nature of the invention, the time that has elapsed since grant, what the patentee or any licensee has already done to make full use of the invention and the ability of the applicant to work it to the public advantage and the risks to him, three purposes are stated to be the aim of the power: to secure full use quickly, to give the patentee "reasonable remuneration" and to protect anyone working or developing an invention in the United Kingdom from unfair prejudice.[14]

This contemplates qualifying the patentee's potential market power in two ways. First, the pressure that it imposes upon him to establish manufacturing facilities in the United Kingdom may prevent him from producing where he can do so most cheaply and efficiently. Secondly, the requirement that working be to the fullest practicable extent appears to contemplate that price ought to be reduced to satisfy larger demand, even if the monopoly profits will in consequence be reduced.[15] (On this front, the application will only take place if the patentee will not grant a voluntary licence on acceptable terms.)

7-053   But because the comptroller must still leave the patentee with "reasonable remuneration," the licence must not venture too far in either of these directions. The courts have had little enough opportunity to indicate how far it is proper to go. As far as manufacturing in the United Kingdom is concerned, the patentee will not protect himself against any grant at all simply by showing that present costs of foreign manufacture

[10] Demaret, *Patents, Territorial Restrictions and EEC Law* (1978) p. 86, n. 30.
[11] [1982] R.P.C. 361.
[12] CPC Arts. 47, 82. There is a 10-year transitional option.
[13] *cf.* the list of factors in *Brownie Wireless' Appln.* (1929) 46 R.P.C. 457 at 473.
[14] See PA 1977, s.50. The factors are to be weighed at the time of making the application; the patentee may not fudge the issue by hasty last minute activity: *McKechnie's Appln.* (1943) 51 R.P.C. 461 at 467.
[15] The unadorned case that the patentee's own prices are in the U.K. too high and that therefore a compulsory licence should be granted, seems rarely to have been presented: but note *Robin Electric's Petition* (1915) 32 R.P.C. 202 (minimum price clause in voluntary licence required licensee to charge higher prices in U.K. than abroad; held unobjectionable, since prices "not so high as to be a serious burden on the consumer or to be unreasonable"). Such an issue is examinable by the Monopolies Commission, if the general conditions for a reference to it are satisfied. In essence such an issue was dealt with by the Commission in its report criticising the pricing by the Hoffmann-La Roche group of its tranquillisers trade-marked "Librium" and "Valium": for this, see below, § A1-012, where the consequential powers in PA 1977, s.50 are also mentioned.

abroad are lower; there must be an historical inquiry to see whether he "used his monopoly fairly as between home and foreign trade," *i.e.* to determine whether his efforts to build up foreign manufacture did not prejudice the chance of doing so in Britain.[16] As far as concerns "further markets," where the foreign patentees of copying machinery had sold to a limited field of British customers, a compulsory licence was granted to a British company upon their prediction that they could sell to an extended range of customers.[17] Even when the comptroller decides to grant the licence, its terms (particularly the rate of royalty) will influence the licensee's decisions about selling price and hence quantity; which in turn will influence the patentee's remuneration. The royalty rate, however, is most likely to be fixed by comparison with any relevant rate charged by the patentee or others in the industry for similar licences.

A compulsory licence system which is directed at one or other form of insufficient exploitation, and which thus requires careful investigation of the circumstances before grant, is not likely to be much used. This is indeed borne out by British and other experience.[18] How far the threat of applying to the Comptroller enhances the bargaining position of would-be voluntary licensees cannot be measured. Neither can it be discounted.[19] But in many cases it will not be strong: for the licensee may also need know-how to get started: and the licensor cannot be obliged to provide that under the present rules. Britain's membership of a growing EEC, moreover, reduces the number of cases in which the threat has any meaning.[20]

The provisions in the 1977 Act should be contrasted with a system in **7-054** which licences are available as of right—subject only to preliminary, or even subsequent, argument about the rate of royalty. Such an arrangement has, for instance, been part of the transitional provisions affecting the extension of term from 16 to 20 years in the 1977 Act.[21] It is one or other scheme of this class which policy-makers usually have in mind when they discuss reducing the reward for invention to the profits that can be collected from licensees of right. Such ideas meet marked hostility

[16] Parker J., *Hatschek's Patent* (1909) 26 R.P.C. 228 at 243; see also *Johnson's Patent* (1909) 26 R.P.C. 52; *Bremer's Patent* (1909) 26 R.P.C. 449 at 465.
[17] *Kallè's Patent* [1966] F.S.R. 112. A number of grounds were alleged by the applicant. In a case where the circumstances were rather special (*Cathro's Appln.* (1934) 51 R.P.C. 75) it was said that demand must be actual not potential. But the Act now refers to "a" rather than "the" demand, and other cases, including *Kallè*, making nothing of the point: see also *Boult's Patent* (1909) 26 R.P.C. 383 at 387; *Fabricmeter's Appln.* (1936) 53 R.P.C. 307 at 312; *Kamborian's Patent* [1961] R.P.C. 403 at 405. As to sub-licensing, see Hilti's Patent [1988] R.P.C. 51.
[18] Between 1959 and 1968 an average of 1.5 were applied for in the U.K. per annum under the general provisions; only two were granted for the whole period; for the special food and drugs provision average applications were 4.1 per annum; four were granted in toto: Banks Report (Cmnd. 4407, (1970), App.D(*d*)).
[19] The Banks Committee thought there was enough indirect effect to justify retaining the provisions on compulsory licensing in general: Chap. 12; but it shared the hostility of leading pharmaceutical firms towards the compulsory licensing provision (PA 1949, s.41—abandoned in PA 1977) that allowed the grant of licences save in exceptional circumstances: Chap. 14. See further, below, n. 22.
[20] See above, § 7-051.
[21] See below, § A2-002.

from those with patenting interests[22]: to such a degree as to provide a testament of faith in the market power that patents may generate for successful inventions.

5. CROWN USE

7-055 The kind of compulsory licence mentioned in the previous paragraph is now exemplified in the British patent system in the Crown use provisions.[23] These empower the Crown to make or sanction use of a patented invention without previous licence, subject only to an obligation to pay compensation for doing so. Originally the Crown was in no sense bound by Letters Patent: for one thing, classic theory relieved "the Crown"— not just the sovereign in person—of civil responsibility imposed by courts of justice.[24] Compensation for use of patented inventions was paid *ex gratia*. In 1883 came a change. In principle the Crown was made subject to patents, but was given the benefit of Crown use provisions that were the ancestors of the present law.[25] Compensation became a matter of legal entitlement; but the Crown could, of course, claim that it was not within the scope of monopoly or that the patent was invalid.[26]

The obvious justification for the Crown use provision lies in national security.[27] But central government acts in many other spheres besides defence and the wider potential of its powers was dramatically demonstrated in 1965: the House of Lords held that the Ministry of Health might authorise an importer to bring in drugs not made by the patentee for use in the NHS hospital service.[28] In the cases to which it is applicable, the Crown's ability to override the patentee's decisions on exploitation may prove a decisive counterweight to full monopoly power. Because of this, it tends to be viewed critically, particularly in EEC and other countries which do not allow their governments so wide-ranging a weapon.[29] In response, it can be said that if a government department decides to take up an invention, it may well be providing an exceptionally large market for it, one that it might take much greater effort to establish in the private sector. As an incentive to invent and innovate, therefore, the prospect of securing compensation for Crown use may in

[22] Witness in the U.K. the campaign (ultimately successful) to abolish PA 1949, s.41 (see above, n. 19) and more recently to prevent the licence of right in the extension of term (above, § 7-045) from affecting pharmaceutical and other patents (which succeeded with CDPA 1988, s.293, 294). See also the Report of the Economic Council of Canada, the Government White Paper thereon, and the reactions to both above, §§ 3-012—3-013.
[23] PA 1977, ss.55-59.
[24] *Feather* v. *R.* (1865) 6 B. & S. 257.
[25] Patents, Design and Trade Marks Act 1883, s.27.
[26] Validity may also be challenged in proceedings for compensation: s.74(1)(*c*).
[27] In times of national emergency, the Crown's powers become very wide indeed: see PA 1977, s.59.
[28] *Pfizer* v. *Ministry of Health* [1965] A.C. 512; [1965] R.P.C. 261.
[29] See, *e.g.* Demaret, *Patents, Territorial Restrictions and EEC Law* (1978), 12-17, 87-89 (On the "reasonable reward" theory also applied by British legislation to compulsory licensing, and on the impact of compulsory licensing and Crown use provisions in the *Sterling Drug* case: see above, § 7-047.

many instances be broadly as attractive as full monopoly profits from other sources. Whether this sort of justification has a sufficient basis in historical fact deserves examination: this it has never had.

The special powers of the Crown to use and then pay compensation are governed by three principal factors:

(i) The acts performed must be "for the services of the Crown."[30]   **7-056**
    They do not have to be done by a government department. Anyone authorised to act on the Crown's behalf is included,[31] but still the aim must be to fulfil a Crown service, whether the benefit goes to the Crown or to members of the public. By the Crown is meant the executive government of the United Kingdom and its services are those supplied by Crown servants under the direction of a minister.[32] This excludes services provided by other agencies of government or supported by public finance: the nationalised industries, independent authorities such as the Post Office, local government, universities and so forth. It does, however, cover the supply of anything for foreign defence purposes (*i.e.* arms to foreign governments), the supply of scheduled drugs in the Health Service, and research into, and supply of, atomic energy.[33] But why, it may be asked, central government and not the rest? Which leads back to the question: apart from defence, has central government (and through it the public) such a claim to cheap inventions that the incentive device provided by the patent system deserves to be substantially qualified?

(ii) Not every act which would otherwise amount to infringement falls within the Crown use exemption. In particular, while acts of manufacture, use and associated activities of keeping and importing are within the exemption, selling and offering to sell fall outside, save exceptionally: as an incident of making, using or importing; in contracts to supply arms to foreign governments; in supplying scheduled medicines through the NHS pharmaceutical services; and in disposing of things no longer required.[34]

(iii) The rate of compensation is not dictated by the Crown but will, if it cannot be agreed, be settled by the court.[35] The Crown is entitled to put itself in the position of a licensee. If it causes loss of manufacturing or other profit, it is obliged to compensate for this.[36] Other benefits from government departments have to be

[30] PA 1977, s.55(1).

[31] *Ibid.* The authorisation must be in writing; but it does not have to be given until after the event: s.55(6). Normally the patentee or an exclusive licensee needs no authority, and so obtains no right to compensation; but see the exceptions in s.57(3),(4); Ency. PL, § 9-018.

[32] *Pfizer* v. *Ministry of Health* (above, n. 28) at 295, 301, 306.

[33] s.56(2)-(4).

[34] s.55(1).

[35] s.55(4). The obligation may run from the date of publishing the application; or, if revealed without obligation of confidence to a government department before that, from the priority date. Note that the government department concerned is under (sanctionless) obligation to notify the patentee of use, unless contrary to the public interest: s.55(7).

[36] CDPA 1988, Sch. 5, s.16, belatedly abrogating *Patchett's Patent* [1967] R.P.C. 237 (C.A.).

brought into consideration and there is a curious provision which possibly means that the patentee may have his compensation reduced if he would not accept a reasonable offer from the Crown.[37]

Where these rules cover the operation, there are a variety of provisions which override ancillary rights: terms in licences, assignments and agreements restricting working or requiring payments are of no effect[38]; copyright in certain models and documents is not infringed[39]; subsequent acquirers are treated as if the Crown were the patentee.[40] In addition, the Crown is made free of all obligations not only if it has undertaken prior use but even if the invention has been merely recorded for the Crown before the priority date of the patent.[41]

---

[37] s.58(3). There are a number of provisions limiting the right to compensation on grounds similar to those limiting claims to damages for infringement of rights in patents and applications: see s.58(6), (8), (10).

[38] s.57(1), (2).

[39] s.57(1). By contrast, registered designs are subject to Crown use provisions, similar to those applying to patents: see Registered Designs Act 1949, s.12, Sched. 1. Rights in confidential information cannot be overridden (PA 1977, s.55(10)), save in the cases covered by the Defence Contracts Act 1958, ss.2, 3.

[40] s.55(8).

[41] s.55(4). As to the scope of this, see Ency. PL, § 9-019.

Part III

CONFIDENCE

CHAPTER 8

CONFIDENTIAL INFORMATION

1. INTRODUCTION

(1) Nature of the liability

A person ought to keep a secret if he has said that he will do so. In recent decisions English courts have translated this simple moral precept into a legal principle of considerable breadth.[1] The development runs counter to the judges' traditional reluctance to adopt broad propositions as ground rules for the imposition of liability, and they are now having to face some of the difficulties inherent in their unusual course.[2]

8-001

All sorts of information may be imparted or gathered in confidence; the degree of secrecy required may be partial or total. The fashioning of the law into more specific rules is accordingly difficult and much of what follows may appear as imprecise as the subject-matter is ephemeral. In contrast with many other legal systems, English law does not distinguish between types of information that may be protected against breach of confidence: technological secrets, such as chemical formulae and mechanical techniques,[3] commercial records such as customer lists and sales figures,[4] marketing, professional and managerial procedures,[5] and equally information of political significance[6] and about personal relationships, such as the Duchess of Argyll's tales to the Duke of her earlier sentimental journeys[7]—all have been treated as protectable.

English law has proved unwilling to include a "right to privacy" among its pantheon of protectable values, fearing that so broad a concept

8-002

[1] The subject has generated a considerable literature. See esp. Jones (1970) 86 L.Q.R. 463; North (1971) 12 J.S.P.T.L. 149; Finn, *Fiduciary Obligations* (1977) Chap. 19 and (1984) 58 A.L.J. 497; Vaver (1979) 1 E.I.P.R. 301; English Law Commission, Report No. 110, *Breach of Confidence* (Cmnd. 8388, 1981); Gurry, *Breach of Confidence* (1984); Ricketson (1984) Chaps. 42–45. Turner, *Law of Trade Secrets* (1962) is an idiosyncratic comparison of U.K. and U.S. law.
[2] As to the moral basis of the cause of action, see *House of Spring Gardens v. Point Blank* [1983] F.S.R. 213 at 253; [1985] F.S.R. 327 at 335 (Irish S.C.).
[3] Many of the cases concern this variety of "know-how," as examples below will show.
[4] *e.g. Robb v. Green* [1895] 2 Q.B. 315; *Lamb v. Evans* [1893] 1 Ch. 218.
[5] *Stephenson Jordan v. McDonald and Evans* (1951) 68 R.P.C. 190 (but note the traditional reluctance to recognise that business management techniques deserve protection: Evershed M.R., same case (1952) 69 R.P.C. 10 at 14); *Thomas v. Mould* [1968] 1 All E.R. 963; *Interfirm Comparison v. Law Society of N.S.W.* [1975] R.P.C. 137.
[6] *Fraser v. Evans* [1969] 1 All E.R. 8 (C.A.); *Att.-Gen. v. Jonathan Cape* [1976] Q.B. 752 (Q.B.D.) (Cabinet papers); *Att.-Gen. v. Guardian Newspapers (No. 2)* [1988] 3 All E.R. 545 (H.L.) (*"Spycatcher"*).
[7] *Argyll v. Argyll* [1967] Ch. 302.

would unduly prejudice competing interests in freedom of information and expression and in a free press.[8] Some of the potential territory is covered by a breach of confidence action, which extends to personal as well as economic subject-matter. But even so, its keystone is the undertaking to preserve confidence, which is either given directly by the defendant, or by someone from whom the defendant derives his information. Invasions of privacy which lie outside this limit remain open to civil or criminal redress only if some general tort, crime or other wrong has been committed. Confidence protection thus plays an important role in achieving a sensitive political balance. We shall return to its relationship to the legal protection of privacy when we consider proposals for reform at the end of the Chapter.[9]

(2) Confidence and patents

8-003   Given the range of subject-matter it is important to compare the protection of confidential information with that provided by patents and by copyright. In the realm of technical ideas confidence cannot play any long-term role unless the information can be put to commercial use without at the same time becoming public.[10] A mechanical device will almost always reveal its workings to experts once it is marketed; but a process of manufacture may not be similarly detectable. In the latter case, an inventor may secure a patent that gives him monopoly protection even against independent devisers of the same invention; but it is for a limited period, and on condition that the invention is sufficiently described in the specification. Accordingly, to keep this invention secret through obligations of confidence is for him an alternative, not an additional, form of protection—an alternative that is not tied to specified time periods but which is good only against those who receive the information directly or (in some cases) indirectly from him. Many countries have accepted that this choice should be provided, however much it may detract from the incentive to publicise that is one root purpose of the patent system. Even in the United States, where alone the matter has been extensively debated, the outcome has been to permit the alternatives. For it was finally decided that industry must be assured the opportunity of conserving new technology that was not necessarily patentable by means of

---

[8] By contrast, the idea took root in the U.S. from the passionate and celebrated article by Warren and Brandeis (4 Harv. L.R. 193 (1890)) and the advocacy of Prosser (esp. 48 Calif. L.R. 383 (1960)). For the comparison, see, *e.g.* R. Wacks, *The Protection of Privacy* (1980) Chap. 1.

The U.K. is bound, as a state adhering to the European Convention on Human Rights, to observe the right to respect for private and family life, home and correspondence contained in Art. 8 (subject to certain exceptions). The Convention does not however give rise to directly enforceable rights of the kind that might override breach of confidence law: *Malone* v. *Commissioner of Police* [1979] 2 All E.R. 620 at 647–649. But *cf.* the Strasbourg Commission's subsequent Report on this same case, 26 D. & R. 105; and see generally, Fawcett, *The Application of the European Convention on Human Rights* (1987), pp. 210–235.

[9] Below, § 8-045.

[10] In the short term—until a patent application can be filed—obligations of confidence prevent the danger that revelation of the invention will destroy its novelty: see above, § 5-012.

confidence; and to insist that patentable inventions should only be protected by patents would be to introduce a distinction that it would be difficult and cumbersome to draw.[11]

In actual practice, patents are often secured for a central invention, 8-004 while much that is learned in the process of bringing it into commercial production is tied up as secret "know-how" by means of confidence undertakings.[12] The distinction, as we have noted, is marked in licensing practice[13]—bare patent licences are very different from operational production packages. The question to be considered here is how far the non-patentable "know-how" is really capable of protection against those who seek to make use of it without consent, as distinct from those who will pay for a licence to obtain it. The problem most commonly arises when managers and other employees of a concern seek to take the "know-how" off to a rival business. We shall see that the courts have been particularly reluctant to saddle ex-employees with obligations that will prevent them from disposing of their general knowledge and skill to their best advantage.[14] Against them, breach of confidence proceedings are hard to maintain, and in this oblique fashion the courts have checked the ability of breach of confidence protection to make real inroads into the territory of the patent system.

(3) Confidence and copyright

In principle copyright is capable of helping to resist invasions of 8-005 privacy. But the intrusion must take the form of making at least one copy, or of giving a performance in public, or of doing one of the other acts specified as constituting infringement. Coupled with this, there must be a copying of the manner of expression and not merely the information contained in the copyright work. The proceedings moreover must be brought by those with title to the copyright.[15] Breach of confidence protection resembles copyright in that the information which the defendant seeks to deploy must derive from that which the plaintiff seeks to protect. But confidence protection is not generally tied to particular ways of using the material.[16] It is concerned with the information in substance and not in form,[17] and only the person to whom obligations of confidence are owed will be entitled to sue.[18]

[11] In the wake of the *Sears* and *Compco* cases (above, § 1-001) doubts about trade secrets protection were raised in *Lear* v. *Adkins* 395 U.S. 653 (1969), and finally disposed of by *Kewanee* v. *Bicron* 416 U.S. 470 (1974).

[12] The patent has, of course, to satisfy the requirement of sufficient disclosure: see above, §§ 5-058—5-063. [13] Above, § 7-052.

[14] Hence the fact that licensees may be willing to pay for know-how does not necessarily demonstrate that the know-how amounts to more than an employee is entitled to treat as general skill and knowledge: see *Potters-Ballotini* v. *Weston-Baker* [1977] R.P.C. 202 (C.A.); *Yates Circuit Foil* v. *Electrofoils* [1976] F.S.R. 345; and see below, pp. 277–280.

[15] See below, §§ 12-002 *et seq.*

[16] But where the confidentiality relates to the way in which ideas are expressed (*e.g.* in a set of precedents or a questionnaire), a breach which does not result in use of the same expression may give rise only to nominal damages: *Interfirm Comparison* v. *Law Society* (above, n. 5).

[17] Nor does the information have to exist in recorded form: see *Printers & Finishers* v. *Holloway* [1965] R.P.C. 239. 255.

[18] *Fraser* v. *Evans* [1969] 1 All E.R. 8 (C.A.) (see below, n. 85).

Thus, if a secret society has rules written for it by a functionary, who does nothing to dispose of his copyright in them, a renegade member intent on "exposing" the society to the public may be in breach of confidential obligations to the society, however he chooses to summarise the rules; he will infringe the author's copyright in the rules only if he substantially reproduces their content. If he pleads "public interest" in defence, the concept is probably the same in each case; but for copyright there are further statutory defences of "fair dealing" that may be apposite.[19]

(4) Historical and doctrinal

8-006   The jurisdiction to restrain breach of confidence has its roots in equity, partly because the remedy most often sought has been the injunction, and partly because the subject-matter occupies the same moral terrain as breach of trust.[20] The scope of the modern law began to be settled around 1850 with *Prince Albert* v. *Strange*[21] (literary material, at once royal and private, on the borders of copyright) and *Morison* v. *Moat*[22] (recipe for a medicine). In both cases, injunctions were granted against indirect recipients of the confidential information, and the jurisdiction was said, rather prodigally, to arise by virtue of property, agreement, confidence, trust and bailment. But it was left uncertain then (as it remains now) in what circumstances direct and indirect recipients of information would have liability imposed upon them. In the period after the Judicature Acts, there were some attempts (typical of their period) to confine the equitable wrong to cases in which the original disclosee agreed by contract, express or implied, to respect confidence[23]; with the apparent consequence that an indirect recipient, not being privy to the contract, would be liable only if he deliberately or recklessly induced breach of that contract.[24] Contract and tort would thus subsume the whole field between them.

8-007   More recently, contract has ceased to be treated as the universal touchstone of liability (though its role in determining what obligations or

---

[19] For these defences, see *Hubbard* v. *Vosper, Beloff* v. *Pressdram, Commonwealth* v. *Fairfax* below, §§ 8-017, 8-018.

[20] The old couplet, "Three things are to be helpt in Conscience, Fraud, Accident and Things of Confidence," attributed to Sir Thomas More (see *Coco* v. *Clark* [1969] R.P.C. 41 at 46) suggests how long the connection has stood.

[21] (1849) 2 De G. & Sm. 652; Mac. & G. 25. Before this there had been a number of cases in which injunctions had been granted to prevent the publication of unpublished letters, plays and other literary works; these were based on a "common law right of property" that a majority of the judges found to exist in *Millar* v. *Taylor* (1769) 4 Burr. 2303, and *Donaldson* v. *Beckett* (1774) 2 Bro.P.C. 129; see below § 9-003.

[22] (1851) 9 Hare 241.

[23] Contractual language reaches a climax in *Vokes* v. *Heather* (1945) 62 R.P.C. 135 (C.A.). *cf. British Celanese* v. *Moncrieff* (1948) 65 R.P.C. 165, 167 (C.A.). The approach produced nice conundrums: see *Triplex* v. *Scorah*, below, n. 6. But *Robb* v. *Green* [1895] 2 Q.B. 315 (C.A.) put the jurisdiction in both contract and equity and this conceptual casualness has been echoed more recently, *e.g.* in *Nichrotherm* v. *Percy* [1957] R.P.C. 207 (C.A.) and *Ackroyds* v. *Islington Plastics* [1962] R.P.C. 97.

[24] *British Industrial Plastics* v. *Ferguson* [1940] 1 All E.R. 479 (H.L.).

confidence exist may still be crucial).[25] Starting with *Saltman* v. *Campbell*,[26] the courts have recognised a wider equitable jurisdiction, based, it is said, "not so much on property or on contract, but rather on good faith,"[27] and this approach is now reasonably well entrenched among the judiciary. As a justification for intervening, particularly at this intermediate stage of legal development, "good faith" has a certain forthrightness that is attractive. The issue is not hedged behind conceptual dogma which all too readily states legal results without properly considering their justification. But if the true measure is a simple moral yardstick, the courts have been tantalisingly vague in the matter of how it is calibrated. This casualness has excited scientifically-minded jurists to a rash of disputation: in favour of working out the implications of "good faith" more exactly[28]; in favour of a new tort of breach of confidence[29]; in favour of "equitable property" as the true basis of protection.[30]

In the account that follows we must isolate the points at which these differences of pedigree begin to matter. They are to be found at the fringes of the wrong, and concern in particular (i) the liability of those who in some sense act innocently, (ii) the circumstances in which damages may be awarded for breach, (iii) the possibility of awarding damages for injury to feelings as distinct from economic loss, (iv) the liability of indirect recipients and (v) the effect of dealings that treat the information as property. The most pertinent question to ask about these problems is whether the answers so far given reflect in a realistic sense jurisdiction based on "good faith"; or whether one of the other explanations, although enjoying little popularity with the judges at present, is in fact truer to the results which they wish to procure. 8-008

2. REQUIREMENTS FOR LIABILITY

Megarry J.'s listing of the requirements for an actionable breach of confidence[31] makes a convenient starting-point for analysis: 8-009

[25] As to this, see below, § 8-021.
[26] (1948) 65 R.P.C. 203 (C.A.); and see *Nichrotherm* v. *Percy* (above, n. 23) at 213–214. *Peter Pan* v. *Corsets Silhouette* [1963] R.P.C. 45 and *Cranleigh Precision* v. *Bryant* [1966] R.P.C. 81, are both cases in which jurisdiction is put solely in equity despite the presence of contract. See further Vaver (above, n. 1) at 303.
[27] Lord Denning M.R., *Fraser* v. *Evans* [1969] 1 All E.R. 8, 11; and also in *Seager* v. *Copydex (No. 1)* [1967] 2 All E.R. 415, 417. For a distinguished precursor see Holmes J., *Du Pont* v. *Masland*, 244 U.S. 100, 102 (1917). But in *Att.-Gen.* v. *Guardian Newspapers (No. 2)* (above, n. 6), the House of Lords eschewed the question, while accepting that the jurisdiction in equity extended beyond contract.
[28] Jones (1970) 86 L.Q.R. 463; and see Goff and Jones, *Law of Restitution* (3rd ed., 1986), Chap. 35.
[29] North and Law Commission, above, n. 1.
[30] Ricketson above, n. 1.
[31] *Coco* v. *Clark* [1969] R.P.C. 41 at 47. Approved by the Court of Appeal in *Dunford & Elliot* v. *Johnston* [1978] F.S.R. 143 at 148 (C.A.) at 509; *Jarman & Platt* v. *Barget* [1977] F.S.R. 260 at 276–277; and relied upon in many other cases.

"First, the information itself . . . must 'have the necessary quality of confidence about it.'[32] Secondly, that information must have been imparted in circumstances importing an obligation of confidence. Thirdly, there must be an unauthorised use of that information [possibly[33]] to the detriment of the party communicating it."

Each of these heads will be treated in turn.

(1) Subject-matter capable of protection

(a) *Types of information*

8-010   The breach of confidence action, as already stated, lies in respect of technical, commercial, personal and other information without distinction by subject. A general reservation has been expressed against covering "trivial tittle-tattle";[34] and it has recently been accepted that scandalous or immoral material may be disqualified from protection, just as it is not accorded copyright.[35]

An idea for something yet to be elaborated may attract legal protection as confidential information, where there is nothing that generates copyright. Thus the idea for a television series about a female popgroup, which would draw upon the backgrounds and histories of three actresses intended for the parts, was held capable of protection. The requirements of copyright law to show specific expression of the idea in scenarios or scripts, in writing or other recorded form, were held not necessary in the law of confidence. It was enough that "the content of the idea was clearly identifiable, original, of potential commercial attractiveness and capable of being realised in actuality."[36] This recognises the considerable value that such initial inspirations may now have. Again, technical information does not have to be novel or attain any level of inventiveness[37]:

> "it is perfectly possible to have a confidential document, be it a formula, a plan, a sketch, or something of that kind, which is the result of work done by the maker on materials which may be available for the use of anybody; but what makes it confidential is the fact that the maker of the document has used his brain and thus produced a result which can only be produced by somebody who goes through the same process."[38]

---

[32] This expression is Lord Greene M.R.'s: *Saltman* v. *Campbell* (above, n. 26) at 215.

[33] For Megarry J.'s doubt about detriment, see below, § 8-035.

[34] Megarry J., *Coco* v. *Clark* (above, n. 26) at 48. But trivia worth money are different: see *Argyll* v. *Argyll* (above, n. 7); cf. *Church of Scientology* v. *Kaufman* [1973] R.P.C. 635.

[35] *Stephens* v. *Avery* [1988] F.S.R. 510. However, a lesbian relationship is no longer so unmentionable a subject that it cannot be protected in confidence: *ibid*.

[36] *Fraser* v. *Thames Television* [1983] 2 All E.R. 101; applying *Talbot* v. *General T.V.* [1981] R.P.C. 1 (S.C., Victoria)—where the particular twist to the idea was merely that a programme series about millionaires would include interviews with particular exemplars.

[37] But see *Nichrotherm* v. *Percy* [1957] R.P.C. 207 at 209 (C.A.) where stating the technical problem that called for solution was treated as not protectable.

[38] Lord Greene M.R., *Saltman* v. *Campbell* (above, n. 26 at 215; and see *Ansell Rubber* v. *Allied Rubber* [1967] V.R. 37.

(b) *Information and observation*

Typically, the subject of protection exists as information before the obligation of confidence is assumed. But some cases have concerned events which the person bound by confidence has observed for himself.[39] So far the courts have shown no inclination to treat the two cases differently and indeed to do so would be highly artificial. The consequence, however, is to broaden the role of the confidence action in the field of privacy.

8-011

(c) *Public knowledge*

If information has been made freely and entirely public, either before it was given to the defendant in confidence, or else in the interval between that time and trial of the action, then in many cases nothing protectable will remain,[40] at least if the defendant's breach of confidence is not the cause.[41] (The possibility of publication occurring after the court's order goes to the scope of remedies and is discussed below).[42]

8-012

Where the revelation is by the defendant himself, he has been held to remain liable.[43] However, this problem has yet to receive the full judicial analysis it deserves. It may well be that even in this situation no subject-matter then subsists which can subsequently be the subject of obligation.[44] But there still remains the question of liability arising from the act of revelation, which is itself a breach. It will be seen later that relief may be granted against wrongful use quite independently of wrongful disclosure,[45] and accordingly an injunction to prevent future use may be appropriate. In addition, any pecuniary relief by way of damages or account should bring in the continuing consequences of the unjustified revelation.

The issue is difficult when the relevation is in some sense only partial. If not all the relevant information has been made public, the rest (if it

8-013

---

[39] This was the character of much of the information which the pop-stars were attempting to keep out of the press in *Woodward* v. *Hutchins* [1977] 2 All E.R. 751. The plaintiffs failed for other reasons: see below, n. 63; see also *Printers & Finishers* v. *Holloway* (below, n. 4).

[40] See *Saltman* v. *Campbell* (above, n. 26) at 215; *John Zink* v. *Lloyds Bank* [1975] R.P.C. 385 at 389; *Harrison* v. *Project & Design* [1978] F.S.R. 81 (information becoming public). Note the readiness to take up this sort of explanation in an "unappetising" personal scandal case: *Lennon* v. *News Group* [1978] F.S.R. 573 (C.A.); *cf. Argyll* v. *Argyll* (above, n. 7). See generally, Tettenborn [1982] 11 Anglo-Am.L.R. 273.

[41] The defendant's action may make an injunction purposeless, but damages and other remedies ought to be available. In *Harrison* v. *Project & Design* (above, n. 40), damages were awarded to the defendant for his production during a period of time until the information became public; it is not clear how this publicity came about, if it was not through the defendant's own activity.

[42] §§ 8-039, 8-040.

[43] *Speed Seal* v. *Paddington* [1986] 1 All E.R. 91 (C.A.).

[44] Lord Goff (*Att.-Gen.* v. *Guardian Newspapers (No. 2)* (above, n. 6) at 661–662) criticises the *Speed Seal* case, particularly for its reliance on the view that only revelation by the plaintiff renders confidential information no longer open to protection—for which see below, n. 55.

[45] Below, § 8-033.

can be adequately specified) remains capable of protection.[46] If the information has been given to some of those interested but not to others, there may remain some "relative secrecy"[47]; whether a court will grant any form of relief in such cases seems to depend on the circumstances as a whole.

In this context, the "springboard" metaphor has enjoyed a vogue:

> "A person who has obtained information in confidence is not allowed to use it as a springboard for activities detrimental to the person who made the confidential communication, and springboard it remains even when all the features have been published or can be ascertained by actual inspection by any member of the public ... The possessor of the confidential information still has a long start over any member of the public."[48]

8-014 But this is not an invariable rule which takes no account of subsequent developments and other circumstances: the "springboard does not last for ever."[49] Among other factors that a court is likely to take into account are the following[50]:

(i) How truly did the information become public? Formal tests of publication drawn from patent law are not used.[51] Nor is it enough to show that a product has been marketed which, if dismantled or analysed, would reveal the information.[52] On the other hand, if the plaintiff includes all the information in a patent specification, he is taken to have made it public.[53]

(ii) How likely was it that the defendant would in any event have discovered the information without impropriety, had he not

---

[46] Thus in *Mustad* v. *Allcock and Dosen* (below, n. 53) the House of Lords only refused protection after noting that, on the evidence, the plaintiff's invention had been completely revealed in its patent specification (*cf. House of Spring Gardens* v. *Point Blank* [1985] F.S.R. 327 (Irish S.C.)). The need to distinguish what is protectable as a secret is crucial where it must be specified in an injunction: see Ricketson (1977) 11 Melb. U.L.R. 223, 289 at 291 for the case-law. The fact that a mixture of public and private information has been taken may lead to an award of damages; *cf. Seager* v. *Copydex (No. 1)* [1967] 2 All E.R. 415 at 417 (C.A.).

[47] Cross J., *Franchi* v. *Franchi* [1967] R.P.C. 149; *cf. Dunford & Elliott* v. *Johnston* [1978] F.S.R. 143 at 148 at 155 (C.A.) where the extent of revelation is given as one reason for refusing interlocutory relief. Note also *Foster* v. *Mountford* [1978] F.S.R. 582 (aboriginal tribal secrets); and the case-law in n. 51 below.

[48] Roxburgh J., *Terrapin* v. *Builders Supply* (1959) [1967] R.P.C. 375, 392; first approved in the Court of Appeal, *Seager* v. *Copydex (No. 1)* (above, n. 46) at 417; see also, *e.g. Cranleigh* v. *Bryant* (below, n. 55) and *Ackroyds* v. *Islington Plastics* [1962] R.P.C. 97.

[49] Lord Denning M.R., *Potters-Ballotini* v. *Weston-Baker* [1977] R.P.C. 202, 205: *Harrison* v. *Project Design*, above, n. 40 at 87. See generally, M. Barclay 26 U.C.L.A. Law R. 203.

[50] *cf.* the list given in the American Restatement of Torts Art. 757, referred to in a number of Australian decisions; see Ricketson (above, n. 46) 228.

[51] *Cf.* above, § 5-011; *Yates* v. *Electrofoils* (above, n. 14) at 387; *Interfirm Comparison* v. *Law Society* (above, n. 5).

[52] See *Saltman* v. *Campbell* (above, n. 26) at 215; *Terrapin* v. *Builders Supply* (above, n. 48) at 26; *Conveyor* v. *Cameron* [1973] 2 N.Z.L.R. 38.

[53] *Mustad* v. *Allcock and Dosen* (1928) [1963] 3 All E.R. 416 n. (H.L.); see also *Lysnar* v. *Gisborne* [1924] N.Z.L.R. 13.

received it in confidence from the plaintiff?[54] If it is in fact available in a third party's patent specification, the issue ought to be whether the defendant would have been likely to search for and discover that specification.[55]

(iii) Did the plaintiff believe that he would be injured by release of the information, and that it was not yet in the public domain? According to Megarry J., if this belief was reasonable, the plaintiff ought to be entitled to protect it.[56] This approach may commend itself to future courts for dealing with cases where information has already got into a limited number of hands. There is some danger, however, that it will unduly favour plaintiffs."

(d) *Public interest*

Free speech and freedom for the media are not under English law directly guaranteed as fundamental legal rights.[57] They exist as political freedoms because censorship and fiscal inhibitions on the press were not able to survive the emergence of democracy, and they remain circumscribed by such limits as the law of defamation, the Official Secrets Act and proscriptions upon contempt of court.[58] Breach of confidence, now extended into the field of political and personal information, is the latest weapon in the armoury of those who wish to suppress items of embarrassing news. This development opens up a fundamental conflict of policies which the courts are still searching to resolve. It is well-settled that "there can be no confidence which can be relied on to restrain a disclosure of iniquity",[59] and in this context "iniquity" probably covers criminal, tortious and other legally wrongful conduct, at least if it is serious.[60] Some judges, clearly, consider that, save where the information concerns "misdeeds of a serious nature and importance to the country," they should intervene to preserve confidential obligations.[61]

8-015

[54] On this problem, see especially Megarry J., *Coco v. Clark* (above, n. 31) at 49–50.

[55] In *Cranleigh Precision v. Bryant* [1966] R.P.C. 81 and *Franchi v. Franchi* (above, n. 47), it was. said that the publication in a third party's patent specification should not be treated as determining obligations of confidence. But that seems too indiscriminate an approach. The former case, in particular, did not need to go so far; there were obvious breaches of fiduciary duty. The reasoning in the cases was criticised by Lord Goff; *Att.-Gen. v. Guardian Newspapers* (above, n. 6) at 661–662.

[56] *Thomas Marshall v. Guinle* [1978] 3 All E.R. 193 at 209–210. Particular usage of a trade or industry might also make the information protectable: *ibid.*

[57] The European Convention (for which see above, n. 8), guarantees the right of freedom of speech, subject *inter alia* to the preservation of confidence: Art. 10. In *Att.-Gen. v. Guardian Newspapers* (above, n. 6), Lords Griffiths and Goff considered the qualification discussed under this head to be in conformity with the Article: pp. 652, 660.

[58] See generally Street, *Freedom, the Individual and the Law* (4th ed., 1977).

[59] *Gartside v. Outram* (1856) 26 L.J. Ch. 113.

[60] But note Bankes L.J., *Weld-Blundell v. Stephens* [1919] 1 K.B. 520, 527; *cf. Butler v. Board of Trade* [1971] Ch. 680.

[61] Ungoed Thomas J., *Beloff v. Pressdram* [1973] 1 All E.R. 241, 260–261 (copyright proceedings, treated as subject to the same public interest considerations); and see Megaw L.J., *Hubbard v. Vosper* [1972] 2 Q.B. 84 at 100–101. Revelation of an agreement registrable under the Restrictive Trade Practices Act (*Initial Services v. Putterill* [1968] 1 Q.B. 396) could well fall within this restricted view of public interest. *cf.* also *British Steel v. Granada* (above, § 2-034, n. 97).

8-016   There is now a broader approach which treats "iniquity" as merely
one instance of just cause for allowing confidence to be broken in the
public interest. Lord Denning M.R., a principal proponent of this view,[62]
has, for instance, held that, where pop-stars have deliberately promoted a
glamorous image of themselves, it is permissible to present the less
savoury truth about their style of life to the public, even if confidence has
to be broken in the process.[63] This approach has much in common with
the freedom of speech defence to invasions of privacy in the United
States: that by putting himself forward as a public figure, a celebrity
must be prepared to suffer the exposure of truths about his personal life.

8-017   Other circumstances in which public interest may justify at least
limited publication to an appropriate person to take action might include
matters of public safety and the due administration of justice. Thus in
Lion Laboratories v. *Evans*,[64] a newspaper came by knowledge that a
breathalyser used by the police on suspected drunken drivers gave
inaccurate readings. It was held proper for the newspaper to publish this
generally, because merely reporting the information to the police or the
Home Office might have led to its suppression. However, it is not to be
supposed that English courts readily accept that there is a sufficient
public interest, particularly to justify publication through the media, even
if it is produced by a "whistle-blower" from inside an organisation who
is moved by moral outrage and who may well be jeopardising a career
rather than seeking any payment in return.[65]

In every case, whether the basis is "iniquity" or some other ground,
the court has to balance the competing interests. For instance, the Court
of Appeal restrained a newspaper from publishing allegations about a
leading jockey's involvement in misleading the Jockey Club because the
information had been obtained by private and unauthorised wire-tapping
of a telephone conversation: the dissemination would be too wide, the
breach of confidence too serious.[66] It is clear that Peter Wright could
never have justified his "treacherous" breaches of confidence about his
service in MI5 by a public interest in knowing that he and other officers
attempted to prevent Harold Wilson's re-election and other unscrupulous
operations.[67]

---

[62] *Initial Services* v. *Putterill* (above, n. 18) at 405, *Fraser* v. *Evans* (above, n. 18) at 11,
Hubbard v. *Vosper* (above, n. 61) at 95–96; *Norwich Pharmacal* v. *Commissioners of
Customs* [1972] R.P.C. 743 at 766 (C.A.).

[63] *Woodward* v. *Hutchins* [1977] 2 All E.R. 751; Lawton and Bridge L.JJ. were equally
convinced; *cf. Argyll* v. *Argyll* (above, n. 7) at 331–333; Wacks (1978) 41 M.L.R. 67.

[64] [1985] Q.B. 526 (C.A.); and see *ex p. Smith Kline & French* [1989] F.S.R. 11 (C.A.); *cf.
X. Health Authority* v. *Y.* [1988] R.P.C. 379 (confidence in hospital records of doctors
with AIDS outweighed public interest in knowing that there were doctors with the
disease).

[65] Different attitudes have been expressed about the degree to which the moral scruples of
the revealer are relevant in judging public interest: *cf.* esp. Lord Denning M.R.'s view
that the use made of it by a person receiving the information is relevant, with Lord
Fraser's rejection of that position: *British Steel* v. *Granada Television* [1981] A.C. 1006
at p.1202. Even a professional may be entitled to break confidence in order to secure the
safety of others: *W.* v. *Edgell* [1989] (to be reported) (psychiatrist disclosing violent
character of patient to prison authorities).

[66] *Francome* v. *Mirror Group* [1984] 2 All E.R. 408 (C.A.).

[67] This is made plain in *Att.-Gen.* v. *Guardian Newspapers (No. 2)* (above, n. 6).

Many cases to do with newsworthy information are founded in copyright as well as confidence. In England, the tendency has been to treat public interest as having the same impact in respect of either cause of action. But, as we shall see, in copyright there are other relevant defences provided by statute.[68]

(e) *Government secrets*

An opposite public interest arises when government seeks to protect confidential information. For although it is relying on a private right it does not have the same personal interest as an individual in preventing information from being released or used. It must show—and carries the burden of proof—that the public has an interest in the protection sought, "because in a free society there is a continuing public interest that the workings of government should be open to scrutiny and criticism."[69] Whether there is a sufficient public interest of this sort will depend on all the circumstances. Where the former minister, Richard Crossman, proposed to reveal Cabinet discussions recorded in his diaries, his publishers were not enjoined: the desirability of mutual confidence in Cabinet deliberations was not a sufficient interest when ten years had elapsed in the interim.[70] Where, apparently through a leak from a civil servant, Australian government documents concerning its relations with Indonesia over the East Timor crisis were about to be published, no sufficient reason for restraining their appearance could be found in national security, relations with foreign countries or the ordinary business of government.[71]

8-018

Where the *Guardian* and the *Observer* gave accounts of Australian proceedings to stop the publication of Peter Wright's *Spycatcher*, in which they disclosed some of Wright's allegations about wrongdoing in Britain's MI5, these publications did not amount to actionable breaches of confidence, even though they came through leaks of the book's contents at a time when it had been published nowhere.[72] Equally, after *Spycatcher*'s publication in the United States, Australia and elsewhere, with the consequence that many copies and accounts had entered Britain, even the *Sunday Times*, which held "serial rights" to the book by "grant" from Wright's publishers,[73] could not be restrained from publishing it: the other events had rendered Wright's allegations too widely known for the public to have any further interest to protect.[74] An attempt to show continuing damage to the operations of the Secret Services, if

---

[68] Below, § 11-028.
[69] Lord Goff, *Att.-Gen.* v. *Guardian Newspapers (No. 2)* (above, n. 6) at 660.
[70] *Att.-Gen.* v. *Jonathan Cape* [1976] Q.B. 752.
[71] *Commonwealth of Australia* v. *Fairfax* (1980) 32 A.L.R. 485; and see *Att.-Gen.* v. *Brandon Book Publishers* [1989] F.S.R. 37.
[72] *Att.-Gen.* v. *Guardian Newspapers (No. 2)* (above, n. 6).
[73] It seems that any such "licence" lacked subject-matter since Wright's breach of obligation left him without enforceable copyright: see below, § 11-042.
[74] *The Sunday Times* had perpetrated an actionable breach by publishing a first episode of *Spycatcher* on the eve of U.S. publication, for which they were liable to an account of profits. From this no payment to Wright's publishers under the supposed "licence" would be deductible: *ibid.*, esp. at 645, *per* Lord Keith.

there could not be absolute assurance that its members would observe lifelong secrecy, was not accepted as sufficient in the circumstances.

(2) Confidential obligation

(a) *Confidence in the receipt of information*

8-019   In the usual case, one person supplies information to another on condition that he will keep it secret. Equally the obligation to do so may arise where the first person employs,[75] commissions, or even requests, the second to acquire information and hold it in confidence for him. But—and here arises the whole case for founding the jurisdiction upon the requirements of "good faith"—whether recipient or acquirer, the second is bound only if he accepts that the information is to be treated confidentially. And yet this is tested objectively: "if the circumstances are such that any reasonable man standing in the shoes of the recipient of the information would have realised that upon reasonable grounds the information was being given to him in confidence, then this should suffice to impose upon him the equitable obligation of confidence."[76] Add to this that, once the obligation is assumed, it may be broken by conduct that is neither ill-motivated nor deliberate.[77] It becomes apparent that a somewhat diffuse notion of "good faith" is being employed.

8-020   There is no need to search for an implied contract, if none has been reached expressly: matrimonial and other personal confidences may give rise to obligations[78]; so equally when one party gives another information during negotiations towards a commercial agreement that is never reached[79]; or in circumstances where statute negates the existence of a contract.[80] On the other hand, it is unlikely that one person could oblige another to respect confidence by sending him unsolicited information in a letter marked "Confidential." This is a practical problem of some importance; it is even said that one enterprise may try to foist confidential material on another in order to put difficulties in the way of the latter using it (or something similar), should it be discovered independently.[81] The recipient of an unsolicited confidence should, for his own protection, return the material at once, making it plain that he regards himself as being under no obligation. If he goes on to use the information he is likely, under the objective test, to be held bound.

---

[75] An instance is *Industrial Furnaces* v. *Reaves* [1970] R.P.C. 605.
[76] Megarry J., *Coco* v. *Clark* (above, n. 31); and see *Yates* v. *Electrofoils* (above, n. 14); *Interfirm Comparison* v. *Law Society* (above, n. 5) at 151; *Deta Nominees* v. *Viscount Plastic* [1979] V.R. 167 at 191.
[77] See below, § 8-038.
[78] *Argyll* v. *Argyll* (above, n. 7) at 322 still spoke (unenthusiastically) of an implied contract, but demonstrated the unreality of such language.
[79] As in *Seager* v. *Copydex (No. 1)* (above, n. 46); *Coco* v. *Clark* (above, n. 31); *A.B. Consolidated* v. *Europe Strength* [1978] 2 N.Z.L.R. 520.
[80] *Malone* v. *Commissioner of Police* [1979] 2 All E.R. 620 at 645 (no contract between telephone subscriber and Post Office).
[81] See Law Commission (above, n. 1) at §§ 52, 72, 109–112; Turner [1976] CIPA 293; *Johnson* v. *Heat and Air* (1941) 58 R.P.C. 229 was a case where the defendant could show that he already knew the information when it was revealed to him.

Of course, contracts continue to be of great importance. The circum- **8-021** stances may be such that the reasonable man may freely use the information supplied to him in the absence of an express agreement to the contrary. Thus where a news agency provided stock-exchange and horse-racing results to its subscribers, it was able to prevent the information being passed on to non-subscribers precisely because the subscription contract forbade this being done.[82] Equally, contract may prescribe the extent of the obligation.[83] The purpose of a "know-how" licence is to permit the licensee to make use of the information provided for the purposes of his own business, but normally the agreement will limit the degree to which the "know-how" can be imparted to others, and use by the licensee after termination of the licence may also be circumscribed.[84] Again, contract may settle that the plaintiff is not owed any duty of confidence, but instead owes such a duty himself to a third party; in which case he has no qualification to sue.[85]

(b) *Fiduciary duties*

The relationship between two persons may be such that equity imposes **8-022** a duty upon one to act in the interests of the other rather than of himself. As with contract, the proof of a fiduciary relationship may be the necessary foundation of an obligation of confidence.[86] This fiduciary duty may, for instance, exist between trustee and beneficiary, agent and principal, individual partner and partnership, director and company, responsible employee and employer.[87] The list of relationships is not closed; but there is a reluctance to find it in commercial relationships, *e.g.* from franchisor to franchisee, or licensee to licensor.[88] Nor are the circumstances in which such fiduciaries are obliged to prefer the interests of their beneficiaries precisely defined.[89] The moral impulse from which

---

[82] *Exchange Telegraph* v. *Gregory* [1896] 1 Q.B. 147; *Exchange Telegraph* v. *Central News* [1897] 2 Ch. 48; *cf.* also *Paul* v. *Southern Instruments* [1964] R.P.C. 118 (C.A.).

[83] For instance, by limiting the period during which the defendant is not to use the information: see *Potters-Ballotini* v. *Weston-Baker* (above, n. 49); *cf.* the cases in n. 82.

[84] *National Broach* v. *Churchill* [1965] R.P.C. 61; *Torrington* v. *Smith* [1966] R.P.C. 285.

[85] *Fraser* v. *Evans* [1969] 1 All E.R. 8 (C.A.) (The plaintiff prepared a report for the Greek government to which he owed a duty of confidence; the defendant editor procured the report from a Greek government source. Had it been improperly procured from the plaintiff he might have established the tort of inducing breach of his own contract of confidence. *cf.* the criminal proceedings in *D.P.P.* v. *Withers*, above, § 2-010, n. 57.

[86] *Moorgate Tobacco* v. *Philip Morris* [1985] R.P.C. 219 (Australian H.C.).

[87] On employees, see *Canadian Aero* v. *O'Malley* (1973) 40 D.L.R. (3d) (S.C. Can.). Amongst the category of agents, note in particular professional advisers such as doctors, lawyers and banks. The scope of the obligations of each category is worked out in case law: for which see, *e.g.* *Tournier* v. *National Provincial* [1924] 1 K.B. 461 (C.A.) (banker); *Hunter* v. *Mann* [1974] 1 Q.B. 767 (Div. Ct.) (doctor); *Parry-Jones* v. *Law Society* [1969] 1 Ch. 1 (C.A.) (solicitor). For relation between a solicitor's duty of confidence and his obligation not to reveal privileged communications in litigation without his client's consent, see *Lord Ashburton* v. *Pape* [1913] 2 Ch. 469; *Parry-Jones* v. *Law Society*; *Butler* v. *Board of Trade* [1971] Ch. 680.

[88] *Jirna* v. *Mister Do-nut* (1973) 40 D.L.R. (3d) 303; *U.S.S.C.* v. *Hospital Products* (1984) 58 A.L.J.R. 587; *Moorgate* case (above, n. 86).

[89] Readers unfamiliar with this important equitable duty will find good accounts, *e.g.* in Goff and Jones, *Law of Restitution* (3rd ed., 1986) Ch. 34, Finn, *Fiduciary Duties* (1977) and on company directors, Gower, *Modern Company Law* (4th ed., 1979), 571–613.

this fiduciary duty stems is very similar to that which requires confidence to be respected and often there is an overlap between the principles. But the difference needs to be observed. In the first place, a fiduciary responsibility may be the source of the duty to preserve confidence: the employee who removes a confidential report from his employer's desk[90] will break the confidence that already exists from his duty of fidelity; an outsider who did the same thing would commit a trespass, but he would not be in breach of confidence.[91] Again, the fiduciary duty may be wider in scope than a simple obligation to observe confidence: the fiduciary may, for example, be expected to continue using information for his beneficiary's advantage only, even after it has become public;[92] equally he may be obliged to hold the profits of his breach on trust for his beneficiary.[93] Equity's intervention is to prevent the fiduciary from taking a personal advantage from the possible conflict of interest and duty.

(c) *Employer and employee*

8-023   Where the relationship between supplier and recipient of information is that of employer and employee, a further distinct policy has been pursued by the judges. They have struck a balance between the desire to accord every worker the freedom to dispose of his labour where and when he pleases and the wish to give some protection to valuable pieces of information that a particular employer may possess over his competitors and which an employee might give to a competitor or use himself in competition. While he remains in employment the employee must observe his "duty of fidelity." But once he leaves his employment, the balance rests largely in favour of the employee, who is entitled to make use of all the skill and knowledge that any employee of his kind would have acquired. He is only obliged to respect two specific "interests" of his employer: in "secret processes" that are in a strict sense "trade secrets"; and in the goodwill that exists between the employer and his customers.

8-024   (i) *The employee in service* In a contract of employment, a term will be implied (if it is not expressed) that the employee will act at all times during his service in his employer's best interests. This "duty of fidelity" embraces the protection of trade and commercial secrets, including both information which is given to the employee and that which he generates in the course of his work.[94] But it is wider than a matter of confidence

---

[90] As in *Jarman & Platt* v. *Barget* [1977] F.S.R. 260, 276 (C.A.).

[91] On this problem, see below, § 8-032.

[92] See *Cranleigh Precision* v. *Bryant* (above, n. 55). The obligation extends equally to the personal use of property and to certain competitive activities.

[93] Goff and Jones (n. 89, above), p. 519.

[94] Employment being a contractual relationship, the implied term has been the legal device for imposing the obligation in question: see *Faccenda Chicken* v. *Fowler* [1986] 1 All E.R. 617 at 625. But clearly it bears an affinity to the equitable duty of good faith that is imposed on fiduciaries such as trustees, agents, partners and the like (for which, see above § 8-022). Accordingly, a tendency can be detected towards treating at least senior employees as fiduciaries: *Canadian Aero* v. *O'Malley* (1974) 40 D.L.R. (3d) 371; in England, see *Normalec* v. *Britton* [1983] F.S.R. 318. *cf.* the position concerning patents, above, § 7-004, and copyright below §§ 12-002—12-003.

and may, in some circumstances, embrace a duty not to engage in directly competitive work, either with another employer or on his own account. In *Hivac v. Park Royal*, the plaintiff company, which produced hearing-aids of advanced design, secured an interlocutory injunction to prevent a rival company from giving jobs to some of its technicians by way of "moonlighting" after hours. Since relief was apparently granted whether or not the technicians would be likely to impart confidential "know-how," the decision went a long way; but the plaintiff was constrained by war-time legislation from simply dismissing the technicians, and this condition made it a special case.[95] During the continuance of employment there is certainly an obligation to keep rival research staff from access to technical secrets,[96] and a duty not to provide the employee's own trade union with the employer's commercial information relevant to wage negotiations.[97]

(ii) *The Ex-employee*. In *Faccenda Chicken v. Fowler*,[98] the Court of **8-025** Appeal has recently contrasted the extensive duty owed during the continuance of employment with the more limited responsibility after termination. The principle that the employer may only seek to protect two interests—in his trade secrets and in the goodwill existing with his customers—was developed first in connection with express covenants. Undertakings by the employee that he will not, upon leaving the employment, set up or join a competitive business, solicit former customers or disclose or use trade secrets, are enforceable only if reasonably necessary to protect the employer; otherwise they are an undue restraint of trade and so are void as contrary to public policy. Such covenants by employees are scrupulously tested; they must be no wider in scope (taking account of types of business excluded, duration and area of operation) than is reasonably necessary to give the employer protection of the relevant interest. Much detailed law has developed around this basic rule and it is easy to overstep the mark that it sets.[99] Nonetheless managerial, professional, sales and research staff are often required to enter such covenants. Not only does a covenant make the position a matter of express agreement (with attendant psychological effects) but it may give wider protection than if the employer seeks to rely upon rights arising by operation of the general law. Breach of a covenant not to compete is usually easier to establish than breach of an undertaking not to disclose or use confidential information: it is relatively easy to show that an ex-employee has joined a competitor or set up in business.

---

[95] [1946] 1 All E.R. 350 (C.A.); *cf. Nova Plastics v. Froggett* [1982] I.R.L.R. 146. See also *Reading v. Att.-Gen.* [1950] A.C. 507 (H.L.); *Davies v. Presbyterian Church of Wales* [1986] 1 All E.R. 705 (H.L.). While there is no duty to report his own breaches of contract, the employee is under a duty to report those of a colleague: *Sybron v. Rochem* [1983] 3 W.L.R. 713 (C.A.).

[96] e.g. *Printers & Finishers v. Holloway* [1964] 3 All E.R. 731.

[97] *Bents Brewery v. Hogan* [1945] 2 All E.R. 570 (where the covenant was express). See also below, § 8-026, on the special problem of preparing to leave employment.

[98] [1986] 1 All E.R. 617.

[99] There is no room to review this important doctrine here. See especially Heydon, *The Restraint of Trade Doctrine* (1972) and, for an economic analysis, M. J. Trebilcock.

8-026   The employer who is not protected by covenant is not entirely without remedy. If, for instance, he keeps a list of customers, he is entitled to stop an employee from deliberately memorising it or copying it out in order to make use of it himself once his employment ceases. This, indeed, is an aspect of the employee's implied duty of fidelity during his term of employment.[1] But he cannot stop an ex-employee from soliciting his customers in circumstances where the ex-employee merely remembers the customers' names in the ordinary course of events. If he had a valid express covenant, then he could.[2]

8-027   If there could not be an effective covenant, then, *a fortiori*, the law of confidence cannot be relied upon. For this general law to apply, so the *Faccenda Chicken* case emphasises, a court must be convinced that the employee has departed with information that he ought not to take advantage of.[3] It is not enough to show that this special element was something that the employee was bound to keep "confidential" during his employment. He must have acquired "trade secrets or their equivalent." In investigating this, account will be taken of four factors: the nature of the employment (*e.g.* whether confidential information was regularly handled), the nature of the information at issue, the employer's view of its character, and the question whether it can easily be isolated from other, unprotectable information.[3a] Chemical formulae, details of technical processes, and hard commercial information, such as prices, are considered examples of what, in the light of circumstances, may continue to be protected even after the determination of the job.[4] But within this second category, a distinction is drawn between the discrete "trade secret", which any honest person of average intelligence would regard as such; and more incidental features or expedients, which were peculiar to the former employer's process or factory, but which are not easily to be separated from general knowledge and acquired skill. While information in the first category continues to be protectable under the general obligation of confidence, that in the second calls for an express covenant; but if a covenant has been taken, it is justifiable within the rule of public policy (provided that it is no wider than warranted by the ex-employer's interest).[5] Moreover, if a covenant is taken but it proves to be too widely drawn, there may still be a breach of general obligation to respect confidence if a sufficiently significant trade secret is at issue.[6] Nothing,

[1] See, *e.g. Robb* v. *Green* (above, n. 4); *Baker* v. *Gibbons* [1972] 2 All E.R. 759; *Diamond Stylus* v. *Bauden* [1973] R.P.C. 675. It is difficult to prove the case if the defendant has not removed a copy of the list.
[2] *e.g. Coral Index* v. *Regent Index* [1970] R.P.C. 147.
[3] See also *G. D. Searle* v. *Celltech* [1982] F.S.R. 92 (C.A.).
[3a] See Purvis and Turner [1989] E.I.P.R. 3; Stewart [1989] E.I.P.R.
[4] *Printers & Finishers* v. *Holloway* [1965] R.P.C. 239; and see *Under Water Welders* v. *Street* [1968] R.P.C. 498; *United Sterling* v. *Felton* [1974] R.P.C. 162; *Harvey Tiling* v. *Rodomac* [1977] R.P.C. 399 (S.C., S. Africa); *Yates* v. *Electrofoils* (above, n. 14).
[5] This proposition in *Printers & Finishers*, though not easily reconciled with all of Neill L.J.'s judgment in the *Faccenda Chicken* case, seems ultimately to be accepted there. So it is understood in *Balston* v. *Headline Filters* [1987] F.S.R. 330; and see *Johnson & Bloy* v. *Wolstenholme Rink* [1989] F.S.R. 135 (C.A.) *cf.* Rideout (1986) 15 Ind.L.J. 183.
[6] *Wessex Dairies* v. *Smith* (1935) 2 K.B. 80 (C.A.); *Triplex* v. *Scorah* (1938) 55 R.P.C. 21; *Thos. Marshall* v. *Guinle* (above, n. 56).

therefore, is lost by taking an express covenant, and if it proves valid, much may be gained.

A principle which distinguishes between discrete technical secrets 8-028 (protectable even in the absence of covenant), incidental information known only to the ex-employer (protectable only by covenant) and general skill and knowledge (unprotectable) places a heavy burden of proof on any ex-employer who seeks to rely upon a general obligation of confidence. It is not enough, for instance, to show that others are prepared to pay for a package of know-how and associated rights if it cannot be shown that the defendant is taking a similar package to his new employer, but only rather general information about the kind of plant that both employers are operating.[7] The ex-employer also risks revealing, by his own pleadings and evidence, significant details which the defendant may not previously have appreciated.[8] Yet the courts can offer only limited help towards preserving the secrecy of what he is obliged to reveal.[9]

(d) *Government departments and agencies*

Government authorities—central, local and special—receive a mass of 8-029 information, much of it, at least by implication, for limited purposes only. So far, the equity of confidence appears to apply to them as it would to other disclosees.[10] There may, however, be special reasons for allowing them to disclose or use the information in pursuit of some public interest, such as the enforcement of the civil or criminal law.[11] In this context the impact of the Official Secrets Acts should not be forgotten.[12]

(e) *The indirect recipient*[13]

If A gives B information in confidence and B passes it to C, C—the 8-030 indirect recipient—may take it knowing that it is confidential; or the circumstances may be such that he ought to have known of the confidence; or he may receive it without this knowledge, actual or imputed, only to be informed subsequently of the true position; in which case, he may initially have purchased it or he may have had it as a gift. The courts undoubtedly wish to protect confidence to the extent of making indirect recipients liable in some of these circumstances; but

[7] Thus evidence that visitors were not restricted in their inspections, or that the employee was never told of the secrecy, are likely to tell against the employer: see *e.g. United Sterling* v. *Felton* [1974] R.P.C. 162; *Aveley/Cybervox* v. *Boman* [1975] F.S.R. 139 at 144.
[8] See *Yates* v. *Electrofoils* (above, n. 14) at 394–395; and see *Potters-Ballotini* v. *Weston-Baker* (above, n. 49) at 206.
[9] In lieu of particulars, the court may order that an independent expert be appointed to inspect the plaintiff's plant on condition that he reveals his findings only to the defendant's legal advisers and destroys any notes; in this procedure it is for the plaintiff to point out to the expert the features that he regards as secret: *Printers & Finishers* v. *Holloway* (above, n. 4) at 248; see also *Terrapin* v. *Tecton* (1968) 64 W.W.R. 129.
[10] This seems to be accepted, *e.g.* in *Butler* v. *Board of Trade* (above, n. 60), *Norwich Pharmacal* v. *C.C.E.* (above, n. 62).
[11] As in *Butler* and *Norwich Pharmacal.*
[12] See *Halsbury's Laws of England* (4th ed.), Vol. 11, §§ 899 *et seq.*
[13] See Stuckey (1981) 4 U.N.S.W.L.R. 73.

which? It is here that doubts are thickest and doctrinal differences headiest.

The deliberate or reckless recipient would in many circumstances be liable under the general law of tort: for inducing or procuring breach of contract, unjustifiably interfering with business relations or conspiracy[14]; if not, his bad faith would easily justify equity's intervention.[15] Other recipients, who at most have only been negligent, are not themselves usually regarded as acting in bad faith. However, obligations of confidence are apparently imposed on direct recipients under an objective test and this may perhaps be justified by saying that it is too much to expect the plaintiff always to establish fraud.[16] The same approach might equally be applied to the indirect recipient. But if the non-negligent recipient is ever to be held liable, it cannot be because of his own default. It must either be because confidential information has been dignified with the status of "property," or else the court's intervention is to secure the information against breach of the obligation of good faith originally assumed by the first recipient.

8-031   The few judgments recently touching the matter seem prepared to impose liability on an innocent recipient from the time when he is informed of the breach of confidence.[17] In *Wheatley* v. *Bell* one defendant acquired confidential knowledge about franchising local business guides and proceeded to sell it to other defendants as franchisees in a different place. The latter, though initially innocent, were enjoined.[17a] Assuming that it is the proper approach—and it seems sensible—then relief ought not to extend to damages for past innocent use; and it would be open to a court to refuse or limit any injunction in light of the extent to which the indirect recipient would be disadvantaged: taking account not only of whether he has paid a purchase price, but whether he could be reimbursed for that expenditure and any consequential investment intended to exploit the information.[18] If confidential information has become property, it is either property at common law which all must respect (save to the extent that the innocent are to be excused damages for past injuries)[19]; or it is property in equity, in which case the bona fide purchaser bears no responsibility but the innocent volunteer does. The difficulty with these stereotypes is that they each take a rather inflexible view of the defendant's circumstances. There is very little indication that

---

[14] For these torts, see above, § 2-006; and esp. *British Industrial Plastics* v. *Ferguson* [1940] 1 All E.R. 479 (H.L.) (S.C., New South Wales).

[15] Thus in *Prince Albert* v. *Strange* (above, n. 21), stress is at one point laid on the duplicity of the indirect recipient: see 1 Mac. & G. 25 at 44.

[16] Above, § 8-019.

[17] *Stephenson Jordan* v. *MacDonald & Evans* (1951) 68 R.P.C. 190 at 195; *Printers & Finishers* v. *Holloway* (above, n. 4) at 253 (liability of Vita-Tex); *Malone* v. *Commissioner of Police* (above, n. 80) at 634.

[17a] [1984] F.S.R. 169 (S.C., N.S.W.).

[18] See Jones (above, n. 1) at 477–478; and note Evershed M.R. in the *Stephenson Jordan* case (on appeal) (1952) 69 R.P.C. 10 at 16.

[19] Even if we are dealing with a new form of intellectual "property," the tendency to preclude such damages in other instances must be remembered: above, § 2-027.

English courts wish to apply either theory to subject-matter of such varying character as is currently protectable in the name of confidence.[20]

(f) Absence of any relationship

In *Malone* v. *Commissioner of Police*,[21] an unsuccessful attack was made on the propriety of official wire-tapping (under the Home Secretary's warrant) in order to detect crime.[22] Megarry V.-C. took the view in principle that if one person told a second something in confidence, but a third overheard it, the last was under no legal liability to preserve the confidence. This is a point, so it was held, at which the moral constraints upon an honourable man outstrip those imposed by law. For this the only reason offered was that people (particularly those who use the telephone) know that they risk being overheard.[23] If the decision is good law, only the recipient of the communication and those to whom he passes it directly or indirectly can be the subject of this equity. It cannot stretch to any form of surreptitious intervention by eavesdropping or other snooping, natural or technically aided.[24] The Younger Committee on Privacy and the Law Commission have favoured the creation of a separate form of civil liability which would encompass some activities of industrial and news spies. There are differences of view, however, about whether the improper conduct should be defined relatively specifically (for instance, by limiting only the use of technical devices)[25]; or whether some more general expression (such as "surreptitious obtaining") ought to be used, leaving more to be settled by the courts.[26] On so sensitive a matter, there is great virtue in being as specific as possible.[27] In the *Malone* case, Megarry V.-C. clearly appreciated the embarrassments that

8-032

---

[20] Only the analogy to the tort of conversion as *one* method of assessing damages for breach of confidence (*Seager* v. *Copydex (No. 2)* [1969] R.P.C. 250) gives implied support to the common law property approach. Certainly in *Morison* v. *Moat* ((1851) 9 Hare 241), the bona fide purchaser was treated as exempt, but the proposition has not found clear echoes in England (*cf.* the cases in n. 19 above, which tend the other way). However, the bona fide purchaser has been treated as protected in Canada (*International Tools* v. *Kollar* (1968) 67 D.L.R. (2d) 386 at 391; *Tenatronics* v. *Hauf* (1972) 23 D.L.R. (3d) 60; *cf. Polyresins* v. *Skin-Hall* (1972) 25 D.L.R. (3d) 152).

[21] [1979] 2 All E.R. 620.

[22] The case reviews critically the present arrangement for supervising telephone tapping in Britain: "a subject which cries out for legislation": *ibid.* at 649.

[23] At 645–646. It is remarkable that this is the first occasion on which the general issue has been aired in a modern British case.

[24] If a tort is committed—by trespass to land or to goods, for instance—this may found a civil action. Where one fruit-farmer stole budwood for a new variety of nectarine from his neighbour and then sold the new fruit in competition, he was enjoined; but his liability was related to the equity of breach of confidence and his conduct was condemned as "unconscionable": *Franklin* v. *Giddings* [1978] Qd.R. 72. Private wire-tapping has since been held wrongful: *Francome* v. *Mirror Group* (above, n. 66); and see *Exchange Telegraph* v. *Howard* (1906) 22 T.L.R. 375.

[25] The Younger Committee (Cmnd. 5012, 1972) favoured the creation of criminal offences relating to surreptitious surveillance by means of a technical device (§§ 560–563) and that civil liability should depend upon proof of an unlawful act (§ 632).

[26] The Law Commission put up the alternatives for further discussion (Working Paper No. 58, §§ 135–140).

[27] Note the warning against "wide and indefinite rights" in the *Malone* case (above, n. 21) at 643.

some all-embracing principle of liability might pose for official investigators.[28] Equally there are non-governmental interest groups (such as the press) who can justifiably demand specific guidance upon what they remain free to do.

If no liability can arise in equity for any form of spying or eavesdropping which involves no breach of confidence reposed, the criminal law may impose its own form of sanction and from this may arise liability in tort. If there is a combination to procure information of economic value, it may well amount to a criminal conspiracy to defraud.[29] If pecuniary damage can be shown to follow, this would make the conduct into a conspiracy actionable in tort.[30]

(3) Unauthorised use

(a) Wrongful acts

8-033   The acts that constitute infringement of a patent or copyright are, in different ways, limited by relatively precise criteria: in the case of patents, by confining infringement to certain kinds of industrial use and commercial exploitation within the scope of the claims defining the monopoly[31]; in the case of copyright by the requirements of reproduction or performance, copying of the manner in which ideas are expressed and the taking of a substantial part of the work.[32] The notion of breach of confidence is by comparison loosely defined. It may consist in any disclosure or use which contravenes the limited purpose for which the information was revealed.[33] If the question is one of misuse, it appears not to matter that the use will not disclose the information to further recipients. Not all the information taken has to be used or disclosed before breach occurs, though doubtless the deployment of insubstantial amounts might be disregarded.[34] The information used must come from that disclosed in confidence and not from some other source. This may raise similar difficulties of proof to those arising in copyright; and, as there, courts may want to infer derivation of the idea from the similarity of end products.[35]

---

[28] Note however his criticism of the present administrative practice governing wire-tapping, and his plea for legislation: above, n. 22.

[29] Persons who combined to make surreptitious copies of films in breach of copyright were held to be conspiring to defraud the copyright owner, even though no one was deceived: Scott v. Metropolitan Police Commissioner (above, § 2-010, n. 57); cf. D.P.P. v. Withers (above, § 2-010, n. 61). In this context it should be remembered that to borrow a copy of a film (in order to copy it) is not theft: R. v. Lloyd [1986] F.S.R. 138 (C.A.). For the development of criminal sanctions against misuse of trade secrets in the U.S. see Glancy, (1979) 1 E.I.P.R. 179.

[30] For this tort, see above, § 2-006; and note the other possibilities there canvassed.

[31] See above, § 6-002.   [32] See below, §§ 11-003—11-017.

[33] But not where the information is no more than the knowledge, skill and experience that an employee must acquire in the course of his duties: United Indigo v. Robinson (1932) 49 R.P.C. 178, 189; and more generally, Worsley v. Cooper [1939] 1 All E.R. 290, 306–310.

[34] In Amber Size v. Menzel [1913] 2 Ch. 239 the defendant was restrained from misusing the whole or any material part of the plaintiff's secret process. Contrast the patent law principle which requires all essential integers of the claimed invention to be taken: above, § 6-002.   [35] See below, § 11-003.

(b) *The defendant's state of mind*

The liability of a defendant may turn upon his state of mind both at **8-034**
the time when he receives the information and when he uses or discloses
it. The former has already been discussed, since it goes to the question
whether an obligation of confidence has been assumed or is to be
imposed.[36] When it comes to breach, it appears not to matter that the
defendant acts out of some misguided or well-meaning motive,[37] that he
does not appreciate the confidentiality of a document from which he
takes the information[38] or that he has forgotten the source of the
information and thinks he has thought of it himself. *Seager v. Copydex*[39]
was treated by the Court of Appeal as involving subconscious copying of
this last kind: the defendant's employees were found to have worked out
how to make a carpet grip embodying a basic idea which they had
forgotten being shown by the plaintiff. A recent Australian decision,[40]
however, has applied the notion of subconscious copying only with some
reluctance. It must remain doubtful whether the law—particularly if it is
based upon an obligation of "good faith"—needs to go so far.

(c) *Detriment to the plaintiff*

In *Coco v. Clark*,[41] Megarry J. questioned whether the plaintiff must **8-035**
show that he has or will suffer detriment by the breach of confidence.
The variety of information that may be the subject of confidence makes
this a complex and difficult issue and one that remains unresolved. The
motive for protecting technical and commercial information is normally
to preserve its economic value for the plaintiff. In these cases is the
plaintiff's interest like property[42] in the sense that he is entitled to decide
if another may make use of it, whether or not he exploits the information
himself? Or may he object only to misuses or disclosures of the
information that injure him in trade competition?[43] The motive for
protecting personal information may well be to prevent distress or
embarrassment; though some people want privacy largely so that they
can turn it to their own financial advantage.[44] In these cases, if there must
be detriment, it may perhaps lie in the need to prove that the plaintiff's
sensibilities will be disturbed; and that in turn raises the nice question

---

[36] Above, §§ 8-019, 8-030.
[37] *Nichrotherm* v. *Percy* [1956] R.P.C. 272 at 281.
[38] *National Broach* v. *Churchill Gear* [1965] R.P.C. 61.
[39] *Seager* v. *Copydex (No. 1)* [1967] 2 All E.R. 415 at 418; *cf.* "subconscious copying" in copyright: below, § 11-004.
[40] *General Television* v. *Talbot* [1981] R.P.C. 1; see Ricketson (1980) 2 E.I.P.R. 149.
[41] [1969] R.P.C 41 at 48; *Dunford* v. *Johnston* [1978] F.S.R. 143 at 148 and *Jarman & Platt* v. *Barget* [1977] F.S.R. 260 at 277 assume that detriment is necessary; *cf.* *Nichrotherm* v. *Percy* [1956] R.P.C. 272 at 273.
[42] Talk of property may not seem very helpful in this context. *cf.* the discussion of whether passing off protected the property in a trade mark or only in the goodwill of the business in which it was used: see below, §§ 15-003, 15-005.
[43] If the latter is the rule, what of the case where he wants to exploit a rival invention that he has also devised? *Seager* v. *Copydex* was such a case.
[44] Consider, *e.g. Lennon* v. *News Group* [1978] F.S.R. 573 (C.A.).

whether an objective or a subjective test should be applied.[45] When it comes to governmental secrets, it is necessary to show a sufficient public interest in their protection,[46] and this may be expressed as the need to show detriment.[47]

It is tempting to say that liability ought to follow simply upon the breaking of the confidence without looking also for detriment. But one should remember that a very wide range of subject-matter is involved, and also that there is always some public interest in the freedom to use information. Restriction of that freedom accordingly requires sufficient reason. In this connection, the caution exhibited in two areas of tort deserves mention: most economic torts are actionable only upon proof of damage[48]; and the tort of defamation is confined to statements which tend to lower the plaintiff in the eyes of right-thinking members of the public—an approach which imposes objective standards.

3. REMEDIES

(1) Injunction and other equitable remedies

8-036   The remedies available for infringement of intellectual property rights have been applied to breach of confidence without much difficulty, save in the case of damages.[49] Typically plaintiffs hope to contain the confidence before escape; hence the importance of injunctions. There has been no doctrinal impediment to awarding equity's ancillary forms of relief—account of profits[50] and delivery up or destruction on oath[51]—in appropriate cases.

To the general discussion of these equitable remedies[52] a number of supplemental points may here be added:

(a) Interlocutory injunctions

8-037   In cases where a defendant is seeking to stop general publication in a newspaper or elsewhere, the courts have to decide whether a special policy will apply. Interlocutory injunctions are not granted in proceedings for defamation if the defendant proposes to justify his statements (*i.e.* establish their truth) or to plead fair comment[53]; the press is thus left free to publish at risk of paying damages. In *Woodward* v. *Hutchins*,[54] the

---

[45] Law Commission (above, n. 26), §§ 63, 65.
[46] See above, § 8-018.
[47] So Lord Keith put the matter in *Att.-Gen.* v. *Guardian Newspapers (No. 2)*, [1988] 3 All E.R. 545 at 640; and see Mason J., *Commonwealth of Australia* v. *Fairfax* [1980] 32 A.L.R. 485 at 492–493.
[48] See above, §§ 2-004—2-007.
[49] See below, §§ 8-048, 8-049.
[50] As in *Peter Pan Mfg.* v. *Corsets Silhouette* [1963] R.P.C. 45.
[51] As in *Industrial Furnaces* v. *Reaves* [1970] R.P.C. 605, where the defendant was not trusted to destroy on oath.
[52] Above, §§ 2-023, 2-028.
[53] *Bonnard* v. *Perryman* [1891] 2 Ch. 269; *Fraser* v. *Evans* [1969] 1 All E.R. 8 at 10 (C.A.); the rule survives *American Cyanamid* v. *Ethicon* (for which see above, §§ 2-019—2-021): *Woodward* v. *Hutchins* [1977] 2 All E.R. 751 (C.A.).
[54] See previous note.

Court of Appeal considered that the alleged breaches of confidence were inextricably linked with defamation (though defamation was not pleaded) and so it refused to halt a newspaper story. But the case lays down no general principle equivalent to that for defamation.

In other circumstances, protection of confidence may override the preservation of free expression. In *Schering* v. *Falkman*,[55] for instance, a man who had been hired to assist a drug company in countering adverse publicity about one of its products, Primodos, had subsequently become a journalist. He and a television company were about to show a programme in which the old controversy over the drug was resurrected. The idea came from his association with the company, though the material had mainly been recovered from public sources. The majority of the Court of Appeal gave interlocutory relief restraining the showing in terms which displayed their distaste for the journalist's lack of moral scruple in taking advantage of his earlier connection with the company. Only Lord Denning M.R., dissenting, gave higher value to the need to free the press and other media from prior restraint.[56]

In the *"Spycatcher"* case, high indignation against the breaches of secrecy   8-038
by the former MI5 officer, Wright, led a majority of the House of Lords to continue and to strengthen interlocutory injunctions against three newspapers,[57] requiring them not to publish extracts or accounts from Wright's memoirs, even after publication abroad had made their contents widely known in Britain.[58] The object of this was to leave to the Attorney-General the practical possibility at the trial of arguing that general injunctions against further revelations by Wright or other confidential government officers should be granted in order to preserve the morale of the secret services.[59] In similar proceedings, shortly before the publication abroad, other newspapers had been obliged to respect the injunctions or court liability for contempt.[60] Interlocutory decisions turn ultimately on the particular balance of convenience, and future courts may hesitate before finding it necessary to go as far as the remarkable circumstances of the Wright affair were considered to warrant. Nonetheless, it is now even clearer that in England the freedom of the press to publish is all too readily overridden by obligations of confidence. It is a very different situation from that which prevails in the United States under the First Amendment to the Constitution. There remains a very serious question, which deserves airing under the European Convention on Human Rights, Article 10, whether the present state of the law is justifiable.

---

[55] [1982] Q.B. 1.
[56] He referred to a fine passage of Blackstone (*Commentaries*, IV, 151–152) on the subject, and to modern developments of the theme, including the European Convention on Human Rights, Art. 10, its interpretation in the *Sunday Times* case ((1979–1980) 2 E.H.R.R. 245), and the view of Lord Scarman in *Att.-Gen.* v. *B.B.C.* [1980] 3 All E.R. 161 at 183.
[57] They were strengthened by removing exceptions pertaining in part to reporting the contemporaneous proceedings in Australia.
[58] *Att.-Gen.* v. *Guardian Newspapers (No. 1)* [1987] 3 All E.R. 316; see also *A.G.* v. *Turnaround Distribution* [1989] 1 F.S.R. 169.
[59] An argument which ultimately failed: see above § 8-018.
[60] *Att.-Gen.* v. *Newspaper Publishing* [1987] 3 All E.R. 276; and see *The Times*, May 9, 1989, for trial of the contempt proceedings.

(b) *Discretion to grant injunction*

8-039   There is some evidence that courts consider a wider range of factors in deciding whether to grant a final injunction in a breach of confidence case than in patent or copyright cases. Some judges have seen difficulties in imposing constraints on the defendant when the circumstances, particularly those arising after the confidential disclosure, make it unfair to go so far. In *Seager v. Copydex (No. 1)*[61] the Court of Appeal refused an injunction and left the defendant to relief in damages; in *Coco v. Clark*,[62] Megarry J. speculated upon a number of circumstances in which it might be appropriate to make the defendant pay only for what he had taken. A list of factors militating against an injunction might include: (i) the fact that the defendant was copying only subconsciously or for some reason innocently; (ii) the gratuitous manner of the plaintiff's communication; (iii) the fact that he was not himself utilising the idea but was rather pursuing an alternative in collaboration with another producer; (iv) the extent of the defendant's own contribution to the design of a successful product; (v) whether the information was economic or personal; (vi) the relatively mundane or subsidiary character of what was taken; (vii) the fact that the information had become public; (viii) possibly even the patentable nature of the idea—thus requiring the plaintiff who wants a full right of property to apply for a patent.[63]

8-040   It would be possible for a court to limit the period of an injunction: for instance where it only wanted to deprive the defendant of his head start, or it wanted to leave the defendant free to use the information once it was put into the public domain. Limited injunctions to such ends have certainly been granted or accepted in principle in other jurisdictions.[64]

(2) Damages

8-041   Where a breach of confidence is also a breach of contract or a general tort such as inducing breach of contract, there is no difficulty in awarding damages in accordance with the normal principles applying to these common law wrongs. Where the liability arises only in equity, damages may be awarded "in lieu of or in addition to an injunction," in accordance with the principle of Lord Cairns' Act 1858, "against the commission or continuance of the wrongful act."[65] In other fields, the courts have shown little inclination to read this power in a limited way: such damages lie (i) where the wrongful act is purely equitable, and (ii)

---

[61] Above, n. 39.

[62] Above, n. 41 at 50. The learned judge's remarks are linked to the question of the extent of liability under the "springboard" doctrine: see above, §§ 8-013—8-014. He shows some inclination to regard the liability as being to pay for information used, rather than not to use it. *cf. Terrapin v. Builders Supply* [1960] R.P.C. 128 at 135.

[63] Factors (i)–(iv) and possibly (vii) were relevant to the refusal of the injunction in *Seager v. Copydex.* Concerning (v), Megarry J. considered that personal information might be protectable by injunction, where industrial or commercial was not. (vii), which is speculative, relates to the discussion of the question, above, § 8-003.

[64] See *International Tools v. Kollar* (above, n. 20); *A.B. Consolidated v. Europe Strength* [1978] 2 N.Z.L.R. 520; *General Television v. Talbot* (above, n. 40).

[65] *Saltman v. Campbell* (1948) 65 R.P.C. 203 (C.A.).

whether the injury has already been committed or will be committed in the absence of an injunction.[66] There are also breach of confidence cases where damages were held available for injuries already caused, in addition to an injunction for the future.[67] But if the only likely breach has already occurred, it continues to be doubted whether damages under the Act can be given: there is then no case for the injunction to which they may be a substitute or addition.[68] In the circumstances, such a view seems narrowly historical.

If damages are being given for future injuries in lieu of an injunction, it is said, in *Seager* v. *Copydex (No. 2)*, that their assessment depends upon whether the information could have been acquired by employing a competent consultant, in which case his fee would be an appropriate measure;[69] or whether the information was special—for instance, inventive—in which case, by analogy to the tort of conversion, the sum should represent its price between willing seller and buyer.[70] In the latter case, however, a sale of all the rights (including the right to apply for a patent)[71] may not always be appropriate. Where the plaintiff is exploiting the information himself, or licensing others, a royalty as if for a non-exclusive licence may be the appropriate measure. Altogether, the analogy to damages for misappropriation of a single tangible article is inept, given in particular the more obvious comparison to patents and copyright and the more flexible approach to damages which applies to their infringement.[72]

8-042

There remains the question, as yet unexplored in the case-law, whether damages for injury to feelings are available for breach of confidence, as they are for defamation and copyright infringement.[73] All that can usefully be said is this. Breach of confidence is slowly becoming one of the ways in which the law accords protection to privacy and those aspects of personal reputation that are associated with it. Infringement of copyright and defamation fulfil the same function in ways that are differently limited. But since both allow damages for injured feelings, it would seem quixotic to bar this form of monetary compensation from the third field, for the sake of yet another historical point.

[66] For a full review, see Jolowicz (1975) 34 C.L.J. 224. *cf.* Meager, Gummow and Lehane, *Equity: Doctrine and Remedies* (1975) § 2317; see also *Elsley* v. *Collins* (1978) 83 D.L.R. (3d) 1 at 13 (S.C. Canada); *General Television* v. *Talbot* (above, n. 40).

[67] *e.g. Peter Pan* v. *Corsets Silhouette* (above, n. 50).

[68] *Proctor* v. *Bayley* (1889) 42 Ch.D. 390 at 401; *Nichrotherm* v. *Percy* [1957] R.P.C. 207 at 213–214; *Malone* v. *Commissioner of Police* [1979] 2 All E.R. 620 at 633.

[69] This is equivalent to Jones' suggestion ((1970) 86 L.Q.R. at 488–491) that a *quantum meruit* assessment may on occasion be appropriate.

[70] [1969] R.P.C. 250; followed in *Interfirm Comparison* v. *Law Society* [1975] R.P.C. 137 at 158.

[71] *Seager* v. *Copydex (No. 2)* (above, n. 70). The case has been treated as laying down no general principle: *General Television* v. *Talbot* (above, n. 40).

[72] *cf. Aircraft Heating* v. *Wellington Gas* [1979] N.Z. Recent Law 106, *Whimp* v. *Kawakawa* [1978] N.Z. Recent Law 114. Note that confidential information is not property for purposes of the Theft Act 1968 s.4: *Oxford* v. *Moss* [1979] Crim.L.R. 119; nor is it a criminal offence in Scotland.

[73] Significantly, *Beloff* v. *Pressdram* (below, p. 370, n. 68), where this was the issue, was pleaded only in copyright.

4. CONFIDENTIAL INFORMATION AS "PROPERTY"[74]

8-043   The willingness of the courts to hold indirect recipients responsible shows
that the obligation to respect confidence is not purely personal to the
initial giver of the undertaking.[75] Is it then, in any meaningful sense,
"property?" The root difficulty of such a question is the flexibility of the
property notion in English law and the many ends to which it is
employed.[75] Clearly, those who deal in technical know-how often treat it
as such. While noting this common usage, Lord Upjohn nevertheless
denied that confidential information was "property in any normal sense,
but equity will restrain its transmission to another if in breach of some
confidential relationship."[76]

While this may well be the predominant view, the theoretical question
has rarely been put to specific tests. Three may be suggested:

8-044   (i)   Does possession of the information in private itself generate rights
against those who misappropriate it? Creation and acquisition, not
necessarily by a consensual dealing, are each modes of acquiring
many kinds of property.[77] The little discussed question of rights
against spies has not been looked at in these terms; but the recent
Malone case emphasised the crucial significance of an undertaking
to respect confidence in this context held that no obligation could
arise against a telephone tapper.

(ii) If "know-how" is assigned, does the assignee acquire the
assignor's right to sue direct and indirect recipients who are
breaking the confidence? Lord Upjohn's approach may mean that
the assignee at most has the right to compel the assignor to take
action.

(iii) If a person with "know-how" assigns or licenses it to two
different people in inconsistent dealings, does one have priority
against the other (and if so, on what principle)? An early New
South Wales decision stressed the obligation of good faith that is
equity's apparent starting point and denied that each recipient
would have more than a personal right against his source.[78] This
too seems consistent with Lord Upjohn's position. Confidential
information will only acquire the characteristics of property if
rights are given against third parties in circumstances such as
these.

[74] See above, § 8-031; on the issue generally, *cf.* Ricketson (1977) 11 M.U.L.R. 223, 289;
Stuckey (1981) 9 Syd.L.R. 402; Weinreb (1988) 28 U. Toronto L.J. 117.
[75] Thus in the *Boardman* case (below, n. 76), one question was whether a fiduciary broke
his equitable obligation by using his principal's property (in information) to his own
advantage.
[76] *Boardman* v. *Phipps* [1967] 2 A.C. 46 at 128; *cf.* §§ 3-037, 4-031.
[77] Including intangible property: consider the cases of copyright, the right to apply for a
patent and the claim to be "proprietor" of a trade mark (discussed below, §§ 17-044–
17-045).
[78] *De Beer* v. *Graham* (1891) 12 L.R.N.S.W. Eq. 144. But if the first recipient receives an
undertaking that the provider of the information will give it to no one else, that
obligation of confidence may today be one which a later recipient can be obliged to
respect.

5. FUTURE DEVELOPMENTS

In 1972, the Younger Committee considered that a general right of   8-045
privacy should not be introduced into the law: it might be used too
readily to trespass upon the freedom to receive and make use of
information and to express opinions.[79] Accepting this limitation, the Law
Commission then undertook a review of the law of Breach of Confidence
and published a Working Paper and then, in 1981, a Report and Draft
Bill.[80] The latter proposed that the liability be expressed as a statutory
duty, couched in the concepts and language of tortious wrong. There
would be, first of all, a duty to preserve confidence arising initially out of
a confidential relationship, and extending to indirect recipients once they
knew the true position. There would also be a duty to respect confidence
in information acquired in seven other specified circumstances, including
unauthorised interference with anything containing the information,
being in a place without authority, using devices for surreptitious
surveillance and the like.

The recommendations as a whole are comprehensive and at several   8-046
points they are rather more precise than the current case-law. But at the
really difficult junctures (*e.g.* whether there is an overriding public
interest in publication) much is inevitably left to the tribunal's particular
sense of balance. Accordingly there has been little pressure in favour of
the draft bill and a degree of at least latent hostility from the media and
others who have reason to be suspicious of a codification that carries
legal protection a considerable way. For the foreseeable future, the state
of the law will likely remain with the judges. They have already done
much to give it substance and scope, dispelling fears that the reach of the
law was inadequate. For the future, the governing question ought to be
whether, in the pursuit of good faith, they have become unduly protective
of information that individuals—and in particular, politicians—would
prefer not to have revealed.

---

[79] Cmnd. 5012, 1972.
[80] English Law Commission, Working Paper No. 58 (1974); Report No. 110 (1981).

Part IV

COPYRIGHT

CHAPTER 9

RANGE AND AIMS OF COPYRIGHT

1. HISTORICAL INTRODUCTION

(1) The emergence of copyright[1]

The notion that an author should have an exclusive "copyright" in his creation took firm shape at the beginning of the eighteenth century. But it derived from a confusion of earlier strains and there was still a major evolutionary conflict to come before its modern form was finally fixed. 9-001

From the early years of the first copying industry—printing—a pattern of exploitation had been developing: an entrepreneur, whose calling was typically that of "stationer," became the principal risk-taker; he acquired the work from its author (if he was not reprinting a classic) and organised its printing and sale. The stationers (forefathers of the modern publisher) were the chief proponents of exclusive rights against copiers. Certainly their own practices—their guild rules and the terms on which they dealt with authors—insisted upon this exclusivity; their regime for "insiders" became a source of trade customs from which general rights against "outsiders" might be distilled.[2]

In this objective the stationers early found an ally in the Crown. In 1534 they secured protection against the importation of foreign books; and in 1556, Mary, with her acute concern about religious opposition, granted the Stationers' Company a charter. This gave a power, in addition to the usual supervisory authority over the craft, to search out and destroy books printed in contravention of statute or proclamation. The company was thus enabled to organise what was in effect a licensing system by requiring lawfully printed books to be entered in its register. The right to make an entry was confined to company members, this being germane to the very purpose of the charter. The system of control was equally satisfying to Elizabeth and her Stuart successors, who supervised it through the Star Chamber and the heads of the established

---

[1] The evolution of copyright has attracted scholars of formidable polish. The sketch that follows relies particularly on Scrutton, *Law of Copyright* (1883) Chap. 4; Birrell, *Seven Lectures on Copyright* (1898); Holdsworth, *History of English Law*, Vol. VI, pp. 360–379; Kaplan, *An Unhurried View of Copyright* (1967), pp. 1–25; Patterson, *Copyright in Historical Perspective* (1968); Feather, *A History of British Publishing* (1988).

[2] See Birrell, Lecture 3; Holdsworth, pp. 363–364 (both accounts being based on Arber, *A Transcript of the Stationers' Registers* (1875)).

Church.[3] Governments determined to censor heterodoxy made concert with the established order of the publishing trade.

9-002   But the royal predilection for granting special privileges might interfere with the interests of the stationers. Not only was the sole privilege to print Bibles, prayer books and laws claimed under the royal prerogative; much wider privileges—not confined to particular, or even new, works—were also granted by letters patent. In the long term, it was not the fact of individual grants which mattered,[4] but their cumulative effect. For they might bear the inference that, as with exclusive rights in technical inventions, it needed special authority from the Crown to secure legal protection against imitators.

So long as the licensing system survived, this line of argument was of no great significance. And Stationers' Company licensing had considerable vitality. It outlived the ignominy into which the Star Chamber fell, being kept up by the Long Parliament and confirmed in 1662 after Charles II's restoration. But he allowed it to lapse in 1679; and, while James II revived it for seven years in 1685, it could not last long in the political climate of his dethronement. Parliament finally refused to renew it in 1694. The stationers, who had argued forcibly against their loss of protection, were left with such claim to "copy-right" as they could make out of the customary practices surrounding registration. As they also lost their search and seizure powers, and equity had not yet begun to grant injunctions to protect any interest that they might establish, the only relief they could hope for was damages in a common law suit.[5] Their needs were equally for definite substantive rights and for effective procedures to enforce them and these needs were reflected in the legislation that they secured in the reign of Anne, the Copyright Act of 1709.[6]

9-003   The "sole right and liberty of printing books" that the Act conferred was given to authors and their assigns; but it stemmed nonetheless from commercial exploitation rather than literary creation pure and simple.[7] Enforcing the right depended upon registering the book's title before publication with the Stationers' Company, "as hath been unusual"; and likewise it was enforceable by seizure and penalties.[8] The right lasted for 14 years from first publication "and no longer"; but if the author was still living at the end, the right was "returned" to him for another 14 years.[9] Other "copy-rights" were expressed to be unaffected by the Act. It was not difficult to argue that an author ought to have some protection over his work before it was published. Since this went uncovered by the

---

[3] The regulatory system was brought under a comprehensive Star Chamber decree of 1586; of this there was a new version in 1637.

[4] Many of the publishing patents naturally came into the hands of Stationers' Company members.

[5] On this period, see especially Scrutton, pp. 89–94; Birrell, pp. 78–93.

[6] See Ransom, *The First Copyright Statute* (1956); Feather (1980) 8 Pub. History 19.

[7] See s.1. Booksellers and printers were named as falling among the author's assigns.

[8] ss.1, 2.

[9] s.11. For books already printed on April 10, 1710, the period was 21 years from that date: s.1.

Act, it could only lie in a right of literary property at common law.[10] But much more absorbing was the question whether any common law right survived in perpetuity the act of publication.

At first, in the view of a majority of judges, history and policy demanded the recognition of this complete property right.[11] The Act of Anne was treated as providing supplemental remedies during the period when unfair competition could most readily injure the first publisher.[12] But the great case of *Donaldson* v. *Beckett*[13] narrowly settled the issue the other way: the statute was taken to delimit the scope of rights after publication absolutely. It was a most strategic victory for those who would insist that claims to trading exclusivity must be balanced against public interest in the freedom to exploit.[14] Had the case gone the other way, protection for other forms of intellectual endeavour against "misappropriation" would have been pressed in a host of analogies. But given *Donaldson* v. *Beckett*, new forms of protection had to be secured from the legislature; and even if a lobby succeeded, the most that could be hoped for would be an exclusive right of limited duration.[15]

(2) Additions to copyright: nineteenth century experience
That process had indeed begun already. The engravers had succeeded   **9-004**
in 1734 and 1766.[16] Textile designers secured some very temporary protection by statutes which were the precursors of the present registered

---

[10] The question was not actually decided before *Donaldson* v. *Beckett* (below, n. 13). But then, 9 of the 10 judges had no doubt about its existence.

[11] Especially in *Millar* v. *Taylor* (1769) 4 Burr. 2303, where Lord Mansfield, a great champion of authors, led the majority. But the same assumption had been made in the 1730s when Chancery began to grant interlocutory injunctions concerning books no longer within the fold of the statute. And the booksellers found some favour from the King's Bench judges in an action (collusive and so ultimately abortive) begun in 1760. The whole tale is ebulliently told by Birrell (above, n. 1), Lecture 4; and see Feather (1987) 22 Pub. History 5.

[12] There were other ways in which the statute was read as protecting only the most serious invasions of the publisher's interests: thus neither translations nor "fair" abridgements at this stage constituted infringements: *Burnett* v. *Chetwood* (1720) 2 Mer. 441; *Gyles* v. *Wilcox* (1740) 2 Atk. 141, 3 Atk. 269; *Dodsley* v. *Kinnersley* (1761) Amb. 403. For the relation of these decisions to the scope of the common law right, see Kaplan (above, n. 1).

[13] (1774) 2 Bro. P.C. 129, 4 Burr. 2408, 17 Hansard Parl. Hist. 953. Lord Mansfield did not participate.

[14] Its tone found sympathetic resonances in the century to come. A notable reiteration came in *Jeffreys* v. *Boosey* (1854) 4 H.L.C. 815. Here the issue took the form: if statute did not allow copyright to a foreign author, was he nonetheless protected at common law. On consulting the judges the House of Lords found that a majority of them favoured the common law right. But the Lords unanimously agreed with Pollock C.B.'s positivist view of copyright as "altogether an artificial right, not naturally and necessarily arising out of the social rules that ought to prevail among mankind, but . . . a creature of the municipal laws of each country, to be enjoyed for such time and under such regulation as the law of each state may direct" (at 935).

[15] *cf.* above, § 8-007.

[16] Engraving Copyright Acts 1734 and 1766 (and further enactments in 1777 and 1836). The term was 28 years.

design system.[17] In 1798 and 1814, sculptures were protected[18]; and eventually—as the technical possibilities for reproducing artistic works expanded—the Fine Arts Copyright Act 1862 brought in paintings, drawings and photographs.[19]

The term of the statutory right in published books was extended to 28 years or the author's life, whichever was longer, in 1814.[20] But Sergeant Talfourd's attempts to have it again extended—for a period of perhaps the author's life and 60 years—ran into the shoal of "economical" argument, put in particularly telling form by T. B. Macaulay.[21] His view of copyright as "a tax on readers for the purpose of giving a bounty to authors" meant that in 1842 the period was extended only to 42 years or the author's life and seven years, whichever was longer.[22] That compromise was to last until international pressures obliged Parliament to revise its views in Talfourd's direction.[23]

9-005   The commercial interests of book publishers had called for a "copyright";[24] and much the same applied to artistic works. But in the arts of drama and music, exploitation occurred as much through performance as through the sale of copies. Playwrights, composers and their commercial associates sought a "use" right upon each public performance of the work. In 1833 this distinct performing right was given in dramatic works[25] and in 1842 extended to musical works.[26] Despite the nature of the performing right, the wider term, "author's right," was never introduced into English usage, as it was in most other languages, in place of "copyright." The difference reflects the accretive historical process by which the British law developed. But equally it carries another overtone: a change to "author's right" might well symbolise some preference for creator over entrepreneur. That is something which has rarely attracted much ardour in Britain.

The same point is underscored in another way. The relation between author and exploiter offers many opportunities for tension and disagreement. In continental Europe the need to safeguard the artistic integrity of the author in the course of such relations was eloquently argued, particularly in the latter nineteenth century; and in many copyright laws the author was accorded moral rights which were entrenched by making

---

[17] An Act of 1787 gave protection against the printing, working or copying of an original pattern for certain types of textile. But it lasted only for two months from publication (in 1794 extended to three)—giving at most a bare head-start.

[18] These Acts extended only to sculptures, etc., of the human figure; the term was 14 years from publication with a further 14 years for authors who were living and had kept the copyright themselves.

[19] Here the term was the author's life and seven years.

[20] Copyright Act 1814, s.4.

[21] Macaulay, *Speeches* (1866) pp. 109–122.

[22] Literary Copyright Act 1842, s.3.

[23] See below, § 9-011.

[24] There had been no difficulty in extending the Act of Anne to sheet music (*Bach* v. *Longman* (1777) 2 Cowp. 623); as for maps, see *Sayre* v. *Moore* (1785) 1 East 361n.

[25] Dramatic Copyright Act 1833; for its history, see McFarlane, *Copyright: the Development and Exercise of the Performing Right* (1980), Chaps. 3–5. Lectures in public were specially treated by the Lectures Copyright Act 1835.

[26] Literary Copyright Act 1842, s.20; see further Lahore, § 225; McFarlane, (above, n. 25).

inoperative any surrender of the rights in advance of the time when the author might want to rely upon them. These typically might include: the right to decide to make the work public; the right to be named as author; the right to object to revisions affecting honour or reputation. Some systems have gone to the extent of adding a right to have the work withdrawn upon payment of compensation; and the right to object to destruction.[27] In Britain, this sort of demand seems scarcely to have surfaced at all. Instead, in the high age of contractual freedom, relations were left to be determined by agreement, supported by such terms as the court might imply in the name of business efficacy and subject to the torts of defamation, injurious falsehood and passing off.[28]

(3) International relations and the Act of 1911

Britain could not however afford to reject entirely the ideals of those   9-006
for whom copyright was a practical expression of reverence for the act of artistic creation. Her commercial position made her a considerable exporter of copyright material and she had a strong interest in reciprocal copyright arrangements with other countries and their colonies. On the question of protecting foreign works it was possible to take a number of attitudes: the French, for instance, granted protection to all authors of works published in France and to works of Frenchmen published anywhere. The Americans, by contrast, first underlined their independence from Britain by confining copyrights to citizens and residents; and, a century later, while conceding some place to foreign authors, country by country, Congress required all legitimate copies of various types of work to be produced in the United States (under the controversial "manufacturing clause").[29] The British, true to their own tradition of giving first consideration to home publishers, admitted foreign authors to copyright upon condition that the work was first published within the country.[30]

With protectionist America, the hope of satisfactory mutual arrange-   9-007
ments was slender; but with continental Europe and elsewhere the prospects were brighter. A number of bilateral arrangements were worked out. Then, by the Berne Convention of 1886, a multi-national system of equality, under which either the personal connection of the author with a member state, or first publication in a member state, was to secure copyright in the other.[30a] But this in turn raised questions about the scope of rights offered in each state. At the Berlin Revision of the Convention in 1908, Britain was obliged to accept the majority consensus on two matters: protection was to arise out of the act of creation itself, without any condition of registration or other formality—which obliged

[27] See, below, § 12-019.
[28] There is no mention of the subject, for instance, in the Reports of the Royal Commission of 1875–1878 and the Committee of 1909.
[29] There were a series of later modifications to the manufacturing clause, see Nimmer, *Copyright* (1979 ed.), §§ 722–723.
[30] For parts of this story, see Nowell-Smith, *International Copyright Law and the Publisher in the Reign of Queen Victoria* (1968), Chaps. 1, 2.
[30a] For the history of the Berne Convention, Ricketson (1987) Chap. 1.

Britain to abandon even the traditional requirement of Stationers' Company registration before suing[31]; and the period of protection for most types of work was to be at least the author's life and 50 years—that quasi-proprietary right against which Macaulay had persuaded Parliament 70 years before.

These changes were adopted in the Copyright Act 1911, the first British legislation to bring the various copyrights within a single text, and at the same time to put rights even in unpublished works on a statutory footing.[32] There was, however, some concession to public interest arguments: in the later years of the copyright in published works there were certain provisions for automatic licences.[33]

9-008   If the author gained by this intrusion of foreign ideals, the entrepreneur was by no means forgotten. The 1911 Act gave the producers of sound recordings their own exclusive right to prevent reproductions of their recordings (and, as the courts later held, also to prevent public performances of them).[34] The right was indiscriminately labelled copyright, even though it was conferred not upon the executant artist whose performance was recorded but upon the business which organised the recording. It was thus not an author's right at all, but something which continental theory would scrupulously distinguish as a "neighbouring right." An important precedent was set for an age that was to see a great increase in the technical possibilities for artistic expression.

---

[31] After 1842, registration was no longer required before publication, but only before suing on the copyright. Accordingly the requirement served no obvious function, and came in for a good deal of domestic criticism.

[32] Common law copyright in unpublished works was abolished: C.A. 1911, s.31.

[33] C.A. 1911, s.3, provided that, after 25 years from the death of an author of a published work, anyone might reproduce it for sale upon payment of a 10 per cent. royalty to the copyright owner. S.4 added a special power (first introduced in 1842) to seek a licence from the Privy Council, which in fact went unused. The Gregory Committee found that this machinery played no significant part in securing cheap republications. In order to satisfy the unqualified requirements of the Berne Convention in its 1948 revision (Brussels), the Committee recommended abandonment: see Cmd. 8661, §§ 20–23. This was effected in 1956.

The provisions just mentioned were often linked with the reversionary interest rules introduced in 1911, though these were motivated by a concern for authors and their dependants vis-à-vis their entrepreneurs. s.5 rendered ineffective an inter vivos assignment by an author of his copyright in a work, and equally his licence to publish such a work, so far as concerned the period from 25 years after his death. While this limited reversionary right was abolished after July 1, 1957, it continued to affect assignments and licences entered into before that date: (C.A. 1956, Sched. 7, § 28(3); Sched. 8, § 6). Numerous musical works which have a recurrent popularity were dealt with in ways which allowed the legatees of composers (at least when moved by others to act) to claim back the last 25 years of the copyright. The precise impact of the reversionary right provision has accordingly been the subject of complex dispute: see Redwood Music v. Francis Day [1981] R.P.C. 337 (H.L.); Harris (1983) 30 J.Cop.Soc. 544.

[34] C.A. 1911, s.19(1); Gramophone Co. v. Cawardine [1934] Ch. 450.

(4) Developments since 1945

(a) *The 1956 Act*

In the post-war period, there has been constant activity on the   9-009
international scene. But alterations in domestic law have derived more
from pressures at home and these may be dealt with first. The Copyright
Act 1956 was a complex piece of draftsmanship which elaborated many
rules at perplexing length while neglecting to spell out basic principles in
the clear order appropriate to a real code.[35] The Act was most notable for
adding three new forms of entrepreneurial copyright—in cinematograph
films (hereafter "films" for short), broadcasts and the typographical
format of published editions—to the 1911 copyright in sound recordings.

Equally significant in terms of new technique was the creation of a
Performing Right Tribunal. In the inter-war period, it had been shown by
the Performing Right Society (PRS) that joint action was a feasible
method of turning the right of public performance in copyright music
into something of real value[36]; and the record companies had followed
suit, once they succeeded in establishing their own performing right,[37] by
setting up Phonographic Performance Ltd. (PPL). The aggregation of
copyrights that such organisations acquired brought a measure of power
over their markets which, as the Gregory Committee found, was capable
of being exercised in controversial ways: in particular PPL had been
prepared to refuse or limit licences to, for instance, dance-halls, in order
to sustain the employment of live musicians.[38] The Performing Right
Tribunal was accordingly created to hear disputes over performing right
licences from authors' collecting societies, and recording and broadcasting organisations.[39] Its services have been used on a number of important
occasions and it is now being looked to as a model for controlling the
activities of licensing bodies which have been or may be established to
deal with reproduction rights, as distinct from performing rights.

Those who contributed to the production of recordings, films and   9-010
broadcasts as performing artists gained no part in the proprietary rights
of the new Copyright Act. The argument against them was that to give
them copyright would make for disproportionate complexity in the
handling of rights and that they could properly be left to protect
themselves by contract.[40] However, even in 1925, it had been admitted
that performers deserved some form of added help against strangers who
misappropriated their performances: but they were only allowed the
assistance of the criminal law.[41] The same system was continued in a
series of statutes somewhat extending the original range. The Performers'
Protection Acts 1958–1972 established summary offences against making

---

[35] It was used as a text-book example of how not to proceed by Dale, *Legislative Drafting*
(1976), Chap. 1.
[36] In the nineteenth century, the copyright owners of dramatic works had for some time run
a Dramatic Authors' Society: see McFarlane (above, n. 25) at 65 *et seq.*
[37] See above, n. 34.
[38] See Cmd. 8662, §§ 140–157.
[39] C.A. 1956, Pt. IV; see below, pp. 399–402.
[40] See the Gregory Report, Cmd. 8862, §§ 165–176.
[41] Dramatic and Musical Performers' Protection Act 1925.

non-private records or films of performances, performing them in public, and broadcasting performances, without the performers' written consent. As the volume of "bootlegging" (surreptitious recording of performances) grew, this half-way house became much less satisfactory protection. There were attempts to persuade courts that the Acts conferred civil rights of action. This produced only slow progress and the issue became one of the many pressures upon the government for the legislation which would eventually emerge as the Copyright, Designs and Patents Act 1988.

(b) *International developments*

9-011   (i) *The Universal Copyright Convention (UCC).*[42] The desire to bring the United States within a general network of international copyright relations was strong. So also was the wish to maintain the basic tenets of the Berne Convention; indeed its revision at Brussels in 1948 only served to strengthen its force. After that event UNESCO took the initiative by promoting the Universal Copyright Convention of 1952. This also guaranteed the principle of national treatment, but on less stringent conditions about the term of protection, the types of work protected and the extent of protection. There was, for instance, no mention of any moral right. The United States was able to join the new Convention, while retaining her copyright term of two periods of 28 years[42a] and introducing a simple requirement of notice on published works of foreign authors not first published there: the symbol ©, together with the name of the copyright owner and the year of first publication.[43] Subsequently, in 1973, the U.S.S.R. joined the UCC and there are now a significant number of states which belong only to the less demanding of the two general Conventions.[44]

9-012   (ii) *The Stockholm and Paris Revisions of Berne and UCC: the developing countries.* Copyright was the first field of intellectual property in which the developing countries sought to have their needs recognised as a special case. The shock waves of the initial confrontation were considerable: the concessions in favour of developing countries were originally moulded into a Protocol to the Berne Convention at the Stockholm Revision in 1967. But these proved more than the traditional publishing states (led by the British) could take. The Protocol allowed developing countries to reduce the term of copyright in their national law; to authorise translations into their national languages; to authorise publishing for educational and cultural purposes and to exclude from the scope

[42] See Bogsch, *Law of Copyright under the Universal Copyright Convention* (3rd ed., 1972).
[42a] The UCC, Art. 4(2), provided for a minimum term of the author's life and 25 years, unless a country already measured by a term of years from publication; in that case the period had to be 25 years or more.
[43] This common marking is not needed to secure protection in any member state of the Berne Union, such as the U.K. For the recent adherence of the U.S. to Berne, see below, § 9-014.
[44] A Berne member may not leave and then rely upon the protection flowing from the UCC, unless it is a developing country: see UCC Art. 27 and Appendix Declaration, as revised in 1971.

of infringement reproduction for teaching, study or research; and to limit the scope of the right to broadcast. As it became clear that the Stockholm version would not be supported, a further revision conference was called (in Paris, 1971).[45] This toned down the special concessions in a new Appendix to the Berne Convention.

The limitations which developing countries[46] are entitled to introduce into national law have been restricted to two. First, once three years have passed since first publication, a competent authority in the country may be empowered to license a national to translate a printed work into a national language,[47] and publish it, for the purpose of teaching, scholarship or research[48]; in the alternative, the country may take advantage of an older Convention provision[49] allowing the termination of the translation right, once 10 years from first publication have elapsed without the copyright owner publishing his own translation. Secondly, if the copyright owner or an associate does not publish the work in a country within a set period[50] after first publication, the competent authority can license a national to publish.[51] But the copies in both cases must be confined to the national market. Any licence must be upon terms of just compensation, judged by the standard of usual royalty rates between the two countries.[52]

9-013

At the same time, rather similar compromises were reached for the UCC. As far as translations are concerned, this Convention did not previously have the 10-year exception as in Berne, but instead allowed (in any country) a compulsory licence of a published "writing" after a seven-year period.[53] On top of this, the developing countries are permitted the post-three-year compulsory licence to translate as in Berne.[54] They also have equivalent rights to allow compulsory licences to reproduce.[55]

9-014

The process of reaching an international consensus on these points has become laborious and complex. The results may do something to colour the political climate in which publishing by foreign houses is conducted in developing countries. But even in those countries which have set up

---

[45] While the administrative provisions of Stockholm have been accepted and brought into force, the rest of Stockholm including the Protocol has ceased to be open for ratification or accession, now that the later Paris Act is in force (since October 10, 1974): see Ulmer (1972) 19 J. Cop.Soc. 263; Toups (1982) 29 J. Cop.Soc. 402; Teran (1982) 30 J. Cop.Soc. 129; Ricketson (1987) Chap. 11.

[46] i.e. countries so regarded in U.N. practice: Appendix, Art. 1(1).

[47] i.e. one in general use there, or in use in a region or by an ethnic or governmental group or in education: see Lahore, § 1728.

[48] Appendix, Art. 2. See also Art. 2(9) allowing a similar licence to a broadcasting organisation.

[49] Convention, Art. 30(2), App., Art. 5.

[50] These periods differ with the type of work, the period for scientific and technological works being as little as three years from first publication: App., Art. 3(3).

[51] App., Art. 3.

[52] App., Art. 6; note the compromise on currency restrictions affecting compensation: Art. 4(6). There are a number of provisions on formalities and further qualifications; for which see Ricketson (1987) Chaps. 13, 14.

[53] UCC, Art. 5.

[54] Art. 5ter.

[55] Art. 5quater.

licensing procedures in pursuance of their Convention entitlements, there is little evidence that local publishers are taking advantage of them.

By the 1988 Act, the United Kingdom has put itself in position to ratify the Paris Revisions of the Berne Convention and the UCC. This is not before time. As it is, it will coincide with United States adherence (at long last) to Berne,[56] thus cementing the commitment of two major producing countries to the senior of the two Conventions.[57] This will help to sustain a wider belief in the value of both, making international collaboration in the field of copyright more positive than is currently the case for industrial property.

9-015   (iii) *Protection of performers, recorders and broadcasters.* The 1956 Act strongly confirmed the United Kingdom's interest in supporting the entrepreneurs of the entertainment industry; and more guardedly the claims of performers have also been acknowledged.[58] The country was accordingly a strong supporter of international collaboration against the piracy of performances, particularly through the media of records and broadcasts. A first drive resulted in the Rome Convention on the Protection of Performers, Producers of Phonograms and Broadcasting Organisations of 1961.[59] The Convention requires a member to provide[60]: for performers, power to prevent the fixation or broadcasting of their live performance (but not a recorded performance)[61]; for record makers, the power to prevent reproduction of their records[62]; for broadcasting organisations, the power to control re-broadcasting and public performance for an entrance fee (but not diffusion by wire).[63] It was indeed ambitious to try to secure international protection for rights of three groups who also have such evident conflicts of interest amongst themselves. The Convention has only attracted adherents slowly. It proved necessary in 1971 to sign a second "Phonograms" Convention, dealing only with mutual protection against the unauthorised commercial copying of sound recordings.[64]

In the field of broadcasting likewise, separate links have been forged, mainly through the activities of the European Broadcasting Union. In particular, the Agreement on Television Broadcasts 1960[65] goes some way

[56] As to which, see Brown (1988) 33 J. Cop.Soc. 196.
[57] For considerations of the future of the Berne Convention at its centennial point, see Ricketson (1987) Pt. III; and the contributions of Davis, Phillips and Koumantos to (1986) 11 Col.-VLA J. Law of A. 33, 165, 225.
[58] See above, § 9-010.
[59] See Davies (1979) 1 E.I.P.R. 154.
[60] In each case, for the benefit of nationals of other member states and for specified activities carried on in those states: see Arts. 4–6.
[61] See, in full, Arts. 7–9.
[62] See Arts. 10–12.
[63] Art. 13. The term must be at least 20 years from performance, fixation or broadcast: Art. 14.
[64] The United Kingdom is also a member of this. See Ulmer (1972) 3 I.I.C. 317; Stewart (1973) 9 Copyright 110.
[65] Made permanent by a Protocol of 1965. Like the Agreement on Television Films of 1958 this agreement was secured by the Council of Europe, through its expert committee on broadcasting.

in continental Europe towards limiting the freedom to pick up broadcasts from another member country and diffuse them by cable (Britain has been able to take advantage of an exception about this).[66] The Satellites Convention (1974) seeks to deal with people (particularly "pirate" radio stations) who might otherwise take the signals of transmissions from point-to-point satellites and broadcast or diffuse them locally. For various reasons Britain has not joined this arrangement.[67]

(iv) *The EEC.* In the field of copyright, Community intervention has advanced slowly. However, a study by Dietz explored the prospects for harmonising Member State laws concerning "classical" copyright[68] and the EC Commission, after long deliberation, has produced a Green Paper of its own. This, however, deals with the particular issues where technological advance demands legal change if copyright is to continue as an effective base for Community trade.[69] Some at least of the Commission's thinking accords with solutions adopted in the new British Act.   **9-016**

(v) *Piracy and the GATT.* In the Uruguay Round of negotiations of the General Agreement on Tariffs and Trade (GATT), the United States has led other industrial countries in demanding that broad and effective intellectual property laws should become a condition of the package of mutual concessions that are to be agreed.[70] Above all the aim is to ensure workable copyright laws which can be used against the large-scale piracy of records, films, books and other copyright material in some 20 countries which are at present in reality non-copyright countries, whatever their international obligations. The Berne and Universal Conventions contain no operative machinery for securing a ruling that a country is not adhering to its obligations, while the GATT appears to offer more hope, since it has been slowly building its own dispute settlement procedure. This attack is not likely to have much direct effect on the law of industrial countries such as Britain, but could have an impact on British-owned copyright in many parts of the developing world.[71]   **9-017**

(c) *The Copyright Designs and Patents Act 1988*
The pressures which contributed to the making of this major enactment have accordingly been heterogenous. By the 1970s it was becoming clear that if copyright was to survive the impact of modern technology — photocopying, audio and video taping and computing each on small-scale and large — adaptations of law and practice would be needed. At the   **9-018**

[66] However, the Whitford Committee (Cmnd. 6732, §§ 70–75) recommended that Britain should abandon this and most other exceptions that were inserted at her behest.
[67] See on this the Whitford Report, §§ 76–81.
[68] *Copyright in the European Community* (English version, 1978) (cited as "Dietz") and see Dietz [1985] E.I.P.R. 215.
[69] *Copyright and the Challenge of Technology* (Com(88)172). See further, below, § 13-013.
[70] On the legal relations of this move to the existing Convention framework for intellectual property, see Kunz-Hallstein in Beier and Schricker (eds.) *GATT or WIPO* (1989, forthcoming).
[71] For a manifestation of the same attitude in the new Copyright Designs and Patents Act 1988, see s.155: this allows the government to withdraw protection from a Convention country to the extent that it does not provide equivalent protection to British authors. Thus has one country built reprisals into international copyright diplomacy.

same time, the unique, ill-considered experiment of using copyright to protect industrial design was disturbing relations in a wide span of industries.[72] In 1974 the Whitford Committee began the considerable task of reviewing the whole range of copyright and designs law in the United Kingdom. Its Report in 1977,[73] for the most part welcomed as an important step forward, nevertheless would remain in limbo for a decade while different parts of government produced their own views and reactions in a series of papers,[74] and the various interest groups engaged in a ferment of proposition and counter-proposition and also secured a number of specific changes: to improve the remedies against pirates[75] to provide copyright in cable-casts and to reinforce it to computer programmes. Because, thanks to the adventure over industrial design, copyright has been drawn so far into the realm of industrial production, the question of reform fell to be assessed with the intellectual property regimes considered as a whole.[76] That is why the eventual Act does a number of things. It restates the statutory law of copyright, on the whole in a plainer and more logical manner than the 1956 Act. At the same time it introduces a number of changes—in particular, the granting of a rental right in certain subject-matter, the creation of moral rights for authors and directors, the extension of control over collecting societies by means of a Copyright Tribunal, and the conferment of a quasi-copyright on performers and their exclusive contractors. The Act also completely revises the law affecting industrial designs; and it changes various details of patent laws, including the establishment of a county court jurisdiction for patents[77]; and extends the liabilities of trade mark infringers. Its details are the substance of the ensuing chapters.

(d) Copyright and unfair competition

9-019   An exclusive right which strikes only at copying is particularly suited to claims that a person is taking something for nothing—that he is reaping fruits sown by the creativity of others. Nonetheless British copyright law has on the whole conformed to the prescription that new rights should not be conceded without making a political case and securing legislation. Indeed, statute has increasingly been used to define not only the duration of the various copyrights, but their subject-matter, the exclusive rights to which they give rise and the exceptions that may be admitted. The refusal to allow any general principle of unfair competition that will extend to the misappropriation of ideas means, however, that no limited, short-term form of liability may be imposed upon even the most sycophantic purveyor of other people's ideas and

---

[72] See below, §§ 14-001 et seq.
[73] Copyright and Designs Law, (Cmnd. 6732, 1977).
[74] See esp. Green Paper, Reform of the Law relating to Copyright, Designs and Performers' Protection (Cmnd. 8302, 1981) and White Paper, Intellectual Property and Innovation (Cmnd. 9712, 1986).
[75] See esp. Copyright (Amendment) Acts of 1982 and 1983; Cable and Broadcasting Act 1984, esp. Sched. 5; Films Act 1985; Copyright (Computer Software) Act 1985.
[76] Note the Report of the Government Chief Scientist, Innovation and Intellectual Property Rights (Cmnd. 9117, 1984).
[77] See above, § 6-017.

enterprise. Accordingly there is always some desire to press the existing concepts of copyright into service. Lord Devlin, for example, once said:

"Free trade does not require that one should be allowed to appropriate the fruits of another's labour, whether they are tangible or intangible. The law has not found it possible to give full protection to the intangible. But it can protect the intangible in certain states, and one of them is when it is expressed in words or print. The fact that that protection is of necessity limited is no argument for diminishing it further, and it is nothing to the point to say that either side of the protective limits a man can obtain gratis whatever his ideas of honesty permit him to pick up."[78]

But this is not an attitude which has been maintained with consistency. There has been some tendency to look upon copyright as typically concerned with established forms of aesthetic activity; and so there are decisions making it difficult to use artistic copyright against the copying of a dress design, or to claim that a suite of furniture amounts to a "work of artistic craftsmanship."[79] In line with such caution, and very significant in its impact, was a tradition (reversed surprisingly in 1968) of excluding artistic copyright from the sphere of mass-produced goods, so as to leave the registered design system as sole occupant. **9-020**

In a sense, the origins of registered designs stretch back to the earliest period of industrialisation in some parts of the textile industry.[80] But the real impetus towards the modern system came in the 1830's. The poor quality of British industrial design, particularly when compared with the achievements of the French, incited middle-class radicals to press for a system of training designers, and manufacturers to demand a more substantial legal monopoly.[81] The system of registration that evolved under statutes of 1839 and 1842 gave a form of protection particularly directed towards preserving the original design-owner's headstart; the term was short but the design was kept confidential in the registry throughout the period.[82]

As we shall see, in 1911 artistic copyright was deliberately excluded from much of the industrial design field, and the same policy of preventing cumulative protection was pursued in 1956 under a rather more complete and satisfactory formula.[83] But the registered design system, with its patent-like preliminary examination and its requirement of novelty or originality, was too limited and cumbersome for many industries. They secured from the Johnston Departmental Committee in 1962 a recommendation of a simpler form of protection against copying. This would last for a relatively short period; but the interests of the rest **9-021**

[78] *Ladbroke v. Hill* [1964] 1 W.L.R. 273 at 291; see further, below, § 11-006. Contrast the thrust of these remarks with the well-known dictum of Dixon J., quoted above, § 1-008.
[79] See below, §§ 10-012—10-014.
[80] See above, § 9-004.
[81] See Prouty, *The Transformation of the Board of Trade 1830–1857* (1957), pp. 18–27.
[82] Copyright of Designs Act 1842, s.17; and for subsequent Acts and further details, see Cmnd. 1808, 1962, App. B.
[83] Below, §§ 14-003—14-005.

of industry demanded as a prerequisite that a person claiming such a right should deposit his design in an official register.[84]

Even this balancing of interests was by-passed in the Design Copyright Act 1968, which was meant to secure such groups as jewellery-, furniture- and toy-makers against the unfair competition of free copying. The particular manner in which artistic copyright was introduced into the sphere of industrial production, however, was ill-thought-through. So in various respects it went much beyond the apparent intentions of its sponsors. Just what has happened must be left until later.[85] But the overall effect of allowing registered design and copyright protection to accumulate was very considerable. At least where a design originated from two-dimensional drawings or plans, to copy them (directly or indirectly) in three-dimensional products was likely to infringe copyright in them; and mostly it made no difference that shape is a consequence of function. Copyright invaded the sphere of technical design with an efficacy and simplicity that has been truly dramatic.

9-022   As a form of protection against design misappropriation it was for a number of reasons, extreme. The very substantial reduction in scope, embodied in the 1988 Act, is largely placed outside the frame of copyright and in the separate folds of registered and unregistered design. The point of doing this, rather than adapting copyright, has been to avoid the international obligations of the latter.

2. ECONOMIC PERSPECTIVES[86]

(1) Market power and individual works

9-023   Even so brief an historical outline will suggest the range of industries that copyright now serves. Starting from the production of books, it has moved out into the modern media of instruction and entertainment—through stage performances to recordings and broadcasting; and with its incursion into the field of industrial design it is now providing a form of "industrial property" comparable in importance to the patent system and the protection of confidence. As with patents and confidential information, copyright may provide the legal foundation upon which monopoly profits can be generated, provided always that the market contains sufficient demand for the product. The ability of patented goods to produce this effect largely depends upon their technical efficiency, judged in economic terms by comparison with any alternative products that are available. But many copyright works gain their uniqueness through the dictates of fashion, as moulded by advertising and other promotion,

---

[84] Cmnd. 1808, esp. §§ 47–48.
[85] See below, § 13-001.
[86] Substantial treatment of aspects of the economics of copyright is to be found particularly in Plant (1934) 1 Economica 167 and The New Commerce in Ideas and Intellectual Property (1953); Breyer (1970) 84 Harvard L.R. 281; Tyerman (1971) 18 U.C.L.A. Law Rev. 1100, 19 Bull. U.S. Cop. S. 99; Economic Council of Canada, Report on Intellectual and Industrial Property (1971), and the Canadian White Paper, From Gutenberg to Telidon (1984).

criticism, the reputation of the author's previous works, the shortage of new material[87] and other factors.

There are examples enough of the manner in which publishers and other producers of copyright material have taken a monopolist's advantage of their exclusive position: the practice of publishing hard-back editions before paperbacks, for instance,[88] or that of showing films at expensive inner-city cinemas before allowing suburban release and then television showing.[89] That such practices should follow from the conferring of copyright is not of itself a ground for criticism. The very purpose of the protection is to allow recoupment for the initiative of creating the material and the investment risked in producing and marketing it. In most instances a copyist could produce a directly competing product at a much lower cost if copyright did not restrain him.[90] Nonetheless, the "tax upon the public" should be broadly commensurate with the objectives of conferring copyright. The obvious economic test of this is: what measure of protection is needed to bring about the creation and production of new works and other material within the copyright sphere? Since any answer must be a rough one, the issue is largely a matter of the duration of copyright. Should it last for the relatively short period for which a patent or registered design is thought to be needed as an industrial incentive? Or is there justification for the very much longer period currently allowed for copyright?

9-024

In seeking an answer, the original Statute of Anne has an interesting suggestiveness. As will be recalled, it first gave a copyright period that was clearly related to the entrepreneur's needs: its term of 14 years from first publication came from the analogy of patents for inventions. But the Act proceeded to distinguish a further interest of the author. It gave him a further 14 years copyright if he was still living at the end of the first period. In subsequent statutory developments, the usual pattern has been to provide an undivided period of entitlement; and the publisher has been left free to take an exclusive assignment or licence of the whole from the author.[91]

---

[87] In his 1954 lecture (above, n. 86, p. 33) Plant commented upon the insatiable appetite of television for expensive novelties.

[88] A practice which, in one instance, brought about the intervention of the EEC Commission's Competition Directorate: see *Jonathan Cape—Penguin Books, "The Old Man and the Sea"* [1977] 1 C.M.L.R. D121. Examples of international price discrimination built upon copyright are to be found in the old British publishing practice of producing cheaper "colonial editions"; and in the pricing of books in Canada (see Economic Council of Canada (above, n. 86) App. B) and in Australia (see the *Time-Life* Case, below, § 12-009, n. 35). Sometimes the organised power of a group of buyers may lead to raised retail prices, as was at one time the case with circulating libraries (see Plant, 1934, n. 86 above, pp. 186–187).

[89] See *Coditel* v. *Ciné Vog* (below, § 12-032, n. 42), which is based upon the assumption that such a system of exploitation is in principle legitimate.

[90] For examples relating to American book publishing, see Breyer (above, n. 86). In film production, comparable figures would be dramatic indeed.

[91] But note the reversionary right in published works that arose under the 1911 Act, s.5: see above, n. 83.

9-025   Economic critics of the present approach stress the disadvantages to the consumer which flow from this ellision of the distinct interests of author and entrepreneur. Plant is surely correct in suggesting that few publishers (or, for that matter, record producers or film makers) calculate how much to risk in a particular venture by reference to likely returns over more than a few years.[92] To shorten the present copyright period is accordingly unlikely to produce any noticeable effect upon the amount of copyright material which they are prepared to put out for consumption. Instead, works that prove to have lasting popularity provide them with bonuses. One justification commonly offered for this is that it induces entrepreneurs to take greater risks in promoting works for which there may be no sufficient demand. That is an attractive argument so long as one restricts attention to things scholarly or acceptably cultural. But the copyright system leaves to the entrepreneur the choice of what to select from the pool of works otherwise uneconomic. A more satisfactory method of choosing what is most deserving (whatever the criteria may be) would be through some form of government or other subsidy,[93] a technique which would prevent the cost having to be borne by the readers of successful books.

9-026   The public is supplied with copyright material through the co-operation of entrepreneur and author, and it may be that there are cases where the very long period of copyright makes it worth an author's while to embark upon a particular project.[94] But this economic calculation can scarcely have stood high amongst the jumble of motives which have led to the current legal protection offered to authors. Their case has been borne along rather by special admiration for aesthetic creativity and the associated desire (often expressed in the rhetoric of natural justice) to provide authors with fruits for their labour which have the character of inheritable property.

Even admitting the force of this attitude, the encouragement of entrepreneurs may still call for separate treatment from the rewarding of authors. Plant's proposal for book publishing was to reduce the period in which a publisher could enjoy exclusive rights; thereafter the copyright owner would be entitled to a statutory royalty on the net selling price of any competitor who chose to exploit the work.[95] For this approach there has been a precedent concerning the "mechanical right" in copyright music—which was introduced in 1911, though it has now been abolished

---

[92] Above, n. 86 (1954) at 15.

[93] As it is, authors themselves, or learned societies or other patrons, often underwrite publishers in the pursuit of a risky venture.

[94] But a far more likely way of inducing a successful author to keep writing would be to reduce the tax burden on his initial returns: see Plant (above, n. 86 (1954)) at 13.

[95] See above, n. 86 (1934) at 194–195; and (1954) at 15–18. An additional theoretical argument is this: a risk-taking entrepreneur must bring his costs into account in determining his most advantageous price and size of production. Since the author, who is taking a royalty on sales, is not concerned with costs, his return will be more if price is lower and production greater than the position that is most advantageous to the publisher: *ibid*. (1934) at 185–186.

in the 1988 Act.[96] But despite Plant's advocacy, there has been no serious political pressure in Britain to carry the idea into other fields of copyright.[97] The overall result is scarcely congruous.

Britain's principal collaborators in the Berne Convention have shown little sympathy for provisions which qualify the entrepreneur's chance of taking exclusive rights throughout the duration of copyright.[98] The industrial states have however been obliged to make the concessions that are now found in the Paris Revisions of Berne and the UCC in favour of developing country members. As already noted,[99] these new qualifications also turn to the compulsory licence as the modifying technique, however unsatisfactory to each side the particular form adopted may prove to be.

(2) Collective enforcement

So far we have considered the market power that may stem from demand for an individual copyright work. A different monopoly effect— and one that is likely to have graver impact—can arise if rights in a whole class of works come under single control. The markets for the distribution of copies of copyright works have not so far been subject to much "cornering" of this sort, at least in Britain. But the opposite is true for performing rights, as has already been mentioned.[1] Composers of most music, and their publishers, found it impossible to enforce their performing rights, work by work, against users such as concert promoters and theatre proprietors. The only practicable system was to found a single organ—in Britain the Performing Right Society—for the collective enforcement of rights. It then became possible to organise licensing schemes for the different categories of user and to set various rates for them.

While this accumulation of rights quite properly obliges users to respect copyright, it at the same time deprives them of the opportunity to object to the licence fee for one piece of music by playing another that is cheaper. The rights society gains not only some power to set prices high but also to discriminate between users and to demand that performances be of a particular kind—most commonly that they be live rather than recorded. For the moment it is enough to draw attention to this type of problem. We shall return subsequently to the role that the Copyright Tribunal is to play in disallowing practices by collecting societies it deems to be an abuse of their market position. Equally we shall see that the

9-027

9-028

---

[96] Below, § 12-019.
[97] Instead, the weak provisions for reversion and compulsory licensing during the last 25 years of copyright, which were part of the 1911 Act scheme (see above, n. 33), were abandoned in 1956. Some members of the Gregory Committee (Cmd. 8662, §§ 22–33) thought that the provisions had no "decisive" effect in securing the production of cheap books and must be given up in obeisance to Berne Convention obligations. The same international pressure was treated as a sufficient answer to Plant's case for a more limited term of copyright: §§ 18–19. cf. also, the Whitford Report, Cmnd. 6732, §§ 625–637.
[98] By contrast, in its 1976 law the U.S.A. has insisted on retaining a provision for a reversion to the non-hired author for the last 25 years of copyright: see Nimmer, Copyright (1979), Chap. 11.
[99] See above, §§ 9-011—9-015.
[1] See above, § 9-010.

Tribunal fulfils the role of arbitrator in disputes where it cannot be said that there is much difference in the bargaining power of owner and user. For instance, PRS and PPL have as substantial a concern to see that their material is broadcast by the BBC and commercial stations as the broadcasting organisations have to secure the right to do so.

As we shall also see,[2] the collective enforcement of rights and the collective distribution of funds to individual right-owners are being introduced as the principal means of arousing copyright from its present impotence against the reprographic copier and the sound and video recorder. As we acquire systems of blanket licensing for single or multiple copying of things readable, audible or viewable, questions about abuses of market power and about the settlement of other disputes between collective groups of owners and users will follow. Similar arrangements are beginning to be established in other countries.[3] In the coming years a great deal of attention will be given to the criteria upon which to determine "fair" rates and conditions for block licensing. A branch of "economic" law is solidifying from a shadowy form.

Entrepreneurs and authors

9-029   Another type of collective organisation deserves to be noted. Various commercial groups in the copyright industries have joint associations to watch over their mutual interests.[4] In the past at least, some of these associations have agreed that members would deal with outsiders only upon terms falling within certain limits. Thus publishers might agree upon the maximum rate of royalty that each would offer authors for certain types of copyright exploitation.[5]

Until quite recently creators have not had much reason for forming groups that will negotiate with entrepreneurial associations for collective guarantees of minimum terms in contracts to publish or use works.[6] Rather, successful authors and composers have negotiated better contracts individually, in some fields using agents, such as the literary agents who are so prominent a feature of English language publishing. This kind of practice probably explains why in Britain there has been relatively little demand that authors should have legal guarantees against unfair contract terms. We shall see that only in relatively extreme cases of exploitative harshness are the courts at present prepared to qualify the rule of contractual sanctity[7]; and so far there has been no intervention by legislation.[8]

[2] Below, §§ 13-007 et seq.   [3] Ibid.
[4] For instance, at the national level in Britain, the Publishers Association, the British Phonographic Industry Copyright Association and the Music Publishers Association; at the international level, the International Federation of the Phonographic Industry. With the growth of commercial piracy to these have been added organisations such as the Anti-Counterfeiting Group and FAST.
[5] However, since the extension of the British trade practices legislation to services (see App. 1, § A1-006), there is now a question whether such agreements would be legitimate.
[6] Which is not to say that mutual interest groups have not existed; witness, for instance, the Society of Authors, Playwrights and Composers and the Songwriters' Guild of Great Britain.
[7] See below, § 12-018.
[8] cf., e.g. the provisions of the French Copyright Law 1957 and the West German Publishing Law 1901.

There are, however, a number of developments that make the collective   9-030
organisation of authors a factor likely to grow in significance. Already
their pressure has played a large role in securing the special scheme for
public lending rights,[9] and since this turns upon a government subvention
the organisation will continue to be needed as a pressure group on this
front. If schemes for block licensing or raising a levy on equipment are
introduced for reprography and domestic recording, there are important
issues about distribution of revenues which will also draw authors into
negotiations as a group.[9] Collective labour relations are already an
established feature of arts administration where performers are concerned, whether or not contracts are for employment in a strict sense or
for independent services. It seems likely that writers, composers and
artists are now beginning to engage in collective bargaining on much the
same basis. An important new dimension is being added to the relationships under which copyright is exploited. It will in consequence have to
be settled whether arrangements between creators and entrepreneurs are
in character equivalent to the agreements between "undertakings" that
fall within the EEC's rules of competition; or whether the proper analogy
is to labour relations, which are outside that policy. For some arrangements at least, the latter analogy seems attractive.[10] So far the issue has
been debated in relation to the rules of performing right societies.[11] But
there the issue is complicated by the fact that those rules are likely to
deal with a tripartite relationship between authors, publishers and users.
The question as a whole is unresolved.

3. THE 1988 ACT AND PRE-EXISTING WORKS

One technical matter may serve as a link between this introductory   9-031
chapter and the next. The current copyright law of the United Kingdom
is now almost entirely contained in the Copyright Act 1988 and the case
law pertaining to it. The 1988 Act repealed virtually all the 1956 Act,
just as that Act had repealed the 1911 Act and the 1911 Act had largely
replaced the common law and statutory rights that preceded it.[12] The
commencement date of the 1988 Act was August 1, 1989; that for the
1956 Act was June 1, 1957; that for the 1911 Act had been July 1,
1912.
   The three Acts introduced basic changes. In particular, each added to
the bundle of rights that constituted copyright. For instance, the 1911
Act specified that literary, dramatic and musical works were infringed by
making a film, record or other "contrivance" for mechanical performance,[13] while the 1956 Act introduced infringement by broadcasting and

[9] See below, §§ 13-037—13-039.
[10] See Van Isacker (1971) 61 UFITA 49; *cf.* Mestmäcker, *Copyright in Community Law*
(1976) 46; Dietz Report, §§ 35–43, 570.
[11] The decisions are mentioned below, §§ 12-024—12-027.
[12] See C.A. 1956, Sched. 9 and C.A. 1911, Sched. 2.
[13] C.A. 1911, s.1(2)(*d*).

by diffusing to subscribers.[14] The 1988 Act has created a rental right in respect of sound recordings, films and computer programs[15]; and is noteworthy in particular for its introduction of moral rights for authors.[16] Again, statutory rules about initial ownership of the copyright were changed on each occasion,[17] as were the "qualifying factors" by which foreign publication or authorship might bring about the acquisition of British copyright.[18] Since the duration of copyright is so substantial (particularly after the extensions of 1911), there remains a range of questions about works that were in existence before commencement of the 1988 Act, the 1956 Act, or even the 1911 Act. A work produced early in an author's life, which acquired copyright until 50 years after his death, could well have a copyright life of 80 years and might last more than 100 years.[19]

9-032   The transitional arrangements in each Act for existing works must be separately considered. Both the 1956 Act and the 1988 Act operate upon the presumption that they apply to things in existence at commencement as they apply to things brought into existence subsequently, subject to the particular modifications specified in Schedule 7 and Schedule 1 respectively.[20] Thus under the 1988 Act, the question of whether the work had copyright under the 1956 Act is not in issue.[21] To this, however, the prime exception is that subsistence of copyright in an existing work is determined by the legal position immediately before commencement.[22]

There are a considerable number of other qualifications and exceptions spelled out in Schedule 1. During the immediate period of transition these are of particular importance and they will be mentioned at numerous points in the next four Chapters. Where the new Act introduces enhanced rights, by and large it extends them to existing works. Where it alters or cuts down rights, the position under the 1956 Act may be conserved wholly or in part. Thus although the rules on first ownership of a work have changed in both the 1956 and 1988 Acts, the issue is determined by the law in operation when the work was made.[23] Equally, where the length of protection accorded to unpublished literary, dramatic and musical works, engravings and photographs is cut down by the 1988 Act, there are exceptions directed to eliminating any unfair prejudice to the owners of existing copyright.[24]

---

[14] See now, CDPA 1988, s.20.
[15] CDPA 1988, s.18(3); below, § 11-021.
[16] CDPA 1988, Part 1, Chap. IV; below, §§ 11-047—11-059.
[17] See C.A. 1911, s.5; C.A. 1956, s.4; CDPA 1988, s.11, below, §§ 12-002—12-005.
[18] For "qualifying factors," see below, §§ 10-020—10-021.
[19] For the term of copyright, see below, §§ 10-027—10-030.
[20] C.A. 1956, Sched. 7, § 45; CDPA 1988, Sched. 1, §§ 3, 4.
[21] Under the 1911 Act, s.24, subject-matter that was protected immediately before its commencement received the rights substituted by that Act, and this remains the position: CDPA 1988, Sched. 1, § 2(2).
[22] CDPA 1988, Sched. 1, § 5. For exceptions see § 5(2).
[23] Below, § 12-002.
[24] Below, §§ 10-027—10-028.

CHAPTER 10

SUBSISTENCE OF COPYRIGHT

1. THE GENERAL PICTURE

The first difficulty of the student of copyright law is to distinguish the **10-001** different types of copyright and to understand the essential questions surrounding them: Is the material of the kind that attracts copyright? If so, for what duration? Who initially is entitled to ownership? What acts constitute infringement? An overview is given in the Table on the following pages. This should be understood for what it is. It does no more than highlight the starting points in discovering the relevant legal rules. Some further factors (*e.g.* the various exceptions to infringement) are too complex to include conveniently. The Table must be read in conjunction with the main text.

The 1956 Act was built upon a distinction between the Part I copyright of creators in literary, dramatic, musical and artistic *works* in Part I; and the Part II copyright (or, as it should be, "neighbouring right"), given in other *subject-matter* to entrepreneurs who produced sound recordings, films, broadcasts, cablecasts and published editions.[1] This division has been obliterated in the 1988 Act. Instead—for better, for worse—the two types are listed indiscriminately. In each case the copyright is in a *work* and it is granted initially in most cases to an "author" who "creates" it; and all is resolved in a grossly misshapen definition of the "creator," (see the Table, line 3). The shift is typical of that old strain of common law thought which sees no difference of kind between true creators and investors in the creations of others; and which is inclined to prefer the latter to the former. The Table gives a column each to the varieties of copyright "work," grouping together (i) literary, dramatic and musical works, and (ii) broadcasts and cable-casts, because of the similarities in their treatment.

Much of this chapter concerns the criteria for deciding whether a work attracts copyright. These criteria are of two principal kinds:

(i) The nature of the material (line 1) and the intellectual or **10-002** entrepreneurial activity that produced it (line 2). These factors, in certain respects closely interwoven, are analysed together in sections 2 and 3 below.[2]

[1] See above, § 9-009.
[2] §§ 10-003—10-019.

BASIC STRUCTURE OF COPYRIGHT UNDER THE 1988 ACT

	Literary, Dramatic, Musical Work	Artistic Work	Sound Recording	Film	Broadcast; Cablecast	Published edition
1. Nature of work	*Literary:* work that is written, spoken or sung, not dramatic or musical; includes table, compilation, computer program *Dramatic:* includes dance or mime *Musical:* work consisting of music — not associated words or actions (s.3(1)) Secondary activities (translating, editing, adapting etc.) may attract their own copyright.	(a) "graphic work," "photograph," "sculpture," collage (b) work of architecture being a "building" or model thereof (c) work of artistic craftsmanship. Only works within (a) are protected "irrespective of artistic quality" (s.4(1))	Reproducible recording of sounds or literary dramatic or musical work (s.56)	Recording on any medium from which a moving image may be produced (s.5(1))	*Broadcast:* transmission by wireless telegraphy capable of lawful public reception or transmitted for public presentation (s.6(1)) *Cablecast:* cable programme service, by non-wireless telecommunication, for reception at 2 or more places or for public presentation (with exceptions) (s.7(1),(2))	Typographical arrangement of a published edition of literary, dramatic or musical work (s.8(1))
2. Originality or Equivalent	Work must be "original" (s.1(1))	Work must be "original" (s.1(1))	No copyright in recording that is a copy (s.5(2))	No copyright in film that is a copy (s.5(2))	Copyright in repeat expires at same time as in original (s.14(2))	No copyright in reproduction of typographical arrangement of previous edition (s.8(2))
3. Author	Creator of work (s.9(1))	Creator of work (s.9(1))	Person undertaking arrangements necessary for making recording (s.9(2))	Person undertaking arrangements necessary for making film (s.9(2))	Person making the broadcast or providing the cable programme service (s.9(2))	Publisher (s.9(2))
4. Qualifying Factor	Unpublished work: status of author. Published work: either country of first publication or status of author at date of first publication or, if already dead, status at death, (s.151–	As for literary etc. work	Status of "author" at date of making; country of first publication (s.151–153)	As for sound recording	Status of "author" when broadcast or cable-cast; Country from which broadcast or sent (s.151, 154)	Status of "author" at date of first publication; country of first publication (s.151–153)

					of architectural work or incorporation of artistic work into building is equivalent to publication. (s.168)
available to the public by means of an electronic retrieval system (s.168)					
6. Duration	Until end of fiftieth year from author's death (special cases: computer-generated works; unknown and joint authorship; Crown, Parliamentary and international organisation copyright). (s.12)	As for literary etc. works	End of fiftieth year from making; or fiftieth year from release if release within fifty years of making. (s.13)	As for sound recordings	End of fiftieth year from first transmission (s.14)	End of twenty-fifth year from first publication (s.15)
7. Scope of Monopoly (primary infringement)	(i) Copying; (reproducing in a material form, storing electronically); issuing copies to public; adapting. (Computer programs: renting to public). (ii) Performing in public; broadcasting, cablecasting (s.16-21)	(i) Copying; issuing copies to the public (ii) Broadcasting, cablecasting (s.16-20)	(i) Copying; issuing or renting copies to the public (ii) Playing in public; broadcasting; cablecasting (s.16-20)	(i) copying; issuing or renting copies to public (ii) Playing or showing in public; broadcasting or cablecasting (s.16-20)	(i) copying; issuing copies to public (ii) Playing or showing in public; broadcasting or cablecasting (s.16-20)	Making a facsimile copy of the typographical arrangement (s.16, 17)
8. First Owner (Subject to assignment of future copyright)	Author or, if made in course of employment, employer (s.11)	As for literary etc. works	"Author" (s.9, 11)	"Author" (s.9, 11)	"Author" (s.9, 11)	Publisher (s.9, 11)

(ii) The qualifying factor, which brings into account international considerations stemming from the copyright conventions and similar arrangements (line 4, considered in section 4, below).[3] In part the qualifying factor depends upon what constitutes publication (line 5, discussed in section 5 below).[4]

Publication is also germane to the factor considered in the final section of this chapter, the duration of the copyright term (line 6).[5] The other lines of the table are taken up in succeeding chapters: the scope of copyright (line 75) is dealt with in general terms in Chapter 11, and particular aspects are considered in Chapter 13. Authorship (line 3) and initial ownership (line 8) are discussed in Chapter 12.

2. THE TYPE AND QUALITY OF SUBJECT-MATTER

(1) Original literary, dramatic, musical and artistic works

10-003   Each of the types of work accorded copyright by the 1988 Act is further defined to some extent by statutory provisions or case-law and this is discussed below. Behind this lies the root requirement that sufficient "skill, judgment and labour," or "selection, judgment and experience," or "labour, skill and capital,"[6] be expended by the author in creating the work. In other words, not only must creative intellectual activity produce the right kind of work, but the input must satisfy a certain minimum standard of effort. Otherwise, there is nothing that can be treated as a work; or—closely associated with this—the work will not be regarded as "original." In the next paragraphs the application of these concepts to the four classical types of copyright work will be discussed. Another basic axiom is that copyright protects the expression of an idea rather than the idea itself. In the case of literary, dramatic and musical works this leads to difficult questions about the need to record the expression in some permanent form; these are also considered.[7]

(a) Literary works[8]

10-004   The expression "literary work," said Peterson J., covers "work which is expressed in print or writing, irrespective of the question whether the quality or style is high. The word literary seems to be used in a sense somewhat similar to the use of the word 'literature' in political or electioneering literature, and refers to written or printed matter."[9] As well

---

[3] §§ 10-020—10-022.
[4] §§ 10-023—10-026.
[5] Below, §§ 10-027—10-030.
[6] This last formulation, employed by Lord Atkinson in *Macmillan* v. *Cooper* (1923) 93 L.J.P.C. 113 at 117, has particular point when the aesthetic merit counts for little beside the investment in effort; see below, § 10-005.
[7] Below, §§ 10-018—10-019.
[8] See CDPA 1988, ss.1(1)(a), 3. The expression is defined as any work which is written, spoken or sung, other than a dramatic or musical work, which does at least distinguish the separate copyright in the words of a song (see below, § 10-009). It includes tables, compilations and computer programs. For the last, see below, §§ 13-016 *et seq.*
[9] *University of London Press* v. *University Tutorial Press* [1916] 2 Ch. 601 at 608.

as works embodying the fruits of considerable creative or intellectual endeavour, copyright has been allowed in such mundane compilations of information as a timetable index,[10] trade catalogues,[11] examination papers,[12] street directories,[13] football fixture lists,[14] a racing information service[15] and the listing of programmes to be broadcast.[16] The principle that there must be sufficient "skill, judgment and labour" accordingly operates as a proviso *de minimis*, excluding as insufficient only those cases where the degree of literary composition is slight. Thus in particular instances courts have refused to recognise as literary works a card containing spaces and directions for eliciting statutory information[17] and an advertisement consisting of four commonplace sentences.[18] In most cases, the titles of books—and equally of plays, films and the like—are treated as insufficiently substantial to attract copyright themselves.[19] The same is true of a trade mark or name, so copyright is not a means of preventing a well-known mark from being applied to an entirely different product or service.[20]

"Literary work" also covers secondary work on existing sources, **10-005** provided that it in turn involves literary "skill, labour and judgment." The following may all suffice: translation,[21] editorial work that involves amendment,[22] critical annotation or explanation,[23] compilation,[24] selection and abridgment.[25] The same *de minimis* principle applies: gathering together existing tables for the front of a pocket diary was held insufficient in one House of Lords decision[26]; likewise the mere extraction of the time of local trains from a general timetable.[27] It makes no difference to the position whether the material taken from elsewhere is in or out of copyright.[28]

[10] *Blacklock v. Pearson* [1915] 2 Ch. 376.
[11] *Collis v. Cater* (1898) 78 L.T. 613; *Purefoy v. Sykes Boxall* (1955) 72 R.P.C. 89 (C.A.); and see Copinger, §§ 122–126.
[12] *University of London Press* case (above, n. 9).
[13] *e.g. Kelly v. Morris* (1866) L.R. 1 Eq. 697.
[14] *Football League v. Littlewoods* [1959] Ch. 637; *Ladbroke v. Wm. Hill* [1964] 1 W.L.R. 273 (H.L.).
[15] *Portway Press v. Hague* [1957] R.P.C. 426.
[16] *Independent Television Publications v. Time Out* [1984] F.S.R. 64.
[17] *Libraco v. Shaw* (1913) 30 T.L.R. 22.
[18] *Kirk v. Fleming* [1928–1935] Mac. C.C. 44.
[19] See Lord Wright, *Francis Day v. Twentieth Century Fox* [1940] A.C. 112 at 123; Lord Hodson, *Ladbroke* case (above, n. 14) at 286; Copinger, §§ 741–743. As a corollary, merely copying the title of a literary work would rarely be a substantial enough taking to constitute infringement: see generally below, § 11-006.
[20] *Exxon v. Exxon Insurance* [1982] R.P.C. 69 (C.A.).
[21] *Byrne v. Statist Co.* [1914] 1 K.B. 622; *Cummins v. Bond* [1927] 1 Ch. 167.
[22] *e.g.* an edited version of a trial transcript: *Warwick Film v. Eisinger* [1969] 1 Ch. 508.
[23] *Macmillan v. Cooper* (1923) 93 L.J.P.C. 113: the notes appended to a condensed text showed sufficient literary skill, taste and judgment; *cf.* below, n. 26.
[24] *e.g.* the football pool cases, above, n. 14; *Portway Press v. Hague*, above, n. 14.
[25] *Macmillan v. Cooper* (above, n. 23): condensation of a single text may not be sufficient, but collecting an anthology of verse would likely be: *Sweet v. Benning* (1855) 16 C.B. 459.
[26] *Cramp v. Smythson* [1944] A.C. 329; and see *Rose v. Information Services* [1987] F.S.R. 254.
[27] *Leslie v. Young* [1894] A.C. 335 (H.L.); *cf. Blacklock v. Pearson* [1913] 2 Ch. 376.
[28] *Ashmore v. Douglas-Home* [1987] F.S.R. 553.

In deciding whether there has been sufficient skill, the courts take account not just of skill in literary expression or presentation, but also of commercial judgment. A fixed-odds football pool form attracted copyright even though it only consisted of a compilation of 16 known forms of bet. Account was taken of the skill deployed in selecting these particular forms of wager, as distinct from the simple labour of compiling them on the pool form.[29] The process was treated as analogous to that of the compiler of a selection of poetry, even though in that case there is literary skill in the selection.[30] Likewise in a random choice game in a newspaper where the only literary material comprised grids of letters printed on cards, some set out in each day's paper.[31]

10-006   The requirement that a literary work be "original" was only added to statutory copyright law in the Act of 1911. The adjective has been read in a limited sense. It is treated as bringing out one characteristic of the requirement of "skill, labour and judgment"—that the work must originate from the author and not be copied by him from another source. In a much repeated passage, Peterson J. said:

"The word 'original' does not in this connection mean that the work must be the expression of original or inventive thought. Copyright Acts are not concerned with the originality of ideas, but with the expression of thought, and, in the case of 'literary work,' with the expression of thought in print or writing. The originality which is required relates to the expression of the thought. But the Act does not require that the expression must be in an original or novel form, but that the work must not be copied from another work—that it should originate from the author."[32]

This has obvious significance for works that derive in some sense from an earlier source.[33] A piece of historical writing, a news report, a street directory and a selection of poetry all attract copyright once the choice and arrangement of source material is more than minimal. If the source or sources are still in copyright and they are reproduced to a substantial extent in the final work, a number of distinct copyrights will exist in it. If the rights are owned by different people, the permission of all will be needed for reproducing it and doing the other acts within the copyrights.

10-007   The strictly limited level of "original" achievement that is required in order to attract literary copyright can be explained in two ways. First, it reduces to a minimum the element of subjective judgment (and attendant

[29] Ladbroke v. William Hill above, n. 14: "An anthology of saleable poems is as much entitled to protection as an anthology of beautiful poems": Lord Develin at p. 290.
[30] The distinction drawn in Purefoy v. Sykes Boxall (above, n. 11) between the skill in selecting goods and in writing a catalogue of them needs to be read in context: the causal connection for infringement (see below, § 11-003) was at issue; cf. Ladbroke case (above, n. 14) at 284, 287.
[31] Express Newspapers v. Liverpool Daily Post [1985] F.S.R. 306; and see Mirror Newspapers v. Queensland Newspapers [1982] Qd.R. 305; Kalamazoo (Aust.) v. Compact (1985) 5 I.P.R. 213.
[32] University of London Press (above, n. 9) at 608.
[33] On derivative works in comparative perspective, Goldstein (1983) 30 J.Cop.Soc. 209.

uncertainties) in deciding what qualifies for protection. Secondly, it allows protection for any investment of labour and capital that in some way produces a literary result: this is true equally of the compiler of mundane facts and of the deviser of a football pool form whose real effort is in the market research determining the best bets to combine. Here copyright is being used to compensate for lack of a roving concept of unfair competition.[34] It is noteworthy that in cases of this kind where copyright is found to exist, the defendant tends to be a direct business competitor. Where some other form of relief is available against the unfair competition (as in the case of titles), copyright tends to be denied.[35]

(b) *Dramatic works*

These are defined as including a work of dance or mime. They include **10-008** the scenario or script for a film, the copyright in the film itself being separate.[36] The general principles concerning literary works apply to this closely analogous category. Nice questions can arise over the copyright entitlement of those who provide "secondary" contributions to scripts written by other playwrights. In *Tate* v. *Thomas*, for instance, a person who supplied a number of ideas, including key lines, which were to be worked out by others secured no part in the eventual copyright.[37] Scenic effects and costumes are only the subject of copyright if they are artistic works. Like literary works, dramatic works have to be "original" in the limited sense which that adjective has acquired in this context.

The exclusion of most titles from the scope of copyright applies equally here.[38] This is linked with preclusion of any copyright in the names of characters or in the typical manner in which characters behave.[39] These can only be protected if sufficient trading reputation with the public gives rise to a form of passing off.[40]

(c) *Musical works: type and quality*

The term "musical work" is defined in the Act only as a work **10-009** consisting of music, exclusive of any words or action intended to be sung, spoken or performed with it.[41] It has long been accepted in British law that where words are set to music, the two remain distinct works for copyright purposes. If there is copyright in each, and lyric writer and composer are not the same person, the two copyrights will usually expire on different dates: Gilbert and Sullivan, for instance, were not co-morientes.

[34] On which theme, note Lord Devlin, *Ladbroke* case (above, § 9-019).
[35] See *"Exxon"* case above, n. 20.
[36] CDPA 1988, s.1(1)(a), 3(1), following Berne Convention, Art. 2(1).
[37] [1921] 1 Ch. 503; see also *Tate* v. *Fullbrook* [1908] 1 K.B. 821 (C.A.); *Wiseman* v. *George Wiedenfeld & Nicolson* [1985] F.S.R. 525; *Ashmore* v. *Douglas-Home* [1987] F.S.R. 553.
[38] See above, § 10-004.
[39] See, *e.g.* Maugham J., *Kelly* v. *Cinema Houses* [1928–1935] Mac. C.C. 362 at 368.
[40] *cf., e.g. Samuelson* v. *Producers' Distributing* (below, § 16-035); *Shaw Bros.* v. *Golden Harvest* (below, § 16-005).
[41] CDPA 1988, ss.1(1)(a), 2(1).

Again general principles discussed in relation to literary and dramatic works will apply. "Secondary" activities which have been held to attract their own musical copyright include arranging music (by adding accompaniments, new harmonies, new rhythms and the like), and transcribing it for different musical forces. There has been little consideration of what minimum effort will suffice for musical copyright. Certainly, "secondary" activity such as selecting and arranging older tunes or scores,[42] orchestrating or making a piano reduction[43] may qualify for its own copyright. But equally, there is very little content in what is sometimes said to be "arrangement,"[45] and this may mean that the requirement of originality is not met.

(d) *Artistic works*

10-010   (i) *General.* Here the tension between different conceptions of copyright becomes marked. Some types of work are treated as artistic only if they bear a distinctive element of aesthetic creativity, others gain protection simply because labour and capital ought not to be freely appropriable.

Artistic works must be "original,"[46] but as for literary works, this contemplates only that they will not be copied. In every case, the threshold measure of labour, skill and judgment must be present. Thus where the subject-matter was designs for "Lego" toy bricks, and those designs which simply repeated earlier designs with indications of minor variations in words and figures (which are themselves not artistic works) the drawings did not have distinct copyright.[47] However, if artistic skill is required to make the copy, it seems that this may supply originality: as where a photograph is taken from a picture,[48] or a coin is engraved in three dimensions from a drawing.[49] It is not therefore the requirement of originality which brings about the differences of approach so much as the manner in which the different categories of artistic work are listed in the Act.[50] These are: (a) irrespective of artistic quality, a graphic work, photograph, sculpture or collage[51]; (b) works of architecture (buildings or

---

[42] *Austin* v. *Columbia* [1917–1923] Mac. C.C. 398.

[43] *Metzler* v. *Curwen* [1928–1935] Mac. C.C. 127.

[44] *Wood* v. *Boosey* (1868) L.R. 3 Q.B. 223; *Redwood Music* v. *Chappell* [1982] R.P.C. 109.

[45] Claims by such arrangers may be excluded for not involving sufficient skill. But the argument that any copyright which they do attract adheres to that of the original composer runs counter to the whole development of British law on the subject: see Cornish [1971] J.B.L. 241; *cf. Performing Right,* November 1971, p. 34.

[46] CDPA 1988, s.1(1)(a).

[47] *Interlego* v. *Tyco* [1988] R.P.C. 343 (J.C.).

[48] *Graves' Case* (1869) L.R. 4 Q.B. 715.

[49] *Martin* v. *Polyplas* [1969] N.Z.L.R. 1046. It was conceded that this activity was "engraving." See also *Arnold* v. *Miafern* [1980] R.P.C. 397; *Wham-O* v. *Lincoln* [1985] R.P.C. 127, discussed below, § 14–022.

[50] CDPA 1988, s.4.

[51] "Graphic works" includes (a) a painting, drawing, diagram, map, chart or plan; and (b) an engraving, etching, lithograph, woodcut or similar work. "Photograph" means a recording of light or other radiation on any medium on which an image is produced (or from which it can be produced) which is not part of a film. "Sculpture" includes a cast or model made for the purposes of sculpture.

models of buildings)[52]; (c) works of artistic craftsmanship not within (a) or (b).[53]

The requisite "skill, judgment and labour" is thus affected by the 10-011 meaning of the various types of work and by the fact that only category (a) secures copyright "irrespective of artistic quality." In the first category, most of the decisions set the minimal level of effort low: a simple drawing of a human hand showing voters where to mark their cross on a voting card,[54] the label design for a sweet tin,[55] the arrangement of a few decorative lines on a parcel label,[56] have all been accorded copyright. (We shall see that, by way of counterbalance, the scope of infringement is narrowly defined in such cases).[57]

As with literary works, judgment that does not go to the degree or amount of artistic skill may be brought into account in deciding whether the minimum requirement for copyright is satisfied. Even three concentric circles may suffice if they are drawn to precise measurements because they are a plan for a technical device.[58]

(ii) *Architectural works and models.*[59] An architect's plans fall within 10-012 category (a) above.[60] It is the actual structure or a model of it which is separately treated in the second category. By implication, some consideration must be given to artistic quality. It may well be enough to show "something apart from the common stock of ideas."[61]

(iii) *Works of artistic craftsmanship.*[62] A considerable miscellany of 10-013 artefacts—jewellery, furniture, cutlery, toys, educational aids and so on— may claim to rank as "works of artistic craftsmanship" within (c).[63] As we shall see, the scope of this category is likely to be of increased importance in the new provisions on industrial design in the 1988 Act.[64] The criteria which a court should apply in deciding whether an article earns this description were intensively canvassed in *Hensher* v. *Restawile*[65] (where the subject-matter was a prototype for a suite of furniture of distinctly low-brow appeal).[66] But the speeches in the House

---

[52] Including any fixed structure—so this may cover a bridge or a dam.
[53] C.A. 1956, s.3(1).
[54] *Kenrick* v. *Lawrence* (1890) 25 Q.B.D. 99.
[55] *Tavener Rutledge* v. *Specters* [1959] R.P.C. 355 (C.A.).
[56] *Walker* v. *British Picker* [1961] R.P.C. 57. An unreported decision held that there was artistic copyright in a signature, see Copinger, § 82.
[57] Below, §§ 11-011—11-012. Copinger, §§ 107, 108 claims that *Bauman* v. *Fussell* (1953) [1978] R.P.C. 485 (C.A.) casts doubt on the subsistence of copyright in snapshots of natural scenes. But the passages quoted are concerned with infringement alone.
[58] *Solar Thomson* v. *Barton* [1977] R.P.C. 537 at 558; and see *Ladbroke* case, above, n. 14.
[59] See Greenwood (1986) 16 Queensland L.Soc.J. 221.
[60] *cf. Chabot* v. *Davies* (1936) 155 L.T. 525.
[61] For this distinction, *Blake* v. *Warren* [1928–1935] Mac. C.C. 268 (decided under the 1911 Act, s.35(1) and concerned in any case with drawings).
[62] See R. G. Kenny (1984) 13 U. Queensland L.J. 206.
[63] Note that if a three-dimensional object can be described as a "sculpture" or an "engraving" it comes within category (a): *cf.* n. 49 above.
[64] See below, Chap. 14.
[65] [1976] A.C. 64; [1975] R.P.C. 31.
[66] *Ibid.* (R.P.C) at pp. 62, 70, 72.

of Lords display no uniformity of approach. Three factors warrant attention: (i) Is it the craftsman's intention to create something artistic that counts or rather the perception by the public of artistic quality in the article? (ii) What level of artistic aspiration or attainment must be shown? (iii) Is it for the judge to make up his own mind on the question, or is his function to weigh the relative strength of expert and other testimony given to the court?

Concerning (i), the House of Lords rejected the Court of Appeal's approach. This was to ask whether the public would purchase the thing for its aesthetic appeal rather than its functional utility.[67] Lord Simon of Glaisdale drew attention to the English aesthetic tradition (stemming from Ruskin, Morris and the Arts and Crafts movement) which eschewed any dichotomy between artistic appeal and functional value, seeking rather to derive the one from the other; indeed, the admission of "works of artistic craftsmanship" into the fold of copyright had been a response to that very movement.[68] Lord Reid, however, still attached first importance to the attitude of the public: a work of craftsmanship would be artistic if a substantial section of the public admired and valued it for its appearance.[69] Lord Kilbrandon, on the other hand, laid emphasis on the conscious intention to produce a work of art,[70] and Lord Simon took a similar starting point, though he also brought into account the result achieved.[71] Less specifically Lord Morris would give primacy neither to the intent of the artist nor the priorities of an acquirer, calling instead for a detached judgment of the thing itself. Viscount Dilhorne appears to take a similar view.[72] Walton J. has since held that, despite Lord Reid's reservation, the proper approach is to consider whether the maker of the object had the conscious purpose of creating a work of art.[73]

10-014   Concerning (ii), at first instance Graham J. was satisfied that the prototype furniture qualified for copyright because it had distinctive characteristics of shape, form and finish, and resulted in articles that were much more than purely utilitarian.[74] But since the House of Lords were unanimously of the opinion that it did not qualify, it seems clear that some higher level of artistic intent or attainment is necessary; this indeed is the real significance of the case. There must be sufficient craftsmanship as well as artistry. Accordingly, Lords Reid and Morris doubted whether a mere prototype, not intended to have value or permanence in itself, could count.[75]

[67] Ibid., at p. 47.
[68] Ibid. at pp. 65–67. One purpose of Lord Simon's disquisition was to emphasise that a work could not be excluded from consideration merely because it was machine-made, rather than hand-crafted. But Lord Reid seems to disagree: cf. p. 53.
[69] Ibid. at p. 54. The same approach is found, e.g. in Cuisenaire v. Reed [1963] V.R. 719 (coloured sticks for mathematical teaching method neither craftsmanship nor artistic); cf. also Cuisenaire v. South West Imports [1968] 1 Ex. C.R. 493.
[70] Ibid. at p. 72.
[71] Ibid. at p. 70; see also Hay v. Sloan (1957) 16 Fox P.C. 185.
[72] [1975] R.P.C. at 57, 62–63.
[73] Merlet v. Mothercare [1986] R.P.C. 126 (raincape not a work of artistic craftsmanship; point not at issue before C.A.).
[74] [1975] R.P.C. at 40; taken by the C.A. to be the same test as whether there is novelty enough to secure a registered design: ibid. at 47. For this, see below, § 14-010.
[75] Ibid. at 53, 56.

Concerning (iii), Lord Kilbrandon emphasised the place of the judge's own evaluation by treating the question as one of law.[76] But Viscount Dilhorne said that it was a question of fact to be decided on the evidence[77] and Lord Simon laid stress on expert evidence—from those who are acknowledged artist-craftsmen or who train such people.[78] Yet again, Lord Reid's view calls for proof that a substantial section of the public regard the article as artistic.[79] At least a person seeking to prove this form of copyright should be permitted to lead both kinds of evidence: expert and (if positive) non-expert.

One problem which the House of Lords judgment does not touch is the question whether there can be a work of artistic craftsmanship when one person supplies the artistic idea and another the craftsmanship. Clauson J. once considered that there could not then be copyright (the two people in question being the designer and the seamstress of a dress).[80] More recently other judges have shown some coolness towards this distinction.[81] Even if in itself it is a bad point, the *Hensher* decision nonetheless requires the designer's contribution to give serious aesthetic significance to the end product. This category of copyright is not a ready tool against unfair imitation.

For the most part, the author of a literary, dramatic, musical or artistic **10-015** work is its creator in a real sense. He or she (but not it) is the person who, by exercising labour skill and judgment gives expression to ideas of the appropriate kind. But even at this juncture, a certain notionalism begins to appear. For the act acknowledges that works of all these types may be computer-generated; and it provides that, where the circumstances are such that there is no human author of such a work, the author shall be taken to be the person by whom the arrangements necessary for creation of the work are undertaken.[81a]

(2) The entrepreneurial copyrights

The copyrights in (i) sound recordings, (ii) films, (iii) broadcasts, (iv) **10-016** cable-casts and (v) typographical format are all carried forward in updated form from the previous legislation.

The subject-matter in the first categories has been re-defined to take account of major technological advances. "Sound recording" covers any recording of literary, dramatic or musical work or other sounds (birdsong, the noises of a motor-race, etc.),[82] regardless of medium, and so

---

[76] *Ibid.* at 72.   [77] *Ibid.* at 62–63.
[78] *Ibid.* at 69–70.   [79] Above, at n. 69.
[80] *Burke* v. *Spicers Dress Designs* [1936] 1 Ch. 400; *cf.* Graham J., *Restawile* case [1975] R.P.C. at 40. And see Eder (1976) 5 CIPA 270; Gibbins and Hobbs (1979) 1 E.I.P.R. 8.
[81] *e.g.* Oliver J., *Spyrou* v. *Radley Gowns* [1975] F.S.R. 455; Fox J., *Bernstein* v. *Sydney Murray* [1981] R.P.C. 303; Walton J., *Merlet* v. *Mothercare* [1986] R.P.C. 115 at 123–124.
[81a] CDPA 1988, s.9(3), 178 "computer-generated." This conception will not always be easy to apply. When a subscriber to a service such as "Lexis" has the results of a search printed out, is this "computer-generated", and if so by whom?
[82] CDPA 1988, s.5(1). Both examples have a commercial value. Note that film sound-track now falls to be treated as a sound recording, rather than as part of the film: the rule applies to existing and new films: Sched. 1 para. 8. Under the 1956 Act the converse applied.

will include an ordinary disc, cassette tape, compact disc, digital audio tape and future technical developments.

"Film" means a recording on any medium (including, therefore, the old celluloid form and the video-tape) provided a moving image can be produced from it.[83] There is, however, no copyright in a sound recording or film which is a copy of another, authorised or unauthorised.[84]

"Broadcast" is a transmission "by wireless telegraphy" of visual images, sounds or other information which is capable of lawful reception by the public (in particular through use of decoding equipment made available through the person transmitting in encrypted form), or which is for presentation to the public.[85] This covers both terrestrial and satellite transmission and takes account of the forms of satellite broadcasting which may be directly received by individuals or may be received by subscribers who obtain a decoder. The definition, however, excludes the familiar satellite transmission that is only for reception and re-transmission by a local broadcasting station. For all these forms, the transmitting of signals to the satellite (the "up-leg") is treated as the act of broadcasting.[86]

"Cable-cast" is not a statutory term but is used here as a compendious abbreviation for "any item included in a cable programme service" as elaborately defined in the 1988 Act.[87] Such a service is one which consists wholly or mainly in sending visual images, sounds or other information by a non-wireless telecommunications system, either to two or more places[88] or for presentation to the public. Excepted from this are interactive services; internal business services; individual domestic services; services on single-occupier premises otherwise than by way of business amenity; services for those running broadcasting or cabling services or programmes for them.[89] There is no copyright in a cable-cast that consists of reception and immediate re-transmission of a broadcast.[90] Neither a broadcast nor a cable-cast acquires copyright to the extent that it infringes another broadcast or cable-cast.[91]

The typographical arrangement copyright arises in respect of a published edition of the whole or part of one or more literary, dramatic or musical (but not artistic) works, provided that it does not simply reproduce the typographical arrangement of a previous edition.[92]

---

[83] CDPA 1988, s.5(1). Note that films made before June 1, 1957 continue to be protectable as under the 1911 Act, i.e., as dramatic works or photographs: Sched. 1, § 7.

[84] s.5(2).

[85] s.6(1). The reception may be by means of a telecommunications system: s.6(4). Broadcasts made before June 1, 1957 acquire no copyright, though later repeats do so: Sched. 1, § 9.

[86] s.6(3).

[87] s.7. Cable–casts made before January 1, 1985 acquire no copyright, though later repeats do so: Sched. 1, § 9.

[88] Not necessarily at the same time: s.7(1).

[89] s.7(2). The list is variable by order of the Secretary of State: s.7(3), (4).

[90] s.7(5)(a); but this activity may constitute infringement of copyright in the broadcast, etc.

[91] s.6(5), 7(6)(b).

[92] s.8.

As will be seen from the Table (line 3), the "creator-author" of these rights not the person who by labour, skill and judgment puts the recording, film, broadcast, cable-cast or printed format into its particular form. He, or she, or (most likely) it, is the person in charge of the undertaking: the person who makes the necessary arrangements for a sound recording or film, the person making a broadcast or providing a cable programme service, the publisher or a typographical format. Despite their new guise, these rights remain in truth neighbouring rights. In the fundamental structure of the law, this deserves never to be forgotten.[92a]

3. FORMALITIES AND PERMANENT FORM

(1) Absence of formalities

Originally British copyright law required registration of works with the **10-017** Stationers' Company as a condition, first of acquiring, later of enforcing, copyright in published works. But that had to be abandoned once the Berne Convention conceived copyright as a property flowing "naturally" and without formality from the act of creation.[93] Since the 1911 Act, neither registration nor any formal notification of the claim to copyright on copies of Berne Convention works has been a prerequisite either of copyright itself or the entitlement to institute proceedings for infringement. As already explained,[94] the "copyright notice" on published works (©, name of copyright owner, year of first publication) appears in order to attract copyright in non-Berne countries—including, until recently, the United States—which accept this as a sufficient formality; they do so in general because they belong to the UCC which provides that this shall be sufficient.[95]

Since these Conventions only cover literary, dramatic, musical and artistic works and films, the same constraints do not apply to other copyright material. But sound recordings no longer require marking, as they did under the 1956 Act, in order to attract their own copyright.

(2) Permanent form for the work

Nonetheless it is an assumption of British copyright legislation that all **10-018** subject-matter requires to exist in some permanent form before it gains copyright. It is possible to look upon this as a corollary of the principle that the protection goes only to the particular expression of ideas. Thus in the case of most artistic works it is only when the particular painting, photograph or other work is executed that idea is transmuted into expression; the act of creation and the "fixation" of the work are indivisible.[96]

[92a] S.9(2).

[93] See above, § 9-008; and note Berne Convention, Art. 5(2). Note that copyright does not depend upon the obligation of every publisher in the U.K. to supply a copy of a published book to the British Museum and five other libraries: see C.A. 1911, s.15 (unrepealed).

[94] Above, § 9-011.   [95] See UCC, Art. 3(1).

[96] Fixation and permanence can give rise to nice issues in the sphere of artistic activity. Adam Ant's face make-up did not have permanence enough for copyright: *Merchandising Corp. of America v. Harpbond* [1983] F.S.R.. 32 (C.A.); nor did a device containing sand and glycerine for making "sand pictures" by moving it: *Komesaroff v. Mickle* [1988] R.P.C. 204.

But literary, dramatic and musical creativity admits of more stages. A man may conceive a speech in his mind and deliver it from memory without ever writing it down. Indeed, some composers, lacking musical literacy, can only get their works into permanent form by dictation or recording. So long as there is no fixation, they have no copyright and must seek legal protection elsewhere, particularly through performers' protection legislation and contract.[97]

10-019   The 1988 Act fills a previous lacuna in the law: it specifies that a literary, dramatic or musical work is not the subject of copyright unless and until it is recorded, in writing or otherwise (for instance, by tape recording or filming); and that it is immaterial whether the author gave permission for the recording or not.[98] It has long been accepted that a person who arranges for a stenographer to take down his speech is the author of the resulting work, for it has merely been recorded by an amanuensis.[99] What, then, of a reporter who records a politician's speech, acting on his own initiative or that of his employer? The new provision appears to treat the politician—the creator of the words—as the author of the literary work thus generated. The provision, however, is not to affect the question whether a distinct copyright exists in the record. If the reporter has used an audio-tape, clearly there is a sound recording that will be the subject of a separate copyright (with, of course, its own limited scope, probably not extending to acts of copying the speech as a written text).[1] But if the record was in writing—for instance, by short-hand—the old case of *Walter* v. *Lane*[2] may still apply. This treated the reporter as entitled to literary copyright in the speech by virtue of his skill and labour in reducing it to permanent form. That decision was reached before the statutory requirement of "originality" was included in the law. How far it remains applicable has since been questioned and a distinction suggested between one who uses an aesthetic skill to make a record (*e.g.* the folk-song hunter) and one who uses standard technique (certainly, the interviewer armed with a tape-recorder; more doubtfully, the stenographer).[3] It would be rational in future to give the recorder *literary* or *musical* copyright only when he has exercised sufficient "labour, skill and judgment"; and it would make more sense than to say that the existence of this copyright depends on whether the actual creator claims any copyright in the material—an approach which finds authority in *Walter* v. *Lane*.[4]

[97] The copyrights in sound recordings, films and typographical format concern fixed subject-matter. Broadcasts and cable–casts, however, are essentially transient activities which are nevertheless protected as such.
[98] CDPA 1988, s.3(2), (3).
[99] Lord James of Hereford, *Walter* v. *Lane* [1900] A.C. 539 at 554. *cf.* the "ghost writer" who is the author giving expression to the teller's ideas: *Donoghue* v. *Allied Newspapers* [1938] 1 Ch. 106; and note *Evans* v. *Hulton* [1923–1928] Mac. C.C. 51. See also the entertaining cases on spiritual communication: *Cummins* v. *Bond* [1927] 1 Ch. 167; *Leah* v. *Two Worlds* [1951] Ch. 393.
[1] See below, § 11-021.
[2] [1900] A.C. 539; *cf.* the copyright in a street directory, *e.g.*, *Black* v. *Stacey* [1929] 1 Ch. 177; and see also *Sands McDougall* v. *Robinson* (1917) 23 C.L.R. 49 at 54–55 (H.C. Australia).
[3] *Roberton* v. *Lewis* (1960) [1976] R.P.C. 169.
[4] But see the *Roberton* case (above, n. 3) at 175.

4. QUALIFICATION

One quintessential purpose of the Berne and UCC Conventions is to **10-020**
secure the principle of national treatment: the works of authors connected with any one member state are to receive the same copyright
under the law of each other member state as do the works of authors
connected with the latter state.[5] The connection may arise by virtue of
the author's personal relationship to a country—his status—or because
the country is the place of first publication. While a work remains
unpublished, of course, the connection can only concern personal status.

Accordingly, the United Kingdom Act first prescribes the factors (of
status and first publication) that will give sufficient connection with
Britain, and with the few dependent territories to which the 1988 Act is
extended.[6] Then, as a consequence of British membership of the two
Conventions, the Act is *applied* to works and Part II subject-matter,
which are connected by the same factors to other Convention countries.
The legal machinery for this step is found in section 32 and the Orders in
Council made in implementation of it.[7]

A complication arises because countries adhere to the Conventions at
different dates. If a country is only a UCC member, then works published
before the country joined do not gain British copyright.[8] But the method
of the Berne Convention is partly retrospective. Once a country joins,
works that are connected with it and are still in copyright under its
domestic legislation acquire British copyright. But persons who have
incurred expenditure or liability for reproduction or performance of such
a work before this copyright took effect can be enjoined only upon
payment of compensation.[9]

(1) Qualification by personal status

If the connection is directly to the United Kingdom, it is necessary to **10-021**
ask whether the "author" is a "qualifying person." He will be if he is a
British citizen or person within certain other categories of the British
Nationality Act 1981[10]; a person domiciled or resident in the United

---

[5] Berne Convention, Arts. 3–5; UCC, Art. 2. Both conventions cover literary, dramatic, musical and artistic works and films: see, respectively, Arts. 2(1), 1.

[6] These include the Isle of Man, the Channel Islands and colonies such as Hong Kong: see CDPA 1988, s.155 and Orders in Council thereunder. Formerly the notion of extension was important since it was the foundation of "Imperial copyright" operating throughout the British Empire. But former British possessions, even if they have stayed within the Commonwealth, have not wished to preserve an essentially uniform copyright law. They are connected today only through the medium of the international conventions, if they have become members.

[7] In the 1988 Act, even the British have ceased to accord protection to authors who are "British Commonwealth citizens."

[8] See   . But unpublished works already in existence may acquire copyright by virtue of personal connection with the UCC country.

[9] Berne Convention, Art. 18;

[10] *i.e.* a British Dependent Territories citizen, a British National (Overseas), a British Overseas Citizen, a British Subject or a British Protected Person: see generally C.A. 1956, s.152(1).

Kingdom; or a body incorporated in part of the United Kingdom.[11] If the connection comes by application of the Act to Convention countries, it will be necessary to show the status called for in the Copyright (International Conventions) Order 1979: the relevant person must be a citizen or subject, domiciliary or resident, of a scheduled Convention country, or a company incorporated there.[12]

In either case, this question has to be asked at the "material time." For unpublished literary, dramatic, musical and artistic works that is the date of making the work. Where the work has been published, it is the author's status at the date of first publication that is in issue; or, if the author died before publication, his status at the date of his death. By way of contrast, the material time for other copyrights does not change: it is the personal status of the "author" of a sound recording or film at the time of its making, that of the broadcasting or cable-casting organisation at the date of transmission and, for typographical format, that of the publisher at publication.[13]

(2) Connection by publication

10-022   First publication is not only a point in time for considering personal status; it is also a connecting factor in its own right.[14] This is so both directly under the Act and through its application to the Convention countries.[15] If publication occurs in two countries within 30 days, the second may be treated as first publication, if this helps: the two are thus deemed simultaneous.[16]

The combined effect of these principles deserves illustration. After "commencement" of the new Act, if an author is a Malaysian subject who resides there at the time that he writes a book, he acquires no British copyright, since Malaysia is not a Convention country. So the position remains while the work stays unpublished (unless Malaysia joins either Convention).[17] But if he has it published (first) in England or Holland (a Convention country) he acquires British copyright by that action. So also if he publishes only in Malaysia, but before doing so he becomes a resident or national of Britain or Holland.

This represents a more restricted principle than formerly. If the work had been created or published before "commencement," the author, as a Commonwealth citizen, would have enjoyed British copyright, even though a British author would have enjoyed no reciprocal status under Malaysian copyright law.

---

[11] In the last two categories, the connection may equally be to a country to which the Act extends.
[12] CDPA 1988, s.152(2).
[13] CDPA 1988, s.152(4), (5).
[14] For the meaning of "publication" see the next section.
[15] CDPA 1988, s.153.
[16] s.153(3), following Berne Convention, Art. 3(4).
[17] Note that for their own purposes, the Conventions define "publication" in terms broadly similar to those of British law: Berne Convention, Art. 3(3); UCC Art. 6.

5. PUBLICATION

What amounts to publication can be significant in establishing a qualify- **10-023** ing factor. "Publication" is also important in measuring the term of most kinds of copyright and it may occasionally be relevant at other points in the law.

In the law of defamation, "publication" means communication to any person other than the person defamed.[18] In the law of patents, it covers making information available to any person free in law and equity to use it as he wishes.[19] As a term of art in copyright law it comes closer to ordinary understanding: in general, it means issuing copies of the work to the public in quantities intended to satisfy reasonable public demand; and, in the case of literary, dramatic, musical and artistic works it includes making the work available to the public through an electronic retrieval system.[20] It does not include performing a literary, dramatic or musical work, or broadcasting or cable-casting it; exhibiting an artistic work; or issuing graphic works or photographs of sculptures, works of architecture or works of artistic craftsmanship. Unauthorised acts are not brought into account.[21]

All this raises technical questions at the margins. Where the require- **10-024** ment is that copies be issued to the public this refers to first putting them into circulation presumably by sale, hire or gift.[22] Publication takes place wherever the publisher invites the public to acquire copies, not where the copies are received. To hold the contrary would make the country of first publication dependent on where shipments happen first to be received.[23] Whether publication is to be accounted more than "merely colourable"[24] depends primarily on the intent of the publisher at the date in question. The Court of Appeal held it enough to put six copies of the sheet music of a song on sale at a time when the song was not known—it was not necessary to promote it first.[25] Some account was taken of the publishers' readiness to fulfil demand when the song did become highly popular[26]; this is best viewed as confirmation of the original intention to supply whatever demand there was.[27]

[18] See, e.g. Clerk and Lindsell on Torts 16th ed., 1989.
[19] See above, §§ 5-010—5-011.
[20] CDPA 1988, s.152(1). Construction of a building is the equivalent of publishing the architectural work it embodies: s.152(3). There is also a definition of "commercial publication": s.152(2).
[21] See s.168(6). Joint authors, etc., are not specifically dealt with. But probably all must consent before a publication is authorised.
[22] See Megarry J., British Northrop v. Texteam [1974] R.P.C. 57 at 67.
[23] Ibid., and see McFarlane v. Hulton [1899] 1 Ch. 884; "Oscar" T.M., note by Pearson (1980) 2 E.I.P.R. 236.
[24] The phrase is used in s.49(2)(b) in contradistinction to an intent to fulfil the reasonable requirements of the public.
[25] Francis Day v. Feldman [1914] 2 Ch. 728 (C.A.); and see Bodley Head v. Flegon [1972] 1 W.L.R. 680.
[26] In Copex v. Flegon (The Times, August 18, 1967), it was argued, but not decided, that there could be no publication of a work in its original Russian where the intent was merely to secure the copyright in subsequent translations. The two purposes, however, are not incompatible.
[27] See below, pp. 357–358.

10-025   We shall see that Part I copyright gives the right not only to stop unauthorised reproductions of the work in its original form but also in other "material" forms, and it gives protection against adaptations (*e.g.* turning a book into a ballet, a novel into a play, a work in Polish into a work in English, a song into an orchestral number, a drawing into a three-dimensional object).[28] If the author, or someone with his permission, converts an unpublished work into one of these new forms and makes copies of the result available to the public, will this have the effect of publishing the original work? The Act gives no plain guidance; but the answer may well turn on the distinction between reproduction (in any material form) and adaptation,[29] publication being primarily concerned with issuing copies to the public. Thus it was held that a drawing was published by issuing three-dimensional embodiments of it to the public, because the definition of "reproduction" specifically include converting a 2D work into 3D and vice versa.[30] By parity of reasoning, it would seem that issuing a work on film or in any other "material" form of "reproduction" would suffice for publication.[31]

10-026   "Adaptation," which is distinguished from reproduction among the acts restricted by literary, dramatic and musical copyright, is concerned with reworking material in a manner which normally involves enough to add a further adapter's copyright. This may well constitute sufficient reason for not treating publication of the adaptation as publication of the original. If this is right, consider its impact upon translations—an important form of adaptation. If a work is written by a resident Chinese (the People's Republic not being a Convention country), and is then sent to the West for publication there in translation, only the particular translation will acquire Convention copyright. There will be nothing to prevent a British publisher from publishing a new translation from the original Chinese.[32]

6. TERM OF COPYRIGHT

10-027 The Act measures the duration of copyright from the end of the year in which a triggering event occurs, such as the author's death, or the making or publication of a work or an edition. In the interests of brevity, this added factor (which usefully simplifies proof) will not in each case be spelled out as the text proceeds, but taken as read.

[28] For this point, see Lahore, §§ 614–617.

[29] See the definitions, text above at nn. 20–21.

[30] *Merchant Adventurers* v. *Grew* [1973] R.P.C. 1 at 10; *British Northrop* case (above, n. 22) at 65. This question became significant once artistic copyright in industrial designs was recognised: see below, § 000. Whether these decisions remain good in relation to design documents within the exclusion of CDPA 1988, s.51, is a question of great obscurity.

[31] A further historical pointer is that, before 1911, publication consisted in principle of communicating a work to the public in any manner, including even by performance. The various specific exceptions operate to reverse this old presumption.

[32] Hence the practice of publishing at least a limited edition of the original first, in order to provide a qualification through first publication for Convention copyright in it. This was the nub of the dispute in *Copex* v. *Flegon*, above, n. 26.

The term required by the Berne Convention for the classic forms of copyright is the author's life and 50 years thereafter.[33] This is the measure which has been maintained in successive British Acts since 1911. Copyright pressure groups seek from time to time to argue that the balance should be tipped further in favour of the author's property, and away from the public interest in the free use of material[34]; and in a few West European states the general term has been extended beyond the Berne minimum.[35] But the case has not so far found favour in the United Kingdom. Indeed, in one respect the 1988 Act has cut back the copyright term. Under the 1911 and 1956 Acts, so long as a literary, dramatic or musical work, an engraving or a photograph remained "unpublished"[36] after the author's death, the 50-year term did not begin to run. Thus the law in some measure conferred a moral right to decide against publication and, more generally, contributed to the protection of posthumous privacy. In the 1988 Act this has been considered over-scrupulous, and (for the future) the term of all literary, dramatic, musical and artistic works, even when unpublished, becomes the author's life and 50 years thereafter.[37] In the case of joint authorship, the term is measured from the death of the last to die.[38] Computer-generated works receive copyright treatment, having copyright which lasts 50 years from making.[39] Anonymous and pseudonymous publications raise special considerations, as do Crown and similar copyrights, and these are dealt with later.[40]

One consequence of these changes in term is the transitional arrange- **10-028** ment for "existing works" that were not "published" at the author's death and accordingly took the longer period under the old law. If they are still unpublished at the 1988 Act's "commencement," they are accorded a term of 50 years from that date. But if publication (or one of its analogues) occurred between the author's death and "commencement," the 50-year period which then began to run delimits the copyright term.[41]

The most significant extension of term that has occurred in the 1988 Act concerns photographs. Because British copyright has never sought to restrict photographic copyright to work of artistic quality,[42] there has been some unease about keeping all photographs (include those of great and continuing public interest) under copyright protection for long periods: such a reward for a photographer who perhaps by chance was in the right place at the right time can easily seem disproportionate. Accordingly, under the 1911 Act, photographs were protected for 50

---

[33] See Ricketson (1987) Chap. 7.

[34] Thus the well-known advocate of birth control, Dr. Marie Stopes, advocated perpetual copyright before the Gregory Committee: see Cmd. 8862, § 16, 17.

[35] In West Germany, the general term became the author's life and 70 years in 1965.

[36] i.e., not published, so far as concerned engravings and photographs; and not published, publicly performed, offered for sale on a record, broadcast or cable-cast: C.A. 1956, s.2(3), 3(4).

[37] CDPA 1988, s.12(1).

[38] Ibid., s.12(4) and see below, § 12-010.

[39] Ibid., s.12(2).

[40] See below, § 10-030.

[41] CDPA 1988, Sched. 1, § 12(4).

[42] See above, § 10-010.

years from making, under the 1956 Act, for 50 years from publication—terms which are retained for photographs made during the currency of each Act.[43] But under the 1988 Act, new photographs are to enjoy the same term as other artistic works.[44]

10-029   The period now conferred for other copyrights is indicated in the Table (line 6). For sound recordings and films this becomes 50 years from making, or if "released"[45] within that period, 50 years from release.[46] This too represents some redirection in the treatment of material that remained long unpublished. For existing sound recordings and films still unpublished at "commencement," a period of 50 years' protection is allowed from that date.[47] The copyright in broadcasts and cable-casts continues to endure for 50 years from first transmission,[48] that in typographical format for 25 years from first publication.[49]

From the rules so far mentioned there are two important variations:

10-030   (i) *Anonymous and pseudonymous works* The Berne Convention imposes twin obligations on member countries: first, an author of a work within the Convention should be entitled to copyright in a publication while preserving anonymity.[50] This moral imperative is not easily realised in a system which measures the copyright term by the life of the author. Hence the second requirement: the publisher of an anonymous work should be able to enforce the author's rights as his deemed representative.[51]

It is no precondition of British copyright that the author be named in any publication; and the Act includes a presumption, until the contrary is proved, that, if a work is published in the United Kingdom without attribution but with the name of a publisher, that person shall be taken to be the owner of copyright at the date of publication.[52] If someone other than the publisher then seeks to assert copyright in the publication, he must either show that his right derives from the publisher or else he must rebut the presumption. He will not succeed in the latter endeavour merely by showing an assignment from the alleged author.[53]

Moreover, as long as a literary, dramatic, musical or artistic work remains of unknown authorship,[54] its copyright is measured without reference to the author's date of death. Instead it has copyright for 50

[43] CDPA 1988, Sched. 1, s.12(2).
[44] *Ibid.*, § 12(1).
[45] *i.e.* first published, broadcast, cable-cast, or, for film or film soundtrack, shown in public.
[46] CDPA 1988, s.13(2).
[47] *Ibid.*, Sched. 1, ss.12(5).
[48] *Ibid.*, s.14.
[49] *Ibid.*, s.15.
[50] Art. 7(3). For the history of the provision, see Ricketson (1987).
[51] Art. 15(2).
[52] CDPA 1988, s.103(4).
[53] *Warwick Film* v. *Eisinger* [1969] 1 Ch. 508. It must be doubted whether this truly gives effect to the Berne Convention, Art. 15(2), since the publisher is by no means necessarily representing the author and enforcing his rights. By confining the presumption to publication in the U.K., the Act may also be failing to fulfil the Convention.
[54] Once the identity of the author, or of one among joint authors, becomes known it cannot subsequently be a work of unknown authorship: CDPA 1988, s.7(4), (5).

years from being made available to the public.[55] The duration may not be increased by revealing the author's name once this period has expired.[56] But, by implication, if the name is disclosed before the expiry of the 50 years, this will have the effect either of extending or of foreshortening the copyright, depending on whether publication or its equivalent was before or after the author's death. This is the one case under the 1988 Act where (of necessity) copyright remains indeterminate until "publication."

(ii) *Crown and Parliamentary copyright* The Crown has a special **10-031** copyright in works made by an officer or servant of the Crown in the course of his duties, and in Acts and Measures. The Houses of Parliament have Parliamentary copyright in bills and other works prepared under their direction and control. The 1988 Act has introduced substantial changes on this subject which will be discussed later. Here it should be noted that Crown copyright in literary, dramatic, musical and artistic works lasts for 50 years from publication or 125 years from creation, whichever is the shorter;[57] Parliamentary copyright in Bills covers only their duration as such, but in other works of the same type, it lasts for 50 years from making.[58]

---

[55] CDPA 1988, s.12(2). "Made available to the public" includes, as well as publishing, performing in public, broadcasting and cable-casting (literary, dramatic and musical works); and exhibition in public, showing a film in public, broadcasting and cable-casting (artistic works).

[56] *Ibid.*

[57] Accordingly, the only transitional provision needed is to extend the triggering act from publication *simpliciter* to the list indicated in n. 6. This applies to existing works if not published before "commencement": CDPA 1988, Sched. 1, § 12(3).

[58] Other points about Crown copyright are discussed below, § 13-038 — 13-039.

CHAPTER 11

INFRINGEMENT OF COPYRIGHT AND MORAL RIGHTS

1. IINFRINGEMENT: BASIC CONCEPTS[1]

11-001 The Copyright Act defines in some detail the types of activity which constitute infringement of the various forms of copyright. As the Table indicates (line 7), the rights of the copyright owner may be roughly classified into "reproduction" rights and "performing" rights. The more detailed statutory categories that can be placed under these heads will be considered later,[1a] as will certain special forms of infringement, defences and remedies.[2] But first, there are four basic matters to discuss: copyright must be distinguished from rights in the physical embodiment of the original work; then come two aspects of the subject-matter improperly taken—the need to show that the defendant has misappropriated the actual work and that this has been to a substantial extent; the last concerns the infringer—the degree to which he may infringe by authorising the acts of others.

(1) Ownership of the original work
11-002   Copyright in a work gives rights that are distinct from ownership of the physical embodiment of the original work—the manuscript, letter, painting or whatever. When one person sends another a letter, he will normally be taken to intend a gift of the paper on which it is written and the recipient becomes its owner. Only if conditions of confidence exist, can the author prevent it being shown, given or sold to others.[3] But sending a private letter implies no assignment or licence of the copyright in it and the recipient has no right to make copies or give performances

---

[1] Dworking and Taylor, Chaps. 5, 6, 10; Hart [1989] E.I.P.R. 113.
[1a] Below, §§ 11-018—11-025. Note that the new law of infringement applies to existing works in respect of acts done after commencement: CDPA 1988, Sched. 1, § 14. There are special provisions affecting rental rights, subsequent dealings in copies made under an exception, typefaces, reconstruction of buildings, libraries, pre-1912 dramatic and musical works, statutory recording, and licences: § 15–23.
[2] Partly discussed below, §§ 11-026—11-046, and partly in Chap. 13.
[3] See, e.g. Pope v. Curl (1741) 2 Atk. 341; Gee v. Pritchard (1818) 2 Swans. 402; Philip v. Pennell [1907] 2 Ch. 577; Hauhart (1984) 13 U.Balt.L.R. 244.

of its content.[4] The same is true of artistic works. The artist's lack of rights in the original painting or sculpture, once he disposes of it, is often a considerable economic disadvantage and has led a few legal systems to introduce a special right to share in the proceeds of certain re-sales.[5] But such a sale assigns no copyright unless this is separately expressed or can be implied from the purpose of the transaction.[6]

(2) Misappropriation

(a) *Causal connection*

The plaintiff must prove that, directly or indirectly, the defendant's **11-003** alleged infringement is taken from the work or subject-matter in which he claims copyright.[7] This is fundamental to the whole concept of copyright, and distinguishes it from the "full" monopoly of the patent system. (Despite the very term, copyright, the legislation has, until 1988, mostly avoided reference to "copying." Now that word is used in relation to the making and marketing of reproductions. But equally there must also be copying in a general sense for infringement of the performing rights.) The owner must show that this causal connection is the explanation of the similarity between the work and the infringement—the other possibilities being that he copied from the defendant, that they both copied from a common source, or that they arrived at their results independently.[8] On the other hand, he does not have to show that the defendant knew that his copying constituted an infringement. As with other rights of property recognised at common law, the primary exclusive rights may be asserted against even the defendant who honestly believes that he purchased the right to reproduce the work.[9]

If the evidence shows that there are striking similarities between the two works, that the plaintiff's was the earlier in time and that the defendant had the opportunity to get to know the plaintiff's work, then a court may well find copying proved in the absence of any convincing explanation to the contrary by the defendant.[10] But the judges have hesitated to fetter the assessment of each case on its facts by the introduction of rules formally shifting the burden of proof from plaintiff

[4] *cf.* a letter to the editor. Under a will a bequest of an unpublished manuscript or artistic work is now to be construed as including the copyright: CDPA 1988, s.89. *cf.* the 1911 Act, s.17(2), restrictively construed in *Re Dickens* [1935] Ch. 267 which still applies to wills that took effect before the 1956 Act: CDPA 1988, Sched. 1, § 29.
[5] For this *droit de suite*, see below, §§ 13-041—13-042.
[6] In any case an implied licence (exclusive or non-exclusive, according to circumstances) may be a more reasonable implication.
[7] *cf.* the "exclusive right" and the basic statement about infringement in C.A. 1956, s.1(1), (2); and s.21(1), (2), (3).
[8] See Sargant J., *Corelli* v. *Gray* (1913) 29 T.L.R. 570; Diplock L.J., *Francis Day* case (below, n. 13) at 625; see also Learned Hand J., *Fisher* v. *Dillingham*, 298 Fed. 145 at 150 (1924).
[9] *Mansell* v. *Valley Printing* [1908] 2 Ch. 441; *Byrne* v. *Statist Co.* [1914] 1 K.B. 622; Copinger, § 410. Innocent defendants may be protected from liability for damages: see above, § 2-027.
[10] If the question is whether the defendant's work has come from the plaintiff's or from independent sources, the defendant may find it difficult to explain the presence of the plaintiff's errors or idiosyncrasies in his text: see, *e.g.* *Harman* v. *Osborne* (below, n. 12).

to defendant at any stage of the trial.[11] Some subject-matter, such as factual and historical information, may well derive from independent effort or a common source.[12]

(b) Subconscious copying

11-004   Particular difficulty arises when the defendant denies any intention to copy and the court believes him. Some judges have accepted that copying could occur subconsciously where a person reads, sees or hears a work, forgets about it but then reproduces it, genuinely believing it to be his own.[13] In such a case, proof of copying is said to depend on "a number of composite elements: The degree of familiarity (if proved at all, or properly inferred) with the plaintiff's work, the character of the work, particularly its qualities of impressing the mind and memory, the objective similarity of the defendant's work, the inherent probability that such similarity as is found could be due to coincidence, the existence of other influences on the defendant . . . the quality of the defendant's . . . own evidence on the presence or otherwise in his mind of the plaintiff's work."[14]

(c) Indirect copying

11-005   It has long been accepted that a work may be copied by imitating a copy of it: "to hold otherwise would be to open the door to indirect piracies, which I am not at all disposed to do."[15] If the plaintiff owns a copyright drawing and then turns it into a three-dimensional article and this is copied in three dimensions by the defendant, the "causal connection" for indirect copying of the drawing will be established.[16] Likewise if the defendant takes a photo of the plaintiff's three-dimensional article, or his own.[17] If a novel is turned into a play, which is in turn converted into a ballet, the same will apply. But the causal chain must run in the right direction. In *Purefoy* v. *Sykes Boxall*, P made a trade catalogue with illustrations of his products and D also published a catalogue with pictures of his own products, which were copied from P's products. In this alone there was no infringement of P's catalogue, for it was not that

---

[11] See especially the *Francis Day* case (below, n. 13).

[12] See, *e.g.* *Poznanski* v. *London Film* [1936–1945] Mac. C.C. 107 at 108; *Harman Pictures* v. *Osborne* [1967] 2 All E.R. 324 at 328.

[13] *Rees* v. *Melville* [1911–1916] Mac. C.C. 168; *Ricordi* v. *Clayton & Waller* [1928–1935] Mac. C.C. 154; *Francis Day* v. *Bron* [1963] Ch. 587, *per* Willmer L.J. (*cf.* 622, 626–627, *per* Upjohn and Diplock L.JJ.); *Industrial Furnaces* v. *Reaves* [1970] R.P.C. 605 at 623. The notion has actually been applied in *Sinanide* v. *Kosmeo* (1927) 44 T.L.R. 371 and the breach of confidence cases, *Seager* v. *Copydex* and *Talbot* v. *General Television* (above, § 8-010).

[14] *per* Wilberforce J., *Francis Day* v. *Bron* (above, n. 13) at 614.

[15] Lindley L.J., *Hanfstaegl* v. *Empire Palace* [1894] 3 Ch. 109 at 127; and see, *e.g.* Blackburn J., *ex p. Beal* (1868) L.R. 3 Q.B. 387 at 394. The leading modern authorities are *King Features Syndicate* v. *Kleeman* [1941] A.C. 417; *British Leyland* v. *Armstrong* [1986] R.P.C. 279 (H.L.). The principle now has statutory force: CDPA 1988, s.16(3).

[16] The great significance of this example for the law of industrial design is discussed below, §§ 14-003 *et seq.*

[17] *Dorling* v. *Honnor Marine* [1965] Ch. 1.

catalogue but the products which were the starting point in the chain.[18] On the other hand, if the plaintiff's parts were reproductions of copyright drawings, the defendant's illustrations would derive from those drawings. But to establish the linkage is not enough. It is also necessary to show that the defendant's ultimate use is a substantial reproduction of the plaintiff's work—this is simply the general requirement discussed in the next paragraph. In providing that infringement may be direct or indirect, the 1988 Act also renders it immaterial that any intervening act does not itself constitute infringement.[19]

(3) Substantial taking

Where there has been copying and all or virtually all of a work is 11-006 taken without emendation, the proof of infringement is straightforward; difficulties arise to the extent that this is not the case. The Act in effect requires that a substantial part must have been copied.[20] This test is a major tool for giving expression to the court's sense of fair play. So "the question whether the defendant has copied a substantial part depends much more on the quality than the quantity of what he has taken."[21] Likewise it has often enough been insisted that the copying must be of the expression of ideas, rather than just of the ideas. But that is a distinction with an ill-defined boundary. Judges who incline to the view that "what is worth copying is prima facie worth protecting"[22] may well stretch the notion of "expression" a considerable way. Once convinced that the defendant unfairly cut a competitive corner by setting out to re-vamp the plaintiff's completed work, they will not easily be dissuaded that the alterations have been sufficient.[23] In this approach the taking of ideas alone is confined to cases where the defendant does not start from the completed work at all, save in the sense that he goes through a similar process of creation: as where he paints for himself the scene that the plaintiff painted,[24] or draws his own cartoon for the same basic joke.[25]

The assessment of each case turns a good deal on its own circumstances. But there are some general considerations which may well have a bearing on the result. These are worth illustrating.

[18] (1954) 71 R.P.C. 227 at 232; 72 R.P.C. 89 at 99 (C.A., which found nonetheless against the defendant; a degree of both direct and indirect copying of the catalogue was proved).
[19] CDPA 1988, s.16(3). It might have been better to say that the act need not involve the making of anything that could be a copyright work.
[20] C.A. 1988, s.16(3)(a).
[21] Lord Reid, *Ladbroke v. William Hill* [1964] 1 W.L.R. 273 at 276; and see Lord Pearce at 293.
[22] Peterson J., *University of London Press* case [1916] 2 Ch. 601 at 610; quoted by Lords Reid and Pearce in the *Ladbroke* case (above, n. 21) at 279, 293. See Christie (1984) 10 Monash L.R. 175.
[23] For a striking example, see *Elanco v. Mandops* (below, n. 37).
[24] cf. e.g. *Krisarts v. Briarfine* [1977] F.S.R. 537; and see, as to indirect copying of a drawing for an object: *Ward v. Richard Sankey* [1988] F.S.R. 66.
[25] *McCrum v. Eisner* [1917–1923] Mac. C.C. 14. On the whole question see further, Laddie et al., §§ 2.50/66.

(a) *Unaltered copying*

11-007   If the defendant has copied without additions or alterations to the part taken, the proportion of that part to the whole of the plaintiff's work need not be large: a short extract from a poem, a recognisable segment of a painting, the refrain of a pop-song. The issue is not much contested, but, given the new copying technology, its practical importance is considerable.[26]

(b) *Extent of defendant's alteration*

11-008   Where the defendant has reworked the plaintiff's material there comes a point beyond which the plaintiff has no claim. Whatever may have been the position in the past, the fact that the defendant has himself added enough by way of skill, labour and judgment to secure copyright for his effort does not, under the present law, settle the question whether he has infringed; rather the issue is whether a substantial part of the plaintiff's work survives in the defendant's so as to appear to be a copy of it.[27]

Particular difficulty arises when the plaintiff's work is taken with intent to satirise—whether the butt in mind is the work itself or some quite different object.[28] In *Glyn* v. *Weston Feature*[29] a filmed burlesque (or, in today's language, "send-up") of Elinor Glyn's once notorious novel, *Three Weeks*, was held not to infringe because very little by way of incident was taken over from novel to film. Likewise in *Joy Music* v. *Sunday Pictorial*,[30] a song lyric had been parodied in pursuit of Prince Philip; but only one repeated phrase was taken, and that with pointed variation. Again there was no infringement. In both decisions it was asked whether the defendant had bestowed such mental labour on what he had taken and subjected it to such revision and alteration as to produce an original work.[31] This must be understood as a way of emphasising that nothing substantial must remain from the plaintiff's work.[32] While in the past, English judges have seemed loathe to find sufficient copying in borderline parody cases,[33] they have now also to consider the moral right of integrity, which is discussed later.[34]

11-009   A rather similar difficulty relates to résumés—summarised plots of plays, abridgments of novels, headnotes of law reports, and so on. There

---

[26] See below, §§ 13-007—13-014; equally in the field of performing rights.
[27] *Redwood Music* v. *Chappell* [1982] R.P.C. 109 (adaptation of song—generous view of difference).
[28] See Ramey (1984) 31 Cop.L.Symp. 1.
[29] [1916] 1 Ch. 261. The plaintiff's claim also failed for its "grossly immoral" tendency: see below, §§ 11-041, 11-042.
[30] [1960] 2 Q.B. 60.
[31] This derives from Lindley L.J., *Hanfstaegl* v. *Empire Palace* [1894] 3 Ch. 109 at 128; and the *Glyn* case (above, n. 29) at 268; *United Feature* v. *Star Newspaper* (1980) 2 E.I.P.R. D 43 (S.C., N.S.W.).
[32] *Schweppes* v. *Wellington* [1984] F.S.R. 210 ("Schlurppes" label intended as joke; plaintiff not amused); *Williamson Music* v. *Pearson Partnership* [1987] F.S.R. 97; Phillips (1984) 43 Camb. L.J. 245.
[33] Younger J., in the *Glyn* case above, n. 29, at 268) notes the absence of decisions finding infringement in "burlesque" cases.
[34] See below, §§ 11-055—11-057.

has been a tendency to treat a really substantial précis of contents as permissible—because it is useful or because it is no serious interference with the plaintiff's interests.[35] To this end it has been asked whether the defendant has really produced a "new work."[36] In this context the phrase seems to indicate a very substantial condensation and revision of the material. With this should be contrasted the Court of Appeal's grant of an interlocutory injunction in *Elanco* v. *Mandops*.[37] The defendants first copied the plaintiff's instruction leaflet for a weed killer and had to withdraw it; they then produced a revision giving the same detailed information in other words. This was held to create an arguable case of infringement because the defendants were not entitled to make use of the plaintiff's skill and judgment in securing the information.

(c) *Character of plaintiff's or defendant's work*

Certain types of work are treated as having a particular value; to appropriate this feature is accordingly of qualitative significance. This is particularly true of dramatic works and films. In periods when stock dramas made the staple of so much English theatre, there were frequent allegations of improper borrowing. After 1911, a series of cases[38] settled that "if the plot of a story, whether it be found in a play or in a novel, is taken bodily with or without some minor additions or subtractions for the purposes of a stage play or cinema film, there is no doubt about the case."[39] It was not necessary to copy the actual words used to work out the plot.[40] This approach shows the concept of mere ideas being confined to "starting point" conceptions—it would be no more than an idea, for instance, to conceive of a play about the return of a husband who has been presumed dead.[41] But where the works in question are both non-dramatic, probably more by way of detailed incident and language must be taken before there is substantial copying.[42] Where the works are artistic, and the court is testing sufficient similarity by appeal to the eye, stress is sometimes laid upon the "feeling and artistic character" of the plaintiff's work.[43]

11-010

---

[35] Cases on the subject decided before the modern notion of infringement had fully appeared must be treated with caution. But see *D'Almaine* v. *Boosey* (1835) 1 Y. & C. Ex. 288; *Dickens* v. *Lee* (1844) 8 Jur. 183; *Tinsley* v. *Lacy* (1863) 1 H. & M. 747; *Valcarenghi* v. *Gramophone* [1928–1935] Mac. C.C. 301.

[36] Jervis C.J., *Sweet* v. *Benning* (1855) 16 C.B. 459 at 483.

[37] [1980] R.P.C. 213; Dworkin [1979] E.I.P.R. 117.

[38] *e.g. Corelli* v. *Gray* (1913) 30 T.L.R. 116 (C.A.); Scrutton L.J., *Vane* v. *Famous Players* [1928–1935] Mac. C.C. 6 at 8 (particularly significant in the age of silent film). One earlier decision at least had required appropriation of actual dialogue: *Scholtz* v. *Amasis* [1905–1910] Mac. C.C. 216; *cf.* also *Chatterton* v. *Cave* (1878) 3 App. Cas. 483.

[39] Maugham J., *Kelly* v. *Cinema Houses* [1928–1935] Mac. C.C. 362; *Dagnall* v. *British Film*, *ibid.* 391.

[40] In *Fernald* v. *Jay Lewis* (1953) [1975] F.S.R. 499, even the taking of one episode out of an episodic novel for a film was held to infringe when the literary characteristics of the episode were all copied and there were some startling similarities of dialogue.

[41] An example given by Scrutton L.J., *Vane* case (above, n. 38) at 8–9; and see *de Manduit* v. *Gaumont British* [1936–45] Mac. C.C. 292.

[42] Copinger, § 480 suggests that the same may be true where a non-dramatic work is turned into a drama; but *cf.* the *Corelli* and *Vane* cases (above, n. 38); Lahore, § 1144.

[43] *e.g.* Somervell L.J., *Bauman* v. *Fussell*, (1953) [1978] R.P.C. 485 at 487.

(d) *Nature of plaintiff's effort*

11-011   In some cases, the plaintiff's "skill, labour and judgment" form a distinct part of the whole result. This may well be so where the effort consists of such secondary work as editing, compiling or selecting material. A court will treat the whole work as the subject of copyright.[44] But whether there is substantial taking falls to be judged by reference to the plaintiff's contribution. In *Warwick Film* v. *Eisinger*,[45] an author published an edited version of Oscar Wilde's trials, a transcript of which had earlier appeared. He acquired copyright in the whole from his work in selection and providing linking passages. But a defendant who took from it passages of the transcript but very little of the author's editing was held not to infringe.

This neatly adjusts the scope of protection to the author's literary effort. The same approach can be seen to apply to some cases where the real skill lies in some commercial assessment distinct from the expressive content of the work: thus in the football pool coupon cases,[46] where it is the particular selection that is so significant, protection goes to taking the selection more or less as a whole. This correlation of protection with achievement is not easily made in all such cases. Where, for instance, the skill consists in recording someone else's performance,[47] it is arguable that there should be infringement only where some considerable part of the whole is taken. The same might be said of the entrepreneurial copyrights—particularly that for typographical format, since it is not associated with the artistic execution of performers, directors or the like. But this sort of consideration is at present speculative.[48]

(e) *Extent of plaintiff's effort*

11-012   If the plaintiff's labour, skill and judgment have only been just enough to earn him copyright, infringement may arise only where there is exact imitation of such features as are of some individuality. In *Kenrick* v. *Lawrence*,[49] the plaintiff claimed copyright in a simple drawing of a hand, made with the intention of showing voters where to register their vote on a ballot form. But it was held that only an exact copy of the drawing would infringe, if the plaintiff were not to be conceded a monopoly in drawings of hands for this and other purposes. Through this consideration also the court is able to take account of the merit overall of the plaintiff's work.

(f) *Manner in which the defendant has taken advantage of plaintiff's work*

11-013   Where the plaintiff's work records information, the use that a defendant may make of it for his own purposes has been carefully circumscribed. The defendant is entitled to use the plaintiff's work as a source

---

[44] *Ladbroke* case (above, n. 31).

[45] [1969] 1 Ch. 508; see also *John Fairfax* v. *Australian Consolidated Press* (1960) 60 S.R. (N.S.W.) 413.

[46] Above, § 10-006.

[47] In so far as this is properly the subject of copyright: *cf.* above, § 10-019.

[48] See further below, § 11-022.

[49] (1890) 25 Q.B.D. 99. Contrast the cases on the plays and novels: above, text at n. 38.

of ideas or information if he takes it as a starting point for his own collation of information or as a means of checking his own independent research.[50] But he is not entitled to copy what the plaintiff has done as a substitute for exercising his own labour, skill and judgment. And he will not escape having his conduct so regarded merely by taking the plaintiff's work and checking that its contents are accurate. Thus it was improper to compile a street directory by sending out slips for checking, which contained entries from the plaintiff's directory.[51] Equally, it is wrong to adopt the same quotations which have been selected for a critical edition of a Shakespeare play,[52] or an account of historical incidents which digest the available sources.[53] In such cases, a defendant who is shown to have adopted the plaintiff's imaginative embellishments or plain errors will be in particular jeopardy.[54]

(g) *Whether the defendant's use will seriously interfere with plaintiff's exploitation of his work*

While infringement may occur even if there is no likelihood of **11-014** competition between plaintiff and defendant, the possibility of such competition or its absence may nevertheless be treated as a relevant factor. This factor undoubtedly played a more significant role while copyright was still in the process of acquiring its character as a full right of property, and before substantial taking was distinguished from notions of "fair use."[55] But it remains a practical consideration that courts are unlikely ever entirely to discount.[56] Thus it is referred to by Farwell J. in deciding that four brief lines from a popular song did not infringe when taken as a heading for a serial story in the *Red Star Weekly*.[57]

(h) *Reproduction by the original author*

Suppose that an author creates a work, and subsequently, at a time **11-015** when he does not own the copyright,[58] he reproduces it in a second work.

[50] See *Jarrold* v. *Houston* (1857) 3 K. & J. 708; *Pike* v. *Nicholas* (1869) L.R. 5 Ch. App. 251; *Hogg* v. *Scott* (1874) L.R. 18 Eq. 444.

[51] *Kelly* v. *Morris* (1866) L.R. 1 Eq. 677; see also *Morris* v. *Ashbee* (1868) L.R. 7 Eq. 34 (poacher turned gamekeeper). The Whitford Committee (Cmnd. 6732, §§ 862–863) considered that new versions of the Ordnance Survey would be infringed if details were systematically copied onto other maps; see also *Sands & McDougall* v. *Robinson* (1917) 23 C.L.R. 49 (H.C., Aust.).

[52] Collins M.R., *Moffatt & Page* v. *Gill* (1902) 86 L.T. 465 at 471; and see *Blackie* v. *Lothian* (1921) 29 C.L.R. 396 (H.C., Aust.).

[53] *Harman* v. *Osborne* [1967] 2 All E.R. 324; *Ravenscroft* v. *Herbert* [1980] R.P.C. 193.

[54] *Harman* case (above, n. 53).

[55] Thus initially such activities as translation and abridgment did not count as infringement.

[56] *Chappell* v. *Thompson* [1928–1935] Mac. C.C. 467 at 471. Note also Parker J., *Weatherby* v. *International Horse Agency* [1910] 1 Ch. 297 at 305: " . . . the nature of the two publications and the likelihood or unlikelihood of their entering into competition with each other is not only a relevant but may even be a determining factor in the case. But . . . an unfair use may be made of one book in the preparation of another, even if there is no likelihood of competition between the former and the latter. After all copyright is property . . . ."

[57] *Chappell* v. *Thompson* (above, n. 56); and see *Ravenscroft* v. *Herbert* [1980] R.P.C. 193.

[58] If he has given up rights by assignment, his freedom to copy the work may be governed by its express terms.

Some concession in his favour seems called for, in order to allow him to continue doing the kind of work at which he is proficient. But across the spectrum of copyright activity it is difficult to know how far judges would accord him any greater freedom than is permitted to others. In respect of artistic works, a special compromise is embodied in legislation: the artist may make substantial reproductions, even using the same mould, sketch or similar plan, provided that the subsequent work does not repeat or imitate the main design of the earlier work.[59] Where other types of work are concerned, a similar approach might well be adopted: the relation between the two end products would be considered rather than the relation between the first work and what has been copied from it. The fact that the author made his reproduction unconsciously (if he can be believed) would probably enhance any claim not to have infringed.[60]

(4) Infringement carried out by others[61]

11-016   Infringement of copyright being a tort, in the ordinary run of things an employer will be vicariously liable[62] for any infringement committed by an employee in the course of his employment and for the acts of independent contractors which he specifically requested. Under earlier law, these principles seem to have delimited the scope of one person's liability for infringements committed by another.[63] But, in contrast with the case of patents,[64] judges have more recently been ready enough to extend the scope of responsibility for the infringement by others of Part I copyright.

In this they have been assisted by the legislature, which has introduced three forms of infringement: (i) "authorising" infringement by others[65]; (ii) "permitting" a place of public entertainment to be used for performance of a work[66]; and (iii) providing apparatus for performing, playing or showing a work, etc.[67] (of these, (ii) and (iii) are now forms of secondary infringement which require proof of the defendant's complicity in ways which will be described later).[68]

"Authorise" has been read as bearing its dictionary meaning of "sanction, countenance or approve."[69] In line with these broad synonyms,

---

[59] C.A. 1988, s.64, based upon *Preston* v. *Tuck* [1926] Ch. 667.
[60] On the difficulties of deciding this, see *Industrial Furnaces* v. *Reaves* [1970] R.P.C. 605 at 623–624.
[61] See Stuckey [1984] U.N.S.W.L.J. 77.
[62] For vicarious liability, see above, §§ 2-003—2-004. To tell a servant not to infringe will not affect this liability if he defies instructions in the course of employment: *PRS* v. *Mitchell & Booker* [1924] 1 K.B. 762; *cf. PRS* v. *Bradford Corp.* [1917–1923] Mac. C.C. 309.
[63] See especially *Karno* v. *Pathé* (1909) 100 L.T. 260—film distributor did not "cause" representation of a play in public by supplying theatre operator with film of it; only the operator infringed. *cf. Falcon* v. *Famous Players* [1926] 2 K.B. 474.
[64] See above, §§ 6-001—6-006, 6-013—6-014.
[65] Now C.A. 1988, s.16(2).
[66] Now C.A. 1988, s.25. This relates only to literary, dramatic and musical works; a defence concerning non-profit activities has been dropped.
[67] Now C.A. 1988, s.26.
[68] See below, § 11-022.
[69] Tomlin J., *Evans* v. *Hulton* [1923–1928] Mac. C.C. 51; Bankes L.J., *Falcon* v. *Famous Players* (n. 63, above) at 491.

it has been said that "indifference, exhibited by acts of commission or omission, may reach a degree from which authorisation or permission may be inferred."[70] Accordingly in a case concerning performing rights (which has been the commonest field of application for these provisions) both authorising and permitting may be alleged, and they amount to much the same thing. "Permitting" performance is expressly stated to be subject to the defences of reasonable innocence and absence of profit-making[71]; "authorising" is not the subject of specific exceptions, but the meaning given to the word excludes liability when the defendant could not reasonably expect that another would infringe.[72] It is also necessary to show an act of infringement that had occurred as a result of the authorisation.[73]

To take some examples: People who organise public entertainments by **11-017** hiring musicians as independent contractors are likely to be authorising or permitting infringement if they simply leave the choice of music to the musicians.[74] Accordingly they ought to procure an appropriate licence from the Performing Right Society themselves or require the musicians to do so. Where the defendant is not the organiser of the entertainment, but only, for instance, the owner of the hall, he is unlikely to be held culpable if he is simply "indifferent" to the choice of music.[75]

In other fields, authorising may also occur by implication. A person who transfers the serial rights in a book authorises their publication in that form, since the specific intent is apparent.[76] An Australian university was held to have authorised infringement by allowing library readers to use its copying machine without giving precise information about the limits to copying within the copyright legislation and without attempting any supervision to prevent infringement: the degree of indifference was too blatant to escape liability.[77] On the other hand, those who provide the copying machinery or the material for home taping will rarely be found to have the necessary control over what is then done, to be "authorised."[78] The manufacturer of a twin-deck cassette recorder did not

---

[70] *PRS v. Ciryl* [1914] 1 K.B. 1 at 9; *Moorhouse v. University of N.S.W.* (1975) 6 A.L.R. 193; [1976] R.P.C. 157; Catterns (1976) 23 Bull. U.S. Cop. 213.

[71] See C.A. 1956, s.5(5) for complete definition.

[72] See *Ciryl* case (n. 70, above).

[73] *RCA v. Fairfax* [1982] R.P.C. 91 (newspaper article suggesting the possibility of home taping); *WEA International v. Hanimax* (1988) 10 I.P.R. 349.

[74] *PRS v. Bradford Corp.* (n. 62, above); *Australasian PRA v. Canterbury-Bankstown Club* [1964–1965] N.S.W.R. 138; *Australasian PRA v. Miles* [1962] N.S.W.R. 405; *Australasian PRA v. Koolman* [1969] N.Z.L.R. 273; *cf. Monaghan v. Taylor* (1885) 2 T.L.R. 685 (entrepreneur present); *PRS v. Bray UDC* [1930] A.C. 377 (entrepreneur approved list).

[75] *Vigneux v. Canadian PRS* [1945] A.C. 108 at 123 *cf. Winstone v. Wurlitzer* [1946] V.L.R. 338; *Adelaide Corp. v. Australasian PRS* (1928) 40 C.L.R. 481 (despite knowledge that infringement likely); *Ciryl* case (n. 70, above) (defendant only managing director of entrepreneur company); *Performances (N.Z.) v. Lion Breweries* [1980] F.S.R. 1.

[76] *Evans v. Hulton* [1923–28] Mac. C.C. 51; and see *Falcon v. Famous Players* (above, n. 63).

[77] *Moorhouse* case (above, n. 70); in another context, see *Standen Engineering v. Spalding* [1984] F.S.R. 554.

[78] See *A. & M. Records v. Audio Magnetics* [1979] F.S.R. 1; *CBS v. Ames* [1981] R.P.C. 407.

authorise infringement of particular copyrights, even though he advertised the capabilities of his product, since he also drew attention to
copyright obligations.[79]

2. CLASSES OF PROHIBITED ACT

11-018 The 1988 Act defines the "acts restricted by the copyright" in general
terms, each type applying to the various categories of work unless a
specific exception is given. The 1956 Act, by contrast, took each category
of subject-matter and listed the relevant acts of infringement. The new
technique seems rather more straightforward. In the Table (line 7) the
restricted acts are listed in two groups, the first being concerned with
making permanent reproductions, adaptations and the like, the second
with transient activities involving a performance or broadcast.

In British patent law, as we have seen, the monopoly right was
extended to use, as well as manufacture and sale, thus enabling the
patentee and his associates to exercise whatever control over their own
products seemed advantageous. In British copyright law, the same basic
assumption has not been made.[80] The typical act of infringement has been
the making of copies. Control over them and their contents once
legitimately made has been conceded only on a case-by-case basis: the
rights over public performance and broadcasting are one form of control
over use; the newly created rental right in sound recordings, films and
computer programs is another.[81]

Often enough the various rights that make up copyright are separately
assigned or made the subject of an exclusive licence.[82] The assignee or
exclusive licensee is then entitled to sue only in respect of his own part
and it may be necessary to decide just what his part is. If the division up
has been made by reference to the different acts listed in the statute, then
the question will turn on the meaning of the statutory words.[83] If some
other, more specific right has been conceded (such as the right to
translate into French, or the right to engrave a picture for a particular
book) then the particular assignment or licence will require
interpretation.

(1) Rights concerned with reproduction and adaptation
11-019   The 1988 Act distinguishes two broad categories of infringement:
restricted acts (or primary infringement) which occur without regard to
the defendant's state of mind; and secondary infringements which are

---

[79] *CBS U.K.* v. *Amstrad* [1988] R.P.C. 567; and see below, § 13-013.
[80] The supposed *droit de destination* in French and Belgian copyright law fulfils much the
same function as the British patent law doctrine; it allows, for instance, a rental right to
be read into the law without specific provision: see E.C. Commission, Green Paper,
Copyright and the Challenge of Technology (Com.(88)172) 146.
[81] See below, § 11-021, and consider also the special scheme for the public lending of
books: §§ 13-037—13-039.
[82] See below, §§ 12-006 *et seq.*
[83] See, *e.g. Chappell* v. *Columbia* [1914] 2 Ch. 124.

committed only if the defendant knew or had reason to believe a defined state of affairs relating to infringement. Under each of the following heads primary and secondary infringement will be considered separately.

(a) *Primary infringement*

Copyright in a work may be infringed by copying it; issuing copies of 11-020 it to the public or by making an adaptation of it.[84] Copying a work, so far as concerns literary, dramatic, musical and artistic copyright, means "reproducing the work in a material form"—a formula introduced in the 1911 Act.[85] Some of the material forms are specifically listed: storing the work in any medium by electronic means—which clearly covers computer storage and presumably extends to the incorporation of the work in a record or film,[86] converting a two-dimensional artistic work into three dimensions, and vice versa.[87] But other changes of form may also count: for instance, turning a story into a ballet,[88] copying a photograph by painting,[89] making a knitting pattern into a fabric,[90] and turning a drawing, such as a cartoon, into a revue sketch.[91] Novel analogies can be made, subject always to the need to satisfy the test of substantial taking.

Quite apart from this, certain acts of adaptation constitute infringement: turning a literary work into a dramatic work or vice versa; translating either kind of work or turning it into a picture form (such as a comic strip); arranging or transcribing a musical work (by, for instance, harmonising or orchestrating it).[92]

The new Act is not so specific as its predecessor about what acts of 11-021 "copying" infringe sound recording, film, broadcasting and cable-casting copyright. Presumably, as before, this includes making recordings or films that are substantial copies; but could it now also cover the transcription into written form of the material on (say) a recording?

Copying also includes specific cases. Making a photograph of the whole or a substantial part of any image forming part of a film, broadcast or cable programme—for instance for a post-card or poster—is such an infringement.[93] And the publisher's copyright in typographical

---

[84] CDPA 1988, ss.16–18, 21.

[85] s.17(2). It makes no difference that the copies are transient or incidental: s.17(6).

[86] *cf.* CDPA 1956, s.48(1) "reproduction," which specified these cases.

[87] CDPA 1988, s.17(3). Converting a literary work (*e.g.* a knitting pattern) into a three-dimensional work (*e.g.* a jumper) is not, however, a reproduction: *Brigid Foley* v. *Ellot* [1982] R.P.C. 433; *Duriron* v. *Hugh Jennings* [1984] F.S.R. 1.

[88] *Holland* v. *Van Damm* [1936–1945] Mac. C.C. 69.

[89] *Bauman* v. *Fussell*, above, n. 43 (C.A.); *Hanfstaegl* v. *W.H. Smith* [1905] 1 Ch. 519.

[90] *Lerose* v. *Hawick Jersey* [1974] R.P.C. 42; *cf. Dicks* v. *Brooks* (1880) Ch.D. 22 (pre-1911 legislation).

[91] *Bradbury, Agnew* v. *Day* (1916) 32 T.L.R. 349 (*cf.* the pre-1911 position in *Hanfstaegl* v. *Empire Palace* [1894] 2 Ch. 1). Note the absence of a general performing right in artistic works.

[92] The final clause of s.21 suggests that these forms of infringement are closely related to infringement by reproduction in a material form: "No inference shall be drawn from this section as to what does or does not amount to copying the work."

[93] CDPA 1988, s.17(4), giving statutory effect to *Spelling Goldberg* v. *BPC Publishing* [1981] R.P.C. 280 (C.A.).

format is infringed (solely) by making a facsimile copy, even if it is enlarged or reduced.[94]

Issuing copies of a work to the public is the form of primary infringement which relates only to first putting the copies in question into circulation, and not, in general, to subsequent distribution, sale, hiring, loan or importation into the United Kingdom[95] (since these acts fall under the heading of secondary infringement). However, to this there is now one important exception. In respect of sound recordings, films and computer programs, it is an act of primary infringement to rent copies to the public, and this includes not only supplying a copy on terms that it will or may be returned for payment or as part of the services or amenities of a business, but also lending by public libraries whether or not for a charge.[96]

(b) Secondary infringement

11-022   Infringement of all forms of copyright may be committed by a defendant concerned in the commercial exploitation of copies, if he knows or has reason to believe that the copies were infringements when they were made.[97] In the case of imported copies this includes "notional infringements," i.e. copies that would have infringed if they had been made in Britain or would have constituted a breach of an exclusive licence agreement relating to that work.[98] The stages of exploitation in question are: importing, possessing in the course of a business, selling, letting for hire, offering or exposing for sale or hire, and exhibiting in public in the course of a business, and distributing either in the course of a business, or otherwise to an extent that prejudicially affects the copyright owner.[99]

As to the defendant's state of mind in secondary infringement, the previous law required it to be shown that the defendant had knowledge that the copies in issue were infringements.[1] But that had been read as requiring only that he had "notice of facts such as would suggest to a reasonable man that a breach of copyright was being committed."[2] The new phrase, "knew or had reason to believe," for all its apparent subjectivity, is likely to be understood in the same sense.

---

[94] CDPA 1988, s.17(B), 168 "facsimile copy."
[95] s.18.
[96] s.18(2), 168 "rental"; [and see Sched. 7, §§ 6, 8, 34 (a disgracefully obscure extension)].
[97] CDPA 1988, ss.22–24, 27. As already noted, the person who first puts copies into circulation commits the primary infringement of issuing copies to the public: above, § 11-021. For infringement by telecommunication of text (s.24(27), see below, §13-026).
[98] s.27(3); see below, § 12-009.
[99] CDPA 1988, s.23.
[1] CDPA 1956, ss.5, 16.
[2] Harvey J., Albert v. Hoffnung (1922) 22 S.R. (N.S.W. 75 at 81; followed by Whitford J., Infabrics v. Jaytex [1978] F.S.R. 451 at 464–465; and see at 467: was the defendant's selector "put on inquiry?" Did he turn "a blind eye to an inquiry which he should have known he ought to have made?" Once apprised of the truth he was allowed a number of days to make his own inquiries: Van Dusen v. Kritz [1936] 2 K.B. 176.

(2) Rights concerned with performance and broadcasting

(a) *The various performing rights*

The extension of copyright from the making of copies to the giving of **11-023** public performances began in 1833. With modern technology, this has grown into a bundle of related aspects of copyright that can be loosely grouped as "performing rights." These are listed in the Table (line 7): performing, playing or showing a work in public; broadcasting it or including it in a cable programme (cable-casting).[3]

The possibilities of infringement in this field have become complex. If, for instance, a copyright musical work is performed to a public audience at the same time as being televised, both the performance and the broadcast require licence. If the broadcast is received and shown publicly this calls for licence of the copyright in the music, and (save where the showing is free) of that in the broadcast.[4] If the original performance was recorded this will be either in the form of a sound recording or a film with associated sound track (each of which will be a form of reproduction). If either the recording or the film is broadcast, this needs a licence. But the owner of copyright in the sound recording or film (as distinct from that in the musical work) has no right in respect of free public playings or showings of the broadcast.[5]

Performance is too ephemeral a phenomenon for it to be easy for **11-024** copyright owners to enforce their performing rights individually. Those who have copyright in musical works and associated lyrics have been leaders in establishing societies for the collective enforcement of their rights. The great proliferation in the exploitation of music through recordings and broadcasts has made this economically feasible in many countries and an international network of performing right societies now exists.[6] In Britain, where record companies have performing rights in their recordings, they have a separate collecting society to assert their rights.[7] In various countries, indeed, the economic power of collecting societies has become suspect: the case for public surveillance is discussed in the next chapter.[8]

(b) *Performance in public*

It has been left to the courts to draw the line between performances in **11-025** public and in private. In 1884, the Court of Appeal characterised as "quasi-domestic"—and therefore private—an amateur performance of a

[3] CDPA 1988, ss.19, 20.
[4] *Cf.* s.71.
[5] See below, § 11-033.
[6] For the history, particularly of the British organisation, the Performing Right Society (PRS), see Peacock and Weir, *The Composer in the Market Place* (1975); McFarlane, *Copyright: the Development and Exercise of the Performing Right* (1980), Chaps. 6–11. The PRS collects on behalf of foreign societies for British use of their repertoires, and it has arrangements to receive equivalent royalties from the foreign societies on its own members' behalf. The Confédération Internationale des Sociétés d'Auteurs et Compositeurs (CISAC) has played an important role in settling the terms of the international system of collection and distribution.
[7] Called Phonographic Performance Ltd. (PPL). See above, § 9-024.
[8] Below, § 12-022.

play in Guy's Hospital to an audience of doctors and their families, nurses, attendants and students.[9] But this was regarded (even in the decision itself) as marking the extreme outpost of free territory. To be in public a performance does not have to be to a paying audience or by paid performers[10]; it is enough that entertainment is being offered as an incident of some commercial activity (such as running a hotel, or even a shop that is seeking to sell the records being played)[11] or of industrial production ("music while you work").[12] Even such worthy institutions as a Women's Institute and a football club's supporters' association engage in public performance, whether they restrict audiences to their own members or allow in guests[13]; and the Act makes clear that a school play or other performance will not be exempt if parents or friends are present.[14] Greene M.R. laid particular stress on the need to consider the relationship of the audience to the owner of the copyright rather than to the performers.[15] This is one way of emphasising the primacy of the owner's entitlement to an economic return from his proprietary rights; the fact that an organisation is socially desirable does not normally give it a claim to free use of copyright material. The one general exception concerns the sound recording right (as distinct from copyright in music and words) where records are played at a charitable or similar club or organisation.[16]

3. "Fair Dealing" and Like Exceptions

11-026 The requirement of "substantial taking" prevents the owner from objecting to minor borrowings from his copyright work. And, as we have just seen, the requirement that a performance be in public means that his licence is unnecessary for a private performance, even of the complete work. In the modern Copyright Acts, other exceptions from the scope of copyright have been specified and the 1988 Act now has a lengthy list. Some of them, such as those relating to education, concern important conflicts of interest, and they will be discussed in their own context in the next chapter. Here they are listed in order that they can be compared in the round.

---

[9] *Duck* v. *Bates* (1884) 13 Q.B.D. 843; under the 1833 Act, the requirement was in any case that the performance be in a "place of public entertainment."
[10] *PRS* v. *Hawthornes Hotel* [1933] Ch. 855; and see *Harms* v. *Martans Club* [1927] 1 Ch. 526 (dance club).
[11] *PRS* v. *Harlequin Record* [1979] F.S.R. 233.
[12] *Ernest Turner* v. *PRS* [1943] Ch. 167.
[13] *Jennings* v. *Stephens* [1936] Ch. 469; *PRS* v. *Rangers Club* [1975] R.P.C. 626; *APRA* v. *Canterbury Bankstown Club* (above, n. 74).
[14] CDPA 1988, s.34(3).
[15] In the *Jennings* and *Turner* cases, above, nn. 12, 13.
[16] So a PRS licence remains necessary, though a PPL licence is not: s.67. Note also the special provision to allow adaptations of broadcasts and cable-casts for the deaf, hard of hearing and handicapped: s.74. Below, § 11-029.

Fair dealing[17]

The three most important of these exceptions turn upon a qualitative **11-027** assessment. They exempt copying for certain purposes if it amounts to no more than "fair dealing." In these cases the courts are left to judge fairness in the light of all the circumstances. But other exceptions are more factual; for instance, unduplicated copying in the course of instruction is exempt irrespective of the amount copied.

Before the 1911 Act, the three main "fair dealing" exceptions were foreshadowed in the case-law as forms of "fair use," a concept that was not clearly distinguished from "insubstantial taking." If there is substantial copying, it is a nice question today whether the use could nevertheless be justified for a reason beyond the confines of the statutory exceptions. Certainly this would be difficult if the case was closely analogous to one of the statutory exceptions but just outside it; the more so if the statutory exceptions are to be strictly construed as limitations upon property rights.[18] Nonetheless a "defence" of publication in the public interest has been recognised to exist and now has a place in the statute.[19] In Australia it has been held that it is less extensive than in a claim based on breach of confidence[20]; but in England the tendency has been to treat the two cases alike.[21]

The first fair dealing exception is that covering purposes of research or **11-028** private study,[22] which now applies to the copyright in literary, dramatic, musical and artistic works, and published editions. With this must be read the more specific exceptions covering certain librarians and archivists[23]; the exception for the inclusion of short passages of literary and dramatic works in collections for schools[24]; and the exceptions for copying and photocopying works in the course of instruction and examination and performing, playing or showing works in certain circumstances at schools, etc.[25]; and for recording broadcasts and cablecasts.[26] The role of these defences is primarily in the field of education and it is in that context that they will be discussed in more detail.[27]

The second fair dealing exception permits all works other than photographs to be used for reporting current events.[28] Photographs have

---

[17] See Puri (1983) 13 Vict.U.Wellington L.R. 277.

[18] This approach was taken in *Hawkes* v. *Paramount* [1934] Ch. 593 (C.A.) to a fair dealing exception in the 1911 Act.

[19] CDPA 1988, s.171(3), preserving rules of law preventing or restricting the enforcement of copyright, on grounds of public interest or otherwise. See further below, § 11-041.

[20] *Commonwealth of Australia* v. *Fairfax* (1980) 32 A.L.R. 485; see also *Kennard* v. *Lewis* [1983] F.S.R. 346 (right-wing criticism of C.N.D. pamphlet).

[21] *e.g. Hubbard* v. *Vosper* [1972] 2 Q.B. 84 (C.A.); *Beloff* v. *Pressdram* [1973] 1 All E.R. 241.

[22] CDPA 1988, s.29.

[23] ss.37–44.

[24] ss.33, 36.

[25] ss. 32, 34.

[26] s.35.

[27] Below, § 13-007.

[28] s.30(2), (3). This may be in a newspaper or magazine, in which case sufficient acknowledgement is required; or in a sound recording, film, broadcast or cable-cast, where acknowledgement is not called for.

been differently treated in order to preserve the full value of holding a unique visual record of some person or event. To come within the exception, the event itself must be current and not the pretext for reviving historical information: the death of the Duchess of Windsor did not justify an exchange of letters between her and the Duke being published without copyright licence.[29] The exception must be read in conjunction with a number of cognate provisions.[30] Together they are of particular importance to the public affairs media and they will be related to that field later.[31]

But it is the third fair dealing exception that is most general of all, allowing works to be used for purposes of criticism or review (of themselves or another work), one precondition of fairness being that the source should be sufficiently acknowledged.[32] Despite its potential range, the defence has not been much elucidated in the case-law. The Court of Appeal has held that the criticism or review may concern the ideas expressed as well as the mode of expression.[33] It has also been said that it cannot be "fair" to publish an unpublished work for this purpose, at least if it is known to have been improperly obtained.[34] And the courts will not permit wholesale borrowing to be dressed up as critical quotation.[35] Lord Denning M.R.'s remarks stressing that fair dealing is inevitably a matter of degree can usefully be applied not only to this head but in spirit equally to the other two:

> "You must consider first the number and extent of the quotations and extracts. Are they altogether too many and too long to be fair? Then you must consider the use made of them. If they are used as a basis for comment, criticism or review, that may be a fair dealing. If they are used to convey the same information as the author, for a rival purpose, they may be unfair. Next, you must consider the proportions. To take long extracts and attach short comments may be unfair. But short extracts and long comments may be fair. Other considerations may come to mind also. But, after all is said and done, it must be a matter of impression."[36]

Beyond these cases of "fair dealing" and the like, there are numerous exceptions which, as a whole, are not easily classified.

(1) Exceptions designed to encourage collective licensing schemes

11-029   As a matter of practicality, the new Act aims to foster the administration of copyright through licensing schemes which are conducted for

---

[29] *Associated Newspapers* v. *News Group* [1986] R.P.C. 515.
[30] Especially s.31 (incidental inclusion); s.58 (record of spoken words); s.62 (artistic works on public display).
[31] Below, § 13-004.
[32] s.30(1).
[33] *Hubbard* v. *Vosper* [1972] 2 Q.B. 84 at 94–95, 98.
[34] *British Oxygen* v. *Liquid Air* [1925] Ch. 383 at 393; but *cf. Beloff* v. *Pressdram* [1973] 1 All E.R. 241 at 264.
[35] *Mawman* v. *Tegg* (1826) 2 Russ. 385; *cf.* Megaw L.J., *Hubbard* case (above, n. 33) at 98.
[36] *Hubbard* case (above, n. 33) at p. 94.

groups of right-owners. Of the five specific cases, three prescribe an exception to infringement which is to operate in the absence of a certified licensing scheme covering the proposed use. These are: (i) recording of broadcasts, cable-casts and material contained in them for the purposes of an educational establishment[37]; (ii) copying and issuing copies of the published abstracts of scientific or technical articles in periodicals[38]; and (iii) making and issuing copies of broadcasts and cable-casts with sub-titling or other modifications for the special needs of the deaf and handicapped, where this is done by a body specially designated by the Minister.[39] In a fourth case—reprographic copying by educational establishments—the same result is achieved by conferring a limited freedom to copy if no certified scheme is offered.[40] In the fifth case—the new rental right as it affects legitimate sound recordings, films and computer programs—the Minister has power to convert the exclusive right into a right to a reasonable royalty, set, if necessary, by the Copyright Tribunal.[41]

(2) Exceptions concerning artistic works

There are carried forward into the new Act a number of provisions **11-030** affecting artistic works: sculptures, building models and works of artistic craftsmanship, if permanently situated in public, may be represented in a graphic work—photographed, filmed, broadcast or cable-cast without licence; likewise buildings wherever situate.[42] An artistic work may be copied, and those copies issued to the public, when advertising its sale— an exception important to auction houses.[43] An artist may copy his own earlier work, provided that he does not repeat or imitate its main design.[44] A building may be reconstructed without infringing copyright in it or the original drawings or plans.[45]

In addition there are exclusions and limitations which are crucial to the new scheme of protection for industrial design, which are reserved for discussion in Chapter 14.[46]

It is at this juncture that one meets the strictly limited rights recognised **11-031** in a typeface as a form of artistic work.[47] The copyright is restricted to making, importing and dealing in machines and other articles specifically designed or adapted for producing material in the typeface. It does not extend to using the typeface itself. The right in relation to machines lasts for 25 years from the first marketing of the machines.[48]

[37] s.35.
[38] s.60.
[39] s.74.
[40] s.36; see below, §§ 13-010—13-012.
[41] s.66; see below, § 13-013.
[42] s.62; extending to certain consequential acts: s.62(3).
[43] s.63—not extending to subsequent dealings for any other purpose.
[44] s.64.
[45] s.65.
[46] ss.51 and 52 are discussed at §§ 14-021—14-025.
[47] This is assumed in the Act from *Stephenson Blake* v. *Grant Legros* (1916) 33 R.P.C. 406.
[48] ss.54, 55. This will enable the U.K. to ratify the so-far inoperative Vienna Convention on Typefaces of 1973.

(3) Broadcasts and cable-casts

(a) Re-cabling

11-032   Where a broadcast is immediately re-transmitted by cable within the area of reception for the broadcast, the cable-casting is not an infringement of the broadcast, provided that it is not encrypted or by satellite; nor is it infringement of any work included in the broadcast.[49] This exception, in its present version limited mainly to cases where poor reception is averted by cabling, is contested by some copyright owners as a derogation from the Berne Convention obligation to accord an exclusive right in the consequent cabling of a broadcast,[50] but that obligation may be conditioned by national legislation, as it is here.

(b) Free public showing

11-033   Where a broadcast or cable-cast is shown or played to a non-paying audience,[51] there is no infringement of copyright in the broadcast or cable-cast, nor in any sound recording or film contained in them.[52] This exception extends to provisions for residents or inmates of a "place" (e.g. a hotel, holiday camp, hospital or prison) and for members as an incident of membership of a club or society.

(c) Time-shifting

11-034   By way of considerable variation on the former law, a broadcast or cable-cast may be recorded for private and domestic use (as distinct from research and private study) in order to view it or listen to it at a more convenient time; the exception now extends to the works included in the transmission as well as the transmission itself.[53]

(d) Various

11-035   There are also provisions covering: incidental recording in the course of making a licensed broadcast or cable-cast of a work[54]; recordings by the supervisory bodies for the purpose of controlling broadcasting and cable-casting[55]; for making private photographs from television broadcasts or cable-casts[56]; for sub-titling broadcasts and cable-casts to the deaf, hard of hearing and handicapped[57]; and for archival purposes.[58]

(4) Public administration

11-036   The new Act contains a much expanded list of excepted activities connected with government. These include things done for the purpose of

---

[49] s.73. There is also an exception in respect of material which the Cable Authority requires to be included in a cable-cast (i.e. those granted rediffusion licences), which in turn is subject to special provision on damages: s.73(3).
[50] Art. 11bis (1), (2); Ricketson (1987) at 455–476.
[51] This concept is elaborately defined.
[52] s.72. Note the counter-provision on damages: s.72(4).
[53] s.70; see below, § 13-013.
[54] s.68.
[55] s.69.
[56] s.71.
[57] s.74.
[58] s.75.

Parliamentary and judicial proceedings, Royal Commissions and statutory inquiries,[59] and extend to direct reports of any of them. In addition various public records and other types of official information may be copied without licence in given ways.[60] The development is a counterpart to the new restriction in scope of Crown copyright, and it is discussed further in that context.

(5) Miscellaneous

(a) Anonymous and pseudonymous works

There is an ultimate exception, already discussed in relation to these types of work, where it is reasonable to suppose that copyright has expired.[61]   **11-037**

(b) Extracts in recital

A solo reading or recitation of a reasonable extract from a literary or dramatic work may be made in public with sufficient acknowledgment; and a recording, broadcast or cable-cast may be made of it, if mainly of material not covered by the exception.[62]   **11-038**

(c) Folksong recordings

A designated non-profit organisation may record a song for an archive, and make copies available for private study or research, even though there is copyright in the words or music, provided that the words are unpublished and of unknown authorship.[63]   **11-039**

(d) Works in electronic form

Where the purchaser of a legitimate copy of, say, a computer program, is entitled himself to make further copies, he transfers this additional power when he transfers the copy to another, unless there are express conditions to the contrary.[64]   **11-040**

4. PUBLIC POLICY

In contradistinction to the statutorily defined defences just mentioned, the judges have kept the power to refuse protection to a copyright owner on public policy grounds,[65] and these we may divide into two kinds.

---

[59] ss.45, 46.
[60] ss.47–50; below, §§ 13-044 et seq.
[61] s.57; for joint authorship see s.57(3).
[62] s.59.
[63] s.61. This should be related to the special arrangements under s.169 for according overseas protection authorities to exercise copyright in respect of folksongs that are part of their national heritage.
[64] s.56; see below, § 13-019.
[65] See now CDPA 1988, s.171(3).

(1) Policy against legal protection

11-041   A line of cases justifies the refusal of relief on a variety of grounds which express disapproval of the content of the work: because it is obscene, sexually immoral, defamatory, blasphemous, irreligious, or seriously deceptive of the public.[66] Thus Elinor Glyn's *Three Weeks*, however opaque its voluptuousness may seem today, was condemned in 1916 as a "glittering record of adulterous sensuality masquerading as superior virtue."[67] A trade catalogue which contained misleading statements about the plaintiff's patents and the size of his premises was not protected.[68] While the power to refuse the assistance of the court survives, it is likely to be exercised today only in clear cases; in particular, some of the early nineteenth century decisions should be treated with caution.[69]

(2) Policy favouring dissemination

11-042   The ability to protect confidential information, it will be recalled, is qualified by considerations of public interest. The same considerations were held in *Beloff* v. *Pressdram* to affect copyright; they created a defence arising outside the statute and based on a general common law principle.[70] In that case, the work consisted of a journalist's private memorandum to colleagues about a Cabinet Minister's view on the succession to the leadership of the Conservative Party. A narrow view was taken of what might be justified in the public interest: it was necessary to show an "iniquity" or "misdeed," and so the defence did not succeed on the facts.[71] But some of the breach of confidence cases already discussed take a broader view of the general principle.[72] These would seem equally applicable to copyright.

5. ACTIONS FOR INFRINGEMENT

11-043   Copyright infringements give rise to a range of remedies, civil, criminal and administrative as well as of self-help. These have been mentioned in the introductory chapter on the subject.[73] All are today important, particularly given the very considerable quantity of pirate copying that

[66] See Phillips (1977) 6 Anglo-Am.L.R. 138; and for the same factors in breach of confidence, above, § 8-010.

[67] *Glyn* v. *Weston Feature Film* [1916] 1 Ch. 261 at 269–270; *cf.* now *Stephens* v. *Avery* (above, § 8-010, n. 35).

[68] *Slingsby* v. *Bradford Patent Truck* [1906] W.N. 51 (C.A.); and see *Wright* v. *Tallis* (1845) 1 C.B. 863 (book passed off as the work of a well-known author; no cause of action to protect copyright in it).

[69] See Younger J., *Glyn's* case (above, n. 67) at 269. During Lord Eldon's Chancellorship, this form of "negative censorship" went particularly far: as in *Murray* v. *Benbow* (1822) Jac. 474n (Byron's "Cain" refused protection); *Lawrence* v. *Smith* (1822) Jac. 471. *cf.* also *Stockdale* v. *Onwhyn* (1826) 5 B. & C. 173 ("memoirs" of a prostitute). For further case-law, see Copinger, §§ 182–187.

[70] [1973] 1 All E.R. 241 at 259.

[71] *Ibid.* at § 261.

[72] Above, §§ 8-011—8-018.

[73] Above, Chap. 2.

continues to plague the record, film and television industries; and none more so than the recently developed *Anton Piller* order for inspection.[74] The whole territory will not be traversed again, comment being restricted here to a number of special provisions affecting civil actions.

(1) Damages

Copyright is a property right invaded by the particularly unfair step of **11-044** copying. At the same time, to some extent it serves to protect an individual's desire to keep his affairs private. Until the 1988 Act this was reflected particularly in the exceptional entitlement to "conversion damages"—essentially for the value of infringing copies as property—as distinct from "infringement damages." This advantage came, however, to be considered too draconian, and conversion damages were abolished by the 1988 Act. The new law, however, expands the possibility of claiming "additional damages" and delivery up for disposal, both of which are discussed below.[75]

The usual basis for claiming substantial damages for infringement relates to the commercial value of the work[76]: as with patents, the claim is either for compensation for lost profits—because the defendant's infringements have lost the plaintiff his own opportunities for sale. How far this will be assumed from the very fact of the defendant's piratical sales depends on the particular circumstances.[77] Alternatively, the claim is for the misappropriation—because the plaintiff has lost the chance of licensing or selling his copyright to the defendant.[78] As part of such a claim, the plaintiff is entitled to show that the cheap or vulgar form of the defendant's piracy injured his reputation and so lost him sales,[79] indeed it has been presumed, in the absence of explanation from the defendant, that a film's lack of success was due to the existence of poor quality copies on the market.[80]

Injury to reputation may, however, have little or nothing to do with **11-045** the commercial popularity of the work; the psychological effect, the injury to feelings, may be much more significant. The 1988 Act allows a court to award damages "in addition to all other material considerations," having regard to the flagrancy of the infringement and any benefit to the defendant, and this is now possible without having to consider whether effective relief is otherwise available.[81] In light of the rule that damages must normally be compensatory rather than punitive,[82] it has been said that "additional damages" under the Copyright Act are to be so regarded, being designed to assuage the extra injury to the defendant's

---

[74] See above, §§ 2-029—2-033.
[75] See Whitford Report, § 701, 702. CA 1988, Sched. 1, § 30(2): actions claiming conversion damages under CA 1956, s.18, must have been begun before August 1, 1989.
[76] But this approach may not always be followed: see Bowen C.J., *Interfirm Comparison* v. *Law Society* (1975) 6 A.L.R. 445 at 446–447.
[77] *Columbia Pictures* v. *Robinson* [1988] F.S.R. 531.
[78] Above, §§ 2-023—2-026.
[79] Lord Wright M.R., *Sutherland* v. *Caxton* [1936] Ch. 323 at 336.
[80] *Columbia Pictures* case (above, n. 77).
[81] CA 1988, s.96(2); *cf.* CA 1956, s.17(3).
[82] Above, § 2-025.

feelings from the aggravating circumstances of the infringement.[83] On this basis, "additional" damages may lie against a professional photographer for supplying the press with a wedding photo which included a man subsequently murdered, without any consent from the member of the man's family who owned the copyright[84]; or against a lampooning magazine which published a confidential memorandum written by a journalist to her colleagues, thereby damaging her reputation as a Parliamentary correspondent.[85] But an exemplary award could still be made where the infringement was intended to be specially profitable.[86]

(2) Presumptions in copyright infringement actions

11-046   It is no longer provided in the 1988 Act that, if the defendant wishes to dispute the subsistence of copyright or the plaintiff's title, he must put the matter in issue by pleading it. They accordingly take their place alongside all other assertions which the plaintiff makes and must, if necessary, prove. There are, however, statutory presumptions which throw the legal burden of proof upon the defendant to infringement proceedings. Where literary, dramatic, musical or artistic copyright is concerned these are:

(i) that a person named as author is the author of a work; and that he did not produce it in circumstances (such as the course of employment) which would deprive him of the copyright initially.[87] If this does not apply, then:

(ii) that if first publication of a work qualifies it for copyright, copyright subsists and was owned at first publication by the person named as publisher.[88] In any case:

(iii) that, where the author is dead or unidentifiable when the action is brought, the work was original and was first published where and when the plaintiff alleges.[89]

As regards copyright in sound recordings, films and computer programs, there are presumptions that statements naming the copyright owner, and, or giving the date or place of first publication, are true.[90]

---

[83] Lord Kilbrandon, *Cassell v. Broome* [1972] A.C. 1027 at 1134; Ungoed Thomas J., *Beloff v. Pressdram* (above, n. 70) at 265; and see *Prior v. Lansdowne* [1977] R.P.C. 511 (S.C. Victoria); *Herbert v. Ravenscroft* [1980] R.P.C. 193 at 208.

[84] As in *Williams v. Settle* [1960] 1 W.L.R. 1072 (C.A.), which however was decided as a case on exemplary damages. For ownership of copyright in these circumstances today, see below, and for the consequential right of privacy, § 11-059.

[85] *Beloff* case (above, n. 70) at 264–272; but the plaintiff failed for want of title (below, §§ 12-003 — 12-070).

[86] The Whitford Committee, § 704, treated s.17(3) as conferring the power to award exemplary damages.

[86] *cf.* CA 1956, s.20(1).

[87] s.104(2); and for the same presumptions in relation to each of joint authors, s.104(3).

[88] s.104(4). This affects anonymous works: see above, § 10-030.

[89] s.104(5).

[90] s.105. The statements are also admissible as evidence of the facts stated and may apply in relation to infringements occurring before the publication or similar act.

6. MORAL RIGHTS[91]

This chapter ends with a return to basic principle. The authors' rights of **11-047** continental Europe grew from a deep respect for intellectual creativity and so looked to protect moral integrity as much as economic return. The moral rights of the author were the first object of the law and only when they were secure was it proper to turn to the economic rights[91a]: Anglo-American tradition viewed the matter more from the market-place, and, by refusing to adopt positive rules, manifested a certain scepticism towards the author, composer or artist who failed to look after his own reputation and integrity.[92]

Since most of the practical problems arose between the author and those with whom he dealt in exploitation of his work, the author could provide much of what he might want by contractual stipulation. Beyond that he might be helped by the law of confidence, defamation, passing-off, injurious falsehood, and the general economic torts. Thus, in *Humphreys* v. *Thompson*,[93] a jury found an authoress to have been defamed by a newspaper serialisation of her story in which the names of the characters were simplified, passages of description were omitted and "curtains" were added at the beginning and end of each episode to what readers' appetites. Her reputation had thus been lowered in the eyes of right-thinking members of the public. In *Samuelson* v. *Producers Distributing*,[94] the defendant put out a film of a revue sketch, wrongly claiming it to be the plaintiff's. Because the plaintiff's piece was well-known, thanks to its inclusion in a royal variety performance, this constituted a form of passing-off. Subsequently the Copyright Act 1956, section 43, by creating a tort of misattribution, extended the range of legal protection, since it eliminated the need to show any established reputation with the public. Otherwise, the legislature in 1956 followed the Gregory Committee's view of *les droits moraux* as suspiciously foreign.[95] It felt no need to confer an explicit *droit de paternité* (right to claim authorship) or *droit au respect de l'œuvre* (right of integrity), let

---

[91] See Dworkin and Taylor Chap. 8; and *cf.* Copyright Law Review Committee (Australia), *Report on Moral Rights* (1988); Parliamentary Sub-Committee (Canada) *A Charter of Rights for Authors* (1985); Vaver (1987) 25 Osgoode Hall L.J. 749.

[91a] High thinking led to a division between the "dualist" theory of moral and economic rights, allowing the former to be perpetual as well as inalienable; and the "monist" theory which subjects both to the same essential characteristics. The French adopted the first, the Germans the second, theory. For the entire history, see the magisterial Stromholm, *Le droit moral de l'auteur* (1967).

[92] For "moral rights" at common law see Dworkin (1981) 12 I.I.C. 476; [1986] E.I.R. 329; and for comparisons between the U.S. and France, Sarrauté (1968) 16 Am. J. Comp.L. 465, Treece, *ibid.* 487.

[93] [1905–1910] Mac. C.C. 148; and see *Lee* v. *Gibbings* (1892) 67 L.J. 263; *Frisby* v. *B.B.C.* (above, n. 23).

[94] Below, § 16-035; for a similar case in defamation, *Ridge* v. *English Illustrated Magazine* [1911–1916] Mac. C.C. 91.

[95] See Cmd. 8662, 1952, § 222.

alone to enshrine these rights, or other manifestations of the same idea,[96] as inalienable and incapable of waiver in advance of actual publication or other use of the work. Yet the United Kingdom, unlike the United States at that juncture, was preparing to ratify the Brussels Act of the Berne Convention; and Art. 6*bis* of that Convention had come to require, at least during the author's lifetime, that these two forms of moral right should be part of a member country's copyright law (and now by its Paris Act, the Convention requires the rights to extend for the duration of the economic rights).[97]

11-048   In 1977, the Whitford Committee accepted that these moral rights should be translated into British law to a reasonable extent.[98] This proposal set in train the search for a formulation which would retain due respect for freedom and sanctity of contract and would protect entrepreneurs in their turn from being held to ransom as infringers of moral rights at a time when it would be difficult and expensive to rectify the wrong.[99] It was this overbearing potential in foreign laws which had for long fuelled the common law antagonism towards them.

In the upshot, the 1988 Act defines four distinct moral rights, the first two of which are in fulfilment of Berne obligations: the right to be identified as author or director (the right of paternity), the right to object to derogatory treatment of a work (the right of integrity); the right against false attribution of a work; and the right to privacy in private photographs and films. Each has its own incidents, but all adopt one basic characteristic of such rights in other systems: that they are inalienable to others while being transmissible on death. Where they depart from more severely protective systems, is in the extent to which they may be compromised in advance.

(1) Right to be identified

(a) *Entitlement and duration*

11-049   The right to be identified as author is given to the creators of literary, dramatic, musical and artistic works, and also to the director of a film, despite the fact that he enjoys no copyright.[1] It is not accorded to any

---

[96] Some systems carry moral protection much further: including also a right of divulgation (to decide when a work should be handed over or made public), a right of withdrawal (generally subject to compensation), a right to insist on completion if others are involved in realisation; and a right even to object to criticism by a person who at the same time exploits the work; see *e.g. Eds. Gallimard v. Hamish Hamilton* [1985] E.C.C. 574 (France).

[97] For Art. 6*bis.*, see especially Ricketson (1987) at 455–476; Plaisant (1986) 11 Col.–VLA J.L.A.A. 157.

[98] Cmnd. 6732, §§ 51–57, drawing attention to the Dutch law as a model.

[99] As where a minor author of a film script might object to his omission from the credits on the eve of the premiere.

[1] CDPA 1988, s.77(1); for joint authors and directors, see s.88(1), (5).

person who is treated by the Act as an "author" for copyright purposes. Here is a first indication that the moral rights are not simply an aspect of copyright, and accordingly need to be treated separately. Subject to a number of exceptions, this moral right applies to works existing at "commencement" in relation to publication, public exhibition and other acts done subsequently.[2]

The right inures only if the work itself is copyright—so the same qualification rules apply as for copyright. It lasts for the same period as the copyright.[3]

(b) *Assertion*

It is a pre-condition of the right that it be asserted. In general, this may **11-050** be done as a statement in an instrument assigning copyright in the work or by any other instrument in writing signed by the author or director during the life of the right.[4] If it is made as part of an assignment, the assertion binds the assignee and anyone claiming through him, with or without notice; whereas if it is made by another instrument, it binds only those with notice of it.[5] Thus an assertion has in principle only to be made in the required form to any exploiter of the work for it to impose on him the obligation to identify the author or director; but delay in making the assertion is to be taken into account in determining whether an injunction shall be granted and also, it seems, in settling damages and other relief.[6]

(c) *Preclusion*

In contradistinction with truly protective regimes of moral rights, it is **11-051** possible for the person who would otherwise enjoy any of the four rights to surrender it in advance of the time when an issue actually arises—such as, for instance, a publisher's decision to exclude an author's name from a pending publication. The waiver may be by instrument in writing signed by the person giving up the right, and it may relate not only to a specific work in existence, but to a class of works or even works in general, and to future works. It may be the subject of a condition and it may be revocable.[7] Such express consent does not require contractual consideration. But an informal waiver may also be operative under general principles of contract or estoppel.[8] So conduct of an author or director on which another person relies in the belief that identification will not be insisted upon (whether or not there has already been an assertion) may well preclude any subsequent enforcement of the moral right.

[2] Scheds. 1, 22, 23. The main exceptions are: of the work of an author dead at commencement, works whose initial copyright invested in someone other than the author; films made before commencement; and anything done in pursuance of a licence or assignment by an author-owner. Because of the complete exclusion of films, there is no scope for using this right to object in the U.K. to the coloration of black-and-white movies.

[3] s.86.

[4] s.78(1), (2). There are additional provisions concerning the assertion of the right in relation to public exhibition of an artistic work: s.78(3).

[5] s.78(4).

[6] s.78(5).

[7] s.87(1)–(3).

[8] s.87(4).

(d) *Acts covered*

11-052   The occasions on which an author or director may insist upon
identification are so defined as to incorporate a "disc-jockey" exception.
Thus the author of most literary, dramatic and artistic works and
directors of films may require identification upon copies being published
commercially, copies or a sound recording or film being issued to the
public, performance or showing in public, broadcasting or cable-casting.[9]
However, authors of musical works, and of words intended to be sung or
spoken with music, do not have the right in respect of public performances, broadcasting and cable-casting.[10] In each case, the identification
has to be likely to bring the identity to the attention of those acquiring a
copy, listening to a performance, etc.[11]

There are other special cases. In particular, although copyright itself
does not extend to the public exhibition of artistic works, there is a right
to be identified as artist at a public exhibition.[12] For this purpose,
moreover, the right is sufficiently asserted by attaching an identification
to the work or a copy when the author or other first owner of copyright
parts with possession of it, or the assertion is included in a licence to
make copies of the work; in either case notice is not necessary to bind
third parties.[13]

11-053   Equally, there is a substantial list of exceptions. There is no right of
identification in computer programs, computer-generated works, or typefaces, or works which are Crown or similar copyright.[14] Where a work or
film is made in the course of employment, the employer as first owner of
the copyright, is not obliged to make the identification; nor is anyone
else who acts with his authority.[15] Publication in a newspaper, magazine
or periodical, or in an encyclopedia or similar work, is excluded.[16] A
number of the exceptions applicable to copyright also apply to the right
to be identified: fair dealing for the purpose of reporting current events
in a sound recording, film, broadcast or cable-cast, incidental inclusion in
an artistic work, sound recording, film, broadcast or cable-cast; the
exclusion and limitation of artistic copyright in the sphere of industrial
design; and other more specific cases.

(e) *Impact*

11-054   The right to be identified is inherently more likely to be of importance
to those who have a reputation still to establish than those whose name
will attract attention on a publication or through other exploitation. The
right does however extend not only to failure to name anyone but also to
plagiarism of work under the name of another, and here even the famous
may have occasion to complain.

---

[9] s.77(2), (3).
[10] See s.77(7), for a full definition of sufficient identification; and s.77(8) for the form to be
adopted.
[11] s.77(4)(a). For works of architecture, sculptures and works of artistic craftsmanship, see
s.77(4)(c).
[12] ss.78(3), 78(4)(c), (d).
[13] s.79(2), (7).
[14] s.79(3).
[15] s.79(6).
[16] s.79(4).

Among lesser authors and directors, it is those who provide work for others in some capacity, without becoming employees[17], who are most likely to be aggrieved by non-identification. There will be some circumstances where by implication the right has been contractually excluded.[18] The person who is commissioned to act as ghost-writer for another would be presumed to accept the consequences. But that is not necessarily the implication between members of a research team in writing up the results. Equally the photographer who supplies material for a book or a film may well have done nothing to raise the belief that he would not claim to be identified.

(2) Right to object to derogatory treatment[19]

(a) Entitlement and duration

As in the previous case, this is given to authors in respect of literary, **11-055** dramatic, musical and artistic works, and to directors in respect of their films, to the extent that they are the subject of, and remain in, copyright.[20] It is a right which draws upon the Berne Convention, Article 6*bis*, though it is in apparently narrower terms. Objection may be raised to "derogatory treatment" of the work, which requires demonstration (a) that the work is subject to addition, deletion, alteration or adaptation; and (b) that this "amounts to distortion or mutilation of the work or is otherwise prejudicial to the honour or reputation of the author or director.[21] It is not an infraction of this right to place a work in a context which subjects it to criticism or ridicule—for instance, using a painting in an exhibition deliberately to show up the superiority of other paintings or to cast aspersions on the artist's life-style. There will, of course, be borderline cases: a production of a sentimental comedy in a vein of social criticism intended to deride the genre will offend, provided that the text is altered or explicit stage instructions are defied.

The right does not depend upon any pre-condition, such as assertion. But, as with the other moral rights, it can be precluded by consent or other waiver.[22] However, those who seek to achieve this by an advance provision in a contract of exploitation will need to express themselves in unequivocal terms; for it is inherently unlikely that an author or director will be wishing to expose himself to alterations even if they are prejudicial to his honour and reputation.[23]

(b) Acts covered

In general authors and directors may object to derogatory treatment **11-056** occurring in copies being published commercially, copies of a sound

---

[17] In general, employees in any case do not have the right: above n. 15.
[18] Since the new British law will still be less categoric than in other systems, the question of which law governs, *e.g.*, assignments and licences will remain important; see, the French Cour d'Appel's decision in *Rowe* v. *Walt Disney* [1987] F.S.R. 37.
[19] See Goldstein (1983) 14 I.I.C. 43.
[20] s.80(1); for the term, s.86(1). As to joint authorship and direction, see s.88(2), (5).
[21] s.80(2). Article 6*bis* refers to "distortion, mutilation or other modification of, *or other derogatory action in relation to,* [the work]" (italics added).
[22] s.87.
[23] See, *e.g. Frisby* v. *B.B.C.* [1967] Ch. 932 (below, § 12-006).

recording or film being made available to the public, performance, playing and showing in public, broadcasting and cable-casting.[24] There are, however, some major exceptions and limitations. The right does not apply in relation to translation, or transposition of the key or register of a musical work[25]; to computer programs or computer generated works; to any work made for the purpose of reporting current events; to publication in a newspaper, magazine or periodical or encyclopedia or similar work, or any unmodified subsequent publication therefrom.[26] In the case of a work of architecture, the architect has no right other than to have his identification as architect removed from the building.[27] In the case of works made in employment, or which are Crown or similar copyright, an author or director who is identified may only insist upon a sufficient disclaimer of association with the work as altered.[28] The broadcasting authorities also have power to make excisions and alterations in order to stop the broadcasting of anything offensive to good taste and decency, or which could encourage or incite to crime, lead to disorder or offend public feeling.[29] In the clean new world of broadcasting, this may be a provision which is relied upon with some frequency.

(c) *Impact*

11-057   It will be plain that many of the recurrent circumstances in which anxiety and objection arise over derogatory treatment have been excised or anæsthetised, so far as the new right is concerned, particularly through the provisions relating to employment, the press, current affairs and, above all perhaps, translation. In the past, directors of films have been known to complain about the manner in which producers intent on maximising the commercial potential of their investment have compromised the artistic integrity of the film by subsequent cutting or interpolation. Doubtless in the future they will use express stipulations to procure the ability to do the same. But to the extent that they do not, the director will have a power of objection more readily enforced than the vestigial possibilities at common law of suing for defamation, trade libel or some form of passing off. But at the end of the day in court, he may secure no more than an order that the work be published with a disclaimer dissociating him from it.[30]

(3) False attribution

11-058   This moral right is the converse of the right to be identified. It is an amplification of rights contained in the Copyright Act 1956, section 43. A person to whom a literary, dramatic, musical or artistic work is attributed as author, or to whom a film is attributed as director, has the

[24] s.80(3)–(6); and note s.80(7) on parts of works previously treated by others.
[25] s.80(2)(a).
[26] s.81(2)–(5).
[27] s.80(5).
[28] s.82.
[29] s.81(6) (and for the Independent Broadcasting Authority, see the Broadcasting Act 1981, s.4(1)). The right to alter in order to avoid commission of an offence or in compliance with statutory duty is general.
[30] See s.103(2).

right to object when that attribution is false.[31] The objection may be in relation to the issue of copies to the public, public exhibition of an artistic work (or copy of it), public performance or showing, broadcast or cable-cast of a literary, dramatic or musical work or a film.[32] Here there is also a secondary wrong (requiring proof of knowledge or reason to believe that there is false attribution) which consists in possessing or dealing with a copy of the work in the course of business: also in the case of an artistic work, dealing with it in business as the unaltered work of the artist, when in fact it was altered after leaving his possession.[33] These rights endure for 20 years from the year of death of the subject of the false attribution.[34]

(4) Right to privacy

This, the first acknowledgement in English law of any right to privacy, **11-059** operates only in strictly delimited circumstances, and is a corollary of shifting the first ownership of certain artistic works from the person who commissioned them to the person who created them or his employer.[35] Under the new Act, where a person commissions a photograph or a film for private or domestic purposes, and that work attracts copyright, he has the right to object to issuing copies to the public, public exhibition or showing, broadcasting or cable-casting.[36] To this there are certain exceptions which also apply to copyright, of which the most general is incidental inclusion in an artistic work, film, broadcast or cable-cast.[37]

The right lasts as long as the copyright and is given independently to each joint co-commissioner.[38] It will be of value in those cases where a wedding group or party picture contains someone who subsequently becomes newsworthy, and will be assertable both where copyright is in a commercial photographer or film-maker, or in a relative or friend who undertakes the task for nothing, since the commission does not here have to be for money or money's worth. Like all rights accorded to protect privacy, it has the potential to become a right to share in the publicity value of the work; just as much as the copyright owner, the commissioner may choose to sell his power to consent to publication or other use. In recent tragic circumstances, the issue arose (under the 1956 Act) whether a wife, who had suffered a brain haemorrhage and was being kept alive to give birth, was the joint commissioner with her husband of their wedding photographs. The husband sought to grant exclusive rights in them to one newspaper; the action was to prevent another from using them when it procured copies from the photographer.[39] It remains to be seen, under the new law, whether the commissioner's action for breach of

---

[31] s.84(1); in relation to joint works, see s.88(4), (5).
[32] s.84(2).
[33] s.84(3).
[34] s.86(2).
[35] See below, §§ 12-002 et seq.
[36] s.85(1).
[37] s.85(2).
[38] ss.86, 88(6).
[39] *Mail Newspapers* v. *Express Newspapers* [1987] F.S.R. 90.

statutory duty will be treated as akin to a proprietary right to exploit publicity value, and, if so, how it will operate as between joint commissioners and on the death of a commissioner.[40]

---

[40] Note in this connection that the right is probably intended to survive the commissioner's death since it is given for the long period of the photographer's death and 50 years thereafter. For a comparison with the much more developed concept of privacy/publicity in the U.S., see Buchanan [1988] E.I.P.R. 227, (1988) 16 Golden Gate U.L.R. 30.

CHAPTER 12

PROPERTY RIGHTS AND EXPLOITATION

In English law, the rules concerning ownership of copyright function **12-001** within a frame of freedom of contract. The starting point of any inquiry must therefore be with any express agreement on the subject, for if this exists it will govern (subject to very limited exceptions).[1] The Act contains rules for determining who is the initial owner in the absence of agreement.[2] These too are important: much copyright, after all, is created without there being any contract concerning its exploitation; and much else arises under contracts which are obscure on the question.

This chapter deals with the question of first ownership, then with methods of dealing by assignment and licence and finally with some public policy rules (including those of the EEC) which impose constraints upon free bargaining.

1. INITIAL OWNERSHIP

(1) Literary, dramatic, musical and artistic works

(a) *Legal framework*

Because copyright arises upon creation of the work, the question of **12-002** initial ownership is not complicated, as is the case with patents and registered designs, by any need to apply for a grant. In literary, dramatic, musical and artistic works, first ownership rests in the author or co-authors unless the exception concerning employment applies.[3] This is a simpler rule than under the 1956 Act which also contained special provisions concerning employed journalists and certain artistic works made under commission.[4] It is not, however, the solution proposed by the

---

[1] For which see below, § 12-018.
[2] Below, §§ 12-002—12-006.
[3] CDPA 1988, s.11; and for the concept of authorship (s.9), see above §§ 10-003, 10-016. Crown and Parliamentary copyright is also subject to special rules: s.11(3); see below, § 13-044. Co-authorship is discussed below, § 12-010. See generally Stephenson (1980) 2 E.I.P.R. 19.
[4] CA 1956, s.4; preserved for works made before "commencement" of the 1988 Act, by the latter's Sched. 1, § 11. .

Whitford Committee, since it allows the copyright owner to have all the rights even when an unintended exploitation of the work materialises.[5]

(b) Employment

12-003   For the types of work under consideration, an employer becomes the initial owner of the copyright if it is made by his employee in the course of the employment and in the absence of contrary agreement.

What falls within the scope of the employment will depend upon the nature and terms of the job and the relation of the work to it.[6] But while it is often clear whether or not an invention relates to an employer's business, with copyright material the issue may well be obscure. A senior executive in a firm of management consultants wrote public lectures about the budgetary control of firms; he was held entitled to the copyright in them.[7] So also was a journalist who undertook a piece of translation and editing from the Portuguese as a special task outside his normal hours of employment; it made no difference that the piece was for an advertisement in his employer's newspaper.[8] But another journalist who wrote an internal memorandum to her colleagues about a possible article was held to be acting strictly within the course of her employment.[9]

The distinction between servants and independent contractors— between those under contracts of service and contracts for services—is a familiar part of the principles governing vicarious liability (in which context it has already been discussed)[10] and it has become increasingly important with the growing variety of labour laws. It was in the context of copyright ownership that Denning L.J. suggested that the old test of whether the person contracting for the work could exercise control over how it was done was becoming obsolete; the question ought rather to be whether the person performing it was doing so as an integral part of the business.[11]

Under the former law, the employed journalist was permitted to have copyright in exploitations of his work beyond the purpose for which it was created, and there was some case for making this a general rule.[12] Instead, amid loud cries of "anomaly," from the newspaper industry, the exception was cut away and all employees were left to bargain for special arrangements.

[5] See further below, § 13-006.
[6] CDPA 1988, s.11(2). The distinction is essentially similar to that concerning patent rights: see above, §§ 7-003–7-005.
[7] Stephenson Jordan v. McDonald & Evans (1951) 69 R.P.C. 10 (C.A.); but the employer was allowed copyright in a chapter written as part of an assignment for a particular client of the employer; see also Re Beeston [1913] 2 Ch. 279.
[8] Byrne v. Statist Co. [1914] 1 K.B. 622.
[9] Beloff v. Pressdram [1973] 1 All E.R. 241. The special rule for journalists could not apply because the memo was not for publication.
[10] Above, § 2-004.
[11] Stephenson Jordan case (above, n. 7) at 22.
[12] CA 1956, s.4(2); the Whitford Committee (Cmnd. 6732, 1977, § 574) looked with favour on a scheme of "compensation" for authors, similar to that affecting inventors; for which, see above, §§ 7-008 et seq.

(c) *Contracts to the contrary*

Where an employer is surrendering the initial copyright given him by **12-004**
law, the agreement does not have to be in any particular form and may
therefore be deduced from conduct and surrounding circumstances.
Where, however, an author is arranging that another person (such as a
commissioner of the work) shall have copyright in it, to confer that legal
title he must execute an assignment which complies with the formalities
required for an actual or a future work.[13] However, an informal
agreement, or indeed circumstances which give rise to fiduciary obligation, may have the effect in equity that the author from the outset holds
the copyright in trust. Thus, in the "Spycatcher" case, the ex-MI5 officer,
who wrote memoirs in flagrant breach of confidence owed to the Crown,
was said by members of the House of Lords to be under such an
obligation.[14]

In applying these flexible rules, it may well be important to know
whether the relevant presumption can be excluded by implication. If an
employed teacher writes a textbook for his subject, he may be entitled to
the copyright because he is employed to teach, not to write textbooks.[15]
But if writing the book is within the course of employment, he may
nevertheless be able to show that an authority employing him has not
claimed copyright from him in the past, or has not done so from other
teachers who have written similar books. From such evidence an agreement that any copyright is to be the teacher's could well be applied.

(2) Entrepreneurial copyright

The Part II copyrights are conferred initially upon the "author- **12-005**
creators" who are responsible for organising production of the material
(see the Table (§ 10-003), lines 4 and 8). This has already been
discussed.[16]

2. ASSIGNMENTS AND LICENSING

(1) The distinction

The most lucrative copyright works are often exploited in a number of **12-006**
ways. Take a popular novel: there are the volume rights, the serial rights
(in newspapers and magazines), the translation rights, the film rights, the
dramatisation rights (play, opera, musical, ballet); soon there may need
to be electronic rights to call it up from store. Add the fact that for some
of these it may be desirable to split the rights of exploitation language by
language; and there is the possibility of dealing with each national
copyright separately. The result is an elaborate concoction of prospects.

[13] For the requirements, see below, § 12-007.
[14] *Att.-Gen.* v. *Guardian Newspapers (No. 2)* [1988] 3 All E.R. 545 at 645 (Lord Keith),
647 (Lord Brightman); *cf.* 604 (Lord Goff). Note, in the context of good faith, the moral
right of privacy in certain photographs and films, above, § 11-059.
[15] It seems that university teachers (or at least Cambridge professors) are to be so regarded:
Lord Evershed M.R., *Stephenson Jordan* case (above, n. 7) at 18; see also *Warner* v.
Gestetner (1989) (to be reported).
[16] Above, § 10-016.

As far as British copyright is concerned, the Act permits the various rights bundled together as copyright not only to be licensed but also to be assigned separately.[17] It is possible to assign for a limited term within the copyright period.[18] Often, therefore, there is a choice whether to grant rights by assignment or by exclusive licence. Provided the contract in which the grant is made is clear about consequential matters, it makes no difference which type is used.[19] But if ambiguities are left, their resolution may be affected by the fact that an assignment is in essence a transfer of ownership (however partial), while a licence is in essence permission to do what otherwise would be infringement.[20] Thus a licensee's freedom to make alterations in the work may be more restricted than an assignee's[21]; the licensee may well not be entitled to assign or sub-license his interest,[22] while his licensor will retain the right (so far as he has not promised exclusivity to the licensee) to grant licences to others.

(2) Formal requirements

(a) *Statutory provisions*

12-007   Assignments of copyright (*i.e.* the legal right of ownership) only take effect if they are in writing, signed by or on behalf of the assignor.[23] Once this is complied with the assignment is effective against all subsequent takers of conflicting interests. There is no public register of copyright transactions and any assignee takes the risk that there are no prior assignments of which he does not know. If there are, his only recourse may well be against his assignor.[24] Agreements to assign future copyright which are signed by or on behalf of the prospective owner have the effect of automatically vesting legal ownership in the assignee. But there must be no other person with a superior equity.[25]

---

[17] CDPA 1988, s.90. The right assigned can be part of a head (such as the right of reproduction or of publishing) in the list of exclusive rights. Thus the right to reproduce a book in French translation may be separately assigned. Terms purporting to giving exclusive rights over acts beyond the scope of copyright can take effect only in contract.

[18] s.90(2)(b)—but no longer for part of the U.K.: an EEC influence.

[19] A not uncommon practice has been to blur the boundary by "giving" (not "granting") the exclusive right to (say) publish. It is then a question of construction to decide which is meant. Failure to use an appropriate technical word does not preclude a finding of assignment: *Chaplin* v. *Frewin* [1966] Ch. 71 at 94 (C.A.); and see Lahore §§ 949–950.

[20] But if more than a bare permission, it will acquire the status of a property right: see further, esp. on the licensor's consequent power of revocation, Lahore §§ 922, 928 *et seq.*

[21] See below, § 12-016.

[22] See below, § 12-014.

[23] s.90(3); *Roban Jig* v. *Taylor* [1979] R.P.C. 130 (C.A.). Agreements which do not comply with the formal requirements may still be effective to transfer an equitable interest: *Warner* v. *Gestetner* [1989] to be reported. But an assignment of a purely equitable interest must satisfy the formal requirements of the Law of Property Act 1925, s.53(1)(*c*): *Roban Jig* case.

[24] By way of action for breach of condition of good title or for money paid upon a total failure of consideration.

[25] s.91(1), (2). The assignment probably has to be for valuable consideration; and see *Wah Sang* v. *Takmay* [1980] F.S.R. 303 (C.A., H.K.).

Licences do not in principle have to take any particular form. But an exclusive licensee will have no right to sue infringers unless the licence complies with similar formalities to those for assignments.[26] Licences bind all successors in title[27] to the licensor's interest except a purchaser in good faith for the valuable consideration and without notice (actual or constructive) and those who take from such a person.[28]

(b) *Implied licences*

Licences are frequently to be implied from the circumstances in which **12-008** copyright material is handed over. A commission to prepare the work may well carry this inference, at least to the extent that is customary. In *Blair v. Osborne & Tomkins*,[29] an architect was hired to prepare plans for the submission of a planning application and was paid for the work to this point. After securing permission, the landowner built in a way that reproduced the plans, and was held to have an implied licence to do so even though he had not employed the architect to supervise construction of the building. But if the architect charges a nominal fee, rather than a proportion of the full scale fee, for his work up to the planning permission stage, and he makes it clear that no licence is being conferred for actual construction, he will not be held to have conferred one (at least in the absence of further factors).[30]

There may also be an implied licence without any initial commission from the licensee. A "letter to the editor" on a theme of public interest is taken to be intended for publication,[31] so also is a submission of material to a magazine, subject to any customary royalty.[32]

(c) *Trans-national movement of goods*

Expressly or impliedly, a licence may confer authority to produce copies **12-009** of copyright works in one country and then to transship them to another, whatever the prohibitions in the copyright law of the second against importation. It will be recalled that in our law, imports into the United Kingdom will infringe if, had the goods been made in Britain, they would have infringed copyright or breached an exclusive licence, to the importer's knowledge or reasonable belief.[33] Thus, provided that the goods are actually made outside Britain, it is not relevant to consider whether they were legitimately made under the copyright law of that place.

---

[26] ss.101, 102; see above, § 2-002.

[27] This does not clearly cover a later licensee, when one or other licence is exclusive; but he ought to be similarly treated.

[28] s.90(4). Licences of future copyright are similarly treated: s.91(3).

[29] *Blair v. Osborne & Tomkins* [1971] 2 Q.B. 78 (C.A.); and see *Beck v. Montana Constructions* [1964–1965] N.S.W.R. 229.

[30] *Stovin-Bradford v. Volpoint* [1971] Ch. 1007 (C.A.); *cf.* also *Netupsky v. Dominion Bridge* (1969) 68 W.W.R. 529; *Barnett v. Cape Town Foreshore Board* (1960) [1978] F.S.R. 176.

[31] *Springfield v. Thame* (1903) 89 L.T. 242; the editor may also alter such a letter in order to fit it in. See further *Roberts v. Candiware* [1980] F.S.R. 352.

[32] *Hall-Brown v. Illiffe* [1928–1935] Mac. C.C. 88; *cf. PRS v. Coates* [1923–1928] Mac. C.C. 103.

[33] CDPA 1988, s.22, 27(3); see above § 11-022. It is now less clear that before that the defendant should have known all the necessary elements of deemed circumstance.

The extensive scope of British patent rights (which in principle cover even the subsequent resale and use of goods first marketed by the patentee) led, by way of counterbalance, to the presumption of a broad implied licence. If the patentee disposes of the goods without limiting the manner in which they may subsequently be dealt with, the implication is that there is no restriction on their circulation or use; but the contrary might be inferred from all the circumstances.[34] What, then, of a sale abroad of "legitimate" goods embodying copyright? Since copyright does not embrace subsequent sale and use, arguably the implied permission to export is the stronger. But in *Time-Life* v. *Interstate Parcel*[35] the High Court of Australia has refused to draw this analogy. Time-Life was exploiting its Australian copyright in certain cookery books by licensing it exclusively to a Dutch subsidiary, which in turn sub-licensed an exclusive distributor in Australia. A parallel importer bought its copies in the United States which were first marketed there by Time-Life.[36] The unconditional sales in America were held to carry no implied licence to import into Australia.[37] It was not therefore necessary to show either an express limitation ("Not for sale in Australia" or the like) or surrounding circumstances (such as knowledge of the exclusive distributorship) which would negate the implied licence.

An English court might be persuaded to draw the analogy to the patent cases which the High Court rejected. Even so, it will be seen that the argument is only about implied intent and the need to give sufficient notice that goods are not to be transferred from one national market to another. It is not about public policy rules overriding the copyright owner's wish to preserve price differentials between different countries by means of copyright.[38] Within the EEC, of course, the required free movement of goods is one such converse policy. Its impact upon national copyright law is discussed later[39]: for the moment the point to be taken is that the latter contains no general concept of international exhaustion.

As to the notional inquiry, would the making of the goods in Britain have constituted infringement, or breached an exclusive licence?: one must assume the act of manufacture to have been by the very person who performed it.[40] If this proves to be the world-wide copyright owner, the result used to be that the imports must be permissible, even though he

---

[34] See above § 6-011, n. 49. Note also that the implied licence was less embracing when the marketing abroad was by a licensee under the foreign patent.

[35] [1978] F.S.R. 251; Cornish and McGonigal (1981) 12 I.I.C.

[36] The parallel importers sold in Australia for just over half the exclusive distributors' retail price.

[37] An argument based upon the warranty of quiet possession got no further.

[38] Note, however, Murphy J.'s reference to possible breaches of the Trade Practices Act 1974 (Commonwealth): [1978] F.S.R. at 287–288.

[39] See below, § 12-031.

[40] *CBS U.K.* v. *Charmdale* [1980] 2 All E.R. 807; not following *Albert* v. *Fletcher* [1976] R.P.C. 615 (S.C.N.Z.) and distinguishing the terms of the Australian Copyright Act 1968, ss.37, 38. But the N.Z. courts continue their own course: *Barson Computers* v. *Gilbert* [1985] F.S.R. 489.

had granted an exclusive licence there; hence the additional inquiry, added in 1988: could such a licence have been broken? There are still difficulties for the copyright owner who exploits all markets himself and wishes to stop parallel importing into Britain.

(3) Co-ownership of copyright

Co-ownership may come about in two ways: because the copyright 12-010 material is produced by joint authors or because an interest is assigned to more than one person.[41] In each case, there are circumstances to be distinguished. Joint authorship does not arise where a creative work is compounded of parts that demand discrete forms of mental activity: the text and music for a song or opera; script, scenery and costume design for a play; an original text and a translation of it.[42] In such cases there are distinct copyrights, each with its own duration measured by relation to the life of the relevant author, each requiring for its exploitation the assent of the owner of that particular right.[43]

Co-authorship occurs when collaborators have worked to produce copyright work of a single kind "in prosecution of a preconcerted joint design."[44] It does not arise where one author writes a play, and another subsequently adds a scene to it; rather the first author brings into existence a copyright in what he has written, and likewise the second.[45] In the latter case, infringement of each copyright is a question whether there has been substantial copying of the work that each covers; neither derives advantage from the other's contribution.[46]

Co-ownership by assignment does not arise when different aspects of the copyright (publishing rights, performing rights, film rights, etc.) are transferred to different people: each has the exclusive right over his apportioned subject-matter.[47]

In contrast with patents, it has been held that a joint owner of copyright or a part of it is not entitled to do acts within its scope without securing permission from his fellows.[48] Equally a licensee needs

---

[41] In the case of assignment, whether the co-owners become joint tenants or tenants in common depends on the terms of the assignment. Joint authors have interests as tenants in common: *Lauri* v. *Renad* [1892] 3 Ch. 402; *Redwood* v. *Feldman* [1979] R.P.C. 1; Copinger § 372.

[42] See CDPA 1988, ss.3, 10.

[43] See also, above, § 10-009.

[44] *Levy* v. *Rutley* (1871) L.R. 6 C.P. 523 at 528, 529.

[45] Note the case of correcting and editing a text in the course of its production, which is treated as producing a joint work if the editor's contribution is sufficient to attract copyright at all: *Springfield* v. *Thame* (1903) 89 L.T. 242; *cf. Samuelson* v. *Producers Distributing* (1931) 48 R.P.C. 580 at 586.

[46] *e.g. Warwick Films* v. *Eisinger* (above, § 11-011).

[47] See s.90(2)(a).

[48] *Cescinsky* v. *Routledge* [1916] 2 K.B. 325, refusing to hold that the plaintiff (co-owner author) should be protected against the defendant (co-owner publisher) by necessary implication from the royalty clause in their publishing agreement. Arguably, this approach would have been sounder, leaving the basic rule as for patents (for which, see above, § 7-018).

permission from all his owners.[49] This can cause problems when it is not clear how many authors contributed to a joint work; for one thing, nice distinctions may have to be drawn between authors who participated in actually making the copyright work and preliminary contributors who put up starting ideas.[50]

3. DEALINGS BASED ON COPYRIGHT

12-011 Although copyright is in character a negative right, a large part of lawyers' business in the field is concerned with putting the protected subject-matter to positive use through contracts of exploitation. The various business organisations that make use of copyright material obtain it quite as much from freelance authors as from employees. One result is a great deal of contracting, some of it tailor-made, but much more standard or semi-standard in form. While large, well-established enterprises generally work with written agreements that deal explicitly with most of the likely legal issues, others prepare the ground less carefully. In their way, contracts exploiting copyright involve relationships over time that can be as complex as those arising from technology licences. In what follows attention will be given to the obviously important questions in this sort of contracting, taking by way of example the contract between publisher and independent author. The governing considerations for other types of copyright agreement naturally vary with the channels of exploitation that are relevant to the kind of subject-matter. Information about them must be sought in specialised works.[51]

(1) Considerations in a publishing contract

(a) *Author's basic obligations*
12-012 These are normally two: to deliver the completed work; and to assign to the publisher so much of the British and foreign copyright as is agreed, or to grant him a licence to publish (frequently exclusive).[52] If the work is still to be written its nature, content and length will need to be defined as clearly as possible.[53] Consideration must be given to whether all rights of publication are transferred or whether the right is restricted to (say) publication in volume form (as distinct from serial form)[54] and, if so,

---

[49] *Powell* v. *Head* (1879) 12 Ch.D. 686; *Mail Newspapers* v. *Express Newspapers* [1987] F.S.R. 90 (one co-owner clinically dead). As a corollary, one joint owner can sue without having to join others.

[50] *e.g.* if a ghost writer is commissioned to write up a celebrity's memoirs he alone is the author: *Evans* v. *Hulton* [1923–1928] Mac. C.C. 51; and see *Kenrick* v. *Lawrence* (above, § 10-011, n. 54); *Tate* v. *Thomas* (above, § 10-008, n. 37); but remember now the copyright of the speaker who is recorded: above § 10-019).

[51] In addition to the standard texts, see Flint, *A User's Guide to Copyright* (3rd ed., 1989) and Clark, *Publishing Agreements* (3rd ed., 1988).

[52] It is common practice for book publishing agreements in Britain to give only an exclusive licence, while the publishers of music generally take an assignment.

[53] If illustrative material is to be supplied by the author and he is not the artist or photographer, separate copyright arrangements may have to be made.

[54] See, *e.g. Jonathan Cape* v. *Consolidated Press* [1954] 1 W.L.R. 1313.

whether both as a hard back and a paperback. Beyond this there is the right to translate into, and publish in, foreign languages; and the rights to dramatise the work for the stage, film and broadcast, and to turn it into a strip cartoon.[55] Since English language publishing is frequently undertaken by separate publishers in Britain and North America,[56] the publisher who takes complete and exclusive rights needs to ensure that he has a sufficient power to sub-license his transatlantic partner.

(b) *Publisher's basic obligations*
These will concern producing the work and paying the author. If the **12-013** work already exists, the publisher may well undertake to publish.[57] If it has still to be created, he may reserve the freedom not to publish. In the latter case he must ensure that there is some sufficient consideration on his part to render the contract binding, *e.g.* in the form of an advance payment. The publisher may be prepared to agree to a time limit within which to take up any option that he may have—over whether to publish at all, or in a particular form,.[58]

His undertaking to pay will likely involve either a lump sum (or sums) or else royalties on sales. If royalties are payable they will usually differ for hardback and paperback versions,[59] and for the publisher's receipts from publishers sub-licensed abroad and enterprises sub-licensed to exploit through films and the like.

The author should consider what will happen if the publisher is unable or unwilling to publish and a third party wishes to acquire the rights. Where the publisher initially takes an assignment from the author, the latter may protect himself by making the publisher's ability to assign or to license the third party conditional upon his consent; likewise if the publisher is a licensee and wishes to assign his licence or grant a sub-licence. If nothing is said specifically about the matter, an assignee is free to act as he likes.[60] A licensee may not assign or sub-license where the licence is read as creating purely personal rights between licensor and licensee; this may, for instance, be spelled out of an arrangement to share profits, or the continuing relationship of remuneration by royalty and involvement of the author in the course of production and preparation of subsequent editions.[61]

One important reason for the author to keep control over any grant of **12-014** rights by his publisher to a third party is that otherwise he may be left with no direct right to claim royalties from the third party.[62] In *Barker* v.

[55] See CA 1956, s.2(5).
[56] See below, § 12-031.
[57] If nothing is said, an assignment implies no undertaking to publish: *Nichols* v. *Amalgamated Press* [1905–1910] Mac. C.C. 166.
[58] An option not conditioned in the author's favour in this way may contribute to a finding that the agreement is contrary to public policy: see below, § 12-018.
[59] Special provisions for complimentary copies and discount sales are usual.
[60] *Messager* v. *BBC* [1929] A.C. 151 at 156.
[61] *e.g. Stevens* v. *Benning* (1854) 1 K. & J. 168; *Hole* v. *Bradbury* (1879) 12 Ch.D. 886; *Hales* v. *Fisher Unwin* [1923–1928] Mac. C.C. 31.
[62] Equally the author may well not be able to hold the third party to other conditions in the original contract, *e.g.* over alterations to the work.

Stickney,[63] the author assigned rights to a publishing company in return for shares in the company and a royalty on all copies of the book sold.[64] The defendant bought the particular copyright as part of an assignment from the company's receiver, in the knowledge of the company's obligations to the author. Even so, this knowledge could not serve to impose an equivalent obligation upon him since he was not party to the initial contract. Nor could the author claim a lien equivalent to that of the vendor in a contract for the sale of goods: he had taken as his consideration a purely personal right to receive royalties.

(c) *Consequential responsibilities*

12-015   It will be the publisher's responsibility to arrange for the printing, binding and distribution of the work, and many of the detailed decisions that this involves will likely be left unspecified in the contract with the author. But arrangements about proofs are often dealt with, the author being placed under an obligation to read and return them within a specified time, and perhaps to pay for additions and corrections to the version originally submitted and set.

(d) *Special protection*

12-016   The author may seek to protect himself against particular forms of prejudice. Thus he may exclude any possibility of modification to his text apart from normal editorial work; as we have seen,[65] if he does not deal with alterations specifically in the contract, he may now be able to rely on his moral right to object to derogatory treatment; but there are numerous exceptions and qualifications. Even an express clause about alterations may not be easy to apply. In *Frisby* v. *BBC*,[66] the question was whether the BBC, which had a limited licence to broadcast a play, would be making a "structural" alteration if it deleted a particular line. The contract allowed the author to object to such an alteration and on the particular facts he succeeded in interlocutory proceedings. If the matter is left entirely to implication, all the circumstances in which the contract was made will be brought into account.[67] But if the exploiter has only received a licence and not an assignment, Goff J. said in the *Frisby* case[68] that the court will be ready to imply a term limiting the "right" to make alterations.

The publisher may require a warranty against liabilities that the author's actions may impose on him: against infringement of another author's copyright in the work[69]; against defamatory and obscene

---

[63] [1919] 1 K.B. 121 (C.A.).

[64] The author would have been in a worse position if the publisher's only obligation was to pay on copies sold by him.

[65] Above, §§ 11-055—11-057.

[66] [1967] Ch. 932.

[67] An example is *Joseph* v. *National Magazine* [1959] Ch. 14: author of an advertisement in the form of a connoisseur's article entitled to object to substantial rewriting; and see *Frisby* v. *BBC* (above, n. 66) at 948.

[68] Above, n. 66 at 948–949.

[69] *e.g.* because the name of a co-author has been withheld or because there is plagiarism of another work amounting to infringement.

material; and against breaches of confidence. Frequently the author is obliged to give an indemnity against losses to the publisher from these causes.

(e) *The longer term*

The two sides will need to consider whether there should be specific **12-017** undertakings about the preparation of second and subsequent editions, particularly if these are going to need a revision of the text. Then it is advisable to prescribe who is to organise the work in the event of the author being unable or unwilling to do it himself. There may also be an important question over the author's next or subsequent books: the publisher may well want an option giving him a right of first refusal over them.

(2) Restraint of trade and unconscionable bargaining

A new degree of protectiveness, qualifying the old respect for sanctity **12-018** of contract, is now beginning to appear, which has had a most striking manifestation over a publishing contract. In *Schroeder* v. *Macaulay*,[70] the House of Lords refused to enforce a music publisher's exclusive agreement with a songwriter. This contract—in standard form—assigned to the publisher copyright throughout the world in every composition of the songwriter composed over a 10-year period.[71] The publisher's only positive obligations were to pay an initial £50 and royalties on such songs as it decided to promote. The House applied the public policy rule against enforcing contracts in unreasonable restraint of trade, although an exclusive undertaking by an outside author to supply a publisher had not previously been characterised as involving any such restraint. It was unreasonable since the obligations imposed on the songwriter were found to be unfairly onerous: because of the length of the tie; because of the disparity between each side's obligations; and—at least as preliminary indicator—because the standard form offered the composer the chance only to take the contract or leave it (whereas special terms might be negotiated with composers who were already successful). Subsequently the Court of Appeal reached the same conclusion over similar publishing contracts with two composers in the "Fleetwood Mac" pop-group.[72] Lord Denning M.R. emphasised that the jurisdiction was part of a general power to adjust transactions where "the one was so strong in bargaining power and the other so weak that, as a matter of common fairness it was not right that the strong should be allowed to push the weak to the wall."

It is not clear whether this jurisdiction would allow a court to order the re-assignment of copyright in songs already transferred to the

---

[70] [1974] 3 All E.R. 616. On general aspects of the case, see Trebilcock (1976) 26 U. Toronto L.J. 359; and for the restraint of trade doctrine, above, § 8-025.

[71] The publisher had an option to extend the contract from five to 10 years if the royalties in the first five years exceeded £5,000. This had been exercised.

[72] *Clifford Davis* v. *WEA Records* [1975] 1 All E.R. 237. This links with Lord Denning M.R.'s determination to revive a general jurisdiction to moderate unconscionable bargaining: see, *e.g. Lloyds Bank* v. *Bundy* [1975] Q.B. 326.

publisher. If that were to be required, the composer would effectively be given power to bargain afresh for better terms across the market.[73]

If the reposing of personal trust has meant that a transaction is tainted with undue influence—as where a young composer and performer put his faith in his manager—a court will go to considerable lengths to achieve "practical justice" in unravelling it, even after is has been completely executed.[74] It will take an account of profits made, less an allowance for work done by the fiduciary, if this was in good faith.[75]

4. CONTROL OF MONOPOLY

(1) The 1988 Act

12-019   As already noted, the chance of extracting oppressive returns from copyright in particular works is less likely than from a patented invention. There is no longer any rule allowing for the grant of compulsory licences of copyright in general, equivalent to those for patents,[76] nor for that matter is the Crown permitted to use on special terms. In the early stages of sound recording, it was feared that the mechanical right to record copyright music might be used extravagantly. In the 1911 Act, a statutory right was given to others in certain circumstances to make their own recordings of such music upon payment of a set royalty. This was continued in 1956, but has now been repealed, there being no sufficient case for singling out the recording of music as suitable for "equitable remuneration."[77]

The most considerable danger of monopoly in the copyright sphere comes from the collective administration of rights, because their accumulation carries an ability to cut a user from access to much of the material that he may wish to exploit. Copyright collecting societies, in Britain as elsewhere, first grew into permanent institutions for the enforcement of performing rights in music—in halls, theatres, hotels and the like, and then by broadcasting. In this country, the Performing Right Society (PRS) was formed in 1914.[78] The record companies followed suit with a separate collecting society, Phonographic Performance Ltd. (PPL), for the performing right in sound recordings.[79]

[73] cf. foreign systems which allow royalty re-adjustments for suprise successes: e.g. West German Copyright Law 1965, Art. 36.

[74] O'Sullivan v. Management Agency & Music [1985] Q.B. 428 (C.A.).

[75] It will not, however, be at a rate that might have been bargained in an arm's length transaction with independent advice.

[76] But the general provisions for control by reference to the Monopolies and Mergers Commission apply to copyright, as they do to patents and to the design rights: s.144; and see §§ A1-011—A1-013.

[77] For the abolition of the statutory licence to record a work bearing musical copyright, see CDPA 1988, Sched. 1. § 21. Note however the sanction against abuse of rental right in s.66; above, § 11-029.

[78] See above, §§ 9-027, 9-028.

[79] Neither was concerned with the right to record (the mechanical right) or the right to include on film sound-track (the synchronisation right).

By developing a set of licensing arrangements for the different types of 12-020 music user (concert promoters, broadcasting organisations, dance hall proprietors, juke-box providers, the owners of shops with piped music, etc.) it became feasible to administer this aspect of copyright effectively. Only few performing rights could be covered by direct arrangements between owner and user (*e.g.* in plays, operas and musicals).[80] After the record companies established by litigation that a performing right was part of their sound recording copyright,[81] they followed suit with a separate collecting society, Phonographic Performance Ltd. (PPL). Neither organsation was concerned with reproduction rights: the "mechanical right" to make a recording of copyright music, the "synchronisation right" to incorporate a record into a film soundtrack, and so on. To enforce these, other joint organisations such as the Mechanical Copyright Protection Society developed.

After the Second World War, there was a current of resentment, particularly from major copyright users, over the terms on which these performing right societies were prepared to do business. On the recommendation of the Gregory Committee,[82] the 1956 Act established a Performing Right Tribunal (PRT), specially charged with power to review the licences and schemes collecting societies in this one field by reference to the criterion of "reasonableness." For this there was already a Canadian precedent; and in turn the lead was followed in other countries, for instance, Australia, the United States, and to a lesser degree in some European countries, such as West Germany.

Now that new technology is so rapidly amplifying the ability to copy material, collective administration is spreading also to cover reproduction rights, and in turn this has raised the need for wider public interest controls. Following proposals of the Whitford Committee,[83] the PRT has been converted by the 1988 Act into a Copyright Tribunal. Contemporaneously with the passage of the Act, the overall justification for the existence of PPL was raised before the Monopolies and Mergers Commission at the behest of local radio stations. The Commission's Report has recognised the economic necessity of collecting societies in the performing rights field.[84] Accordingly the established model for collective administration and its control goes forward into the new era with its foundations reinforced.

(a) The Copyright Tribunal

The Tribunal is now to be composed of a chairman and two deputy 12-021 Chairmen, who will be legally qualified, and between two and eight ordinary members.[85] It will normally sit in panels of three and work according to rules which, more than in the past, will encourage the use of written procedures.[86]

---

[80] Performing right societies have an interest in seeing that they are not by-passed by an extension of bilateral arrangements outside these traditional fields: see below, § 12-026.

[81] Above, § 9-008, n. 34.

[82] Above, § 9-028.

[83] Cmnd. 6732, 1977.

[84] Report on Collective Licensing (Cm. 530, 1988).

[85] CDPA 1988, Part I, Chap. VIII. The Lord Chancellor will appoint the legal members, the Secretary of State the others.

[86] Some proceedings of the PRT have been criticised as unduly lengthy.

The Tribunal may consider two principal categories of case: licensing schemes and licences. A scheme sets out "the classes of case in which the operator . . . is willing to grant licences" and the terms for doing so. Licences are permissions which fall outside this definition.[87] While a tariff offered by one of the performing right societies to all dance hall proprietors is typically a scheme, being "in the nature of a standing invitation to treat,"[88] it is the government's view that the licence for reprographic copying in schools which the Copyright Licensing Act now offers to local education authorities is not. The correctness of this assumption may one day fall to be questioned, since it is only in the case of schemes that representative bodies of users have the right to bring a case before the Tribunal.

The Tribunal's jurisdiction does not extend to all copyright licences; it would be contrary to the Berne Convention to place under public control the licences and licensing schemes offered by individual right owners of literary, dramatic, musical and artistic works and films. Equally it has not been thought necessary to cover publishing, as distinct from copying, these works. Accordingly, in respect of these works, jurisdiction relates to licences and schemes of a licensing body, i.e. a society or other organisation with a main object of negotiating or granting licences, including licences covering works of more than one author. In other cases—relating to neighbouring rights and the new rental rights—the licences and schemes do not have to be from a licensing body.[89]

The Tribunal does not act of its own motion but on the complaint of, or on behalf of, licensees, actual or potential. They may raised objections before they enter a licence, or against the refusal to grant them one, but not afterwards, save in one special case concerning expiry[90]; sanctity of contract is not to be compromised by a running ability in an individual licensee to seek a re-writing of his terms. As far as concerns schemes, so long as they are not yet operational, it is for a representative organisation of potential licensees to make the reference.[91] Once the scheme takes effect, the right covers both such an organisation and a person claiming a licence.[92] Once an order has been made, the scheme may be referred again by its operator, a claimant for a licence or a representative organisation.[93] As regards separate licences, it is the person seeking the licence who may refer the case.[94] In the past there have been cases concerning schemes raised before the PRT by organisations of dance hall proprietors, cinema operators, and bingo-hall enterprises.[95] The second

[87] s.117.
[88] PRS v. Workmen's Club Union [1988] F.S.R. 586.
[89] s.116.
[90] See s.126 for this case.
[91] s.118.
[92] s.119.
[93] s.120; but subject to limitations designed to prevent constant harassment.
[94] s.125.
[95] See cases 1/1958, 9/1960, 11 and 12/1962, 13/1963, 21/1966, 23/1971, 27/1973 and 28/1975. On the scope of jurisdiction, see Reditune v. PRS (PRT Cases, 30–32/1977).

kind of application has been important for broadcasting organisations and there have been references by the BBC, Manx Radio, and the Association of Independent Radio Contractors.[96]

The legislation defines one main criterion by which the Tribunal is to **12-022** decide whether it will confirm or vary a scheme, or vary or impose a licence—reasonableness in the circumstances. But is is obliged to take account of all relevant considerations,[97] and in every case it must have regard to the availability of schemes or the grant of licences to others in similar circumstances, and the terms offered them, exercising its power so as to prevent unreasonable discrimination in the scheme or licences of the organisation in question.[98] In various instances more specific matters are also listed for consideration: in respect of reprography licences,[99] educational taping of broadcasts,[1] conditions imposed by promoters of events,[2] payments in respect of underlying rights,[3] and works included in re-transmissions.[4]

The actual orders of the PRT show that it has often acted in a generally similar manner to a labour arbitrator who is dealing with a conflict about future terms and conditions of employment, rather than about existing legal rights. (Indeed, in so far as the PRS represents authors rather than entrepreneurs, their role is comparable to that of a trade union in negotiating on behalf of the labour force that it represents; the comparison becomes blurred because the Society also represents music publishers.) Thus where the prime issue is a tariff—or in other words what the licensor ought to be able to demand for its members— the Tribunal's starting point will be the difference between asking-price and offer. It will then look to see what justifications can be offered for fixing upon one point rather than another between these poles. If there has been a previous agreement, comparisons with this tariff as the "fair price" for its own time will obviously have some relevance. Equally, it may serve a purpose to compare the rates agreed with other categories of user.[5] This, after all, is often as close as the Tribunal can get to a market comparison, and even so there will be no competing sellers.

A few cases have raised issues of whose interests it is legitimate for a **12-023** licensor to protect; and these resemble questions about abuse of market power. Thus it was not proper for the PRS to offer film exhibitors licences at discriminatory discounts, depending on whether an exhibitor belonged to one or other trade association; the PRS got nothing in

---

[96] See cases 17 and 18/1964, 24/1971 and 35/1978.
[97] s.135.
[98] s.129.
[99] s.130; below, § 13-011.
[1] s.131.
[2] s.132.
[3] s.133.
[4] s.134.
[5] Where the circumstances are similar, availability and terms must be taken into account: s.129. For a decision that there was no sufficient similarity see Case 38/1978 (independent local radio/PPL).

return that could justify this preference.[6] On the other hand, it was proper for PPL to impose some limit on a local radio station's proportion of "needle time" (the amount of records broadcast compared with the amount of live music): the record companies were found to have a legitimate long-term interest in the continued employment of live performers who would act as the source for their future business.[7]

The PRT proved itself useful in resolving basic and difficult conflicts of interest in the entertainment industries. Its successor will in all likelihood have difficult tasks in larger, unexplored terrain. The need for it in an age of increasing collectivisation for authors and their entrepreneurs is inescapable.

(2) Dominant position in the EEC

12-024   The Performing Right Tribunal is primarily concerned with the licensing activities of the performing right societies rather than their constitutional arrangements. Yet there are numerous ways in which a society may want to strengthen its economic position through its rules and their effect on members. Take, for instance, the record companies: they have a performing right in their own records, exploited through PPL. They have an interest to see that the authors and publishers do not secure an undue proportion of what users will pay overall for performing rights in recordings of copyright music; and they may want to protect live performers against too high a proportion of "needle time"—in broadcasting, dance halls or wherever. An authors-and-publishers' society like the PRS may therefore be significantly affected, if record companies can become members of it, for instance by setting up a publishing operation. Not surprisingly, therefore, such societies tend to take counteractive steps at least to limit the rights of record company members.[8]

12-025   The EC Commission, which can intervene only within the terms of its competition rules, investigated the organisational structure of the West German collecting society, GEMA,[9] and found a number of its restrictive rules and practices to constitute an abuse of its dominant position, contrary to the Rome Treaty, Article 86.[10] The basic objectives of joint

---

[6] Case 9/1960. Another case concerned the PRS's insistence that Southern Television pay royalties on emphemeral recordings made in the course of broadcasting despite the explicit exception of this activity from infringement (CA 1956, s.6(7); see now above, § 11-035); the Tribunal disapproved: Case 2/1958. *cf.* the practice mentioned in the Whitford Report §§ 389–394.

[7] Case 18/1964; and see also case 35/1978.

[7a] Below, §§ 13-011, 13-013. This prospect adds significance to decisions on performing rights issues that have been reached elsewhere: see *e.g. Swedish Group of Int. Fed. of the Phonographic Industry* v. *Sveriges Radios* (Swedish Supreme Court, 1965); *Commercial Broadcasters Fed.* v. *Phonographic Performances (N.Z.)* (New Zealand Copyright Tribunal, 1977); Both hold *inter alia* that manufacturers' rights are not to be valued at lower rate than composers' rights, an opinion also shared by the PRT in Case 35/1978. See also Court (1987) 11 Syd.L.R. 348.

[8] Thus the PRS has rules restricting the number of directors from "user-owned" publishers and foreign publishers. For the German society, GEMA, see below, § 12-026.

[9] *Re Gema (No. 1)* [1971] C.M.L.R. D35; and generally, Mestmäcker *Copyright in Community Law* (1976) pp. 60–69. At the same time other national collecting societies within the then EEC were investigated, but no decisions were issued. In the U.S., similar collecting societies have had their activities circumscribed by anti-trust proceedings.

[10] For Art. 86 in general, see above, § 1-025.

collecting societies were accepted to be legitimate—and in a later case, the European Court of Justice has agreed.[11] It is proper for individual members (composers, associated authors and publishers) to protect their interests against major music users (such as broadcasting organisations and record companies) by assigning rights to a joint association. But nevertheless anti-competitive arrangements must not be made if they are beyond what is required "for the association to carry out its activity on the necessary scale."

In particular, three aspects of GEMA's rules were criticised: **12-026**

(i) Rules which followed from the arrangement amongst national collecting societies that each would have only its own nationals as members were disapproved.[12] It is true that these rules limited members' ability to express dissatisfaction with their national society by joining the society of another EEC state and taking whatever advantages it offered its members: the effect of such a transfer of allegiance would be to make the national society a mere collecting agency on its own territory for the foreign society which the author had joined. The Commission's decision amounts to an insistence that members should not be deprived of this measure of ultimate independence. In reality habit makes them unlikely to take advantage of such a power.[13]

(ii) Since GEMA acted as licensor not only of performing rights, but also (among other things) of the mechanical right to record music, it required a transfer of exclusive rights of all aspects of copyright, at home and abroad. It accordingly had a strong interest in preventing individual authors from being drawn out of membership and into direct relationship with a user such as a record company. This objective it pursued by a variety of measures: requiring a long period for notice of withdrawal, taking the right to future works even after resignation, paying loyalty bonuses and paying out of its social fund only to members of twenty years' standing. The Commission insisted that the rules should not oblige members to assign rights for territories in which it did not act directly; nor should it take over all aspects of copyright in the territories in which it did operate.[14] Likewise it ought to be possible to resign at the end of any year—a demand which the Commission was later to soften to three years in return for further concessions on the range of rights transferable to the society.[15]

(iii) GEMA had prevented record companies from acquiring influence by excluding them from membership as publishers.[16] This the Commission also objected to, while recognising that it would be proper to restrict the voting rights of such members when they had a conflict of interests

---

[11] *Belgische Radio* v. *SABAM* [1974] E.C.R. 51 at 313; [1974] 2 C.M.L.R. 238; note also *Greenwich Film* v. *SACEM* [1980] 1 C.M.L.R. 629.

[12] See [1971] C.M.L.R. at D47; and see *Gesellschaft für Verwertung von Leistungsschutzrechten* [1983] 3 C.M.L.R. 695. The international arrangements concerning performing rights are mentioned above, § 11-024, n. 4.

[13] Rules making it difficult for publishers with foreign connections to become ordinary members were criticised as tending to hinder the formation of a Community-wide market: [1971] C.M.L.R. at D47–48.

[14] [1971] C.M.L.R. at D48–50.

[15] *Ibid.*, at D50; *Re Gema (No. 2)* [1972] C.M.L.R. D115.

[16] *cf.* the rules of the PRS on the matter, mentioned above, n. 8.

(*e.g.* over the licence rate for the mechanical right to record musical compositions).[17]

A number of GEMA's commercial practices were also characterised as abusive: for example, the tariff on the mechanical right was found to discriminate in favour of German-produced records, and that on recording equipment in favour of German manufacturers[18]; and it was improper for the mechanical right fee in effect to require payments for works not under the society's control.[19]

12-027 The types of investigations that are conducted, on the one hand by the Copyright Tribunal, and on the other by the EC Commission follow from the different powers with which they are invested. The case for the British approach is that an organised arbitral body, independent of governmental influence, provides a satisfactory means of controlling a monopoly that is in other respects efficient from the point of view of both owners and users.[20] On the other hand the likelihood that many licensing negotiations will lead to a reference or application to the Tribunal has been criticised: the extra time and expense that are used up is said to distort the ability of the licensing societies to react to inflation, causing them to press cases earlier and harder than would probably be the case if voluntary bargaining were the sole route to settlement.[21] The stand taken by the EC Commission has shown collecting societies that the manner in which they organise their activities is not above scrutiny in the public interest. In a field where conflicts of interest are complex and the stakes are considerable, this makes a deal of political sense.

5. FREE MOVEMENT OF GOODS AND COPYRIGHT[22]

12-028 In *Deutsche Grammophon* v. *Metro*,[23] the EC Court of Justice received a reference concerning the "neighbouring right" of a sound-recording enterprise under German law.[24] The plaintiff was seeking to prevent the resale in Germany of records originally marketed in France by a subsidiary and thereafter brought into Germany by a parallel importer. The Court directed that it would be contrary to the Treaty of Rome for a German court to enforce the neighbouring right against these goods.[25]

---

[17] [1971] C.M.L.R. at D51–52; and see the later negative clearance [1982] 2 C.M.L.R. 482.
[18] For this special levy on equipment, see below, § 13-013.
[19] [1971] C.M.L.R. D53–55.
[20] Wallace (1973) 4 I.I.C. 280; see also Joliet (1973) Europarecht 17; de Freitas (1987) 34 J.Cop.Soc. 148; Deringer and Mestmäcker [1985] Int. Bus. L. 65, 71.
[21] The lengthy proceedings between PPL and the ALRC (above, n. 7) have given force to these concerns; hence the hope that the Copyright Tribunal will operate more expeditiously: above, § 12-021.
[22] See generally, Korah (1982) 14 Case Western J.I.L. 7; Dietz (1983) 30 J.Cop.Soc. 517; Ubertazzi (1985) 16 I.I.C. 46.
[23] [1971] E.C.R. 487; [1971] C.M.L.R. 631.
[24] *i.e.* a right equivalent to the sound recording copyright of C.A. 1956, s.12.
[25] It was not at this stage clear whether German law applied to this right an international, or a purely national, concept of exhaustion: for the application of the decision by the German court, see [1972] C.M.L.R. 107.

This was the first occasion on which the Court resorted to the free movement of goods policy as a basis for limiting the scope of a national intellectual property right, since there was no restrictive agreement to bring the competition rules into play.[26] Though sometimes regarded as a decision in which the plaintiff had no equivalent protection in the country of first marketing (France), it is better treated as one in which a less satisfactory measure of protection (through unfair competition principles) was available there.[27] The Court attached no significance to the question, and the decision gave birth to the "consent" basis for applying Articles 30–36: if the initial marketing was with the plaintiff company's consent, whether it had then been afforded an equivalent opportunity to earn profits above the competitive level was irrelevant.[28]

Since the sound-recording right protects an investment rather than an **12-029** aesthetic achievement, it was argued that different considerations apply to authors' rights because of their greater inherent value.[29] This the Court has not accepted, applying the same principle of free movement to cases of copyright in crockery design and recorded music.[30]

In *Musikvertrieb Membran* v. *GEMA*,[31] this view was applied with **12-030** severe consequences. Because of the then statutory right to record copyright music in the United Kingdom at a royalty of $6^{1}/_{4}$ per cent. of net selling price, the voluntary licences which rightowners granted for that country contained a $6^{1}/_{4}$ per cent. royalty clause. In Germany the GEMA, as collecting society for mechanical rights there, charged 8 per cent. and sought to collect the difference as a condition of allowing in parallel imports from Britain. It was held to be contrary to Article 30 to use German copyright to resist importation except on the demanded terms. It would appear, however, that if the rightowner had granted no licence for the United Kingdom, but had left the record company to assert its statutory entitlement, the records would have been produced under compulsory licence and not with consent, as in *Pharmon* v. *Hoechst*,[32] and so would not be "free goods" in the hands of a parallel importer. Thus the "consent" test has a certain arbitrariness to it.

[26] The initial marketing being by a subsidiary of the right owner: Had there been an agreement between potentially competing enterprises to divide markets, this would have been caught by Article 85: *cf. Time-Life* v. *SABAM* [1979] 2 C.M.L.R. 578 (C.A., Brussels). It may be that the competition rules now being applied to patent licences by the E.C. Commission (see above, §§ 7-030—7-040) will be adapted to copyright licences that have a significant effect on their particular market. But defining markets for copyright material is particularly hazardous.

[27] See Gibbins [1980] 2 E.I.P.R. 42 at 45.

[28] Per contra, the free movement policy has no application against sound recordings which are manufactured and sold in a member state without any licence from the originator of the recording, because no sound recording right exists in that state or because it has expired there: *EMI Electrola* v. *Patricia* [1989].

[29] *Dansk Supermarked* v. *Imerco* [1981] E.C.R. 181. Note the application of the doctrine equally to registered designs (*Keurkoop* v. *Nancy Kean Gifts* [1982] E.C.R. 2853) and to industrial design protected through unfair competition law against slavish imitation (*IDG* v. *Beele* [1982] E.C.R. 707).

[30] *Membran* case (below, n. 31).

[31] [1981] E.C.R. 147.

[32] See above, § 7-044, n. 67.

Yet here, as in relation to other forms of intellectual property, it is no longer being pressed to the same extremes as seemed imminent in the early 1970s. As with patents, if the aspect of copyright in question is a substantive rule which applies equally to domestic and imported goods, it will not be abrogated so far as the latter are concerned by Treaty of Rome considerations.[33] Thus, where Danish law provided a rental right in respect of films, at a time when British law did not, an act of rental in Denmark required a copyright licence even for video tapes which had been imported from the United Kingdom, after manufacture and marketing there with the copyright owner's consent.[34] Where French law provided, rather than a sound recording right, a mechanical reproduction right in copyright music which was separate from the performing right in the music, that right could be the subject of a charge by SACEM, the French collecting society, even on legitimate records imported from a member state which did not have such a right.[35] The charge, which was regarded as a normal form of copyright exploitation,[36] was levied, not in respect of importation, but for an act of performance that took place subsequently.

12-031   In the field of English language publishing the impact of free movement of goods poses difficulties. Traditionally the following arrangement has been typical: an author's copyright has been divided so as to give a United States publisher exclusive rights to the North American market, a British publisher has had the "traditional British market"[37] to himself, while both have enjoyed licences in continental Europe.[38] Moreover, since copyright is such a long-lasting right there are a great many publishing agreements already in existence on these terms which will remain important for considerable periods. If the free flow of goods doctrine applies without modification to such a case, the American licensee may market in (say) Holland and a parallel importer may then import and sell in the United Kingdom.[39] This, it is alleged, would allow a more powerful set of competitors outside the EEC to drive British publishers into insolvency. The case, of course, awaits full and detailed argument. But, as Dietz has emphasised, the threat is to an industry which plays a special cultural and political role; so there are strong reasons for not

---

[33] See above, §§ 7-045—7-046.
[34] *Warner Bros.* v. *Christiansen* [1988].
[35] *Basset* v. *SACEM* [1987] 3 C.M.L.R. 173; and see Davies and Rauscher auf Weeg, *Challenges to Copyright in the European Community* (1983) Pt. IV, Chap. 1.
[36] It was accordingly not open to objection under Art. 86, despite the monopoly position of SACEM.
[37] *i.e.* in the main, British Commonwealth territories, current and former, other than Canada. See generally Publishers' Association, *Memorandum on European Community Law and Copyright in Literary Works* (1980).
[38] Formerly publishers agreed collectively to abide by this division in their contracts for publishing particular works. But this has come under anti-trust attack from the U.S. Department of Justice. The joint agreement has been abandoned in a consent decree: see *United States* v. *Addison-Wesley* 2 Trade Cases (CCH) 70 (1977) 640.
[39] Or, if it is proper to apply the "common origin" notion of *Van Zuylen* v. *Hag* (below, §§ 18-007, 18-008; and see above, § 7-048), the American may produce in Holland and import into Britain himself; if so, how much of the production process has to be in Holland for it to count? Merely binding up loose sheets?

judging the issue by narrow criteria of competitive effectiveness. It is by no means clear how this might be achieved. But the Court is moving gradually towards a greater readiness to balance competing considerations in applying the free movement policy; in a rule of reason approach may lie the answer. Thus it may prove possible to distinguish between genuine products of another member state and goods from outside the Community which had had a mere "stop-over" in a first member state.

6. FREE PROVISION OF SERVICES AND COPYRIGHT

Because of its performing right aspect, copyright is a form of intellectual **12-032** property that is concerned with providing services as well as marketing goods. This has led to the question whether Articles 59–66 of the Rome Treaty, which concern the free provision of services,[40] operate in a manner equivalent to Articles 30–36 on the free movement of goods. Article 59 requires the removal of restrictions on freedom to provide services in respect of nationals of member states who are established in a state other than those for whom their services are intended. This, however, is subject to reservations: notably that it shall not prejudice the applicability of provisions imposed by law, regulation or administrative action providing for special treatment for foreign nationals on the grounds of public policy ("ordre public"), public security or public health.[41] *Coditel* v. *Ciné Vog (No. 1)*[42] dealt with territorial limitations that were brought about in two ways: on the one hand, the copyright owners of a French film had granted exclusive rights to a Belgian distributor to organise its showing in cinemas in Belgium and subsequently on television there; on the other, its emission by television broadcast on the first German channel was restricted to the reception areas of that channel's transmitters. Was a Belgian cable television company then entitled to pick up the German broadcast and transmit it to its subscribers by diffusion within the Belgian distributor's territory? The Court of Justice held that the free provision of services by a national of one member state in the territory of another, required by Article 59, did not override the normal operation of Belgian copyright law, under which the cable diffusion in Belgium of the German broadcast required the licence of the copyright owner.

The Court carried over the phraseology of Article 36 in confining the limiting effect of Article 59 to cases where intellectual property is being applied as a means of arbitrary discrimination or a disguised restriction in the economic relations between member states.[43] However

---

[40] These articles form part of the Foundation of the EEC devoted to the free movement of persons, services and capital.
[41] Art. 56, as applied by Art. 66 (*cf.* Art. 36). See also *Procureur du Roi* v. *Debauve* for the refusal to hold that Art. 59 qualified a Belgian law against broadcast advertising.
[42] [1980] E.C.R. 881.
[43] Judgment, § 15.

it refused to attribute this character to the exclusive contractual arrangements by which the author and his assignees sought to procure revenue from performances of the film. It treated the condition preventing the Belgian distributor from licensing a television transmission for the first 40 months as part of the "essential function" of copyright.[44] It also stressed that the apparently territorial character of the television licences was largely the consequence of the legal monopolies over transmission.[45]

12-033   In subsequent proceedings concerning the potentially anti-competitive effects (under Article 85) of the limited distribution agreements, the Court directed that the trial instance must decide whether the exclusive right to exhibit the film created artificial and unjustified barriers in relation to the needs of the film industry and associated issues, including whether an excessive rate of return in relation to investment was being extracted.[46] These are difficult and time-consuming questions for a non-specialist court.

[44] *Ibid.*, § 14. The question whether these agreements offended Art. 85 was not referred to the Court of Justice. Had it been, the Court might have been tempted to say (as did the Court of Appeal of Brussels) that the agreements lay outside Art. 85's ambit since they concerned an aspect of the "specific subject-matter" of copyright. But this would amount to nothing other than a rather obscure way of saying that any distortion of competition stemmed from the intellectual property right rather than the agreements.
[45] *Ibid.*, § 16.
[46] *Coditel* v. *Ciné Vog (No. 2)* [1982] E.C.R. 3381, esp. at 3402.

Chapter 13

COPYRIGHT: PARTICULAR CASES

More than other types of intellectual property, copyright has burgeoned 13-001
into a separate varieties, related but distinct. The preceding chapters have
emphasised the principles that identify the species as a whole. It is
important to start with these common characteristics. For one thing they
focus attention on why copyright is so often the form adopted when new
circumstances call for protection: a right against copying appears proof
against unduly wide monopoly and it makes others accountable where
the claim is most evidently justifiable. But the point has been reached at
which we must turn to the many differences of detail in the various
copyrights. This chapter is not intended to be exhaustive. Rather it takes
up a number of subjects where the impact of copyright is currently
significant and controversial. The first section deals with the role of
copyright in the politically sensitive area of the news media. The
following sections (2–4) are concerned with technological advances that
affect the dissemination of information, culture and entertainment: visual
and aural reprography; computers; and the diffusion of broadcasts and
other material by wire and by satellite. Sections 5–8 concern claims to
new forms of right: by performers; by writers against public lending; by
artists for a share in resale prices; and by those who would like to see
encouragement of the arts enhanced out of royalties from works no
longer in copyright. Finally the special position of Crown and Parliamentary copyright is treated (section 9). The now reduced role of copyright
in the protection of industrial design is reserved for the next Chapter.

1. THE MEDIA AND THE PUBLIC INTEREST IN NEWS

Producing the news of the day generates many tensions. Between rivals in 13-002
the media there is constant pressure to stay in the van, and if at all
possible to get ahead with a scoop—whether it is the first story or the
most captivating photograph. A journalist may meet all sorts of difficulties in extracting information, which will cost time and money to
overcome. Obligations of confidence may hinder him even when he has
acquired it. We have already seen that the judges have fashioned a
defence of public interest which may limit rights in confidential information; the same general defence may be raised to claims of copyright.[1] In

[1] Above, §§ 8-015—8-018, 11-041.

any country which seeks to conserve the independence and freedom of action of its press and other media there are nice balances to be struck. Here we explore the extent to which copyright gives rise to exclusive rights in news reports; and the degree to which it can hamper the revelation of material by anyone other than its owner.

(1) Copyright in news

13-003   There will be no copyright in news until there is a work or other subject-matter capable of protection; and then only to the extent that the particular type of copyright may be infringed.[2] Once a story is turned into a literary work or illustrated by an artistic work there may be infringement in the form of reproduction in another paper or inclusion in a broadcast. This is equally so, where the literary work is the script of a news broadcast and the copyist works from the legitimate broadcast. But if a broadcast is verbatim and there is no initial work, the copyright in the broadcast may be of no help.[3] For this special copyright probably does not cover any literary or pictorial reproduction of its content as such[4]; and even the right to prevent rebroadcasting may well not extend to the case where the material is taken down and a different news-reader broadcasts it afresh.[5] In these cases, the broadcast copyright is clearly infringed only if the copyist can be shown to have made an intermediate recording.

In the *INS* case,[6] the Supreme Court of the United States was moved to provide a remedy against the systematic and damaging misappropriation of news by one agency from the newspapers supplied by a rival. But there the limited scope of American copyright law made it impracticable to seek copyright protection. In Britain or any other Berne Convention state, copyright arises upon the creation of a literary or artistic work and is enforceable without formalities: its potency is accordingly the greater and the need to qualify it in the public interest may be more pressing.

Walter v. *Steinkopff*[7] illustrates the basic approach. The *St. James' Gazette* copied a number of extracts from *The Times* almost word for word, including some two-fifths of an article by Rudyard Kipling. This was held to infringe *The Times'* copyright in its pieces. It made no difference that *The Times* had itself borrowed some of the information, that the *St. James' Gazette* was not a direct competitor (since it gave the news only later), that the source was acknowledged or that the editor of *The Times* did not at once object. North J. sought to dispel any

---

[2] The Brussels version of the Berne Convention (Art. 9(3)) allowed member countries to create exceptions from copyright for the "news of the day"; but the more recent Paris version does not go so far. Nor does British law.

[3] The broadcast copyright covers filming, re-broadcasting and certain types of public performance: see Table, above, § 10-003, line 7.

[4] The 1956 Act clearly excluded such forms of infringement; but the 1988 Act refers to "copying a work" (including a broadcast), without offering further definition, save that "reproduction in a material form" is not a form of copying that apparently applies to a broadcast.

[5] The new Act does not deal with the point specifically, nor did the old.

[6] Above, § 1-007.

[7] [1892] 3 Ch. 489.

implication that copyright might confer exclusive rights in the news itself by stressing the dichotomy between unprotectable idea and protectable expression. In other contexts, the courts have shown some willingness to treat the taking of detailed information as infringement, even when the actual expression of the ideas has been worked out afresh.[8] Given the general interest in making news available through channels on which the public relies, it may well be that copyright in news is confined to substantial reproduction of the actual language used to write it up. But a defendant who systematically starts from a particular source will probably fare less well than one whose "borrowings" are part of a standard practice of monitoring the stories of all other rivals. Today this sort of question may arise equally under one of the "fair dealing" defences discussed in the next section.

(2) Fair dealing and recording speech

The two forms of fair dealing that are germane to the news media[9] are: **13-004**
(i) use of any work for purposes of criticism or review of it or another work or a performance of either[10]; and (ii) use of any work other than a photograph for the purpose of reporting current events.[11] The exception for "on-the-spot" photographs leaves the law affecting them as it was previously.[12]

A court must consider all the circumstances of the "dealing" in the light of the purpose for which alone it is permitted.[13] The proportion of the work that has been copied is one starting point. No question of fair dealing arises unless there has been "substantial taking"; but even when this point is passed, questions of quantity may well be less significant than quality. There may be occasions upon which it is proper to take the whole work.[14]

Equally the precise manner in which the work is used for criticism, review or reporting current events will be important; it is obviously germane to ask whether the defendant could have made his point effectively without any "substantial taking." This judgment will in some cases be influenced by the fact that the work was private or was given to a person in confidence. This, however, is simply a further consideration, since the defences are not confined to published material.[15] As *Beloff* v.

---

[8] The broadcasting media may also benefit from the exception concerning incidental inclusion: C.D.P.A. 1988, s.31; above, § 11-028.

[9] See especially *Elanco* v. *Mandops*, above, § 11-006.

[10] CDPA 1988, s.30(1); "sufficient acknowledgment" (see s.178) is a prerequisite.

[11] CDPA 1988, s.30(2). Again there must be "sufficient acknowledgment" save in a sound recording, film, broadcast or cable-cast: see Berne Convention, Art. 10*bis*.

[12] See C.A. 1956, s.9(3), a more restricted exception.

[13] As far as criticism or review is concerned, this may relate to the content, as distinct from the style of a literary (or other) work; as for current events, they may not be a pretext for reporting something else: see above, § 11-028.

[14] *Hubbard* v. *Vosper* [1972] 2 Q.B. 84 (C.A.) at 98; *Beloff* v. *Pressdram* [1973] 1 All E.R. 241 at 263.

[15] *Beloff* v. *Pressdram* (above, n. 14) at 263, refusing to give any firmer meaning to Romer J., *British Oxygen* v. *Liquid Air* [1925] Ch. 383 at 393.

Pressdram emphasised, the press is accustomed to rely upon leaks of information in advance of formal publication. Ungoed Thomas J. refused to draw any distinction between leaks to a newspaper from another newspaper and from some other source. Since he found the publication of a memorandum to be unfair chiefly because it was not intended for publication and had been leaked in breach of confidence, a newspaper which publishes a leaked document of any kind may have difficulty in making out such a defence.[16] Only if it is able to rely on factors which pertain to the public interest—and which might be raised under that separate but related head[17]—will it be on surer ground. That might be so, for instance, if the document revealed criminal activities or a serious threat to public safety or health.

13-005   Economic considerations will include the amount of damage that the defendant may inflict on the plaintiff, and the extent to which the defendant will get for nothing something which in usual business practice he would expect to have to pay for. These are factors illustrated by the *INS* and *Steinkopff* cases mentioned above.

The express acknowledgement that a speaker may acquire copyright from the recording of his statement, if the result is an original work, has an immediate importance to both the written and the broadcast media, since they make wide use of interviews. The problems which those interest groups foresaw led to an exception in addition to the general fair dealing provisions. The 1988 Act, section 58, provides for two distinct exceptions: a record of spoken words that is made for reporting current events may be used for that purpose; and a record for the purpose of broadcasting or cable-casting may be used for that (but not one for the other). Moreover, it must be a direct record, not prohibited by the speaker, not an infringement of any other copyright, not a use prohibited by the speaker; and it must be a use permitted by the possessor of the record (not a leak). The limits should be observed: if a celebrity gives someone an interview about his private life (not a current event), which is reproduced verbatim he becomes the owner of the copyright. He may therefore have a moral right to object to derogatory treatment by alteration or omission, though this will not normally extend to press publication. In this latter case, he might object by demonstrating breach of the moral right against false attribution.[18]

(3) Organisation and Journalist

13-006   Since most of the material supplied to newspapers and news programmes comes from employed journalists and reporters, their copyright

---

[16] *Beloff* v. *Pressdram* (above, n. 14) at 264; and, for the facts, see above, § 11-041. Whether it could make a difference that the information was secured by theft rather than by breach of confidence was left open.

[17] Above, § 11-041.

[18] See above, §§ 11-055—11-058; *Moore* v. *News of the World* [1972] 1 All E.R. 441.

relationship to their employer is important. Previously newspaper journalists presumptively enjoyed a special division of the copyright, which went to the employer only for press use. But this has disappeared in the 1988 Act. The copyright in the work of all employed journalists now resides initially in their employers for all purposes, unless they can extract an express contract to the contrary.[19]

Where the employer has the copyright, the employee will not enjoy the moral right to be identified.[20] Indeed, so great was the press fear of the need to name contributors that this moral right does not arise over any publication in a newspaper, magazine or similar periodical, even where the material comes from a non-employed person.[21] It does, however, apply to broadcasts, to the extent that the exception for fair dealing in reporting current events does not operate.[22] Doubtless waivers will be extracted in many cases. The moral right to object to derogatory treatment may be claimed by an employed journalist, or by anyone else who is published in a newspaper, magazine or periodical, if the work was prepared for such a purpose.[23]

Where the material being used consists of a photograph or film, it may not be sufficient to secure the licence of the copyright owner. If the work was commissioned for private and domestic purposes, then the commissioner enjoys the special right of privacy given by section 85, and may *inter alia* object to inclusion of the material in a newspaper, broadcast or cable-cast.

2. REPROGRAPHY AND RECORDING: EDUCATIONAL AND PRIVATE COPYING

At the beginning of this century, the techniques for copying (except by 13-007 hand or typewriter) were still limited to complex and technical procedures like printing. Even photography of the printed page or picture required the subsequent intervention of a person able to develop negatives and make prints. The vast improvement of mechanised techniques for producing copies of material written and drawn—photocopying or (to initiates) reprography—has been matched by an equally startling advance in simple means for recording musical and dramatic performances—in sound and now, with video-cassettes, in sight. The characteristic of these developments which most threatens the copyright system is the ease with which one or more copies can be produced. The upsurge in commercial

---

[19] CA 1956, s.4(2); *cf.* CDPA 1988, s.11; see above, § 12-003.
[20] CDPA 1988, s.79(3).
[21] s.79(6).
[22] s.79(4). There must in any case be an "assertion."
[23] s.81(4).

piracy of books, recordings, films, computer games and other programs directly undermines the economic interest of the original producers. It has had to be met by much more intensive policing of activities which for the most part constitute the most direct and incontrovertible imitation; sometimes, also, as where the entire get-up and trade-marking is also counterfeited, it is a source of ready deception to consumers. In the counter-attack, the courts have made a distinct contribution, as in the development of the *Anton Piller* and allied orders; and so equally have administrative officers, where trading standards authorities have taken action under the Trade Descriptions Act.

Where individuals make single copies for their own use the balance of conflicting interests between copyright owners and users is much more even. Each act, at least if viewed in isolation, is only a slight threat to the copyright owner's economic concerns; and the educational or personal value of being free to copy in this way is not to be discounted as insignificant.

This section is accordingly concerned with the proposals that have been pressed, particularly over the last decade, to deal with the phenomena of private copying and home taping; and then with the solutions which the government eventually saw fit to offer in the 1988 Act.

(1) Visual copies of literary and other material[24]

13-008   The world's early copyright systems naturally concentrated their fire upon the multiplication of pirated copies. In most, including the British, little attention was given to the question whether making a single copy counted as an infringement, or whether, on the contrary, such a private use was an exploitation of knowledge and ideas which ought to be left free for all. In 1911, when the "fair dealing" exceptions were first spelled out in statutory terms, "private study" and "research" were included in the list of permitted purposes[25] without the problem having surfaced in previously reported litigation. Nor was there much consideration of the matter afterwards. It was held, not surprisingly, that an infringing publisher could not justify his book by saying that readers would use it for private study.[26] But otherwise the courts were not asked to say how much could be taken; nor what purposes constituted private study or research[27]; nor whether multiple copying could ever be justified under this head.

13-009   The 1956 Act revision left "fair dealing for purposes of research or private study" as an exception and added provisions concerning educational instruction and examination, the making of anthologies and, above

---

[24] See generally Kolle (1975) 6 I.I.C. 382; Kerever [1976] Copyright 188; Ricketson (1982) 10 Aust.B.L.R. 31; Nevins (1985) 7 E.I.P.R. 222.

[25] CA 1911, s.2(1)(*i*).

[26] *University of London Press* v. *University Tutorial Press* [1916] 2 Ch. 601; and see now *Sillitoe* v. *McGraw-Hill* [1983] F.S.R. 545.

[27] Consider, for instance, copies for the professional information of businessmen or government servants.

all, copying in non-profit libraries.[28] There were a number of indications within them that the notion of fair dealing in this context was restricted to the taking of single copies by or for individuals and did not extend to multiple copying for (say) members of a class or choir.[29] The libraries exception, moreover, indicated that copying of a single article from a periodical was permissible, but that copying of substantial extracts from books required permission of the copyright owner where that could reasonably be obtained.[30] Beyond this, the British Copyright Council, on behalf of publishers and authors, at one stage issued its own interpretation of permissible maxima.

For a long period, publishers in the United Kingdom contemplated possible solutions to the mounting tide of photocopying without arriving at any clear policy. The prospect of finding a technical device which would prevent machines from being used to reproduce copyright work mostly looked unpromising, and in any case would have led to an undesirable embargo on something which large numbers of readers wished to do. The field was not one in which government was likely to be persuaded that a levy on copying machines or the paper used in them should be introduced: for one thing much photocopying involves no copyright infringement. The Whitford Committee treated the question extensively and with considerable sympathy for the difficulties faced by authors and publishers, taking the view that the scholar had no better claim to the free provision of copies of intellectual material than he did to free pens and paper.[31] The Committee's solution was to propose the introduction of appropriate blanket licensing arrangements through collecting societies of right-owners. The government would supervise the establishment and organisation of these societies, using by way of sanction the withdrawal of reprographic copyright for any sector which failed to act. Where proper licensing arrangements were in place, the fair dealing exception for research or private study would no longer avail, so that the licence would be needed for single as well as multiple copying of copyright material in all institutions, organisations, offices and even private homes. This, however, proved too aggressive a disturbance of the existing compromise to be politically acceptable.[32]

During the 1980s, publishers have begun to press more vigorously for **13-010** licensing arrangements. The music publishers launched proceedings against a school and a local authority for substantial photocopying of scores which otherwise they would have had to purchase[33]; book publishers proceeded against a university for multiple copying. Authors and book publishers formed the Copyright Licensing Agency to set up blanket licensing arrangements with major users, and succeeded, first with Scottish local education authorities and then with their English counter-

[28] CA 1956, s.6(1), 9(1), 41, 6(6), 7.
[29] Esp. s.41.
[30] s.7.
[31] Cmnd. 6732, 1977, Chap. 4.
[32] The libraries and educational organisations offered strong resistance to the idea.
[33] The effects of photocopying have been particularly hard on the publishers of sheet music.

parts.[34] Lengthy discussions with the Committee of Vice-Chancellors and Principals have led to an experimental scheme at some universities, which is likely to blossom into permanent and general arrangements.[35]

The 1988 Act has a range of provisions designed to encourage this evolutionary process by means of a relatively light legislative hand.[36] Fair dealing for purposes of private study and research remains a defence and it is now specified that someone other than the scholar or researcher may copy on his behalf.[37] Since after substantial debate, the government agreed that those in commerce and industry who undertake research and private study should not be excluded, it must be their view that the exception is of rather broad scope. But it remains for the courts to decide how far business, and for that matter government, should be able to take single copies without licence by claiming to need them for these purposes.[38] It is made clear that "systematic single copying" (for instance all the members of a class requesting the same material at once) is not within the exception.[39] No more specific guidance is given on what measure of single copying is "fair" than under the previous Act.[40] As before, there are separate provisions concerning copying by the librarians of prescribed (i.e. non-profit-making) libraries. Provided they are supplying individuals for research or private study at cost and in accordance with regulations, they may copy up to one article in an issue of a periodical and a reasonable extract from any other publication. In the latter case it is no longer necessary to seek permission of the copyright owner if that is reasonably obtainable.[41] These "library" arrangements are now essentially by way of supplement to the fair dealing provision, since a librarian may also rely upon the latter, when supplying a researcher or student.

13-011   Copyright accordingly is much more likely to be infringed by multiple copying (including colourable disguises for it). Only for purposes of examination are schools and other prescribed "educational establishments"[42] entitled to copy by means of a reprographic process.[43] But in order to encourage the organisation of general licences, the Act says this: until they become available, these institutions are permitted to copy very small amounts of literary, dramatic and musical works and typographical

---

[34] Beginning in 1986–1987, the scheme now produces over £1 million in revenue each year, which is distributed on the basis of sampling. See generally Clark (ed.) *Publishing Agreements* (3rd ed., 1988) 206–210.

[35] The royalty of 2·5p per page is being charged for individual copying, with an enhanced rate for copies that are being placed in libraries.

[36] See Dworkin and Taylor, pp. 169–178.

[37] CDPA 1988, s.29.

[38] *Cf.* the disagreement over the legitimacy of government copying in *Williams & Wilkins* v. *U.S.* 487 Fed. 2d. 1345 (1973).

[39] s.29(3)(b); applied to the library exceptions by s.40.

[40] See above, §§ 11-027, 11-028.

[41] ss.38–40. See also s.41 (one library supplying another); s.42 (replacements); and s.43 (copying by librarians and archivists of unpublished works); note also s.44 (copy necessary before export of an article of cultural or historical importance).

[42] The category may be expanded beyond schools by Ministerial order: s.174.

[43] s.32(3)—even then there is an exception in respect of musical works, because of the widespread sale of examination pieces.

arrangements for purposes of instruction—1 per cent. per quarter of the year.[44] The licences have to allow at least as much copying as this. Moreover their terms are subject to the jurisdiction of the Copyright Tribunal, which is specifically directed, in all cases to deal with reprography, to have regard to (a) the availability of the published edition, (b) the proportion being copied and (c) the nature of the use.[45] It is not clear how far weight should be given to evidence that (say) students are unlikely to buy a book if they cannot have a photocopy of some section of it, but it is surely a relevant factor.

There are three other provisions which aim to assist the creation of licensing arrangements. First, reprography schemes and other licences are subject to a statutory implied indemnity by the licensor covering infringement of any work which the licence purports to cover in its "blanket" but which it is in fact not within the licensor's authority to grant.[46] Secondly, in relation to instruction in educational establishments, the Secretary of State has power to order the extension of a licence or scheme to cover works which are similar and are unreasonably excluded.[47] Thirdly, also in respect of such instruction, the Secretary of State may establish an inquiry to decide whether a scheme or general licence should be established for a category of literary, dramatic, musical or artistic work not currently covered.[48] If the recommendation favours such a step, but it is not organised by right-owners within a year, a royalty-free licence takes effect.[49]

In the 1950s the publishers saw the approaching revolution in repro- **13-012** graphy and successfully lobbied for a distinct "publishers' right" to be included in the 1956 Act—the copyright in typographical arrangement of a published edition of a literary, dramatic or musical work.[50] While in this first form, much was left unsaid about the scope of protection, the version to be found in the 1988 Act is a considerable improvement. The right is given to the publishers for 25 years from publication of any edition of a literary, dramatic, musical or artistic work, which is not merely a re-publication.[51] It is infringed by making a facsimile copy of the typographical arrangement—the means of doing so is no longer limited by definition.[52] The work that has been published does not have itself to be in copyright; indeed the particular value of the right is in relation to

---

[44] s.36.

[45] s.130; and see above, §§ 12-021—12-023.

[46] s.136.

[47] s.137; it is necessary to find that adding the works would not conflict with normal exploitation and would not unreasonably prejudice legitimate interests. For variation, discharge and appeal, see ss.138, 139.

[48] s.140; again subject to the condition concerning normal exploitation and unreasonable prejudice.

[49] s.141.

[50] CA 1956, s.15.

[51] CDPA 1988, s.8. Artistic works are still not included, for reasons that remain obscure: Dworkin and Taylor 30. Electronic publishing is probably included.

[52] As copying techniques develop to include means of modifying what is copied, the term "facsimile" may prove restrictive.

new editions of old works, where the publisher nonetheless has a setting cost to retrieve. It is made manifest that where there is fair dealing for purposes of research or private study, this special copyright is not infringed: and that is likewise so in respect of the acts of copying permitted by librarians.[53] This repairs a curious lacuna in the 1956 Act.

(2) Audio and video copying

13-013 Audio- and video-cassette recorders are standard equipment for much of today's population. What minute proportion of them have any idea how frequently they are infringing copyright by their copying? The legal position under the 1956 Act in the United Kingdom was that copying of copyright material remained an act of primary infringement, for all that it took place in the home for private enjoyment, unless it was a fair dealing for purposes of research or private study. The one exception was that to make a copy of a broadcast did not infringe the broadcaster's copyright—though it would still infringe copyright in any work or film included in the broadcast.[54]

Very little home taping could be justified as fair dealing for research or private study, for that exception does not, even under the 1988 Act,[55] extend to sound recording and film copyright. Some of the home taping of sound undoubtedly deprives recording manufacturers of sales that they would otherwise have máde, but it is very difficult to determine how much; the claims of the manufacturers and the counterclaims of blank tape manufacturers show stark differences of opinion.[56] Probably little of the present copying of television broadcasts (including broadcast films) by means of VCRs deprives owners of sales of film video tapes, though it must deprive them of a certain revenue arising indirectly from hiring through rental shops. Much of this type of copying involves the "time-shifting" of broadcasts for viewing at a more convenient moment, the copier then wiping the tape by recording something else. Moreover, VCRs at present allow recordings only from broadcasts, not from other tapes, where as with sound both activities are common. These differences between audio and video recording are important in assessing the impact of the Berne Convention, which appears to disallow any general exception for domestic copying if it would deprive the owner of just remuneration.[57] This has necessarily been a basic consideration for government in deciding what should be done on the matter in the 1988 Act. Copyright owners have campaigned on two main fronts in recent debates: to prevent the introduction of exceptions which would legitimise all domestic copying of recordings and films (even though this would make honest people of the many who can only infringe when they copy); and to secure an actual return by a sales royalty or levy on recording equipment or tapes or both. No copyright issue has been more hotly debated than

[53] ss.29(1), 38(1), 39(1), 41(1), 42(1).
[54] See CA 1956, s.14(4).
[55] CDPA 1988, s.29(1). See generally, Dworkin and Taylor, Chap. 3.
[56] For the debates, see e.g. Davies, *Private Copying of Sound and Audio-Visual Recordings* (1984); Home Taping Rights Campaign Office, *The Case for Home Taping* (1987).
[57] Berne Convention (Paris Act) Art. 9(2); Ricketson (1987). 479–489.

this proposed royalty-cum-levy. On no other matter did the British government swing so evidently in the wind. As is now well-known, one school of thought believed in the royalty as the least compensation to which producers were entitled; but it succumbed to a higher school which sensed the levy to be an interest-group tax and so a political danger. Britain therefore has not for the moment followed the lead set by West Germany, Austria, France, the Iberian countries and most Scandinavian countires.[58] The government's refusal received contemporaneous support from the EEC's Green Paper on copyright issues, which blew hot and cold on the levy concept and warmed instead to the idea of spoiler devices.[59]

As we have seen, right-owners have been attempting to persuade courts that those who supply recording equipment are authorising or inciting infringement. But in the celebrated "Betamax" case, a majority of the United States Supreme Court refused to find private recording from television, largely for "time-shifting," to be anything other than "fair use" (according to American doctrine).[60] In England, equally, there were rejections of other cases and finally, in CBS Songs v. Amstrad, the House of Lords refused to find infringement or other wrong in marketing a twin-deck tape recorder, for all that it would likely be used for taping copyright music and sound recordings without licence.[61] Now, where material is copied from a broadcast or cable-cast, the new Act has in any case introduced an exception for time-shifting, which affects all copyrights in the material transmitted as well as in the transmission itself.[62] Record and film companies will scarcely set about home copiers, requiring them to prove their intent to view or listen at a more convenient time; so this is very close to an exemption of all domestic copying, provided that it comes from a broadcast or cable-cast. The Government thought that the Berne Convention allowed it to go so far.

With these avenues closed, right-owners in the United Kingdom have had to rest content with two provisions. The first is the introduction of the rental right as part of the copyright in sound recordings, films and computer programs.[63] It is a right against the business activity of making copies available for a payment in money or money's worth) on terms that they will be returned.[64] It is not yet clear what licensing arrangements will be made for hire-shops. But if the entitled manufacturers do demand this tribute for hiring, schemes and general licences will be subject to the

---

[58] Cf. the Government's pro-levy stand in its White Paper (Cmnd. 9712, 1986), Chap. 6.
[59] Copyright and the Challenge of Technology (Com(88)172) Chap. 3.
[60] Sony v. Universal City Studios 104 U.S. 774 (1984); Ladd (1983) J.Cop.Soc. 421; Leete (1986) 23 Am.Bus.L.J. 551.
[61] [1988] R.P.C. 57; and see above, § 11-017. Cf. the position of a library which supplies a photocopying machine for use by readers: Moorhouse v. University of NSW [1976] R.P.C. 157.
[62] CDPA 1988, s.70, covering private and domestic recording of a broadcast or cable programme solely for the purpose of enabling it to be viewed or listened to at a more convenient time.
[63] s.18(2) proviso.
[64] s.179 "rental"; but the concept is extended to all lending of this material by public libraries: see above, § 11-021.

jurisdiction of the Copyright Tribunal[65]; and if they refuse to license rental shops they face the threat of a Ministerial order reducing their right to one of equitable remuneration.[66]

13-014   The second provision is aimed, in the coming era of highly efficient copying equipment, to support the fitting of spoiler devices which will prevent the making of useable copies. Once such techniques are adopted the problem becomes the elimination of anti-spoiler devices. Section 296 gives a new right to a person who issues copies of copyright works to the public with built-in "copy-protection." He is entitled to proceed against anyone who "knowingly" makes, imports or markets equipment designed to circumvent the copy protection.[67] This is a civil right of action which may lead to an injunction, monetary relief, delivery up and direct seizure, as with copyright piracy. But it is not necessary for the right-owner to show that his own works were likely to be copied on defendants' machines. In this respect, the protection is wide. At last right-owners have secured one form of relief against marketers of copying hardware.

    Its significance, and that of the rental right, will have to be tested against rapidly developing technical possibilities. It is the shift towards digital, as distinct from analogue, recording, already manifest in the compact disc and digital audio tape (DAT), that is transforming the present position. The characteristic of the new technology that is most threatening to copyright interests is its ability to produce unlimited copies, which are for practical purposes perfect, without any loss of recording quality. In Japan, where DAT is more widely available than elsewhere, there has in consequence been an upsurge in rental-shops for sound recordings. When digital transfer of videos becomes possible (as is doubtless inevitable) it can be expected that there will be much hiring for the purpose of making home copies; small-scale pirates can be expected to spring up everywhere. This is what gives urgency to the search for effective spoiler devices and for ways of suppressing counter-measures against them. Many battles still lie ahead before some kind of workable compromise settles in the industries concerned. Can it in the end be that right-owners will be able by a technical device to prevent the public at large from using machines for convenient copying to which they have become accustomed on a very large scale?

3. COMPUTERS: SOFTWARE, DATA BASES, OUTPUT

13-015 The efficiency of computers in storing, retrieving, selecting and manipulating information no longer inspires the awe that it did a quarter-century ago. Even so computer science remains still in its vigorous infancy: far more complex prospects, in which computers are linked in networks, are beginning to develop; so also are the limited and simplified

[65] Above, §§ 12-021—12-023.
[66] s.66(1)–(4).
[67] It also extends to those who publish information intended to aid or assist such circumvention. See generally, Davies [1986] E.I.P.R. 155.

possibilities provided by the micro-processor. The industry attracts immense investment—in machinery for use (hardware), programs to direct operations and their accompanying documentation (software) and research concerning both.[68] There have certainly been efforts directed to employing intellectual property in the protection of this investment. But more immediately striking is the fact that comparatively little emphasis has been placed on such rights. In truth the industry is developing so rapidly that it has managed by and large with the short-term aids of contract and attendant confidence. Those who supply computer services have mostly directed their attention to their legal relations with their own clients. Much, for instance, has been lately heard of "shrink-wrap" licences on the outside packaging of software; these are intended to bind those who break the packet open.[69] As the computer art becomes more mature, and certain operations at least are performed in much the same way over longer periods of time, interest in rights of property that are good against competitors will undoubtedly increase.

As this happens, the main interest is likely to focus upon programs and other software, since it is their use which most often bears profitable repetition and so opens the way to imitation by rivals. The growth of separate "software houses" over the past decades has made this sort of competition a real danger. We have seen already that most national and regional authorities have been reluctant to admit patents for computer programs, though some change seems now to be occurring.[70] While it is commonly accepted that copyright is a more useful implement in this field, there has been growing discussion about a special system to meet the needs of the computer industry. In this section we are first concerned with the present application of British copyright law to computer programs and then with possible modifications and alternatives for the future. But programs are not the only subject-matter which may create copyright problems: something must also be said of the data used and produced in the course of computer operations.

(1) Computer programs[71]

As in the working out of complete copyright works such as plays or symphonies, the program which instructs a computer to perform the desired operation often goes through a series of evolutionary steps from preliminary conception to detailed and complex expression. In this process (which varies from case to case) a crucial stage in the conception is often the expression of the basic steps to be executed—the algorithm—in the form of a flow-chart or other logical flow diagram. Thereafter the statement of instructions in a computer language is relatively unskilled **13:016**

---

[68] See Whitford Committee Report, Cmnd. 6732, § 477.
[69] How far they are enforceable is a difficult issue of contract and confidence: Smith (1985) Comp.L. & P. 128; Maher (1987) 35 J.Cop.Soc. 292.
[70] Above, §§ 5-046 et seq.
[71] The literature is now immense: note particularly: Ulmer and Kolle (1983) 14 I.I.C. 159; Karnell [1985] E.I.P.R. 126; Brown (1986) 3 Comp.L. & P. 45; Cline (1987) 75 Calif.L.R. 633; Bainbridge (1987) 50 M.L.R. 202; H. Carr, *Computer Software: Legal Protection in the United Kingdom* (1987); Dworkin and Taylor, Chap. 15.

though it may be very laborious. The detailed writing will likely be in a so-called "high level" language (such as Fortran or Cobol), giving the program in source code. The computer itself then converts this into operational terms of object code, by means of a separate "system control" program.

13-017   Since the advent of the micro-computer, producers of software, some of it the result of very large investment indeed, have become most anxious to prevent imitations appearing on the mass market. They have turned to copyright as the form of intellectual property most immediately adaptable to their purpose and have striven to establish, country by country, that the generation of a program is considered the creation of literary work. In some countries this result has been achieved by court decision. But two hazards in particular have emerged. First, there has been a counter-argument that, at least when the program reaches electronic form, it has become a means of operating the machine and is no longer appropriate subject-matter for copyright protection.[72] This is a particularly damaging view, given that many programs are now written entirely on computer, rather than first on paper; and given, as a corollary, that copies of the program in machine-readable form may not be regarded as "reproduction in a material form" for purposes of infringement.[73] Secondly, in countries which require a sufficient level of originality to be shown, there might be no protection for a program involving only humdrum writing skills.[74]

Partly because of these considerations, there have been contemporaneous attempts to procure legislation specifically incorporating programs into the copyright fold, mainly as literary works. While in the United Kingdom, the judges showed no tendency to resist this deployment of copyright,[75] an Act was nevertheless procured in 1985 which sought to forestall any lapse into apostasy.[76] Now in the 1988 Act, that position has been reaffirmed and indeed carried somewhat further in matters of important detail.[77]

[72] So the High Court of Australia by majority held in *Computer Edge* v. *Apple Computer* [1986] F.S.R. 537, joining in the revival of Davey L.J.'s dictum, (refusing to find copyright in a chart for making a shirt-sleeve): "a literary work is intended to afford either information and instruction, or pleasure, in the form of literary enjoyment" (*Hollingrake* v. *Truswell* [1894] 3 Ch. 420; and see *Exxon* v. *Exxon* [1982] R.P.C. 69). But "instruction?" For the opposite view, in the U.S. and Canada: *Apple Computer* v. *Franklin* 714 F.2d 1240 (1984); *Whelan* v. *Jaslow* 797 F.2d 1222 (1986), [1987] F.S.R. 1; *Broderbund Software* v. *Unison World* 684 F.Supp. 1127; *Apple Computer* v. *Mackintosh Computers* (1986) 28 D.L.R. (4th) 178; Hoffman *et al.* [1988] E.I.P.R. 337.

[73] In the *Apple* case, the Australian High Court did not need to reach this question. If the copy was not "reproduction," it was unlikely to be held a "translation" or any other form of "adaptation."

[74] See, for instance, the German Supreme Court's decision, *In Kasso-Program* [1986] E.I.P.R. 185. Inevitably, its meaning is the subject of hot debate: see Lehmann (1988) 19 I.I.C. 473.

[75] Thus there were interlocutory decisions in which copyright protection was assumed: *e.g. Sega Enterprises* v. *Richards* [1983] F.S.R. 73; *Thrustcode* v. *W.W. Computing, ibid.* 502.

[76] Copyright (Computer Software) Amendment Act 1985, applying the 1956 Act to programs as it applies to literary works.

[77] Dworkin and Taylor, Chap. 15; Perry (1988) 4 Comp.L. & P. 33; Millard, *ibid.* 66.

(a) *Existence of copyright*

"Literary work"—which in general is any work that is not dramatic or **13-018** musical and which is written, spoken or sung—now explicitly includes a computer program.[78] The program must therefore be in writing, but this is defined to include writing in code, not necessarily by hand, and "regardless of the method by which, or medium in or on which, it is recorded."[79] This presumably is wide enough to embrace storage in a computer. There will still be the general copyright considerations: has there been sufficient labour, skill and judgment to satisfy the requirement of originality, and in the case of very simple programs—perhaps to control a watch or telephone—it may not be possible to surmount this hurdle. But the low threshold set by this requirement means that it will pose only minimal difficulty.

(b) *Exclusive rights*

As to infringement, the restricted act of "copying a work" is stated to **13-019** include storing the work in any medium by electronic means,[80] and that will apply as much to the infringement of a program as to the storing of data in a computer. The conversion of a program from one computer language or code to another counts as "translation" and therefore as the restricted act of "adaptation," except where this occurs incidentally in the course of running the program.[81] More importantly, perhaps, organising the circulation of copies of a program for sale may infringe, and acts of selling and other marketing may amount to secondary infringement.[82] In parallel with the neighbouring rights in sound recordings and films, the new rental right also embraces computer programs.[83] This extends not only to rental in the usual sense but even to free lending by public libraries.[84] Also, as with neighbouring rights, there are no moral rights of paternity and integrity in computer programs.[85]

The government refused to introduce a general exception allowing those who obtain legitimate copies of programs to make back-up copies of them. It would admit only one statutory addition to the operation of contractual terms: if any work in electronic form is sold on terms that it may be copied or adapted, the right to do so passes to any subsequent tansferee of any of the copies.[86]

(c) *Substantial taking*

As elsewhere in copyright law, the scope of the right remains largely a **13-020** matter for judicial decision. Right-owners naturally wish to be able to

---

[78] CDPA 1988, s.3(1)(b). There is no definition of "computer" or "program."
[79] s.178 "writing," "written."
[80] s.17(2); note also s.17(6) covering transient copying.
[81] s.21(4).
[82] s.18, 22 *et seq.*
[83] s.18(2); this right endures for 50 years from first legitimate marketing of the program: s.66(5). Like other rental rights, it is liable to be reduced to a right to equitable remuneration by ministerial order: s.66(1).
[84] See above, § 11-021.
[85] s.79(2), 81(2): the same is true of computer-generated work.
[86] s.56.

prevent not only direct piracy but also more sophisticated re-creations of programs, and indeed to be able to proceed against borrowings that are put to other uses by additions, deletions and other changes. It is often straightforward to "deconstruct" a program from its object code version and then substantially to rewrite its detailed steps in other ways. There are then considerable difficulties in showing that enough of the original has been taken, in accordance with general principles of copyright law. While the owner has only to demonstrate substantial copying (judged by quality rather than plain quantity), nevertheless it is taking of expression and not merely idea which is in issue. In the United States, some courts have been convinced by expert witnesses that this is an appropriate case to look beyond literal reproduction of programming instructions to the "look and feel" of the program as a whole.[87] This is a view which confines "idea" to the basic purpose for writing the program and allows considerable scope for a finding of infringement where there has been reverse engineering and adaptation.[88] The reasoning resembles that which English courts have applied, for instance, in cases on stealing the dramatic structure of a play.[89] It is to be predicted therefore that here also the courts will be prepared, as they receive similar cases, to go some distance down the same path. Thus in a recent interlocutory decision, Falconer J. found that an arguable case of infringement of a computer-language translation program had been made out by showing a small proportion of actual line similarity, structural similarities and the occurrence of the same errors in both programs.[90] How far this reasoning will be carried will doubtless depend upon the degree of deliberate corner-cutting which a particular defendant has exhibited.

(2) Data bases

13-021   The ability of the computer to store large amounts of information for selective retrieval at a later stage is only beginning to be realised. Ultimately this may become a form of holding which replaces the books of a library, just as already it is replacing the documents of a business or government record office. When, if ever, the scholar will set to work with display panel and print-out facility can only be a matter of speculation. But it suggests the potential importance of knowing whether the act of feeding a work into a computer store and the step of retrieving it, or some part of it, are to fall within the scope of copyright.

The act of storing now falls within the scope of copyright under the new British law.[91] As far as actual use of the stored material is concerned, general principle would suggest that only if a print-out of a substantial part of the work is taken is there an act of reproduction. As with programs, there seems no good reason for introducing a special "use"

---

[87] Notably, *Whelan* v. *Jaslow* (above, n. 72); see Stern [1986] E.I.P.R. 195, [1987] E.I.P.R. 125.

[88] *Cf.* the topography right, below §§ 14-034—14-035.

[89] See above, § 11-010.

[90] *MS Associates* v. *Power* [1985] F.S.R. 242.

[91] C.D.P.A. 1988, s.17(2), following a Whitford Committee recommendation, Cmnd. 6732, §§ 505, 508.

right that would be broader in scope. If the provider of a data base wishes to charge in proportion to his client's use of the data, he can arrange this by contract; against a stranger the right would appear to have little practical value.

(3) Output

Where a computer is utilised to produce material that is recognisable **13-022** as a "work" in any copyright sense, the question of copyright in that output can also arise. According to the Whitford Committee, "the author of the output can be none other than the person, or persons, who devised the instructions and originated the data used to control and condition the computer to produce the particular result. In many cases it will be a matter of joint authorship."[92] This analysis may fit expectations when an individual or an organisation is responsible for its own data and program. But where a software house is commissioned by a client to provide the program, it may well be reasonable for the client to assume that it holds copyright in the output.

In seeking a workable solution, the 1988 Act has introduced the "computer-generated work," *i.e.* a work generated "in circumstances such that there is no human author."[93] In some of the situations described by the Whitford Committee (*e.g.* word-processing, data manipulation), there will be a human author who can be identified with some ease. The borderland may prove difficult. Where, however, the work is computer-generated, the copyright endures for fifty years from making the work[94] and is accorded initially to "the person by whom the arrangements necessary for the creation of the work are undertaken."[95] These rules make plain the borrowing from ideas affecting the older neighbouring rights, particularly in films. But their transposition to this new field is less than happy. As between the provider of a data base (such as "Lexis") and a user who extracts information from it, who undertakes the arrangements for creation? Perhaps this is a case of joint authorship, as Whitford suggested—but is there really a "common design"?

(2) A future regime

The fashioning of copyright law to protect investment in computer **13-023** technology has followed in the wake of a lusty new industry which had been advancing with such rapidity that ideas and products must have a brief life. But middle age will settle eventually and with it will come a re-examination of regimes of rights. It may not be long before the weight of opinion comes to perceive that the copyright adaptation, together with a measure of patenting for the most substantial breakthroughs, has only been a makeshift solution. In particular, the resort to literary copyright,

---

[92] Cmnd. 6732, §§ 514, 515; see also National Commission on New Technological Uses of Copyrighted Works (CONTU), Final Report 43–46; Hewitt [1983] E.I.P.R. 308.
[93] CDPA 1988, s.178.
[94] s.12(3).
[95] s.9(3); for the exclusion of moral rights, s.79(2), 81(2).

with its long personal period of protection must in principle be unaccept-able for a technique intimately connected with the operation of machines—the very perception which made some hesitate about the very use of copyright in this way. It is likely however that in relation to programs in the future it will continue to be thought that a right dependent upon proof of copying will for most material be the proper base of operation. What needs then to be done is to shape protection as an acknowledged neighbouring right, with a term of "industrial" dura-tion, a rule conferring initial ownership on the enterprise or organisation financially responsible for generating the material and a number of adaptations to fit the particular subject of protection. The 1988 Act indicates some movement in this direction. Over the next few years it is likely that the same evolution will be carried further as other countries adapt their legislation, and international discussion progresses.

4. CABLE AND SATELLITE TRANSMISSION

13-024 Broadcasting by Hertzian wave opened the first great opportunity of relaying performances to truly mass audiences. The resultant copyright issues were resolved over time, first, as with public performance, by treating broadcasting as an act of infringement—broadcasters as users of copyright works had therefore to seek copyright licences; and secondly, by making the act of broadcasting an activity which itself attracted copyright—those who relayed or re-transmitted the broadcast then needed a licence (unless they could claim some special exemption). By 1956, the use of wire to distribute broadcasts from a receiving antenna or to transmit other programmes was sufficiently advanced for cable-casting to be made a restricted act for literary, dramatic and musical works. A European Television Agreement of 1960, sponsored by the Council of Europe, aimed to prevent a person receiving a broadcast from another state in order to diffuse it by cable. To this the British have been parties, but subject to significant reservations.[96] A separate right in cable-casts that were not mere relays had to wait until 1984, when the technical possibilities of co-axial cable were considered to herald a communication revolution in the United Kingdom as in other countries.[97]

13-025 In the last decade, rapid advances in the use of satellites for inter-national communications has also promised many novelties, and these are coming to fruition.[98] In part they concern broadcasting activities. Fixed satellite service (FSS) systems operate by securing that the transmission is received from the satellite by a station and the programme is then distributed (typically) through a cable system. Direct broadcasting by

---

[96] Some but not all of these are being withdrawn in the light of the 1988 Act.
[97] Cable and Broadcasting Act 1984, s.57, Sched. 5, §§ 6, 7.
[98] Much information about these developments can be found in the EEC Green Paper, *Television without Frontiers* (1984). See also Abrahams (1984) 32 J.Cop.Soc. 173; Bate *Television by Satellite: Legal Aspects* (1987).

satellite (DBS) systems operate to individual receivers, such as dishes, without the intervention of earth station and cable. With the development of encrypting techniques, an operator can limit direct reception so that it is available only to those who have the requisite decoding receiver. Other elements discriminating between recipients can be added, such as language and advertising. At the same time, the distinction between FSS and DBS has been blurred by the possibility of receiving the same broadcast can be received directly or through a station. Mixed systems of this kind began to be licensed in the United Kingdom from 1985 onwards and are the basis of the pay-TV services, now being introduced in Britain and elsewhere in Europe.

Cable and satellite are between them opening many new communications prospects apart from broadcasting and cable-casting, such as relaying a meeting, speech or performance to limited numbers of people in a different place or places; transmitting the content of documents so as to produce facsimiles at the point of reception; and providing access to information services and arranging the consequent placing of orders.

In determining how far these activities should be the subject of copyright, the new legislation proceeds by reference to general precepts. The distinction between reproduction and performance rights is observed. Thus "faxing" involves copying upon reception, and a special provision makes it secondary infringement to transmit a work by telecommunication system knowing or having reason to believe that such a copy will result.[99] Broadcasting and cable-casting, however, are acts of performance which accordingly require dissemination to sufficient numbers before they are covered. Hence the definition of "broadcast" which requires a transmission by wireless telegraphy capable of being lawfully received by members of the public, but includes one in encrypted form for which the programme provider has made decoding equipment available to the public.[1] Hence also the definition of "cable programme service" which covers the sending of information by a "non-wireless" telecommunications system, either to two or more places or for presentation to the public, but excepting from this a variety of limited, "closed-circuit" possibilities, which have been mentioned earlier[2]; and also by excluding services (like tele-shopping) so far as they are inter-active.

Beyond this, there are a number of crucial provisions determining the **13-026** basis on which right-owners can assert economic interests. Thus "broadcaster" is defined (so as to affect both rights and liabilities) to cover those who share responsibility for programme content, but to exclude

---

[99] CDPA 1988, s.24(2).

[1] s.6(1), (2). Note the provisions designed to reinforce the position of those who supply encrypted services: s.297 makes it a summary offence fraudulently to receive such a programme; and s.298 gives civil remedies against a person who makes or provides equipment for fraudulent reception.

[2] s.7; see above, § 10-015. Note, however, that the cabling of broadcasts within hotels, institutions and the like is no longer an excepted activity. It needs its own licence: cf. CA 1956, s.48(3).

carriers who merely provide some part of the transmission service (such as satellite access).[3] Satellite broadcasting occurs at the stage of the "up-leg" to the satellite, rather than the subsequent "down-leg" for reception—and this is so whether the primary arrangement is for FSS or DBS transmission.[4] Thus if the programme is transmitted from the United Kingdom, copyright licences are needed there and deserve to be rewarded at a rate which takes account of audiences wherever they are being reached.

The right of a copyright owner to a return in respect of the immediate re-transmission of a broadcast by cable has continued, as before, to be limited. In particular, diffusion service licensees in Britain do not need separate licence of either copyright in the broadcast or in works, recordings or films transmitted, because of their statutory responsibility to carry all BBC and IBA programmes[5]; nor do those who provide cable service in the area intended for reception of the broadcast (where the object of cabling will normally be to overcome some reception difficulty).[6] In these cases, the right-owner of material broadcast must expect his return through the royalty paid by the broadcaster, subject only to an ultimate provision concerning enhanced damages for any infringement in both the broadcast and the cable re-transmission.[7]

5. Rights in Performances

13-027 Performers engage in activities which are more immediately artistic and re-creative than the entrepreneurs who enjoy copyrights in sound recordings, films, broadcasts and cable-casts. Yet there has been considerable reluctance to give performers an equivalent property right, which has in the past been sustained principally by these very entrepreneurs. It is said that performers are protected indirectly by the entrepreneurial rights, that those financially responsible are best placed to pursue imitators, and that to give copyright to all performers in a play, a film or an orchestra would lead to quite unnecessary complexity.[8] However, some right to stop the unauthorised appropriation of performances has long been needed to cover, in particular, covert recording of the performance itself.

---

[3] s.6(3).

[4] s.6(4). This accepts a solution which makes for commercial convenience, but the question has been the subject of hot debate at the international level.

[5] s.72(2), (3).

[6] *Ibid.*; but this applies only if the transmission is not by satellite and is not encrypted.

[7] See s.73(3) proviso. Right-owners have argued that this limitation is inconsistent with the Berne Convention Art. 11*bis* (1) which distinguishes acts of radio-diffusion and acts of communicating a radio-diffusion of a work to the public, "whether over wires or not". This position has considerable strength, given the specific language of the text. But the U.K. government has not agreed.

[8] So the Gregory Committee were persuaded: Cmd. 8662, Pt. VII.

This was achieved through Performers Protection Acts,[9] which carefully restricted the available sanctions to criminal penalties and conferred no civil rights of action by their explicit terms.

Although the United Kingdom was a prominent proponent of the Rome Convention for the Protection of Performers, Producers of Phonograms and Broadcasting Organisations (1961), it made sure that the right guaranteed to performers in contracting states went only to the "possibility of preventing" a list of acts, and gave no "right to authorise and prohibit," as it did for sound recordings and broadcasts.[10] Thus the approach through the criminal law could continue to be justified.

Over the last two decades, the "bootlegging" (surreptitious recording) of performances by pop-stars and others has grown considerably and parts of the music industry have become particularly concerned. The Whitford Committee was convinced that performers should enjoy a civil right of action to injunction and damages, though it considered that this should not amount to copyright, even though it did not vouchsafe what limitations ought to be imposed to this end.[11] During the long shelf-life of that Report, a string of cases were brought in an effort to establish that "bootlegging" was actionable by inference from the Performers' Protection Acts. The Courts demonstrated themselves to be torn between a desire to put down an obvious act of unfair competition[12] and a nervousness over taking a step which Parliament had evidently refrained from; and which if allowed in this case might lead to other implications of civil statutory duties in less justifiable circumstances.[13] By 1987 the outcome of this process was that a performer could proceed for an injunction or damages as one of a class specifically protected by the Acts[14]; the recording company with whom he had an exclusive contract could not.[15] These tortuous decisions may now be regarded as a prelude to the provisions of the 1988 Act, Part II.

Following the lead of the Whitford recommendation, this creates a **13-028** dual form of "quasi-copyright" in performances, not only of dramatic, musical and literary material but also of "a variety act or any similar presentation."[16] The dual form arises because one right is conferred on

---

[9] Initially the Musical Performers' Protection Act 1925; subsequently the Performers Protection Acts 1958–1972.

[10] Cf. Art. 7 with Arts. 10, 13. For the position in the EEC as a whole, see Gotzen, *Performers' Rights in the EEC* (1977).

[11] Cmnd. 6732, § 412.

[12] Manifest particularly in *Island Records* case, where the C.A. was eager to grant an *Anton Piller* order against a bootlegger.

[13] The reluctance to do this in other circumstances was particularly apparent in *Lonrho* v. *Shell* [1982] A.C. 173, where Lord Diplock cast doubt on some of the reasoning in *Island Records*, while indicating that performers might have the special case afterwards acknowledged in *Rickless* (below, n. 38).

[14] *Rickless* v. *United Artists* [1987] F.S.R. 362 (C.A.).

[15] *R.C.A.* v. *Pollard* [1983] Ch. 135.

[16] s.180(2), explicitly including dance and mime. The extension to variety acts would cover circus turns, skating and possibly gymnastics, but not sporting activities which pay no tribute to graceful execution.

the performer personally,[17] and a second right on any record or film producer who has an exclusive contract[18] to make a record of the performance with a view to commercial exploitation.[19] The performer's own right is not capable of assignment and after his death may be exercised only by a person specifically nominated in his will or else by his personal representative.[20] By contrast the person with an exclusive recording contract may assign that contract, and with this the performance right goes to the assignee.[21]

13-029   Why, in the light of this, the performer is not allowed a full "property" right is obscure. In some European jurisdictions, the copyright author is accorded a non-assignable right in recognition and support of his special position as an artist. Here, however, the intention was apparently to place the performer in some lesser position than the author of a copyright work. This is also reflected in an ultimate power of the Copyright Tribunal to override a performer's refusal of consent, if it is being unreasonably withheld, or he or she cannot be identified.[22] This rather cumbersome procedure is directed particularly at the triangle-player in an orchestra or the spear-carrier in a play, whose consent to recording has not been procured and who seeks at a late stage to maximise his consequential power.

13-030   The dual rights do not attach to "works" made by "authors," but in other respects they are defined by factors which bear a family resemblance to those of copyright:

(i) *Duration*: the rights last for 50 years from the end of the year of performance.[23]

(ii) *Qualification for protection*: This is important just because the Rome Convention has relatively few signatory states and the granting of protection is confined to those states and to any other designated state which is considered to afford reciprocal protection to British performances.[24]

The qualification rules are different for the two rights. First, the performer's own right: infringement can occur only in respect of a "qualifying performance."[25] This is one made by a "qualifying individual" (the subject, citizen or resident of a "qualifying country") or one made in a "qualifying country." The qualifying countries are: the United Kingdom and other EEC states, Rome Convention countries and designated countries affording reciprocity.[26] Secondly, the exclusive recorder's

[17] For this right in general, ss.181–184.
[18] Exclusive, that is, even of the performer him- or herself: s.185(1). For the right in general, ss.185–188.
[19] By selling, hiring, or showing or playing in public: s.185(4).
[20] s.192.
[21] s.185(2). The right may also be licensed and that licence assigned: s.185(3).
[22] s.190.
[23] s.191.
[24] ss.206–210. Note that the Channel Islands, the Isle of Man and British colonies will be included only if designated by Order: s.208(5).
[25] s.181.
[26] s.206(1).

right: this can be infringed only if that person, or one of his licensees[27] is a "qualifying person" *i.e.* a "qualifying individual" (in the same sense as for performer's right) or a body corporate sufficiently connected with a qualifying country.[28]

(iii) *Remedies for giving rise, it would seem, to injunction, damages and account of profits, infringement.* The rights are enforceable as breaches of statutory duty. Because this is territory where immediate remedies are needed, the right-owner is given similar powers to those conferred on copyright owners: to engage in seizure against traders without premises, to have orders which include delivery up and disposal, and to proceed by way of prosecution for a range of statutory offences.[29]

6. PUBLIC LENDING RIGHT

(1) Background

To some extent the economic protection of copyright extends beyond reproduction to cover use. Public exploitation of works—by performance, broadcasting and the like—has been made part of the exclusive right for all the relevant types of copyright.[30] Equally the rental of sound recordings, films and computer programs has been covered as some compensation for the growth of home taping. Rather earlier, there was a long-running campaign to secure authors a distinct return on the borrowing of their books from libraries.[31] The nub of the argument is that organised borrowing eliminates the sale of copies to those readers who would otherwise buy their own, and it increases the number of people who benefit from the book without bringing any return to the author save his share in sales to libraries. In the United Kingdom, as in a number of other countries (West Germany and the Netherlands, the Scandinavian countries and Australia) this demand has been crowned with success. The Public Lending Right Act 1979 creates a special regime outside copyright to meet the case, which is directly funded by central government.

13-031

The problems begin with the basic conflicts of interest. On the claimants' side, there are authors and publishers. Accordingly there is the question whether both should be entitled to a share; and if so whether the rules for employed and independent authors should differ. There is also the international question, how far should foreign authors or their publishers be entitled to participate? On the user's side, there are the libraries and their borrowers. Libraries are maintained by local and central government, by educational establishments (public and private) and by private organisations (some of them profit-making). There are difficulties in determining which of them should be the subject of recoupments for borrowing and who should pay them.

[27] s.185(3).
[28] s.206(1).
[29] See generally, ss.194–202; and above, §§ 10-020—10-022.
[30] See above, § 2-009.
[31] See especially Findlater (ed.), *Public Lending Right—a Matter of Justice* (1970).

In Britain, the public libraries have attained a position of special importance in the recreational, cultural and educational life of the nation.[32] Accordingly, the campaign for an authors' lending right centred upon them. Authors' representatives, determined to keep apart from publishers, accepted that the only attainable scheme was accordingly one funded by the taxpayer, not the borrower. This in turn has dictated an administration managed by a Registrar and team of civil servants.

(2) The Public Lending Right Act 1979 and the Scheme

13-032   The right created by the Act covers books (but nothing else)[33] lent out to the public by local library authorities[34] in the United Kingdom. It is given to the authors of the books; but as it is assignable without restriction,[35] it is clearly open to publishers to negotiate with their authors an interest in it. Nothing is said about employed authors, so common law principle may dictate that presumptively they hold their interest in trust for their employers, where the work is prepared in the course of employment. By analogy to copyright, the entitlement lasts at most for the author's life and 50 years.[36]

While the Act speaks of "authors" of books without qualification, it leaves it to the Secretary of State, in drawing up his Scheme, to define the "classes, descriptions and categories" of books that qualify.[37] So also with the scales of payment; but entitlement must be "dependent on, and its extent ascertainable by reference to, the number of occasions on which books are lent out from particular libraries, to be specified in the scheme or identified in accordance with provision made by it."[38] This expresses preference for monitoring actual borrowings rather than taking sales to libraries as the base: it is a solution closer to the object of the Act and was reckoned to cost no significantly greater amount.[39]

13-033   The Scheme established under the Act applies to books of at least 32 pages, which are written by authors who are EEC nationals, or British or West German residents.[40] Works by more than two co-authors are excluded. The sum to be divided has become in 1989 £3.5 million per annum, of which some 20 per cent goes in administration.[41] Part of this is

---

[32] The British make 600 million or more borrowings of books from public libraries a year; the West Germans only 160 million and the Americans 450 million.

[33] So records, cassettes, video-tapes and toys are all outside the scheme. The creators concerned did not press a case, and to cover them would have added a new range of practical problems. But see the impact of the 1988 Act, below, n. 44.

[34] As defined in s.5(2).

[35] See s.1(7)(b).

[36] s.1(6). The entitlement starts with first publication or registration, whichever is later. The scheme may alter the periods. The analogy to literary copyright is not exact, since post-mortem publication does not extend the duration of public lending right.

[37] s.1(1), (2).

[38] ss.1(2), 3(3).

[39] See the papers of the Technical Information Group of March 1975 and March 1976.

[40] 24 pages for poetry and drama.

[41] PLR Scheme (Commencement) Order 1983 and subsequent Orders of 1983. The inclusion of West German authors follows from a mutual recognition of rights. This has been possible despite the fact that German protection is given as part of copyright, while this is not so in Britain.

expended on the sample of borrowings from selected libraries, which determines the distribution among authors.[42] There is however a ceiling of £6,000 per author, which prevents the most popular writers from scooping a distinctly shallow pool. Even among those who do register, the scheme provides little more than a pourboire, but for the moment authors take it as a token of justice.

(3) Public "rental"

The 1988 Act has created a rental right in sound recordings, films and **13-034** computer programs, where the hiring is by a business for money or its equivalent.[43] By sleight-of-hand in an obscure Schedule, the government has extended this right to lendings by public libraries of these types of material, not only where a charge is made but when the loan is free.[44] So the copyright owners of this material—by definition entrepreneurs, save in the case of the occasional computer program—have protection within the framework of copyright and may extract what they can from the libraries (who in turn must decide what they will pass on to borrowers), subject only to the threat of Copyright Tribunal proceedings, or the imposition of an equitable remuneration scheme[45] if these demands prove too strident. Foreign owners will in many cases qualify under general Convention obligations. Perhaps this surreptitious change presages an abandonment of the special public lending scheme for the authors of books. It is certainly ironic that they should have been cast the sop of a non-copyright solution, while the big producers of records, films and programs have been allowed under the copyright net.

(Artists' Resale Right)

7. Droit de Suite

The special value of some artistic works lies not in the capacity to **13-035** multiply copies but in the uniqueness of the original. This is true of many paintings and sculptures. As an artist acquires a reputation, works of this kind accelerate in value. Then his death may add to the element of scarcity, and the effect will be marked in the resale prices of his works. Since the artist and his estate normally benefit only from the first sale of the work, they receive no return from subsequent increases in capital value. A *droit de suite*, which is provided by the laws of a number of states,[46] but nowhere in the common law world, requires a proportion of

[42] See Ministerial Report, H.C. 4, 1988–1989.
[43] See above, § 11-021.
[44] CDPA 1988, Sched. 7, § 8, amendment to the Public Libraries and Museums Act 1964, s.8(6).
[45] Under CDPA 1988, s.66; above, § 11-029.
[46] Within the EEC, Belgium, France, West Germany, Italy and Luxembourg; and in some 10 states elsewhere. See generally, Plaisant (1969) 5 Copyright 157; Ulmer (1975) 6 I.I.C. 12; Nordemann (1977) 13 Copyright 337.

resale prices[47] to be paid during the copyright period to the artist or his successors.[48] As an "author's right" it is the antithesis of "copyright"; but it shares the same moral justification.[49]

In its path, however, stand various political or practical objections. According to the Whitford Committee,[50] which refused to recommend its introduction, these are:

13-036   (i) Any form of *droit de suite* chiefly benefits the artist's estate after his death; yet "the present climate of opinion is against inherited wealth."[51]

(ii) To have much meaning, the right would have to be made inalienable, after the fashion of a moral right—otherwise any well-advised purchaser would require its assignment at the very stage of the artist's career when he lacks the power to resist; yet this would be "contrary to normal practice" in British copyright law.[52]

(iii) Logically all sales ought to be subject to the levy; yet it would be virtually impossible to enforce in the case of private sales and would tend to drive business from the auctioneers and other dealers in Britain.[53]

(iv) Again, logically it ought to apply to all kinds of artistic works and to the original manuscripts of other works—there might also be a case for including limited editions; but these prospects are said to create "practical difficulties."[54]

(v) It would be desirable to restrict the amount to a proportion of the resale profit in excess of inflation; but that would be complicated to administer.[55]

(vi) The right would appropriately be limited to the artist's life and 50 years; yet the Committee thought it "purely fortuitous" whether sales giving rise to a claim would actually take place in that period.[56]

(vii) There was little demand for the right, which had not produced much for artists in countries where it existed.[57]

Nevertheless the right exists, at least in form, in five EEC states.[58] So on paper the market in works of art between member states is distorted.

---

[47] The proportion in existing schemes has been between one and five per cent. Frequently there is a minimum value by way of starting point.

[48] See generally, Price (1960) 77 Yale L.J. 1333; Plaisant (1969) 5 Copyright 15; Lahore, *Copyright and the Arts in Australia* (1974), pp. 83–86.

[49] Hence it has attained a place in the Berne Convention (Brussels, Art. 14*bis*; Paris, Art. 14 *ter*); but it is left to member states to decide whether to confer it.

[50] Cmnd. 6732, Chap. 17.

[51] *Ibid.*, § 802.

[52] *Ibid.*

[53] *Ibid.* Most existing systems restrict the right to public sales. The special position of British houses in the world of international art dealing makes it likely that there would be strong resistance to a *droit de suite* in domestic law.

[54] § 803.

[55] §§ 799, 803.

[56] § 802.

[57] §§ 797, 798. It seems that the right produced only £47,000 in France in 1966 and as little as £100,000 in the whole world in 1972.

[58] See n. 46 above.

However, in reality, there are West European countries, such as Switzerland, which do not have the right and which might acquire much
European art business if the right were introduced throughout the EEC.
Accordingly it is not to be expected that there will be Community action
on the subject.

8. DOMAINE PUBLIC PAYANT

This system aims to provide funds earmarked either for the support of **13-037**
authors in some kind of social need or to promote the arts. It calls for
the payment of royalties upon exploitations of works, after their
copyright has expired, into a joint fund.[59] It could operate for a limited
period or in perpetuity.

It is a proposal which attracts distinguished advocates from time to
time, particularly amongst authors who feel some uneasiness about the
extent to which the arts are dependent upon government grants.[60] But if
an "independent" fund is raised from royalties upon deceased authors'
works, the amount of support allowed out of general revenue is likely to
be modified. Accordingly, even those who would most like to see more
resources devoted to the arts are faced with a difficult bit of political
guesswork. In terms of method, the choice is between a tax on those who
acquire or enjoy works during the term of a *domaine public payant* and
a tax raised on the public as a whole. In terms of amount, the choice
concerns the degree of dependence on decisions of the government of the
day. In terms of distribution, the difficulties of establishing a "fair" body
for making decisions arise under either system. One uncalculated uncertainty is the cost of collecting royalties if there were to be a *domaine
public* payment. Without dismissing the case out of hand, the Whitford
Committee found it unproven.[61] But it may well merit closer investigation
in future.

Again there is an EEC dimension. Italy has an established *domaine
public payant* and France has engaged in a number of experiments.
Germany extended its copyright period to the author's life plus 70 years
rather than confer such a right.[62] Dietz has proposed a *domaine public
payant* as one way of resolving the discrepancies in the terms of
copyright within the Community,[63] for there may be grave political, or
even constitutional, difficulties in reducing a period of copyright protection for the future. But because the question of duration is as a whole so
sensitive, it has not been covered in the EC Commission's Green Paper
on Copyright. The whole matter is one on which national preferences are
likely to continue unfettered for a long time.

[59] Which could be administered by the state or by an authors' collecting society.
[60] It was proposed to both the Gregory and Whitford Committees, and rejected by both:
Cmd. 8661, § 24; Cmnd. 6732, §§ 643–647; and see n. 14 below.
[61] Cmnd. 6732, § 646.
[62] See generally, Mouchet (1970) 6 Copyright 197.
[63] Dietz, §§ 434–437.

9. CROWN AND PARLIAMENTARY COPYRIGHT

13-038 Under the 1956 Act, there were sweeping provisions giving copyright in literary, dramatic, musical and artistic works to the Crown if they were either made under its direction or control, or were so published.[64] Thus, for instance, a patent specification, drafted by a patent agent for a client, ceased to be a copyright of either and became the Crown's when the Patent Office published it. The Whitford Committee criticised the reach of these provisions, but at first it appeared that the government was not to be shifted on the subject. However, more temperate attitudes in the end prevailed, and the Crown's claims have been largely aligned with those of employers.[65] In the wake of this it has been necessary to confer a separate copyright on Parliament in respect of documents and other material emerging from its proceedings[66]; and also to confer immunity from infringement where a public office or person in authority is producing information in which there is a special public interest.[67] In approaching the subject, the lawyer needs to remember that Crown and Parliamentary copyright remain distinctive creatures. Among their characteristics, those concerning duration of the rights have already been mentioned.[68]

Crown copyright under the 1988 Act arises where a work is made by an officer or servant of the Crown in the course of his duties.[69] Parliamentary copyright is, in the main, given to whichever House has, by its direction or control, had the work made; or to both, if they are jointly responsible.[70] But while the old formula of "under direction or control" is still used in respect of Parliamentary copyright, it is explicitly limited to work made by an officer or servant of the relevant House in the course of his duties, and to any sound recording, film, live broadcast or live cable-cast of proceedings.[71] It is not sufficient that a House commissions a report from an outside person, such as Specialist Adviser to a Select Committee. These copyrights take effect without the need to comply with the usual rules for qualification.

13-039　　As regards the acts permitted in the interests of public administration,[72] the Crown is entitled to make copies[73] of a literary, dramatic, musical or

[64] C.A. 1956, s.39. For egregious consequences, see, e.g. Ironside v. Att.-Gen. [1988] R.P.C. 197.
[65] CDPA 1988, ss.163, 164; cf. above, § 12-003. For the copyright which may by Order be conferred on international organisations, see s.168.
[66] ss.165–167.
[67] ss.47–50.
[68] Above, § 10-031.
[69] The old test (was the work made under the Crown's direction or control?) was in some respects wider. By the relevant transitional provision, it would appear that a work which was Crown copyright under the old law, but not under the new, ceases at "commencement" to be Crown copyright and becomes (presumably) that of the author, or his employer, or the assignee of either and has the duration of ordinary copyright: Sched. 1, § 40.
[70] s.165, and see s.166 for the special copyright in Bills.
[71] s.165(4).
[72] Note also s.47, allowing the person duly authorised to permit copying of the content of a public register, but not for publication; similarly, under s.49, for public records; and under s.50 for acts specifically authorised by statute.
[73] And to issue the copies to the public.

artistic work communicated to it in the course of public business, but only when it does so for the purpose of the communication to it, and only if no breach of confidence is involved.[74] By this, the Crown recovers some of the ground which it surrendered in accepting a more limited concept of Crown copyright. But not all: in particular, in the material that no longer belongs to it, it has no proprietary right to prevent publication, politically embarrassing though that may be. This perhaps explains (while it certainly does not excuse) the recent insistence of government departments that they be given contractual powers to decide if and when reports of research which they have commissioned shall be published.[75] The United Kingdom is not a country in which ideas of free access to, and free use of, government information flourish with any vigour.[76] Were this so, there would have developed, as in the United States,[77] much more embracing notions of public domain material in which no copyright may be claimed. As it is, in Britain, the Crown has copyright even in Acts of Parliament and Church of England Measures.[78] For these, as for delegated legislation and official reports, the government will doubtless continue to specify by Treasury Circular how far it will countenance free copying by others.

Of particular interest to lawyers in this context is copyright in law reports. While it is to be assumed that no judge would hold himself to be a servant of the Crown, he or she is appointed by royal authority and is therefore probably an officer of the Crown.[79] Accordingly under the new test, judgments fall within the scope of Crown copyright[80] and this must extend to extempore oral pronouncements, provided that a record of them is made by someone.[81] While copyright is not infringed either by anything done for the purposes of judicial proceedings, or for reporting them, the latter exception does not extend to the copying of work which is itself a published report of the proceedings. This proviso appears to apply to the Crown copyright in the judgment as well as any copyright which an agency recording the judgment may have.[82]

---

[74] ss.47, 171(1)(e).

[75] Under the old law, where copyright lay in the Crown, the DHSS and some other Departments nevertheless conceded in research contract conditions that the researchers should be entitled after notice to publish. One argument in 1987 for changing this provision, was that the Crown needed to control publication in order to "protect Crown copyright." So little is the nature and purpose of copyright understood that many must have been misled by this piece of self-serving mystification.

[76] *Pace* Lord Goff, above, § 8-018.

[77] For which see, Nimmer, *Copyright* § 5-06.

[78] s.164.

[79] s.45, also covering Parliamentary proceedings; and see s.46 in relation to proceedings of royal commissions and statutory inquiries.

[80] Under the old law, it was not entirely straightforward to say that judgments were by the direction or control of the Crown; accordingly this is one point at which Crown copyright has been broadened in the new Act. See generally, Taggart (1984) 10 Syd.L.R. 319; von Nessen (1985) 48 M.L.R. 412; Tapper (1985) 11 Monash U.L.R. 75.

[81] For the new law of fixation, see above, §§ 10-018—10-019.

[82] The distinction is important in English practice, where judgment reporting has in large measure been a private service.

Part V

TRADE MARKS AND NAMES

CHAPTER 14

INDUSTRIAL DESIGN

I. BACKGROUND

So far as industry is concerned, easily the most significant changes 14-001
introduced into intellectual property law by the Copyright, Designs and
Patents Act 1988 concern design elements in industrially produced
articles.[1] Thanks to the history of this vexed question over the last 20
years in the United Kingdom and other Commonwealth countries, many
industries, whether their production concentrates upon machinery or
upon decorative articles, have come to rely upon copyright protection
against imitations of the form and appearance of their products. They
will look eagerly at the new dispositions to discover what aid is to be
had in the future. In many cases they cannot expect as generous a
coverage as has recently been available. The general scope of the law has
been brought back roughly to where it is in other countries. But it must
be understood that there are difficulties here which all countries find
hard to resolve.[2]

From the tortuous history of the subject certain salient features can be
picked out.

(1) Origins of design registration

The registration system was the nineteenth-century answer to demands 14-002
for protection of the design elements in articles mass-produced by an
industrial process.[3] Initially it gave only a very short term of protection to
cover the lead-time in introducing a new product on to the market.

(2) Copyright Act 1911

This introduced the concept of infringement of an artistic work by 14-003
"reproduction in a material form," including the conversion of a two-
dimensional design into a three-dimensional article.[4] In order to sterilise
the potency of this new notion in the field of industrial design, section 22
excluded all copyright in designs capable of being registered under the
registration system, which were used or intended to be used as models or

---

[1] See Dworkin and Taylor Chap. 12; Lane [1988] E.I.P.R. 370.
[2] See, for comparisons, Reichman [1983] Duke L.J. 1143; 31 J.Cop.Soc. 267; Perot-Morel
[1984] E.I.P.R. 129; Krüger (1984) 15 I.I.C. 168; Fellner, *The Protection of Industrial
Designs in the EEC* (1985).
[3] See below, § 14-008.
[4] Including infringement by indirect copying of the article legitimately made from the
design: see *King Features* case (below, n. 89a).

patterns to be multiplied by any industrial process.[5] This had the effect of keeping copyright out of most industrial territory, though its effect did not extend to designs which were originally intended for a non-industrial process, such as comic strip illustration. Because of this difference the section was eventually judged unsatisfactory, though it has continued to be the rule affecting pre-1957 designs.[6]

(3) Copyright Act 1956

14-004   This set out to eliminate dual protection by copyright as well as registration on a different, highly complex basis. The essential feature of section 10 was that while copyright now subsisted in designs of all kinds, industrial application of them would not amount to infringement if a registered right had been applied for, or if the copyright owner had used the design on industrially produced articles. In the regrettable decision of *Dorling* v. *Honnor Marine*,[7] the Court of Appeal chose to distinguish between designs capable of registration which were subject to section 10, and designs which were not (chiefly because they were functional) and so bore full-term artistic copyright even in industrial applications.

(4) Design Copyright Act 1968

14-005   The 1956 Act provision was modified in 1968, by a terse Act,[8] which in essence put off the moment for excluding copyright in industrial applications of a design until 15 years from first authorised marketing of articles bearing the design. Despite the best efforts of Whitford J.,[9] this was held to continue the *Dorling* distinction between registrable designs (now able to enjoy 15-year copyright) and non-registrable, functional designs which endured for the designer's life and 50 years thereafter.[10]

(5) British Leyland v. Armstrong.[11]

14-006   Because this disproportion produced extreme results affecting so much industrial production, the House of Lords were moved to intervene in advance of new legislation. In the *British Leyland* case they had to consider a copyright claim to the design of the exhaust pipes for certain

---

[5] For a long period there was little consideration of which designs were capable of registration. Latterly, it was held that, while they might not be registrable because solely functional (see below, § 14-016) they did not lose this quality because in the particular case they were not "new or original": see *Interlego* v. *Tyco* [1988] R.P.C. 343 (and, for the equivalent point under the 1956 Act, *Interlego* v. *Alex Foley* [1987] F.S.R. 283). In the *Tyco* case the point was part of an argument of considerable audacity (which failed).
[6] See now CDPA 1988, Sched. 1, § 6.
[7] [1965] Ch. 1.
[8] Introduced as a Private Member's Bill, it was intended to improve the position of the designs of furniture, jewellery, toys and the like. Its impact on functional design went unappreciated during its enactment.
[9] *e.g. Hoover* v. *Hulme* [1982] F.S.R. 565; overruled (quite unnecessarily) by the C.A. in *British Leyland* v. *Armstrong* [1986] R.P.C. 308–309, 315–316. The issue was not taken to the H.L.
[10] A distinction labelled by the Whitford Committee, "bizarre": Cmnd. 6732, 1977, § 96.
[11] [1986] R.P.C. 279; Tettenborn (1986) 45 Camb.L.J. 216.

BL cars, which was being asserted against spare part manufacturers. Exhaust pipes had the characteristics (i) that they must assume a given shape in order to fit the particular contours of the underbody, and (ii) that they needed quite regular replacement. The market was accordingly lucrative, and much more so to BL if its licence was needed for all pipes made to its designs.[12] The majority of the House of Lords were attracted by the notion that the sale of a car carried with it implied licence to use BL designs in the course of repairing the car.[13] But they saw the need to go beyond the idea of implied licences[14] and instead imported the land law concept that a person may not derogate from his grant. From this they drew the conclusion that BL could not object to anyone, including a spare parts manufacturer, using the designs to make things which would go to repairing their cars. To transplant so basic a notion into a new field raises various uncertainties about its potential, and the decision was subject to a good deal of purist criticism. Certainly it should not be forgotten as a conceptual tool which may have effects on the law after the 1988 Act reforms.[15] What should be understood, however, is that the House of Lords cleared a path through an oppressive jungle of legislation and interpretation, which indicated the extent to which proper legislative pruning should be carried. Without the decision to fortify the government, who can tell what rights design-owners might have managed to retain when the long-delayed reform of industrial designs law came in the recent Act?

In tackling the 1988 Act, the new must be set alongside the continuing **14-007** and the old. The next section is a description of the traditional scheme for protecting designs by registration, which highlights both the inherited characteristics of that system and the modifications introduced by the 1988 Act. The following section outlines the succession of attempts to preclude or limit the role of artistic copyright in the sphere of industrial protection, as part of a policy which, until 1968, strove (not entirely successfully) to avoid cumulative protection. The final section deals with the new strategy of 1988: the preclusion of artistic copyright once more from much of the field; the introduction of an unregistered design right of strictly limited duration in the area vacated; and the continuance of registered design partly in the territories of copyright and unregistered design, but partly in its own exclusive field.

---

[12] The "Euro-defence" of abuse of dominant position (Treaty of Rome, Art. 86) was dismissed in the litigation in a manner amounting virtually to incomprehension: see the C.A. judgments, above, n. 9.

[13] Lord Griffiths' interesting dissent would have gone so far as to deny that a design for a functional part could be infringed by three-dimensional, indirect copying. This solution would have removed much artistic copyright from industrial production; the majority judgments are confined to cases of spare parts.

[14] The difficulties with "implied licence" were of making it extend to protect a parts manufacturer and of preventing its exclusion by express statement to the contrary in the initial contract of sale.

[15] See CDPA 1988, s.171(3), Sched. 1, § 19(9).

2. Registered Designs

14-008 The origins of design registration have already been mentioned.[16] Although initially conceived as some form of copyright protection, the need actually to prove that an alleged infringement was copied was gradually obliterated. The history is rather obscure,[17] but it is one part of the process by which design registration acquired characteristics of the patent system. Both called for an initial application and grant of rights, and in 1875 the Patent Office took over the administration of designs. Thereafter the governing legislation was brought together in a single statute (the Act of 1883, maintained in 1907). Only in 1949 were the systems separated into parallel Acts. Designs are still protected under the Registered Designs Act 1949; but that Act has been amended at a number of points in 1988, in order to fit the system into the new order.[18]

(1) **Requirements for a registrable design (validity)**[19]

14-009 "Design"—the fundament of the system—is defined thus:

> "features of shape, configuration, pattern or ornament applied to an article by any industrial process, being features which in the finished article appeal to and are judged solely by the eye."[20]

The design is not something distinct from the article to which it is applied; nor does the manner in which it is applied affect the issue.[21] What is depicted and described in the registration is the article with the design incorporated. So the design must be registered separately for different kinds of article.[22] The features that are applied to the article must appeal to the eye, in the sense of catching or attracting the eye— particularly the eye of a potential buyer. They may be decorative elements ("pattern," "ornament") added to the article or they may be part of the very structure ("shape," "configuration").[23] To this basic definition, there are a set of exceptions. Among them it is important to distinguish those which were part of the original 1949 Act from those which have been added in 1988.[24] And in relation to the latter, it is useful to mark points of comparison with unregistered design right, since there are designs which qualify for both types of protection.

---

[16] Above, § 14-002.

[17] CDPA 1988, s.268, at last eliminates the confusing phrase "copyright in the design."

[18] Major amendments, and the transition to them, are contained in CDPA 1988, Pt. IV; further amendments are added by Sched. 3, and the RDA 1949 in its new form is given in Sched. 4 (but without the transitional provisions). References here are to the R.D.A. in this amended version.

[19] See generally, Blanco White (1974), §§ 8–102—109, 8–201, 208; Russell-Clarke, Chaps. 2–4.

[20] RDA 1949, s.1(3).

[21] Note on this the Copyright (Industrial Designs) Rule 1989.

[22] See below, § 14-025.

[23] See especially *Amp v. Utilux* [1972] R.P.C. 103, at 107, 112 (H.L.).

[24] Unless the contrary is indicated, references will be given to the amended version of the 1949 Act set out in CDPA 1988, Sched. 4.

(a) *Novelty*

Designs are not registrable unless they are "new." This is a 1988 **14-010** variant of the 1949 requirement that the design be "new or original."[25] The concepts of novelty in patent law and originality in copyright law are quite distinct, and the 1949 requirement never received a full analysis which would have demonstrated how near "new or original" was to either. The main emphasis in the case law was upon "new," and it is simpler, and probably no great change, to make "new" the sole criterion. (Note, however, that the equivalent adjective in the unregistered design right is "original"—a distinction not without resonance).[26]

In the law of registered designs, the requirement of novelty is amplified by a number of matters. It is to be tested against designs for any kind of article (not just articles for which registration is sought) that have been published or registered in the United Kingdom.[27] For this the criteria draw to a considerable extent on patent law. If the prior publication is in the document, there must, it seems, be clear and unmistakable directions to make an article bearing the design. It is not enough simply that it is an artistic work.[28]

Equally the publication may arise out of embodiment in an actual article. If the document or the article is made available to the public, rather than kept secret, it will anticipate.[29] Indeed, as for patents, it seems that to disclose the design to one specific person who is under no obligation of confidence to the discloser will amount to publication.

In addition, it is stated that differences in "immaterial details or in features which are variants commonly used in the trade" are not sufficient to render the design "new."[30] The designer must have applied some further skill and labour of a draftsmanlike nature.[31] In the 1988 simplification, this serves to carry novelty a little beyond precise anticipations and suggests comparison with inventive step by reference to common general knowledge in the law of patents. But common trade usage is not the only criterion for judging the novelty of registered designs.

Where the application is to register a design corresponding to an artistic work, and it is made by or with the consent of the copyright owner, the fact that the artistic work itself has previously been used (and therefore published) is not of itself a sufficient anticipation. Only if the work had been applied industrially as a design to articles which were

---

[25] RDA 1949, s.2.

[26] See below, § 14-026.

[27] RDA 1949, s.1(4). Novelty is judged at the date of application, save that a Paris Convention applicant who first applied for protection in another Convention country not more than six months before may claim priority back to the date of this application: ss.13–16; *Deyhle's Applcns.* [1982] R.P.C. 526. For the addition of designs containing non-essential variations, see s.4.

[28] *Rosedale* v. *Airfix* [1957] R.P.C. 239 at 244, 249; and see *Bessell's Design* [1964] R.P.C. 125 (publication must be as a design, not merely in an advertisement); *Bampal Materials Design* [1981] R.P.C. 44.

[29] See RDA 1949, s.6(1); and note the further exceptions in s.6(2), (3).

[30] RDA, s.1(4); and see Lord Moulton, *Phillips* v. *Harbro Rubber* (1920) 37 R.P.C. 233 at 240.

[31] Farwell J., *Re Calder Vale* (1934) 53 R.P.C. 117 at 125.

then marketed could it found an attack on novelty.[32] Here we meet three concepts which have been crucial in defining the relation between registered designs and artistic copyright:[33]

14-011   (i) *Corresponding design*: in relation to an artistic work, this means a design which, if applied to an article, would produce an infringement of copyright (now within the terms of the 1988 Act)[34];

(ii) *Applied industrially*: an activity which is defined by rule; in the past it has meant application of the design to more than 50 articles (not forming a set, as in a canteen of cutlery) or to non-hand-made goods manufactured in lengths or pieces, such as textiles and wallpaper.[35]

(iii) *Articles excluded from registration*: these too are prescribed by rule,[36] and have in the past covered much sculpture,[36] wall plaques and medals and printed matter primarily of a literary or artistic character.[37] It is to be expected that in any new definition of "applied industrially" these applications of artistic works will be excluded.

(b) *The whole article and parts*

14-012   The 1949 Act has always provided that an article for which a design may be registered includes "any part of an article if that part is made and sold separately."[38] The limiting effect of this has been that to an extent it was not possible to acquire a registered design for each of the component elements of a machine or decorative artefact which a competitor might choose to copy, perhaps in the course of supplying replacement parts. But if this was a deliberate policy it was less than fully effective. While there could be no registered design in, for instance, the cover for an ammeter (as distinct from the ammeter as a whole),[39] there could be in a light fitment for a car, if it was supplied to the car manufacturer by an outside component-maker: and there could be in a side-panel for a car, since it would also be sold separately as a spare. Accordingly, the registered design system has offered some scope for protecting integral parts; though latterly there has been the question whether a manufacturer of the larger article is not pre-empted by his duty "not to derogate from his grant"[40] from afterwards asserting registered design rights in parts of the complete article which he marketed, and now he will also be pre-empted by considerations of "must match" and immaterial appearance.[41]

---

[32] RDA 1949, s.6(4), (5).
[33] See also below, § 14-023.
[34] RDA 1949, s.44(1).
[35] RDA 1949, s.6(6) and see Copyright (Designs) Rules 1957.
[36] *i.e.* sculpture other than casts or models used or intended as models or patterns to be multiplied by any industrial process.
[37] A long list was given. See generally Designs Rules 1949, r. 26.
[38] RDA 1949, s.44(1) "article."
[39] See *Sifam* v. *Sangamo* [1973] R.P.C. 899.
[40] Following the reasoning in the *British Leyland* case (above, n. 9).
[41] See below, §§ 14-014—14-015.

(c) Construction method

Associated since 1949 with the exclusion of functional designs has **14-013** been the exclusion of a "method or principle of construction."[42] The concept has received little interpretation in English courts. In *Swain* v. *Barker*[43] it was said that, where the sides of a wire filing-tray were in half circles, making it impracticable to include corner supports, their absence was said to be a design feature that could not be considered as it arose from the construction adopted.

(d) "Must match"

To secure conformity with unregistered design right, the 1988 Act **14-014** excludes consideration of features of shape and configuration which are "dependent upon the appearance of another article of which the article is intended by the author of the design to form an integral part."[44] The scope of this formula will be discussed later.[45] Whatever its precise effect, it would seem to cover items such as the side-panels for cars which are sold as spares and so are not excluded by the no-separate-sale factor.[46]

(e) Immaterial appearance

The 1988 Act also adds an exclusion where "the appearance of the **14-015** article is not material, that is, if aesthetic considerations are not normally taken into account to a material extent by persons acquiring or using articles of that description, and would not be so taken into account if the design were applied to the article."[47] This perhaps does no more than give statutory effect to *Amp* v. *Utilux*.[48] It ensures that any judgment about aesthetic content is made from the perspective of a purchaser. It is not relevant—as it is for a work of artistic craftsmanship in copyright—to consider the intention of the designer.

(f) Functional features

A registrable design does not include features of shape or configuration **14-016** which are dictated soley by the function which the article has to perform. This 1949 provision was at one time thought to exclude only articles which assumed the sole shape possible for the particular purpose. But in *Amp* v. *Utilux*,[49] the House of Lords extended its ambit by reading it together with the requirement of "eye appeal." An electrical terminal for washing machines was held unregistrable because a potential customer would decide to buy it solely for its utility and not because of any attraction in its shape. Strictly utilitarian articles were thus excluded from registration (and in consequence the scope of full-term copyright protection was increased).

[42] RDA 1949, s.1(1)(a).
[43] [1967] R.P.C. 23.
[44] RDA 1949, s.1(1)(b)(ii).
[45] Below, § 14-027.
[46] Above, § 14-012.
[47] R.D.A. s.1(3).
[48] Below, n. 49.
[49] [1972] R.P.C. 103; see also *Kevi* v. *Suspa Verein* [1982] R.P.C. 173.

Even so the boundary-line was imprecise. In the earlier case of *Cow* v. *Cannon*,[50] a hot-water bottle was constructed with a series of thick ribs which had an insulating function similar to that of a separate cover. The Court of Appeal upheld the design registered for vertical ribs, because they might have been incorporated using different patterns — horizontal or diagonal lines, for instance, or some more elaborate conformation. It is unclear whether that design remained registrable after *Amp* v. *Utilux*; a set of ribs designed to represent a teddy bear doubtless would not be regarded as solely functional.[51]

(2) Proprietorship and dealings

14-017   The commissioner of a design for money or money's worth is the person primarily entitled to apply for registration; if the design is not so created, the right is in the employer of the designer, where it is created in the course of employment; but otherwise the right belongs to the designer.[52]

These rules are the same for unregistered design right.[53] Indeed there is a presumption that any dealing with the latter also covers a registration relating to it[54]; and the Registrar is not to register a person's interest in a registered design unless satisfied that it is also held in the corresponding unregistered design right.[55]

The right to apply may be transferred by assignment, transmission or operation of law. As with patents, access to the system is open to all, regardless of nationality. The preference accorded to nationals of Paris Convention countries is the six-month priority affecting the question of novelty. Here there is a direct contrast with the qualification conditions imposed on unregistered design right.[55a]

(3) Registration and term[56]

14-018   It follows from the definition of "design" that the application must be to register for a specified article,[57] and registration can become expensive if the design is intended for a considerable range of goods. Where the articles are of the same general character ordinarily on sale or intended to be used together (*e.g.* cups and saucers) a single registration for the set of articles is permitted.[58]

The Registry searches through previous registrations to discover anticipations.[59] If the application is accepted,[60] the design is registered and

---

[50] [1961] R.P.C. 236.
[51] Note that the unregistered design right at this point has a more precise exclusion, the so-called "must fit" provision; see below, § 14-026.
[52] RDA 1949, s.2(1)–(1B).
[53] Below, § 14-031.
[54] CDPA 1988, s.224.
[55] RDA 1949, s.19A.
[55a] Below, §§ 14-028 — 14-029.
[56] See Blanco White, (1974) §§ 8–110/123; Russell Clarke, Chap. 5.
[57] Design Rules, r. 13.
[58] *Ibid.* r. 12; and see RDA 1949, s.44(1).
[59] s.3(2).
[60] The Registrar is left with an ultimate discretion: s.3(3) and note s.43(1).

made public.[61] An interested person may not oppose the application but may seek cancellation after grant before the Registrar[62] or the High Court.[63] From the Registrar appeal lies to the Registered Designs Appeal Tribunal[64] (which is similar to the former Patents Appeal Tribunal).

The term of a registered design is measured from date of application.[65] Under the 1949 Act, the duration was a maximum of three periods each of five years. In the 1988 Act, this has been extended to five periods, making a maximum of 25 years.[66] This possibility of extension applies to existing registrations that are still current, if they were applied for up to January 12, 1988. But if they were applied for after that date, but before "commencement," it is necessary to consider whether they would have been precluded from registration by the exceptions being added to the system in the new Act—the "must match" and the "appearance immaterial" exceptions described above. After "commencement," such cases are to be entitled only to unregistered design right; and correspondingly these intermediate registered designs have their term restricted to 10 years from commencement, with licences of right available throughout that period.[67]

(4) Infringement[68]

The exclusive right given by registration covers manufacture and commercial dealing in the United Kingdom, but not (in general) use. More specifically infringement may be committed by doing any of the following acts with an article bearing the design, or one not substantially different: (i) making, or (ii) importing it for sale, hire or use for the purposes of a trade or business; (iii) selling, hiring, or offering or exposing it for sale or hire.[69] One "contributory" step towards manufacture is also covered: making anything for enabling the article itself to be made.[70] This relates to moulds, plates, dies and the like that will directly produce the designed article, but it has been said not to extend to a kit of

14-019

---

[61] See s.17, ss.22–24; for secrecy directions in the interests of defence, s.5. There is an obligation to register changes of ownership and grants of interest (licences, mortgages, etc.): ss.17, 19.

[62] s.11(2).

[63] There is a special provision for a certificate of contested validity in High Court proceedings: s.25.

[64] s.28 (as amended).

[65] s.3(5).

[66] s.8. Provisions are added, equivalent to those in P.A. 1977, ss.25(4), 28, allowing the restoration of a registration which has lapsed through non-payment of renewal fees: ss.8(4), 8A, 8B. The lengthened term is equivalent to that for copyright in articles that are artistic works: see below, § 14-025. Note that if the design derives from an artistic work, and is registrable only by virtue of s.6(4), the registered design may last only as long as copyright in that artistic work: s.8(5).

[67] CDPA 1988, ss.265(2), 266—these transitional provisions are not included in the revised RDA.

[68] Blanco White (1984), §§ 8–209/215; Russell Clarke, Chap. 7.

[69] s.7(1), (2).

[70] s.7(3).

parts for making the article (let alone such miscellanea as screws and glue).[71]

In testing whether an article infringes a registered design for that article, the normal starting point is the design as a whole. The protection is for the entire thing and not for its separate parts by themselves.[72] But in many cases, the applicant is required to file a statement of novelty,[73] drawing attention to the special features which form the kernel of the designer's conception. In any case, particular attention is given to the design of the striking, or commercially significant, features of an article, such as the whistle of a whistling kettle.[74] It is proper to take account of imperfect recollections that a consumer may have, provided that he is a person interested in design features.[75]

The comparison between design and alleged infringement determines whether or not there are substantial differences between them. It is an inquiry of the same order as that to decide whether the design is novel in light of the prior art. Even if the registered design itself does pass this test the extent by which it does so is important in deciding what infringes it. If the distance is a small one, a defendant will not infringe who introduces small variations himself.[76] Moreover, the two things are not solely to be compared side by side.[77]

(5) Control of monopoly[78]

14-020   A compulsory licence of a registered design may be granted by the Registrar (*i.e.* the Comptroller) on one broad ground: that the design is not being applied in the United Kingdom to such an extent as is reasonable in the circumstances of the case.[79] No further formula is given by way of guide towards the proper exercise of this discretion. Some assistance may be available from the comparable provisions on patents,[80] though they are much more elaborate. The power is certainly more limited than the licences of right now available in respect of unregistered design right.[81]

The Crown is entitled to use (or authorise the use of) a registered design for the services of the Crown.[82] The conditions are similar to those

---

[71] Harman L.J., *Dorling* v. *Honnor Marine* [1964] R.P.C. 160 at 166; *cf.* Danckwerts L.J., at 170; both agree that, in order to infringe, the making of parts must be for an article that will itself be marketed, rather than that put together by a private, do-it-yourself completer, a view confirmed by the 1988 version of s.7(1)(a).

[72] See Lord Westbury, *Holdsworth* v. *McCrea* (1867) L.R. 2 H.L. 380 at 388.

[73] See Design Rules, r. 14.

[74] *Best* v. *Woolworth* [1964] R.P.C. 232 (C.A.).

[75] *Sommer Allibert* v. *Flair Plastics* [1987] R.P.C. 599 (C.A.).

[76] See Luxmoore J., *Dean's Rag Book* v. *Pomerantz* (1930) 47 R.P.C. 485 at 491.

[77] See, *e.g. Valor Heating* v. *Main Gas Appliances* [1972] F.S.R. 497 at 502; *Benchairs* v. *Chair Centre* [1974] R.P.C. 429 at 442 (C.A.).

[78] Blanco White (1974), § 8–124 and Chap. 11; Russell Clarke, pp. 79–80, 126–127.

[79] RDA 1949, s.10.

[80] See above, §§ 7-054 *et seq.*

[81] For control over abuse of monopoly, as with the other rights applicable to designs, see s.11A.

[82] RDA 1949, s.12, Sched. 1, now amended to include compensation for loss of profit provisions, as with patents: see above, § 7-056, n. 36.

applying to patents. Compensation must be paid unless the Crown had already recorded or applied the design otherwise than in consequence of the registered proprietor's communication before the date of registration.[83]

3. ARTISTIC COPYRIGHT

(1) The exclusion of design documents and models

Under the 1988 Act, as before, copyright in a drawing arises irrespec- **14-021** tive of artistic quality, provided that there is sufficient labour, skill and judgment to give originality. It may be infringed by reproducing it in a three-dimensional article; and it matters not whether the act of copying is direct or indirect.[84] The main object of section 51 is accordingly to limit the application of that principle by stating that the act of making an article from a "design document or model" which records or embodies a design cannot after all constitute infringement. This applies where the design is "for anything other than an artistic work or a typeface." "Design" has a restricted meaning: "the design of any aspect of the shape or configuration (whether internal or external) of the whole or part of an article, other than surface decoration." However, one point should be kept in mind: it is not copyright in the design, but copyright in the design document or model, which is affected by the new limitation.

Section 51 undoubtedly excludes from the sphere of copyright much of what, under the previous law, has been considered to fall within it: blue-prints for pumps, car exhausts or taps must count as design documents for non-artistic works, and this is so whatever the form of record — whether it is "a drawing, a written description, a photograph, data stored in a computer or otherwise." The material thus excluded can only be protected as a registered or an unregistered design, if the conditions governing those rights are met. Previously there was no such limitation and artistic copyright ranged across much of the industrial landscape. A degree of uncertainty infects the penumbra of section 51, as can be seen if each of its requirements is further examined.

(i) *"Design for anything other than an artistic work"*

If the design document is for a piece of jewellery, the design is in all **14-022** likelihood for a "work of artistic craftsmanship." It could accordingly be infringement of copyright in the drawing to make up the jewellery from it (direct), or from jewellery made from it (indirect); and in the latter case it would also be infringement of copyright in the jewellery (and the authors of these two copyrights may well be different people: designer and silversmith respectively).

The category, "works of artistic craftsmanship," is a limited one, as the House of Lords demonstrated in *Hensher* v. *Restawile*.[85] Copyright is

[83] Sched. 1, § 1(2), (3).
[84] See above, § 11-005.
[85] See above, §§ 10-013—10-015.

not in this case accorded "irrespective of artistic quality." But among those things which are protected without regard to artistic quality, as well as drawings, are sculpture, engravings and etchings. None of these artistic works is further defined, save that "sculpture" includes a cast or model. The consequence of treating drawings in this way is well-established: no matter how technical their content, they attract artistic copyright. Can the same approach be taken to the other categories? In *Wham-O Manufacturing* v. *Lincoln*[86] the New Zealand Court of Appeal accepted its logic in relation to "plastic 'Frisbees,'"—*i.e.*, the wooden models, plastic injection moulds and the final products themselves were all considered to be "engravings," and the first two things were also "sculptures." In part, this outcome depended on statutory provisions equivalent to those in the United Kingdom Act of 1956, which have not been retained in the 1988 Act.[87] But the differences need not affect the central questions, so an English court might still reach an equivalent result. However, the New Zealand court refused to hold that the "Frisbees" themselves were "sculptures," because a sculpture must express in three-dimensional form an idea of the sculptor, and the court could not find this to be present in the result of injecting plastic into moulds. It is possible in future that, by similar reasoning, artistic intent will be treated as a necessary element in "sculpture," "engraving" and "etching", so as to give them narrower scope. Otherwise, artistic copyright will continue to apply to every artefact made by injection moulding (and who knows what else?).[88] That can scarcely have been intended as part of the new reduction in scope for copyright. An indication that English courts may draw back can be found in *Davis* v. *Wright Health Group*,[89] where Whitford J. refused to apply the *Wham-O* rationale to dental casts. They were not "casts for the purposes of sculpture,"[89a] since they were not intended to have any permanent existence.

(ii) *"Design document or model recording or embodying a design for anything"*

14-023   Use of the preposition "for" in this phrase may bring into consideration the intention or purpose for which the design was recorded. Take the classic example—the cartoon character, Popeye, and his merchandising as a doll.[90] Initially the drawings were *for* a comic strip, not for making articles. Read naturally, section 51 would appear not to touch such a case, leaving the merchandising of such a figure to the sphere of

---

[86] [1985] R.P.C. 127.

[87] Thus there is no longer a provision concerning the ownership of commissioned works which led to the view that "engraving" included the plate from which they were produced (see also *James Arnold* v. *Miafern* [1980] R.P.C. 397); and engraving no longer includes "print," so that it may not be possible to conclude that the object produced from the mould is also an engraving.

[88] Thus the *Wham-O* concept has been applied in New Zealand to plastic boxes for packing kiwi fruit: *Plix Products* v. *Winstone* [1986] F.S.R. 63.

[89] [1988] R.P.C. 403.

[89a] These are specifically within the definition of "sculpture"—see now CDPA 1988, s.4(2).

[90] *King Features Syndicate* v. *Kleeman* [1941] A.C. 417.

copyright (and thus in effect returning to a basic distinction under the 1911 Act). However, it would be possible, if strained, to read the section as extending to any subject-matter capable of being turned into an article. In which case, Popeye and his ilk would be covered by it, so far as concerns the production of articles. Later, if the owner decides to engage in marketing, he may have a design document or model prepared. Either would itself be affected by section 51. But again, read naturally, the section would not touch the original drawing. If it is substantially reproduced in the article finally made by the defendant (even if the causal connection must be traced through a design document or model), copyright in it would be infringed.

(iii) *"Any aspect of shape or configuration . . . other than surface decoration"*

It will be a nice question whether a feature of a design is for surface **14-024** decoration, so that a design document embodying it may bear artistic copyright; or whether it is for some other element of shape or configuration, when that consequence is excluded by section 51. In a registered design case, the Court of Appeal held that ridges moulded into plastic chairs were features of shape and configuration, even though they were intended to add decorative or ornamental value to the chair; they were not merely features of two-dimensional pattern or ornament added at a later stage.[91] Since the Copyright Act draws on exactly this terminology, this interpretation ought to apply equally to it. What, then, of a dress? Are sleeves and pleats configuration, while buttons and bows mere surface decoration?

(2) The new limitation of period

In any case where section 51 does not apply to a design, copyright will **14-025** continue to be infringed by making three-dimensional copies of it. But once any artistic work has been used in industrial production with the copyright owner's authority, the duration of this aspect of the copyright is foreshortened by section 52.[92] It ceases to be infringement to make articles of any description (other than those of a primarily literary or artistic character)[93] which copy the copyright work, after 25 years from the end of the year in which industrially produced articles from the work were first marketed anywhere in the world by or with the authority of the copyright owner. The same concept of industrial application of a corresponding design is found here as applies to registered designs.[94] The section embodies the obligation under the Berne Convention to accord at

---

[91] *Sommer-Allibert* v. *Flair Plastics* [1987] R.P.C. 599 (the issue arose because the statement of novelty relied on shape and configuration). Equally in *Cow* v. *Cannon* (above, n.50), the ridges on the hot-water bottle had been held to be shape or configuration. And note the general reliance on Luxmoore J., *Kestos* v. *Kempat* (1936) 53 R.P.C. 139 at 152.

[92] *cf.* CA 1956, s.10, after its amendment by the Design Copyright Act 1968: both excluded one application of copyright from infringement; but the period before this happens is now 25, not 15 years; and there is no longer a distinction between designs that could, and could not be, registered.

[93] Above, § 4-018.

[94] See the Paris Act of the Convention (1971) Art. 2(4); Ricketson (1987).

least 25 years protection to a work of applied art so far as it is copyright.[95] At the same time it rids copyright of its most egregious excess in entering the realm of industrial property.

Apart from this limitation of term in relation to industrial exploitation, copyright principles apply as before. Qualification extends to persons connected by personal status to prescribed Convention countries—an important contrast, it seems, with unregistered design right. First ownership of a work made under commission belongs to the artist who creates the work (unless there has been an express assignment)—a contrast with both registered and unregistered design right.[96] The artist, moreover, will benefit from the moral right to be identified (subject to the duration limit of section 52) and the right to object to derogatory treatment. These could be of some assistance to designers who are not employees.

4. (UNREGISTERED) DESIGN RIGHT

(1) Subject-matter

14-026   The unregistered "Design Right" accorded by Part III of the 1988 Act is defined in terms co-ordinate to those which limit the scope of copyright in the sphere of industrial production. Nevertheless, the new right is a hybrid displaying characteristics both of copyright and registered design law. Accordingly one must be wary of transposing assumptions from either field without careful examination.

The right arises in an "original design," comprising "any aspect of the shape or configuration (whether internal or external) of the whole or part of an article" which is not "surface decoration."[97] "Original" probably introduces the copyright notion of "not copied," rather than the concept of novelty used for registered designs where the equivalent adjective is now "new." The difference could be important.[98] The right is not restricted to designs applicable to the article as a whole ("any aspect . . . whole or part").[99] But, as with registered designs, a method or principle of construction is excluded.[1] In addition there are two specific exceptions which were included to prevent the new right after all from affecting replacement parts. These are: "features of shape or configuration which

(i) enable the article to be connected to, or placed around or against, another article so that either article may perform its function, or
(ii) are dependent upon the appearance of another article of which the article is intended by the designer to form an integral part."[2]

---

[95] cf. below, § 14-028.
[96] cf. above, § 14-017; below, § 14-031. Note that the designer of material in a design document that has applications precluded from copyright by s.51 has no moral right to be identified in those applications; but he does retain a right to object to derogatory treatment: cf. ss.79(4)(f), (g); 80, 81; and see generally, above, §§ 11-055 et seq.
[97] CDPA 1988, s.213(1), (2), (3)(c).
[98] See, e.g. below, § 14-030.
[99] cf. above, § 14-012.
[1] CDPA 1988, s.213(3)(a).
[2] s.213(3)(b).

The first of these is a "must fit" exception, but in terms more limited than the "purpose dictated solely by function" exception of registered design law.[3] The exception here requires that the article including the design must take its place "so that" one or other article may perform its function. If the handle for a jack has flanges which fit into grooves on the jack itself, the flanges would not provide design right features because they enable the jack to be wound up. But does a car exhaust pipe, contoured to fit the underside of a particular chassis, assume its shape so as to enable fumes to be expelled or the car to operate? Although this was the topical example of the need for a "must fit" exception, it is by no means clear that it has been covered by the final drafting. The exception is certainly narrow. It does not prevent there being design right in an electrical connector, except to the extent that the connector has (say) rods which fit into a wall-socket. Yet such a connector was refused a registered design in the leading case of *Amp* v. *Utilux*.[4]

The second exception—"must match"—has been added in the same **14-027** terms to registered designs law.[5] The typical case was thought to be the panel for a car door, and in all likelihood that example is within the exception. The requirement that the shape or configuration be intended by the designer to form an integral part of something else was included in order to prevent the exception from extending to things intended to be made in sets, such as cutlery or glasses.

It must be noted that, because of international obligations or in pursuit of reciprocity, the Secretary of State may make different provision for different descriptions of design or article, or exclude acts from the scope of infringement.[6] This will allow the special topography right already operating to continue in the form dictated by the United States.[7]

(2) Qualification

One important motive in creating a separate unregistered design right **14-028** has been to preclude foreigners from entitlement, in a way that was difficult to introduce while protection was accorded under copyright.[8]

The explicit provisions on qualification for unregistered design rights are expressed to relate to the United Kingdom, other member states of the EEC, the colonies and like territories to which Part II may be extended, and countries which accord reciprocal protection to British designs.[9] "Qualifying individuals" are citizens, subjects or habitual residents of one of these countries; and "qualifying persons" are these individuals together with corporate bodies incorporated in, or carrying on substantial business in, such a country.[10] Qualification also turns on the circumstances in which a design is made. If not made under

[3] Above, § 14-016.
[4] Above, n. 49.
[5] Above, § 14-014.
[6] s.245.
[7] See below, §§ 14-034—14-035.
[8] Because of the Berne Convention (Paris Act), Art. 2(4); above, § 14-025.
[9] These countries will be specified by Order under s.256.
[10] CDPA 1988, s.217.

commission or in employment, the designer must be a qualifying individual (or qualifying person, where the work is computer-generated).[11] In the excepted cases, it is the commissioner or employer who must be a qualifying person.[12] If there is no qualification according to these rules (and there may well not be), then it may arise from first marketing by a qualifying person with exclusive marketing rights in the United Kingdom, its extended territories, or the EEC.[13]

In this form, the qualification provisions amount to an attempt by this country to follow the path of reciprocity which it has long since abandoned in established fields of intellectual property, but to which it has recently been led in the cognate field of computer chip topography by pressure from the United States.[14] It is not clear what degree of reciprocity it is intent on securing. Will it treat as a reciprocating country one in which industrial designs are protected by an extension of unfair competition doctrine to cover the misappropriation of product ideas?[15] Or is it striving to tell the world that unfair competition protection is not direct enough? These uncertainties at least will be resolved in time. What must remain unsettled, since it is an inherent defect of the reciprocity approach to international relations throughout this field, is the train of reaction in other countries which may follow.

14-029   The Paris Convention for the Protection of Industrial Property, of which the United Kingdom has been a member for more than a century, has as its object "patents, utility models, industrial designs . . . " and requires that "industrial property" be understood in its "broadest sense."[16] Accordingly it is arguable that, once the United Kingdom institutes a specific scheme for the protection of industrial designs, even though this does not require registration, it is obliged to provide equal treatment to nationals of Paris Union states. The Government, it appears, is sufficiently uncertain of its position to have taken power to do this.[17] After all, it may choose to by-pass the narrowly calculating approach of reciprocity. Such a step would improve its moral position *vis-à-vis* those countries which still refrain from joining the major intellectual property conventions and prefer to think in terms of bilateral negotiation. But it would make rather ridiculous the whole cumbersome edifice of unregistered design right.

(3) Exclusive right

14-030   The operative concepts here are akin to copyright, rather than to registered design. Primary infringement (which occurs irrespective of the defendant's culpability or innocence) consists either of making articles to the design for commercial purposes or making a design document in

---

[11] s.218; for joint designers, see s.218(3), (4).
[12] s.219.
[13] s.220.
[14] See below, §§ 14-034, 14-035.
[15] For the extent to which unfair competition laws give protection against "slavish imitation" in Western Europe, see Fellner, above, § 14-001, n. 2.
[16] Art. 1(2), (3).
[17] s.221.

order to make such articles. What must occur is reproduction of the design, *i.e.* copying the design, directly or indirectly, so as to produce articles exactly or substantially to that design.[18] The right given is only against copying, not against independent creation.

Secondary infringement, which can occur only where the defendant knows or has reason to believe that he is dealing with an infringing article, may be constituted by unauthorised importation for commercial purposes, possessing for commercial purposes, and selling, letting for hire, or offering or exposing for sale or hire, in the course of a business.[19]

The right of action is akin to that for copyright infringement and is supported by equivalent provisions concerning additional damages, delivery up, disposal of infringing articles, exclusion of damages for innocent infringement, exclusive licensees, and joint ownership.[20] There is, however, no right to engage in self-help seizure.

In unregistered design cases, the plaintiff is given one exceptional advantage which is not accorded in copyright. Once he shows that an alleged "infringing article" has been made to a design in which the right subsists or has subsisted at any time, it is for the defendant to prove that the article was made at a time when design right did not subsist.[21] That seems a fair presumption when the duration of the right itself is not in issue and the only question is the date on which the defendant acted. If however there is contention over the date on which the plaintiff's design was first recorded, or on which the plaintiff first authorised marketing of articles to the design somewhere in the world—both of which will affect the duration of the right—the defendant is put to proof of matter which cannot be in his own knowledge. The inherent unfairness of the provision might be limited if the plaintiff were first obliged to show that his design was not copied from another source. This at least could oblige him to give details of its creation, if not of its first marketing. It is accordingly desirable that "original" should be so understood.

Unregistered design right is subject to Crown use on terms of compensation. The rules are as for registered designs.[22]

(4) Authorship and first ownership

The rules concerning authorship and first ownership run in tandem 14-031 with those for registered designs and differ from those for copyright.[23] If a design is made under a commission for money or money's worth, first ownership is accorded to the commissioner; if that is not the case, where it is made by an employee in the course of employment, it belongs to the employer; failing this, the designer—*i.e.* the creator—becomes the first owner.[24] Any of these, when prospective owner of a design to be created, may assign it by agreement in writing, signed by both parties, so as to

[18] s.226.
[19] s.227; s.228 applies to unregistered design right the same rules concerning importation as for copyright: see above, § 12-009.
[20] See ss.229–235.
[21] s.228(4).
[22] ss.240–244, 252.
[23] *cf.* above, §§ 12-002—14-017.
[24] ss.214, 215.

vest the right on creation in the assignee.[25] Thus for both types of design right, a commissioner acquires first ownership by rule of law, whereas in copyright ownership goes to the author. Given that there are various circumstances where it is currently difficult to know whether there are copyright or only design rights in the industrial exploitation of the design of an article, the question of ownership needs to be resolved by express contract; failure so to provide may lead to awkward dispute.

(5) Duration and licences of right

14-032   The period for which unregistered design right subsists has been limited so as to make the right less valuable than that arising under copyright or the registration system. The main thrust of the system is to give protection to functional objects and parts against imitation in the early years of their exploitation. Design right expires 15 years after first recording of the design in a design document or the first making of an article to the design, whichever is earlier; or—a further limitation—if articles to the design are legitimately marketed anywhere in the world to the design within the first five years of recording or making, then the period is 10 years from first beginning this activity. The latter circumstance is likely to be the most usual.[26]

Moreover, during the last five years of the right—in most cases, after five years from first legitimate marketing—others are entitled to a licence of right for the design, its terms to be settled (if necessary) by the Comptroller, with appeal to the Designs Appeal Tribunal.[27] In exceptional cases, after reference to the Monopolies and Mergers Commission and a finding by it that design right is being asserted in a manner contrary to the public interest, the Minister may order (*inter alia*) that licences of right be available even before the last five-year period.[28] In recent years, there have been two Reports of the Commission which have criticised aspects of design copyright exploitation by car manufacturers—reports which have been influential in settling the terms of the 1988 New Deal.[29] In future, there will be legislative machinery for giving effect to the Commission's decisions, whether they relate to patents, copyright, registered designs or unregistered designs.[30] The application for a licence of right in the final five years may be made up to one year before commencement.[31] Once the final five-year period is reached, an alleged infringer who undertakes to obtain a licence of right cannot be the subject of an injunction or delivery up order; and damages against him

[25] s.223.
[26] s.216.
[27] s.237. Categories of design may be excluded from this provision by Order, because of a convention obligation or in order to secure or maintain reciprocal protection of British designs: the obvious case will be the topography right in semiconductor chips; for which see below, § 14-035.
[28] s.238.
[29] *Car Parts*, H.C. 18, 1983; [1983] F.S.R. 115.
[30] For the equivalent provisions, see CDPA 1988, ss.144, 270.
[31] s.247.

are limited to double the rate of royalty set in the licence of right.[32] In arriving at an appropriate royalty rate, the Comptroller will be seeking to evaluate the design element in the plaintiff's product as a contributory factor both to its development cost and to its success in the market.[33] In some circumstances, there may be evidence of royalty practices in voluntary licences and these may indeed burgeon as the new regime comes to be understood.

Behind the availability of licences of right may well lurk issues of subsistence of the right, its terms and first entitlement. Save in infringement proceedings and other actions where they arise incidentally, these issues can be raised only in proceedings before the Comptroller, subject to reference or leave by him, or appeal from him, to the High Court or proceedings brought there by agreement of the parties.[34] The controversial presumption in the plaintiff's favour which arises in relation to "infringing articles" does not seemingly apply in such proceedings, a matter which design copiers would do well to note.

(6) A brief comparison

By way of summary, let us conjure the vision of a table lamp 14-033 consisting of a base modelled as a mermaid and a lampshade in the form of a water-lily. The whole lovely complement could be the subject of a registered design, claiming its novelty in aspects of shape and configuration, and perhaps pattern and ornament as well. That right could endure for 25 years from registration.

Equally the lamp might attract artistic copyright: as a whole, because it had the quality to rank among works of artistic craftsmanship; or because copyright can be traced back to a drawing that was not for an industrial design; in part, because one or other element constitutes a sculpture or perhaps an engraving—the base or (particularly if it is moulded) the shade. In these cases the protection will last for 25 years from the first legitimate marketing of products embodying the copyright work.

Such copyright can subsist beside any registered design that there may be. But to the extent that there is copyright there can be no infringement of unregistered design right in any element of shape or configuration.[35] There may, however, be elements, such as the bulb-holder, which will at most attract this lesser form of protection (with its normal maximum of 10 years, subject to licences of right in the last five). Moreover, the essentially utilitarian bulb-holder could not attract the lesser design right so far as it was a commonplace in the trade, nor so far as its shape was formed to receive the bulb ("must fit"). The scope for discriminatory argument seems altogether without bounds.

---

[32] s.239.

[33] In exercising his discretion as to terms, the Comptroller is given little statutory guidance. Some of the considerations which have been brought to bear on patent licences of right (see § 7-054) may well prove germane.

[34] s.246.

[35] s.236. Since, thanks to the different rules about ownership of commissioned works, there may be disputes about ownership, the presence or absence of copyright may frequently fall to be tested.

(7) Topography right

14-034   Finally in this chapter we reach a juncture where the special demands of computer technology meet more general concerns over the protection of industrial design. The semiconductor chip gives effect to program instructions through a circuitry fixed on semiconductor material in layered form. The familiar ROMs, RAMs and EPROMs that are the basis of software packages are forms of such chips. Their mass-production is frequently the result of major investment in design, so there has been great pressure for legal means to prevent their imitation.

In the United Kingdom, there was some chance that, because design copyright under the 1956 Act (as amended) was such an extended notion, the layered circuitry, taken from a design, could be treated as copyright. This was probably a forlorn hope, because of the requirement under the old law that a non-expert be able to recognise that the alleged infringement was a reproduction of the work.[36] In other countries even this prospect was not open and the sole chance lay in an extension of unfair competition law. The United States, with the largest investments at risk, insisted that there be rapid legislative intervention. Its own Semiconductor Chip Protection Act 1984 created a *sui generis* right in original "mask" works.[37] At the same time, it announced that, if other countries wished their nationals to enjoy this new protection in the United States, they must provide equivalent protection for American mask works in their own territories. The EEC, by Directive to member states, led the scramble to comply with this edict, though it has been far from clear why, in the state of the computer industry world-wide, it should hasten to confer rights which overall would be of greater benefit to Americans than would the reciprocal benefits in the United States to its own firms.

The obligation under the Directive was met in the United Kingdom by subsidiary legislation under the European Communities Act 1972. The Topography Right conferred by the Products (Protection of Topography) Regulations 1987, lies in the pattern fixed, or intended to be fixed, in or upon a layer of a semiconductor product, or in the arrangement of the layers of a semiconductor product; and a semiconductor product is:

"an article the purpose, or one of the purposes, of which is the performance of an electronic function and which consists of two or more layers, at least one of which is composed of semiconducting material and in or upon one or more of which is fixed a pattern appertaining to that or another function."[38]

To acquire protection the topography must be "original," *i.e.* the result of the creator's or creators' own intellectual effort or combined efforts. It

---

[36] CA 1956, s.9(8), not continued in the 1988 Act. Despite this, the U.K. secured temporary reciprocity from the U.S.A. on the basis of this supposed protection.

[37] So called from the masking technique which is one method of producing the circuitry on the chip surface. See Ladd, *et als., Protection of Semiconductor Chip Masks in the United States* (1986); Hart [1985] E.I.P.R. 258; Lang [1986] Utah L.R. 717.

[38] r. 2(1). It is created when first expressed in a form which can be reproduced: r. 2(2). In its own sphere this form of protection predominates; artistic copyright is excluded: r. 9.

must, moreover, not be "commonplace among creators of topographies or manufacturers of semiconductor products."[39]

The period of protection is 10 years from the year of first commercial 14-035 exploitation anywhere in the world, or 15 years from creation, whichever is the shorter.[40] It is given to United Kingdom and EEC citizens and residents, and to those of countries designated as offering reciprocal protection.[41] In addition it is given upon first commercial exploitation in one of those countries by a qualifying person. It is an exclusive right in respect of commercial production, exploitation and importation of reproductions of the topography protected.[42] Accordingly copying is an element in the wrong.[43]

The United States Act is echoed not only in these provisions but above all in a limitation concerning reverse engineering. It is permissible to reproduce the topography for the purpose of analysing or evaluating it, or analysing, evaluating or teaching the concepts, processes, systems or techniques embodied in it[44]; and as a result of such steps, it is permissible to create another original topography.[45] This in effect substitutes an older test of copyright infringement for the one that currently prevails in that sphere. For topography right, it would seem, the question is how much original work has been done in addition by the alleged infringer, not, as in current copyright law, how much of the old can be traced in the new. There is less scope for notions of taking the "look and feel" of expression, which is such a current issue in the United States law relating to copyright in computer programs and is likely to have a place in the British approach.[46]

More generally it will be seen that much of the unregistered design right now introduced in the 1988 Act derives from the Topography Regulation. The two main points of difference are the absence from the latter of licences of right in the last five years and the absence from the former of the reverse engineering defence. There will be an order which ensures that topography right continues to keep its special contours, set according to the American mould.[47] How far unregistered design will be given a similar shape by judicial decision is one of the current imponderables.

---

[39] r. 3(3).
[40] r. 5.
[41] While the Regulation is less than clear, it appears to adopt the principle that the right belongs to a commissioner or an employer, if there is one, otherwise to the creator. In the former cases it is the status of the commissioner or employer as a qualified person which is relevant: r. 3(1), (6).
[42] r. 3(2). There is an elaborate definition of what constitutes "commercial exploitation": r. 2(3), (6).
[43] r. 4 defines the exclusive right, r. 6 the act of infringement (here as elsewhere the drafting is extraordinarily cumbersome) authorising others to do a restricted act constitutes infringement: r. 6(1). Acts of dealing are secondary infringement in the sense of needing proof of knowledge or reason to believe that they constitute infringement: r. 6(3). There is an exception for private and non-commercial use: r. 4(2)(a).
[44] r. 4(2)(b).
[45] r. 6(2).
[46] See above, § 13-020.
[47] Under CDPA 1988, ss.221(2), 237(3), 245(1).

CHAPTER 15

COMPETITOR AND CONSUMER

1. UNDERLYING THEMES

15-001 This final Part focuses attention upon rights long associated with intellectual property, which nevertheless are concerned with methods of promoting and selling goods and services. Once more the purpose of legal intervention is to give protection to information. But trade marks, names and other such symbols have a less finite character than the information protected by patents, copyright and confidence. In an economy where the general understanding is that most goods and services come from competing enterprises, trade mark owners typically use their marks to indicate the origin of what they have to offer. Their hope is that this will trigger off an association in consumers' minds between origin and good value. But what the consumer understands by the cypher depends on his previous knowledge and experience.

Two themes underlie the detailed law that is the subject of the following chapters. The first was raised in Chapter 1[1] and need not be dwelt upon at length at this point. It is the question, how far should traders be invested with power to sue upon the unfair business practices of their competitors? We have already noticed the traditional British reluctance to go further than to give protection against promotional tactics that will harm one rival in particular, for instance by passing off goods as his. The fact that most West European countries know an unfair competition action of much greater range has now become of more than academic interest, since the attainment of uniform or harmonized laws in this field is a natural concern of the EEC. We may reserve discussion of the new proposals until after describing the extent of competitors' actions in present English law.[2]

The second basic theme concerns the uses to which trade marks are put and the scope of legal protection that ought in consequence to be accorded to them. Over the last century these uses have increased in diversity, which has raised conflicts with policies directed towards the welfare of consumers. The historical section which follows will provide some introduction to the interplay between business demand and legal response in Britain and other countries. Then some attempt will be made to present the controversies surrounding trade mark protection at the present day.

[1] See above, §§ 1-005—1-006, 1-012.
[2] Below, § 18-019.

392

2. HISTORICAL DEVELOPMENT

(1) Judicial protection

As modern capitalism has grown, the drive to sell products and 15–002
services by means of some mark, brand or name has invaded more and
more fields. Some foods and a few other staples are still frequently sold
to the consumer without branding, but the tendency is consistently
towards labelling to indicate source.[3] Before industrialisation, there were,
of course, instances of traders or trader-groups who deployed marks of
various kinds to distinguish their products. The hallmarks of goldsmiths
and silversmiths and the marks of Sheffield cutlers are English examples
which have survived as distinct systems.[4] But the demand for general
legal protection against unfair imitation of marks and names is a product
of the commercial revolution that followed upon factory production and
the growth of canals and railways. That demand has swelled immensely
with the development of modern advertising and large-scale retailing.
Most advertising teaches the consumer to buy by product mark or house
name and it keeps reiterating its message in the hope of stopping buyers
from defecting to rivals. Trade marks and names have become nothing
more nor less than the fundament of most market-place competition.

In the English case law demands for legal protection against the 15–003
imitation of marks and names were being made and acceded to from the
early years of industrialisation. The courts of equity took the lead
because plaintiffs wanted injunctions. They intervened when one trader
represented to the public that he was selling the goods or carrying on the
business of another.[5] Soon afterwards, similar actions for damages at
common law are found, the action on the case for deceit being held to lie
at the instance of a competitor.[6]

That extension bore its own limitation, for deceit required proof of
deliberate fraud.[7] The courts of equity, however, being concerned primarily with a forward-looking remedy, did not feel the same constraint.
Impelled by their sense of the injury that could be caused by passing-off,

[3] Even the "corner-shop" may now be run under a business name sufficiently impersonal
that, if a rival copies it for his business, the public may think that a new branch has been
opened.

[4] British hallmarks are now regulated by the Hallmarking Act 1973. Cutlers' marks are
now dealt with in the Trade Marks Act 1938, s.38, Sched. 2 and Trade Marks Act Rules,
rr. 95–100, the Cutlers' Company still having charge of a Sheffield Register. See Kerly,
Chap. 6; and for the history, Schechter (below, n. 5), Chap. 5.

[5] The possibility of such an action seems recognised by Lord Hardwicke L.C. in *Blanchard*
v. *Hill* (1742) 2 Atk. 485. The older, obscure case at common law, *Southern* v. *How*
(1618) Popham 144, is treated as allowing an action on the case for a fraudulent design
"to put off bad cloths . . . or to draw away customers from another clothier" (*i.e.* a
competitor's, as well as a consumer's, action); thereafter see *Hogg* v. *Kirby* (1803) 8 Ves.
215; *cf. Longman* v. *Winchester* (1809) 16 Ves. Jun. 269; *Crutwell* v. *Lye* (1810) 17 Ves.
Jun. 335. See generally Schechter, *The Historical Foundations of the Law Relating to
Trade Marks* (1925), Chap. 6.

[6] *Sykes* v. *Sykes* (1824) 3 B. & C. 541 (the basic principle appears already to be
established); *Blofeld* v. *Payne* (1833) 4 B. & Ad. 410.

[7] See *Pasley* v. *Freeman* (1789) 3 T.R. 51; *Derry* v. *Peek* (1889) 14 App.Cas. 337(H.L.);
Clerk and Lindsell on Torts, Clerk & Lindsey 16th ed., 1989, §§ 1629 *et seq.*

they would enjoin even a defendant who had adopted the mark or name in all innocence: the goodwill at risk was easily characterised as "property," the deception of the public was in itself "fraud."[8] Other potential limitations were by-passed: the common law courts had no scruple in holding it actionable for a manufacturer to supply a retailer with "the instruments of fraud"[9]; or for one trader to pass off goods as another's even if they were not of inferior quality.[10] Westbury as Lord Chancellor insisted that a mark or name was protectable even though the public did not know the producer as such but used the connection with a trade source simply as a sign of quality.[11]

15–004   By the 1850s, public agitation about the extent to which food, drugs and other commodities were sold in an adulterated state was beginning to run high. It mixed with the complaints of established competitors that they were being undercut by such practices, by cheap imports that did not declare what they were and by the false imitation of brands, marks and names.[12] To some extent, purchasers found a market remedy—by lending their custom to the new retailing co-operatives.[13] But there were also calls on their behalf for legal protection, the criminal law being envisaged as the principal machinery.[14]

Important commercial interests, however, wanted Britain to adopt a system of registering trade marks—after the model, for instance, of the French law of 1857.[15] In part their concern was domestic. The passing-off action, though useful, depended on proving in each case that the plaintiff had a trade reputation with the public. That could sometimes be costly and laborious. If there were a register, the issue could be reduced to the question: was the defendant imitating the mark in a manner liable to deceive? But in part, it was from international trade that the demand arose. Prussian and American counterfeiters were said to be passing off their own "Manchester" textiles and "Sheffield" cutlery in various parts of the world.[16] The hope of stopping foreign imitations of British marks seemed to lie in also establishing a register. Mutual protection of foreigners' marks in Britain could then be offered as a *quid pro quo.*

15–005   There was considerable "liberal" suspicion of this idea for a new property right: a first entrant might be able to appropriate ways of marking his goods that could pose difficulties for later competitors. The Merchandise Marks Act 1862, which included "forging a trade mark"

[8] *Millington* v. *Fox* (1838) 3 My. & Cr. 338; *Edelsten* v. *Edelsten* (1863) 4 De G.J. & S. 185. But for the adventures of "property" in this subject-matter, see below, §§ 16-001—16-003.

[9] *Sykes* v. *Sykes* (above, n. 6).

[10] *Blofeld* v. *Payne* (above, n. 6).

[11] *Hall* v. *Barrows* (1863) 4 De G.J. & S. 150 at 157.

[12] See, *e.g.* E. W. Stieb, *Drug Adulteration* (1966), Chaps. 8–11.

[13] See, *e.g.* G. D. H. Cole, *A Century of Co-operation* (1945); C. R. Fay, *Co-operation at Home and Abroad* (5th ed., 1948).

[14] One record of this political activity is the Report of the Trade Marks Bill Select Committee PP 1862 (212) XII.

[15] For this step and its consequences in French trade mark law, see Beier (1975) 6 I.I.C. 285 at 294–298.

[16] See the many complaints in evidence to the 1862 Committee (above, n. 14).

prominently amongst its prohibitions on the false marking of goods, was solely a criminal statute, and deliberately so.[17] A pattern of considerable moment was thus established: the criminal law was to provide the general machinery against misdescription of wares. The normal principle that any citizen might prosecute was to apply—indeed in the 1862 Act it was encouraged by the old device of sharing the penalty between prosecutor and Crown. But competitors were not to have the weaponry of civil suits to deal with a wide range of misleading trade descriptions. The Merchandise Marks legislation grew in completeness with a revised statute of 1887. This was to continue in force (with amendments) until the Trade Descriptions Act of 1968.[18] But its actual enforcement was to remain extremely patchy. For unlike the neighbouring legislation on food and drugs and weights and measures, local authorities were not placed under any duty to provide inspectors and others who would see to observance. And in practice competitors showed little interest in putting their resources to the task.[19]

(2) The trade marks register

Traders kept up pressure to have the protection of trade marks made secure. In 1875 the campaign for a registration system succeeded so far as marks for goods were concerned.[20] But the new system acquired from the start a number of characteristics which stamped it as a special privilege conceded with some misgiving: **15–006**

(1) For the first 30 years of the register's operation, only a limited range of symbols might be registered as trade marks[21];

(ii) Registration was not simply a matter of deposit but was subject to an official examination and open to opposition by third parties after advertisement of the application;

(iii) Not only prior registrations but also prior use of the same mark or one deceptively similar would prevent registration.

There was, however, no obligation to use the mark in all cases before registering it. This gave businessmen an important measure of security when launching a new product.

---

[17] See the Report of the 1862 Committee (above, n. 14) at vii.

[18] Enacted in the wake of the Final Report of the Malony Committee on Consumer Protection, Cmnd. 1781 (1962). Its operation, and the additions to it (especially by the Fair Trading Act 1973), are mentioned below, § 18-019.

[19] Occasional prosecutions reached the law reports, e.g. where a name of geographical origin was in issue: see e.g. Holmes v. Pipers [1914] 1 K.B. 57; Corke v. Pipers, referred to in Vine Products v. Mackenzie [1969] R.P.C. at 18–19. The failure of criminal proceedings against the importers of "Spanish Champagne" (see [1961] R.P.C. 116 at 119) underlines the standard of proof required.

[20] Trade Marks Registration Act 1875; amended in 1876 and 1877 and then incorporated into the Patents Designs and Trade Marks Act 1883.

[21] In 1875, these were: name of individual or firm specially printed, etc., written signature, distinctive device, mark, heading, label or ticket; to which certain other matter might be added: see s.10, slightly expanded in 1883 and 1888 (Patents Designs and Trade Marks Acts).

For a time it was not clear whether the registrable types of mark could be protected only after registration.[22] But the judges were sympathetic to the view that goodwill acquired through actual trading should have the first call on legal protection. Common law and equity were held still to give relief against passing off, even if it was effected through imitating a mark that might have been registered.[23] The methods of protection became cumulative, not alternative.

15–007 As quite recent developments in France and Benelux have shown,[24] a trade mark registration system may work on different premises: registration may be allowed without any substantive examination for conflicting interests beforehand; and as a corollary protection is made conditional upon registration, so that industry has an official record of all marks already in existence. The British system has continued to build upon its Victorian foundations. The cumulative relation between common law and statutory rights and the existence of a pre-grant examination allowed the categories of registrable marks to be expanded. By the Act of 1905, where there was some inherent objection to a mark (particularly because, being a word, it had some other meaning) this might be overcome upon proof of sufficient use as a trade mark to distinguish the origin of goods.[25] Furthermore in 1919 the register was divided into Parts A and B in order that certain marks could be given not quite complete protection before they had been used enough to overcome all doubts.[26] But service marks were never brought into the system, thus leaving one whole field exclusively to common law protection.

The 1905 Act tied the statutory privilege to actual trading by making non-use for the previous five years a ground upon which a person with an interest could have a mark removed from the register.[27] In a different way, the courts insisted on the same connection: under the 1905 Act, they treated registration as expungeable if the mark had been licensed[28]; for that rendered obscure whether the mark indicated a connection in trade with registered proprietor or licensee. They would not consider the registered right as a discrete part of the trader's property which might be dealt with by him without reference to the public's understanding of its meaning.

15–008 The scale of business organisation in the twentieth century, following the lead of the American "trusts," has led to many shifts in trading practice. The spread of production, the growth of a popular press with its immense prospects for advertising, the increase of trans-national

---

[22] The 1875 Act, s.1 (and its amendments in 1876) provided that "proceedings to prevent the infringement of any trade mark" should not be brought unless the mark was registered.
[23] See especially *Great Tower* v. *Langford* (1888) 5 R.P.C. 66; *Faulder* v. *Rushton* (1903) 20 R.P.C. 477 (C.A.). In the U.S.A. the existence of common law rights alongside the federal system of registration has also been important, though with somewhat different consequences: see McCarthy, *Trade Marks and Unfair Competition* (2nd ed., 1984), Chap. 1.
[24] For which see Beier (above, n. 15) at 297–298.
[25] On this see further, below, §§ 17-015—17-024.
[26] Below, §§ 17-025, 17-026, 17-068.
[27] For the present law, see below, §§ 17-050—17-052.
[28] Below, § 17-056.

business in successful products and the consequent need to shield high-priced markets against parallel imports from elsewhere were all characteristics of the new era. Brand advertising on a large scale by manufacturers replaced goodwill that was principally associated with retail outlets, and this only increased the commercial significance of the trade marks around which it revolved. There was considerable pressure to be able to license and assign marks more freely than was possible under the British system. This stemmed not only from the spread of corporate groupings under parent holding companies and the increase in licensing of technology and business "packages." One particular advantage, it was hoped, was that if the same trade mark was in legally distinct ownership in different countries, the rights could be employed to deter parallel importing.[29] An elaborate and not very satisfactory compromise over assignment and licensing was embodied in the presently governing statute, the Trade Marks Act 1938.[30]

New advertising techniques also led to pressure on the registration 15–009 system to compensate for the absence of a general unfair competition law. The 1938 Act contained two concessions in this direction.[31] Very well-known trade marks became registrable "defensively" for goods in which the owner did not trade, in the hope of preventing others from annexing any of their notoriety. But the judges treated this arrangement coldly and it has not had much impact.[32] Owners of Part A trade marks were also enabled to object to comparative advertising and similar practices which attempted to take the benefit of the advertising without paying for it. Again, some judges found the expansion of the law unpalatable and the provision has had an uncertain effect.[33]

In 1974, the Mathys Departmental Committee reported on the British system under the 1938 Act in terms of general satisfaction with the British way of doing things.[34] After that much would begin to happen which would cast increasing doubt on those inherent virtues, which will be discussed in the next section. One result has been that the Trade Marks (Amendment) Act 1984 has extended the registration system to service marks for businesses, so that it is no longer necessary to prove passing off in order to protect the name, symbol or get-up of a business. The new section of the Register was opened in October 1986.

(3) Trade marks in international commerce

The case for a registration system succeeded largely because of the 15–010 needs of British exporters. It had proved difficult to negotiate bilateral arrangements with other countries when their nationals could not be offered the protection of a registered right in Britain.[35] The 1875 Act gave

[29] For the fate of this device in recent times, see below, §§ 18-001—18-005.
[30] Below, §§ 17-057—17-062.
[31] Both following recommendations of the Goschen Committee, Cmd. 4568 (1934), §§ 73–77, 184–185.
[32] Below, §§ 17-046—17-048.
[33] Below, §§ 17-076, 17-077.
[34] Cmnd. 5601, esp. § 46; see below, §§ 15-011, 15-012.
[35] See Schechter (above, n. 5) at 140.

British manufacturers the increasingly important hope of protection abroad, and there was then no difficulty in supporting the provisions on trade marks in the Paris Convention on Industrial Property of 1883. These were modest, consisting mainly of the principle of "national treatment"[36] and a short period of priority stemming from the filing of a first application in one member state.[37]

There was no provision for any form of international application which would ease the procedure for securing registrations in a number of countries. A movement to this end succeeded with the signing in 1891 of the Madrid Agreement on the International Registration of Trade Marks. This allows an applicant who has registered a mark in his home or business country to deposit an international registration with an international office (now WIPO). The mark will then be registered in the other member states that are designated unless a state raises an objection under its national law within 12 months.[38] The British have so far declined to join in this arrangement.[39] It would indeed give foreigners who have quick and easy access to property rights at home presumptive access to British protection, while the British manufacturers would be left to face thorough and deliberate examination by their own Registry before they could take advantage of the arrangement.[40] But now that EEC developments are affecting the future shape of the British system, the prospect of joining Madrid has come more into focus.[41]

15–011   This outcome is one consequence of the battle of the systems. But there remains a substantial demand from trans-national businesses for a simpler system of securing trade marks because of the basic role of marks in marketing strategies. In 1973 a Trademark Registration Treaty was signed in Vienna by the United Kingdom and United States as well as leading Madrid Agreement countries. This Treaty would provide for a single initiating application by which the process of securing a trade mark can be opened in designated member countries simultaneously. Each country will then follow national laws and procedures in dealing with the application.[42] Only the period of initial registration and renewals would be standardised—at 10 years. It would seem, however, that the TRT was an effort in vain.[43]

---

[36] See above, § 3-010, n. 45.

[37] For international priority and trade mark applications, see below, § 17-035. The Convention now contains a number of other guarantees: e.g. protection abroad may not be made dependent upon having filed at home (Art. 6(2)) and well-known marks must be protected to the extent required by Art. 6bis.

[38] It remains open to "central attack" in its home territory, an idea received with suspicion by non-participants; but see Tatham [1985] E.I.P.R. 91.

[39] The main participants have been countries of continental Europe and North Africa. There is also a Pan-American Agreement: for its history, see Ladas, *International Protection of Trade Marks by the American Republics* (1929). The U.K. is a party to the Nice Agreement of 1957 on classifying goods and services for registration purposes.

[40] The financial arrangements also disadvantage a country with a strict examination system; see Mathys Report, Cmnd. 5601, 1974, § 32.

[41] As well as the U.K., Denmark, Ireland and Luxembourg are the EEC states not in Madrid. For the complexities of a decision to join, see Llewelyn [1986] E.I.P.R. 74.

[42] There would be strict time limits for processing the application. See generally, Derenberg (1973) 63 T.M.R. 531.

[43] As to a possible TRT II, see Sommers [1985] E.I.P.R. 136.

On the whole, the British registration scheme has not led to serious dissatisfaction among traders or consumers. There has in particular been no widespread concern over the annexation of all potentially good marks; this is a much more likely consequence of a deposit system or one that contains no obligation at all to use the mark. Certainly the two modern examinations of the British system by official committees have led to recommendations of little besides some measure of extension and liberalisation.[44] The Mathys Committee's most substantial proposal was accordingly to permit the registration of marks for services as well as goods.[45] The whole report still awaits implementation.

Membership of the EEC, however, brings the prospect of more fundamental change. Where trade marks have been deployed to prevent the movement of goods between Community states, Treaty of Rome principles have already overridden many restrictive effects of national trade mark laws.[46] At the same time, a plan to establish an EEC-wide registration system has been fostered: a first draft was completed in 1964,[47] but only revived in 1974 in train of the successful patent negotiations.[48] As with patents, the Community register is envisaged as an alternative to the national systems, not as a replacement. But since attitudes among member states to the role of the register and to the consequent place of unfair competition principles is so different, the project is obviously a complex one and involves the imposition on national systems of a number of co-ordinate provisions. These have already been agreed in a Directive of December 21, 1988. When implemented, there will have to be substantial changes in the British system of registration.

The Community mark project is also well advanced though the site of 15–012 the Community Trade Mark Office is still in the political air. It is likely to become operative as part of the drive towards 1992.[49] But there remains a question whether the advantage of a single route to protection throughout the Common Market is not outweighed by the costs of a new bureaucracy and the myriad legal complications that will arise in the course of adjustment. It seems likely, after all, that many trade marks will continue to be chosen on a national basis because of differences in languages; and many more will belong to purely national businesses—the more so in that service marks are becoming, or are likely to be made, registrable. As with the EEC's initiative on aspects of unfair competition law, discussion of the Community trade mark project is best postponed

[44] The first, the Report of the Goschen Committee (above, n. 31), led to the amending legislation of 1937–1938.
[45] Cmnd. 5601, § 70.
[46] This complicated issue is taken up later: see §§ 18-006—18-012.
[47] The Report (by a Working Party chaired by de Haan) was not published till 1973: see Department of Trade and Industry, *Proposed European Trade Mark*. On the subject generally, see also Delgado [1977] Patent L.R. 43; Franceschelli [1977] 8 I.I.C. 293; UNCTAD, *The Role of Trade Marks in Developing Countries* (1979); Michaels (1980) 2 E.I.P.R. 13.
[48] For which, see above, §§ 3-019, 3-020.
[49] See Report of S.C. on European Communities, 21/82 (H.L.); Kaufmann (1987) 25 J.C.M.St. 223.

until the British system has been dealt with.[50] There will then be some interesting comparisons to draw.

3. The Purpose of Protecting Trade Marks[51]

15–013 With the immense growth in the scale of business, and the advertising that accompanies it, modern customers rarely have that personal knowledge of suppliers which is the hallmark of a village economy. Even so, their interest in source of supply has not in essence changed. Information about origin is only a means towards an end: their main concern is in the quality of what they are buying. In the case of some goods, part of that quality may be bound up with source in a specific way: as, for instance, when the goods will need servicing and the manufacturer or supplier is looked to for the service. But in a great many cases source, particularly when indicated by a cypher such as a product mark or get-up, does not have even this significance. What it does is to enable the purchaser to link goods or services to a range of personal expectations about quality which derive from previous dealings, recommendations of others, attractive advertising and so on. Nor should it be forgotten that, however persuasively the advertiser may seek to promote this sort of symbol, it retains a neutral character in one sense: once a consumer learns that he does not want particular goods, the mark, name or get-up becomes a significant warning signal.

15–014   It is a basic assumption in a competitive economy that the consumer benefits by being able to choose among a wide range in the quality and price of goods and services. But once a range of alternatives is offered, he can choose rationally only if he knows the relevant differences. Acquiring all the appropriate information is in many cases too time-consuming and costly, so risks have to be taken. This is particularly so over qualities that cannot properly be checked or tested before purchase, but have to be taken on trust. How willing a purchaser is to take the risk of buying something unknown in place of something known will depend on many factors: for instance, how satisfied he is with the known, and how serious the consequences will be for him if the unknown turns out unsatisfactory. It is one thing to experiment with a washing powder, but another with a drug or with decaffeinated coffee.

The seller's interest is to emphasise qualities (including price) that differentiate his product from those of his competitors. Inevitably, if those differences are in reality slight, he will be tempted to exaggerate them, or to bolster them with appeals to sentiment of one kind or another. There is a strong case for controlling the claims of advertisers and this has become a recent preoccupation of Western societies as part

[50] See below, §§ 18-014—18-018.
[51] There is a growing body of literature on the economics of information which pertains to the following discussion. References to it, and an attempt to extract its relevance to the policy issues surrounding trade marks can be found in Cornish and Phillips, (1982) 13 I.I.C. 41; Landes and Posner (1987) 30 J.L. & Econ. 265.

of the movement for consumer protection. The approach may be by persuasion[52] or by legal prohibition. In either case, it will probably aim first to eliminate factual inaccuracies, then points of spurious differentiation and ultimately the more oppressive manipulations of feeling—naked appeals, for instance, to fear or aggression.

In such laudable pursuits, the continuing importance of being able to 15–015 distinguish the source of goods and services should not be forgotten. To remove the possibility of differentiation (save for goods that can be tested by inspection) is, indeed, to eliminate the incentive to provide goods of superior quality.[53] If the consumer cannot trust the information that he receives he will tend to buy things of lower quality, although overall he may be less satisfied with the results. He may even feel compelled into extraordinary measures in his own defence. To take an extreme but telling example: developing countries have become alarmed by the high price of pharmaceuticals and the amount of advertising—filled with claims difficult to check—which accompanies their marketing. There has accordingly been a temptation to outlaw the sale of drugs by trade mark. Where this has been tried, however, without at the same time giving the state control over quality in the market, suspicion of the efficacy and genuineness of what is on offer soon runs high. So do black-market prices for products still bear trustworthy trade marks.[54]

A law protecting marks, names and get-up, accordingly, seems unavoid- 15–016 able in a capitalist economy. In various aspects, however, these laws have tended to develop in a manner that may appear to confer power without responsibility. The trade mark owner acquires the all-important right to stop imitations of his indication of source, but his own use is conditioned by few limitations or positive requirements. It is perfectly possible for the public to be taught that a box bearing a particular mark and get-up contains 500 grams of chocolates and then, by discreet expansion of the packaging, to reduce that amount to 475 grams. Customarily the way of providing against such conduct, if it is shown to mislead the public, is to penalise it through criminal laws, such as those in Britain against false and misleading trade descriptions; or to enjoin it through laws on unfair competition (if they extend to such cases).[55]

As a further sanction, should such a trader be deprived of his trade 15–017 mark, or refused the right to enforce it? The main consequence of doing so would be to open the door to imitators of the mark,[56] thus compounding the existing confusion by the prospect of other imitators. Moreover,

[52] As in the self-regulation systems so characteristic of British business, such as the Advertising Standards Authority; for which see above, § 2-014, below, § 18-019.
[53] On this, see especially Akerlof (1970) 84 Q.J. Economics 488; Heal (1976) 90 Q.J. Economics 499 (with reply by Akerlof).
[54] The country in question was Pakistan: see UNCTAD Secretariat, "The Impact of Trade Marks on the Development Process in Developing Countries" (TD/B/C/, 6A/C3.3, 1977) at 266.
[55] It would of course be possible to include such powers in trade mark statutes, if it were thought important enough to insist upon.
[56] Theoretically, it would be possible to enjoin the misuser from all uses of the mark in future, not just misleading ones. But that would be extreme.

if uncovering the deception had led to adverse publicity, there will then be sectors of the public who want the mark to continue in use in order to know what to avoid.

In practice it is difficult to show that conduct of the kind just illustrated is definitely misleading. The qualities indicated by a trade mark are rarely definable with sufficient precision for it to be possible to say that if they are changed there is definite deception. The best hope of securing more reliable and relevant information for the buying public is by specifying the characteristics that must be given in labelling and advertising. Marketing which does not comply with the requirement can then be directly penalised or prohibited. To threaten deprivation of trade mark rights will in practice rarely be of assistance.

In recent discussions about trade marks there has been a quite distinct reason for insisting that their prime function, indeed the only function with which the law should concern itself, is to designate the trade origin of goods. We have seen that, particularly in the inter-war period, trade mark interests sought extensions of protection that would (i) cover forms of unfair competition such as indirect "dilution" and comparative advertising,[57] and (ii) erect trade marks into barriers against the international movement of an enterprise's products. One way of arguing for such extensions was to play up the role of origin as a mere means towards indicating quality, and to suggest that the "real" function of trade marks in modern commerce was either to guarantee quality, or to protect the investment which went into advertising, whether the public understood the trade marks advertised in terms of origin or quality or both. But, as we shall see, there has been a strong judicial reaction against the use of trade marks as legal barriers between price-differentiated markets, not only within the EEC but also in international trade generally.[58] It is this which has induced the recent apologia for trade marks as indicators purely of origin.[59] It is a theoretical concern with "function" that is essentially defensive. It arises from a fear that trade marks may cease to be protected even against piratical imitations, that most "essential" of objectives in the current law.

---

[57] Above, § 15-009. "Dilution" is a somewhat emotive term used to describe borrowing a well-known mark for use in a different field. "Defensive" registration was intended in part to provide a remedy: see below, §§ 17-046—17-048.

[58] See below, §§ 18-001—18-005.

[59] A good sample can be found in Union des Fabricants, *Marque et Droit Economique* (1976) 85 *et seq*. Note also the Confederation of British Industry's study on consumer attitudes to trade marks (1976).

CHAPTER 16

COMMON LAW LIABILITY

1. PASSING-OFF[1]

The passing-off action was first developed to meet a classic case. As Lord **16-001** Halsbury put it: "nobody has any right to represent his goods as the goods of somebody else."[2] The same has been held of representations about services; and a defendant may also be liable for passing off one class of the plaintiff's goods as another.[3] His means may consist of misappropriating the plaintiff's mark, business name or get-up; or he may simply supply his own goods when he receives an order for the plaintiff's.[4] In all such cases the plaintiff loses the customer because the latter is misled by a competitor. The seriousness of such a threat is recognised in legal principle: at least so far as an injunction is concerned, the action will lie even where the defendant is innocent[5]; and relief may be granted without proof of actual damage, but simply because of the likelihood of future injury.[6] This, as we have seen, carries passing-off further than most other economic torts.[7] And because it is in this sense a wide-ranging form of liability, the judges have in the past been careful to ensure that it is not applied indiscriminately to analogies which fall outside the classic cases.

This caution is for instance expressed in the refusal to treat rights **16-002** arising from use of a trade mark as giving a fully-fledged right of property in that mark. All that the common law protects through its passing-off action is the goodwill between a trader and his customers which the mark helps to sustain.[8] His rights against imitators last only so long as he does not abandon his business; and he cannot by assignment give another trader the power to sue for passing-off unless he assigns his

---

[1] See, generally, Kerly, Chap. 14; Young, *Passing Off* (2nd ed., 1988); Drysdale and Silverleaf, *Passing Off* (1986); Morison (1956) 2 Syd. L.R. 50; Cornish (1972) 12 J.S.P.T.L. 126; Gummow (1974) 7 Syd. L.R. 224; Dworkin [1979] 1 E.I.P.R. 241.
[2] *Reddaway* v. *Banham* [1896] A.C. 199 at 204; 13 R.P.C. 218 at 224.
[3] See below, n. 31.
[4] As in *Bostitch* v. *McGarry* [1964] R.P.C. 173.
[5] See below, § 16-017.
[6] See below, §§ 16-024—16-029.
[7] Above, §§ 2-006, 2-007.
[8] See especially *per* Lord Parker, *Burberrys* v. *Cording* (1909) 26 R.P.C. 693 at 701; *Spalding* v. *Gamage*, (below n. 31) at 284; and see *Singer Mfg.* v. *Loog* (1882) 8 App. Cas. 15; *Reddaway* v. *Banham* (above, n. 2); *Star Industrial* v. *Yap* [1976] F.S.R. 256 (J.C.); *Erven Warnink* v. *Townend* (below, n. 12).

business at the same time.[9] Moreover, this principle restricts the tort to injury in the course of trade. One person cannot object if the name by which his house is known is used on the house next door.[10]

16-003   Even if attention is confined to cases where customers are misled, there are forms of unfair competition which are not yet known to give a competitor a civil right of action. In particular, if one trader misdescribes some physical quality of his own goods in a way that brings in customers, this may well expose him to criminal sanctions and to contractual or even tortious liability to those actually deceived, but not to an action by other members of the trade.[11] One explanation for this may be that none of them suffers in a special degree more than the others. But we shall see that this has ceased to be a categorical point of distinction. For in *Erven Warnink* v. *Townend* (the "Advocaat" case)[12] the House of Lords has accepted that where a group of traders share a reputation in a trade name that describes a type of product, any one of them may sue an outsider who uses it for goods which are not properly so described. For this Lord Diplock offered a broad justification in terms of policy. After noting the wider ambit of criminal offences in the Merchandise Marks Acts and even more rigorous later statutes, he said:

"Where over a period of years there can be discerned a steady trend in legislation which reflects the view of successive Parliaments as to what the public interest demands in a particular field of law, development of the common law in that part of the same field which has been left to it ought to proceed upon a parallel rather than a diverging course."[13]

Yet on the heels of this encouragement came a warning. In *Cadbury-Schweppes* v. *Pub Squash*,[14] unfair trading was alleged to lie in the defendant's advertising which had adopted the general tenor of the plaintiff's successful campaign to stress both the masculinity and the nostalgia attending the drinking of lemon squash. But there was no confusion between the trade marks or the get-up of the actual products themselves and so no passing-off, Lord Scarman remarking on the importance of not stifling competition by undue redress, and refraining from deciding whether any cause of action could lie in the absence of such confusion.[15] Accordingly there are some difficulties in describing the present scope of the cause of action.

[9] See below, §§ 16-014—16-016.
[10] *Day* v. *Brownrigg* (1878) 10 Ch.D. 294. The same notion is expressed in the requirement of likely damage: see *Street* v. *Union Bank* (1885) 30 Ch.D. 156; *Hall of Arts* v. *Hall* (1934) 51 R.P.C. 398.
[11] See above, § 2-008.   [12] [1980] R.P.C. 31.
[13] *Ibid.* at 405—406. He also notes that the statutes do not themselves give rise to any civil action for breach of statutory duty: see above, § 2-011. Is the field then really "left" to the common law?
[14] [1981] R.P.C. 429 (J.C.); and see *Adidas* v. *O'Neill* [1983] F.S.R. 76 (Irish S.C.); but *cf. Elida-Gibbs* v. *Colgate-Palmolive* [1983] F.S.R. 95.
[15] [1981] R.P.C. at 490—491. The caution in this opinion has been reflected in the unwillingness of Australian judges to use a statutory tort of deceptive trading (Trade Practices Act 1974, s.52) as a vehicle for overrunning the bounds of passing-off. This result is lamented by Blakeney (1984) 58 A.L.J. 316, but rather approved by Cornish (1985) 10 Adelaide L.R. 32.

In the "Advocaat" case, Lord Diplock defined the necessary elements of a passing-off action as follows:

"(1) a misrepresentation (2) made by a trader in the course of trade, (3) to prospective customers of his or ultimate consumers of goods or services supplied by him, (4) which is calculated to injure the business or goodwill of another trader (in the sense that this is a reasonably foreseeable consequence) and (5) which causes actual damage to a business or goodwill of the trader by whom the action is brought or (in a *quia timet* action) will probably do so."[16]

These five characteristics fall to be analysed by reference to the plaintiff's reputation, the defendant's act and the likelihood of damage.

(1) The plaintiff's reputation

(a) *Not just confusion*
    In the normal case of passing-off, the plaintiff has to prove a **16-004** reputation sufficient for members of the public to be misled by the defendant's conduct into thinking that they are securing the goods or services of the plaintiff. It is not enough for the public simply to be confused about whether it is getting the plaintiff's or the defendant's goods: such might be the case, for example, where both start trading at virtually the same time with confusingly similar names[17]; or where a mark will not suggest either of them to the public because instead it carries an association with some third party. The makers of "Evian" water-bottles (for their "Evian" bicycles) could not stop a rival from selling bottles under the same name; the mark on the bottles was likely to be understood as referring to a third party, the marketers of "Evian" mineral-spring water.[18]
    Accordingly, the plaintiff will demonstrate the volume of his sales and advertising expenditure and will supplement this by evidence from traders and public of the meaning that they attach to the distinguishing features of the plaintiff's goods or business: saying for instance that they have long understood the trade mark "XXXX" to denote goods of the plaintiff's manufacture. At the end of the day, the plaintiff must show that it is his reputation that is being misappropriated by the defendant. Otherwise it may well be a case of "the unknown seeking remedies against the known."[19]

[16] Above, n. 12, at 93; see also Lord Fraser at 105–106, who adds that the reputation must be with the English public as the result of trading in England: see below, § 16-012.
[17] But a head-start of three weeks was enough to secure an interlocutory injunction against a deliberate imitator in *Stannard* v. *Reay* [1967] R.P.C. 589; cf. *Compatibility Research* v. *Computer Psyche* [1967] R.P.C. 201 (logo for computer dating not sufficiently established in short period of use).
[18] *Evian* v. *Bowles* [1965] R.P.C. 327 and see *Rolls Razor* v. *Rolls (Lighters)* (1949) 66 R.P.C. 137 (suggesting, in the case of each product, "in the Rolls-Royce class").
[19] Harman J., *Serville* v. *Constance* (1954) 71 R.P.C. 146 at 149.

(b) *Distinguishing feature*

16-005		The plaintiff must have some badge of recognition upon which to found his reputation. Commonly this is a trade mark (whether it be a word, or a symbol such as a "logo") or a corporate, business, professional or philanthropic name specially adopted. But it need not be: it may simply be a personal name—in full or abbreviated, actual or assumed[20]; or the name of a place where the person does business; or the "get-up" in which goods or documents are packaged,[21] or, of course, any combination of mark, name and get-up. In one extreme case, the very shape of the product itself (laundry blue with a stick in it) was held to have come to indicate the plaintiff's goods.[22] In another, extreme in a rather different way, the plaintiff company was held to have a trading reputation in lemon juice sold in life-size plastic lemons, even though these also bore labels with its mark "Jif"; and the defendants' lemons amounted to passing-off even though they bore the mark, "ReaLemon."[23] Also controversial has been a decision that the green-and-black colouring given to a well-known patented tranquilliser could not be imitated by a compulsory licensee because the public recognised it as a brand rather than an indicator of type.[24] There have been others, which can be kept for later discussion, in which the reference to the plaintiff is decidedly indirect.[25]

In the case of literary and other artistic works, and of performances, the reputation may lie in the work or performance itself, or in a

[20] Thus journalists and performers have protected their noms-de-plume and stage names: e.g. Landa v. Greenberg (1908) 24 T.L.R. 441 ("Aunt Naomi"); Hines v. Winnick [1947] Ch. 708 ("Dr. Crock and his Crackpots"); Marengo v. Daily Sketch (1948) 65 R.P.C. 242 ("Kem" the cartoonist); Sykes v. Fairfax [1978] F.S.R. 312 (S.C., N.S.W.). Note also cases where the name of someone else is used; as in Franke v. Chappell (1887) 57 L.T.(N.S.) 141 (impresario protected "Richter Concerts," named after the great conductor).

[21] This may even consist of the colouring of a container: Sodastream v. Thorn Cascade [1982] R.P.C. 459 (C.A.).

[22] Edge v. Niccolls [1911] A.C. 693 (H.L.)—despite the possible effect of raising the cost of production for any other competitor: see at 709. But that is an unfortunate consequence, avoided in later cases by making it difficult to prove the necessary reputation, e.g. Hawkins v. Fludes Carpets [1957] R.P.C. 8; British American Glass v. Winton [1962] R.P.C. 230; Gordon Fraser v. Tatt [1966] R.P.C. 505; Jarman & Platt v. Barget [1977] F.S.R. 260 at 272 (C.A.); Rizla v. Bryant & May [1986] R.P.C. 389; but note Combe International v. Scholl [1980] R.P.C. 1. See Evans (1968) 31 M.L.R. 642; Walton [1987] E.I.P.R. 159. cf. now the protection of industrial design by copyright and registered and unregistered design: above, Chap. 14.

[23] Reckitt and Coleman v. Borden [1988] F.S.R. 601 (C.A.). Although the defendant's mark was very well-known as such in the U.S., there was evidence that in the U.K. shoppers took it to be descriptive of the product.

[24] Hoffmann-La Roche v. DDSA Pharmaceuticals [1972] R.P.C. 1. Since this is a substantial barrier against a policy of encouraging generic substitutes for original proprietary drugs, it is important to note a certain readiness to distinguish the case; e.g. Roche Products v. Berk Pharmaceuticals [1973] R.P.C. 473—colouring of pills not distinctive of plaintiff's product; John Wyeth v. M. & A. Pharmachem [1988] R.P.C. 26—colouring denoted different dosages; Boots v. Approved Prescription Services [1988] F.S.R. 45— quality differences prevented through Medicines Act approval, so no argument for interlocutory relief; and cf. Smith Kline & French v. K. V. Higson [1988] F.S.R. 115— arguable that colouration not likely to be taken as use of a registered trade mark. See Llewelyn (1981) 12 I.I.C. 185.

[25] See below, §§ 16-030—16-032.

"character" drawn from either. In this way, subject-matter which may have no copyright receives protection: thus for a defendant to suggest that his film was yet another in a successful series concerning the "One-armed Swordsman" was held actionable at the suit of the producer of the series.[26]

It is the plaintiff's reputation as a source of goods or services that is in **16-006** issue. The courts have not required that he make his identity plain by, for instance, giving full name and address. It is enough that a trader uses a mark, name or device of any kind as a cypher by which to teach the public how to get his goods.[27] Nor have the courts required that this connection be of any particular kind: he may be the manufacturer, wholesaler, retailer, selector or distributor of goods.[28] For example, a supermarket chain which offers its "own brand" lines has a reputation in both the goods and the business. An importer who provides all the advertising, sales and servicing for a product in his own name may well acquire the reputation even against the manufacturer.[29] If the plaintiff's reputation is adequate for the purpose, even to suggest that goods are made under his licence or some other trading arrangement giving him a means of control over them would be actionable.[30]

Accordingly the starting point for deciding whether there has been a **16-007** misrepresentation amounting to passing-off is the understanding that the plaintiff has built up with the public. Thus if his mark is used on one product of a particular quality, the defendant may not use the mark in trade for other goods, even if they emanate from the plaintiff. In *Spalding* v. *Gamage*,[31] for instance, the defendant was held not entitled to sell the plaintiff's "Orb" footballs as his "New Improved Orb" footballs. But in such cases it has been said that there must be two distinct classes of the plaintiff's goods: a songwriter could not prevent an early work from being passed off as a new work where the court could draw no clear dividing line in quality between the older and the more recent.[32]

However, where a mark (whether it is a product or a house mark) is built up by an international group of companies, it may well signify the group as a whole, rather than individual members of it. This may limit the opportunity of using passing-off proceedings to prevent the parallel importing of the group's products. To this we return later.[33]

---

[26] *Shaw Bros.* v. *Golden Harvest* [1972] R.P.C. 559 (S.C. Hong Kong); *cf. Producers' Distributing* v. *Samuelson* [1932] 1 Ch. 201, below, § 16-035.

[27] *Powell* v. *Birmingham Vinegar* [1897] A.C. 710; 14 R.P.C. 720; *cf. Politechnika* v. *Dallas Print Transfers* [1982] F.S.R. 529 ("Rubik's cube").

[28] In Hong Kong, reputation as a buyer has been protected: *Penney* v. *Punjabi Nick* [1979] F.S.R. 26; *Penney* v. *Penneys* [1979] F.S.R. 29.

[29] For the problems that arise between rival claimants to a single reputation, see below, § 16-010.

[30] So said in *H. P. Bulmer* v. *Bollinger* [1978] R.P.C. 81 (C.A.). But a majority of the court refused to believe that the use of "champagne perry" led to the belief either that the drink was champagne or was endorsed by any champagne house. For attempts to apply similar arguments to "merchandising rights," see below, §§ 16-035, n. 64; 17-036, n. 73.

[31] (1915) 32 R.P.C. 273 (H.L.); and see *Robinson* v. *Wilts United Dairies* [1958] R.P.C. 94 (C.A.); *Colgate Palmolive* v. *Rockwell* (1989, C.A.), to be reported. The same applies where secondhand goods are called new, or imperfect goods perfect; see Kerly, § 16–26.

[32] *Harris* v. *Warren* (1918) 35 R.P.C. 217; *cf.* Dworkin (1979) 1 E.I.P.R. at 245.

[33] See below, §§ 18-001—18-002.

(c) *Secondary meaning*

16-008   If the plaintiff has used a mark or name which has some other connotation for the public, then he faces the special difficulty of establishing that the public does understand the word or symbol to indicate that goods or services come from him. The other meaning may exist quite independently before he starts to trade: it may be a word or phrase which describes the goods or services, in particular or in general, or it may have a geographical significance. The plaintiff must then establish that his use of the term as an indicator of source has given it a "secondary meaning." How difficult it will be to do this depends on the particular circumstances. If the term precisely describes the product, then the secondary meaning has to be proved up to the hilt. In *Reddaway* v. *Banham*,[34] for instance, the mark "Camel Hair Belting" had just this character. But, as the House of Lords insisted in that case, there is no absolute rule that traders are not entitled to protection if they use such terms. Other traders' interests are considered to be sufficiently protected by the form of injunction that will be granted. This requires the defendant not to use the descriptive term in such a way as to mislead the public into thinking that it is getting the plaintiff's goods or services.[35] Where the plaintiff is the first to develop a market, or has a legal monopoly of it (for instance, through a patent), the courts show great reluctance to treat the name of the product or service offered as bearing a secondary meaning: "oven chips" and "Chicago pizza" have provided recent examples.[36]

The same approach applies to geographical names. The makers of "Glenfield" starch sued a defendant who set up his starch-making business in Glenfield and then used the name as a trade mark. They secured an injunction in similarly qualified terms.[36a] Again, where one trader has had the field to himself and has built up quality associations as an element in his get-up—such as different packet colouring for different qualities of cigarette paper—he cannot prevent a second entrant into his market from adopting the same indicators together with a different trade mark.[37]

(d) *Personal names*

16-009   Special considerations apply when the plaintiff establishes a reputation in a word that is the defendant's personal name. It is the present rule "that a man must be allowed to trade in his own name and, if some confusion results, that is a lesser evil than that a man should be deprived

---

[34] *Reddaway* v. *Banham*, above, n. 2; *cf. Cellular Clothing* v. *Maxton* [1899] A.C. 326; 16 R.P.C. 397, and for further case-law, Kerly § 16–35.

[35] *Reddaway* v. *Banham* (above, n. 2) at 221, 231, 234. When the meaning is only "secondary," the defendant may more readily be held not to be causing confusion: see below, § 16-022.

[36] See *McCain International* v. *Country Fair Foods* [1981] R.P.C. 69 (C.A.); *My Kinda Town* v. *Soll* [1983] R.P.C. 407 (C.A.).

[36a] *Wotherspoon* v. *Currie* (1872) L.R. 5 H.L. 508 (H.L.), where Lord Westbury first used the phrase "secondary meaning" (at 521); *cf.* the special facts of the "Stone Ale" case: *Montgomery* v. *Thompson* [1891] A.C. 217 (H.L.).

[37] *Rizla* v. *Bryant & May* [1986] R.P.C. 389.

of what would appear to be a natural and inherent right"[38]; but he must act honestly,[39] not setting out deliberately to take advantage of another's reputation. Moreover, the exception is confined to the naming of a business. It does not justify the use of a personal name as a mark for goods, if the result will be confusion with the established reputation of another.[40] In modern times most judges have felt that some other mark can always be found for goods.[41]

Company names are deliberately adopted in a way that personal names are not (unless they are assumed).[42] Nevertheless if a company originally takes its name honestly and then conducts business under it for a period, it will be entitled to continue using it for the business (but not as a mark for goods) as if it were an individual using a personal name.[43] A new company cannot claim this privilege, even if its name is taken chiefly from that of a person, unless it has taken over an existing business and is continuing to use its name.[44]

(e) Mark becoming descriptive

A mark may initially be used to distinguish the origin of goods. But if **16-010** it proves highly successful the public may begin to use it as a generic term for the kind of article to which it has been applied. Marks of this sort—the advertiser's dream so long as they remain within the range of protection—are most commonly associated with products that have some really novel property or technical construction.[45] The company making "Corona" cigars proved that some purchasers treated this as a brand,

[38] Lord Simonds, *Marengo v. Daily Sketch* (1948) 65 R.P.C. 242 at 251. But first names and nicknames are not specially privileged: *Biba Group v. Biba Boutique* [1980] R.P.C. 413.

[39] Seeking out an individual with an appropriate name in order to lend colour to the imitation of a rival's name is not likely to be found honest. Likewise where the name of a person genuinely associated with an enterprise is nevertheless used as part of a scheme to suggest an association with the plaintiff which does not exist: as in *Bentley v. Lagonda* (1947) 64 R.P.C. 33; (below, § 17-068, n. 55).

[40] The distinction was clearly drawn by Romer J., *Rodgers v. Rodgers* (1924) 41 R.P.C. 277 at 291, and accepted, *e.g.* in *Baume v. Moore* [1958] R.P.C. 226 (C.A.) and by a majority of the House of Lords in *Parker-Knoll v. Knoll International* [1962] R.P.C. 265 at 279, 284, 287.

[41] The earlier case law tended to treat the right to one's name as a higher right even in relation to selling goods: see, *e.g.* *Burgess v. Burgess* (1853) 3 De G.M. & G. 896; *Turton v. Turton* (1889) 42 Ch.D. 128. A turn in the tide is discernible in Buckley L.J.'s judgment in *Brinsmead v. Brinsmead* (1913) 30 R.P.C. 493 at 507–509; but there have been modern supporters of the older approach: Lord Greene M.R., *Wright v. Wright* (1949) 66 R.P.C. 149, 151–152; Lord Denning, *Parker-Knoll v. Knoll* (above, n. 40) at 277.

[42] Curiously, some uncertainty surrounds the question whether a person who has honestly taken up an assumed name can continue to use it for his business: see Kerly, § 16–89.

[43] *Parker-Knoll v. Knoll* (above, n. 40); *Anderson & Lembke v. Anderson & Lembke* [1989] R.P.C. 124; But *cf.* cases where there is a dispute over entitlement to the reputation of a single business: below, § 16-011.

[44] *Dunlop Pneumatic v. Dunlop Motor* (1907) 24 R.P.C. 572 (H.L.); *Waring v. Gillow* (1916) 33 R.P.C. 173; *Hawtin v. Hawtin* [1960] R.P.C. 95; *Fine Cotton Spinners v. Harwood Cash* (1907) 24 R.P.C. 533; *Kingston Miller v. Kingston* (1912) 29 R.P.C. 289; *Fletcher Challenge v. Fletcher Challenge* [1982] F.S.R. 1.

[45] For instance, in English courts, "Linoleum" was found non-distinctive (*Linoleum Co. v. Nairn* (1878) 7 Ch.D. 834); but the registration of "Vaseline" as a trade mark survived: *Cheseborough's T.M.* (1901) 19 R.P.C. 342 (C.A.).

others as an indication of size and shape. The plaintiff was entitled to a limited injunction against selling cigars not made by the plaintiff without making clear that this was so; only if the defendant proved that the word had wholly lost its original meaning, it seems, would he be entirely free to use it. But if the way in which he uses the term must make plain to his customers that he is adopting the descriptive sense, he will not be enjoined.[46]

(f) Concurrent reputation

16-011 If two separate businesses have honestly acquired a reputation in a single mark or name, some of the public may associate it with the one, some with the other, some with both. This has not prevented the courts from holding that each has a sufficient reputation to take action against the outside interloper who attempts to take advantage of it.[47] Recently the same principle has been extended to the case where numbers of manufacturers have a joint reputation in the name for a product with particular qualities. The question, according to the House of Lords, is whether the class of traders can be defined with reasonable precision. The test can be satisfied by showing that a word connotes recognisable and distinctive qualities in goods. All who supply them then share in the reputation[48]; "champagne," "sherry," "Scotch whisky" and "advocaat" have all been held examples.[49] In the first of these instances there were at least 150 shippers, each of whom was entitled separately to sue.[50]

Contrast with these cases of shared reputation, the difficulties that may arise between two traders each of whom has built up an independent reputation quite honestly in the same or a similar mark. If one can show that he has the reputation in a business name for a particular area, the other will not be permitted to use the name in that area, however much he may enjoy a reputation in the name in some other part of the country.[51] But if each has built up his reputation in a particular locality and argument arises because both are expanding business into intermediate territory, neither may be able to show that the public there associates the name with him so as to lead to passing-off by the other.[52] Likewise if

---

[46] Havana Cigar v. Oddenino [1924] 1 Ch. 179 (C.A.).

[47] Dent v. Turpin (1861) 2 J. & H. 139 (single business divided among successors); Southorn v. Reynolds (1865) 12 L.T. 75; Dunnachie v. Young (1883) 10 S.C. (4th) 874.

[48] Erven Warnink v. Townend [1980] R.P.C. 31. On the nature of the reputation raised in these cases—an issue at the frontier of passing-off—see below, § 16-032. For the relation to other forms of protection, see Appendix 3.

[49] Bollinger v. Costa Brava [1960] R.P.C. 16, [1961] R.P.C. 116; Vine Products v. Mackenzie [1969] R.P.C. 1; John Walker v. Ost [1970] R.P.C. 489. See also Pillsbury Washburn v. Eagle 86 Fed. Rep. 608 (1898).

[50] "The larger [the class] is, the broader must be the range and quality of products to which the descriptive term used by the members of the class has been applied, and the more difficult it must be to show that the term has acquired a public reputation and goodwill as denoting a product endowed with recognisable qualities which distinguish it from others of inferior reputation that compete with it in the same market.": Lord Diplock, Warnink case (above n. 12), at 95.

[51] Cavendish House v. Cavendish-Woodhouse [1970] R.P.C. 234 (C.A.); Levey v. Henderson-Kenton [1974] R.P.C. 617.

[52] Evans v. Eradicure [1972] R.P.C. 808; City Link v. Lakin [1979] F.S.R. 653.

two companies have previously enjoyed a shared reputation through an element of joint ownership, and that connection is severed, for instance, by the nationalisation of one of them.[53]

(g) Geographical considerations

In the ordinary case, the plaintiff's reputation lies with the public **16-012** within the jurisdiction and the defendant's passing-off is directed at that public. But English courts have not hesitated to extend their protection to certain aspects of foreign trade: relief will be granted against supplying the "instruments of fraud" in Britain for the purpose of deceiving a foreign populace.[54]

A more difficult case arises where the plaintiff's business is one which is run abroad but has an international reputation which extends to this country. The courts insist that what is in issue is the plaintiff's reputation with the English public bred from business conducted in England.[55] If the plaintiff, without having any business establishment in England, nevertheless does some business there, this will suffice: it was enough that the "Sheraton" hotel group had bookings taken in Britain for hotels which were entirely foreign.[56] By contrast in *Bernardin* v. *Pavilion Properties* it was held that for protection to be granted the reputation in England must be based upon some user there: the proprietor of the internationally known "Crazy Horse Saloon" in Paris was thus unable to enjoin an imitator in London from cashing in on the reputation of the name and "get-up."[57] Some decisions have treated this dividing-line as too categorial. But it was re-affirmed in the "Budweiser" case, where the American and Czech enterprises, which each traded under this mark in selling lager in their domestic and other markets, were seeking to launch their own products in Britain at much the same time. The Americans sought to claim prior reputation by virtue of sales in service-base shops to United States forces; but the Court of Appeal refused to bring this reputation into account: it did not amount to carrying on a business in the country.[58]

(h) Temporal considerations

Again, in the straightforward case, the plaintiff's reputation arises from **16-013** trade or business that he has built up and is continuing. If his business

---

[53] *Habib Bank Ltd.* v. *Habib Bank AG* [1982] R.P.C. 1.

[54] *Johnston* v. *Orr-Ewing* (1882) 7 App. Cas. 216 (H.L.); *John Walker* v. *Ost* (above, n. 49).

[55] See esp. *Erven Warnink* v. *Townend* (above, n. 12) at pp. 105, 106 *per* Lord Fraser; *Anheuser-Busch* case (below, n. 58).

[56] *Sheraton* v. *Sheraton Motels* [1964] R.P.C. 202; or if a commercial importer buys abroad and sells in Britain: *Panhard* v. *Panhard* [1901] 2 Ch. 513; 18 R.P.C. 405; and see *Poiret* v. *Jules Poiret* (1920) 37 R.P.C. 177; *Globelegance* v. *Sarkissian* [1974] R.P.C. 603 (foreign reputation "tacked onto" small English reputation); *Home Box Office* v. *Channel 5* [1982] F.S.R. 449; *Esanda* v. *Esanda Finance* [1984] F.S.R. 96 (S.C., N.Z.).

[57] [1967] R.P.C. 581.

[58] *Anheuser-Busch* v. *Budejovicky Budvar* [1984] F.S.R. 413 (C.A.). As a result, the Americans were unable to establish passing-off by the Czechs; and see *Bernardin* v. *Pavilion Properties* [1967] R.P.C. 581.

has ceased, his reputation may nevertheless survive. He will, however, only be able to succeed if he can also show that he has not abandoned the name or mark[59]; in other words that he intends to do business with it again in the future.[60] So the name-owner may preserve his interest while his business is temporarily closed during a change of premises.[61] The owner of the "Ad-Lib Club" was able to assert its notoriety even though it had been closed for five years (because of an injunction against noise); no alternative premises had since been found on which to re-open it, but that remained his intention.[62] The reputation must survive, however. Use at one period gives no property right of indefinite duration.[63]

From the other end of the spectrum, a sufficient reputation through publicity may be shown even before the plaintiff starts trading. The BBC succeeded in demonstrating such a reputation from the media interest in its "Carfax" traffic information system for cars.[64]

(i) Dealings in trade reputation

16-014 In different ways the preceding paragraphs have drawn attention to the fact that in a passing-off action what is being protected is the trading reputation built with the public, not some larger and more permanent right of property. This factor becomes specially significant when we turn to attempts to assign and to license "common law" marks.

First consider a common occurrence in international trade: a foreign enterprise sets up a distributing agency in Britain[65]; success makes it desirable to manufacture here[66]; eventually the British enterprise, for whatever reason, acquires independence that is economic as well as legal. At different stages the question may arise, which has the better right to the marks and names: foreign "originator" or local trader? A prime issue is: what have the British public been taught to understand by the reputation? If the mark is built up as the original manufacturer's mark and the goods still come from him, then the reputation must be his[67]; but the contrary is true where it becomes known as the importer's or local manufacturer's, however much the other may have desired and supposed that the mark would remain his.[68]

---

[59] *Maxims* v. *Dye* [1977] F.S.R. 321; *C & A Modes* v. *C & A (Waterford)* (below, n. 24).
[60] *Star Industrial* v. *Yap* [1976] F.S.R. 256 (J.C.).
[61] *Berkeley Hotel* v. *Berkeley International* [1972] R.P.C. 673.
[62] *Ad-Lib Club* v. *Granville* [1972] R.P.C. 673.
[63] *Norman Kark* v. *Odhams* [1962] R.P.C 163 ("Today" as a magazine title held not to survive seven years' non-use).
[64] *BBC* v. *Talbot* [1981] F.S.R. 228; but note *My Kinda Bones* v. *Dr. Pepper's Stove* [1984] F.S.R. 289.
[65] The agency may not start as a distinct legal entity; or it may be a subsidiary; or it may be an independent entity taking its own commercial risks.
[66] The starting point may be with the establishment of manufacturing arrangements in the country.
[67] *e.g. Imperial Tobacco* v. *Bonnan* (1924) 41 R.P.C. 441 (J.C.) (not passing-off to import genuine "Gold Flake" cigarettes into India, despite the creation of an exclusive distributorship there); *Sturvenant Engineering* v. *Sturvenant Mill* (1936) 53 R.P.C. 430 (end of market-splitting agreement).
[68] *Oertli* v. *Bowman* [1959] R.P.C. 1 (H.L.) (manufacturing licensee); *Diehl's T.M.* [1970] R.P.C. 435 (distributor's registered mark—unregistered mark should be similarly treated).

If the marks have been transferred together with the business that uses **16-015** them then they must belong to the transferee. An extreme case is this: where the marks of a German company's British subsidiary were transferred to an unconnected entity as a measure of wartime expropriation, the new owner was able to restrain passing-off by the German company.[69]

If the original owner believes it advantageous to "transfer" the marks without the accompanying business, he may instead create grave jeopardy: he himself will have abandoned his interest, however much his reputation lingers[70]; the "assignee" will have no reputation of his own on which to sue.[71]

Before the Trade Marks Act 1938, these sorts of difficulties affected registered trade marks as well as unregistered.[72] The Act accordingly allowed the originator to license (and thus keep ultimate control of) registered marks and to assign them even without goodwill.[73] The courts have not, however, been prepared to adapt the law affecting "common law" marks in order to bring about a comparable development. In *Star Industrial* v. *Yap*, a company manufacturing "Ace Brand" toothbrushes in Hong Kong stopped importing them into Singapore after an import duty was imposed on them, and it abandoned its business there. The Privy Council held that it could not, three years later, assign its Singapore rights in the mark to a part-owned subsidiary; nor, more than five years later, could it secure relief against passing-off by a competitor.[74]

To businessmen who have not secured registration for a mark, this rule **16-016** may present an unexpected obstacle to a profitable transaction. But the rule only emphasises a policy to which the courts have consistently adhered: the passing-off action should extend only to the protection of subsisting goodwill; beyond this other traders should be free to use the names and marks that are to their best advantage.[75] The concession allowing the assignment of registered marks is indeed some derogation from that policy, and one that is likely to be carried further when the

---

[69] *Adrema* v. *Adrema-Werke* [1958] R.P.C. 323; if the two concerns remain connected, the contrary may well be true: see below, §§ 18-001—18-005. If the goods are being imported into the U.K. from another EEC state, the result of the *Adrema* case will now be affected by the Rome Treaty, Arts. 30, 36; see below, §§ 18-007—18-009.

[70] See above, n. 62.

[71] At least until he builds up his own trade: see *Pinto* v. *Badman* (1891) 8 R.P.C. 181.

[72] Hence cases on registered and unregistered marks were decided on a similar basis. *Pinto* v. *Badman* in fact concerned the former. Probably the marks associated with a distinct part of the business could be assigned with that part alone; but this could not give cover to the assignment of one out of several marks with which the assignor labelled a single type of goods: see *Sinclair's T.M.* (1932) 49 R.P.C. 123; Kerly, §§ 13–02/09; and below, § 17-056.

[73] But subject to certain controls discussed below, § 17-056—17-062. To a limited extent it also became possible to assign unregistered marks together with those that were registered; but the effect of the provision is obscure: T.M.A. 1938, s.22(3); below, §§ 17-057—17-058.

[74] [1976] F.S.R. 256; *cf. Coles* v. *Need* [1934] A.C. 82 (J.C.).

[75] If they do so in a way which misleads consumers into connecting their goods with a former user of the mark, the public interest may be protected through the Trade Descriptions Act's machinery.

legislation is revised.[76] Meanwhile the gap between registered and unregistered rights has been narrowed by the introduction of registration for service marks.[77]

(2) Defendant's representation

(a) Defendant's state of mind

16-017   It has long been settled that, where the defendant is perpetrating the passing-off himself, the fact that he does not realise it is no defence against the grant of an injunction.[78] But whether a defendant must pay more than nominal damages for injuries caused while he remains innocent remains unsettled.[79] As we saw earlier,[80] the tendency in intellectual property is to give reasonably innocent defendants this measure of protection. There seems no reason to adopt a different approach for passing-off. Where the defendant is alleged to have supplied others with the instruments for defrauding subsequent customers he is liable only when his mark is calculated to deceive.[81] If a producer's mark is not likely to cause confusion when an ultimate customer sees it, the fact that a retailer might keep it hidden when supplying an order for the plaintiff's goods will not render the producer liable.[82]

(b) Form of passing-off

16-018   As already noted, it does not matter what means the defendant uses to represent his goods or business to be another's. He may simply supply his own in response to an order for the plaintiff's, without ever making a positively misleading statement. Or he may imitate the badge which the plaintiff has used to implant reputation in the public mind. Nor does it matter what misrepresentation about trade is made: falsely to claim to be a manufacturer's authorised agent may be actionable.[83]

(c) Likelihood of confusion

16-019   In a case where there is something to be said in the defendant's favour, the most frequent issue is whether his way of doing business is sufficiently likely to confuse the public. If he has imitated the plaintiff's mark or other badge exactly, the only question left is whether he has done enough else to dispel the otherwise misleading effect of his imitation: has he said with sufficient prominence, "No connection with the plaintiff"? It

[76] See below, § 18-018.
[77] See below, §§ 17-001—17-003.
[78] See above, § 16-001, and for further case-law, Kerly, § 16–15.
[79] The issue is deliberately reserved by the H.L. in *Marengo* v. *Daily Sketch* (1948) 65 R.P.C. 242 at 247, 251, 252, 254; Goddard L.J. in *Draper* v. *Trist* (1939) 56 R.P.C. 429 at 443–444, appears to be against any liability other than nominal damages; *cf.* Clauson L.J. at 441; there is a difference of view in *Henderson* v. *Radio Corp.* (1960) [1969] R.P.C. 218 at 229, 244; *cf.* Kerly, § 16–106.
[80] See above, § 2-027.
[81] See, *e.g.* *Payton* v. *Snelling* [1901] A.C. 308; 17 R.P.C. 628 at 635, 636; Kerly, § 16–75. It is presumably this principle that Lord Diplock had in mind when listing the characteristics of passing-off: for which, see below, § 16-030.
[82] *e.g. Schweppes* v. *Gibbens* (1905) 22 R.P.C. 601 (H.L.).
[83] *Sony* v. *Saray Electronics* [1983] F.S.R. 302 (C.A.).

is an unusual case in whch a trader attempts to do this; even more rarely will he do enough.[84] "Thirsty people want beer not explanations."[85] Despite which, judges and legislators sometimes treat the ability to add distinguishing information as a practical possibility.[86]

If the defendant's marking or naming is not an exact imitation, the first question is whether he has sailed too close to the wind, or has shown a true mariner's judgment. This has to be decided largely in light of the particular circumstances. But the comparison to be made must be emphasised: it is between the manner in which the plaintiff's reputation has been acquired in actual trade and the trading practice in which the defendant is indulging or threatens to indulge.[87]

The question is: what impact would the defendant's mark be likely to have on probable customers, given the expectations they already have and the amount of attention that they will pay.[88] All the circumstances in which goods are actually sold, or business conducted, will be considered: will an appeal be made to the same set of customers? Will orders be in writing or by word of mouth? Will there be sales among ill-educated or illiterate customers?[89] Will marks be used in clearly legible and striking form?[90] If the goods themselves can be inspected before purchase, will this reveal a difference in kind?[91]

Normally the customer will not have the opportunity of seeing the two **16-020** marks side by side. So, in comparing their visual appearance, it is necessary to allow for imperfect recollection by a person of ordinary memory.[92] A court will concentrate on the aspect of the mark that is most likely to be memorable, the "idea of the mark" as it is sometimes called. Thus to mark cigarettes "99" was held not to pass them off as

---

[84] One instance is where the defendant is understood to be using the plaintiff's mark only to indicate that he is selling the same sort of product: "a substitute for 'Yeastvite,'" "Claret style," and a host of nicely nuanced variants. On this sort of comparative reference, see below, §§ 16-043—16-045.

[85] Lord Macnaghten, *Montgomery* v. *Thompson* (1891) 8 R.P.C. 361 at 368. And see *McDonald's* v. *Burgerking* [1986] F.S.R. 45 ("It's not just Big, Mac"—taken to arouse associations with plaintiff's product).

[86] See below, § 17-002, n. 16.

[87] Compare the test of whether a registered trade mark has been infringed: below, § 17-067. In general the principles here discussed apply equally in comparing marks on an application to register and in deciding upon infringement of a registered mark. For greater detail, see Kerly, Chap. 17.

[88] Good examples may be found in the cases concerning newspaper titles; *e.g. Borthwick* v. *Evening Post* (below, n. 8); *D. C. Thomson* v. *Kent Messenger* [1974] F.S.R. 485; *Morning Star* v. *Express Newspapers* [1977] F.S.R. 113 (see especially at 117; if "only a moron in a hurry would be misled" the case is not made out).

[89] *e.g. Edge* v. *Niccolls* [1911] A.C. 693 (H.L.); *Johnston* v. *Orr-Ewing* (1882) 7 App. Cas. 219 (H.L.) (yarn for the "natives of Aden and India").

[90] Think of signs on petrol stations and marks on watches: *e.g. British Petroleum* v. *European Petroleum* [1968] R.P.C. 54; *"Accutron" T.M.* [1966] R.P.C. 152 at 155.

[91] *e.g. Turner's Motor* v. *Miesse* (1907) 24 R.P.C. 531; the question is closely related to the need to prove likely damage.

[92] See especially *Aristoc* v. *Rysta* [1945] A.C. 68 (H.L.) and Luxmoore L.J. in C.A. (1943) 60 R.P.C. 87 at 108 (registration case).

"999"; the idea of the latter was triplication.[93] But to use a lion's head on a soap wrapper may well be actionable if someone else is already known for his "Lion" or "Red Lion" soap.[94] If phonetic similarity is important, account must be taken not only of the different ways in which customers and sales staff might pronounce a word but also of slovenly speech: consider, for example, the possibilities inherent in "Rysta," when compared with "Aristoc," for stockings[95]; or "Piquant" and "Picot" for cosmetics.[96]

(d) Descriptive connotation

16-021   Where the key to the plaintiff's reputation is alleged to lie in some word or other symbol that describes some quality of the goods or services, the defendant may avoid liability by relatively minor differentiation. Thus in a leading case, "Office Cleaning Association" was held sufficiently distinct from "Office Cleaning Services."[97] There has been much concern to ensure that a plaintiff is not unfairly enclosing part of "the great common of the English language."[98] Accordingly, whether the action succeeds is likely to depend on proof of actual passing-off—proof that there were people who both took the word or phrase as indicating the plaintiff and were misled by the defendant's imitation; or at least that the defendant adopted his name in the hope of producing this result.

(e) Responsibility upon the defendant

16-022   In the context of passing-off,[99] the courts have felt no hesitation in pinning responsibility upon a person who enables the injury to occur. A manufacturer or wholesaler who provides retailers with the means of deception will be liable without proof either that the retailers knew that they were passing-off or that actual passing-off was taking place.[1]

---

[93] *Ardath* v. *Sandorides* (1925) 42 R.P.C. 50; *Johnston* v. *Orr-Ewing* (above, n. 89) provides a good example where the mark is compounded of picture and words; *Lever* v. *Goodwin* (1887) 36 Ch.D. 1 (C.A.) is useful on general get-up. Whether there are similarities in colour may be important in passing-off cases, because the actual usages are being compared; *cf.* the position with a registered trade mark: below, §§ 17-014, 17-068.

[94] *Hodgson* v. *Kynoch* (1898) 15 R.P.C. 465 (note that the evidence was held to establish passing-off but not trade mark infringement).

[95] Above, n. 92.

[96] *Picot* v. *Goya* [1967] R.P.C. 573.

[97] *Office Cleaning Service* v. *Westminster Cleaners* (1946) 63 R.P.C. 39 (H.L.). For further examples, see Kerly, § 16–51. Likewise if the plaintiff's mark is close to a descriptive word, the courts look with care at evidence of actual confusion, particularly if it is secured by a trap order: *Fox's Glacier Mints* v. *Jobbings* (1932) 49 R.P.C. 352 (local use of "glassy mints").

[98] Cozens Hardy M.R., *Crosfield's Appln.* (1909) 26 R.P.C. 837 at 854.

[99] *cf.* the position over patents (above, §§ 6-013—6-015) and copyright (above, §§ 11-016—11-017).

[1] *Singer* v. *Loog* (1880) 18 Ch.D. 395; *Lever* v. *Goodwin* (1887) 36 Ch.D. 1 (C.A.); *Draper* v. *Trist* (1939) 56 R.P.C. 429 (C.A.); and see the cases on foreign passing-off, above, § 16-012. It is different when goods leave the defendant in "innocent" condition and a subsequent seller misuses them.

[2] [1930] 1 Ch. 330; *cf. Champagne Heidsieck* v. *Scotto* (1926) 43 R.P.C. 101.

But the plaintiff, rather than the defendant, may be primarily responsible for the confusing state of affairs, as when he puts similar labels on products of different quality. In *Champagne Heidsieck* v. *Buxton*,[2] the plaintiff sold different types of champagne in France and England under similar labels. It was not open to him to say that an importer who brought the French goods into England for resale passed them off. It was for the plaintiff himself to make the difference plain. This concept would seem to place a particular difficulty in the way of using the passing-off action against a parallel importer and in that context we shall return to it.[3]

(f) *Proof of likely deception*
The plaintiff is not required to show actual deception in order to **16-023** succeed. But if he can do so, his case will be much advanced.[4] Likewise, at least in order to get an injunction, he is not obliged to show that the defendant was acting dishonestly.[5] But if there is a question whether the public will be deceived, proof of actual fraud carries him a long way (without being necessarily conclusive): "Why should we be astute to say that [the defendant] cannot succeed in doing that which he is straining every nerve to do?"[6]

There has been very little discussion of how many people must likely be deceived.[7] It seems that their number must be "substantial"; even 20 cases of actual deception were once disregarded, where the plaintiff's case went to loss of reputation rather than to direct competition.[8] The Court of Appeal has been prepared to take account of a survey of opinion, after allowing for expert criticism of the manner in which it was conducted.[9] Clearly there are difficulties in devising investigations that are not biassed, particularly if left to the parties; they are also expensive. But they can bring an element of objectivity into an inquiry that otherwise leaves a judge to his own hunch amid a welter of conflicting affidavits.

(3) Likelihood of damage

(a) *Likely damage*
Because the "property" is in the goodwill or business of the plaintiff, **16-024** and not in his mark, name or get-up, he has to show, if not actual injury,

---

[3] See below, §§ 18-001—18-005.
[4] See Kerly, §§ 16–77, 17–38.
[5] See above, § 16-017.
[6] Lindley L.J., *Slazenger* v. *Feltham* (1889) 6 R.P.C. 531 at 538 and see Kerly, §§ 16–87, 17–39.
[7] e.g. *Globelegance* v. *Sarkissian* [1974] R.P.C. 612; *Wienerwald* v. *Kwan* [1979] F.S.R. 381.
[8] *Borthwick* v. *Evening Post* (1888) 37 Ch.D. 449 (C.A.).
[9] "GE" *Trade Mark* [1970] R.P.C. 339 at 370, 383, 386 (not the subject of comment on further appeal); cf. Graham J. [1969] R.P.C. 418 at 446–447; *Stringfellow* v. *McCain Foods* (below, n. 18).

then at least some likelihood of injury that is more than the mere imitation. The mark or other symbol, in other words, is not simply a licensable commodity. In "ordinary" passing-off between competitors who are selling the same or substitutable products or services, likelihood of damage is the corollary of demonstrating likelihood of confusion. This third element assumes a distinctive role when the case is not one of simple diversion of customers from one rival to another.

(b) *Goods or business not the same*

16-025   In *Walter* v. *Ashton*,[10] the defendant, who had been responsible for a successful sales campaign to sell "Daily Express" bicycles with the co-operation of that newspaper, launched a new campaign to sell "The Times" bicycles, but without having any connection with "The Times." Byrne J. required the existence of a "tangible probability of injury" to the plaintiff's property and found it thus: the representation that "The Times" had a business responsibility for the sale of the cycles exposed it at least to the risk of litigation and possibly (if the newspaper did not take steps to disconnect its name) even to liability. This test, though occasionally criticised,[11] has often been the touchstone of later cases.[12]

Another form of probable injury is damage to trade reputation from the assumed connection, such as suggesting that a nightclub had begun an escort agency[13] or that the Queen of department stores had stooped to moneylending (as conducted by the defendant).[14] Again, the plaintiff may be injured by losing the chance to expand his business into the field that the defendant has occupied, if the latter is not restrained. A plaintiff who sold "Marigold" rubber gloves and the like secured an interlocutory injunction against a defendant who began using the mark on toilet tissues, the plaintiff stating that he was planning to use the mark upon very similar goods.[15] In contrast, there have been numerous cases in which, because the goods or businesses are not the same, the plaintiff has failed, either at the interlocutory or the final stage. For instance, the "Albert Hall Orchestra" (organised by Albert Edward Hall) was allowed to continue using this name over the objection of the proprietor of the Royal Albert Hall, there being no actual or reasonable danger of

---

[10] [1902] 2 Ch. 282.
[11] *Harrods* v. *Harrod* (1924) 41 R.P.C. 74 at 78; *cf.* 86–87.
[12] The requirement is strongly reaffirmed in *Erven Warnink* v. *Townend* [1979] F.S.R. 397.
[13] *Annabel's* v. *Shock* [1972] R.P.C. 838.
[14] *Harrods* case (above, n. 11). See also *Hulton Press* v. *White Eagle* (1951) 68 R.P.C. 126.
[15] *L.R.C.* v. *Lila Edets* [1973] R.P.C. 560. An extreme example is *Eastman Photographic* v. *Griffiths* (1898) 15 R.P.C. 105 ("Kodak" for bicycles, when cameras were being specially sold for bicycles: the prospect of the plaintiffs actually applying their mark to bicycles seems to have been supposition). Another is *Lego System* v. *Lego M. Lemelstrich* [1983] F.S.R. 155 (plastic gardening equipment likely to be associated with the well-known "Lego" toys; name adopted perfectly properly in Israel and elsewhere).

damage.[16] The makers of "Zoom" iced lollipops could not obtain interlocutory relief against the marketing of "Zoom" bubble gum.[17] The night-club "Stringfellows", could not object to oven chips sold by that name.[18] The copyright owners of the "Wombles" books and television series had no "merchandising rights" that were good against a company that leased "Wombles" rubbish skips.[18a]

(c) Not trading in the same geographical area

The same considerations apply when the plaintiff establishes a business 16-026 reputation in one place and the defendant then sets up a similar business in another so as to suggest that the plaintiff has opened a new outlet. In *Brestian* v. *Try*, for instance, the plaintiff had hairdressers' shops in London, Wembley and Brighton; the defendant was restrained from using the same name for hairdressing in Tunbridge Wells. But Jenkins L.J. was careful to find "that damage would probably ensue" because customers might go to the defendant instead of the plaintiff; and Romer L.J. pointed to evidence that the plaintiff's credit and reputation might be endangered.[19] More recently a business with "Chelsea Man" shops in three cities was held entitled to a country-wide injunction, because of its intention to extend business beyond these places.[20]

This ought to be the appropriate principle for dealing with cases where a plaintiff has built up a reputation by business abroad and the defendant imitates him so as to lead customers to believe that the plaintiff has come to Britain.[21] If there is a tangible risk that the plaintiff's good name will be hurt by the poor quality of what the defendant provides or adverse publicity about him,[22] or if the plaintiff has plans to come to Britain which will be jeopardised,[23] these should provide a sufficient basis for his claim. But it would be a new departure to give such a plaintiff relief merely because the defendant was taking advantage of his reputation.[24]

---

[16] *Hall of Arts* v. *Albert Hall* (above, n. 10).

[17] *Lyons Maid* v. *Trebor* [1967] R.P.C. 222.

[18] *Stringfellow* v. *McCain Foods* [1984] R.P.C. 501.

[18a] *Wombles* v. *Womble Skips* [1977] R.P.C. 99. See below §§ 16-035—16-036.

[19] [1958] R.P.C. 161 (C.A.); and see also *Outram* v. *Evening Newspapers* (1911) 28 R.P.C. 308 (papers of same name in Glasgow and London: no likelihood of pecuniary loss from confusion); *The Clock* v. *Clock House* (1936) 53 R.P.C. 269 (confusion of road houses, the proximity (5 miles) being stressed).

[20] *Chelsea Man* v. *Chelsea Girl* [1987] R.P.C. 189 (C.A.).

[21] *cf.* the discounting of foreign reputation in *Bernardin* v. *Pavilion Properties* and *Anheuser Busch* v. *Budeforicky Budvar* (above, n. 58).

[22] *cf. Annabel's* v. *Shock* (above, n. 13).

[23] A nice question is, how definite must the plaintiff's plan to expand be? What is to be done about the business which tries to secure the name or brand of a transnational company before the latter moves into a particular market? Note that in the *Alain Bernardin* case, the proprietors of the French business had no plans to set up in Britain, so the refusal of relief may well have been correct on the facts.

[24] *Maxim's* v. *Dye* (above, n. 59) appears to come close to this; but the defendant did not appear at the hearing. *cf. C & A Modes* v. *C & A (Waterford)* [1978] F.S.R. 126 (Irish S.C.), where it was insisted that "goodwill does not necessarily stop at a frontier", but that the plaintiff's goodwill must nonetheless be liable to be damaged by the passing-off. Both decisions were criticised in *Athletes Foot* v. *Cobra Sports* [1980] R.P.C. 343; which held that the plaintiff must have at least a customer in Britain; see also *Metric Resources* v. *Leasemetrix* [1979] F.S.R. 571; *Lettuce* v. *Soll* (see (1980) 2 E.I.P.R. at 170–171).

(d) *Not trading: other sufficient reputation*

16-027　Professional and charitable institutions may have a reputation that will be protected in passing-off proceedings if it is likely to be injured by the defendant's activities. Again courts have been careful to state what it is that creates a tangible probability of injury: in the case of a professional association it may be that the passing-off will induce members to leave and potential members not to join[25]; in the case of a charity that regularly appeals for funds, it may be the danger to its reputation, should the defendant ever fall into financial difficulties.[26]

(e) *Not trading: sponsorship*[27]

16-028　The practice of having celebrities lend their names to the commendation of products or services is an advertising device with a long history. For the most part this kind of sponsorship is arranged by contract, and in advertising circles it is considered improper to use a person's name without his consent for this purpose.[28] However unethical it may be, it is not settled how far it is actionable. Consider two cases:

(i) The value in taking the alleged "sponsor's" name lies in his expert knowledge of the product or business in question and it can be shown that his professional reputation will be damaged by the association that is wished upon him. Typically a doctor's name is taken to promote a medicine. In such a case there should be no obstacle to the grant of relief. The bulk of dicta seem to be in favour, though there is no authority clearly in point.[29]

(ii) The value in taking the alleged sponsor's name lies either in his own expertise or simply in the glamour of the association; but there is no evidence that any professional reputation will suffer or that there will be any other form of financial loss.[30] It was in this context that Wynn-Parry J. insisted that, for the grant of an injunction, there be "a common field of activity in which, however

[25] *e.g. Society of Accountants* v. *Goodway* [1907] 1 Ch. 489; 24 R.P.C. 159; *B.M.A.* v. *Marsh* (1931) 48 R.P.C. 565; *cf. British Assoc. of Aesthetic Plastic Surgeons* v. *Cambright* [1987] R.P.C. 549.

[26] *British Legion* v. *British Legion Club* (1931) 48 R.P.C. 555; *Dr. Barnado's* v. *Barnado Amalgamated* (1949) 66 R.P.C. 103.

[27] See Murumba, *Commercial Exploitation of Personality* (1986) Pt. II.

[28] See below, n. 40.

[29] See, *e.g.* Lord Cairns, *Maxwell* v. *Hogg* (1867) L.R. 2 Ch. App. 307 at 310; Maugham J., *BMA* v. *Marsh* (1931) 48 R.P.C. 565 at 574; Sugerman J., *Henderson* v. *Radio Corp.* [1969] R.P.C. 218 at 221. In the old case of *Clark* v. *Freeman* (1848) 11 Beav. 112 a doctor, who objected to being associated with a quack medicine, failed to secure an injunction before his case had been put to a jury in a trial at law. But that only reflected the general practice before the Chancery reforms of the 1850s; Lord Langdale M.R. expressly left open the possibility of an injunction after a verdict for the plaintiff. But *cf. Dockrell* v. *Dougall* (1899) 80 L.T. 556; and see McClelland (1961) 3 Sydney L.R. 525; Mathieson (1961) 39 Can B.R. 409; Treece (1973) 51 Texas L.R. 637.

[30] Exceptionally, the use of a person's name as a sponsor may be found to carry an innuendo that will support a defamation action: the suggestion, for instance, that an amateur sportsman was in fact taking money for his sponsorship: *Tolley* v. *Fry* [1931] A.C. 333 (H.L.). If a popular personality has already contracted exclusively to sponsor another trader's product and this is known, the tort of interfering with business relations might apply.

remotely, both the plaintiff and the defendant were engaged."[31] In *McCullough* v. *May*, he held that "Uncle Mac," the children's broadcaster, could therefore not restrain the use of "Uncle Mac" as a trade mark for shredded wheat. The appearance of certainty about this test has appealed to some judges as a reason for refusing relief[32]; to others it has seemed unduly mechanical, leading apparently to a denial of relief even where it is likely that the plaintiff has, or will, suffer damage.[33] At root the question is whether the right to one's own name (and to such other indicia of personality as sound of voice and appearance)[34] deserves to be a full property right. In *Henderson* v. *Radio Corporation*, the Supreme Court of New South Wales considered that a professional dancing couple could enjoin the unauthorised use of their photograph upon a record sleeve without proof of any likely financial loss[35]; the Ontario Court of Appeal has recognised that a professional player may sue for the "appropriation of his personality."[36] No English court has been prepared to go even so far,[37] let alone to address the question whether an unknown person can object to the use of his "personality" (name, photograph, etc.) in commercial or other propaganda without his permission.

The common law has remained unwilling to prevent all unwanted **16-029** personal publicity under the rubric of a "right of privacy" or a "personality right." As we have noted already,[38] there must be some more specific form of injury: for instance, through a breach of confidence or a defamatory statement. In its recommendations the Younger Committee on Privacy adhered to this pragmatic, case-by-case approach. It attached weight to the counter-interest in freedom of expression, about which it heard a good deal from the press and other media—interest groups whose position would be substantially jeopardised by a roving liability for invasions of privacy. Nonetheless there is a good case for saying that the use of a person's name, appearance or voice in commercial publicity without his permission is a particular type of conduct that should be actionable.[39] Since the public interest in information as news is not at

---

[31] (1948) 65 R.P.C. 58.

[32] See, *e.g.* Walton J., *Wombles* v. *Wombles Skips* (above, n. 18a).

[33] *e.g.* in *Henderson* v. *Radio Corp.* (below, n. 35); *Totalizator Agency Board* v. *Turf News* [1967] V.R. 605.

[34] Such as the voice of a well-known actor: *Sim* v. *Heinz* [1959] R.P.C. 75; *Lloyd* [1961] C.L.P. 39.

[35] [1969] R.P.C. 218.

[36] *Krouse* v. *Chrysler* (1973) 40 D.L.R. (3d) 15 (claim failed on facts); *Athans* v. *Canadian Adventure Camps* (1978) 80 D.L.R. (3d) 583.

[37] *cf. Lyngstad* v. *Anabas* [1977] F.S.R. 62 (doubt in interlocutory proceedings whether real prospect of the pop-group Abba succeeding at trial in preventing use of the name and likenesses on T-shirts, jewellery, etc.); *Harrison* v. *Polydor* [1977] F.S.R. 1 (no real prospect of preventing use of photos of The Beatles on sleeves for record of interviews with them).

[38] Above, §§ 8-002, 11-059.

[39] The problem was not, however, important enough to be dealt with by the Younger Committee.

stake, it is hard to see why a person should have to put up with public exposure that he may find embarrassing or distressing, merely because he cannot prove likely injury to an economic interest. Significantly, advertising which makes use of unauthorised sponsoring is not permitted in the voluntarily-enforced British Code of Advertising Practice.[40]

(4) The proper scope of passing-off

16-030   The action labelled passing-off is not confined to misrepresentations that the defendant's goods or services are those of a trade competitor. Expansion of the tort is aided by the unspecific terms in which the elements of reputation, confusion of customers and likely damage are indicated in Lord Diplock's five characteristics.[41] A number of key issues deserve to be reviewed, some connected with cases already decided, others of a more speculative nature.

(a) *Nature of the deception*

16-031   Trade marks and names, which traders employ as indications of origin, are, so far as customers are concerned, a means of identifying qualities that they more or less consciously link with origin.[42] Because of this, it seems natural to allow passing-off to be extended to other indications which give consumers similar information about quality, either *in toto* or in some specific respect. While there have been cases which have confined passing-off to misrepresenting indications of origin, a number of other decisions have been more liberal. For instance, the following have been treated as actionable: inserting pages of advertisements into a magazine, thus making it less attractive to other advertisers[43]; "misappropriating" commendations from customers of another trader's goods[44]; advertising goods to be "as shown on television," when it was really the plaintiff's goods that had been shown.[45] Contrast with these the decision (now of doubtful standing) that no action lay against selling one collection of Hazlitt's Essays as the book set for a particular examination, when in fact it was another collection (the plaintiff's) that was set.[46]

16-032   The line between quality and origin is also blurred in cases where plaintiffs share a reputation in a name that is descriptive such as

---

[40] (6th ed., 1979), § 4.7.

[41] *cf.* the remark of Romer L.J., below, § 16-003.

[42] See above, §§ 15-013 — 15-014.

[43] *Illustrated Newspapers* v. *Publicity Services* (1938) 55 R.P.C. 172; and see *Mail Newspapers* v. *Insert Media* [1987] R.P.C. 521.

[44] *Plomien Fuel* v. *National School of Salesmanship* (1943) 60 R.P.C. 219. Possibly cases of "inverse" passing-off, where the defendant takes the result of the plaintiff's work and says that it is his own, could be similarly treated: *cf. Bullivant* v. *Wright* (1897) 13 T.L.R. 201; and see Borchard (1977) 67 T.M.R. 1.

[45] *Copydex* v. *Noso* (1952) 69 R.P.C. 38.

[46] *Cambridge University Press* v. *University Tutorial Press* (1928) 45 R.P.C. 335. A similar attitude is to be found in older cases in which the defendant laid claim to prizes, medals or patents properly belonging to the plaintiff, but the latter could not prove that the public therefore throught that it was getting his goods: see *e.g. Batty* v. *Hill* (1863) 1 H. & M. 264 (where the transient value of the reputation was stressed); *Tallerman* v. *Dowsing Radiant* [1900] 1 Ch. 1; *Serville* v. *Constance* (1954) 71 R.P.C. 146. They might be differently decided today: see Kerly, § 16–24.

"champagne" or "Scotch whisky." In its "Advocaat" decision, the House of Lords refused to confine the kind of description that would suffice to special cases, such as appellations of origin which indicate that a product has physical properties associated with its place of primary production.[47] But there is another, even more striking, respect in which these cases have extended the notion of deception. In the cases concerning the defendant's use of "Spanish Champagne," "British sherry" and the like,[48] the addition of the national adjective must have told the cognoscenti that they were getting a substitute; only those who wanted "the real thing" without knowing what it was would not pick up the distinction.[49] Relief was given to protect the proper meaning of the words against dilution even by a technique that would confuse only those with little idea of that meaning and so of the plaintiff's reputation.[50] The cases have been treated as properly decided.[51] They suggest that the plaintiff's reputation may lie in qualities or commendations which he ought to be able to keep for himself. Thus the true winner of a prize or medal for particular goods ought to be able to stop another from claiming it.[52] Possibly, there must be some sector of the British public which already appreciates the true meaning of the word or other indicium: the reputation must not be solely potential.

(b) *Nature of the injury*

16-033 The other direction in which the "drink" cases extend concepts concerns the likelihood of damage. "Classic" passing-off involves a plaintiff who is peculiarly injured because it is his exclusive goodwill which is misappropriated. But in the cases concerning a shared reputation it is not necessary to show that the plaintiff suffers more than others with whom he shares the goodwill.[53] This carries passing-off some way towards providing a general unfair competition action against all mis-descriptive promotion of products and services. It would seem no substantial step after these cases to allow any one trader whose goods have a particular quality from objecting when another advertises his goods as having the quality when they do not. In the "drink" cases, it is true, qualities were subsumed within a word describing the product as a whole. But "advocaat" was held properly to describe an egg-and-spirits drink, whereas the defendant's product was composed of egg and fortified wine. A similar outcome might well have been reached if the misdescription had been directly of the contents of the drink.

It would be going further again to give a competitor an action where his product does not contain the quality which the defendant inaccurately

---

[47] "Champagne" and "sherry" were appellations of origin in this sense. The C.A. in "Advocaat" took the narrower view. See generally, Appendix 5.

[48] Above, n. 49.

[49] See [1961] R.P.C. at 127, [1969] R.P.C. at 23.

[50] See especially [1969] R.P.C. at 23.

[51] See *Erven Warnink* v. *Townend* [1980] J.R.P.O. 31; *Bulmer* v. *Bollinger* [1978] R.P.C. 79 (C.A.).

[52] *cf.* the cases mentioned in n. 46 above.

[53] See above, §§ 16-010—16-011.

claims for his own. This would indeed make the mere fact of being a competitor a sufficient ground for objecting to misleading advertising. This is often permitted in legal systems which have a general concept of unfair competition,[54] and the traditions of other EEC states in the matter may eventually exert their own influence upon developments in Britain.[55]

Many would identify the interest of competitors and consumers in preventing misrepresentative marketing. Accordingly they would welcome the provision of competitors' actions as an effective method of policing from within an industry. But before accepting this unthinkingly, it is as well to reflect upon the reasons that may in the past have led the judges to move with circumspection in this field. Competitors furnished with a right of civil action that includes the chance of stopping a rival by injunction have a powerful weapon at their command. Some indication of that power has already been outlined in Chapter 2. In the cut and thrust of competitive marketing, the threat of intervening when a rival is launching an advertising campaign can inflict grave injury. That of course is justified when the defendant is plainly in the wrong. But there will be many cases when the issue is not easily determined; and others again when the plaintiff's concern for the welfare of the consumer might seem rather heavily spiced with self-interest. No one can weigh in advance the respective benefits and costs of making the content of each competitor's advertising and labelling the subject of actionable criticism by the rest of his industry. No one can predict how far a penchant for competition by litigation might develop. But with the growth of European and other foreign penetration of the British Market, the predispositions of non-domestic enterprises in this direction might have a significant influence.

16-034　　The British approach to date has been largely to rely upon a set of criminal sanctions aimed directly at protecting the consumer, and, since 1968, enforced principally through the trading standards departments of local authorities.[56] The procedures of the criminal law do not normally allow for rapid preventive action and they require a high standard of proof. At least in England, competitors are as free as other private citizens to launch such prosecutions. But it seems that they do so only occasionally when they feel their own interests to be particularly threatened. Accordingly, as these laws operate in their modern context (given also the possibility of improving this in ways that will be mentioned later),[57] they provide a reasonably adequate means of combatting the serious cases of malpractice. There is certainly some wisdom in the courts' reluctance to give competitors the additional chance of bringing a civil suit, with the inherent danger of self-serving interference that this would import.

[54] In the U.S., see *Restatement of Torts*, § 761; Lanham Trade Mark Act 1946, s.43(a).
[55] However, the EEC Directive on Misleading and Unfair Advertising (84/450; O.J. L.250, p.17) did not in the end require that competitors be accorded such a right of action.
[56] See above, § 2-013.
[57] See below, § 18-019.

(c) *Character merchandising*[58]

In *Samuelson v. Producers Distributing,*[59] the defendant held out his **16-035** film as containing a popular revue sketch written by the plaintiff, when in fact it did not. (If it had, liability in copyright would have arisen.) The plaintiff's copyright included the exclusive right throughout its duration to authorise filming of the sketch. In granting relief, the Court of Appeal in effect treated this aspect of the property as equivalent to goodwill built up through trade. Romer L.J. pointed out that injunctions granted to restrain "classic" passing-off were "merely instances . . . of a much wider principle . . . that the Court will always . . . restrain irreparable injury being done to the plaintiff's property."[60]

There is no copyright in a fictional character or a performer's act outside the confines of the particular texts or scenarios in which they are developed. Copyright does not extend to Biggles, or the character repeatedly played by Charlie Chaplin, whatever they are made to do or say. Accordingly to put these characters into new books, plays or films cannot be treated as damaging "property." But an action may still be grounded upon an injury to goodwill. The plaintiff may, for instance, show that he is likely to lose sales of his own books or theatre tickets from the competition.[61]

However, where the character is deployed in some way that does not compete with a business run by those who originally exploited it—as may well be the case where its name is applied to T-shirts or sweets or other such merchandise[62]—it is not easy to demonstrate any sufficient likelihood of damage and English judges have shown no readiness to enforce "merchandising rights" in this sort of case. Thus the exploiters of those once-popular denizens of children's television, The Wombles, could not secure an interlocutory injunction against using "Wombles" on rubbish skips.[63] Attempts to suggest that the relevant goodwill in this sort of case arises from the public's belief that creators do grant licences to use the name and that this acts as a guarantee of quality have not so far been believed in English actions,[64] though in a case concerning the "Muppets" in Australia it did for once succeed.[65]

---

[58] See genrally Adams, *Merchandising Intellectual Property* (p. 198); Vaver [1978] 9 I.I.C. 541; Wood and Llewelyn [1983] E.I.P.R. 298; Mostert (1986) 17 I.I.C. 80.

[59] [1932] 1 Ch. 201; *cf. Ormond v. Knopf* (1932) 49 R.P.C. 634.

[60] *Samuelson* case (above, n. 59) at 210. This dictum was used in cases such as "Champagne" to justify a broad view of passing-off.

[61] Illustrations are *Shaw Bros. v. Golden Harvest* (above, § 16-005, n. 26) and *Marengo v. Daily Sketch* (1948) 65 R.P.C. 242 (H.L.) (cartoonist's nom-de-plume).

[62] If an artistic work is reproduced on the product, the copyright owner's licence is necessary for 25 years after he first authorises its use on articles of any kind: CDPA 1988, ss.51, 52; above, §§ 14-021—14-025.

[63] *Wombles v. Womble Skips* [1977] R.P.C. 99.

[64] See *ibid.* and *Tavener Rutledge v. Trexapalm* [1975] F.S.R. 479 at 485–486 (outsider built up substantial trade in "Kojakpop" lollipops, so-called after the television character; entitled to prevent "licensee" of owner of television rights from entering same market.)

[65] *Children's Television Workshop v. Woolworths* [1981] R.P.C. 187; *cf. Lorimar Productions v. Sterling* [1982] R.P.C. 395 (S.C., S. Africa); *Grundy Television v. Startrain* [1988] F.S.R. 581.

16-036   Here again, English law is more limited in scope than many jurisdictions that actively foster a law of unfair competition. In arguing the case for extension, one writer has recently claimed that this would "reflect the habits of fair commercial men and public expectations, without any recognisable public interest weighing against it."[66] The case can of course be put attractively. The desire to exploit a character on merchandise stems from its success with the public in the originaZl fictional entertainment. For that success the author or performer and his associates are responsible and they claim in effect that merchandising rights should become part of their property.[67]

But the corollary of property is potential market power. The claim to merchandising rights is made at a time when the popularity of the character would give an opportunity to charge monopoly prices if the rights were conceded. Far from there being no public interest against according the rights, there seems to be a strong case for preserving competition. At least the argument is close enough to militate against extending the law by judicial decision. Major additions to copyright are today generally made by Parliament and, as we have seen, this is the way in which some forms of reaping without sowing have recently been made actionable.[68] The same ought to apply to the claim to merchandising rights.[69] If such a change were introduced, it would presumably also include merchandising rights in the names and pictures of real people such as pop stars. As already suggested, their claim seems rather stronger.[70]

What ought perhaps to be of concern is not that someone who does not trade should have the right nevertheless to license. Rather the law should let all competitors come onto the market until such time as one of them shows that the name definitely indicates goods originating from him to a substantial sector of the public. This is partly a question of preventing registered trade mark rights from being too readily acquired— an aspect that will be reviewed later.[71] But if the issue is raised in passing-off proceedings, a question of secondary meaning arises, since the character's name has non-trade mark associations.[72] This, equally, deserves to be dealt with by demanding clear proof that the name has nevertheless come to be recognised as indicating a trade connection.[73]

---

[66] Vaver above, n. 58.
[67] The manner in which other jurisdictions approach the question is described in several articles in [1978] Ann.I.P.L.
[68] It is noteworthy that attempts to include a merchandising right in CDPA 1988 did not succeed.
[69] Though not, presumably, in copyright legislation, since characters have not been thought an appropriate sub.ject-matter for copyright; certainly the Whitford Committee (Cmnd. 6732, 1977) § 909, thought an unfair competition law was the appropriate framework for any development, rather than copyright.
[70] See above, § 16-028.
[71] See below, § 17-044.
[72] cf. "Tarzan" T.M. (below, § 17-020, n. 3).
[73] On this, note the facts of the "Kojakpops" case (above, n. 64) where intially there were a number of competitors exploiting the name but they all faded away save the plaintiff, who proved very substantial goodwill.

2. Injurious Falsehood[74]

(1) Elements of the tort

The tort of injurious falsehood is sometimes available to deal with **16-037** forms of unfair trading that do not amount to passing-off. These may consist of false claims to legal rights (including, of course, intellectual property rights) and other false statements, such as disparaging criticisms of a competitor's goods or business. But, in contrast with passing-off, at the end of the nineteenth century, the courts deliberately confined this tort to those circumstances whch were most incontrovertibly unjustifiable. Their caution stands as one of the chief barriers to the adoption of any broad conception of unfair competition.[75]

In *Ratcliffe* v. *Evans*, Bowen L.J. declared written or oral falsehoods to be actionable "where they are maliciously published, where they are calculated in the ordinary course of things to produce, and where they do produce, actual damage."[76] This formulation, which encapsulates the tort in its modern form, is broad so far as types of falsehood are concerned, but narrow in its requirement of malice and special damage (the latter being now modified by statute in many cases). Each of these elements calls for separate consideration.

(a) *The falsehood*

The first actionable falsehoods concerned slanders of title to land. In **16-038** the course of the last century, the tort came to cover other misstatements—especially about property and business—until any falsehood was encompassed; but the requirement of pecuniary damage has served to limit successful claims mainly to falsehoods about property, profession, trade or business. The plaintiff must show that the statement is false: true statements, however disparaging and harmful, are not actionable.[77]

The damaging untruth may arise by implication from what is actually said. To state, for instance, that a man is working for a particular organisation may suggest to the hearer that he is no longer working in his former business and so deprive him of orders.[78] Equally for a defendant to claim to be the sole agent for particular machinery may imply that the plaintiff is no longer, or never was, such an agent.[79] If a statement is not explicitly about the plaintiff, whether it must nevertheless be taken as referring to him depends on the particular circumstances. In this connection, the courts have held that an untrue claim to a title of any kind, or to be an inventor or designer, is a falsehood that may be actionable at the instance of the person properly entitled. To this extent

---

[74] See generally, Wood (1942) 20 Can.B.R. 296; Prosser (1959) 59 Col. L.R. 425; Morison (1959) 3 Sydney L.R. 4; Heydon, *Economic Torts* (2nd ed., 1978) 81–86.

[75] See below, §§ 17-076, 17-077, for "importing a reference" to a registered mark.

[76] [1892] 2 Q.B. 524 at 527.

[77] The onus of proof, moreover, lies upon the plaintiff: see *Burnett* v. *Tak* (1882) 45 L.T. 743; *Anderson* v. *Liebig's Extract* (1882) 45 L.T. 757; *cf. Hargrave* v. *Le Breton* (1769) 4 Burr. 2422 at 2425.

[78] *cf. Balden* v. *Shorter* [1933] Ch. 427.

[79] *Danish Mercantile* v. *Beaumont* (1950) 67 R.P.C. 111. Consider also *Liebig's Extract* v. *Anderson* (1886) 55 L.T. 206.

relief is available against what is sometimes called "inverse" passing-off.[80] But there must be some reason to link the statement with the particular plaintiff, rather than with all traders of his class.[81]

(b) Malice

16-039   There are occasions when "malice," as a legal term of art, has a broad, objective sense, indicating circumstances when a person has done something which has no sufficient justification or excuse; and there have been suggestions that this is what the term means in the law of injurious falsehood.[82] But most modern decisions agree that here it refers to the defendant's state of mind. Did he know his statement to be false? Did he act with some "by or sinister purpose"[83] or (to put it less pungently) some "indirect or dishonest motive."[84] Stable J. has summarised the case law thus: if the defendant knows the statement to be untrue, it is malicious whether or not the defendant intended to benefit himself (or someone else) rather than injure the plaintiff; if, however, the defendant does believe his untrue statement, but nevertheless he makes it for the purpose of injuring the plaintiff, that too will suffice.[85]

(c) Special damage

16-040   Until Parliament intervened, the courts required proof of special damage—proof, for instance, that property had lost its value, or a business its custom or a source of supply, as a consequence flowing naturally from the false statement.[86] But, in trading cases at least, they did not always restrict this to unequivocal proof that the plaintiff had lost particular transactions or profits. Where a defendant said in a press report that the plaintiff had gone out of business, then it might well be sufficient for him to prove that his sales overall had forthwith fallen, if his customers were normally unknown and changing; but not if they were regular and known.[87] What evidence will suffice must depend on the whole circumstances; a plaintiff who fails to follow up a reasonable prospect of furnishing concrete proof may severely weaken his case.

The Defamation Act 1952, s.3, has abrogated the need to prove special damage if the words in question (a) were calculated to cause pecuniary damage to the plaintiff and were published in writing or other permanent form, or (b) were calculated to cause pecuniary damage to the plaintiff in respect of any office, profession, calling, trade or business, held or carried

---

[80] e.g. Serville v. Constance [1954] 1 All E.R. 662; Customglass Boats v. Salthouse [1976] 1 N.Z.L.R. 36, [1976] R.P.C. 589 and cf. Bullivant v. Wright (1897) 13 T.L.R. 201.

[81] cf. cases cited in n. 78, above.

[82] e.g. Lord Davey, Royal Baking Powder v. Wright Crossley (1900) 18 R.P.C. 95 at 99; and see Newark (1944) 60 L.Q.R. 366; Wood (above, n. 74) at 319.

[83] Harman J., Serville v. Constance (above, n. 80) at 665.

[84] Scrutton L.J., Greers v. Pearman (1922) 39 R.P.C. 406 at 417.

[85] Wilts United Dairy v. Robinson [1957] R.P.C. 220 at 237. A less limited approach may possibly develop through the impact of liability for negligent misstatements. Note the suggestive decision in Ministry of Housing v. Sharp [1970] 2 Q.B. 223; Mesher (1971) 34 M.L.R. 317.

[86] Haddan v. Lott (1854) 15 C.B. 411.

[87] e.g. Ratcliffe v. Evans (above, n. 76); Greers v. Pearman (above, n. 84).

on by him at the time of the publication.[88] The phrase "calculated to cause pecuniary damage" is probably not to be understood as a reference to the defendant's state of mind but rather in an objective sense, "calculated" being synonymous with "likely."[89] It is not, in other words, a specific part of the requirement of malice, but is akin to the requirement of likely damage in the tort of passing-off.[90]

(2) Particular aspects

(a) *Relation to other torts*
If the defendant's statement represents that his goods or business are 16-041 those of the plaintiff it is an injurious falsehood that amounts to passing-off. So it is actionable despite lack of malice.[91] If the statement tends to lower the defendant personally in the eyes of right-thinking members of society then it is actionable as defamation: proof of intent to defame is then, in principle, irrelevant; and it is for the defendant to excuse himself by proving the truth of the statement or establishing some other defence such as fair comment on a matter of public interest or one of the forms of privilege. It is not defamation, but only injurious falsehood, to disparage a trader's goods, business or property, save where there is also an imputation of undue "carelessness, misconduct or want of skill."[92] This may, of course, be the innuendo behind a statement about the goods or business. But unless this is so, honest disparagement is not actionable at common law.[93]

(b) *False claims of infringement*
Because intellectual property is protectable by litigation alone, and not 16-042 also by possession, the ability to assert rights is crucial. And equally, as earlier noted,[94] because it often takes time and expense to settle whether there has been infringement of a valid right, a threat to sue can do immense commercial harm, particularly to a manufacturer whose customers receive the threats. In this connection, the limited scope of injurious falsehood deserves special note. For it is only if a person

---

[88] This was recommended by the Porter Committee on the Law of Defamation (Cmd. 7536, 1952), §§ 50–54. A defamatory statement that is in the same form or of the same character as the cases covered by s.3 is actionable in defamation without proof of special damage. The Faulks Committee on Defamation (Cmnd. 5909, 1975, §§ 584–589) have since recommended that the remaining distinction between the written and the spoken word should be abolished.

[89] So held in New Zealand: *Customglass* case (above, n. 80) at 603.

[90] See above, §§ 16-023 *et seq.*

[91] An instance where both were successfully pleaded is the *Wilts United Dairy* case (above, n. 85).

[92] *Linotype* v. *British Empire Type-Setting* (1899) 81 L.T. 331; *Griffiths* v. *Benn* (1911) 27 T.L.R. 346. Each must in consequence be separately pleaded *A & M Records* v. *Audio Magnetics* [1979] F.S.R. 1 at 9. The distinction nonetheless did not appeal to forthright minds: see Lord Halsbury in the *Linotype* case at 333.

[93] But see below, §§ 17-075 — 17-077.

[94] See above, §§ 2-043 — 2-045.

untruthfully and maliciously asserts to a rival's customers that they are receiving infringing goods that the rival has any cause of action under the general common law. Hence the introduction of the special statutory action for threats of patent and registered design infringement; and the question whether the same should apply to other threats of litigation. These have already been discussed.[95]

(c) *Comparative advertising*[96]

16-043   Comparison—explicit or implied, specific or vague—lies at the root of modern advertising. Where there is price competition, the cheaper rival may seek to stress similarities in his comparison with the more expensive; where there is not, he may emphasise some point of differentiation, more or less genuine and useful to the consumer. In the absence of passing-off, the only weapon which the common law provided against any sort of comparative advertising was restricted to disparagements that amounted to injurious falsehood. And at an early stage of both the modern tort and modern advertising, the courts showed particular reluctance to allow such actions to succeed.

Not only must there be malice and untruth in the comparison, but, where the two are distinct, the misstatement must be about the plaintiff's goods and not about the defendant's.[97] In *White* v. *Mellin*[98] the House of Lords held it not actionable for a retailer to attach stickers puffing his "own brand" to tins of the plaintiff's baby food; all the stickers said was that the "own brand" was "far more nutritious and healthful than any other preparation." Lord Herschell, in particular, feared a flood of litigation over the rival merits of products and the deployment of judicial decision as a means of advertisement.[99] In *Hubbuck* v. *Wilkinson*,[1] the Court of Appeal treated even an advertisement purporting to set out the results of chemical tests as no more than a statement that the defendant's paint was equal to, or somewhat better than, the plaintiff's.

16-044   Actions have occasionally succeeded for specific and damaging lies, such as that the defendant's newspaper circulation was 20 times that of any local paper (*i.e.* the plaintiff's).[2] The present test has been stated thus: there must be a real disparagement or untrue statement that a reasonable man would take to be a serious claim.[3] Hyperbolic puffing, in

[95] See above, §§ 2-044—2045. Note that one effect of emphasising the balance of convenience in proceedings for an interlocutory injunction may be to undermine the requirement of malice in injurious falsehood: see *Jaybeam* v. *Abru* [1976] R.P.C. 308. But *cf. Polydor* v. *Harlequin Records* [1980] F.S.R. 26 (C.A.); *Crest Homes* v. *Ascott* [1980] F.S.R. 396.
[96] See Dworkin (1979) 1 E.I.P.R. 41; Ollett (1980) 9 C.I.P.A. 142; Symposium (1977) 67 T.M.R. 351.
[97] *Canham* v. *Jones* (1813) V. & B. 218; *Young* v. *Macrae* (1862) 3 B. & S. 264. *cf. Western Counties Manure* v. *Lawes* (1874) L.R. 9 Ex. 218, which was criticised in *White* v. *Mellin* (below, n. 98) at 164.
[98] [1895] A.C. 154 (H.L.).
[99] *Ibid.* at 164.
[1] [1899] 1 Q.B. 86; and see *Alcott* v. *Millar's Karri* (1904) 21 T.L.R. 30.
[2] *Lyne* v. *Nicholls* (1906) 23 T.L.R. 86.
[3] *De Beers Abrasive* v. *International General Electric* [1975] F.S.R. 323.

other words, will be discounted for what it is.[4] There has been very little chance to see whether, in an age of consumer testing, the judges remain as reluctant as their predecessors to find that the "reasonable man" takes comparisons seriously. But the stress on an objective test should be noted.

The reluctance to find comparative advertising actionable has, however, been reversed by one piece of statutory intermeddling. The Trade Marks Act 1938, section 4(1) provides that a mark registered in Part A may be infringed by "importing a reference" to it.[5] This has particular relevance to comparative advertising, covering as it does not only disparaging differentiation ("their 'X' is not half so effective") but also sycophantic assimilation ("just the same as an 'X' and half the price"). But "X" must be a Part A mark. This change was introduced at a time of growing protection for established business against competitive pressures. Parliament went out of its way to make one particular form of "unfair" competition actionable.

Comparative advertising is a matter on which competitors' and con- 16-045 sumers' interests by no means coincide. True and informative comparisons are to the consumer's advantage. Accordingly there is an argument for repealing the Trade Marks Act provision, which we shall consider again later. What is interesting in this field, however, is that legal controls seem to be of little practical importance. Even before 1938, comparative advertising seems to have played a very minor role in Britain: very largely a "dog-bites-dog" attitude among advertising agencies and their clients kept "knocking copy" out of the British press. In the new atmosphere of "consumerism," the advertisers and the media have found it circumspect to agree in principle that "fair" comparisons ought to be allowed,[6] and (despite the Trade Marks Act provision) they are now a regular feature of some industries' advertising. This only strengthens the case for returning the law to the discriminating attitude found in the cases on injurious falsehood. But it would be naïve to suppose that this discrimination is easily practised. For an advertiser who compares with his rivals will be selecting the features for emphasis that suit him best. Deciding whether he has been "unfair" in the process is a matter on which the most conscientious judges will differ. If the issue is taken seriously, it must bring in spurious differentiations that do not refer to other products specifically, but only to the products or services that are in any way competitive ("The only washing-machine on the market that boils your clothes," etc.) But this, if false, is unfair competition with the rest of the trade. Once more, it must be doubted whether it should be actionable at the suit of any one competitor, rather than through the machinery of prosecution.[7]

---

[4] "Advertisements are not to be read as if they were some testamentary disposition in a will": Whitford J., *McDonald's* v. *BurgerKing* [1986] F.S.R. 45 at 58.

[5] Discussed more fully below, §§ 17-075 — 17-077.

[6] What is regarded as unjustifiable is outlined in the British Code of Advertising Practice (6th ed., 1979), II, 11–14.

[7] In the U.S.A., the Federal Trade Commission has already travelled some distance in this direction, taking objection to misleading claims to unique qualities, to implied representations that matters are significant when they are not and to a great variety of failures to state factors which may strike consumers as significant disadvantages: see, *e.g.* Howard and Hulbert, *Advertising and the Public Interest* (FTC Staff Report (1973)).

CHAPTER 17

REGISTERED TRADE MARKS

1. REGISTERED MARKS AND COMMON LAW RIGHTS[1]

(1) The cumulative principle

17-001　After an initial period of doubt it was accepted that the registered owner of a trade mark for goods also retained his rights to protect any reputation acquired through use by means of a passing-off action.[2] Since the extension of the Register to cover service marks the same is true for them. Actual goodwill in trade remains the fundamental value to be protected and registration is conceived merely as a heightened form of protection for certain cases, which in some respects remain rather narrowly defined. These limitations make it important that common law rights should survive undiminished. For it is easy under such a system for a trader's actual goodwill to outstrip the range of protection that he has acquired through registration. The disadvantage of the present "cumulative" approach is, of course, that a trader contemplating the adoption of a new mark has no complete register of prior rights to consult. Some countries which use a more embracing approach to what may be registered and what rights are thereby given, also insist that registration must be a prerequisite to protection of anything that they define as a trade or service mark.[3]

When we consider the future of the British system and the likely introduction of an EEC trade mark we shall return to this difference of approach. But it is useful to note even at the outset. For it suggests that a satisfactory system for protecting trade marks depends upon a nice balance in the relationship between a number of concepts. We can see a little more of these relationships (before moving on to detail) if we list some of the main differences between common law protection and the rights given by registration.

---

[1] The leading textbook is *Kerly*, which sets out the Trade Marks Act 1938, as amended, in separate versions as it applies to trade marks (for goods) and service marks. As to the latter, see also Morcom, *Service Marks* (1987).

[2] See above, § 15-007; the right of action against passing-off goods is preserved by TMA 1938, s.2. There is no necessary inconsistency between a finding that passing off has occurred, and that there is no trade mark infringement, even where the defendant has used an essential feature of the plaintiff's mark: *Lee Kar Choo* v. *Lee Lian Choon* [1967] 1 A.C. 602 (J.C.).

[3] This is the principle of the French Trade Mark Act 1964 and the Benelux Uniform Law, operative from 1971. But it does not mean that a trader who establishes substantial reputation with the public loses out to one who registers before he does: see generally, Beier (1975) 6 I.I.C. 285 at pp. 294–298.

(i) Registration may take place before any reputation has been acquired **17-002**
in the mark through actual trade: it is enough, when the mark is
inherently distinctive, to have a bona fide intention to use it as a mark
for the goods or services in question.[4] Though marks which are not
clearly distinctive can only be registered after proof of sufficient use,[5]
thereafter the registered proprietor may proceed against infringers without the uncertainty and expense of having each time to prove his actual
trading reputation. These are the main respects in which protection is
"heightened" by registration.[6]

(ii) Registration is in principle permitted only for the goods or services
in which the registered proprietor (or user)[7] trades or for "goods or
services of the same description."[8] If registration is secured for other
goods or services it is to that extent open to the removal from the
register, upon the application of an interested person, by proving either
no bona fide intention to use or non-use for the previous five years.[9]
There are, however, certain grounds of excusal, including use upon goods
or services of the same description. Moreover, infringement can occur
only where the defendant is using the mark in relation to the goods for
which it is registered. This cluster of rules form the major constraint
upon the scope of the registration system. In consequence, any injury
occasioned by a practice such as using a well-known trade mark for a
wholly different line of goods is actionable only at common law.[10] In
such a case there must be an investigation of the actual position in trade.

(iii) The other important limitation on the scope of the registration
system at present lies in the concept of protected marks. This has been
considerably expanded since 1875. In particular the recent extension of
the system to service marks has carried the whole system into wider
realms. Even so, there are a number of limitations which preserve a
significant place for passing-off.

(iv) Registration is not a purely formal act, as it generally is in
countries which make it a precondition of protection. On the contrary,
the examination is one of the most complete amongst trade mark systems
of the world. Not only is distinctiveness assessed by the registrar, but a
search and examination of prior registrations for the same goods or
services and those of the same description is made ex officio.[11] In
addition, third parties are entitled to oppose an application on any

[4] See below, § 17-044.
[5] See below, § 17-015.
[6] In addition, to some extent, the comparison to be made in a trade mark infringement
action is simplified artificially, whereas in passing off it is between the manner in which
plaintiff and defendant actually trade: see below, § 17-067.
[7] For registered users, see below, § 17-058.
services or goods.
[8] This is not a broad conception: see below, § 17-003. Distinguish the classification of
goods, which has an administrative purpose: below, § 17-006.
[9] There are exceptions: see below, §§ 17-050—17-051.
[10] See above, § 16-025; but note the special provisions for defensive registration, below
§§ 17-046—17-048.
[11] See below, § 17-007. Examination systems such as the German leave it to owners of
conflicting marks to raise their own objections: see below, § 582.

relevant legal ground. This includes in particular their own prior use of a mark that is liable to confuse, whether or not it is upon similar goods or services.[12]

(v) In determining whether a mark that is not initially distinctive has acquired that character through use, essentially the same considerations are brought into account in common law proceedings and during an application to register. But in extreme cases, marks may be deemed so inherently non-distinctive that they can never be registered, even though their "secondary meaning" might support a passing-off action.[13]

In the hope of expediting the registration of "difficult" marks, a Part B was added in 1919 to the old Register (which became Part A). Registration in Part B has only to satisfy a somewhat lower standard of distinctiveness.[14] As a consequence, it is supposed to give a rather lower level of protection: a defendant may bring into account against a Part B (but not a Part A) mark other indications on his goods that will distinguish them from the plaintiff's.[15] This, however, is more a legislator's distinction than a businessman's. Indeed, the whole division of the register stands under suspended sentence of death from a recommendation of the Mathys Committee.[16]

(vi) In response to commercial pressure, registered marks became capable of assignment and licence separately from the goodwill of the business for which they were acquired, subject to certain administrative safeguards.[17] Apart from one obscure exception,[18] common law rights remained closed to the same sorts of dealing. Their protection goes only to the trade reputation that is part of business goodwill.[19]

(vii) There are various forms of unfair competition outside the classical type of passing off where the common law has afforded only limited relief. In the hope of providing readier protection, the registration system has been extended in three ways. First, against the fear that well-known trade marks will be "diluted" if an unconnected trader uses them on different goods, defensive registration has been introduced for invented words. Secondly, against the threat of comparative advertising which makes use of a Part A mark, the definition of infringement has been extended to cover "importing a reference" to the registered proprietor a registered user for their goods or services. Thirdly, to give protection to the kind of mark that indicates that goods have a particular quality or composition, registration of certification marks has been permitted under special Department of Trade supervision. The first two of these extensions are considered in the course of the text[20]; the third is outlined in Appendix 3.

[12] See below, § 17-030.
[13] See below, §§ 17-021 — 17-023.
[14] See below, § 17-026.
[15] See below, § 17-068.
[16] Cmnd. 5601, § 124.
[17] See below, §§ 17-056 — 17-062.
[18] See below, § 17-057.
[19] See above, §§ 16-014 — 16-015.
[20] Below §§ 17-046 — 17-048, 17-075 — 17-077.

(2) "Goods and services of the same description"

This expression occurred in the preceding paragraphs as a concept **17-003** delimiting the scope of rights in the registration system. A person may, for instance, register a mark for the goods in which he trades and for goods of the same description. It is thus a conceptual tool that needs some introduction at the outset. The first question will be whether two kinds of goods are the same.[21] It is only if they are normally described by different words that the question is reached, are they nevertheless goods of the same description? It seems to be necessary, but not sufficient, first to find a generic term that could supply this single description.[22] But, particularly if that word or phrase proves to be unusual or too general, the courts look at the issue from a business and practical point of view, taking account of similarities in nature and composition, in uses and in distribution channels. There is authority favouring a liberal approach[23]: and so rum and rum cocktails were treated by the House of Lords as goods of the same description.[24] Even so, the results of some cases seem fairly cautious: shoes and shoe polish were held not to be of the same description[25]; ice cream and jellies were on the borderline.[26] Certainly it is not enough that the public would likely assume that there was a trade connection between the two types of goods if they bore the mark or marks in question.[27]

What has so far been said applies equally to services of the same description. In addition the provisions on the subject are now extended to services associated with the goods or goods of the same description and vice versa. Association occurs when "it is likely that the goods might be sold or otherwise traded and the services might be provided by the same business."[28]

2. ORIGINAL REGISTRATION

(1) Procedure for registration

In 1875, Parliament expressed its hesitation over a register of trade **17-004** marks by imposing bureaucratic control. Today the Registrar (who is the

---

[21] Occasionally even this can give rise to difficulties: *e.g. Everest* v. *Camm* (1950) 67 R.P.C. 200 (C.A.); and see *"Tornado"* T.M. [1979] R.P.C. 155.

[22] See the leading modern authorities: *Lyons' Applcn.* [1959] R.P.C. 120 (C.A.) (where the issue was non-use); *"Daiquiri"* T.M. [1969] R.P.C. 600 at 620 (H.L.) (mark becoming descriptive—s.15).

[23] Lord Wilberforce, *"Daiquiri"* case (above, n. 22), following Lord Herschell, *Powell's* T.M. (1894) 11 R.P.C. 4 at 7.

[24] *"Daiquiri"* case, overruling a more scrupulous Court of Appeal.

[25] *Jellinek's Applcn.* (1946) 63 R.P.C. 59.

[26] *Lyons' Applcn.* (above n. 22). But examples should not be read out of context of the evidence given. This should be borne in mind when considering the lists of articles held to be, or not to be, goods of the same description in Kerly, § 10–14/15.

[27] That is the test for registering a defensive mark, and it is taken to be wider: see *Ferodo's Applcn.* (1945) 62 R.P.C. 111; below, §§ 17-046—17-048. *cf.* the narrower proposition of Kay J., *Australian Wine Importers'* T.M. (1889) 41 Ch.D. 278 at 281.

[28] TMA 1938, s.68(2A).

Comptroller-General of Patents)[29] is obliged to consider not only the distinctiveness of a mark for which registration is being sought,[30] but also its capacity to deceive[31] and any other ground of objection.[32] In difficult cases, he may consult informed bodies, such as trade associations. Indeed, the system is open to political intervention above the level of the Patent Office.[33]

17-005 　In addition, third parties are given the right to oppose registration before it is accorded, and this lets in information (particularly about trade marks and names in use) that will not be revealed in the Office's search of its register. The onus of proof, moreover, is firmly upon the applicant; if the Registrar is left in doubt about an application it is his duty to refuse it.[34] As a corollary of this strict examination of applications, once registration is allowed, there is a prima facie presumption that the original registration is valid.[35]

Here are some basic points about the stages in an application for an ordinary trade mark to be registered in Part A or B:

(a) *Application*

17-006 　The applicant must claim to be the "proprietor" of the mark.[36] In any one application he may only seek registration for goods or services within a single class of the 42 in Schedule 4 of the Trade Mark and Service Mark Rules. More than one application (with attendant fees) may accordingly be needed. The application may subsequently be amended with the consent of the Registrar or an appellate tribunal.[37]

The classification is an administrative measure, designed to aid the process of searching in Britain and abroad. There is no need to register for the whole of a class (some of which are very broad).[38] Classification has nothing to do with the principle that a trader may register only for the goods in which he trades and goods of the same description.

[29] TMA 1938, s.1(1).
[30] See below, §§ 17-015—17-026.
[31] See below, §§ 17-027—17-039.
[32] See below, § 17-042—17-048. The Registrar may require the applicant to seek the consent of another registered proprietor of a similar mark. But if the consent is given, this is only one factor in assessing whether there is a real likelihood of deception or confusion. The Registrar may not use the consent to justify what is otherwise objectionable: "Velva-Glo" T.M. [1961] R.P.C. 255 at 261; Kerly, §§ 4–18, 10–07/08; cf. the proposed EEC system, below, § 18-016.
[33] Note the power given in TMA 1938, s.19(1).
[34] Eno v. Dunn (1890) 15 App.Cas. 252, 7 R.P.C. 311; Australian Wine Importers' T.M. (1889) 41 Ch.D. 278, 6 R.P.C. 311; Kerly, § 10–06.
[35] So also subsequent assignments and transmissons: TMA 1938, s.46. After seven years, Part A marks secure a higher measure of protection from attack: see s.13, below, § 17-049.
[36] See below, § 17-044.
[37] s.17(7). Before making an application a person may apply to the Registrar for preliminary advice on the inherent distinctiveness of a proposed mark. For this and its consequences, see s.42.
[38] The classification of the TMA 1938, Sched. 4, was first agreed at an international conference in 1934. It is revised from time to time and has acquired eight new classes for service marks. See further, Kerly, Chap. 5.

(b) *Examination*

The registry conducts a search of existing registrations and pending **17-007** applications to see if any provide a ground of objection. All grounds are considered, including distinctiveness, deceptiveness and special reasons for refusing the application under the general discretion.[39]

(c) *Conditions, limitations, disclaimers*

The Act permits the Registrar to offer registration subject to condi- **17-008** tions, limitations or disclaimers of the exclusive right in some part of the mark.[39] Such arrangements can dispose of potential objections without the application being totally refused. Thus the registration may be limited to use in a particular colour or colours.[40] Or it may impose on the proprietor an obligation not to use the mark on certain goods within the registration because, for instance, such a use would be potentially deceptive. Thus "Domgarden", which was thought to have a German ring about it, was capable of registration for wines only with a condition that it be used exclusively for German produce.[41] The registration is put in this convoluted form in order to give the proprietor the right to pursue an infringer who is using the mark to misdescribe his goods.

The most frequent form of limitation upon the exclusive right given by registration is a disclaimer, the purpose of which is to make plain that in some respect the proprietor's ability to sue others for infringement is restricted.[42] In a straightforward case, some part of the mark will be disclaimed. A composite device mark may, for instance, include stars which are already a common feature of labelling in the trade; these may have to be disclaimed.[43] In nicer instances, the disclaimer has to be worded so as to ensure that the proprietor has a right only in a particular version of a picture, device or word.[44]

Disclaimers, conditions and limitations may be required not only during the Registrar's first consideration of the application, but during opposition and after registration,[45] particularly upon applications to expunge and to register a user agreement.[46]

[39] See below, § 17-042.
[40] TMA 1938, ss.14, 17(2), Kerly, Chap. 9.
[41] For the consequences, see s.16.
[42] *"Domgarden" T.M.* [1982] R.P.C. 155.
[43] While a disclaimer will limit the registered proprietor's exclusive right, the disclaimed matter will, it seems, be treated as part of the mark when considering whether a later mark should be registered: *"Granada" T.M.* [1979] R.P.C. 303. It has been said that a disclaimer should be required only "for some good reason": *Albert Baker's Appln.* [1908] 2 Ch. 86 at 104–105; *Cadbury's Appln.* [1915] 32 R.P.C. 456 at 462; but *cf. Eclipse* v. *Registrar* (1957) 99 C.L.R. 300 at 315, 320–321.
[44] Thus in *Diamond T's Appln.* (1921) 38 R.P.C. 373, a device including "Diamond T" in a diamond border was allowed with a disclaimer of the border and the word "Diamond."
[45] *e.g. Bagots Hutton's Appln.* (1915) 32 R.P.C. 333.
[46] See TMA 1938, ss.14(1), 17(2), 18(5), 18(7), 15(2)(b), 26(2), 28(5), 32, 33. Note that under s.34(1)(e) the proprietor may himself apply to have a disclaimer or memorandum not extending his rights added to the register.

(d) *Association of marks*

17-009   One special limitation which the Registrar may impose is to require that certain marks be treated as "associated." These are marks which are the same or are confusingly similar and are held by a single proprietor for the same goods or services, or those of the same description.[47] The effect of declaring them associated is that they may only be assigned as a bundle.[48] This avoids the dangers that might follow from divided ownership.[49] Notice, however, that this procedure does not apply to marks, even if they are identical, when held for goods or services not of the same description.

There are various reasons why a proprietor may want to hold closely related marks for the same kinds of goods. With changes in advertising and labelling fashions he may want to modify his first mark.[50] Where the essential part of the mark is difficult to register (because, for instance, it is a name or initials), it may first be necessary to make this part of some more elaborate device; with successful trading it may later prove possible to register simpler versions.[51] For various export markets it may be desirable to use slightly different versions of the mark.[52]

(e) *Subsequent steps*

17-010   If the applicant is unwilling to accept an objection raised by the Registrar, he may, within one month, ask for a hearing. At this he may present evidence (normally by statutory declaration).[53] If the applicant objects to a decision of the Registrar (who acts through a senior officer), he may appeal either to the Department of Trade[54] or to the Chancery Division of the High Court.[55]

17-011   Once the mark is accepted by the Registrar (albeit subject to limitations) it will be advertised by him in the Trade Marks Journal.[56] This gives notice to the world of its impending registration. Persons who object to the registration[57] may enter an opposition. This may be upon

---

[47] Including those goods and services which are themselves "associated": TMA 1938, s.23(1), (2), 68(2A). Association can occur at any time and lasts until dissolved: see s.23(5).

[48] s.23(1). Use of an associated mark may save a mark from removal for non-use: s.30(1), below, § 17-052.

[49] For possible consequences of assigning some only of similar marks, see below, §§ 17-054—17-055.

[50] If he does not want also to retain his original registration, he may apply to alter it under s.35 (for procedure, see TMA 1938 Rules, rr. 89–92).

[51] Where these simplifications mean that the new registration is for part of the earlier mark (assuming that goods of the same description etc. are involved) it must be registered under ss.21(1) and 23(3) as associated.

[52] Where the variations concern statements about the goods, number, price, quality or names of places or other non-distinctive matter, the versions may be included as a series in a single registration (thus saving fees): ss.21(2), 23(4).

[53] TMS 1938, ss.43, 55.

[54] The Department appoints a senior member of the patent bar to hear these appeals. It may, however, refer the matter to the court: s.53.

[55] For time limits and other procedural details, see Kerly, §§ 4–38 *et seq.*

[56] TMA 1938, s.18(1): note the proviso allowing advertisement before acceptance.

[57] They do not have to be "persons aggrieved" (*cf.* s.32(1)). A mere consumer may well be entitled to oppose: see s.18(2). For procedures, see TMA 1938, s.18(3)–(5), (11), Rules 1986, rr. 46–58, Kerly, §§ 4–30 *et seq.*

any of the substantive objections to registration, including the objection that the Registrar should exercise his discretion against the application. The proceedings again take place before the Registrar. Either side may appeal against an unfavourable decision, but in this case only to the High Court.[58]

Whether they take place before the Department of Trade or the Court, appeals are in the nature of a rehearing. New grounds and evidence can normally be admitted only when they would be admitted in other civil appeals, subject to considerations of public interest.[59] If the basis of the case has not changed, considerable respect is normally accorded to the experience of the hearing officer.[60]

(f) Registration

Upon surmounting all objections to it[61] the mark will be registered, the **17-012** date of application being deemed to be the date of registration.[62] It is registered for seven years and is thereafter renewable for periods of 14 years.[63] The precise date of registration can be important for such matters as periods of non-use.[64]

3. CONDITIONS FOR SECURING REGISTRATION

(1) "Trade mark," "service mark"

The perimeter of the registration system is set by these terms: A "trade **17-013** mark" is

" . . . a mark used or proposed to be used in relation to goods for the purpose of indicating or so as to indicate, a connection in the course of trade between the goods and some person having the right either as proprietor or registered user[65] to use the mark, whether with or without any indication of the identity of that person . . ."[66]

"Service mark" is similarly defined as

"a mark . . . used or proposed to be used in relation to services for the purpose of indicating, or so as to indicate, that a particular person is connected, in the course of business, with the provision of those services, whether with or without any indication of the identity of that person."

---

[58] TMA 1938, s.18(6)–(11).

[59] See Kerly, § 4–46.

[60] Lord Dunedin, *Banham* v. *Reddaway* (1927) 44 R.P.C. 27 at p. 36: "unless he has gone clearly wrong, his decision ought not to be interfered with"; *Broadhead's Appln.* (1950) 67 R.P.C. 209.

[61] TMA 1938 s.19(1), (2). For proof of registration, see s.58.

[62] *Ibid.* s.19(1) prescribes the procedure for terminating applications that are not being proceeded with.

[63] *Ibid.* s.20(1), (2). For lapse and restoration, see s.20(3), (4).

[64] See *"Bon Matin" T.M.* [1988] R.P.C. 553.

[65] For the concept of registered user, see below §§ 17-058—17-059.

[66] TMA 1938, s.68(1). Certification trade marks for goods (not services) are separately defined; they are dealt with in Appendix 3, below, §§ A3-010—A3-011.

Before service marks became registrable, service organisations, providing for instance banking, insurance or professional advice, sought marks for printed matter and the like, where the intention was to use the mark on material provided in the course of such services without being distinctly sold, *e.g.* bank cards and insurance policies. These marks for goods were refused and would still be. But now, of course the mark could in many cases be registered for the service.[67]

Services may, however, be rendered to goods. So long as the services are performed in the process of preparing goods for their initial marketing, the person who renders them is entitled to register a trade mark for the goods. This may be used to indicate that he has altered the goods physically (*e.g.* by dyeing or some other chemical treatment) or that he has selected them. But once they reach the consumer, they cease to be "in the course of trade." Hence a goods mark cannot be registered to indicate a repair or reconditioning service.[68] A service mark may now be available if the service is for money or money's worth. Supermarkets and other retailers have wished to register their own names and logos for "retailing" services, since this would allow them to cover all their merchandise by a single registration. But so far it has been held that the ancillary activities of a retailer are too indefinite to allow for the services to be adequately specified in such a registration.[69]

17-014   The Act adds a further definition of the word "mark," which includes "a device, brand, heading, label, ticket, name, signature, word, letter, numeral, or any combination thereof."[70] "Get-up," in the sense of the shape of goods, or the shape of a container for them, is not registrable. Thus, the House of Lords has refused to permit registration of the "Coca-Cola" bottle.[71] However, in an earlier decision, the House took the opposite view of colour arrangements applied to a pharmaceutical capsule.[72] It is hard to see that there is any sensible distinction between the two. In "Coca-Cola" objection was taken to registering features of

[67] See *Bank of America's T.M.* [1976] F.S.R. 7 (Irish S.C.); *Royal Inns of America's T.M.* [1977] F.S.R. 14 (Irish Controller); *"Airco" T.M.* [1976] F.S.R. 401 (S.C. Bermuda); *"Wells Fargo" T.M.* [1977] R.P.C. 503. *Aliter* where travellers cheques and credit cards were sold: *"Visa" T.M.* [1985] R.P.C. 323. Titles for journals distributed free have been refused registration in the U.K.; *"Hospital World" T.M.* [1967] R.P.C. 595; *"Update" T.M.* [1979] R.P.C. 166; *cf. "Golden Pages" T.M.* [1985] F.S.R. 27 [Irish S.C.].

[68] *Aristoc v. Rysta* [1945] A.C. 68 (H.L.) ("Rysta" not registrable for repairing stockings. The decision insisted that, however much the concept of a trade mark has been broadened in 1938, in this respect the system remained limited in scope). Equally, it would seem likely that a "union label," intended to indicate that goods were manufactured in a trade union closed shop, would not be a trade mark—should these ever come back into fashion: *cf. Att.-Gen. for N.S.W. v. Brewery Employers Union* (1908) C.L.R. 469 (H.C. Aust.).

[69] *Dee Corporation's Application* [1989] F.S.R. 267; and similarly *Action Bolt v. Tool Wholesale* [1989] F.S.R. 274 (S.C., S. Africa), see Hodkinson [1987] E.I.P.R. 73; Olsen [1987] E.I.P.R. 251.

[70] TMA 1938, s.68(1); for service marks, "brand . . . ticket" is omitted.

[71] *Coca-Cola's T.Ms.* [1986] R.P.C. 421.

[72] *Smith Kline & French's Appln.* [1976] R.P.C. 511; applied in *Unilever's (Striped Toothpaste No. 2) Appln.* [1987] R.P.C. 13. *cf.* Windeyer J., *Smith Kline & French v. Registrar* [1972] R.P.C. 519 (H.C. Aust.). It is also necessary for such marks to satisfy the requirement of distinctiveness, which in most cases will be difficult to make out: *Unilever* (above) and *John Wyeth's Coloured Tablet T.M.* [1988] R.P.C. 233.

this kind for their "monopolistic" tendencies, though just what these consist of is unclear.

(2) Distinctiveness

The very purpose of a mark is to distinguish the goods or services of **17-015** one trader or businessman from those of another. In discussing passing off we have seen that some marks are well-suited to this role—because they have not been used by others in that field for any purpose, and because they convey no other meaning and so are not words or devices that others could have a legitimate interest in using: an invented word, new-minted for the occasion, is the obvious example. On the other hand, marks which already have a meaning, or are in common use, are ill-adapted to be a particular proprietor's mark. The British registration system, with its careful preliminary examination, has been constructed as a graded filter. Certain marks are not allowed through to the register, even though they may have been so extensively used as to have acquired a "secondary meaning."[73] Other marks, to which objection is less categorical, will pass upon proof of sufficient use. But as the register currently organised, they may first have to spend a period in Part B, until further use allows them into Part A. It is not permissible to admit marks to Part B which could never be accepted for Part A because of their inherent lack of distinctiveness. We shall consider first the test of distinctiveness for Part A, before proceeding to the somewhat lighter criterion for Part B.

(a) Part A distinctiveness: basic principle

Section 9(1) requires that a Part A mark contain or consist of one of **17-016** five categories of "essential particulars."[74] The first four of these concern particular kinds of words. But the fifth—"any other distinctive mark"—admits any mark that satisfies the criterion specified in section 9(2): the mark must be "distinctive" in the sense of being "adapted to distinguish" goods or services with which the proprietor . . . is . . . connected in the course of trade or business from those with which he is not. A tribunal assessing this has to consider both whether the mark is inherently adapted[75] to distinguish the goods or services and whether it is adapted to distinguish them in fact, i.e. from its actual use as a mark and any other circumstances.[76]

---

[73] Thus the plaintiffs in *Reddaway v. Banham* (above, § 16-008, n. 35) would have been most unlikely ever to secure registration of "Camel Hair Belting."

[74] The concept of "essential particulars" stretches back to the 1875 Act, when it defined in a relatively limited way what could be registered as a trade mark: see above, § 15-006, n. 21.

[75] "Inherent adaptability" was added to the statutory formula in the 1938 Act, following Lord Parker, *Registrar of Trade Marks v. W. & G. Du Cros* (below, n. 80 (R.P.C.)) at p. 672.

[76] s.9(3). The section says that the tribunal "may" have regard to the extent of both these characteristics. Despite this permissive form, the House of Lords has held that there are cases where the inherent lack of adaptability cannot be made up for by proof of use: see the *Yorkshire* and the *"York"* cases below, ns. 21, 22.

Where the mark is to be used in Britain, it is its distinctiveness there that is in question. Accordingly evidence that it is used or registered abroad by the applicant or an associate has little significance, if any.[77]

(b) Non-word marks for Part A

17-017   For a non-word mark, the issue is not complicated by further statutory requirements. It is left to the Registrar (under the supervision of appellate tribunals) to decide how far general rules can be enunciated and how much must be left to the particular circumstances. If a device is something—stars or diamond shapes, for instance—that is common to the trade, they will not be "adapted to distinguish" a particular trader's goods. Whether they are will depend on evidence and this may be found in the marks already on the register.[78] It is a matter on which first impressions are particularly important.[79]

A useful illustration is the use of letters of the Roman alphabet (i.e. when used as initials or in some other way that will not be taken as a word). A single letter would be regarded as inherently non-distinctive, and it used to be thought that the same applied to two initials. However, occasionally—upon proof of very substantial use as a trade mark—such marks have been registered.[80] Three letters require substantial prior use, and thereafter the case becomes progressively easier to make.[81] Though there has been less discussion, Arabic numerals are apparently treated in much the same way.[82]

(c) Word marks for Part A

17-018   The "essential particulars" that form the first four cases of section 9(1) refer to categories of word marks. The first two, despite their position, are special forms of marks involving names (business names particularly represented, and signatures); they are reserved for consideration with surname marks.[83] The next two categories are of general importance. They are: invented words (category (c)), and words that are not directly descriptive or geographical, and are not surnames (category (d)). There is a relationship between them, which in broad terms is this: if a word is newly coined and as such conveys no obvious meaning it is "invented"

---

[77] *Impex* v. *Weinbaum* (1927) 44 R.P.C. 405 at p. 410; *Ford-Werke's Applcn.* (1955) 72 R.P.C. 191; *Gaines' Applcn.* (1951) 68 R.P.C. 178 at 179; Kerly, § 8–67.

[78] Thus in *Bass Ratcliffe & Gretton's T.M.* [1902] 2 Ch. 579, 19 R.P.C. 529 (C.A.) the owners managed to justify the registration of a simple diamond shape, despite the use of more complex diamond devices on other labels. Particular versions of emblems and quasi-national symbols may likewise become registrable: "*Welsh Lady*" T.M. [1964] R.P.C. 459 at 461. The same consideration arises in relation to word marks: see generally Kerly, § 8–70.

[79] *Celine's App.* [1985] R.P.C. 381.

[80] The difficulty is particularly acute if the letters are not depicted in monogram or script form, or accompanied by any other device: see *British Petroleum* v. *European Petroleum Distributors* [1968] R.P.C. 54; cf. *Registrar of Trade Marks* v. *W. & G. Du Cros* [1913] A.C. 624; 30 R.P.C. 660 (H.L.); "*Vew*" T.M. [1986] R.P.C. 82.

[81] See further "*GI*" T.M. [1986] R.P.C. 100.

[82] For instances, see *Ardath* v. *Sandorides* (1924) 42 R.P.C. 50 ("999"); *Reuter* v. *Muhlens* (1953) 70 R.P.C. 235 (C.A.) ("4711").

[83] See below, § 17-025.

within category (c). If it is not invented it falls into category (d) unless it is descriptive, geographical or a surname. If it comes within this exception, it can qualify only under category (e); and because its other meaning must render to mark to some extent not inherently adapted to be a trade mark, evidence is required of its adaptability in fact.[84] This evidence (normally of use as a trade mark) must be sufficient to overcome the initial objection to the mark. There are some marks so inherently unsuitable as trade marks that even proof of "100 per cent. distinctiveness in fact" will not suffice for registration in Part A.[85] Words in categories (c) and (d) do not normally have to be shown to be distinctive in fact, and that is the advantage attaching to them. But still the root test is that they must be "distinctive."[86] So in particular cases there may be an initial objection requiring evidence to overcome it. "Chin Chin" for alcoholic beverages was held to be non-descriptive and so within (d), but nonetheless to be inherently non-distinctive.[87] A number of aspects call for detailed consideration.

(i) **Invented words.** Whether a word is invented depends upon two **17-019** factors, one subjective, the other objective: the word must have been newly coined and it must convey no "obvious meaning to the ordinary Englishman."[88] First, therefore, it is necessary to consider how the word was derived: if it was not new-minted but was instead derived from a surname[89] or a foreign word,[90] it may not qualify for this reason. Then it is necessary to consider the ordinary Englishman's understanding (but not that of someone particularly learned).[91]

Here, however, the courts have distinguished between mere changes of spelling and more substantial changes from words in the existing vocabulary. Mispelling—slight ("Trakgrip")[92] or gross ("Orlwoola")[93]—do not bring the privilege attaching to invention, however common a technique this has been for telling the public that it is dealing with a trade mark. But compounding words so as to leave some indirect suggestion—for instance some   "covert   and   skillful   allusion   to   the   character

[84] See the proviso to s.9(1)(c).
[85] See below, §§ 17-021—17-023.
[86] "*Chin Chin*" T.M. [1965] R.P.C. 136; "*Livron*" case, below, n. 16.
[87] Parker J., *Phillipart* v. *William Whiteley* [1908] W Ch. 274 at 297; approved in *de Cordova* v. *Vick* 68 R.P.C. 103 at 108 (J.C.).
[88] *cf.* "*Buler*" T.M. [1966] R.P.C. 141; it could even include spelling a surname backwards: *Cording's Applcn.* (1916) 33 R.P.C. 83 at 95 (C.A., approved on other grounds in H.L., *ibid.* 325).
[89] "*Diabolo*" for a game: *Phillipart* case, above, n. 87 (where the two factors are taken together); "Bioscope," mainly used abroad for cinematographic device: *Warwick* v. *Urban* (1904) 21 R.P.C. 240.
[90] A person who may recognise that a coined word is in fact an unusual foreign word: the fact that "solio" is the Italian for "throne" did not prevent the word from being treated as invented: *Eastman Photographic* v. *Comptroller* [1898] A.C. 571, 15 R.P.C. 476.
[91] *Dunlop Rubber's Applcn.* (1942) 59 R.P.C. 134.
[92] "*Orlwoola*" T.M. [1910] 1 Ch. 130, 26 R.P.C. 850 (C.A.); different again may be spelling out: *e.g.* "*Exxate*" T.M. [1986] R.P.C. 567.
[93] Lord Macnaghten, *Solio* case (1898) 15 R.P.C. at 486.

or quality of the goods"[94]—is nonetheless inventive. The House of Lords held that the test which removes a non-invented word from category (d) into category (e) does not also serve to limit the notion of an invented word. "Solio" was registrable for photographic equipment as an invented word even though it might be taken to allude to the sun.[94] Such conflations as "Coffusa" (coffee + infuser) and "Bitumental" (bitumen + metal)[94a] were likewise accepted under category (c); "VapoRub," however, was disallowed as being insufficiently distinct from the two words of which it was compounded.[94b]

17-020   (ii) Direct reference to character or quality. Words chosen as marks often relate to some quality of the goods. Provided that the word is not "invented," and if the reference to character or quality is direct, then evidence of distinctiveness is a prerequisite of registration. Words such as "Brownie" and "Bullseye" for cameras and films,[95] "Oomphies" for shoes,[96] "Tub Happy" for clothing[97] and even "Dustic" for adhesives[98] have been held to involve no sufficiently direct reference. Contrast "Tastee-Freez" for ice-cream,[99] "Weldmesh" for wire mesh,[1] "Tarzan" for films and toys,[2] and even "Madame" for food.[3] The second group of examples shows considerable variation in the amount of evidence of actual distinctiveness needed to secure their registration. The ultimate question is whether, if registration is granted, other traders would be hampered in making any fair and honest use of the word in their own trade.[4]

17-021   Some marks are so inherently non-distinctive of certain goods that they can never be registered, however well-established the mark may be by use. "Electrix" for vacuum cleaners[5] ("electrics" misspelt) and

---

[94] *Ibid.* It was doubted, in any case, whether there was any sufficiently direct relation to character or quality of the goods.

[94a] The first two illustrations given in the "Wisqueur" (whisky + liqueur) case: *Hallgarten's Appln.* (1949) 66 R.P.C. 105. The next illustration given—"Liviar" (liver + caviare) was accepted only for Part B, the word "probably being regarded as non-invented because it was too close to the word 'liver' alone" (at p. 109).

[94b] *de Cordova* v. *Vick* (above, n. 87)—but held a borderline case. In Australia, a condensation ("Rohoe" for rotary hoe) was similarly treated: *Howard* v. *Webb* (1946) 72 C.L.R. 175. See further, Kerly, § 8–18/29.

[95] *Kodak* v. *London Stereoscopic* (1903) 20 R.P.C. 337.

[96] *La Marquise's Appln.* (1947) 64 R.P.C. 27.

[97] *Mark Foys* v. *Davies Coop* (1956) 95 C.L.R. 190 (H.C. Aust.). The term suggested only "in a vague and indefinite way a gladsome carelessness *à propos* the tub."

[98] *Dundas's Appln.* (1955) 72 R.P.C. 151. See also the "Chin Chin" and the "Solio" cases (above, nn. 86, 90).

[99] *Tastee Freez's Appln.* [1960] R.P.C. 255.

[1] "*Weldmesh*" T.M. [1966] R.P.C. 220 (see further below, § 17-026).

[2] "*Tarzan*" T.M. [1970] R.P.C. 450 (C.A.).

[3] "*Madame*" T.M. [1966] R.P.C. 415. If a word requires translation for its descriptive significance to be appreciated there is no direct reference to character: "*Kiku*" T.M. [1978] F.S.R. 246 (Full S.C., Ire.) (Japanese for chrysanthemum registrable for perfumes).

[4] See, in particular, Lord Parker, W. & G. case (above, n. 80) at pp. 669–670; and the "*Sheen*" case (below, n. 7).

[5] *Elextrix's Appln.* [1959] R.P.C. 283 (H.L.).

"Perfection" for soap[6] (or anything) are well-known examples of words that were incapable of ever qualifying for Part A. But this is so only of a limited number of words. Many more fall into the same class as "Sheen" for sewing cotton: this was found to be a less usual word than "lustre" to describe the quality in question and so was registered upon proof of very substantial use.[7]

A useful example of the operation of this part of the Act is provided by the case of a novel product. The name coined for it may well rank as an "invented" word, even though it contains some element referring to a quality. Or it may be a known word which has no direct reference to character or quality. In either case it will be registrable even before use as a trade mark, provided that nothing has happened to render its distinctive quality questionable. The most likely occurrence of this kind is that the word has been used as a description of the product—the more so if the applicant for registration is still the only marketer of the product. A striking example was the refusal to register marks for new rose varieties because at the same time the words were registered as varietal names with the National Rose Society.[8] Once the word has been used as a mark, this will provide evidence that may overcome any initial objection to registration. But continuing use of the word in a descriptive way will weaken the case for later registration. It is specially provided that the commonly accepted name of a single chemical element or compound cannot be registered for chemical substances or preparations.[9]

(iii) **Geographical names.** If a word is a geographical name "according to **17-022** its ordinary signification"[10] it is registrable only upon sufficient proof of distinctiveness. Again, the legitimate interests of other traders lie behind the special requirement.[11] Commercially valuable associations between a place and type of goods are not infrequently built up by use of the place name. The association may derive from the physical conditions for production of raw material (e.g. wine grapes) or for carrying out a manufacturing process (e.g. Roquefort cheese) or from an established tradition of local craftsmanship. These appellations of origin and indications of source are commonly used by a number of independent traders in the region. One purpose of the rule presently under discussion is to prevent any one of them securing a vital advantage over the others.[12] Their group reputation cannot be protected by individual registration but only through passing-off

---

[6] *Crosfield's Appln.* [1910] 1 Ch. 130; 26 R.P.C. 837 (C.A.). Note that the word was in the form of a noun rather than an adjective; similarly the verbal form, "Uneeda": *National Biscuit Co.'s Appln.* (1902) 19 R.P.C. 281; and the adverbial: *"Always" T.M.* [1986] R.P.C. 93.

[7] *J. & P. Coats Appln.* (1936) 53 R.P.C. 355 (C.A.).

[8] *Wheatcroft's T.M.* [1954] Ch. 210, 71 R.P.C. 43. Now the names of new varieties may be protected under the special machinery for plant varieties: see App. 4.

[9] TMA 1938, s.15(3). *cf.* the problem of a mark which becomes descriptive: see below, §§ 17-052—17-053.

[10] s.9(1)(*d*). The phrase was introduced to reflect the *Magnolia* decision (below, n. 17).

[11] See *Clark Equipment* v. *Registrar of Trade Marks* (1964) 111 C.L.R. 511 ("Michigan" for earth-moving equipment).

[12] Thus in *Thomson* v. *Seppelt* (1925) 37 C.L.R. 305, one of the seven wine growers in a town was not allowed to register the town name as a trade mark for wine.

proceedings,[13] registration of a certification mark[14] or special legislative provision.[15]

17-023   The question whether a word is geographical appears, from the language of the statute, to be judged objectively, "ordinary signification" being a matter of the Englishman's normal understanding. Thus if the geographical use of the word is rare, it will be taken either to be invented[16] or to have some other meaning.[17] Probably, however, subjective considerations cannot be disregarded. If, even though the geographical meaning is very unusual, the trader adopted it because that is where he produced the goods and there are others who may have a similar interest in using it, it would be refused registration, at least without very substantial proof of distinctiveness in fact and evidence that embarrassment to others is likely to be minimal.[18]

At the other end of the scale, there are many words of such geographical importance that they are never registrable in Part A: "Liverpool" for cables,[19] "Glastonburys" for slippers,[20] "Yorkshire" for copper tubes,[21] and "York" for freight containers[22] are standard examples in the case law. In such cases a trader is left to prove passing off before he can secure protection.[23]

17-024   (iv) Surnames. A word which "according to its ordinary signification" is a surname also requires proof of distinctiveness before registration.[24] Many surnames have another meaning either in English or another language. Here at least "ordinary signification" does not amount to "commonest meaning."[25] If the name is used as a surname it will not be regarded as such only if its other meaning is overwhelmingly commoner

---

[13] See above, § 16-011.

[14] See below, §§ A3-010, A3-011.

[15] See below, Appendix 3.

[16] e.g. the word "Livron" was invented for a tonic containing liver and iron, and so satisfied the subjective requirement for that category; but the court found the word, as the name of a French town too well-known to satisfy the objective requirement: Boots' T.M. (1937) 54 R.P.C. 327 (C.A.). There are differences of view in that case about how rare the geographical usage must be before it is discounted: cf. pp. 334, 337, 339. In "Farah" T.M. [1978] F.S.R. 234 Kenny J. preferred the test of Romer L.J. (p. 337): is the word wholly unknown to the ordinary Englishman/Irishman?

[17] e.g. "Magnolia" was sought for a metal alloy; several towns in the U.S. bore that name but the produce was connected with none of them: Magnolia Metal's T.M. [1897] 2 Ch. 371, 14 R.P.C. 621 (C.A.). And see the same case (at 628). " 'Monkey' is not proved to be a geographical name by showing merely that a small and by no means generally known island has been called by that name." cf. the problem discussed below, at n. 25. It is proper to take account of the fact that a name has become geographical between application and hearing: "Avon" T.M. [1985] R.P.C. 43 (naming of new local authority district).

[18] See the Magnolia case (above, n. 17).

[19] Liverpool Electric's Appln. (1929) 46 R.P.C. 99 (C.A.).

[20] Bailey v. Clark (1938) 55 R.P.C. 253.

[21] Yorkshire Copper's Appln. (1953) 71 R.P.C. 150 (H.L.). For further illustration see Kerly, § 8-33—8-37, 8-51.

[22] "York" T.M. [1984] R.P.C. 231 (H.L.).

[23] See above, § 16-009.

[24] s.9(1)(d).

[25] "Cannon" T.M. [1980] R.P.C. 519 (C.A.); the approach is said to apply equally to geographical names.

and better known: examples are "Coup" and "Cheer."[26] Where the other meaning is still the more usual but the gap is not so considerable the word will be treated as a surname and so, until sufficient use is proved, will not be registrable in Part A (though it may be at once registrable in Part B): examples are "Jury" and "Bugler."[27] If the surname has no other meaning (as, for instance "Dabner" or "Crossingham")[28] the question of distinctiveness is similarly approached. Where it is an unusual surname a modicum of use may suffice to secure Part A registration.[29] The commoner the name, the harder it is to establish distinctiveness in fact. But there is no decision holding a very common surname to be so inherently non-distinctive as never to be registrable.

(v) **The special cases.** The first two categories of "essential particulars" **17-025** in section 9(1) are: (a) the name of a company, individual or firm represented in a special or particular manner; and (b) the signature of the applicant or a business predecessor.[30] Each is somewhat different from the category of surnames simpliciter.[31] The word used in either could be purely a surname but is likely to have more to it: a Christian name or initials when it indicates an individual; or a collection of surnames, "& Co.," "Ltd." or something else to show that it is a company or partnership. The advantage of falling within one of these categories is that proof of distinctiveness in fact it is not normally required for registration. Nonetheless if there is an evident difficulty, distinctiveness must still be established: it could not be for "Kwik Kopy."[32] There is probably a corresponding limitation upon the scope of infringement, attention being paid to whether the defendant is imitating the "special or particular manner" in the first case, and the signature in the second.[33] Accordingly, if a business has built reputation enough in its name, or the surname part of it, it is advisable to secure registration of it independently of these special forms.[34]

---

[26] These are the examples given in *Swallow Raincoats' Appln.* (1947) 64 R.P.C. 92 at p. 94. "Swallow" was found to be sufficiently well-known as a surname for account to be taken of this. See generally, *Burford's Appln.* (1919) 36 R.P.C. 139 (C.A.).

[27] (1947) 64 R.P.C. at p. 95.

[28] *Ibid.* at p. 94; and see *"Kreuzer" T.M.* [1978] F.S.R. 239 (H.C., Ire.).

[29] Telephone directories are the usual testing grounds: a few entries in foreign directories will not suffice: *"Farah" T.M.* [1978] F.S.R. 234 (Irish S.C.); *"Ciba" T.M.* [1983] R.P.C. 75.

[30] TMA 1938, s.9(1)(a), (b).

[31] In the second category, the signature must be that of the actual applicant or predecessor (whether real or artificial): see *Macmillan* v. *Ehrmann* (1904) 21 R.P.C. 357. The first by contrast, may cover "names" that are not the real names of the applicant or anyone connected with his business: for instance, "Robin Hood": *Standard Camera's Appln.* (1952) 69 R.P.C. 125; *cf. Holt's T.M.* [1896] 1 Ch. 711, 13 R.P.C. 118 (C.A.) ("Trilby" not a "name of a company," etc., but a fictional character). See Kerly, § 8–08/15.

[32] "Kwik Kopy" T.M. [1982] R.P.C. 102.

[33] See *Crawford* v. *Bernard* (1894) 11 R.P.C. 580; the Registrar may require an admission that the mark confers no rights save in the particular form.

[34] But it may not be essential: the question is whether the public is likely to be confused. As the mark becomes well-known through use, this danger may arise in an increasingly broad band of cases. On the significance in infringement of devices additional to a word mark, see the *June* case, below, § 17-068, n. 54.

(d) Distinctiveness for Part B

17-026   Marks may secure the somewhat lower degree of protection provided by Part B of the register when they do not satisfy the Part A test of being "adapted to distinguish."[35] It is unusual today for an applicant to seek registration only in Part B; normally registration there is offered by the Registrar when he is not satisfied that the mark has yet made the Part A grade.[36] To be registered in Part B it is only necessary to show that the mark is "capable" of distinguishing the proprietor's goods or services from those of other traders or businessmen.[37] The test is whether the mark is inherently and in fact *capable* of distinguishing the goods.[38]

There are two basic questions about distinctiveness for Part B. First, can marks that will never be admitted to Part A nevertheless be accepted for Part B? The requirement for Part A that the mark be inherently adapted to distinguish serves to protect the interest that other traders may have using the mark. In refusing to register "Liverpool" for cables in either Part, Lawrence L.J. stressed that "in neither case is distinctiveness in fact conclusive."[39] The inherent capacity to distinguish, in other words, imports for Part B the same policy considerations as does "inherently adapted to distinguish" for Part A. This proposition has been upheld by the House of Lords in *"York." Trade Mark.*[40]

The second question is this: given that a mark is of the intermediate kind that may eventually secure a place in Part A, what will be sufficient for an earlier registration in Part B? The same kind of balancing of the inherent objection against the amount of use takes place as for Part A, but the balance is set more in the applicant's favour.[41] A mark to which the objection is serious—a common surname, a fairly obvious description—cannot be admitted to Part B merely upon a promise that it will be substantially used. But some weight can nevertheless be given to "the eventualities which are likely to arise in industry and commerce."[42]

(3) Deceptiveness

17-027   A mark which is deceptive at the time of application will not normally be registrable.[43] Two kinds of deceptiveness call for separate treatment: the mark may be identical or closely similar to that of another trader or

---

[35] For the difference in the scope of the right, see below, § 17-068, 17-076.
[36] When Part B was introduced in 1919, a mark could be registered in it only upon proof of two years' use. But this requirement was dropped in the 1938 Act.
[37] TMA 1938, s.10(1).
[38] s.10(2). The proprietor may register the mark (or one that is similar) in both parts of the register—for instance for different goods (s.10(3)).
[39] *Liverpool Electric's Appln.* (above, n. 19) at p. 122.
[40] Above, n. 22; the same principle was assumed in *Yorkshire* and *Electrix* (above, nn. 21, 72). It leaves little of the more equivocal decision in *"Weldmesh" T.M.* [1966] R.P.C. 220. The Irish S.C. have taken the opposite view: *"Waterford" T.M.* [1984] F.S.R. 390.
[41] See generally, the *"Ustikon"* case, *Davis v. Sussex Rubber* (1927) 44 R.P.C. 412 (C.A.); *Liverpool Electric's Appln.* (above, n. 26); Kerly, § 8–73.
[42] Lloyd Jacob J., *Smitsvonk's Appln.* (1955) 72 R.P.C. 117 at pp. 120–121; and see *Quennell's Appln.* (1955) 72 R.P.C. 36 at p. 38. The future of Part B is uncertain: see above § 17-002, n. 16.
[43] For marks which become deceptive only after registration, see below, §§ 17-054–17-055.

businessman; or it may create a misleading impression in some other way about the goods sold under it or the services provided. Both kinds of objection may be taken by the Registrar as well as an opponent, and it is the former's ability to object to conflicts with other marks that gives the British examination its special rigour.[44]

(a) Deceptiveness because of prior marks

A trader or businessman may have a better right than another to the same or a similar mark either because he is the first to register it or the first to use it. In many cases the claim to preference may be founded upon both prior registration and prior use, but the two causes must nonetheless be carefully distinguished. There is in addition the complication that in special circumstances substantial honest use by two people independently may entitle each to be registered. This possibility will be discussed at the end of this section. **17-028**

(i) **Prior registration.** According to section 12(1), a trade mark is not to be registered if a different proprietor already holds a British registration for the same or a confusingly similar mark for the same goods or services, or those of the same description.[45] The inquiry here is to some degree divorced from the realities of business. Not only is it confined to considering registrations that at most cover the limited class of goods or services of the same description,[46] it is also an inquiry into the potential ability to deceive between the marks as registered or proposed for registration: any normal and fair use of them for the goods or services in question is brought into account.[47] The way in which the applicant is using or intends to use his mark is thus only one possibility for consideration. But if it is a deceptive version, this must be regarded as one of the relevant ways in which it could be used.[48] **17-029**

(ii) **Prior use.** An objection based upon prior use of a similar mark arises under section 11, by which it is not lawful "to register as a trade [or service] mark or part of a trade [or service] mark any matter the use of which would, by reason of its being likely to deceive or cause confusion or otherwise, be disentitled to protection in a court of justice. . . ."[49] Here the comparison is between the actual use by the other trader or businessman and any use by the applicant of his proposed mark in **17-030**

---

[44] On this theme, see below, § 18-016.
[45] The onus of proof is upon the applicant: see above, § 17-006. For the residual effect of a mark removed from the register, see TMA 1938, s.20(4).
[46] For this see above, § 17-003.
[47] See Evershed J., *Smith Hayden's Applcn.* (1946) 63 R.P.C. 97 at p. 101. The possibility that the applicant will use get-up that is distinctive is ignored: *Hack's Applcn.* (1941) 58 R.P.C. 91 at p. 103; Kerly, § 10–04.
[48] *e.g.* "Woodies" T.M. [1965] R.P.C. 366: mark refused for confectionary in light of evidence that it would be used on cigarette-shaped sweets; the mark was a well-known abbreviation of the opponent's mark, "Woodbine" for cigarettes, also registered for confectionary.
[49] Normally this will be raised by an opponent rather than the Registrar, who will not have the means of informing himself.

any normal and fair manner. The other trader's use does not have to be upon the same goods or services, or those of the same description.[50] Nor is it necessary to show that the other trader has such a reputation that the applicant's use of his mark would amount to passing off. The section bites if "the result of registration of the mark will be that a number of persons will be caused to wonder whether it might not be the case that the two products came from the same source." Reasonable doubt leading to a "real tangible danger of confusion" is the criterion.[51]

17-031   (iii) **Comparing marks.** The points of departure under sections 11 and 12 are different. But once these have been brought into account, the relevant factors in the comparison are common and bear a family resemblance to the comparison made in a passing-off action,[52] Attention must be paid to the manner in which the two marks are likely to be used in trade, taking the marks as a whole. If words are involved, their look and sound for likely customers are important[53]; likewise the features of the mark most likely to impress themselves on the purchasing public's mind.[54] Where, for instance, a well-established mark consisted of a picture of a milkmaid and the words "Milkmaid Brand" for various drinks, a later applicant was not allowed to register a rather similar picture with the word "Dairymaid"; there was evidence that the first trader's products were sometimes referred to as "Dairymaid" brand.[55] Equally, if a mark, such as "Rus" for bricks, has a strong reputation it may not be permissible for a competitor to register "Sanrus," not because the one will be read or heard as the other, but because the public may believe that the first proprietor has adopted the second mark.[56] Danger of confusion of this kind is particularly likely if the first trader is known to use a series of marks with a common feature: all, for instance, beginning with "Flow—"[57] or ending with "—King."[58]

---

[50] e.g. "Players" T.M. [1965] R.P.C. 363.
[51] Lord Upjohn, "Bali" T.M. [1969] R.P.C. 472 at pp. 496–497, amending the well-known formulation in the Smith Heyden case (above, n. 47) at §§ 16-018—16-020.
[52] So reference should be made to the fuller discussion of the question, above, §§ 16-018—16-020.
[53] On this a passage of Parker J.'s, Pianotist Appln. (1906) 23 R.P.C. 774 at p. 777, is often quoted (he refers to a s.12(1) comparison). For important purchases, sound is today likely to play a less significant role: "Lancer" T.M. [1987] R.P.C. 303.
[54] An aspect of the "idea of the mark": for which see Jafferjee v. Scarlett (1937) 57 C.L.R. 115 at pp. 121–122 (H.C. Australia). Where the goods are to be exported and the mark may create a different impression in the foreign market, the probability of deception in the actual course of trade must be brought into account: ibid. at 124. cf. the suggestion (probably to be read narrowly) that innocent deception in a foreign market is irrelevant: Boord v. Bagots Hutton [1916] 2 A.C. 282; 33 R.P.C. 357 (H.L.).
[55] Anglo-Swiss Condensed Milk v. Metcalf (1886) 31 Ch.D. 454.
[56] See Ravenhead Brick v. Ruabon Brick (1937) 54 R.P.C. 341.
[57] cf. "Flowstacka" T.M. [1968] R.P.C. 66 (existence of series overcame lack of inherent distinctiveness); see also Southern Cross v. Toowoomba Foundry (1954) 91 C.L.R. 592 (H.C. Australia).
[58] cf. "Frigiking" T.M. [1973] R.P.C. 739 at p. 752; see also "Semigres" T.M. [1979] R.P.C. 330.

(iv) **Honest concurrent use.** When the register was first established, **17-032** there were numerous instances where unconnected honest users sought registration for similar marks at the same time. From the outset, the court was given a discretion to admit such users to the register, the practice being to allow up to three but beyond that to treat the marks as "common to the trade."[59] This discretion to permit registration of identical or confusingly similar marks for the same goods and goods of the same description is now given to the Registrar as well as the court "in case of honest concurrent use, or of other special circumstances."[60]

If the rival claims arise in contemporaneous applications, the Registrar will have first to consider whether one is entitled to the exclusion of the other, in accordance with the principles of priority considered below.[61] He may require the parties to take this question to the court[62]; but if he concludes that both should be registered or neither, he may either require the parties to reach an acceptable agreement for registering their marks subject to limitations,[63] or he may himself decide what conditions or limitations shall be attached to the use of either or both of the marks as a method of restricting their capacity to confuse.[64]

If one of the trade or service marks is already registered when the other is applied for, again the first question must concern priorities—in this case, whether the later applicant should seek to have the earlier registration removed from the register.[65] If there is no case for that, then it is for the Registrar to consider whether he can permit the second mark to be registered, if necessary, subject to conditions or limitations (but in such a case there is no room to impose conditions on use of the mark already registered).[66]

How then is it decided whether there is a "proper" case for registering **17-033** the mark of an honest concurrent user? The factors referred to by Lord Tomlin in *Pirie's Application*[67] as germane to the case before him are commonly taken as the starting point:

(i) What degree of likelihood is there that confusion will arise from use of the two marks? If it is only slender this is a potent reason for allowing registration.[68]

(ii) Was the original choice and subsequent use of the mark honest? Knowledge of the opponent's mark at the time that it is selected is

---

[59] *Jelley's Appln.* (1882) 46 L.T. 381n.

[60] For an instance where the use was found honest, but in all the circumstances, the registration was not allowed, see *"Bali" T.M. (No. 2)* [1978] F.S.R. 193.

[61] See § 17-035.

[62] TMA 1938, s.12(2); the application may be for Part A or Part B: *Gedye's Appln.* ("Tiger Brand") (1922) 39 R.P.C. 377.

[63] See TMA 1938, s.12(3), based upon *Bainbridge and Green's Applns.* ("Lion Brand") (1940) 57 R.P.C. 248.

[64] s.12(2). For this discretion when non-use within s.26(1) is proved, see s.26(2)(b).

[65] See below, § 17-035, n. 88.

[66] s.12(2), which if applicable overrides s.11 (but not s.9: see n. 72 below); *"Chelsea Man" T.M.* [1989] R.P.C. 111.

[67] (1933) 50 R.P.C. 147 at pp. 159–160.

[68] For the rule of "triple identity," see Faulkner, *Elements of Trade Mark Law and Practice* (3rd ed., 1971) 13–14; below, n. 75.

an important but not decisive indicator of lack of honesty.[69] If usage is begun in knowledge of the other mark and of objections from its owner, but in the belief that there will be no confusion, the conduct will likely be held honest.[70]

    (iii) How long is the period of use? Five years was sufficient in the *Pirie* case but the Registrar normally expects seven as a minimum. Exceptionally, where the applicant's use was very substantial and there was no evidence of use by the opponents, two years and ten months sufficed.[71]

    (iv) Was there evidence of confusion in actual use?

    (v) Was the applicant's trade larger than the opponents? An affirmative answer may assist the applicant, but, in a number of instances, the fact that his trade is smaller has not been decisive against him.[72]

    Such a list is not conclusive, for the reference to "other special circumstances" in section 12(2) requires that every relevant consideration be brought into the balance[73]: the reasons why there has been a break in continuity of use, for instance, are likely to be important.[74] The Registry's practice of refusing registration in cases of "triple identity" (*i.e.* of marks, goods and areas of sale) should not be applied where there are special circumstances—for instance, because the public has brought about the concurrent use by affectionate abbreviation.[75]

17-034   A delicate balance is involved in deciding whether registration should be permitted under section 12(2). Once it is decided that the marks are potentially confusing, the public interest in not having the marks upon the register has to be set against the legitimate interest of the traders which derives from their actual use.[76] There is no obligation to allow registration despite a high risk of confusion; and if one of the users can prove that the other is passing off in any circumstances, he may sue to prevent it.[77] The exception should, in other words, be regarded not as one in which the public interest gives place to private entitlement, so much as one in which a special concession is allowed if the danger to the public can be reduced to minor proportions.

---

[69] *Pirie's Applcn.* (above, n. 75) at p. 160; and see *Massachussets Saw Works' Applcn.* ("Victor") (1918) 35 R.P.C. 137.

[70] It is not clear how far there must also be evidence (in the form, say, of professional advice or court decisions here or abroad) that the belief was reasonable. These factors were present in *"Bali" T.M. (No. 2)* [1978] F.S.R. 193.

[71] *"Granada" T.M.* [1979] R.P.C. 303; Faulkner (above, n. 68) 14. The very short period that sufficed in *Peddie's Applcns.* (1944) 61 R.P.C. 31 was the product of unusual circumstances.

[72] *e.g. Electrix Ltd.'s Applcn.* [1957] R.P.C. 369 (Wynn Parry J.—for the appeal, see below, n. 78); and note the compromise solution in *Harrods Ltd.'s Applcn.* ("Hyde Park") (1935) 52 R.P.C. 65.

[73] *Holt's Applcn.* [1957] R.P.C. 289 ("English Rose").

[74] *cf. Peddie's Applcns.* (above, n. 71) with the 29-year lapse in *Fortuna-Werke's Applcn.* [1957] R.P.C. 84.

[75] *"Bud" T.M.* [1988] R.P.C. 535.

[76] See Lord Diplock, *"GE" T.M.* [1973] R.P.C. at 326.

[77] A point not acknowledged in Lord Diplock's animadversions on the conflict of policy (see previous note).

Moreover, if there is a separate objection in the public interest—most obviously that the mark sought to be registered does not satisfy the test of distinctiveness—this will prevent registration. The House of Lords[78] found "Electrix" inherently non-distinctive for vacuum cleaners, being the phonetic equivalent of "electrics"; registration had therefore to be refused, despite a finding at first instance of sufficient concurrent use.[79]

The Companies Registry[80] has power to refuse to register apparently conflicting names for businesses and companies. Because service marks are frequently similar to business names, this did a good deal over time to eliminate such conflicts between domestic traders and the introduction of service mark registration has not produced a rush of difficult cases. But the problem of concurrent use will undoubtedly create difficulties in the coming EEC system; and the Draft Regulation makes no provision equivalent to section 12(2).[81]

(v) **Registration and use: priority.** Behind the grounds of objection 17-035 concerning conflicting marks lie certain assumptions about priority. If the conflict is between two claimants to identical or similar marks for the same goods or goods of the same description, neither of whom has used his mark, then the better right lies with the first to register.[82] But account must be taken of any priority gained by virtue of the Paris Convention from foreign applications to register.[83]

It would doubtless be the simplest bureaucratic expedient to give priority to the first to register and that is the basic principle in some countries.[84] But the whole history of the British system leads it to prefer claims that are based upon actual use in trade.[85] Accordingly, if one of the rival claimants begins to use before the other has either used or registered, and he continues this use without interruption, he cannot be sued for infringement[86]; he normally has the better right to register,[87] and, should the other secure registration first, the first user could seek concurrent registration. The Registrar, however, may object to this in the public interest. If he is not willing to allow both marks on the register, he may insist that the earlier user secure the removal of the other mark (relying on section 11) before registering his own.[88]

---

[78] [1959] R.P.C. 283.
[79] Above, n. 72.
[80] For this, see Gower, *Modern Company Law* (4th ed., 1979) at 302–304.
[81] A prior registration in any national system will be one ground of invalidity of the EEC mark: 5865/88, Art. 7, 42.
[82] *i.e.* to apply to register, since registration dates back to the date of application: see above, § 17-012.
[83] The period is six months: PIP Art. 4; Patents and Designs Act 1907–46, s.91. Convention priority is also proof against intervening use.
[84] See above, § 15-007.   [85] See above, § 15-005.
[86] TMA 1938, s.7.
[87] *Leedham & Heaton's Applcn.* (1928) 45 R.P.C. 229; strict priority in time may not always be conclusive: *cf. Notox's Applcn.* (1931) 48 R.P.C. 168 (where the insufficiency of the opponent's use, rather than the fact that it was later, was treated as crucial).
[88] *Fitton's Applcn.* (1949) 66 R.P.C. 110. By contrast, if one person is first user and then first to register, but the second begins his use in the interim, this is not a ground for expunging the first's registration: *"Welsh Lady"* T.M. [1964] R.P.C. 459.

If the first user has not kept his mark in continuous use, or the other claimant's registration came even before his use, his position is less secure. He may well have no ground upon which to object to the other's original registration. If he has not begun to use his own mark by that date, he will have none. If his use has been intermittent or has come to an end, the question is: was his mark known to a substantial number of people in the United Kingdom[89] and does it remains so?[90] And he is given no special protection from his opponent when he subsequently applies to register his own mark; all he can hope for is that his use will be sufficient to permit registration as an honest concurrent user.

(b) *Other forms of deceptiveness*

17-036   The benefits of registration are denied to marks which are likely to deceive for some reason other than their similarity to marks or get-up of other traders.[91] But the risk must be such as to disentitle the applicant from protection in a court of justice.[92] So not every conceivable eventuality will form the basis for an objection[93]; and apparent objections may be discounted if there is evidence enough that the public are not in fact misled.[94] Any prospect of deception may be brought into account, provided that it relates to the mark itself and not to some other aspect of the applicant's trading methods. A number of types are well-known. In the first two listed below, the connection with lack of distinctiveness will be evident.[95]

17-037   (i) Deception concerning quality of the product. If a mark contains a descriptive element, it is liable to mislead if applied to goods which do not fit within the description. Thus one objection to "Instant Dip" for the whole class of cleaning materials was that the registration sought would cover materials that were not dips.[96]

17-038   (ii) Deception concerning geographical origin. Where a trade has no connection with a place whose name is known to the British public it will

---

[89] "*Nova*" T.M. [1968] R.P.C. 357. Again, foreign use is not treated as relevant; so the receipt of foreign journals containing advertising, or small amounts of test or other marketing may well be insufficient: see *Gaines' Appln.* (1951) 68 R.P.C. 178; [1958] R.P.C. 312.

[90] *Hassan-al-Madi's Appln.* (1954) 71 R.P.C. 348 (opponent retained a "residual renown" and was found (rather generously) not to have abandoned the mark).

[91] See *Aristoc* v. *Rysta* (below, n. 99).

[92] TMA 1938, s.11. The meaning of this requirement was elucidated in "*GE*" T.M. (below, § 17-054, n. 89).

[93] *Seligmann's Appln.* (below, n. 7) at 57; and see *Royal McBee's Appln.* [1961] R.P.C. 84 at p. 92.

[94] Thus "National" may carry the suggestion of official approval (*Natonal Galvanisers' Appln.* (1920) 37 R.P.C. 202), unless evidence of actual trading establishes a secondary meaning instead (*National Cash Register's Appln.* (1917) 34 R.P.C. 354 (C.A.)).

[95] Refusal does not of itself prevent use of the mark: see above, § 15-017.

[96] *Seligmann's Appln.* (1954) 71 R.P.C. 52; "Orlwoola" is another well-known example (see above, § 17-019, n. 92); and see "*China-Therm*" T.M. [1980] F.S.R. 21. Note, however, the special practice developed for food and wine marks, mentioned above at § 17-008, n. 42.

be deceptive to adopt that name in a trade mark.[97] The name does not have to be one that has some notoriety for the type of goods in question: an English pharmaceutical concern could not use "Livron" for a tonic, because of the French town of that name where the opponent had works.[98]

(iii) Deception concerning form of trade connection. If the same mark 17-039 is applied to new and secondhand goods there is an evident danger that the public will mistake the one for the other. So long as this remains only a theoretically possible manner of using the mark, no account would be taken of such an objection. But evidence that an applicant intends to adopt the practice renders it unregistrable.[99] The variation in trade connection may, however, be less striking.[1] A person may first have used the mark to indicate that he is the manufacturer of goods and may then use it to indicate a connection as importing distributor. He may moreover do this for all the goods or only for some. Or he may transfer the mark to a distributor who is to import his goods from abroad. According to a provision in the 1938 Act,[2] the later use in these examples is not to be deemed deceptive "on the ground only" that the mark has been, or is, used to indicate a different form on trade connection between goods and the later user or any predecessor in title. This may well mean that such changes in trade connection do not affect registrability unless the public is taught to believe that the trade mark indicates a particular form or trade connection and this is later changed.[3]

(iv) Incorrect suggestion of approval or association. This reason for 17-040 refusing registration is amplified by specific provisions in the rules: if a person is to be named or represented his consent may be required[4]; words such as "Royal" and "Imperial," and arms, representations and devices connected with the Royal Family are not to be included[5]; if the arms or other insignia of states, cities, societies, companies, persons, etc., are to be used, the Registrar may require appropriate consent[6]; and there are special provisions for "Red Cross" and other cross marks and "Anzac."[7] To cases which do not fall within these explicit rules, the general principle of section 11 may be applied: "Vitasafe" for vitamin preparations was refused because it bore the innuendo of an official guarantee.[8]

---

[97] *Hill's T.M.* (1893) 10 R.P.C. 113: "Forrest London" for clocks made in Coventry. There was no connection with Forrest either.
[98] *Boots' T.M.* (1937) 54 R.P.C. 327 (C.A.); but see above, n. 16.
[99] *Aristoc* v. *Rysta* [1945] A.C. 68; 62 R.P.C. 65 (H.L.).
[1] It will be recalled that repairing is not currently an accepted connection in the course of trade in registering a goods mark, rather than a service mark: above, § 17-013.
[2] TMA 1938, s.62.
[3] The issue arises equally when the change comes after registration; and in this context it is discussed below, §§ 17-054—17-055.
[4] Rules 1986 r. 18. If recently dead, consent may have to be sought from his personal representatives.
[5] rr. 15(*b*) and 16; and see *Royal Worcester Corset's Appln.* (1909) 26 R.P.C. 185.
[6] r. 17.   [7] rr. 15(*c*) and 16(*d*).
[8] *"Vitasafe"* T.Ms. [1963] R.P.C. 256; and *cf.* the "National" cases (above, n. 94).

17-041   (v) **Incorrect suggestion about legal right.** There is a particular sensitivity towards marks that indicate the existence of legal rights. The rules give the Registrar the power to exclude such words as "Patent" or "Copyright," or phrases such as "To counterfeit this is a forgery."[9] If "Trade Mark" is included, it must not be used so as to suggest that only part of a mark is within the registration[10]; nor must there be any suggestion that the proceedings will be taken against use on goods for which the mark is not registered.[11]

(4) Other objections to registration

(a) *The Registrar's discretion*

17-042   This is a convenient point at which to note that, over and above the specific statutory grounds for refusing admission to the register, the Registrar has a discretion to refuse an application or to accept it only subject to amendment, modification, limitation or condition, "as he may think right."[12] The discretion must be exercised on judicial principles and affected neither by caprice nor overcaution[13]; the grounds must be capable of being clearly stated and must amount to more than "vague distaste for the applicant and his methods of business."[14] But it is sometimes used to justify an exclusion which does not clearly fall within a specific head. Thus the Registrar refused "Jardex" for poisonous disinfectant, given the existing registration of "Jardox" for meat extract—the consequences of confusion on a shelf could be particularly unpleasant.[15] The existence of the discretion is also important in providing a penumbra to the two statutory grounds that have yet to be mentioned.

(b) *Unlawful, immoral and scandalous marks*

17-043   Section 11 provides that matter contrary to law or morality, or any scandalous design, shall not be registered. This covers only "something intrinsic or inherent" in the mark itself[16]: defamatory, obscene, offensive and so forth. This makes the Registrar judge of matters of opinion that in other legal contexts are well known for their ability to attract controversy. The Registrar has refused the privilege of registration where he considers that a substantial minority of the population is likely to take offence. Here the discretion is taken to justify giving heed to the views of relatively minor groups. On thin evidence, "Hallelujah" was refused for

[9] r. 15(a).
[10] Fry L.J., *Appollinaris' T.M.* [1891] 2 Ch. 186 at 233; *Wills' T.Ms.* [1893] 2 Ch. 262, 10 R.P.C. 269; *Day v. Riley* (1900) 17 R.P.C. 517; and see Kerly, § 10–36.
[11] Fry L.J. *Appollinaris* case (previous n.) at 226. Equally, fraudulent use of "Registered Trade Mark" before registration may be penalised by refusing entry on the register: *cf. Arthur Fairest Ltd.'s Appln.* (1951) 68 R.P.C. 197.
[12] TMA 1938, s.17(2).
[13] Younger J., *Standard Woven's Appln.* (1918) 35 R.P.C. 53 at p. 57.
[14] Cross J., *"Rawhide" T.M.* [1962] R.P.C. 133 at 142; and see further Kerly § 4–07.
[15] *Edwards' Appln.* (1945) 63 R.P.C. 19: there was no objection under s.12 since the goods were decidedly not of the same description; and the Registrar was not armed with evidence of use which might have brought s.11 into play.
[16] *Fairest's Appln.* (above, n. 11) at 208; *"Nova" T.M.* [1968] R.P.C. 357.

women's clothing (religious susceptibilities) under both section 11 and the discretion.[17] If the mark infringes copyright (for instance in a drawing), then it should be refused registration.[18]

If it is the trade in which it is applied, and not the mark itself, which is unlawful, section 11 has no role. But under the discretion a mark was refused for use on football pool coupons, giving evidence that the pool was persistently run in breach of Betting and Lotteries Acts[19]; if the mark were allowed to be described as registered,[20] this might be understood as conferring judicial approval upon the whole operation.

(c) *Proprietorship of the mark*

The right to apply for registration is given by section 17(1) to "the **17-044** proprietor of a trade [or service] mark used or proposed to be used by him." Section 29(1) confirms the principle that the "proprietor" alone may apply by admitting two exceptions: a person may apply where the intended use is to be by a corporation about to be formed; so may a proprietor who accompanies his application with an acceptable application to register another as user of the mark.[21] Consequently an applicant is not entitled if he has no bona fide intention to use the mark at all, or will do so only if current uncertainties are resolved.[22]

These principles place difficulty in the path of authors and their associates who wish to acquire "merchandising rights" in fictional characters and the like through registered trade marks.[23] A corporation which had achieved success with a winsome girl-figure, "Holly Hobbie," on greetings cards and the like in the United States had then "merchandised" it for use on a great many products put out by others there. In expanding this operation to Britain it sought to register "Holly Hobbie" for 12 classes of goods. Since it intended itself to do no more than license the name to others, it provided with each application a user agreement to come into effect with one licensee in each class.[24] This was intended to comply with the second special case in section 29(1) and so to sidestep the rejection of applications which occurred in the earlier merchandising case, *"Pussy Galore" Trade Mark.*[25] But while the *Pussy Galore* applications failed because the applicant did not use or propose to use the mark, the *Holly Hobbie* applications were rejected by the House of Lords[26]

---

[17] [1977] R.P.C. 605; *cf. La Marquise's Appln.* (1947) 64 R.P.C. 27.
[18] *"Karo-Step"* T.M. [1977] R.P.C. 255; *"Oscar"* T.M. [1980] F.S.R. 429.
[19] *Fairest's Appln.* (above, n. 11).
[20] As it had been before registration! But this was excused as a blunder: see above, n. 10.
[21] For the registration of users see below, §§ 17-058—17-059.
[22] As in *"Rawhide"* (above, n. 14), where the title of a U.S. television series was sought for various wares; but the judge doubted whether there was any intent to use if the series was not released in Britain.
[23] A different difficulty concerns distinctiveness and the associated problem of whether any use would be taken to be use as a trade mark: see above, § 17-020, n. 3.
[24] For user agreements—the formal method of trade mark licensing under TMA 1938, s.28—see below, §§ 17-058—17-059.
[25] [1966] R.P.C. 265; for the view that this ground of rejection cannot stand with *"Bostitch"* T.M. (below, § 17-060), see Kerly § 2–04; also *"Dristan"* T.M. [1986] R.P.C. 161 (Indian S.C.); *"Benji"* T.M. [1988] R.P.C. 251.
[26] *"Holly Hobbie"* T.M. [1984] R.P.C. 329; Lane [1985] E.I.P.R. 6.

because of the provision that registered user agreements are not to be registered if they would lead to trafficking in the mark.[27] The applicants sought to deflect this attack by showing that in their user agreements they had the power to control the quality of licensees' products. If they were intending seriously to do this, then indeed they might have demonstrated a sufficient connection with the goods to be using the trade marks themselves. But a quality control clause was not of itself sufficient, where, due to the very size of the merchandising scheme, it was most unlikely to become operative in particular cases. The decision shows the same reluctance as in the current law of passing off to accede to pressure for greater protection just because merchandising has become a lively advertising practice.[28]

17-045   In section 17, the judges have found an answer to a different problem that has grown with international trading. Sections 11 and 12 deal with objections arising from the likelihood of confusion with another mark on the British market—evidence of what happens abroad is not directly relevant.[29] Yet where an enterprise has built a strong reputation in a mark elsewhere, if another is able to register it in the United Kingdom, he may be in a position to block the entry of the foreign user into the British market. In such a case it has been held that the registration by the first can be expunged, either on the ground that he was not the proprietor entitled to apply, or else under the discretion. While the concept of "proprietor" clearly extends to a person who bona fide intends to use, as well as one already using, it does not cover a person who copies another's mark, even if the latter mark is not in use in Britain.[30] Thus a United States shoe manufacturer, whose "Naturalizer" shoes were well-known there, secured the removal of "Naturalizet," which had been derived from it.[31] Two limits, however, have been identified in the case-law. First, a person may appropriate as "his" trade mark the name of fictional character or title, provided that no one has earlier established a reputation in it as a trade mark for the goods in question.[32] This rule of trade mark law does not assist in the elusive search for "merchandising rights." Secondly, a person who invents a mark himself does not lose his right to secure registration of it (or some variant) merely because someone else initially has a prior conflicting application which is not proceeded with.[33] In such circumstances the

---

[27] TMA 1938, s.28(6).
[28] See above, § 15-008. Lord Bridge, however, expressed the opinion that s.28(6) was anachronistic and should be repealed: [1984] R.P.C. at 350–351.
[29] See above, § 17-035, n. 89.
[30] See *Vitamins' Appln.* [1956] R.P.C. 1; *North Shore Toy* v. *Stevenson* [1973] 1 N.Z.L.R. 562; *"Sidewinder"* T.M. [1988] R.P.C. 261.
[31] *Brown Shoe's Appln.* [1959] R.P.C. 29.
[32] *"Rawhide"* T.M. (above, n. 14).
[33] *"Genette"* T.M. [1968] R.P.C. 148; approved, [1969] R.P.C. 189 (C.A.); and note the cases in n. 18. The creative character of the decisions under discussion is emphasised by the different treatment of the problem in Australia: there, in the absence of fraud or breach of confidence, one person may register another's mark so long as its use has been entirely foreign: see *Aston* v. *Harlee* (1960) 103 C.L.R. 391; *Kendall* v. *Mulsyn* (1963) 109 C.L.R. 300 and the case-law there referred to.

latter will continue to have priority only if he has sufficient use in trade to give him the protection of section 11.

(5) Defensive registration

The brand loyalty attaching to the best-known trade marks may give **17-046** considerable drawing-power in the market-place. The owners of such marks may therefore face imitations of them not only on products directly competitive but also upon articles in which they themselves do not deal. There may be greater or less proximity to their own trade: even if the two sorts of goods are quite dissimilar, the person who takes over the well-known mark may find the general association advantageous. As diversification by large firms has become so standard a feature of modern business, some at least of the public may well assume that the original user is extending his business into new territory. Even if they do not draw so specific an inference, they may be attracted to the new goods by the general familiarity of the mark.

However much the first user may object to "dilution" of this kind, he **17-047** cannot claim that it threatens him with direct losses through competition. We have seen that the judges have sometimes been prepared nonetheless to find an indirect risk of damage upon which to afford relief in passing off—from an undesirable association damaging to goodwill or an exposure to litigation.[34] In 1934, the Goschen Committee were persuaded that owners of well-known marks should have surer protection in some such cases[35] and their recommendation led to the introduction of defensive registration in the 1938 Act, section 27.

This type of registration is allowed where (i) the mark is for an invented word or words, and (ii) the mark "has become so well-known as respects any goods in respect of which it is registered and in relation to which it has been used that the use thereof in relation to other goods would be likely to be taken as indicating a connection in the course of trade between those goods and a person entitled to use the trade mark in relation to the first-mentioned goods."[36] A defensive registration is then excepted from the requirement that the proprietor should intend to use it and should use it bona fide for the registered goods.[37]

As already suggested, the public's reaction to the appearance of a well-known mark on novel goods may vary. A defensive registration is allowed only if a fairly specific test is satisfied: the new use must in effect suggest that the first user is extending his business. In *Ferodo's Application*,[38] Evershed J. interpreted this provision somewhat strictly. He recognised that it muse be possible to encompass within a defensive registration goods that are less proximate to the goods traded in than "goods of the same description," since this limited range may properly be

[34] See above, § 16-025.
[35] Cmd. 4568, 1934, §§ 73–77.
[36] s.27(1); the registrations are then treated as associated: s.27(3). For conversion of an ordinary registration, see s.27(2); and for removal where no ordinary registration survives, s.27(5).
[37] i.e. the mark is not open to removal under TMA 1938, s.26 (for which, see below, §§ 17-049 et seq.); but where the requirements of s.27 are no longer satisfied, a person aggrieved may seek expunction: s.27(4).
[38] (1945) 62 R.P.C. 111.

the subject of an ordinary registration. Nonetheless, the implication that the first user is connected in trade with the further goods is more easily drawn when the two types of goods are similar. Proof is required of this particular type of deception and the standard is at a level similar to an investigation of likely deception or confusion between goods of the same kind. The inference is not to be drawn merely from the fact the mark is well-known; it will normally depend on evidence, not from the purchasing public, but from traders dealing in goods of the "defensive" category about two things: the significance of names and brands in their business and their own reaction if they were to see the mark on such articles. On this test it was not possible under section 27 to register "Ferodo" (well known for brake linings and clutches) for pharmaceuticals, smokers' articles and matches.[39]

17-048   It is not clear what advantages a defensive registration gives against later similar applications to register for the same goods.[40] In *Eastex's Application*,[41] Wynn Parry J. took account of the special manner in which the prior mark had been built up into a well-known mark ("Lastex") on the goods for which it was first registered (elastic yarn) in order to limit the scope of its defensive registration (for women's clothing). The particular use of "Lastex" was as a mark on clothing, in addition to the manufacturer's mark, to indicate that they contained "Lastex" yarn. Because of this, there was held to be no sufficient likelihood of confusion to prevent the subsequent registration of "Eastex" for women's coats and the like. In essence, the decision deprived the defensive registration of independent effect *vis-à-vis* the other applicant. Even if correctly decided, it is probably limited in scope to the special type of facts with which it dealt.

The judicial reluctance to give wide effect to section 27 has kept the number of defensive registrations low.[42] The Mathys Committee recommended the abandonment of section 27 except for marks already on the register.[43] In 1984 the section was not extended to service marks. But when the new EEC systems takes effect there will be more general protection open to proprietors of marks, even in respect of their use on dissimilar goods, in order to prevent unfair advantage being taken of their distinctive character or repute or detriment to.[44] This reflects the much greater sympathy with which Continental member states have traditionally viewed "famous" marks, making them willing to provide against dilution.[45]

---

[39] See also *Vono's Applcn.* (1949) 66 R.P.C. 305.

[40] *i.e.* where objection to the later application is taken under s.12(1) (and note generally, s.27(6)).

[41] (1947) 64 R.P.C. 142.

[42] By 1974, there had been some 100 applications (mostly successful) during the entire life of s.27; Mathys Report, Cmnd. 5601, § 102.

[43] *Ibid.* §§ 100–104.

[44] Community Trade Mark Regulation (Draft 5865/88) Art. 8(1)(*d*). Member States are permitted to have a similar provision in their law: First Directive on Trade Marks (December 21, 1988) Art. 5(2).

[45] See Cohen Jehoram (1978) 17 Ind.Prop. 219.

4. Objections to a Trade Mark Once Registered

The British registration system allows considerable range both to official 17-049
and to third-party objections before registration takes place. Once that
event occurs, the mark is presumed valid.[46] Any objector seeking to have
the mark expunged bears the onus of making a sufficient case; before
registration the onus is on the applicant. Moreover, the various grounds
of objection can be raised only by a "person aggrieved," *i.e.* someone
with a sufficient trading interest, current or intended.[47]

Before the House of Lords' decision in *"GE" Trade Mark*,[48] various
aspects of this part of trade mark law were obscure. That decision laid
down three cardinal principles:

  (i) The court and the registrar have jurisdiction over removal when it
      is given by the general provisions of section 32 or a specific
      provision in another section. Section 32 allows objection (*inter
      alia*) to the original registration on the ground that the entry was
      made without sufficient cause or that there was an error or defect
      in it; objections arising subsequently to this date may be raised on
      the ground that the mark is one wrongly remaining upon the
      register. The jurisdiction to remove under the section is
      discretionary.

 (ii) Section 32 is jurisdictional only: it is necessary to find the
      substantive ground of objection in another provision of the Trade
      Marks Act 1938. References in other sections to the act of
      registering may (according to context) be to both the initial act of
      registering and the subsequent maintaining of a mark on the
      register: in particular, as we shall see, this is the sense in which
      section 11 has been read as referring to both these senses.[49]

(iii) Section 13 institutes a limited form of incontestability for Part A
      marks after seven years from their date of registration. But it
      applies only to objections to the original registration, not to those
      arising subsequently, because it says so expressly. Even then there
      are exceptions: where the mark "was obtained" by fraud; and
      where it "offends"against section 11. The use of the present tense
      for the second exception suggests that the objection to the original
      registration must be one that also exists at the date of the
      application to expunge: this, however, is one point that remains
      unsettled.

---

[46] TMA 1938, s.46. But since this throws the onus of proving a negative upon an applicant
to expunge, the burden upon him may not be high: *Re Ellis & Goldstein's T.M.* (1966)
40 A.L.J.R. 418.

[47] See s.32; Kerly, § 11–02/09. A person using the mark when trading in the same or
similar goods has the necessary *locus standi*, and the courts have been reluctant to take
nice points on standing against traders. Non-traders are likely to fail: see, *e.g. Ellis's T.M.*
(1904) 21 R.P.C. 619 (Society of Friends could not object to "Quaker" for spirits).

[48] [1973] R.P.C. 297.

[49] See below, § 17-054.

With this framework of jurisdictional rules in mind, we can turn to the three main reasons justifying removal of a mark: because it has not been used, because it has ceased to be distinctive, and because it has become deceptive.

(1) Non-use

(a) *Basic provisions*

17-050   By section 26, the court or registrar may expunge the registration of a mark for any of the goods or services covered upon two grounds: (i) because initially the registered proprietor had no bona fide intention of using it for the goods or services and has not since done so; (ii) because in the previous five years the mark has not been used bona fide upon the goods or for the services in question.[50] (Note that in each case the period is measured to a date one month before the application to expunge. This gives the person seeking removal time to inform the proprietor that he intends to apply, without allowing the latter to save himself by starting use.)[51] The first of these objections is associated with the requirement that an applicant for registration should have a bona fide intention to use.[52] Taken together these are the chief armour in the Act against stock-piling marks. But an application to expunge after registration can only be made by person with a sufficient trading interest to rank as a "person aggrieved."[53] Such a competitor will not be likely to seek the removal of an unused mark unless he has some investment in his own conflicting mark to protect. Otherwise it is normally simpler for him to choose a different mark.

17-051   We have already said something of "bona fide intention to use" in connection with the right to apply for registration[54]; it is not enough to be seeking "something which may someday be useful."[55] Nor is it permissible, in order to escape the inherent lack of distinctiveness in a mark that is really wanted (such as "Merit" for cigarettes), to register a word sufficiently similar (*e.g.* "Nerit") as a "ghost mark"; and in its desire to put down the practice, the Court of Appeal has disregarded quite substantial test-marketing under the ghost mark as merely colourable.[56]

[50] s.26(1). In this case the section gives its own jurisdiction and there is no need to rely upon s.32. See generally, Llewelyn and Brattne (1982) 13 I.I.C. 319.

[51] Failure to notify in advance could lead to an adverse award of costs: see, as regards proceedings before the registrar: TMA 1938 Rules, rr. 57, 83.

[52] See above, § 17-044. Note the special arrangements upon an application for taking account of intention to use through a registered user. So equally under s.26, the use by such a user is treated as use by the proprietor and will accordingly defeat an application to expunge: see below, § 17-052.

[53] This is specified in s.26; the same principles apply as for s.32 (see above, n. 40). See "Oscar" T.M. [1979] R.P.C. 173; "Kodiak" T.M. [1987] R.P.C. 269 (C.A.); Ritz Hotel v. Charles of the Ritz [1988] F.S.R. 549 (S.C. S. Africa).

[54] See generally above, §§ 17-044—17-045; and Imperial Group v. Philip Morris [1980] F.S.R. 146.

[55] Ducker's T.M. (1928) 45 R.P.C. 105 at p. 115; and see ibid. at p. 397 (C.A.).

[56] Imperial Group v. Philip Morris [1982] F.S.R. 72; and see Levi-Strauss v. Shah [1985] R.P.C. 371; there must be "a real commercial use on a substantial scale."

Under the second head, the applicant to expunge must show that there has been no bona fide use in the five-year period. If the mark owner has supplied goods even on one occasion as part of a genuine attempt to get them on the British market with the mark, this may be enough to protect him;[57] equally if he has instituted an advertising campaign for orders.[58] From this has to be distinguished the purely colourable use of the mark designed primarily to keep rights in it alive. Use that occurs only in brochures or advertisements, without accompanying use on goods may well be looked at with suspicion. On the other hand, if there is substantial use in actual trade, it does not cease to be bona fide because it is undertaken in order to improve the user's position in a conflict with a competitor.[59]

(b) Exceptions

The tribunal is well-nigh obliged to remove the mark once the non-use 17-052 is proved,[60] unless one of the exceptions specified in the section applies.[61] Then there is a discretion not to remove. These are the exceptions[62]:

   (i) Where the failure to use is due to special circumstances in the trade, rather than to an intention not to use or to abandon the mark, that failure is not to be taken into account.[63] Government restrictions preventing the imports or exports that the mark owner would otherwise have made are a straightforward instance of "special circumstances." They may be brought into account even if they do not apply equally to the whole trade,[64] or if they impose a quota (rather than an embargo) at a level not commercially viable for the mark owner.[65] If under free market conditions, the mark owner can show a glut that makes it not worth his while to put out goods, it may be that this also is enough.[66] Since it is unlikely that such an explanation could convincingly be given for a full five years of non-use, the answer to this uncertainty may well depend upon another: do the special circumstances have to apply throughout the whole period of non-use? Under the 1905 Act, the Court of Appeal answered this in the affirmative.[67] But in 1938 the wording was changed somewhat, and the Comptroller has taken

---

[57] Note of Official Ruling (1944) 61 R.P.C. 148; "Vac-U-Flex" T.M. [1965] F.S.R. 176; Ellis & Goldstein's T.Ms. (1966) 40 A.L.J.R. 418; cf. "Nodoz" T.M. [1962] R.P.C. 1; Wills v. Rothmans (1956) 92 C.L.R. 182.

[58] "Hermes" T.M. [1982] R.P.C. 425.

[59] Electrolux v. Electrix (1954) 71 R.P.C. 23 at p. 42 (C.A.).

[60] s.26(1).

[61] There remains an element of discretion to deal with exceptional cases not specified in the statute: Lyons' Appln. [1959] R.P.C. 120 (C.A.); Carl Zeiss' T.M. [1970] R.P.C. 139 (H.C. Australia) and earlier authorities there referred to.

[62] The provision concerning territorial limitation when a competitor establishes a case for concurrent registration (s.26(2)), is dealt with above, § 17-032, n. 64.

[63] s.26(3).

[64] As in Manus v. Fullwood (1949) 66 R.P.C. 71 at p. 79 (C.A.).

[65] As in "Bali" T.M. [1966] R.P.C. 387 at p. 406; see also Crean's T.M. (1921) 38 R.P.C. 155.

[66] See per Chitty J., Mouson's v. Boehm (1884) 26 Ch.D. 398 at 406.

[67] Columbia Gramophone's T.M. (1932) 42 R.P.C. 621.

the view that any excusable period of non-use stops time running against
the proprietor; when that period comes to an end, the measuring must
begin afresh.[68] Another possible reading of the exception is that periods
on either side of the period of excusable non-use may be aggregated in an
attack upon the registration.

(ii) Bona fide use of the mark for goods or services of the same
description as those concerned in the application to expunge may
prevent removal,[69] provided that the registration also covers these
similar goods or services. But this exception cannot apply if the
applicant for removal is himself registered as an honest concurrent
user of an identical or nearly resembling mark for the goods
concerned, or could be so registered. Even if the applicant to
expunge has not in his own trade built up sufficient use to be
classed as an honest concurrent user, still, if his reputation is
already much more substantial for the goods concerned than is the
trade mark owner's for the "goods of the same description," the
discretion not to remove the mark may not be exercised in favour
of the owner of the mark under attack. So in *Lyons' Application*[70]
the registered proprietor's limited use of "Hostess" for jellies was
held insufficient to prevent its removal for ice-cream, on which the
applicant for removal had already begun to use "Hostess" in a
thriving trade.

(iii) There is a discretion to bring into account the proprietor's use of
an associated mark[71] for the goods or services in question, or
(taking this in conjunction with the previous exception) on goods
or services of the same description.[72] The same discretion applies
to use of the mark with additions (but not deletions) not materially affecting its identity. But there will be careful scrutiny of the
reason why the use has been of the associated mark, rather than
the mark under attack. The tribunal has to be satisfied that the
use of the former is "equivalent for" use of the latter. The Court
of Appeal was not satisfied of this, when the mark owner was
reserving the mark under attack for use on cheaper quality goods
than the goods bearing the associated mark.[73]

(iv) Use by a licensee of the mark will count as use by the proprietor if
the user agreement is registered.[74] Where it is not, the position is
uncertain. The question is discussed later.[75]

---

[68] *Marshall's Appln.* (1943) 60 R.P.C. 147 at p. 148; *Zenith's Appln.* (1951) 68 R.P.C.
160. In *"Daiquiri Rum" T.M.* (above, n. 50) it was assumed that "special circumstances"
within a substantial part of the previous five years would found a sufficient explanation.
[69] s.26(1) proviso; it also covers associated services or goods.
[70] Above, n. 61.
[71] For associated marks, see above, § 17-009.
[72] s.30(1); applied in *Morny's T.M.* (1951) 68 R.P.C. 131 (C.A.); *Spillers* v. *Quaker Oats*
[1969] F.S.R. 510.
[73] *Electrolux* v. *Electrix* (1954) 71 R.P.C. 23 at pp. 37–38 (C.A.); see also *"Cal-U-Test"*
T.M. [1967] F.S.R. 39; *Farmer* v. *Anthony Hordern* (1964) 112 C.L.R. 163. For the use
of altered marks, see *"Otrivin" T.M.* [1967] R.P.C. 613; *"Pelican" T.M.* [1978] R.P.C.
316; *"Huggars" T.M.* [1979] F.S.R. 310.
[74] TMA 1938, s.28(2).   [75] Below, § 17-060, n. 26.

(v) As already mentioned,[76] a defensive registration of an invented word is not caught by section 26, so long as a registration of it for goods on which it is well known is maintained.

(2) Mark without distinctiveness

A mark that was descriptive at the date of its registration, and which **17-052** lacked sufficient use as a trade mark by way of counter-balance, would seem, in principle, to have been registered without sufficient cause and therefore to be removable under section 32.[77] But there are two qualifications. First, an objection to the original registration in Part A cannot be raised on this ground after seven years.[78] Secondly, if the mark has become sufficiently distinctive in the period between registration and the application to expunge, the discretion in section 32 is unlikely to be exercised against it.

In section 15(1) and (2), the Act specifies the extent to which a trade mark is to be treated as wrongly remaining upon the register because, in the period since registration, it has been used as the name or description of an article or substance. Objection can be raised only in two cases:

(i) if persons carrying on trade in an article or substance use the word as a name or description for the thing; their usage has to be "well-known and established," but usage by consuming public is irrelevant;

(ii) if the word is the only practicable name or description of an article or substance formerly made under a patent and the patent has ceased to have effect for two years or more.[79]

In the first of these cases, the usage by traders must not be in relation **17-053** to goods of the registered proprietor or a registered user; in the second, this is (obviously) not so. Once it has been shown that a word or words in a registered mark has become a name or description in one or other of these senses, two consequences follow. First, a person aggrieved may apply to have a trade mark consisting of the word removed in so far as it is registered for the article or substance in question or for "goods of the same description"; if the word is only a part of the mark, then the relief may be limited to requiring a disclaimer of any exclusive right in the word.[80] The registration for goods of the same description may be affected in these ways even though the word is not also registered for the

---

[76] Above, § 17-046.
[77] Following the approach in *"GE" T.M.* (see below, n. 89): ss.9 and 10 provide the grounds for saying that the mark should not initially have been registered in Part A or Part B. *Woodward v. Boulton Macro* (1915) 32 R.P.C. 173, lends support to the view that s.11 forms an alternative basis for such an objection; but that decision has been disapproved on other grounds in the *"GE"* case.
[78] By virtue of s.13, see above, § 17-049.
[79] The equivalent provision for service marks relates to the name or description of an activity when used by others who provide services including that activity.
[80] s.15(2). Contrast the case where the registered word is only part of the descriptive phrase. In Australia this has been held to fall outside the scope of the section: *Faulding v I.C.I.* (1965) 112 C.L.R. 537 (registration of "Barrier" not affected by usage of "barrier cream").

article or substance that it describes.[81] Secondly, exclusive rights under the Act or at common law are lost: in case (i) from the date when the use became well-known and established,[82] in case (ii) from two years after the expiry of the patent.[83]

It is possible to imagine cases where marks lose their distinctive character for a reason other than that they come to describe the goods: the creation of a new local government area, for instance, may make a geographical name prominent when previously it was obscure. There is no power to remove them from the Register for such a reason.[84]

(3) Deceptive marks

17-054   At the application stage, registration may be refused because the mark is deceptive, either because of a conflict with another mark in use, or because some other association renders it misleading.[85] But even so, the objection must be strong enough to disentitle it to protection in a court of justice; if a case of honest concurrent use can be made out, this may override the objection.[86] Where, however, a deceptive mark is unjustifiably registered, objection may be taken, it seems, to the original registration afterwards. But in the case of a Part A mark with seven years' maturity, probably the mark must also be deceptive at the date of the application to expunge.[87]

It is possible for a mark to become deceptive only after its registration, either because of the use of another mark or for some other reason.[88] "GE" Trade Mark[89] dealt with the first of these cases. In 1907, General Electric of America registered the two initials "GE" as a monogram in a rondel for various electrical goods. Subsequently the English General Electric Company—an entirely separate concern—made such use of "GEC" in connection with its own name that the House of Lords found that use of the American company's "GE" rondel would lead a substantial portion of the British public to think that its goods came from the English General Electric Company.[90] Even so the House held that there was no sufficient ground for removing the American company's registrations because there was no blameworthy conduct on its part. Section 11,

---

[81] See generally "Daiquiri Rum" T.M. [1969] R.P.C. 600 (H.L.) where that mark for rum was expunged, given the trade use of "Daiquiri" for a rum cocktail (found to be goods of the same description—see above, § 17-003).

[82] cf. above, § 16-010. Particular danger may arise if dictionaries begin to give descriptive meanings to words without listing them as trade marks. See generally on the subject, Holmqvist, Degeneration of Trade Marks (1971).

[83] This danger is avoided by ensuring that a new product has a name that is distinct from the trade mark and sufficiently known. New drugs are normally given a chemical abbreviation that is more of an effort for a doctor to write on a prescription form than the mark.

[84] "York" T.M. [1984] R.P.C. 231 (H.L.); and see Mars v. Cadbury [1987] R.P.C. 387.

[85] See above, §§ 17-015 et seq.

[86] See above, §§ 17-032—17-034; also the "GE" case (below, n. 89) at pp. 325–326, where the evolution of this preference for honest use is surveyed.

[87] Because of s.13; see above, § 17-049.

[88] e.g. because of the way in which the owner assigns or licenses it: below, §§ 17-057—17-062.

[89] [1973] R.P.C. 297 (H.L.); see also above, § 17-049; Bradley (1973) 7 Syd.L.R. 93.

[90] For this form of deception, see below, § 17-067.

certainly, did allow for objection against a subsequently deceptive mark. This followed an investigation of the section's ancestry which convinced Lord Diplock that "register" was used to cover both putting on and keeping up the register.[91] But the requirement that the mark be not only deceptive but in consequence also disentitled to protection gave rise to the qualification that there must have been blameworthy conduct on the part of the proprietor. On the facts, the House of Lords followed the trial judge in finding none.[92] But the Court of Appeal construed certain dealings between the two parties as indicating a determination to use the marks despite inevitable confusion of the public.[93] This provides an example (on the Court of Appeal's assumptions) of a case of deception about origin that might today justify an order to expunge. Other instances could arise from improper dealings in trade mark rights—but these must be reserved for later discussion.[94]

Where the element of deception does not go to the question of origin, **17-055** the test for removal must be at least as severe. If a word suggests certain qualities in the goods, or that they derive from a particular place, and the mark is then used on other goods, a case could be made out. But the blameworthy conduct standard, it may be hazarded, would demand proof of deliberate intention to mislead about a characteristic of significance to the public.[95] If a mark for cigars includes the word "Havana," and it is deliberately used on Brazilian cigars, this could well be enough.[96] Contrast the use by a Swedish manufacturer of his name on milking machines produced in Britain, in circumstances where the public were not shown to attach particular significance to the place of origin.[97] For an intermediate case, consider this: the mark itself is neutral in content, but it has been advertised so as to become associated with the high production standards of a particular country; the country of manufacture is then changed. In Canada such conduct was held to jeopardise the registration.[98] It would probably take a very strong case to convince a British court that it should hold likewise.

This sort of question brings us back to the basic purpose of the registration system, which is to give protection against imitators of the

---

[91] See also above, § 17-049.
[92] Above, n. 89, at 335.
[93] [1970] R.P.C. 339.
[94] See below, §§ 17-061 — 17-062.
[95] If the registered proprietor changes his form of connection with the goods—if he was formerly their importer and he becomes the manufacturer, or vice versa—this is not "of itself" enough to jeopardise the mark, according to s.62. But cf. *Thorne* v. *Pimms* (1909) 26 R.P.C. 221 (mark indicated that its owner was the distributor of a particular maker's whisky; deceptive then to use it as a distributor's mark for other whisky); see also *Diehl's T.M.* [1970] R.P.C. 435 at 446–447.
[96] cf. the denial of relief and registration in a number of such cases: e.g. *Newman* v. *Pinto* (1887) 4 R.P.C. 508 (C.A.); *Fuente's Trade Marks* (1891) 8 R.P.C. 214.
[97] See *Manus* v. *Fullwood & Bland* [1949] Ch. 208; (1948) 65 R.P.C. 329. Disputes between manufacturer and distributor are considered further, below, § 17-067.
[98] *Wilkinson Sword* v. *Juda* (1967) 59 D.L.R. (2d) 418. There was the added fact that at the same time the mark was being assigned to the subsidiary manufacturing in the second country; and the suit was an attempt to stop parallel imports from the original country.

mark. When the confusion is with another registered mark, removal exposes the former proprietor to an infringement suit. But if the deception goes to some quality of the goods or services removing it from the register thereby allows others to use it: the chance of deception may simply be compounded. Only prosecutions under the Trade Descriptions Act or equivalent criminal legislation would act as a direct sanction against such deception. Perhaps removal of the registration should be reserved for cases where the conduct is so obviously improper that a prosecution would be likely to succeed.

5. Assignment and Licensing of Registered Marks

17-056 A passing-off action protects the goodwill built up by actual trading. Only if a newcomer acquires the business to which the goodwill is attached is he entitled to treat the reputation of his predecessor as his own.[99] One reason given for this was that, as the mark or name indicated a particular business, the public could well be deceived if it were simply applied to the goods or business of another.[1] In the Trade Marks Act 1905,[2] the same principle was applied to registered marks.[3] But as methods of business dealing expanded, the demand to be able to treat trade marks as disposable assets grew. Judicial scruples over "fraud on the public" began to appear exaggerated. A feeling developed that objection might be reserved for cases where the assignment or licence was actually likely to deceive.[4] The case-law indeed suggested the variety of circumstances in which the prevailing rule might render an assignment invalid: where the assignor wanted to put one mark out of several held for cigarettes into the hands of a distributor which was a wholly-owned subsidiary,[5] where a retailer wanted to sell a mark for medicines that he had never used,[6] where a French manufacturer wanted to assign its British mark to an exclusive distributor in England in order to prevent parallel imports.[7]

To the pressure for reform, the legislature responded with elaborate provisions that were designed to allow both the assignment and the licensing of registered marks without associated goodwill, but at the same time to preclude the unacceptable instances.

[99] See above, §§ 16-014—16-016.
[1] See Pinto v. Badman (1891) 8 R.P.C. 181 (C.A.).
[2] s.22.
[3] An earlier provision (Patents Designs and Trade Marks Act 1883, s.87) had mentioned the registration of trade mark licences, but this was not repeated in 1905.
[4] For which, see the Goschen Report (Cmd. 4568, 1934), §§ 102–123.
[5] Sinclair's T.M. (1932) 49 R.P.C. 123 (C.A.).
[6] "Mac" T.M. (1937) 54 R.P.C. 230.
[7] Lacteosote v. Alberman (1927) 44 R.P.C. 211. The mark was already well-known as the manufacturer's cf. also Brecks Sporting Goods v. Magder (1975) 17 C.P.R. (2d) 201 (S.C. Canada); Sarco Canada v. Sarco [1968] 2 Ex.C.R. 537.

(1) Assignment

Section 22 of the present Act allows the assignment of a registered 17-057 mark without the goodwill of the business as well as with it,[8] subject to this: the transaction will be invalid if its result would be likely deception or confusion of a specified kind, *i.e.* if more than one person concerned in the transaction would acquire or retain rights (registered or unregistered) to identical or similar marks for the same goods or services of the same description.[9] If the assignment is not with the goodwill, there is also an administrative control. In order to render the assignment effective, it is necessary to apply within six months to the registrar for any directions about advertising the assignment that he may impose and to comply with them.[10] If the assignment involves a geographical division of rights within the United Kingdom, the registrar must first find that it is not contrary to the public interest.[11] Beyond this, the section also offers a positive vetting procedure, under which the registrar's approval—in the form of a certificate of validity—can be secured. This is binding in the absence of fraud or misrepresentation.[12]

The section also deems the assignment of an unregistered mark without associated goodwill to be effective in certain circumstances[13]: it must have been used together with a registered mark for the same goods in the same business,[14] and it must then have been assigned at the same time as the registered mark to the same person. The effect of this is mysterious, since rights in unregistered marks are protected on the basis of actual reputation. Possibly a court would hold that an assignee within the provision[15] can rely upon his assignor's reputation in passing-off proceedings against an imitator of the mark. If not, the assignment can do no more than prevent the assignor from asserting any residual right that he may claim against the assignee.

(2) Registered user agreements

Section 28 allows the licence of a registered mark itself to be registered 17-058 as a user agreement. This may be in respect of all or any of the goods covered, with or without conditions or restrictions concerning the way in which the user may deploy the mark.[16] The consequences of registration include the following. First, the use within the terms permitted by the agreement is deemed to be use by the registered proprietor—rather than

---

[8] s.22(1).
[9] s.22(4) also covering associated services and goods. If the assignment is proper on its face, it is not for the registrar to inquire into facts which might show that it was invalid: *Cranbux's Appln.* (1928) 45 R.P.C. 281.
[10] s.22(7).
[11] s.22(6). It is, however, possible to restrict the different owners, in their use of the mark, to goods for different export markets: s.22(4) proviso.
[12] s.22(5).
[13] s.22(3).
[14] The registration must cover all the goods for which the unregistered mark is used, but the registered mark does not have actually to have been used on all of them.
[15] He would not be within the provision if the assignment resulted in the kind of deception specified in s.22(4): see above, n. 9.
[16] TMA 1938, s.28(1).

by the registered user or anyone else—for all purposes under the Act or at common law.[17] Secondly, the registered user may himself sue an infringer, if the proprietor is not willing to do so.[18] Thirdly, the registered user, if he keeps within the permitted use, cannot infringe another registered mark (though he may commit passing off).[19]

Registration of a user is not a pure formality. The Registrar must decide whether an agreement is or is not against the public interest.[20] The principal determinant of this is whether the proprietor continues to retain a measure of control over the use of the mark by the user.[21] If sufficient control remains, the mark can be said to indicate some connection in the course of trade with the registered proprietor.[22] Hence deeming the use to be his is not artificial, but a reflection of reality. The taint of "trafficking in a trade mark" is removed.[23]

17-059   Control may be retained if it is a condition of the licence that the mark will only be used on goods which satisfy the registered proprietor's standards of quality. These standards he may prescribe by reference to the materials to be used, the process of production, requirements of testing, and so forth. A quality control clause is normally needed for registering a user agreement between independent enterprises. In other cases, the element of "control" may be provided in a different way: as where the proprietor is a parent company and the licensee is subsidiary, or where the trade mark licence accompanies a patent licence. Ultimately the decision lies in the registrar's discretion.

While there are provisions allowing the variation or cancellation of a user's registration on a variety of grounds,[24] there is no regular procedure for ensuring in the public interest that the conditions in the agreement which justified the registration are in fact being observed. Accordingly the Mathys Committee doubted the value of the registrar's initial examination.[24a] It is likely in future legislation that registration will be reduced to a formal procedure, giving the user the right to institute infringement proceedings.[25] But equally it ought to remain a ground of objection to the licensed mark that no quality control is being practised. And it might be particularly difficult to show this where an organisation is seeking to see registered trade mark licensing as the legal basis for "merchandising rights" in fictional characters.

---

[17] s.28(2). See "Off!" T.M. [1981] F.S.R. 314 (S.C. Canada).

[18] s.28(3): the user must give the proprietor two months in which to commence action on his own account. The user's power may be excluded by contrary agreement.

[19] See below, § 17-073, n. 75.

[20] s.28(4), (5).

[21] The Act does not say so; but this is the hallmark of the registrar's practice: see next § If no control is exercised, the user is improperly registered and the mark may be open to attack for non-use: "McGregor" T.M. [1979] R.P.C. 36.

[22] See esp. per Graham J., "GE" T.M. [1969] R.P.C. 418 at p. 454; for "trafficking," "Hollie Hobby" T.M., above, § 17-044.

[23] The Registrar is to refuse to register a user agreement which has this quality—s.28(6); it is not defined.

[24] See ss.28(8)–(10), 32.

[24a] See the Report (Cmnd. 5601, (1974)) §§ 169–180.

[25] The proposals in the Draft EEC Trade Mark Regulation are to this effect: see Arts. 16, 17 (5865/88).

(3) Unregistered licences

It would be reasonable to infer from the registered user provisions that **17-060** Parliament intended them to be the sole route by which a trade mark could legitimately be licensed.[26] Certainly the Goschen Committee recommended their introduction in the belief that a licence would otherwise be held a deception on the public, jeopardising the power to enforce the mark and to maintain any registration of it.[27] But the change in attitude which allowed the introduction of "supervised" licensing in 1938 was by the 1960s considered to justify a more general shift. Where the proprietor of a mark retained control over use of the mark by a licensee, there remained a "trade mark connection," whether or not the licence, or indeed the mark itself, was registered. Accordingly it has been held that licensing of this kind was unobjectionable: a company might license the use of its "house-mark" on such conditions to a jointly-owned subsidiary[28]; an American licensor of know-how and designs might permit its British licensee to apply its mark to goods produced by the latter.[29]

Among the earlier decisions disapproving of licensing, the most diffi- **17-061** cult is *Bowden Wire* v. *Bowden Brake*.[30] The House of Lords treated a trade mark licence as inherently deceptive in leading the public either to believe that goods bearing the mark were its proprietor's when they were not, or that the mark had come through use to indicate the licensee, not the proprietor.[31] That case must now be read in light of the Lords' decision in *"GE" Trade Mark*[32]: a mark will be expungeable for subsequent deceptiveness only if its proprietor has been guilty of blameworthy conduct sufficient to render it disentitled to protection in a court of justice.

Possibly the *Bowden* case, if indeed it has any relevance to the law **17-062** under the 1938 Act,[33] supports the following proposition: where the proprietor of a mark permits another to use it without retaining any power to control the products that are to bear the mark, and there are

---

[26] Note not only s.28(2) (above, n. 17), but the provisions restricting the right of a proprietor to apply to register a mark that he is not going himself to use to the cases prescribed in s.29(1)—which include the case where contemporaneously an acceptable user is to be registered as such: for this, and the problem imposed by the new liberality in the matter of unregistered licensing, see above, §§ 17-044—17-045.

[27] See the Report, Cmnd. 4568, §§ 118–121.

[28] *"GE" Trade Mark* [1970] R.P.C. 339 at pp. 372, 392–95 (C.A.). The conclusion reached by the C.A. is not affected by the summary manner in which the H.L. disposed of the point at issue (see [1973] R.P.C. at p. 336). See also *British Petroleum* v. *European Petroleum* [1968] R.P.C. 54.

[29] *"Bostitch" T.M.* [1963] R.P.C. 183; Melville (1966) 29 M.L.R. 375.

[30] (1914) 31 R.P.C. 385.

[31] The breadth of the decision is emphasised by the presence of a number of features which make the circumstances seem less than heinous to the modern reader: the licence was for the period of certain patents also licensed, wire produced by the licensor was incorporated, at least initially, in the brakes that were marked by the licensee, and the two companies had common directors until after termination of the patents and shortly before the instigation of the litigation. *cf.* the grounds on which the registrar considers a user agreement to be registrable: above, § 17-059.

[32] Above, n. 89.

[33] The restrictive scope of the 1905 Act, under which it was decided, should be recalled: see above, § 17-056.

no countervailing explanations to excuse this, the mark will become liable to removal.[34] This might, for instance, be so if both licensor and licensee continued to produce similar goods under the mark without any quality supervision by the former of the latter,[35] or even if the owner made no real effort to enforce a quality control agreement.[36] On the other hand, there are decisions upholding marks in the following circumstances, which in essence were treated as involving no blame: allowing a retailer to use the name of the supplier of goods on other goods during a period when the supplier was prevented from supplying his own[37]; and allowing a British importing agent to use his foreign manufacturer's mark on goods which he himself made in Britain, the intent being to keep the business alive even though imports were prevented by the war.[38] *A fortiori* it might now be said that there is nothing blameworthy in unregistered licensing under conditions of quality control, as in the cases already mentioned,[39]

6. INFRINGEMENT

(1) Statutory proscription

17-063   Section 4(1) of the 1938 Act provides a definition of trade mark infringement that is "crabbed and involved" and of "fulginous obscurity."[40] It begins with a statement of the "exclusive right" to which the registered proprietor is entitled: to use the trade mark in relation to the goods for which it is registered. "Without prejudice to the generality" of this,[41] it proceeds to define two different forms of infringement. The first covers use by others of the mark (or one deceptively similar) as a trade mark. This is the traditionally recognised form of infringement and the only one covered by the registration system before 1938. The second covers certain uses of the mark, not as the defendant's own, but in order to "import a reference" to the registered proprietor or user or their goods. This was an attempt to remedy the supposed deficiencies of the tort of injurious falsehood by preventing comparative advertising and the like, whether true or false, sycophantic or disparaging, if it involved use of a registered mark.

[34] See the treatment of *Bowden* in *Cluett-Peabody* v. *McIntyre* [1958] R.P.C. 335 at p. 357; and for further case-law, see Kerly, §§ 10–41, 13–23, 13–25.
[35] Even so it must be asked whether it does anything useful to remove the mark from the register: on which theme generally see above, § 15-017.
[36] *Sport International Bossum* v. *Hi-Tec Sports* [1988] R.P.C. 329 (C.A.).
[37] *Coles* v. *Need* [1934] A.C. 82; 50 R.P.C. 379 (J.C.) (business name, but the same ought to apply to a registered mark).
[38] *Manus* v. *Fullwood & Bland* [1949] Ch. 208; 66 R.P.C. 71 (C.A.); *cf.* also *Warwick Tyre* v. *New Motor* [1910] 1 Ch. 248; 27 R.P.C. 161.
[39] Above, § 17-054. *cf.* "*Radiation*" T.M. (1930) 47 R.P.C. 37 (use as a house mark by subsidiaries of a parent company applicant).
[40] *Per* Greene M.R. and Mackinnon L.J. respectively, *Bismag* v. *Amblins* (below, n. 90) at 232, 237.
[41] This obscure phrase suggests that there are acts other than those specified which may also constitute infringement—a point which gave Greene M.R. difficulty in the *Bismag* case see below, n. 90, at 233).

These two forms of infringement call for separate treatment. There is a whole series of consequential statutory provisions in sections 4–8 of the Act, which will be mentioned where appropriate.

(2) Use as a trade mark for the infringer's goods

It is infringement for an unauthorised person[42] to appear to be using **17-064** the mark or one deceptively similar, for goods within the registration "as a trade [or service] mark," i.e. to indicate a connection in the course of trade [or business] with the registered proprietor or user.[43] Registration replaces the need at common law for the plaintiff to prove an actual trade reputation. Yet there are a number of points where common law liability is couched in terms of flexible principle, while statutory protection is more strictly limited by definition. So it is advisable, in discussing this form of infringement, to keep comparisons with passing off in mind.

(a) Defendant's goods or services

To reiterate a basic distinction: infringement under this head can occur **17-065** only where the infringer uses the mark for goods or services within the registration. So there is no scope for argument that the public would suppose that a mark owner is extending his trade, if the mark is used on proximate goods for which he has not secured a registration.[44]

Occasionally, there may be a doubt whether or not the defendant's goods fall within the description registered[45]: the issue will probably be resolved upon evidence from the trade in question. A commoner difficulty arises when marked goods are incorporated into some other finished product. In *Spiller's Application*,[46] the House of Lords took the view that a mark stamped on the side of bread must be treated as a mark for the bread and not the flour from which it was made, despite evidence that the latter usage was quite common in the trade. It is not clear in what circumstances the contrary conclusion could be reached. The speeches suggest that this might be so, either when the thing incorporated retains its own identity[47] or when something other than the final article is obviously meant.[48]

(b) Use as a trade mark

Infringement occurs only if the defendant's use of the mark, or **17-066** something nearly resembling it is "as a trade mark." Thus "Treets" for chocolate bars was not infringed when the defendants described their bars as "Treat Size," since they were not using that expression to indicate

[42] s.4(1) refers to use by the registered proprietor or user: but see s.4(3)(a) (below, §§ 17-069—17-072); note also s.68(2B) stating that marks nearly resemble one another if they are so near as to be likely to deceive or cause confusion.
[43] s.68(1), see above, §§ 17-013—17-014. The scope of the registration is, of course, limited by the conditions (such as disclaimers) or limitations in the registration: see s.4(2).
[44] See above, § 17-002.
[45] cf. above, § 17-003, n. 21.
[46] *Spiller's Appln.* (1954) 71 R.P.C. 234 (H.L.).
[47] *Ibid.* at p. 238 (Lords Oaksey and Reid).
[48] *Ibid.* at pp. 238, 240, 252 (Lords Asquith, Cohen and Keith).

a connection in the course of trade.[49] In producing a book entitled "Mothercare/Other Care," a publisher was indicating its content and not creating the impression that it came from the "Mothercare" shop chain.[50]

(c) *Likely confusion*

17-067   The test of whether the defendant's use has been of a mark identical with, or so closely resembling, the registered mark as to be likely to deceive or cause confusion is to an extent an artificial one. What is compared is the defendant's mark in actual use with any reasonable and honest use that could be made of the plaintiff's mark as it appears on the register.[51] The latter's actual use (if any) is irrelevant; whereas in passing-off proceedings it is crucial. Subject to this, the comparison takes account of the same factors in the main as in passing off. The impressions created by the marks in terms both of sight and sound are judged as they would be thought likely to strike customers in the actual trade. How far beyond this a court will go in taking account of the connections arising by way of influence from "the idea of the mark" is not clear. In *"GE" Trade Mark*, for the purpose of deciding likelihood of confusion under section 11, the House of Lords found the monogram could be confusing because "GE" would mean "General Electric" to the public, and hence probably the British company rather than the American.[51a] Provided that this can apply equally to a question of infringement, the way may now be open to rely upon other inferential factors. If so, the repercussions upon other parts of the system deserve consideration. If the words "Blue Paraffin" may be infringed by selling paraffin coloured blue, the evidence establishing that the mark does distinguish the applicant's goods ought to be more convincing than if infringement is confined to confusingly similar words.[52]

(d) *The difference between Part A and Part B marks*

17-068   The definition of infringement for both A and B marks is the same, subject to one qualification: in the case of Part B marks no relief is to be granted against a defendant who shows that his use "is not likely to deceive or cause confusion or to be taken as indicating a connection in the course of trade between the goods" and the registered proprietor or

---

[49] *Mars* v. *Cadbury* [1987] R.P.C. 387: the defendant's use was held to amount only to "association": *sed quaere.* See also *Unidoor* v. *Marks & Spencer* [1988] R.P.C. 275: "Coast to Coast" on a T-shirt probably not a trade mark use.

[50] *Mothercare* v. *Penguin Books* [1988] R.P.C. 113 (C.A.). This lays to rest doubts stemming from *Bismag* v. *Amblins* (below, § 90); for which see Kerly, § 14–05.

[51] *Saville Perfumery* v. *June Perfect* (see below, n. 54); *Electrolux* v. *Electrix* (1954) 71 R.P.C. 23 at p. 31 (C.A.); *British Petroleum* v. *European Petroleum* (1968) R.P.C. 54 at p. 64 (differences of colour in actual use irrelevant).

[51a] See above, n. 28, at 320–322. Formerly the tendency seems to have been to require proof of passing off in such cases: *cf. Hodgson & Simpson* v. *Kynoch* (1898) 15 R.P.C. 465 ("Lion" not infringed by picture of a lion's head); *Duracell* v. *Ever Ready* [1989] F.S.R. 71 (two-colour mark not infringed by monochrome photograph).

[52] *cf. "Blue Paraffin" T.M.* [1977] R.P.C. 473 at p. 500, where Buckley L.J. considered the only liability for selling blue paraffin would (*semble*) be in passing off.

user.[53] Since proof of this (by the plaintiff) forms the very core of establishing infringement, it must be that for Part A marks, likelihood of confusion about trade source is assessed upon a narrower range of considerations. What these are is clearly explained by Greene M.R. in *Saville Perfumery* v. *June Perfect*.[54] "The statutory protection is absolute in the sense that once a mark is shown to offend, the user of it cannot escape by showing that by something outside the actual mark itself he has distinguished his goods from those of the registered proprietor." There the plaintiff's mark (for perfumery) was "June," somewhat dressed up. The defendant company and an associated business had in all honesty used names that included "June" to market hair curlers. They then (less innocently) introduced goods within the registration by statements such as "A 'June' Hair Curler Product" and "*Perfect* 'June' Hair Curler(s) introduce the *Perfect* lipstick." Once it was shown that the use of "June" here was as a trade mark and not to indicate something else (the court was struck by the deployment of quotation marks) the addition of other words or indications, which might serve to undo the deceptive implications, were irrelevant since the mark was in Part A. They would have been relevant to a Part B mark or for passing off. Yet the difference that separates Part B from Part A is significant only in unusual cases. For, at least where explanatory statements are in issue, if the statement is effective to undo any deception, the use of the mark may well be found not to be "use as a trade mark."[55] The distinction may have more importance where features of the overall get-up of the goods differ markedly and consistently.[56]

(e) *Use in relation to goods*
The defendant's use has to be "in relation to" goods within the 17-069 registration. Since for infringements under this head non-physical as well as physical relations are included[57] (*i.e.* use in advertisements, invoices, etc.,[58] as well as on the goods, the packaging and accompanying publicity), most likely ways of deploying a mark as a trade mark are now covered. But still there must be a "printed or other visual representation

---

[53] TMA 1938, s.5(2).
[54] [1941] 58 R.P.C. 147 at 161 (C.A. subsequently upheld, *ibid.*). What matters is the mark as registered, not how the plaintiff uses it (unless there has been insufficient use of the mark in consequence): *Levi-Strauss* v. *Shah* [1985] R.P.C. 371.
[55] Consider, for instance, the statement in *Bentley* v. *Lagonda* (1947) 64 R.P.C. 33: "It is worth reflection that the products of LAGONDA and the designs of W. O. BENTLEY have not always been large cars." The emphasis given to the two car marks was found to be a deliberate attempt to associate the two as trade marks.
[56] See cases such as *Pirie's Applcn.* (above, § 17-033) where an honest concurrent user was allowed to register. *cf.* Beier (1978) 9 I.I.C. 221.
[57] TMA 1938, s.68(2).
[58] See *Hardmuth* v. *Bancroft* (1953) 70 R.P.C. 179 and Kerly §§ 2–220, 14–10, 14–14. *Reuter* v. *Muhlens* (1953) 70 R.P.C. 235 (C.A.) holds the circulation of the mark on envelopes in the U.K. to be infringement even when the circulator is not trading in the goods there but only abroad. It must be doubted whether this was "in the course of trade" (s.4(1)).

of the mark,"[59] a requirement which does not apply to passing off, and which, with the arrival of commercial radio, seems unduly constricted.[60] The use does not have to be a use in trade. Accordingly, where a government health bureau used "Conquest" as a fictional brand in an anti-smoking campaign, thereby in ignorance using a cigarette manufacturer's registered mark consisting of that word, it was liable as an infringer.[61]

(f) Scope of rights

17-070   The registered proprietor or a registered user acting within the permitted use cannot infringe. Equally if either has applied the mark to goods or services or consented at any time to its use, and has not removed or obliterated it, others who deal in those goods—and so also use the trade mark—are not infringers. These principles, made explicit in section 4(3)(a), express the general rule that prior consent and subsequent acquiescence constitute defences.[62] They have particular importance in determining how far British law subscribes to a doctrine of exhaustion that is international in scope. In that context, the sub-section is discussed in the next chapter.[63]

17-071   If conditions are attached to a licence to use a trade mark, it does not follow that breach of them results in infringement. The purpose of protecting trade marks (under this head) is to ensure that they accurately indicate a connection in the course of trade with the registered proprietor or user. So at most it should only be conditions designed to prevent the mark from being used improperly that would, if broken, have this result. Other breaches can at most be actionable as breaches of contract. Thus if goods bearing the British mark are marketed abroad by the British proprietor subject to a ban on export to Britain, the trade mark right cannot be used to stop their entry. Associated with this are a number of issues which will be discussed in the next chapter.[64]

In section 6 the Act specifies five ways in which properly marked goods may not be subsequently treated, if the mark owner or registered user makes it a condition not to do so. If then, the restriction is broken, the acts are deemed infringement. They are: (i) applying the mark after impermissible alteration of the goods as respects their state or condition, get-up or packaging; (ii) altering, partly removing or obliterating the mark; (iii) removing or obliterating the mark without removing other references to the registered proprietor or user; (iv) applying any other trade mark in addition; (v) adding other written material likely to injure the reputation of the mark.[65] But to have the required effect, the

---

[59] TMA 1938, s.68(2). Held, in South Africa, not to cover a mark electronically recorded on video tape: *Esquire Electronics* v. *Roopanand* [1985] R.P.C. 83—an unnecessarily scrupulous interpretation.

[60] Accordingly, the Mathys Committee (Cmnd. 5601, (1974), § 106) recommended that audible use should also be covered.

[61] *Gallaher* v. *Health Education Bureau* [1982] F.S.R. 464—an Irish case.

[62] Above, § 2-032.   [63] Below, §§ 18-001—18-005.

[64] *Ibid.*   [65] TMA 1938, s.6(2).

condition against doing any of these things must be specified in a written contract between proprietor or user and purchaser or owner of the goods.[66] If binding, the condition affects all owners of the goods who have notice of it, except a purchaser who at the time of purchase did not know of it.[67]

The corollary of this section must be that, in the absence of an advance **17-072** contractual provision, none of these acts would constitute infringement. There is certainly no blanket embargo in British trade mark law upon repackaging and re-marking the "genuine" goods, such as is said by the EC Court of Justice to be part of the "essence" of the trade mark right when it is given in another national law.[68] If in the absence of a binding condition the goods were repackaged, and in the course of doing so they were adulterated, or were re-marked so as to indicate a higher or better quality, this would amount to passing off.[69] It would be for the mark owner to prove this and advocates of a wider right claim that he should not be put to this difficulty. But there is a disadvantage: to restrict the enterprise of middlemen whose re-marking is innocent of all deception may impose discernible restrictions on competition in the course of marketing. Hence the cautious compromise in section 6.[70]

(g) *Prior or concurrent entitlement*

The Trade Marks Act specifies a number of defences to infringement, **17-073** which are discussed under this and the next head. Each turns upon considerations that also arise upon applications to register, so some reference back is called for.[71]

We have already noted the principles that apply when two independent traders lay claim to identical or confusingly similar marks for the same goods or description of goods. If A begins continuous use before B uses or registers, A has a prior right which, *inter alia*, affords him a defence against infringement proceedings by B.[72] If he is not in so impregnable a position, he can seek protection only by applying to be registered as an honest concurrent user: and that requires consideration not only of the applicant's honesty but of the extent of his use and the degree of likely confusion.[73] If he does succeed, he then has an exclusive right on an equal footing with B.[74] If each is registered for the same goods, neither can sue

---

[66] s.6(1). It is only use of the mark in physical relation to the goods that falls within s.6: see s.6(3).

[67] As to sufficiency of notice, *cf.* cases on "limited" patent licensing, above § 6-011, n. 48.

[68] *Hoffman-LaRoche* v. *Centrafarm* (discussed below, § 18-010, n. 42). Even so, the court qualified this aspect of "essence."

[69] See, *e.g. Spalding* v. *Gamage* (above, § 16-007, n. 31).

[70] The Mathys Committee (Cmnd. 5601, 1974, § 87) favoured retaining s.6 as it stands, except that written notice should suffice without proof of contract.

[71] See above, § 17-035.

[72] TMA 1938, s.7.

[73] See above, §§ 17-032—17-034. In an appropriate case, the court may suspend B's injunction against infringement to enable A to pursue such an application: see, *e.g. Electrolux* v. *Electrix* (above, § 17-051, n. 59; and for the unfortunate consequences, § 17-034, n. 78); *cf. Berlei* v. *Bali* [1970] R.P.C. 469.

[74] TMA 1938, s.4(4).

the other for infringement, but only for such passing off as can be proved.[75] If they are registered for different goods (though of the same description), neither person can use his mark to trade in the other's goods without infringing.

(h) *Bona fide use of certain words*

17-074   Whether a word or device is used by the defendant to infringement proceedings "as a trade mark" is judged objectively: the question is whether his use is likely to be so understood.[76] Unless it is there can be no infringement of the kind under discussion. The Act provides that, even if there would be infringement by this test, it is still permissible for a person to make bona fide use of his own name or that of his place of business (or the name or place of business of any predecessor) or to use any bona fide description of the character or quality of the goods.[77] These are all cases where traders are considered likely to have a genuine reason for wanting to use particular words; hence the difficulty of showing sufficient distinctiveness to secure registration.

The bona fides on which these defences turn is a subjective concept: a defendant who believes that there is no likelihood of confusion may rely on them. What he must establish is that he acted "without any intention to deceive anybody or without any intention to make use of the goodwill which has been acquired by another trader."[78]

Once again, the role of passing off needs to be considered. A person who is honestly using his own name as a mark for goods, may still be liable for passing-off, even though he has a defence against infringement of a registered trade mark consisting of the word which is the crux of the misrepresentation.[79]

(i) *Other defences*

17-075   If the plaintiff's trade mark is deceptive or has been used in the course of deceptive trade, his action may be barred. The considerable amount of early case-law on the subject suggests that, if there is some explanation or partial excuse for the deception, it may be disregarded—particularly if it can be characterised as "collateral" to the mark itself. If it is intentional and systematic, the action will fail. Thus where a registered proprietor falsely advertised his medicament "Bile Beans" as containing an Australian herb discovered by a fictitious scientist, he failed against another trader using "Bile Beans," despite the "collateral" character of the misrepresentations.[80]

---

[75] TMA 1938, s.2. If passing off is likely, any concurrent registration will be subject to conditions designed to avoid it.

[76] For an example, see the *Bentley* case, above, n. 55.

[77] TMA 1938, s.8; see Kerly, § 15–30/33. It is not clear whether "place of business" extends beyond particular address to the geographical locality generally.

[78] Danckwerts J., *Baume* v. *Moore* [1957] R.P.C. 459 at 463; and on appeal see Romer L.J. [1958] R.P.C. 226 at 235, stressing that "there is no such thing . . . as constructive dishonesty."

[79] *Parker-Knoll* v. *Knoll International* [1962] R.P.C. 265 (H.L.); *cf.* above § 16-009; and *Parker-Knoll* v. *Knoll Overseas* [1985] F.S.R. 349.

[80] *Bile Bean Mfg.* v. *Davidson* (1906) 23 R.P.C. 725; *cf., e.g. Ford* v. *Foster* (1872) L.R. 7 Ch. 611; and see generally Kerly, §§ 15–48/56.

In addition, the general defences of consent, acquiescence, estoppel and delay may be applicable when the defendant's use has not been objected to over a long period.[81]

(3) Infringement by importing a reference

The second form of infringement specified by section 4(1)[82] is this: using **17-076** the mark or one deceptively similar in trade, "in relation to any goods [or services] for which it is registered,"[83] so as to appear to be importing a reference to some person having the right, as proprietor or as registered user to use the trade [or service] mark or to goods with which such a person as aforesaid is connected in the course of trade [or business]. To fall within this, however, the use must be upon the goods or in physical relation to them [or where the service is provided] or in an advertisement issued to the public—a restriction which excludes use in the private soliciting of orders and in invoices accompanying goods.[84] It also seems that the mark in question must be registered in Part A. When a defendant "imports a reference" he will not be saying that there is a trade connection between his own goods and the registered proprietor (or user). If so, no relief for infringement of a Part B mark can be secured against him.[85]

This addition was first introduced in 1937,[86] in order to render actionable sales techniques which depended upon drawing comparison with well-known branded goods. In 1934 the House of Lords had decided that to advertise a preparation as "A substitute for 'Yeastvite' " (but cheaper) did not infringe the "Yeastvite" mark[87]: there was no attempt to say that spurious goods were "Yeastvite." This then should be taken as the paradigm case of "importing a reference." Although the extended definition of infringement now contained in section 4 has proved antipathetic to some judges,[88] the "Yeastvite" case itself ought today to be decided the other way.[89] The difficulty lies in knowing what

---

[81] See above, § 2-036.

[82] Certification marks are similarly treated: see s.37(3)(b). The only part of the statutory defence in s.8 that is here relevant (use of description of character or quality of the alleged infringer's goods) is excluded: see s.8(b).

[83] For this phrase, see below, n. 95.

[84] s.4(1)(b). In Bismag v. Amblins (below, n. 90) Lord Greene M.R. considered that the "exclusive right" with which s.4(1) starts may cover importing a reference in other circumstances: but that would render the limits specified in s.4(1)(b) purposeless: see above, n. 41, and Kerly, § 14–05.

[85] s.5(2), as interpreted in Broad v. Graham (No. 1) [1969] R.P.C. 286; and Montana Wines v. Villa Maria Wines [1985] R.P.C. 412 (N.Z.C.A.) see Kerly, § 14–40.

[86] On the recommendation of the Goschen Committee (Cmnd. 4568 (1934), §§ 184–185). For a sardonic view of the politics, see the defendant's advertising in Bismag v. Amblins (below, n. 90).

[87] Irving's Yeastvite v. Horsenail (1934) 51 R.P.C. 110.

[88] Mackinnon L.J., Bismag v. Amblins (below, n. 90), whose judgment is more vituperative than analytical, and Simonds J. at first instance. Some rather inconclusive support for the approach of these judgments is to be found in Aristoc v. Rysta (1945) 62 R.P.C. 65 at pp. 77, 79, 85. (But the case concerned registrability; see above, § 17-013, n. 68).

[89] So equally other methods of indicating similarity: "Alligator pattern" (see Young v. Grierson Oldham (1924) 41 R.P.C. 549), "as Broadstel" (cf. Broad v. Graham, above, n. 85); comparative chart of hair dye colours (cf. Clairol v. Thomas (1968) 55 C.P.R. 176 (Ex.Ct., Canada)).

else amounts to "importing a reference." Consider the following examples, "Bongo" being a Part A mark registered for the relevant goods in
all of them:

17-077

(i) A advertises his "Mulga" photographic films as better than
"Bongo" films, to which statement he may or may not add true or
false corroborative details. All such comparisons would seem
equally to "import a reference."[89a]

(ii) A advertises that he has genuine "Bongo" films for sale and also
his own "Mulga" films and he adds a comparative price chart
which suggests that "Mulga" films are the same quality but
cheaper. Such an elaboration on the "Yeastvite" formula was
tested in *Bismag* v. *Amblins*,[90] where a majority of the Court of
Appeal held that one use of the registered mark was to make a
comparison of value in selling the goods which did not bear the
mark and that this was infringement by importing a reference.

(iii) Piles of "Bongo" and "Mulga" films are placed side by side with
the price for each prominently displayed. In the *Bismag* case,
Greene M.R. appeared to regard this as not amounting to infringement.[91] So long as the customer is not specifically told (truthfully
or otherwise) that the quality of the two is the same, or that
"Mulga" films are better, the cross-reference is not sufficiently
"imported."

(iv) A advertises his films as "Made by the former suppliers of 'Bongo'
films"—a true statement, making capital out of a previous business connection. This also infringes.[92] It has been held[93] that there
is no infringement if the former connection is instead indicated by
referring to a business name containing the trade mark ("Made by
the former suppliers to Bongo Films Ltd."). But this has been
doubted[94]: for section 4(1)(b) explicitly states that the reference
may be to the registered proprietor or user, as well as his goods or
services.

(v) A advertises his "Mulga" films as "Suitable for use in 'Bongo'
cameras." It may be that, if "Bongo" is registered by B for
cameras, there is still infringement within section 4(1)(b) even
though the purpose is to relate the mark to another type of
goods.[95] Certainly this seems the intention of the draftsman, since
he provided a defence apparently upon this assumption: a trader is
allowed to show that his goods are adapted to form part of, or be

---

[89a] Cf. *News Group* v. *Mirror Group* [1989] F.S.R. 126—advertising for *Daily Mirror*
infringed *"The Sun"* trade mark by a comparison suggesting that *The Sun* always said
"Yes, Prime Minister," while *The Mirror* said "No."

[90] (1940) 57 R.P.C. 209; see also *Inde Coope* v. *Paine* [1983] R.P.C. 326.

[91] *Ibid.*, at p. 235.

[92] *British Northrop* v. *Texteam* [1974] R.P.C. 57 at pp. 76–79.

[93] *Pompadour Laboratories* v. *Frazer* [1966] R.P.C. 7; *Harrods* v. *Schwartz-Sackin* [1986]
F.S.R. 490.

[94] See Kerly, § 14–27; and *cf.* *"Autodrome"* T.M. [1969] R.P.C. 564.

[95] This is so if the defendant's use of the mark "in relation to any goods in respect of which
it is registered" means, in this context, his reference to the registered proprietor's or
user's goods and not his own: see above, n. 85.

accessory to, other goods by making a "reasonably necessary" reference to another's trade mark.[96] If, then, the defendant's purpose is not to state that the one article may be an accessory to or part of another, but to say, for instance, that they may be used together, the statutory defence may well not apply.[97]

[96] s.4(3)(b).
[97] See Kerly, § 14–34. Could "the Rolls-Royce of beers" possibly infringe "Rolls-Royce" for cars? cf. also Rolls-Royce v. Zanelli [1979] R.P.C. 178.

CHAPTER 18

TRADE MARKS AND THE EEC

1. NATIONAL LAW AND THE TREATY OF ROME

(1) Trade marks in international trade

18-001   Like other rights discussed in this book, trade marks have been used as a means of dividing up the national markets for the similar goods of connected enterprises. But the legal techniques have been more complicated, because trade marks fulfill a different function from intellectual property in a strict sense. At least in many states, the owner of a trade mark has not been able to use his rights to repel the importation of similar goods which he has originally marketed elsewhere. For this there is an obvious reason: the mark does not cease accurately to indicate that the goods originate from him merely because they cross a national frontier. Certainly in British law this general principle is clear.[1]

If the trade mark was placed in different legal hands,[2] the national owner in the country of import could say that the mark had not been applied in order to indicate a connection with him, but rather with the owner in the country of first marketing. But if the legal entities were in fact economically connected—because each was owned by a common parent company, or they were both licensees or distribution agents with a common source—to say so might seem no more than a pretext for dividing markets. Accordingly in some European countries, the courts have refused to allow the local trade mark owner in such cases to preclude parallel imports of "connected" goods.[3]

18-002   In the United Kingdom, where the question has to be worked out in relation both to common law and to statutory rights, the Court of Appeal has decided part of the issue in the same sense.[4] The Revlon group of companies operated in Europe through two subsidiaries, one of which was the owner and the other the registered user of the British mark "Revlon Flex" for (*inter alia*) shampoo.[5] When the parent company

---

[1] At common law: *Champagne Heidsieck* v. *Buxton* (above, § 16-021). For registered marks: TMA 1938, s.4(3)(*a*) (above, § 17-070).

[2] A registration system makes it much simpler to ensure that the rights are in legally distinct hands. What follows will deal primarily with registered marks.

[3] See especially *Cinzano* v. *Java Kaffeegeschäfte* [1974] 2 C.M.L.R. 21 (West German Supreme Court).

[4] TMA 1938, s.4(3)(*a*).

[5] [1980] F.S.R. 85. The proceedings were interlocutory but the Court addressed itself to the substantive issues of law in light of the evidence, under the rubric, is there a serious question to be tried? Followed in *Winthrop Products* v. *Sun Ocean* [1988] F.S.R. 439 (H.C. Malaya); and in *Bailey* v. *Boccaccio* [1986] 4 N.S.W.L.R. 701, where, however, artistic copyright in the label was held to have been infringed by importation.

distributed "Revlon Flex" shampoo in the United States and a parallel importer brought it into Britain for sale, the European subsidiaries were unable to establish that the sales amounted either to passing off or infringement of the registered mark. The reputation relevant to passing off was that built up by the multi-national group, the British public being unaware of which member company made or produced the goods and where they were manufactured. Accordingly there was no misrepresentation in selling shampoo originally put out by the American parent.[6]

As far as concerns the registered mark, there is no infringement where the British proprietor or user has applied the mark to the goods, or has at any time consented to its use.[7] In the view of Buckley and Bridge L.JJ. the European subsidiaries could not be treated as having actually applied the mark to the goods in question,[8] but they must be taken to have consented to its use in relation to them.[9] This implication was spelled out of two factors: the parent company's legal power to impose its will upon all subsidiaries, and the deployment of the mark as a house mark for the whole group.

The Revlon case however leaves a number of questions unsettled. In particular three:

(a) Marketing by exclusive distributor; production by legally independent licensee

Since the Revlon judgments rely partly upon the power of parent over 18-003 subsidiary, the position may differ where the plaintiff is (legally speaking) independent of the distributor of the goods abroad. If a local exclusive distributor has been made responsible for marketing in Britain, his only chance of sustaining a case of passing off against parallel imports of his manufacturer's goods might arise if he had consistently built the mark up as associated entirely with him.[10] Likewise, unless this were so, any registered rights that he has acquired might well be open to the objection that he had "consented" to the marking, or possibly that he was not the proper proprietor.[11]

If the British operation were organised through a licensed manufacturer, he might stand in better case.[12] But still he might need substantial evidence that the British public associated the goods with him rather than with a transnational network of licensees, whose existence and linkages went unappreciated by consumers. Again, if the latter is the realistic picture, an assertion of registered rights might be met by a finding of "consent" to the use of the mark.[13]

[6] Ibid. at 102–104, 112–113.
[7] TMA 1938, s.4(3)(a).
[8] Above, n. 5 at 107. Templeman L.J., however, was prepared to go so far: at pp. 115–116.
[9] Ibid. at 107–108.
[10] cf. the facts of a case such as Re Diehl's T.M. (above, § 16-014, n. 68).
[11] This might be taken under s.11 or s.17(1), but is speculative.
[12] But if the licensor originally operated in Britain himself, an assignment of his rights could be open to attack: see above, § 17-057.
[13] In particular this might be spelled out of arrangements by which the licensor retained power to control the quality of products put out under the mark. cf. the Cinzano decision (above, n. 3) where a manufacturing licensee's product was treated in the same way as a subsidiary's.

(b) *Export embargo*

18-004   Buckley L.J. emphasised in *Revlon* that the parent company's disposal of the goods in the United States had left it unable to object to their subsequent export to the United Kingdom (or anywhere else); and, as part of their "consent" to use of the registered mark, the European subsidiaries were also bound by this.[14] If the parent had explicitly marked the goods, "Not for Export," the subsidiaries might have enforced their registered rights. While it is not clear why this automatically should make a difference, it has been held in subsequent cases that where an export prohibition existed to sustain differences in the quality of products on the two markets, section 4(3)(a) did not apply.[15] Where "Colgate" toothpaste manufactured by a Brazilian subsidiary of Colgate-Palmolive was sold on condition that it would be exported only to Nigeria, and it was of lower quality than any British "Colgate" toothpaste, it infringed the British trade mark to import it here.[15a] This, it seems, was because the act of marking was deemed to be an application of the Brazilian, not the British, mark. Since there was nothing in the mark to indicate this, the distinction was entirely metaphysical and thus of questionable merit in such a context.

At a more technical level, there is the question, what is meant by the parent company having a right to object to export? This would in many cases depend upon the contract, tort or trade mark law of the state in which first distribution takes place.[16] But if the only right is contractual, is it enough that only the first purchaser or other recipient from the manufacturer is bound? In *Revlon* itself, the imported goods may have been given to a charity upon condition that they might not re-sell them.[17] Even if this were so, the Court of Appeal treated it as not relevant to the issue before it but as giving rise at most to some action by the parent against those implicated in the breach of condition. Why should a "No Export" condition give rise to different consequences?

(c) *Differences in quality*

18-005   In the *Revlon* case, the imports were anti-dandruff shampoo, whereas the local products were not. But Buckley L.J. found that no "reasonably perspicaceous member of the public" would be misled about this difference, despite use of the same mark, because the difference was clearly indicated.[18] Had the marketing been similar enough to induce a mistake about different classes or qualities of goods, there would remain scope for a finding of passing off as a quality. More recent decisions have

---

[14] Above, n. 5 at 106.
[15] *Castrol* v. *Automotive Oil* [1983] R.P.C. 315; *Colgate-Palmolive* v. *Markwell* [1988] R.P.C. 283.
[15a] *Colgate-Palmolive* v. *Markwell* (1989, C.A., to be reported).
[16] Under equivalent British law, breach of the stipulation would not be an infringement of the trade mark (unless there was also a breach of TMA 1938, s.6); for which, see above, §§ 17-071—17-072).
[17] As the proceedings were interlocutory, the matter was not investigated.
[18] Above, n. 5, at 104; see also at 113.

refused to take notice of the fact that it is through the plaintiffs' choice of labelling that the confusion comes about.[19]

To a substantial degree, the *Revlon* decision subjects British trade mark law to the principle of "international exhaustion." We shall see in the next section how rules of EEC law have been used to insist upon the same result, in trade between Member States. But this overriding effect is necessary only to the extent that the national trade mark law of a state into which goods are being imported debars their entry. In Britain, as in some other EEC countries, this is often not the case where the goods are "connected" with the trade-mark owner. In these countries, community doctrine has an additional effect only in certain borderland cases.

2. IMPACT OF EEC LAW

Where EEC authorities have been faced with attempts to use the division **18-006** of trade mark rights as a barrier in Common Market trade they have taken a rigorous attitude.[20] In *Consten and Grundig* v. *Commission*,[21] the first case to hold that the organisation of a net of exclusive distributors could offend Article 85,[22] the EEC Court of Justice condemned as part of that arrangement the registration by each distributor in his own country of the mark "Gint."[23] This had been added to the goods in order to render the market division water-tight.[24]

In other circumstances there might be no agreement caught by Article 85, either because the entities were too closely connected[25] or because

[19] *Wilkinson Sword* v. *Cripps & Lee* [1982] F.S.R. 16, *Colgate & Palmolive* v. *Markwell* (above, n. 15a); and note the rather strange *Yardley* v. *Higson* [1984] F.S.R. 304 (C.A.). But *cf. Champagne Heidsieck* v. *Buxton*, above, § 16-022, n. 2. Since the Court stresses the function of registered marks to be to indicate origin (*ibid.* at 106), it would presumably be even more difficult to make out a case on registered rights. *cf.* the *Cinzano* decision (above, n. 3) where the difference in vermouths produced for different national tastes was held something which the associated companies could make plain if they wished.

[20] At one stage there was some tendency to disparage the value of trade marks, at least in comparison with the intellectual property rights: see especially Dutheillet de Lamothe Adv.-Gen., *Sirena* v. *Eda* (below, n. 55) at (C.M.L.R.) 264; "the interests which patent legislation is intended to protect are economically and humanely more respectable than those protected by trade marks."

[21] [1966] E.C.R. 299; [1966] C.M.L.R. 418.

[22] Much of industry had previously supposed that the competition policy was concerned only with inter-brand competition, and that restrictions amongst those marketing a single product could only be regarded as strengthening that form of competition.

[23] To have assigned "Grundig," the mark that was significant to customers, could have provoked the objection that it was well-known as the manufacturer's mark and could not properly signify the distributor.

[24] As was shown by the term requiring assignment to Grundig on termination of the distribution agreement.

[25] In a parent-subsidiary group, agreements or practices which "have the aim of establishing an internal distribution of tasks between the undertakings" are not regarded as having anti-competitive effects, because the control of the parent eliminates any prospect of competition: *Centrafarm* v. *Sterling Drug* (above, § 7-042, n. 60), Judgment § 41). But an agreement to distribute trade marks in a way that will exclude the operations of a parallel importer may be concerned with something different. This could be significant for imports from outside the EEC: see below, §§ 18-011—18-012.

they were not connected at all.[26] Then Articles 30–36[27] were brought into play. Since these in many respects have a more categorical effect they may be examined first.

(1) Free movement of goods

18-007　　The Court of Justice has defined the "specific subject-matter" of trade mark rights thus: it is "the guarantee that the owner of the trade mark has the exclusive right to use that trade mark, for the purpose of putting products protected by the trade mark into circulation for the first time, and is therefore intended to protect him against competitors wishing to take advantage of [its] status and reputation . . . by selling products illegally bearing [it]."[28] Accordingly to use a mark to divide up national markets for goods of the one organisation is a mere "exercise" of them. This cannot be permitted when it prevents the importation of goods into one Member State from another. The contentious issue is, in which cases are the marked goods to be treated as the "same?" In *Centrafarm* v. *Winthrop* the Court said that the holder of the mark in one EEC state may not prevent the importation of goods from another Member State if they were marketed there by him or "with his consent."[29] But in that case, the trade mark "Negram" belonged to different marketing subsidiaries in the countries of export (United Kingdom) and import (Netherlands). It seems that any nice conception of "consent" is not here in order. In all likelihood there is "consent" whenever there is some link between the two mark-owners, whether that link is "legal, financial, technical or economic."[30]

18-008　　This assumption seems safe because the court has insisted on applying the same overriding principle even to a case where no such link existed. *Van Zuylen Frères* v. *Hag*[31] concerned the European fortunes of the well-known mark "Hag" for decaffeinated coffee. Originally acquired in various European states by the German Hag company, the mark for Belgium and Luxembourg later was assigned by that company to its Belgian subsidiary. After the Hitler war, however, the Belgian government sold the Belgian business (including its trade mark) to Belgian owners as an act of sequestration by way of war reparation. Thereafter there was no connection of any kind between the Belgian and German Hag enterprises: within the Common Market these separate concerns had exclusive trade mark rights in different countries.[32] The Court of Justice held that it would contravene the free movement of goods doctrine for

---

[26] As in *Van Zuylen* v. *Hag* (below, n. 31).

[27] For the distinction between the free flow of goods doctrine embodied in these Articles and the competition policy of Arts. 85 *et seq.*, see above §§ 1-023—1-027.

[28] *Centrafarm* v. *Winthrop* [1974] E.C.R. 1183; [1974] 2 C.M.L.R. 480 Judgment § 8 (the trade mark counterpart of the *Sterling Drug* case, above, § 7-042, n. 60.

[29] *Ibid.* § 10.

[30] This encompassing phrase entered the jurisprudence of the court in a negative sense in the *Hag* case (below, n. 31).

[31] [1974] E.C.R. 731; [1974] 2 C.M.L.R. 127.

[32] The particular value of the mark, deriving doubtless from the sensibilities of the consuming public towards such a commodity, was shown by German Hag's unsuccessful attempt first to penetrate the Belgian market under the mark, "Decofa."

the owner of the Belgian mark to use it to stop the importation of German Hag's goods either by a parallel importer who had bought the goods legitimately in Germany or by German Hag itself. No question of consent to first marketing arose: it was enough that the marks had "the same origin."[33] The court swept aside the objection that this result would leave the consumer not knowing which enterprise was the source of particular products: "While . . . the indication of the origin of a trade-marked product is useful, informing consumers thereon can be done by means other than those which would affect the free circulation of goods."[34]

The decision aroused loud protest.[35] At one and the same time, it could be said to show cavalier disregard for the way in which the public relies on such trade marks—to get the same goods as before—and a gross disrespect for the private value derived from a successfully promoted mark. Certainly the idea that some kind of notification could be devised to disabuse customers of their confusion seemed to postulate a public already aware of the difference between the sources, or at least one prepared to digest complex explanations of the facts.[36] The Treaty of Rome undoubtedly obliges the court to balance the value of trade marks against the advantages to consumers of direct competition through the free circulation of products.[37] The court may have believed that the latter benefit could be procured without serious prejudice, and that the two parties could safely be left to differentiate the overall get-up of their products by voluntary action. But why should the newcomer want to engage in this sort of distinguishing? Why should the prior owner be obliged to take action to throw off the association?[38]

The same or similar trade marks may be held by different enterprises **18-009** in different Common Market countries in three circumstances:

(i) where they shared a common origin, but ownership was split up by voluntary assignment; this may have been done either in pursuit of an exclusive distribution system or for some quite different motive, such as realising the best price when its owner wanted or was obliged to sell up.

[33] Judgment, § 12.
[34] Judgment, § 14.
[35] See, e.g. Ladas (1974) 5 I.I.C. 302; Mann (1975) 24 I.C.L.Q. 31; Mak (1975) 6 I.I.C. 29; Waelbroeck (1976) 21 Antitrust Bull. 99; Bellamy and Child, § 9–25/38; cf. Jacobs (1975) 24 I.C.L.Q. 643; Johannes and Wright (1976) 1 Eur. L.R. 230.
[36] This aspect of the decision has sparked considerable discussion of the possibility of undoing potential confusion by "distinguishing additions": for a review, see Beier (1978) 9 I.I.C. 221. There may be circumstances—particularly when it is in any case uncertain how far there will be confusion—for dealing with the matter by requiring such additions: see the British practice on concurrent use (above, § 17-032) and the remarks of the German Supreme Court in the *Terranova* case (1978) 9 I.I.C. 52.
[37] See Ullrich (1975) GRUR Int. 291.
[38] The entire get-up of the two "Hag" packets was apparently the same. To the extent that it is possible under the law of a particular jurisdiction to sue for unfair competition or passing off upon proof of deception in the light of the plaintiff's trade reputation, the *Hag* rule might be distinguished: see Cornish (1975) 38 M.L.R. 329.

(ii) where the marks shared a common origin but they passed into commercially unconnected hands as the result of government intervention—*Hag* was a relatively rare but by no means unique case.

(iii) where the marks were at all times owned and developed by entirely separate enterprises.

For better, for worse, the first two cases are subject to the principle in the *Hag* case.[39] Following the hostile reception accorded to that decision, the Court of Justice held that it did not apply to the third case. Under German trade mark law, the owner of the well-known mark "Terranova," registered for certain building materials, was held entitled to prevent a British firm from using or registering its mark "Terrapin" for prefabricated buildings; and nothing in Articles 30–36 overrode this.[40] The Court could offer no convincing explanation of why this third case should differ from the second,[41] but there it drew the line. The policy of free circulation is not so strong that a bona fide mark owner in one part of the market can use it in another part where a separate enterprise already has conflicting rights: he must instead build up his trade with a new mark.

18-010   Original manufacturers have found obstacles to strew in the way of parallel importers, as two recent decisions demonstrate. Both concern the export of drugs from a cheap market (United Kingdom) to an expensive one (Germany, Netherlands). In the first,[42] the pills—marked "Roche Valium"—were originally sold in lots of 100 or 250. For commercial reasons the parallel importer needed to re-package them in lots of 1000; this it did, relabelling them with the original marks and an indication that it was the marketer. In the second case,[43] a drug company marketed what was essentially the same tranquilliser as "Serenid D" in Britain and as "Seresta" in the Netherlands; there was however some difference in taste. The same parallel importer re-packaged the British product as "Seresta" and sold it in the Netherlands, again indicating that it was the marketer. In each case, the new affixation of the trade mark, albeit to the genuine goods, would be an infringement according to national law.[44]

[39] The first case falls *a fortiori* under Arts. 30–36; see the discussion by Warner Adv.-Gen. in the *EMI* case ([1976] 2 C.M.L.R. at pp. 260–261) of the *Sirena* decision (below, n. 55).

[40] [1976] E.C.R. 1039; [1976] 2 C.M.L.R. 482.

[41] *cf.* Judgment § 6 where the guarantee to consumers in *Hag* is said to have been "already undermined by the subdivision of the original right."

[42] *Hoffman-La Roche* v. *Centrafarm* [1978] E.C.R. 1139; [1979] 3 C.M.L.R. 217; *cf. Boots* v. *Centrafarm* [1979] F.S.R. 613 (Netherlands H.C.).; *Hoffman-La Roche* v. *Centrafarm* [1984] 2 C.M.L.R. 561 (German S.C.).

[43] *American Home Products* v. *Centrafarm* [1978] E.C.R. 1823; [1979] 1 C.M.L.R. 326. For an interesting consequence, see *Septrin* T.M. [1987] R.P.C. 220: in deciding whether to grant a product licence to a parallel importer from another Member State, under the Medicines Act 1968, the DHSS must have regard to whether a necessary re-marking of the product for the British market would be permissible within the *American Home Products* case (see text at n. 50); if on the other hand, this would amount to infringement, the licence should be refused.

[44] How far this would have been true, in the first case, in other states of the Community is the subject of argument. For the plaintiff's expert's view see Beier, [1979] 10 I.I.C. 20; but *cf.* Capotorti, Adv.-Gen., [1979] E.C.R. at 1175 *et seq.* And for the limited power to restrain repackaging in U.K. law, above, §§ 17-071—17-072.

The Court of Justice was asked whether giving effect to the rights would nevertheless conflict with the free movement of goods policy.

It was disposed to accept that "the essential function of the trade mark ... is to guarantee the identity of the origin of the trade marked product to the consumer ... , by enabling him without any possibility of confusion to distinguish that product from products which have another origin"[45]; moreover, "the guarantee of origin would in fact be jeopardised if it were permissible for a third party to affix the mark to the product, even to an original product."[46]

So much could perhaps be treated as "essence" rather than "exercise,"[47] because a new doctrinal qualification was to be introduced: even if the infringement goes to an essential aspect of the mark it has still to be asked whether the rights are not being used as a "disguised restriction in trade."[48] And in answer the court showed itself adept in supplying pragmatic solutions that would do something to lift what would otherwise be relatively simple barriers to parallel imports. In the case of the increased pack size, it indicated that national rights ought not to be available against re-marking that adequately guaranteed no interference with the goods in their original condition: for instance where an inner package was not interfered with[49]; or where a public authority supervised the re-packing.[50] In the case of the different marks, the court made the issue turn on the intent of the mark owner: it was left to the national court to judge whether the purpose of the different names was to divide the Common Market artificially into parts.[51]

(2) Competition Rules

The considerable scope given to Articles 30–36 leaves a relatively **18-011** minor role, in the field of trade marks, for Articles 85 and 86. Still it should be remembered that a division of markets by means of an agreement or concerted practice involving the use of trade mark rights remains unlawful under Article 85 and this provides the Commission with a jurisdiction to intervene and, if necessary, to impose sanctions on the parties.[52] There is, moreover, one circumstance in which the competition policy may have a wider ambit. Article 30 relates only to the

---

[45] *Hoffman-La Roche* case (above, n. 42), § 7; and see *Pfizer* v. *Eurim-Pharm* [1982] 1 C.M.L.R. 406 §§ 7, 8. This clearly reflects the line of theorising about the legal function of trade marks that is mentioned above, § 15-017.

[46] *American Home Products* case (above, n. 43), § 14.

[47] In general attitude, the Court seems now to be at a considerable distance from its *Hag* decision.

[48] *i.e.* the exemption in the first sentence of Art. 36 may always be abnegated by this consideration found in the second sentence: see above, § 1-024.

[49] This was the situation in the *Eurim-Pharm* case (above, n. 45).

[50] Not content with this quasi-legislative exercise in compromise, the court also indicated that the re-packager must notify the trade mark owner in advance of his intention. The inspiration for this came from Danish case-law: see *Hoffman-La Roche* case [1979] E.C.R. at 1175–1176 (above, n. 42).

[51] See *American Home Products* case (above, n. 43), § 23.

[52] For examples, see *Advocaat "Zwarte Kip"* [1974] 2 C.M.L.R. D79; *Tepea* v. *EC Commission* [1978] E.C.R. 1391; *Toltecs and Dorcet T.Ms.* [1983] 1 C.M.L.R. 412; *Sport International Bossum* v. *Hi-Tec Sports* [1988] R.P.C. 329 (C.A.).

movement of goods between Member States: trade mark rights that have
been divided between the Common Market and external territories may
be used by the EEC owner to exclude imports from outside the
community without offending that Article.[53] But if the split is the result of
an agreement to keep out of the Community as a whole goods which
would otherwise enter it in competition, Article 85 may be transgressed.[54]

18-012   This brings us to the following difficulty: a splitting up of national
trade marks creates a division of markets that may need no further
consultation or collaboration to maintain. A trade mark assignment may
itself be completely carried out and yet continue to have anti-competitive
effects for an undefined term. It appeared that, by its elliptical decision in
Sirena v. *Eda*,[55] the Court of Justice was saying that if an assignment
made long before the institution of the EEC originally divided markets, it
must be considered as continuing to do so. This was attacked essentially
for its unfairness in rendering automatically and continuously unlawful
an agreement that in its own time could not have been objected to.[56]
Subsequent decisions, however, have indicated that, for there to be
breach of Article 85, the behaviour of the persons concerned after
execution or termination of the agreement must show "the existence of
elements of a concerted practice and of co-ordination peculiar to the
agreement and producing the same result. . . . "[57] In the Court's view, the
mere assertion of national trade mark rights is not enough to show this.
However, it is relevant to consider whether the outside party is in a
position to use other marks (changing those on his products, if necessary)
in order to enter the Common Market[58]; so that (presumably) if a
successful trade mark stands as a barrier to the entry of others,[59] slight
evidence of concerted intent to use its division to keep an outsider off the
entire market may be enough to show an infringement of Article 85.[60]

3. THE FUTURE OF REGISTERED TRADE MARKS

(1) Mathys Committee Report

18-013   Presented in 1974, this Report[61] was above all a firm endorsement of
the existing structure of British trade mark law and practice. Virtually no
comparisons with other systems were made, save by implication. For
instance, on the question of the examination before registration, a

[53] *EMI* v. *CBS* [1976] E.C.R. 811; [1976] 2 C.M.L.R. 235.
[54] *Ibid.*
[55] [1971] E.C.R. 69; [1971] C.M.L.R. 260; see Ullrich (1972) 3 I.I.C. 193; *cf.* Ladas (1972) 11 Ind. Prop. 208.
[56] And the Treaty of Rome does not have retroactive effect.
[57] *EMI* case, (above, n. 39), Judgment § 31.
[58] *Ibid.* § 32–34. This was said in relation to the "Columbia" mark for records; CBS, the non-EEC owner, had other well-known marks within the Common Market and could (at a price) re-label.
[59] "Hag," for instance: see above, n. 32.
[60] Whether, in light of this test, there was evidence enough to justify the Commission's decision in *Advocaat "Zwarte Kip"* (above, n. 52) is questionable.
[61] *British Trade Mark Law and Practice*, Cmnd. 5601; see also above, § 15-011.

passing reference to "deposit" systems was made in order to underscore the superiority of the full British examination.[62] The Committee viewed registration as a privilege of considerable economic potential—granted, moreover, within a framework of the wider legal protection that the passing-off action gives to actual use in trade.[63] Accordingly, the Report accepted without real discussion the principle that registration should be available only in respect of goods in which the proprietor (or a user) trades or intends to trade and goods of the same description[64]; and it displayed the same attitude to the rule that registration (as distinct from use) gives rise to an objection against a competing application to register only for such goods.[65] The Committee considered the rule that a registered mark can only be infringed by use for the goods covered by the registration necessary in the interests of certainty.[66] Curiously, there was no consideration of the question whether the sanctions against registering for an unduly wide range of goods should be strengthened.

Of the two major proposals of the Report—to allow registration of service marks and to end the Registrar's examination of assignments without goodwill and registered user agreements—the first has been implemented.[67] The second will be considered during the wholescale reaction to European Community developments, which are destined to cause the next upheaval in British intellectual property.

(2) Proposal for a Community Trade Mark

Since the Mathys Report appeared, there has been considerable **18-014** development in the proposal for an EEC trade mark system and is now approaching enactment.[68] When the Regulation takes effect, it will provide an alternative means of securing registered protection within the EEC. But the various national systems are to be adapted, at least to some extent, so as to operate upon similar basic principles to those of the community system. This will be in accordance with the First Directive on Trade Marks, enacted on December 21, 1988. There hangs over the project, and in particular the Regulation, the question of the Community's competence to enact its proposals.[69] These can ultimately be settled only by the EC Court of Justice, which is unlikely to hold that the Treaty of Rome does not confer the necessary power.[70]

---

[62] See §§ 37, 143.
[63] See, e.g. §§ 96, 103.
[64] See TMA 1938, s.17(1), 26; cf. Report, § 166.
[65] See TMA 1938, s.12(1); cf. Report, § 143.
[66] § 75.
[67] See above, §§ 17-002, 17-059.
[68] In 1964, a working group of the EC Commission completed a Preliminary Draft Convention for a European Trade Mark. As in the field of patents the work then came to a halt. The Trade Mark draft was not published until 1973. Thereafter the commission, advised by a new working party, drew up a Memorandum on the Creation of an EEC Trade Mark (SEC (76) 2462); (1976) 7 I.I.C. 367; Danish [1978] Int. Prop. L.R. 533. The two then formed the basis for the draft which the Commission turned into a Regulation proposal and which is in its final stages before the Council.
[69] The Regulation is to be enacted under the Treaty of Rome, Art. 235; the Directive proceeding under Art. 100A.
[70] See H.L. Select Committee, Report on Trade Marks, (H.L. 21, 1982) §§ 58–72.

18-015   Under the proposed Regulation, marks will be registrable for services
as well as goods, and what may constitute a mark will be widely
defined.[71] Even so, it is not proposed that registration will be the only
way of protecting such subject-matter: rights in national law against
passing off or unfair competition may also be used.[72]

There will be an official examination, but it will not be so extensive as
under the present British system. The Community Trade Mark Office will
raise only the "absolute" grounds of invalidity: lack of distinctiveness;
deceptiveness in matters such as nature, quality or geographic origin, but
not because of similarity to another trade mark; mark contrary to public
order or morality.[73] It will be for the proprietor of an earlier trade mark
or similar right to raise the "relative" grounds of refusal,[74] that the mark
in suit is identical to a prior mark and is for identical goods or services;
or that it is so similar to the earlier mark, and the goods or services for
which it is to be used are also so similar, that the public would be misled
as to the origin of the goods or services bearing the mark in suit.[75]

18-016   The community mark is conceived as a unity, effective throughout the
Common Market. Those with a mark already on the community register
or on one of the EEC national registers will be able to oppose an
application and seek cancellation of the mark after registration, provided
they also satisfy the criteria requiring use.[76] After a vigorous campaign,
the British secured acceptance of the view that marks, etc., protected at
common law could form the basis of objection both before and after
grant.[77] Even then the prior right must be of more than local or regional
importance—a requirement that could bear hard on the small business
whose success enables it gradually to expand.

18-017   Under the strict approach of the present British law, registration (as
distinct from use) by one person may found an attack against registration
by others only where the two are for the same goods or services or those
of the same description, and an infringement suit lies only in respect of
the goods for which the mark is registered.[78] A community mark will give
its proprietor somewhat broader rights, employing the same test in the
case of opposition and of infringement.[79] Since the rights may extend to
cases where the goods or services are "similar," there is ample scope for

[71] Regulation (text in 5865/88) Art. 3; similarly in the Directive Art. 2; cf. above,
§§ 17-013—17-014.
[72] Art. 12.
[73] Arts. 2, 6; cf. the Directive, Art. 3, which does not require official examination to be
limited in the same way.
[74] There is to be no arrangement to allow concurrent users onto the register (cf. TMA 1938,
s.12(2), above, §§ 17-032—17-034). They must remain content with such national rights
as they may have. See Beier (1978) 9 I.I.C. 227; cf. (1977) 8 I.I.C. at 25. The earlier
proposal for conciliation boards was subsequently abandoned, was a positive obligation
on all tribunals to make proposals for friendly settlement of disputes; now this remains
only as a discretion given to the Community Office: Art. 35(3).
[75] Art. 7; and see the Directive Art. 4.
[76] Art. 7(1), (2); and see Directive, Art. 4(1), (2), (3). For the requirement of use, see below,
§ 18-018.
[77] Art.7(4). See the H.L. Report (above, n. 70), § 36, 38; also Directive, Art. 4(4).
[78] cf. above, nn. 64, 65.
[79] For the test, see above, n. 75 and Arts. 8, 10; Directive, Arts. 5, 6.

differences of opinion about the circumstances in which the public is likely to be confused as to origin. It is not clear what part the extent and scope of actual use of the registered mark is to play in making this comparison.[80]

Originally, the Commission proposed to enact a general doctrine of international exhaustion. That has now been confined to intra-community exhaustion, following the Treaty of Rome case-law. There is in addition now an exception covering "legitimate reasons to oppose further commercialisation, especially where the condition of the goods is changed or impaired after they have been put on the market.[81] The most significant consequence of this formulation is that it rests with courts to decide how far a trade mark right is exhausted by marketing outside the Common Market.

The new system will contain sanctions that seek to ensure that a registered mark is used, but they are much less rigorous than originally proposed. They will be broadly equivalent to the five-year non-use rule in the British system.[82] There is not to be any requirement (as occurs, for instance, in the United States) of proof of use when the registration is renewed. Accordingly there is considerable scope for stock-piling.

It seems an inevitable price of developing such an institution at **18-018** community level, litigants must contribute handsomely to the development of detailed legal principles. The very general character of the basic concepts proposed for the Community system assumes that the courts are to put judicial flesh upon the legislative skeleton. Yet the differences of detail between the national laws of Member States are considerable; so courts handling infringement and revocation suits after grant may interpret the Regulation in different ways. The European Court of Justice will have an ultimate arbitral function. It may find itself with a heavy caseload.

4. MISLEADING AND UNFAIR ADVERTISING

In 1978, the EC Commission, developing its role in the protection of **18-019** consumers, produced a draft Directive requiring the harmonisation of laws against misleading and unfair advertising.[83] Originally of very considerable scope, it came under sustained attack. The case put by the British advertising industry was that there existed voluntary mechanisms, such as the Advertising Standards Authority[84], which were better able to

---

[80] For criticism of the highly refined reference to actual use in the present German law, see Beier (1975) 6 I.I.C. at 302–303. cf. the present British law of infringement, above, § 17-067.

[81] Art. 11; and see Directive, Art. 7.

[82] Arts. 13, 35(2), 39; cf. Directive, Arts. 10–12.

[83] See Schricker (1977) 8 I.I.C. 185. On unfair competition law in the EEC, see Beier (1985) 16 I.I.C. 139.

[84] See above, § 2-013.

achieve results than the compulsory sanction of legal regulation.[85] The actual Directive which emerged was of more modest proportion. In implementing it by regulation in 1988, the United Kingdom government has added to existing legislation on trade descriptions and related matters[86] only in relatively minor ways.

The Director General of Fair Trading is given the duty of considering complaints about misleading advertisements in the press and in public generally.[87] In deciding how to act he has to bear in mind the interests involved and the desirability of encouraging control by voluntary bodies.[88] If, upon investigation, he is not satisfied, he may seek an injunction from the High Court against anyone concerned with publication of the advertisements. The court may require such a person to substantiate the accuracy of any factual claim. It may grant the injunction without proof of actual loss or damage and irrespective of the intention or negligence of the person responsible.[89] In the field of broadcasting and cabling, equivalent powers are given to the Independent Broadcasting Authority, which may refuse to broadcast an advertisement,[90] and to the Cabling Authority, which may issue a direction not to transmit the advertisement, or to transmit it only in modified form.[91]

What is made clear is that a ground of objection may arise from prejudice to competitors as well as consumers. An advertisement is misleading if it in any way (including its presentation) it deceives or is likely to deceive its recipients, so as to affect their economic behaviour or to injure a competitor.[92] The latter have still not been given a general right of civil action against any misleading advertisement, let alone other unfair competition, which is likely to harm them. Only administrative mechanisms have been somewhat strengthened.

---

[85] See H.L. Select Committee, Report on Misleading Advertising (H.L., 1978); but cf. Dir.-Gen. of Fair Trading, *Review of the Self-Regulatory System of Advertising Control* (1978), taking a less sanguine view of self-regulation.

[86] See above, § 15-005.

[87] Control of Misleading Advertisements Regulations 1988, r. 4, subject to the exclusions of rr. 3, 4(2).

[88] r. 4(3).

[89] r. 6. Note also the Director's powers to obtain and disclose information: r. 7.

[90] rr. 8, 9.

[91] rr. 10, 11.

[92] r. 2(2).

APPENDICES

CONTROL OF MONOPOLIES AND RESTRICTIVE PRACTICES: NOTE ON INSTITUTIONS AND SOME SUBSTANTIVE RULES

The purpose of this Appendix, as explained in Chapter 1, is to give a **A1-001** brief introduction to certain aspects of the competition laws of the EEC and the United Kingdom which have not found a place in the main text. The relation between intellectual property rights and EEC policies has assumed such significance that it has already been dealt with at various points.[1] It remains to say something about the institutional framework for operating the EEC rules. By contrast, the rather pragmatic British system of control has not given rise to the same degree of tension. So it has been left to this note to indicate the legal reasons for this. The discussion of the British legislation concerning restrictive practices in particular is concerned with substance rather than procedure.

1. EEC INSTITUTIONS FOR IMPLEMENTING COMPETITION POLICY[2]

As we have seen, the Rome Treaty's Rules of Competition hinge on two **A1-002** complementary articles: Article 85 is directed against agreements and equivalent practices which prevent, restrict or distort competition; Article 86 against abuse of a dominant position; and in each case it is the effect on trade between Member States which is to be considered. The institutions which decide whether a particular case is to be condemned may have to consider it under both Articles: there is no division of authority such as is found in the United Kingdom system[3]; nor are the two articles mutually exclusive—a practice may offend both.

The principal authority charged with securing observation of the rules of competition is the EC Commission, acting through its Competition Directorate. But the Articles are "directly applicable" in the sense that the rights of private citizens in Member States are affected by them

---

[1] Above, §§ 1-021—1-027, 6-011, 6-012, 7-041—7-049, 12-028—12-031, 18-001—18-013.
[2] See generally Bellamy and Child, *Common Market Law of Competition* (3rd ed., 1987) Korah, *Competition Law in Britain and the Common Market* (3rd ed., 1980); R. Merkin and K. Williams, *Competition Law* (1984).
[3] Below, § A1-005.

without the help of municipal legislation. Accordingly, national courts may be obliged to consider their effect when deciding private suits. An agreement may be held void as restrictive of competition in the Common Market[4]; and action to enforce intellectual property (or other) rights may be lost because the rights are being asserted in pursuance of a restrictive practice or in abuse of a dominant position.[5]

(1) The EC Commission

A1-003   The following features mark the executive role of the Commission:

   (i)   It is armed with considerable powers of investigation into circumstances where it suspects an infringement of either Article.[6] These include powers of entry to examine records and to ask for immediate explanations.

  (ii)   When the Commission does find an infringement of either Article it can require the parties to put an end to it, or to undertake to do so. And for an intentional or negligent infringement it can impose a fine of up to one million units of account or 10 per cent. of an undertaking's turnover, whichever is the greater.[7]

 (iii)   In order to induce the submission of information to it voluntarily, there is a system (prescribed in Council Regulation 17 of 1962) for notifying agreements, etc., either for negative clearance (*i.e.* a declaration that an agreement is not caught by Article 85(1)) or for exemption under Article 85(3). Where it is exemption that is sought, notification carries protection from being fined for implementing the agreement during the interim period (which frequently is substantial)[8]; only if the Commission takes the positive step of indicating, after a preliminary examination, that it considers the agreement to infringe, does this protection cease to operate.[9] Some agreements of relatively minor significance do not even require notification in order to attract the benefits that attach to that step. These include two-party agreements under which an assignee or user of industrial property rights or manufacturing know-how is bound by restrictions, and two-party agreements solely for joint research and development.[10]

  (iv)   The task of granting individual exemption under Article 85(3) to agreements, etc., which contain restrictions indispensable in securing countervailing benefits, is reserved exclusively to the Commission. This power is fundamental to the whole conception of

---

[4] Article 85(2).

[5] See, *e.g. Consten and Grundig* v. *EC Commission* [1966] C.M.L.R. 418; *Application des Gaz* v. *Falks Veritas* [1974] Ch. 381; Bellamy & Child, §§ 1-34—1-40, where the relationship between Community and national law is also discussed.

[6] See generally Bellamy and Child.

[7] See Bellamy and Child §§ 12-012 *et seq.* especially the Table of Fines Imposed.

[8] Reg. 17/62 Arts. 2, 4, 5, 15(5), (6); Bellamy and Child, Chap. 1; Korah, § 11.1.3.

[9] *Bronbemaling/Heidemaatschappij Beheer,* above, § 7-032, n. 92, is an example of this sort of preliminary decision.

[10] See Reg. 17/62, Arts. 4(2), 5(2).

Community competition policy.[11] Enterprises which are prepared to play the game may consult the Commission before ever entering their agreements, or they may notify an agreement already reached and then negotiate the removal or modification of clauses as a precondition to exemption. Exemption is always for a defined period, though it may be renewed in the light of conditions prevailing at the later time.[12]

(v) By its Regulation 19 of 1965, the Council of Ministers gave the Commission power to deal with exemptions on a group basis by specifying in regulations different categories of agreement which would qualify *en bloc*. The Block Exemptions for Patent Licences, for Know-How Agreements and for Franchising Agreements fall under this power.

(2) National courts

The question of infringement of either Article may well be raised in A1-004 national court proceedings, before the Commission has had time to rule upon the agreement or practice in question. If the agreement is "old" and has been duly notified to the Commission it is to be treated by national courts as valid until the Commission decides otherwise. But "new" agreements are not provisionally valid in this sense.[13] This rule was laid down by the EC Court of Justice in order to deal with the considerable uncertainties that existed during the early stages of introducing the competition policy. If it does not give preliminary protection, the national court must itself consider the question of infringement and, to this end, it may be obliged to analyse the structure and operation of the relevant market,[14] a task which cannot be easy for non-specialist tribunals. Behind these basic rules lie many uncertainties of considerable practical importance. For them the reader must refer to books on EC Competition Law.

2. RESTRICTIVE PRACTICES AND MONOPOLIES IN THE UNITED KINGDOM

The United Kingdom legislation has been built upon an institutional A1-005 distinction between two categories. (i) Most restrictive trading agreements fall to be registered by the Director-General of Fair Trading and may

---

[11] *Davidson Rubber* and *Raymond/Nagoya* (above, § 7-032, n. 92) are examples.

[12] See generally Reg. 17/62, Arts. 6–9, Bellamy and Child, Chap. 3, Korah; §§ 9-5 *et seq.* Normally the period of exemption can run only from the date when the agreement is put into a form acceptable to the Commission. To this, however, there are exceptions relating to "old" and "pre-accession" agreements.

[13] *Brasserie de Haecht* v. *Wilkin (No. 2)* [1973] E.C.R. 77, [1973] C.M.L.R. 287. "Old" agreements were those in existence on March 13, 1962. "Pre-accession" agreements, which come within the rules of competition only by virtue of the accession of a state to the Rome Treaty, are probably to be treated as "old" agreements here.

[14] *Belgische Radio en Televisie* v. *SABAM* [1974] E.C.R. 51, 313; [1974] 2 C.M.L.R. 238. The parts of an agreement that are absolutely void under Act. 85(2) may be severable; the rest of the contract will then remain enforceable: see *Chemidus Wavin* v. *S.p.l. Transformation* [1977] F.S.R. 181 (C.A.).

require justification before the Restrictive Practices Court: here the current legislation is the Restrictive Trade Practices Act 1976 and the Restrictive Practices Court Act 1976 with which should be linked the Resale Prices Act 1976, governing resale price maintenance.[15] (ii) Abuses of monopoly power may be referred by the Director-General or the Secretary of State to the Monopolies and Mergers Commission for investigation and report; here the Fair Trading Act 1973 applies. To this structure, the Competition Act 1980 adds a third part, giving the Director-General, and then the Monopolies and Mergers Commission, power to investigate anti-competitive practices falling outside the scope of (i) above.

(1) Restrictive trade practices

(a) Registrable agreements

A1-006   Producers and suppliers of goods in the United Kingdom who carry on business there are obliged to notify agreements under which at least two of them undertake to restrict their conduct in one or more of the ways listed in the Act.[16] Since 1976, the same has been true of the suppliers of services in the case of a similar, but not identical list of restrictions.[17] As issues of public policy are at stake, the parties cannot put themselves beyond the reach of this legislation by agreeing that their "arrangement" is not to be legally binding: if they place each other under purely moral obligations that is an agreement for the Act's purposes.[18] For similar reasons, agreements between suppliers of goods, or between suppliers of services, to exchange information about certain terms on which they deal may also by order be brought within the scope of the Act.[19] If the lists of restrictive items are studied, it will be seen that, although each differs, there is concern particularly with prices and charges; terms and conditions of supply; the quantities, descriptions or geographical area for supplying goods and the extent or scale of services; the persons to or by whom goods or services are to be supplied; and in the case of goods there is explicit reference to their processes of manufacture—a matter of some importance where intellectual property rights are involved.

(b) Exceptions

A1-007   Agreements which relate to intellectual property rights may on occasion fall within these ground rules for registration of restrictive trading agreements. When precisely this is so is a matter of some uncertainty: it is not, for instance, clear whether a patent or copyright licensee who accepts limitations upon price, quantity or field of use is being restricted,

---

[15] For the earlier legislation and its common law background, see Korah §§ 1–3, 11–14; *Chitty on Contracts* (25th ed., 1983), §§ 4001–4010.

[16] Restrictive Trace Practices Act 1976, s.6(1).

[17] s.11. The order bringing this section into effect for services generally, but subject to particular exceptions, is the Restrictive Trade Practices (Services) Order 1976; see Chitty, §§ 4109 et seq.

[18] s.43(1); Chitty, §§ 4031–4045.

[19] ss.7, 12; on the recommendations of trade associations, s.8; Chitty, §§ 4100–4013, 4141. So far the only information order relates to the price of goods.

since without the licence he could not have acted at all[20]; nor is it clear whether a licensor who grants an exclusive licence is accepting a restriction concerning processes of manufacture, by virtue of the fact that he is surrendering his power to license others.[21]

To an extent—but not completely—such issues are avoided when specific exceptions apply. Let us first note these:

(i) Patent, design and copyright licences (and equivalent transactions): A1-008 these are not registrable, if the only restrictions (or information provisions) within the statutory lists concern the invention, articles for which the design is registered or the subject-matter of the copyright.[22] Thus if licensor and licensee each agree to charge standard prices, or to limit their production runs, or to use a patented invention only upon certain kinds of article or in certain forms of service, they fulfil basic conditions for registration; but they are exempt if they do not also do such things as agree prices on non-patented goods or services. Provided that there are only two parties, the exception continues to apply even if each has a patent or design which he is cross-licensing to the other. But this is not so once there are three or more parties, each of whom is granting an interest to one or more of the others in his patent or design: such pooling agreements fall outside the exception and are registrable if at least two parties accept statutory restrictions (or information responsibilities).[23]

(ii) Provided that there is to be an *exchange* of information, a limited exception may apply to agreements concerning information about the production of goods or services: in the case of the supply of goods, the information must concern processes for their manufacture, and the restrictions may only relate to the kinds of goods to be subjected to the processes; in the case of the supply of services, the information must concern techniques or processes to be applied in the services, and the only restrictions must relate to the form or manner in which those services are to be made available or supplied.[24] In these instances restrictions or matters of information pertaining to (say) prices or terms of supply are not exempted.

(iii) Trade mark licences: again with registered user agreements for the licensing of registered trade marks, there is an exception where the restrictions pertain only to the descriptions of goods that are to

---

[20] See below, at n. 26.
[21] Wilberforce, Campbell and Elles, *Restrictive Trade Practices and Monopolies* (2nd ed., 1966), p. 299 seem to treat such an undertaking as restrictive, saying that it is not within the exemption for patent agreements.
[22] Restrictive Trade practices Act 1976, Sched. 3 § 5(1)–(3); Chitty, § 4087.
[23] Sched. 3 § 5(4)–(8), as amended by the Competition Act 1980, s.30.
[24] Sched. 3 §§ 3, 8. The broad definition of "services" (s.20) means possibly that the act of supplying the information is itself a service distinct from any use of the information by its receiver in a service. If this really is so, the usual clauses requiring confidentiality to be observed may make the agreement registrable, the exception in § 5(8) having no relevance. See Chitty, §§ 4111, 4133 Sched. 3, § 4.

bear the mark or the processes of manufacture to be applied to them.[25] There is no exception relating to unregistered trade mark or trade name licences (which could be significant, for instance, for franchising schemes).

A1-009 The extent of these exceptions seems in some respects ill-defined; and more fundamentally, they seem obscure in purpose. As noted before, the question of what should be excepted must depend upon what is otherwise registrable: and it has never been settled whether a licence of intellectual property rights on terms restricting price or field of use is to be regarded as imposing a restriction on the licensee or as allowing limited access into territory otherwise closed.[26] Because, in a two-party agreement, the question cannot arise unless the licensor is himself also accepting restrictions of a specified variety, it has attracted very little attention.

(c) Investigations

A1-010 The duty upon parties to an agreement that has become registrable is to furnish particulars of it to the Director-General.[27] He in turn has certain powers to investigate where he suspects failure to comply, though these powers are less peremptory than those of the EC Commission.[28] Failure to register does not attract fines or other criminal sanctions, nor does executing an unregistered agreement.[29] The agreement is unenforceable and a person harmed by its execution may sue for breach of statutory duty.[30]

It is the Director-General's duty to refer agreements to the Restrictive Practices Court, unless they have been determined, or a stay is desirable in light of EEC proceedings, or the Minister decides that they are not significant enough.[31] The Court decides whether the agreement is contrary to the public interest. In order to submit the question to "justiciable" criteria, an agreement containing any of the prescribed restrictions is deemed to be against the public interest unless it can be justified under a number of "gateways." For instance, it is possible to show a balance in favour of the agreement because of substantial advantages to the purchasers, consumers or users; because it counteracts a monopolist not party to the agreement or a preponderant buyer or seller; because it may

---

[25] Sched. 3, § 4.
[26] The latter approach has been used in relation to the common law doctrine of restraint of trade (*Esso Petroleum* v. *Harper's Garage* [1968] A.C. 269; *Cleveland Petroleum* v. *Dartstone* [1969] 1 All E.R. 201 (C.A.). And there is some authority for using the same approach interpreting the restrictive practices legislation (*Re Automatic Telephone* (1963) L.R. 3 R.P. 462, 483; *Ravenseft Properties* v. *D.G. of Fair Trading* [1977] 1 All E.R. 47). But it is really an approach which makes nonsense of the provisions on, for instance, patent pools: for in a patent pool each recipient is being granted rights that he did not have before. *cf.* also Bellamy and Child, § 9–6. n. 6.
[27] Restrictive Trade Practices Act 1976, s.24; see further, Chitty, §§ 4142–4156.
[28] *Ibid.*, s.36.
[29] Probably an agreement once registered is enforceable until the Restrictive Practices Court declares against it; but the matter is uncertain; see Chitty, § 4152.
[30] s.35.
[31] s.21.

prevent an adverse effect on the general level of unemployment; or because it supports export business.[32]

If an agreement is found to be unjustified, the Court may order that it should not be implemented; failure to respect the order (or an undertaking in lieu) is punishable as contempt of court.[33] Substantial fines have been imposed in several cases.

(2) Investigation of Monopolies

(a) *Reference*

The Monopolies and Mergers Commission, which consists of up to 25 **A1-011** experts drawn from business, industrial and academic circles, reports (*inter alia*) on the ways in which the public interest may be affected by "monopoly situations" achieved in private enterprise.[34] Its investigations into monopolies are usually initiated by a reference from the Director-General of Fair Trading.[35]

The terms of the reference, which may be more or less limited in scope, determine the range of the investigation. There are two restrictions upon the institution of an investigation:

(i) One quarter of domestic or exported goods of any description, or of services of certain descriptions supplied within the United Kingdom, must come from a single business or group of companies, or from a complex of businesses acting together to restrict competition (a "complex monopoly situation")[36]; accordingly, it is the Commission's first task to determine whether a "monopoly situation" within this definition exists.

(ii) In the course of this assessment no account is to be taken of restrictive trading agreements within the definition of the 1976 Act; these are matters for the Restrictive Practices Court, not the Commission.[37]

(b) *Commission's rôle*

Unlike the Restrictive Practices Court, the Monopolies Commission is **A1-012** not conceived to be exercising judicial power.[38] The Commission's task is to investigate and then to report the subject-matter referred to it. It does not itself issue orders intended to rectify abuses. That is left for political action by the Minister. The essence of the Commission's role is to decide

---

[32] ss.10, 19 (services); Korah, Chap. 6.

[33] s.2; see Chitty, §§ 4158–4160, 4169.

[34] First established as the Monopolies Commission in 1948, its jurisdiction and the consequential powers of the Secretary of State are now governed by the Fair Trading Act 1973.

[35] See Fair Trading Act 1973, ss.50, 51.

[36] *Ibid.*, ss.6–8, and see ss.9–11.

[37] s.10(2). Thus professional services have been referrable to the Monopolies Commission because they are explicitly excluded from the restrictive practices legislation.

[38] Its wide powers of investigation have accordingly to be the subject of sanctions enforced by the courts: F.T.A. 1973, s.85. The Commission is not obliged to follow the procedures of a court, but must observe the rules of natural justice: *Hoffmann-La Roche* v. *Sec. of State for Trade* [1975] A.C. 295 at 354, 368. (H.L.).

(given the existence of a "monopoly situation")whether the dominant firm or firms are acting against the public interest by taking steps to exploit or maintain that situation.[39] It is unlikely to condemn conduct that is simply the successful expansion of a business undertaken in time to meet a rise in demand. But it has reported against deliberate action, such as discriminatory price cutting, which is aimed at keeping out competitors[40]; and against advertising expenditure at a level designed to procure the same effect.[41] It has also not been afraid to disapprove of the level of prices for patented goods, even where consequent profits are largely being reinvested in research and development. Such was the upshot of the investigation into the prices of the two patented tranquillisers, "Librium" and "Valium."[42] Equally it has found that Xerox and Rank Xerox together deterred competition and maintained their dominance of the market for plain paper copiers by their patenting activities and restrictive patent licensing.[43]

The Commission's investigation is inevitably much concerned with finding information about the performance of the alleged monopolist or monopolists. But it has also to formulate the underlying issues of public policy, and this it does in a public interest statement.[44] The statement gives the firms under investigation and others interested a basis upon which to present information and views; upon it the monopoly is examined by the Commission and a Report is completed. In this procedure, as events following the *Tranquillisers* Report show, there may well be room for argument over whether those impugned are given sufficient notice of the "case" against them.[45]

(c) *Political consequences*

A1-013   After a report adverse to the monopoly, the Minister will normally first try to reach agreement upon a remedial course of action with the monopolistic enterprise. If these negotiations, which are often undertaken by the Director General's office, are fruitless, the Minister has power to compel an alteration of practice by order—making it, for instance, unlawful to withhold supplies or services, or to take steps such as requiring a "tie-in" in the sale of different products; or requiring the publication of prices or even imposing the prices to be charged.[46] The most extreme power is to order divestiture of part of a business (but only upon the affirmative resolution of both Houses of Parliament), a remedy which is fraught with practical difficulties.[47]

Where patents are involved in the provision of goods or services that is criticised in the Commission's report, the Minister may apply to the

[39] See Fair Trading Act 1973, s.84, which lists particular matters for the Commission to bear in mind.
[40] See Korah pp. 36–37.
[41] Report on Detergents (H.C. 105, 1966).
[42] Report (H.C. 197, 1973).
[43] Report on Supply of Indirect Electrostatic Reprographic Equipment (H.C. 47, 1976–1977).
[44] See generally Korah, pp. 26–29.
[45] See the decision mentioned in n. 38, above.
[46] See generally, Korah pp. 29–35.
[47] *Ibid.,* pp. 34–35.

Comptroller-General of Patents for an order cancelling or modifying restrictive conditions in patent licences or declaring licences under the patent to be available as of right.[48] Such a step has never been taken. But the *Tranquillisers* Report led to the making of orders to cut prices to the very substantial extent recommended by the Commission.[49] Both report and order raise fundamental questions about the purpose and scope of the patent system. Here, in a unique market (the drugs being largely paid for by the government,[50] but ordered on doctors' prescriptions), the patentee was able to derive very substantial profits from its protected position. The Report in effect insists that, even though the power to do so comes from a patent, the patentee may be required to moderate his behaviour: for instance he may be expected to comply with "reasonable" procedures devised by the relevant government department and the industry for negotiating price reductions over the life of the patent.[51]

(3) Anti-competitive practices[52]

The trading agreements that are the target of the 1976 Act involve **A1-014** "horizontal" mutual restrictions. The aim of the Competition Act 1980, in giving a power to investigate anti-competitive practices, is to bring under scrutiny "vertical" agreements between, for instance, a manufacturer and his distributors or trade customers.[53] An anti-competitive practice is a course of business conduct which (taken with or without the conduct of associates) "has or is intended to have or is likely to have the effect of restricting, distorting or preventing competition" in goods or services in the United Kingdom.[54] In particular, exclusive distribution agreements, refusal to supply outlets such as supermarkets, and various forms of price discrimination, through practices like loyalty rebates, are likely to come under review. The precedent set by the EEC competition rules is evident.[55] The procedure will commence with a preliminary

---

[48] P.A. 1977, s.51, as amended by the Competition Act 1980, s.14. Similar orders may be made where the Commission has reported that a merger is against the public interest.

[49] Licences of right were decidedly not the issue. The Patents Act 1949, s.41, provided at that time for compulsory licences of pharmaceutical patents almost as of right. The dispute was hardened by the government's failure to act at once on the Banks Committee's recommendation (Cmnd. 4407, § 410) that s.41 be repealed. This was eventually brought about by P.A. 1977, ss.127, 132(5), Sched. 3(2)(c).

[50] In this field, Crown use powers gave a separate opportunity for limiting the patentee's market power (see above, §§ 7-055). But the government had still to bear in mind the need to support British pharmaceutical industry: see the *Tranquillisers* report (above, n. 46), § 203.

[51] See Rhinelander, (1974) 15 Virginia J. Int. Law 1.

[52] See Dinnage, (1980) 2 E.I.P.R. 157; Korah (1980) 11 I.I.C. 460.

[53] The powers of the new Act do not extend to agreements registrable under the Restrictive Trade Practices Act 1976. One type of agreement which might now be caught is one between foreign enterprises which do not carry on business in the United Kingdom but nevertheless affect competition here.

[54] Competition Act 1980, s.2(1); even competition in the production of goods is covered, which might bring in a case of making goods in a form that could not be combined with the goods of other manufacturers: see Dinnage (above, n. 52) at 160. There is a special provision (s.11) on the supply of goods and services by nationalised industries and other governmental bodies.

[55] The Act is intended as a counter-inflationary measure in substitution for the Price Commission, which it abolishes: s.1.

investigation by the Director-General of Fair Trading, acting "as expeditiously as possible." If he reports that a practice is anti-competitive he will also state whether it is appropriate to refer it to the Monopolies and Mergers Commission.[56] Within a period of 4–8 weeks thereafter he must make any proposed reference, unless in the meantime he has accepted undertakings from those concerned.[57] In its investigation, the Commission applies the same public interest criteria as in monopoly references: indeed, a practice that arises in a "monopoly situation" may be investigated under the Fair Trading Act procedure or under the new Act.[58] If an unfavourable report results, the Secretary of State may request the Director-General to seek undertakings, and, if no acceptable outcome can be agreed, he may ultimately take action of the same kind as on reports concerning monopolies, with the exception of divestiture.[59] If patents are involved there is a similar power of referral to the comptroller.[60]

The Government has published a Green Paper on the future of British restrictive practices law which proposes bringing it into line with the EC Rules of Competition.[61] This has attracted less than universal acclaim and it remains to be seen whether further action is taken in this direction.

---

[56] s.3.
[57] An undertaking cannot at this stage be positively sought by the Director-General; but if he does accept one that is proffered, it must be published: s.4(1)–(4) and note the consequential provisions, s.4(5)–(9).
[58] s.8 and see above, § A1-012.
[59] ss.9, 10 and see above, § A1-013.
[60] See above, § A1-014.
[61] Review of Restrictive Trade Practices Policy, Cm. 331, 1988; a White paper is promised for 1989.

APPENDIX 2

"OLD" PATENTS

Patents granted before June 1, 1978, or granted upon applications for **A2-001**
which the complete specification was filed before that date, are subject to
the Patents Act 1949, as amended by the 1977 Act.[1] In the main text, a
number of contrasts were made between the 1949 Act and its successor,
looking from the "new" perspective. This Appendix, viewing the matter
the other way round, notes the major points at which the law governing
"old" patents is distinct from the new.

1. TERM

The 1949 Act period of 16 years from the filing date, with certain **A2-002**
possibilities for extension,[2] has been changed: one consequence is that
there will be some "old" patents even in 1998. Those which were already
11 years old on June 1, 1978, kept to the 16 years, with the possibility of
extension on the old grounds up to a maximum of 20 years.[3] Those less
than 11 years old were automatically extended to 20 years with no
possibility of longer life.[4] In giving this four-year extension, a number of
qualifications were added to prevent prejudice to the Crown and licensees
where they continued to use the invention after the 16 years ran out; and
licences of right became available during the extra four years.[5] Particularly in the pharmaceutical field, these licences of right have been the
subject of great controversy. In that sphere, and such others as the
Secretary of State may order, the 1988 Act has abrogated the licence of
right provision. The case for doing so was one part of a campaign for
longer term patents for pharmaceuticals, to take account of the delays of
medical testing.[6]

The old law allowed patents of addition to be taken out for modifications or improvements to the main invention; these did not have to show
an inventive step over the main invention, the protection lasted as long as
the main invention and no separate renewal fees were required.[7] In

[1] See PA 1977, s.127; and see generally also s.128 and Scheds. 1–4.
[2] PA 1949, s.23 (inadequate remuneration) and s.24 (war loss); abolished by the 1977 Act.
[3] Formerly extensions could be much longer.
[4] See PA 1977, Sched. 1, §§ 3, 4.
[5] See Ency. PL, §§ 2-020–2-021.
[6] CDPA 1988, s.293, 294; see Dworkin and Taylor, pp. 207–208; Burnett-Hall (1989) 18
CIPA 154.
[7] See Blanco White, *Patents for Inventions* (5th ed., 1983), §§ 5-201–5-209.

applying the transitional rules on extension of term, a patent of addition is treated as part of the main patent, whatever its own date.[8]

2. VALIDITY

A2-003 Pre-grant opposition by third parties (on limited grounds)[9] was abolished in 1978.[10] After grant both the Patents Court and the Comptroller acquired jurisdiction to revoke on the grounds of invalidity specified in the 1949 Act, section 32.[11] These grounds, which contain some crucial differences from the new law, may be summarised thus:

(1) Not an "invention" (manner of new manufacture)[12]

The manner in which the judges allowed expansion of the range of patentable subject-matter is relevant to the new law and is discussed in the text.[13] It is an issue which tends to arise at the application stage rather than after grant, and so is likely now to have only occasional importance for "old" patents.

(2) Lack of novelty[14]

A2-004 Here there are vital differences. In particular for old patents: (i) only what was known and used in the United Kingdom at the priority date is taken into account[15]; and (ii) publications and uses are disregarded for a variety of reasons[16]: publication only in a United Kingdom specification more than 50 years old at the relevant filing date[17]; when the invention was obtained from the patentee or his predecessor, publication in breach of an obligation to that person not to do so[18]; publication in an application that was made in contravention of the patentee's rights[19]; during the year before the priority date, communication to a government department to investigate merits[20]; display or use of the invention within the six months before the British filing at a certified exhibition (a much wider category than under the 1977 Act), consequent publication or unauthorised use[21]; within the six-month period, description in a paper

---

[8] See n. 7.
[9] *i.e.* those in P.A. 1949, s.14(1).
[10] Sched. 3, § 1(2)(a); and note Sched. 4, § 4, § 17(a).
[11] Sched. 1, § 7. In continuing the effect of s.32, the 1977 Act does modify it in a very minor way by abolishing revocation for one kind of false suggestion about priority and non-fulfilment of government orders: PA 1977, Sched. 1, § 6, Sched. 3, § 1(2).
[12] PA 1949, s.32(1)(d); Blanco White, §§ 4-909—4-912.
[13] Above, §§ 0–000.
[14] See generally, Blanco White, §§ 4-101 *et seq.*
[15] PA 1949, s.32(1)(e); *cf.* "the state of the art": above §§ 5-003 *et seq.*
[16] *cf.* the very limited reasons under the new law: above, § 5-013.
[17] PA 1949, s.50(1); see *Thetford* v. *Fiamma* [1988] 3 C.M.L.R. 549, for this rule in relation to free movement within the EEC.
[18] *Ibid.* s.50(2).
[19] s.50(3).
[20] s.51(1).
[21] s.51(2)(a)–(c). The exhibition did not have to fall within the conditions of the International Convention: *cf.* above, § 5-013, n. 48.

read by the inventor to a learned society or published with his consent in its transactions[22]; within a one-year period before the priority date, publicly working the invention for reasonable trial when this was reasonably necessary.[23] Subject to these limitations on the range of relevant material, the substantive issue was approached in a manner that is likely to apply in similar fashion under the new law.

(3) Secret use

Quite apart from the general rule concerning lack of novelty, a use that A2-005 was secret would invalidate, unless it was for reasonable trial and experiment, or by a government department in consequence of the applicant's disclosure, or by some other disclosee without consent.[24] However much there was to be said in principle for a rule that sought to prevent a person from using an invention in secret and then patenting it at a time that suited him commercially, this separate ground of objection finds no place in the new dispensation.[25]

(4) Prior claiming

Under the 1949 Act, only a valid claim to the same invention in a A2-006 British patent of earlier priority date rendered a later claim invalid.[26] Any other part of the contents of the earlier specification had no effect upon the later; if the earlier had not been published at the priority date of the later; it was not deemed to form part of the art for purposes of novelty. A succession of casuistic decisions[27] make it sometimes difficult to tell when there are conflicting claims to the one invention.

(5) Obviousness

As with novelty, the prior art consists only of what was known and A2-007 used in the United Kingdom at the priority date.[28] Apart from this the approach of the old decisions to the substantive question is likely to continue.[29]

(6) Insufficient description or failure to disclosure the best known method of performing[30]

the first of these allied grounds has an equivalent in the requirement of A2-008 clear and complete disclosure under the new law[31]; the second finds no separate place.

---

[22] s.51(2)(d).
[23] s.51(3).
[24] s.32(1)(f), 32(2). see Blanco White; §§ 4-114—4-116.
[25] See above, §§ 5-006—5-007.
[26] s.32(1)(a).
[27] For this case-law, see Blanco White; §§ 4-031—4-311.
[28] PA 1949, s.32(1)(f); and see generally, Blanco White; §§ 4-201—4-228.
[29] Above §§ 5-022.
[30] PA 1949, s.32(1)(h); see Blanco White, §§ 4-501—4-519.
[31] cf. above, 180. The requirements for deposit of micro-organisms apply only to new patents; cf. *American Cyanamid's (Dann) Patent* [1971] R.P.C. 425 (H.L.)

(7) Inutility

A2-009 This likewise is not a distinct ground of objection under the new law.[32] Its meaning under the old has already been considered, in speculating upon how far it may have survived in transmogrified form.[33]

(8) Claim of insufficiently defined scope (ambiguity) or claim not fairly based on the matter disclosed in the specification[34]

A2-010 Here an equivalent objection survives in the new law only during examination of the application and not after grant. In discussing this, the old law has been referred to.[35]

(9) Grant to person not entitled to apply, or in contravention of rights[36]

A2-011 These related, often overlapping, grounds are the basis on which objections to entitlement must be put under the 1949 Act. The right to apply is limited by the Act to the inventor or inventors,[37] their assignees and persons who are making Convention applications within 12 months of their first application for protection in a Convention country.[38] Where a case of contravention of rights is made out, the objector may be allowed to have the priority date of the objectionable application for his own application.[39]

(10) Patent obtained on a false suggestion; primary or intended use contrary to law[40]

A2-012 These are peripheral grounds which have survived, subject to minor change.[41]

If a patentee succeeds in resisting an attack on the validity of his patent, he may secure a certificate of contested validity. The effect of this regarding the costs of subsequent actions is more favourable to him under the new law than the old.[42] It is not clear how far the new law can apply when the patent is old.[43]

3. INFRINGEMENT

A2-013 The 1977 Act's provisions on infringement[44] derive partly from the EPC (especially Article 69 on the scope of protection and the Protocol on its

[32] s.32(1)(g); see Blanco White, §§ 4-401—4-414.
[33] See above, §§ 5-038, 5-065.
[34] s.32(1)(i), Blanco White, §§ 4-701—4-707, 4-801—4-808.
[35] Above, §§ 5-064—5-068.
[36] s.32(1)(b), (c). See Blanco White, §§ 4-601—4-605.
[37] "Inventor" in the old sense, including importer from abroad: see above, § 3-003.
[38] s.1(1), (2). cf. the 1977 Act, where the restrictions apply to the right to grant: see above, §§ 7-001-7-002.
[39] s.53; but there are difficulties in the transition to the 1977 Act: see Ency. PL, § 2-017.
[40] s.32(1)(j), (k); Blanco White, §§ 4-1001—4-1008.
[41] Above, n. 12.
[42] Above, § 2-038, n. 21.
[43] See Ency. PL, § 2-042.
[44] See above, §§ 6-001—60-017.

interpretation) and partly from the CPC (especially the introduction of indirect infringement).[45] It seems clearly to have been the draftsman's intention that these new provisions should apply to acts performed after June 1, 1978 which are alleged to infringe an "old" patent. This must follow from a provision that exempts from infringement under the new law someone who continues to do what under the old law was not infringement.[46] The manner of expressing this objective was convoluted; but the Court of Appeal held firmly to the view that the new law of infringement and associated matters applies to all patents.[47] The result would be a curiously technical difference between old and new patents and one, it is to be hoped, that the courts will avoid. There are, it may be added, similar obscurities in the provisions affecting the actions for declaration of non-infringement and to restrain threats, where the issue is whether an "old" patent infringes under the new law.[48]

4. AMENDMENT

"Old" patents can be amended only in accordance with the 1949 Act's **A2-014** principles. After publication of the complete specification any amendments must be by way of disclaimer, correction or explanation and must not introduce (into description or claims) matter not previously disclosed in substance; nor must they result in a claim not wholly within the scope of any previous claim. The only exception lies in the correction of an obvious mistake.[49] Amendment under both old and new law remains a matter of discretion for the court or Comptroller.[50] This will continue to be exercised in light of the explanations offered for why the amendment being sought was not included in the original specification, or introduced by amendment at an earlier time.[51] But once an amendment is made, in the absence of fraud it is binding and relates back to the grant of the patent. The amendment is not open to a subsequent challenge to its propriety such as is provided under the new law.[52]

[45] See above, *ibid.* in §§ 4-029—4-031.
[46] PA 1977 Sched. 4, § 3(3). The idea of "continuing" to do something creates the same difficulty as that discussed in § 6-016, n. 80, see Ency. PL, § 2–007.
[47] See Ency. PL, § 2–006. There is equal obscurity over whether the Protocol to EPC Art. 69 has any application: *ibid.* But then the Protocol attempts to influence attitude rather than impose hard rule.
[48] See Ency. PL, §§ 2-044, 2-046.
[49] PA 1949, s.31(1). For the meaning given to the various concepts of this rule, see Blanco White, Chap. 6.
[50] PA 1949, ss.29, 30 which confer jurisdiction: as to which see Blanco White, §§ 6-001 *et seq.*
[51] This is discussed above, §§ 4-026—4-027.
[52] *cf.* above, § 4-025.

5. Miscellaneous

A2-015 In a number of important respects the 1977 Act applies its provisions to "old" patents as much as to "new." This is true of the new regime on proprietary interests,[53] the provisions on compulsory licensing[54] and on Crown use.[55]

---

[53] See above, §§ 7-014—7-017.
[54] See above, §§ 7-049—7-054.
[55] See above, §§ 7-055—7-056.

JOINT INTERESTS IN MARKS

As the main text illustrates, there are words and symbols which groups **A3-001** of independent traders, rivals amongst themselves, nevertheless all use to distinguish their products from those of outside competitors.[1] Tradition, fashion or advertising may impart great drawing power to these signs. They cover a whole spectrum of types, of which it is useful to isolate the following examples:

Type 1: Geographical names from products which acquire their particular qualities from being produced in the place designated ("appellations of origin")

This category is largely confined to wines ("Champagne" "Sherry"), **A3-002** though other examples occasionally arise ("Roquefort" cheese, produced in caves of a particular natural formation). The special cachet of these denominations leads to the practice (particularly in countries other than that of production) of selling generally similar products with associative tags of the "Sherry-type," "British sherry" variety; or even to the adoption of the basic name without qualification.[2]

Type 2: Geographical names for products whose qualities are not particularly associated with the place designated (sometimes distinguished from the previous category as "indications of source")

A wider range of food, drink and other products are sold under the **A3-003** name of a town or region with which they have become associated, even though this association depends on local skills rather than on geographical peculiarities.

---

[1] See esp. above, §§ 16-030—16-032.

[2] An agreement for the Protection of Appellations of Origin and their International Registration was reached at Lisbon in 1958, but it has not attracted many states as adherents (the United Kingdom is not a member). A major difficulty in securing international agreement on protection for marks of this type (and the indications of source mentioned next) is that local products (especially wines) may well have come to be described by a name that is taken from a famous European original ("burgundy," "champagne," "Kaiserstuhl," etc.) This usage may well have acquired status enough in the country concerned to make it politically unacceptable afterwards to prohibit it. There are, however, proposals to introduce protection in the Paris Industrial Property Convention. Within the EEC the matter is now regulated expressly and restrictively: see especially Regs. (EEC) 816 and 187/70, discussed in *A. P. Bulmer* v. *Bollinger* [1979] R.P.C. 110; and *cf. EC Commission* v. *Germany* [1975] E.C.R. 181; [1975] 1 C.M.L.R. 340; Beier (1977) 16 Ind.Prop. 152. For the international problem more generally see, *e.g.* Krieger (1974) 13 Ind. Prop. 381; Benson (1978) 17 Ind. Prop. 127; Harris (1979) 1 E.I.P.R. 205.

Type 3: Names or symbols associating goods with production in a particular country or region

A3-004   Most obviously the name of a country as a whole, or of a region, may influence a customer's choice; and other words or symbols may suggest similar associations: tartan with Scotland, Eiffel tower with Paris, etc.[3]

Type 4: Non-geographical names or symbols for products of a particular composition or quality

A3-005   Hallmarks for metals are one instance[4]; "advocaat" for a concoction of brandwijn, eggs and sugar is another.

Type 5: Name or symbol of a trade association or group

A3-006   A well-known example is the "Woolmark." the motive force of such a group will be the mutual self-interest of members. The extent to which they perceive their joint goodwill in the name or symbol to be a substantial weapon in the battle against outside competition will vary; so will their readiness to allow newcomers also to use it.

Type 6: Mark of an agency not directly connected with trading interests which is used to signify that goods have met a standard

A3-007   This may be more or less specific. Design Council awards, for instance, recognise good design in British products of all kinds. BSIs (standards of the British Standards Institution) are much more precise.

There are three important ways in which words and symbols of these types may be legally protected against misappropriation by a trader who is not entitled to use them. These are discussed in the following paragraphs.

(a) *Criminal Proceedings*

A3-008   The Trade Descriptions Act 1968[5] lays down a number of offences relating to misstatements about goods which are germane to the kinds of mark under consideration. Section 1 creates criminal liability for applying a false trade description, or selling goods to which such a description has been applied.[6] A false trade description may concern: quantity, size or gauge; method, place or date of manufacture, production, processing or reconditioning; composition; fitness for purpose, strength, performance, behaviour or accuracy; other physical characteristics; testing by any person and its results; approval by a person or conformity with a type approved by any person; person by whom manufactured, produced,

---

[3] For an example of the sort of conflict which may arise with the interest of an individual trader, see *"Welsh Lady" T.M.,* above, § 17-017, n. 78.

[4] See also above, § 15-002, n. 4.

[5] See also above, §§ 2-008—2-011.

[6] This offence imposes strict liability, though there are important defences contained in ss.23, 24; for which, see, *e.g.* Lowe and Woodruffe, *Consumer Law and Practice* (1980), pp. 181–187.

processed or recondition; other history.[7] The somewhat narrower provisions on false statements relating to services[8] expressly include the examination, approval or evaluation by any person of services, accommodation or facilities provided in the course of trade or business. The range of these offences is extended by a number of definitional provisions,[9] and false statements in advertising are covered.[10]

Other more specific legislation may also be in point. Thus the Food and Drugs Act 1955 makes it an offence to display a label or publish an advertisement which falsely describes the food or drug, or is calculated to mislead as to its nature, substance or quality.[11] Where the safety or life or health is at risk, the procedures of the Consumer Safety Act 1978[12] may be brought into play. These depend upon the Secretary of State making an order covering the type of goods in question. *Inter alia* these orders may require a type of goods to meet a prescribed safety standard, such as one laid down by the British Standards Institution (BSI). It then becomes an offence to deal in goods which do not meet the standard.[13]

In general, these criminal statutes do not directly prescribe any statutory duty for breach of which civil proceedings may be instituted.[14] The possibility of seeking compensation in the criminal proceedings and of suing under the general law of tort should, however, be recalled.[15]

(b) *Civil proceedings at common law*

It will be appreciated, from the discussion of passing off in the text, A3-009 that this cause of action is available in any case of the above types where traders can show a joint reputation that is being misleadingly adopted by a stranger. The "Champagne" and "Sherry" cases were of Type 1; but the recent "Advocaat" decision, with its suggestively wide dicta on the scope of passing off, was a case of Type 3.[16] Those dicta might now allow a court to give civil protection to a certifying agency of Type 5. It remains to be seen how far all the traders of a large region or country could be regarded as having a sufficient joint reputation in a mark indicating merely that goods come from that country.

[7] s.2(1), there being special provisions relating to animals, plants and seeds, and food and drugs. Examples include labelling a Danish turkey, "Norfolk King Turkey" (*Beckett* v. *Kingston* [1970] 1 K.B. 606); labelling wine not from Portugal or Madeira, respectively "port" or "madeira" (Anglo-Portuguese Commercial Treaty Acts, 1914, 1916).

[8] s.14(1): the offence must be committed knowingly or recklessly; see further, Lowe and Woodruffe, pp. 178–181.

[9] See especially ss.3, 14(2), (3).

[10] For goods, by s.5; for services by the general terms of s.14(1). Note that special defence in s.25.

[11] s.6.

[12] Which is in course of replacing earlier legislation of 1961 and 1971: see generally, Lowe and Woodruffe, Chap. 12.

[13] s.2.

[14] See above, §§ 2-011. The Consumer Safety Act, however, is the exception, giving a right of action to any person "affected by" failure to perform an obligation (such as carrying out a test) prescribed under its machinery. A certifying body or competitor might claim to be a person "affected": the issue has not been tested.

[15] See above, §§ 2-005—2-007.

[16] Above, § 16-012.

(c) *Certification trade marks*

A3-010   A person or group who want protection for marks of any of the types
mentioned above may be able to register a certification trade mark.[17] This
will give the proprietor equivalent rights to those of the owner of an
ordinary registered mark against traders who use the mark, or one
deceptively similar, either as their own trade mark or in order to "import
a reference."[18] A proprietary right, enforceable by civil action, is thus
created which does not depend for its enforcement upon proving a
sufficient reputation with the public. Certification marks are broadly
analogous to the "collective marks" found in many European systems.
The distinctive characteristic of the British type, however, is that it is
subject to a measure of political control in the public interest. This is not
usually present in schemes for collective marks.[19]

A certification mark may only be registered in Part A and an applicant
has to satisfy the Registrar that the mark is distinctive for the purpose
intended: it must be adapted to distinguish goods within the registration
as certified by a person in respect of origin, material, mode of manufacture, quality, accuracy or other characteristic from goods not so certified.[20] the applicant must accordingly be the person who will give this
certification and he may not himself trade in the goods in question.[21] In
addition, the mark must pass the other tests of suitability for registration,
in particular that it is not deceptive in the sense of sections 11 and 12.[22]

Once the application is found acceptable on these general trade mark
grounds,[23] it proceeds to the Fair Trading Division of the Department of
Trade for examination of the regulations which must be put forward as
governing its use.[24] The Department has to ensure that the applicant is
competent to give the certification and that the registration is to the
public advantage. In particular it will strive to ensure that the characteristic to be certified is clearly specified, that use will be properly controlled,
that any person complying with the scheme may use the mark and that
there is a right to appeal against refusal to allow use.[25] There are certain
powers after grant to alter the regulations on the application of a person
aggrieved or the Registrar, and the Department may itself remove the
mark for failure to observe the regulations.[26] But no official check is
regularly made on the use of a certification mark.

A3-011   Many of the existing certification marks are used to certify specific
qualities such as technical and safety standards or composition, which are

[17] See especially TMA 1938, s.37, Sched. 1.
[18] s.37(3); and see above, §§ 17-076—17-077. Defences equivalent to s.4(3) and (4) are
found in s.37(5), (6) and ss.7 and 8 apply to certification marks; s.6 however cannot be
used to make conditions governing use bind third parties: see Sched. 1, § 6.
[19] See Joseph (1979) 1 E.I.P.R. 160.
[20] s.37(1), (2).
[21] s.37(1), proviso.
[22] See Sched. 1, § 2. The registration may be subject to limitations or conditions: s.37(4).
[23] Or even before: see Sched. 1, § 5.
[24] s.37(7). Once the Department's approval has been secured, the mark is published and is
open to opposition in the normal way: Sched. 1 § 2.
[25] Sched. 1, § 1(5), as amplified by the Mathys Report (Cmnd. 5601, 1974), § 192.
[26] Sched. 1, §§ 3, 4.

of interest either to the general public or to a sector of industry. In such cases, the proprietor is often a trade association. One of the chief purposes of Department of Trade intervention is to prevent the mark from being turned into an unjustified barrier to entry by further competitors. Hence the emphasis in the Department's criteria upon allowing any person to use the mark whose products have the characteristic being certified. This is the prime difference from the collective marks of foreign systems. Less rigorously tested is the characteristic that the applicant group puts up for certification. An early decision accepted that a union of French syndicates might register "Unis" for all classes of goods in order to indicate they were of French origin[27] (see Type 3 above). The Malony Committee on Consumer Protection criticised the triviality of certifying the place of manufacture in some instances.[28] This, however, continues to be permitted. Provided that there is no real prejudice to existing or future traders, an appellation of origin or indication of source may therefore be protected by a certification mark, provided that it is held by an association which does not itself trade. This was done in the case of "Stilton" for cheese, the certification being proper for cheese made to certain quality standards within 15 miles of Melton Mowbray.[29] Proper control was established by a regulation requiring all certified users to use the mark only on cheese which satisfied these criteria.

---

[27] *Union Nationale Inter-Syndicale's Appln.* [1922] 2 Ch. 653 (C.A.); registered as a "standardisation" mark under the TMA 1905, s.62. Much of this decision was given legislative form in the provisions of the present Act on certification marks.

[28] Cmnd. 1781, 1962, § 330. The Committee also criticised the practice of refusing registration where another mark was already on the register to certify the same characteristic of the goods: §§ 331, 332.

[29] *"Stilton"* T.M. [1967] R.P.C. 173. The word was not properly geographical since the cheese was no longer produced in the village of Stilton, which lay outside the denominated area. This gave rise to a careful investigation of possible prejudice.

APPENDIX 4

PROTECTION OF PLANT VARIETIES

A4-001 The scientific breeding of new plant varieties raises ecological issues that rank in difficulty beside the genetic engineering of animal tissue. Nonetheless it is now carried on by important commercial organisations which have secured legal protection for their substantial capital investment. In the United States the creation of a legislative shield began as long ago as 1930, when plant patents became available for a-sexually reproducing varieties.[1] In the United Kingdom, the Plant Varieties and Seeds Act 1964 introduced an elaborate form of intellectual property right designed to fit the particular case. This was part of a movement in various West European countries which also led to the establishment of the UPOV Convention mentioned below.[2]

(1) A special system

A4-002 The 1964 Act provides for the grant of a full monopoly right, not dependent upon proof of copying, to breeders or discovers of plant varieties.[3] It is not part of the patent system: the grant of rights is made by the Plant Variety Rights Office which has its own Controller.[4] This is in contrast with the United States and some West European countries. As succeeding paragraphs will suggest, there are a number of basic points at which simple adherence to the patent model is unsatisfactory, and it is not easy to judge whether it is better to take that model, varying it where necessary, or to start afresh, in establishing protection for plant varieties. Advocates of the former approach tend to be strong protagonists of effective international protection who see the political advantages of bringing plant variety rights within the structure of the Paris Convention network, and who object to the limited scope of the current schemes. As the matter has so far developed, there has been an international convention in the field since 1961, when national legislation was beginning to

[1] See 35 U.S.C., § 161. Sexually reproducing varieties are now covered by the Plant Variety Protection Act 1970 (U.S.).
[2] For further discussion see Dworkin [1983] E.I.P.R. 270; and Jouffray [1984] E.I.P.R. 283.
[3] Plant Varieties and Seeds Act 1964, s.2(2), (4). As far as concerns priorities, the basic principle is that the first to apply has the better right; but there are arrangements to accord 12-months' priority to applications in countries of the Convention (see next note) in certain circumstances: Sched. 2, Pt. I.
[4] Plant Varieties and Seeds Act 1964, s.1(2), II. The responsible department so far as concerns England and Wales is the Department of Agriculture. Decisions of the Controller are subject to appeal to the Plant Variety Rights Tribunal (s.10, Sched. 4). The Plant Breeders Rights Regulations 1969 provide that any person with a substantial interest may intervene in applications for rights and most other proceedings.

spread,[5] but this convention is separately administered, being merely associated with WIPO.

(2) Official testing

A basic point on which the 1964 Act departs from the patent system is A4-003 that protection is granted only after official testing. This trial is designed to show that the variety has the requisite properties mentioned in paragraph (4) below.[6] The Plant Variety Rights Office continues its testing so long as the variety right endures, and it can revoke the grant should the variety lose its distinctiveness. Several West European systems (whether "patent" systems or not) also have similar testing and this has led to collaborative arrangements between the different countries.[7] There is a saving of effort which is increasing in significance as the number of applications grows. The United States system does not provide for the same tests on a regular basis, and this makes international co-operation difficult.

The process of testing is needed not only to obtain variety rights but also to secure government approval for the marketing of seed: the two requirements thus run in the tandem.

(3) Gradualism with variations

Under the British system protection is available only when a scheme A4-004 has been made by the relevant ministers for the genus or species to which the variety belongs.[8] the point of proceeding by schemes is that adaptations can be made to take account of particular characteristics and requirements. Thus the term of the rights varies from scheme to scheme, being between 15 and 25 years in length[9]; and the scope of the exclusive right is in some schemes specially extended (see below, paragraph (5)).

(4) Criteria of validity

A protectable variety must be new, distinct, uniform and stable. It is A4-005 the last three of these characteristics that are officially tested. *Novelty* has

---

[5] Convention for the Protection of New Varieties of Plants (UPOV), 1961; signed initially by several European states (including the U.K.) and ratified by the U.K. on September 17, 1965; a revised text was signed in October 1978, which in particular allowed countries to offer both patent and variety right to the same invention if this was part of their law upon ratifying. Thus the U.S. was able to join.

[6] Because these trials will take at least two growing years, an applicant for variety rights may apply for a protective direction from the Controller of Plant Varieties: s.1(3), Sched. 1. This gives the applicant the right to prevent others from doing anything that would amount to infringement or wrongful use of the variety name if the rights had been granted; but the applicant must also undertake not to market the variety during the same period: Sched. 1, § 2.

[7] Provided for by the Convention (above, n. 5), Art. 30(2).

[8] s.1(1). The first five were introduced in 1965; the number has now risen to nearly 50 schemes.

[9] s.3. For fruit, forest and ornamental trees the term must be at least 18 years. There is a provision allowing the Controller to make one extension up to a maximum of 25 years on the ground of inadequate remuneration: s.3(5), (8), *cf.* PA 1949, s.23. For surrender of rights, see s.3(6).

a carefully limited meaning, different from that of patent law.[10] Only "prior commercialisation" counts against the applicant. This may be performed by anyone anywhere before the relevant scheme is introduced. But once the scheme exists, only prior sales and offers for sale by the applicant count against him, and even so his sales abroad in the previous four years are disregarded. To be *distinct,* the variety must have one or more important morphological, physiological or other characteristics that differ from other varieties according to common knowledge.[11] Whether the variety is sufficiently *uniform* has to be judged by regard to the particular features of the variety's sexual reproduction or vegetative propagation.[12] It will be *stable* if it remains true to its description after repeated reproduction or propagation. Where the applicant specifies a particular cycle of reproduction, the variety must keep its essential characteristics at the end of each cycle.[13]

If rights have been granted, the Controller must revoke them if he is satisfied that (i) there was prior commercialisation; (ii) the variety is not distinct[14]; (iii) the right-holder is no longer able to supply him with reproductive material for the variety; (iv) prior rights existed in another person, or (v) he was given incorrect information.[15] In addition he has a discretion to revoke on certain grounds concerning the maintenance of stocks, compulsory licences, protective directions and fees.[16] In proceedings for revocation, third parties may intervene, but they have no statutory right to initiate them. Moreover there is no explicit power to plead invalidity as a defence to infringement; nor may a counterclaim for revocation be made.

(5) Rights over reproductive material

A4-006 The rights given by the Act were deliberately limited in ways which sought to curb the right-owner's power to make monopoly profits. Two principles were accordingly adopted:

(i) the rights should extend only to the marketing of reproductive material (seed, tubers, cuttings, etc.) intended for reproduction and not for consumption (*e.g.* grain for milling);

(ii) farmers and other should not have to procure a licence to make their own seed and other material from their previous crop. The exclusive right accordingly covers selling reproductive material and producing it for purposes of sale.[17] Only exceptionally—where plant breeders will not otherwise receive adequate remuneration— may a scheme extend the exclusive right so as to cover producing

[10] Sched. 2, Pt. II, § 2; *Elizabeth of Glamis-Rose* [1966] F.S.R. 265: see Lesser [1987] E.I.P.R. 172.
[11] Sched. 2, Pt. II, § 1; see *Maris Druid-Spring Barley* [1968] F.S.R. 559.
[12] Sched. 2, Pt. II, § 4; *Zephyr-Spring Barley* [1967] F.S.R. 576; *Moulin Wheat* [1985] F.S.R. 283.
[13] Sched. 2, Pt. II, § 5; *Zephyr* case, *ibid.*
[14] But not that it is not uniform or stable.
[15] ss.3(7), (8), 6 (4), Sched. 2, Pt. I § 2 (6).
[16] ss.6(3), 7(7), Sched. 1, § 4(1); Plant Breeders' Rights Regs. 1969, reg. 26(6).
[17] Selling is defined in s.4(6).

or propagating the variety for the purpose of selling cut blooms, fruit and some other part of product.[18] It is expressly provided that if the material is bought abroad (something which is not itself restricted), it is an infringement thereafter to use it for reproduction, or to sell it as such, in Great Britain.[19]

(6) The registered name

For any variety in which rights are granted, the Controller may require A4-007 a name to be proposed.[20] The name if intended to be descriptive of the variety and not distinctive of commercial source in the trade mark sense.[21] The Controller may accordingly refuse to accept a proposed name because of its ability to cause confusion, including confusion with a trade mark or name.[22]

The varietal name, once registered, carries its own right. The proprietor may bring a civil action against anyone who uses the name (or one confusingly similar) for selling any other variety within the same class.[23]

(7) Licensing

The Act permits conditions, limitations and restrictions to be attached A4-008 to licences, in the same way as is possible for other propriety rights.[24] Acts in breach of such conditions which fall within the exclusive right then amount to infringement; there is no principle even of national exhaustion.[25] Where, however, limiting conditions have an appreciable effect on intercommunity trade, Article 85 of the Treaty of Rome may apply. It is necessary to determine whether the various conditions of exclusivity provided for in a licence amount to distortious of competition or means of promoting the exploitation of the new variety.[26]

Given the importance of new plant varieties and the Act's determination to qualify the ability to make monopoly profits out of rights, it is no surprise to find a fairly extensive regime for compulsory licensing.[27] After a period of years which varies from scheme to scheme, the Controller must grant a non-exclusive licence if he is satisfied either that the rightholder has unreasonably refused to grant a voluntary licence or has

---

[18] s.4(1)(c), Sched. 3, § 3. This has been done, e.g. in the case of roses, chrysanthemums and carnations: see S.I. 1965 No. 728, 1968 No. 617 and 1968 No. 624.

[19] s.4(2). Where cut bloom reproduction has been covered by a scheme, there is no equivalent provision affecting the importation for sale of blooms grown abroad. But consider the analogy of the *Saccharin* rule for patents: above § 6-010, n. 45.

[20] s.5; Plant Breeders' Rights Regulations 1969, reg. 18. For the relation to the Indices of varietal names generally, see ss.5(3), 20, 21.

[21] cf. *Wheatcroft's T.M.* (above, § 7-021, n. 8).

[22] Reg. 18 (2).

[23] s.5(6), with a defence of reasonable innocence to a claim to damages. Note also s.5A, making it an offence, save in specified circumstances, to sell reproductive material by a name other than its registered name.

[24] s.4(4). There is an implied licnece (unless expressly negated) on a legitimate sale of reproductive material to re-sell, but not to produce reproductive material for sale: s.4(5).

[25] See s.4(3), allowing a defence to a damages claim only where the defendant had no notice of the conditions.

[26] *Nungessee* v. *EC Commission* above, § 7-033.

[27] s.7.

proffered only unreasonable terms, unless there is good reason to the contrary.[28]

The EEC trade mark system will not itself provide for marks of this character. But the First Directive allows national laws to provide for collective marks, or for certification or guarantee marks, the last being of the same general character without being subject to the same measure of state regulation. It is specifically provided that certification and guarantee marks may designate the geographical origin of goods (as "Stilton"); but they must be open to use by a person properly entitled, provided that his use is in accordance with honest commercial practice.

---

[28] For the various criteria to be balanced by the Controller, see s.7(3), (6); *Cama-Wheat* [1968] F.S.R. 639. There are arrangements to give locus standi to collective organisations which represent right-holders: s.7(5).

INDEX